Women, Gender, and Politics: A Reader

Women, Gender, and Politics:
A Reader

Mona Lena Krook and Sarah Childs, Editors

OXFORD
UNIVERSITY PRESS
2010

OXFORD
UNIVERSITY PRESS

Oxford University Press, Inc., publishes works that further
Oxford University's objective of excellence
in research, scholarship, and education.

Oxford New York
Auckland Cape Town Dar es Salaam Hong Kong Karachi
Kuala Lumpur Madrid Melbourne Mexico City Nairobi
New Delhi Shanghai Taipei Toronto

With offices in
Argentina Austria Brazil Chile Czech Republic France Greece
Guatemala Hungary Italy Japan Poland Portugal Singapore
South Korea Switzerland Thailand Turkey Ukraine Vietnam

Published by Oxford University Press, Inc.
198 Madison Avenue, New York, New York 10016
www.oup.com

Oxford is a registered trademark of Oxford University Press

Library of Congress Cataloging-in-Publication Data

Women, gender, and politics : a reader / Mona Lena Krook and Sarah Childs, editors.
p. cm.
ISBN 978-0-19-536880-2; 978-0-19-536881-9 (pbk.)
1. Feminism—Political aspects—Cross-cultural studies.
2. Women's rights—Cross-cultural studies. 3. Women—Political
activity—Cross-cultural studies. I. Krook, Mona Lena. II. Childs, Sarah, 1969–
HQ1236.W637725 2010
305.42—dc22   2009050172

Printed in the United States of America
on acid-free paper

For our teachers, mentors, colleagues, and students

PREFACE

This reader is just one of the many products that have resulted from our first meeting at a women and politics conference in Belfast in March 2002. Being very young scholars, we booked ourselves into very cheap accommodations and met while roaming the halls for a hairdryer. Keeping in touch over the years, we had our first opportunity for sustained collaboration in 2004–2005, when Mona was an Economic and Social Research Council Postdoctoral Fellow at the University of Bristol, which has been Sarah's home institution since 2003. We spent many afternoons and evenings discussing how to conceptualize and analyze various facets of women's political representation. In 2005, these interests spilled into new collaborations with Karen Celis, at the University College Ghent, and Johanna Kantola, at the University of Helsinki, which has led us to think about "representation" in a much broader sense as occurring in parliaments, but also in social movements, political parties, and the state, as well as through the vehicles of elections and public policy.

When Mona returned to the United States to take up a job at Washington University in St. Louis, our conversations turned as well to questions of how to teach a course on women, gender, and politics. Neither of us felt that existing books were appropriate for a general introduction to the field, as monographs and edited collections tend to focus narrowly on one aspect of women's political participation and/or one particular country or region of the world. This is a well-established norm in scholarly research, but creates a gap for students, both graduate and undergraduate, who seek exposure to a broader range of theoretical ideas and empirical examples. At the same time, we felt that a traditional textbook was inadequate to the task. These are too often overly general, focused on breadth rather than depth and pitched at a very introductory level. Furthermore, in our single- and co-authored research we have become increasingly aware of the need for both students and researchers to be able to access influential pieces "firsthand."

This reader reflects our effort to distill some of the key bodies of research on women, gender, and politics. We focused on selecting both classic and recent contributions in six areas of research: (1) women and social movements; (2) women and political parties; (3) women, gender, and elections; (4) women, gender, and public policies; (5) women, gender, and political representation; and (6) women, gender, and the state. Our aim has been to capture the various ways that research has developed in each of these areas, both thematically and chronologically. To draw connections between the readings, each section includes a short overview of the selections and their relation to one another. Each set of readings might therefore be read as an introduction to general trends in thinking about women, gender, and politics, or alternatively, as an entry into key sets of debates as they have evolved over time.

The resulting volume, as with our other work, is truly "co-authored." Despite the physical distance between us, we really do make decisions together: we engaged in a lot of back and forth exchanges on what to include and exclude, as well as on how the individual chapters and articles should be edited. We hope that the authors feel that we have done justice to their work, in what was—ultimately, and perhaps inevitably—a rather ruthless process. In our efforts to ensure that the reader included both theoretical and empirical work, covered major themes related to gender and politics, and reflected—as far as possible—both temporal and regional variations, we realized that it was impossible to include every influential piece. Although our coverage could not be total, we hope that we have managed to put together a single collection that offers a thorough—if necessarily incomplete—introduction to the study of women, gender, and politics.

In compiling this reader, we became indebted to a number of individuals who helped shape this project and bring it to fruition. We are especially thankful to David McBride, our editor at Oxford University Press, who saw the potential of this reader and offered invaluable advice throughout the process, as well as to his assistant, Brendan O'Neill, for talking us through the details of putting together a volume such as this. In addition, the three anonymous reviewers who read our proposal offered very helpful suggestions for improving the content and flow of the reader, as well as crucial support for the project as a whole. Our students in our courses, "Politics of Gender" at the University of Bristol and "Gender and Politics in Global Perspective" at Washington University in St. Louis, inspired this project and in many ways helped us think through how we might best edit the pieces we have chosen.

Lydia Anderson-Dana, who was at the time an undergraduate student at Washington University, assisted with some of the initial paperwork for the reader. Diana Z. O'Brien, currently a graduate student at Washington University, performed something of a small miracle in helping us obtain clean copies of all the pieces, contact details of authors and publishers, and—at a time when the copy machine at the Department of Political Science was out of service—permission to copy and scan nearly all of our edits in other parts of the university at one point or another. She also became an expert with the fax machine, when it was necessary to send out our edits and permissions that way as well. Emma Qing Wang, currently an undergraduate at Harvard University, stepped in and assisted during the final stages, helping us implement the final edits and reviewing all the notes and references.

For this crucial assistance, we gratefully acknowledge the financial support of the Graduate School of Arts and Sciences at Washington University; the Weidenbaum Center on the Economy, Government, and Public Policy Research at Washington University; and the Radcliffe Research Partnership Program. The time and resources to write the introductory essay were facilitated by Mona's fellowships at Harvard University at the Radcliffe Institute for Advanced Study, as well as the Women and Public Policy Program at the John F. Kennedy School of Government, where the fellowship was funded by The Women's Leadership Board.

Finally, we would like to express an enormous thanks to the authors and publishers who agreed to have their work included. We hope that they can be proud of this reader, and the role that they have played in the development in this field of research, even if in the process we may have cut out the one sentence that they really think is the most important statement of their work. We sincerely appreciate their generosity.

In closing, we would also like to thank our friends and colleagues in the wider gender and politics community, which is in many ways one of the best aspects of being a women and politics scholar. They provide a challenging but supportive—and fun!—environment within which to work on theoretically and substantively important questions in political science. Some of the key networks—always open to new members—include the Women and Politics Research Section of the American Political Science Association, the Women and Politics Specialist Group of the Political Studies Association, the Gender and Politics Standing Group of the European Consortium for Political Research, and the Gender and Politics Research Committee of the International Political Science Association. For these reasons, we would like to dedicate this book to our teachers, mentors, colleagues, and students, who together form part of this growing community. They continually remind us of the value of reading, teaching, and doing research on women, gender and politics.

CONTENTS

1. *Women, Gender, and Politics: An Introduction* 3
   Mona Lena Krook and Sarah Childs

PART I: *Women and Social Movements*

2. *Mobilization without Emancipation? Women's Interests, the State, and Revolution in Nicaragua* 21
   Maxine Molyneux

3. *Beyond Compare? Women's Movements in Comparative Perspective* 29
   Karen Beckwith

4. *Women's Movements and Democratic Transition in Chile, Brazil, East Germany, and Poland* 37
   Lisa Baldez

5. *Protest Moves inside Institutions* 47
   Mary Fainsod Katzenstein

6. *Do Interest Groups Represent the Disadvantaged? Advocacy at the Intersections of Race, Class, and Gender* 55
   Dara Z. Strolovitch

7. *Translating the Global: Effects of Transnational Organizing on Local Feminist Discourses and Practices in Latin America* 63
   Sonia E. Alvarez

8. *Cross-Regional Trends in Female Terrorism* 71
   Karla J. Cunningham

PART II: *Women and Political Parties*

9. *The Dynamics of Gender and Party* 81
   Joni Lovenduski

10. *Theorizing Feminist Strategy and Party Responsiveness* 87
    Lisa Young

11. *Building a Base: Women in Local Party Politics* 89
    Jo Freeman

12. *Women's Political Representation in Sweden: Discursive Politics and Institutional Presence* 97
    Diane Sainsbury

13. *The Problem with Patronage: Constraints on Women's Political Effectiveness in Uganda* 107
Anne Marie Goetz

14. *Feminist Political Organization in Iceland: Some Reflections on the Experience of Kwenna Frambothid* 117
Lena Dominelli and Gudrun Jonsdottir

PART III: *Women, Gender, and Elections*

15. *The Developmental Theory of the Gender Gap: Women's and Men's Voting Behavior in Global Perspective* 127
Ronald Inglehart and Pippa Norris

16. *Puzzles in Political Recruitment* 135
Pippa Norris and Joni Lovenduski

17. *Entering the Arena? Gender and the Decision to Run for Office* 141
Richard L. Fox and Jennifer L. Lawless

18. *Party Elites and Women Candidates: The Shape of Bias* 151
David Niven

19. *Women's Representation in Parliament: The Role of Political Parties* 159
Miki Caul

20. *Explaining Women's Legislative Representation in Sub-Saharan Africa* 167
Mi Yung Yoon

21. *Quotas as a "Fast Track" to Equal Representation for Women: Why Scandinavia Is No Longer the Model* 175
Drude Dahlerup and Lenita Freidenvall

PART IV: *Women, Gender, and Political Representation*

22. *Quotas for Women* 185
Anne Phillips

23. *Representation and Social Perspective* 193
Iris Marion Young

24. *Should Blacks Represent Blacks and Women Represent Women? A Contingent "Yes"* 201
Jane Mansbridge

25. *Preferable Descriptive Representatives: Will Just Any Woman, Black, or Latino Do?* 215
Suzanne Dovi

26. *From a Small to a Large Minority: Women in Scandinavian Politics* 225
Drude Dahlerup

27. *Beyond Bodies: Institutional Sources of Representation for Women in Democratic Policymaking* 231
S. Laurel Weldon

PART V: *Women, Gender, and Social Policies*

28. *Sex, Gender, and Leadership in the Representation of Women* 243
Karin L. Tamerius

29. *Congressional Enactments of Race-Gender: Toward a Theory of Raced-Gendered Institutions* 251
Mary Hawkesworth

30. *Taking Problems Apart* 263
Carol Lee Bacchi

31. *Sex and the State in Latin America* 267
Mala Htun

32. *Beyond the Difference versus Equality Policy Debate: Postsuffrage Feminism, Citizenship, and the Quest for a Feminist Welfare State* 277
Wendy Sarvasy

33. *Is Mainstreaming Transformative? Theorizing Mainstreaming in the Context of Diversity and Deliberation* 283
Judith Squires

PART VI: *Women, Gender, and the State*

34. *The Liberal State* 293
Catharine A. MacKinnon

35. *Gender and the State: Theories and Debates* 299
Johanna Kantola

36. *Gender in the Welfare State* 305
Ann Orloff

37. *Interacting with the State: Feminist Strategies and Political Opportunities* 313
Louise Chappell

38. *Introduction to Comparitive State Feminism* 319
Dorothy McBride Stetson and Amy G. Mazur

39. *State Feminism or Party Feminism? Feminist Politics and the Spanish Institute of Women* 327
Monica Threlfall

40. *When Power Relocates: Interactive Changes in Women's Movements and States* 335
Lee Ann Banaszak, Karen Beckwith, and Dieter Rucht

CREDITS 347

INDEX 351

Women, Gender, and Politics: A Reader

Chapter 1

WOMEN, GENDER, AND POLITICS: AN INTRODUCTION

Mona Lena Krook

Sarah Childs

In recent years, the status of women as political actors has captured the imagination of spectators around the world. The growing number of female presidents and prime ministers, as well as record proportions of women elected to national parliaments, suggest that women have made important gains in the political sphere. Yet the experiences and portrayals of female politicians, in addition to the continued under-representation of women in politics, draw attention to the many ways in which access to political office is still very much stratified by gender. At the same time, women continue to be involved in large numbers in social movements and political parties. However, their participation has increasingly taken new forms, as women have ascended to leadership positions, focused on a wider array of issues, and experimented with new tactics of political protest. Women have also received renewed focus from the media and political elites as voters and candidates. This is due to the increased salience of the gender gap in recent elections in many countries and the dramatic rise in female candidates as a result of newly adopted quota policies. The presence of more women in politics has in turn raised questions about whether or not women make a difference in terms of introducing new policy priorities, proposals, and outcomes. Such a lens suggests that public policies are not gender-neutral, and thus that state actors and agencies play an important role in shaping gender relations in ways that produce and reproduce inequalities between women and men.

To make sense of these developments, this volume seeks to offer an introduction into the broad body of research on women, gender, and politics. This work is informed by feminism, the belief in the social, economic, and political equality of women and men. It is marked by two major contributions to political analysis: (1) introducing the concept of "gender" and (2) expanding the definition of "politics." Although the term "gender" is often elided with "women" (cf. Carver 1996), but it is crucial to distinguish between "sex," normally taken to denote biological differences between women and men, and "gender," referring to the social meanings given to these distinctions. The concept of gender thus makes it possible to move the analytical focus away from biological sex, which treats men and women as binary opposites, to constructed gender identities, which view masculinity and femininity as features that exist along a continuum, often in combination with other identities (Childs and Krook 2006). As such, theories of gender offer a chance to explore masculinities and femininities, as well as the relative status of men and women, in the conduct of political life.

The term "politics," in turn, is often used by political scientists to refer to the formal processes and institutions of government and elections. Women's movement activism in recent decades, however, has inspired feminists to theorize at least two additional meanings. One group expands its range to encompass informal politics and the dynamics of everyday life. Some scholars insist, for example, that social movements are a form of political participation on par with engagement inside the state (Baldez 2002; Beckwith 2007).

At the same time, feminists draw attention to the power relations that permeate all levels of social life, including relations within the private sphere of home and family. For them, "the personal is political" (Okin 1979; Squires 1999). A second group, together with postmodern theorists, has adopted a notion of "politics" as any instance or manifestation of power relations (Butler 1990; Foucault 1995). They are thus interested not only in the politics of the state and the politics of social movements, but also the politics of language, the politics of exchange, and the politics of representation, which they have analyzed using a wide variety of research tools.

Both of these feminist innovations have come under challenge in recent years. On the one hand, there has been increased recognition of the ways in which multiple facets of identity may interact to shape not only personal interactions but also large-scale political outcomes. In these debates, scholars have offered various schemes for analyzing how the dynamics of gender shape and are shaped by other patterns of inequality based on race, class, sexuality, ability, and other features (Hancock 2007; Weldon 2006). For some, this critique means that it is no longer possible to speak of "women" as a group; for others, it simply entails recognizing that there may be strategic value to retaining the category of "women" while also remaining aware of differences among women that may at times make it difficult to generalize about women as a group (cf. Fuss 1989; Squires 1999). On the other hand, increased globalization, combined with decentralization, has posed major challenges to traditional configurations of political organization, creating new opportunities and constraints for feminist change. As a consequence, "politics" is now an even more diffuse entity, with new and developing arrangements that are not yet well understood.

To acquaint readers with this vast literature, this volume brings together classic and more recent contributions on central topics in the study of women, gender, and politics. It is divided into six sections to reflect the range of research in this subfield of political science: (1) women and social movements; (2) women and political parties; (3) women, gender, and elections; (4) women, gender, and political representation; (5) women, gender, and public policies; and (6) women, gender,

and the state. Within each of these sections, readings have been selected to capture the various ways that research has developed in each of these areas, both thematically and chronologically. To aid the reader, each section begins with a short overview of the readings and their relation to one another, as a means to better situate each piece within the context of the whole. Each section might therefore be read as an introduction to general trends in thinking about women and politics or, alternatively, as an entry into key sets of debates on gender and politics as they have evolved over time. To reflect the diversity of trends and approaches, the collection includes readings that, as a group, analyze both developed and developing countries, as well as historical and contemporary examples, and use both statistical and case study methods. This introductory essay provides a brief survey of the state of the art in the six areas covered in this book. It draws out general trends, notes recent developments, and concludes with thoughts as to how a gender lens improves knowledge of both formal and informal political processes.

Women and Social Movements

Social movements have long been a central focus of studies of women, gender, and politics. This is due in part to the fact that women have largely been excluded from other arenas of political participation, like elections, political office, and international politics. While formal barriers like lack of suffrage have been overcome in most countries, informal norms associating women with the private sphere and men with the public continue to exert influence, leading fewer women than men to hold top-level political positions. At the same time, women have also played a major role in many civil society organizations, including churches, choirs, and charities. While social movements form part of civil society, they are distinguished from other voluntary organizations in that they involve "collective challenges, based on common purposes and social solidarities, in sustained interactions with elites, opponents, and authorities" (Tarrow 1998, 4). Given feminists' strong interest in changing the status quo, it is perhaps not surprising that they have been attracted to the study and practice of social movement organizing.

Women's participation in movement activities falls into three broad categories (Beckwith 2000). Women's movements encompass any type of systematic organizing by women. Although this term is most often associated with movements promoting women's rights, including suffrage and women's liberation, it also refers to movements that draw on—and possibly even seek to preserve—more traditional gender roles, like mothers' movements and right-wing women's groups. Some key questions asked by researchers concern definitions of "women's interests" (Molyneux 1985), relationships between women's movements and political parties (Lovenduski and Norris 1993), how political opportunities for women's movements are gendered (Chappell 2002), and determinants of women's movement failure and success (Banaszak 1996).

Feminist movements are often seen as a subset of women's movements. However, they are distinct in that they may include men and, more fundamentally, are informed by a gendered power analysis that aims to overcome women's subordination. Nonetheless, they may be inspired by different types of feminism. Liberal feminism emphasizes equality between women and men and believes that change can be achieved through legal and social reform. Radical feminism, in contrast, stresses differences between women and men and views gender inequality as a basic system of power that organizes human relationships. Socialist feminism combines ideas from Marxism with radical feminist ideas about patriarchy to highlight economic and cultural sources of women's oppression. Finally, postmodern feminism merges ideas about "sex" and "gender" with postmodern or poststructuralist theory to call attention to the multiple and contradictory aspects of individual and collective identity, which undermine the possibility of a unitary category of "women" or "men."[1] Key dilemmas for feminist movements, therefore, include whether to engage or not engage with state actors (Kantola 2006; L. Young 2000), mobilize separately or in coalition with other actors (Beckwith 2000; Molyneux 1998), and emphasize sex and gender over other identities (Goetz and Hassim 2003). A related concern is whether to use the term "feminism" at all, given its various negative connotations in many parts of the world as "man-hating," "bourgeois," a tool

of "colonial oppression," a measure of "Western decadence," and even a type of "forced emancipation" (Basu 1995; Franceschet 2005).

A third subset of this literature concerns women in social movements. While the content of these groups may not relate directly to questions of women or feminism, they are often deeply gendered in terms of their participants, issues, and tactics. Some social movements, for example, tend to attract women, like antinuclear, peace, and environmental groups (Braidotti et al. 1994; Roseneil 1995), while others are dominated by men, like guerrilla and terrorist organizations (Cunningham 2003; Reif 1986). These patterns stem in part from metaphorical associations between women, peace, and care, on the one hand, and men, war, and violence, on the other. Within many groups, further, women have often been relegated to support roles, although this pattern has begun to change in some movements as women have assumed a greater number of leadership positions. However, the enduring tendency to view men, but not women, as political actors continues to play an important role in how various groups have devised strategies and recognized opportunities for mobilization. Indeed, the fact that women are often not seen as "political" has enabled them to protest when members of other groups have been violently repressed (Baldez 2002), as well as—more recently—carry out terrorist attacks because they are less likely to be searched by authorities (Cunningham 2003). In the former case, women often gain moral force by mobilizing as mothers; in the latter, they may draw on maternal imagery—even to the point of posing as a pregnant woman in order to conceal a bomb—as a means to achieve violent ends.

While it is possible to distinguish analytically between women's movements, feminist movements, and women in social movements, there are also important overlaps between these categories. Feminist movements are often viewed as a subset of women's movements; in many cases, they are even seen as synonymous terms. A less well-known connection is that women in social movements often launch women's movements, especially when the movement in question aims to overcome injustice or fight for equal treatment. In some instances, like campaigns for civil or human rights, women gain a gender consciousness after being treated in sexist ways (Bunch 1990; Evans 1979). In others, such as revolutionary or nationalist movements, women experience frustration after being asked to delay their demands for gender equality until the "broader" cause is achieved (Basu 1995; Luciak 2001). The issues that have in turn become central to women's and feminist movements include legal and political rights, employment opportunities and discrimination, reproductive choice and abortion, violence against women, sexual freedom, and women's political participation and representation. Nonetheless, the particular emphasis of individual movements varies across countries and over time.

Differences in priorities may also be debated within movements themselves. In some cases, activists disagree on the best strategies for accomplishing the group's goals. Early suffrage organizations split on several occasions on the question of whether to pursue lobbying or more disruptive tactics (Daley and Nolan 1994). Similarly, while liberal feminists are more open to working inside existing institutions, radical feminists prefer to stay outside on the grounds that engaging with patriarchal structures only serves to legitimate and perpetuate these institutions (Squires 1999). In other instances, there are critiques from within and outside the movement regarding claims to speak for "all women," when in fact these tended to reflect the needs and viewpoints of Western, white, middle-class, heterosexual, and able-bodied women (Mohanty 1988). This tendency, however, is not limited to feminist groups: national organizations that represent marginalized groups are substantially less active on issues affecting disadvantaged subgroups than they are when it comes to issues affecting advantaged subgroups (Strolovitch 2006). These patterns not only pose challenges to articulating "women's interests," but also call attention to the dynamics of power at work within and across groups working for social justice.

Debates over how to define women's movements have led to discussions over the nature and location of social movements. While some argue that a group must be autonomous from other political structures in order to be classified as a women's movement (Gelb 1989; Weldon 2002), others suggest that women's presence and struggles inside male-dominated institutions should

be viewed as a type of social movement activity (Katzenstein 1998; Sainsbury 2004). This boundary has been pushed even further with increased globalization and a concomitant rise in transnational contention, which have served to create new opportunities and constraints in women's movement organizing.[2] On the one hand, local groups have adopted new discourses and practices as a result of increased contacts with other women's groups across national borders. Some have forged new personal bonds of solidarity with others who share locally stigmatized values, while others have learned new strategies for lobbying more effectively for an expansion of women's rights (Alvarez 2000). On the other hand, patterns of governance have shifted with state reconfiguration and increased multilevel governance, such that activists are not limited to petitioning state actors, but may also appeal to—or seek strategic alliances with—international organizations and transnational advocacy networks as a means to achieve policy change (True and Mintrom 2001). At the same time, however, changes in the structures of states have made it less clear which actors have the capacity to implement these reforms in meaningful ways (Banaszak, Beckwith, and Rucht 2003).

Women and Political Parties

A second relatively large literature is research on women and political parties, for some of the same reasons as social movements: until recently, political parties have served as the main avenue for women's participation in the formal political sphere. This work can be divided into three primary areas of research. The first concerns women's modes of participating in the party system. In many countries, women have played an active role inside political parties—in many instances, even before women gained the right to vote. However, they rarely assumed leadership roles and even now still make up a minority of all top party officials (Kittilson 2006). Women have instead often been relegated to more ancillary roles, such as cooking, doing clerical work, and mobilizing female voters, although they have also been involved in giving speeches and writing campaign literature (Bashevkin 1985; Freeman 2000). Their participation has often been facilitated by the presence of women's sections within the parties, although there is ongoing debate as to whether such organizations serve as a platform for formulating women's demands or as a mechanism for marginalizing women and their concerns within the party at large (Sainsbury 2004; Tripp 2001). For some, this insider position has been crucial for gaining greater presence in political decision making and attention to women's concerns in public policy (Lovenduski 1993), while for others it results in cooptation and reduced effectiveness overall (Goetz and Hassim 2003).

A second major topic is interactions between women's movements and political parties. Stemming from concerns about cooptation, a key dilemma in feminist organizing has been whether or not to participate in mainstream power structures. For some, engaging with political parties is the only effective means for promoting women's interests; they believe that change must—and can—come from within existing institutions (Sainsbury 2004). For others, however, true change requires remaining outside the party system; participation, for them, can only serve to legitimize and perpetuate patriarchal power relations (Lovenduski 1986). Although these perspectives are informed by different types of feminism, the strategies of particular women's movements may vary within and across countries, with movements adopting partisan, crosspartisan, or apartisan stances vis-à-vis parties (L. Young 2000), and shift from a separatist toward a more integrationist approach, or vice versa, over time (Britton 2005; Lovenduski 1993). On the occasions where women's groups have decided to engage with political parties, they have tended to do so overwhelmingly with parties of the left (Kittilson 2006; Lovenduski and Norris 1993). However, a growing literature also reveals mobilization by women inside parties of the right (Clark and Schwedler 2003; Wiliarty 2001). The choice to engage, in turn, often creates a new dilemma of "double militancy," namely what to do when there is a conflict between identities as a party versus a movement activist (Beckwith 2000).

A third and related area of research involves the responses by political parties to women's movement demands. One typology discerns two broad categories of responses—representational responsiveness, which entails recruitment of more women to positions of power, and policy responsiveness, which involves greater attention to issues of concern to women—and argues that parties may be responsive, promoting representational and policy concerns; cooptive, recruiting more women but not altering policy priorities; nonresponsive, making no changes in response to feminist demands; and oppositional, outwardly refusing to change their recruitment practices or policy stands (L. Young 2000). Although it does not necessarily adopt this language, much of the literature on this question explains these variations with reference to party ideology, strategy, and structure. In general, scholars find that left-wing parties are more open to feminist demands, being more likely than right-wing parties to nominate female candidates and alter their party platforms (Lovenduski and Norris 1993). In part, this is due to a greater willingness among established left parties to take steps to overcome patterns of exclusion and marginalization, as well as among new left parties to promote new ways of doing "politics" (Kittilson 2006). It is also crucial to note, however, that parties of the right have and can play a role in promoting women's rights; indeed, in several countries they were at the forefront of promoting women's right to vote and equal pay (Wolbrecht 2000). Party strategy also plays an important role: studies find that parties tend to be more willing to respond when they believe they will gain something in return, like electoral benefit (Lovenduski and Norris 1993) or support for an existing regime (Goetz and Hassim 2003). The effects of ideology and strategy, in turn, are affected by the organizational structures of political parties, stemming from their degree of decentralization and party discipline (Caul 1999; L. Young 2000).

The literature on women and political parties thus focuses on gendered patterns in party activities, lobbying, and priorities. Most of this work analyzes trends in established parties, exploring how women's engagement may reinforce or challenge "politics-as-usual" within these organizations. A small number of studies, however, have addressed the phenomenon of women's parties. While rare, these parties have appeared in a wide range of countries and, in various ways, reveal the potential and limits for women to engage with and transform existing party systems. They have appeared in all regions and ideologically are quite diverse: while some are feminist, others claim to be centrist and still others emphasize women's traditional roles (Stokes 2005). Nonetheless, they generally emerge with two basic goals: to increase the number of women in elected office and to insert women's issues onto the political agenda. In most cases, they appear at moments of crisis or change in existing political systems; with few exceptions, they win only a small number of votes. A common approach to explaining their lack of appeal is to argue that "sex" is not viewed as a political cleavage; women do not necessarily identify politically as "women," but rather with a particular set of policy positions. However, the major appeal of women's parties, where they have been successful, is their effort to introduce a new way of doing "politics" by taking decisions by consensus, flattening hierarchies, and rotating positions (Dominelli and Jonsdottir 1988).

Women, Gender, and Elections

Work on political parties links to another major area of study, focused on women, gender, and elections. Although wide-ranging, it can be separated into research on electing versus being elected. The first category can be further subdivided into two sets of concerns: women's right to vote and gender gaps in voting behavior. While today women's suffrage is nearly universal,[3] it was initially viewed as controversial. Opponents expressed concerns that it would bring about the decline of the family, bolster the conservative vote, and usher in prohibition. Supporters, in contrast, suggested that women's suffrage would improve the form and content of politics, even helping to secure world peace (Pateman 1994). The first countries to give women this right were largely peripheral countries within the world system, like New Zealand, Australia, Finland, and Norway. Suffrage then spread to countries around the world, coming in waves after the two major world wars and, later, following independence in many postcolonial states (Daley and Nolan 1994). National and international suffrage alliances acted as crucial motors for change that, over time, resulted in a broader shift in international norms,

such that today the franchise for women is seen as a taken-for-granted feature of political citizenship. All the same, having the same right to vote does not necessarily mean that men and women have equal opportunities to influence political outcomes. Some scholars argue that women's delayed suffrage has had long-term implications for women's status in political life, stemming from the fact that many political institutions—including political parties—predate women's right to vote (Harvey 1998).

Predictions as to how women would use their right to vote were an integral part of debates leading up to women's suffrage. Although many argued that women would be unlikely to vote in a substantially different direction than men, a large number of participants on both sides imputed distinct political preferences to women and men. Early research found that women tended to vote in greater numbers than men for conservative parties, a trend often explained with reference to the belief that women were more religious than men (Duverger 1955). However, this gap began to narrow and then reversed in many countries in the West in the 1980s and 1990s, such that today women appear to give greater support to parties of the left. Whereas the "traditional gender gap" continues to prevail in many non-Western contexts, the so-called modern gender gap has become an enduring feature of the political landscape in the West (Inglehart and Norris 2000). In an effort to understand what drives these gaps, a more critical literature has emerged suggesting that there are important differences among feminists and nonfeminists (Conover 1988), as well as among older and younger women (Norris 1996). At the same time, alternative research designs find that the gender gap credited to changes in women's behavior may in fact be more accurately attributed to men, who have shifted their support in greater numbers to parties of the right (Kaufmann and Petrocik 1999). These patterns indicate that the "gender gap" has been socially constructed as a female phenomenon (Mueller 1988), which has in turn led parties to take steps to appeal more explicitly to female voters out of the belief that their support has the potential to radically alter electoral outcomes.

One way in which parties have sought to appeal to women is by nominating and electing more women to political office. Although women are underrepresented in most elected bodies,[4] there are substantial variations across levels of government, as well as across countries and over time. In many cases, more women win office at the local and regional levels than at the national level (Darcy, Welch, and Clark 1994). In contrast, they have rarely acceded to positions of executive leadership as cabinet ministers (Davis 1997) and as presidents and prime ministers, although their numbers have grown dramatically in recent years (Jalalzai 2008). Most research, however, has focused on women's representation in national parliaments. A starting point for many analyses is the supply and demand model of political recruitment, which proposes that the number of women elected is the combined result of (1) the qualifications of women as a group to run for political office, namely their resources and motivation, and (2) the desire or willingness of elites to select female aspirants, based on elites' perceptions regarding women's abilities and experience (Lawless and Fox 2005; Niven 1998; Norris and Lovenduski 1995). In contrast, scholars largely dismiss arguments about voter bias; although some early work found that the public was reluctant to vote for female candidates, most studies find that voters not only vote for male and female candidates at equal rates, but may in fact vote in greater numbers for women over men (Black and Erickson 2003).

In addition to explanations of why women are underrepresented in general in national parliaments, a large literature addresses crossnational and crosstemporal variations, looking to identify some of the structural and contextual factors that may shape women's access to political office. This work finds that the percentage tends to be higher in countries with proportional representation (PR) electoral systems than in those with majoritarian electoral arrangements (Salmond 2006). Proportional representation systems tend to be organized around multi-member districts, meaning that more than one person is elected, which open the way for women to be included as the total number of seats available in each district increases. In contrast, majoritarian systems resemble a "winner-take-all" situation where only one candidate may win election, reducing the number of opportunities for a diverse group of candidates to be elected (Caul 1999). Correlations are similarly observed

with women's overall rates of education and labor force participation (McDonagh 2002), as well as with levels of national socioeconomic development (Matland 1998), whose effects are generally attributed to modernization processes that enable women to move into higher social and economic roles that lead to greater influence in politics (Inglehart and Norris 2003). Finally, cultural attitudes also appear to be important, as the number of women in politics is typically higher in Protestant countries (Reynolds 1999) and in countries where citizens are more open to women in leadership positions (Inglehart and Norris 2003). Yet, these findings may be case- and time-specific: although some research confirms these findings in non-Western cases (Paxton 1997; Yoon 2004), other work discovers that these same factors appear to play little or no role in developing countries (Matland 1998). More specifically, there are a growing number of developing countries with majoritarian electoral systems, where women have a relatively low status, and/or where the majority religion is not Protestant, but women have made major gains in recent years. At the same time, research examining past trends finds that the effects of PR electoral systems did not surface until recently; before 1970, there were few differences among countries in this regard.

Research on women, gender, and elections has thus been more attentive than some other literatures in terms of recognizing diversity among "women," incorporating men into the analysis, and exploring connections between developments in the public sphere and social, economic, and cultural realms. Even so, there is ongoing debate regarding the nature and importance of the gender gap in voting behavior. In addition to asking why women as a group might have political preferences distinct from those of men (Studlar, McAllister, and Hayes 1998), scholars have probed the content of women's political interests (Campbell 2006) and sought to explain lower levels of political knowledge among women as compared to men, despite changes in the opportunities for women's engagement in political life (Mondak and Anderson 2004). At the same time, a growing literature explores differences among women, in terms of how gender, race, and class may interact to shape women's political priorities (Gay and Tate 1998). Studies of women's election have also developed in new directions over the last few years. Some have attempted to nuance the category of "women" by analyzing differences in access among women of different races and ethnicities (Hughes 2008). Others have observed dramatic shifts in women's representation in recent years and sought to identify new factors that may facilitate women's election to parliament, including the adoption of candidate gender quotas (Dahlerup 2006; Krook 2009; Tripp and Kang 2008), the end of violent conflict (Bauer and Britton 2006), and the mobilization of women's groups, both national (Kittilson 2006) and international (Krook 2006; Paxton, Hughes, and Green 2006). This work suggests that the public sphere, while still heavily gendered, may be shaped in active ways by strategies and opportunities for political change.

Women, Gender, and Political Representation

Women's voting behavior and the election of female candidates are often treated as important questions in themselves. While recognizing that women's participation carries symbolic value for democracy, another line of work seeks to go beyond political priorities and presence to consider what effects these may have on concrete policy outcomes. It addresses the degree to which the presence of women in political office translates into attention to women's concerns in policy making; in other words, the relationship between the "descriptive" and "substantive" representation of women (cf. Pitkin 1967). Political theorists have presented various arguments pointing to women's "interests" and "perspectives" as a means to support efforts to increase women's political representation (Mansbridge 1999; Phillips 1995; Williams 1998; I. Young 2000). Yet, the notion of "women's interests" remains controversial (Celis 2006; Molyneux 1985), and as a result, scholars have identified "women's issues" in a number of different ways in empirical research. They have defined it, variously, to include policies that increase women's autonomy and well-being (Reingold 2000), concerns in the private sphere according to established views on gender relations areas where surveys discover a gender

gap in the population (Schwindt-Bayer 2006), and any issue of concern to the broader society (Mackay 2001).

Scholars have also focused on different aspects of the policy-making process. They have examined legislator attitudes and priorities (Schwindt-Bayer 2006; Swers 1998), patterns of bill introduction and cosponsorship (Franceschet and Piscopo 2008; Swers 2005), and legislative votes (Thomas 1994). Most studies find that women tend to have the greatest impact at earlier stages in the legislative process (Grey 2002; Tamerius 1995). Although some suggest that the best solution is to examine the entire legislative process (Swers 2002), others highlight the numerous elements of contingency that may be responsible for moving an issue to agenda prominence and gaining its passage (Childs and Withey 2006). However, there is some debate on the need to establish differences among women and men in political office. While some claim that women only have an impact when they do not act in the same way as men (Cowell-Meyers 2001), others argue that convergence may occur when the increased presence of women leads men to show more interest in women's issues (Reingold 2000), the presence of antifeminist women and profeminist men evens out the aggregate balance of preferences across women and men (Chaney 2006), and "gendering" processes silence women by pressuring them to conform to positions taken by men or by blocking their opportunities to freely articulate their own views (Hawkesworth 2003). Further, some criticize the focus on "difference" because it retains an emphasis on women as the sex with special interests and experiences.

These concerns intersect with questions about the impact of numbers. Because women constitute a minority in most political bodies, researchers have explored whether a "critical mass" of women is needed before legislative change can occur. The concept was originally invoked to explain why the presence of women did not appear to affect policy outcomes, the argument being that women were unlikely to have an impact until they grew from a few token individuals into a considerable minority of all legislators (Dahlerup 1988). It is supported by evidence showing that legislatures with higher proportions of women tend to introduce and pass more bills on women's issues than their female counterparts in low representation legislatures (Thomas 1994). However, a growing body of research criticizes these assumptions, finding that women make a difference even when they form a small minority (Crowley 2004) or, alternatively, that a jump in the proportion of women may *decrease* the likelihood that individual female legislators will act on behalf of women as a group (Carroll 2001). Further, there are important boundary conditions that may prevent women from pursuing reforms addressing "women's interests." These include diversity among women, in terms of their race, class, and party identities (Barrett 1995; Childs 2004), as well as features of the political environment, such as committee membership (Norton 1995), institutional norms (Kathlene 1995; Mackay 2008), legislative inexperience (Beckwith 2007), and the electoral system (Tremblay 2003). These findings have in turn led many to question the continued utility and relevance of "critical mass" as a concept in research on the substantive representation of women (Childs and Krook 2006; Dahlerup 2006).

The literature on women, gender, and political representation has thus long retained a critical edge, seeking to problematize the concepts of "women" and "gender" and expand the notion of "politics." However, some recent contributions have pushed these challenges even further, to the point of questioning some of the core assumptions behind this work. In terms of research on women's legislative behavior, for example, a growing number of studies document diversity among women in terms of not just their race and party, but also their mechanism of election (Goetz and Hassim 2003; Schwartz 2004), emphasizing that being female may matter less than gender consciousness for achieving feminist outcomes (Archenti and Johnson 2006; Childs and Krook 2006). Further, scholars continue to question the concept of "women's interests," arguing that these may not only vary across countries and over time, but also across groups of women divided by race, class, and other identities; as such, it is crucial to promote the election of women sensitive to the needs of dispossessed subgroups of women (Celis 2006; Dovi 2002). Finally, a new literature has emerged that seeks to open up when and where women's policy representation may take

place, noting that parliaments are only one possible arena among many: actors in social movements, political parties, and the state may also articulate claims, and take concrete steps, to represent women's concerns (Celis, Childs, Kantola, and Krook 2008; Weldon 2002).

Women, Gender, and Public Policies

In addition to studying women's legislative behavior, researchers have also analyzed legislative outcomes by exploring the gendered nature of public policies and the creation and evolution of gender equality policies. With regard to the former, feminists have been particularly interested in exploring how laws—including those on questions not traditionally thought of as "women's issues"—reflect normative interpretations concerning gender relations, in terms of what trends are viewed as "problems" and how these "problems" are framed and translated into policy prescriptions (Bacchi 1999; Elman 2007; Verloo 2007). In revealing how public policies construct "men" and "women" as groups, this work exposes the gendered hierarchies that inform policy making, as well as the frequently contested nature of women's rights around the globe. In addition to legislators, other key actors in policy debates include churches, doctors, lawyers, unions, employer associations, and international organizations (Htun 2003; Norgren 2001), revealing that a host of groups recognize the power of public policy to shape social, economic, and political outcomes. These political struggles, in turn, help explain important differences across countries in terms of policies on the family (Charrad 2001; Htun 2003), property rights (Basu 1995; Tripp 2003), reproduction (Norgren 2001; Stetson 2001), and the labor market (Morgan 2003; Ruggie 1984), to name but a few policy areas. As a result, countries may have varied policy profiles in terms of their articulation of women's rights, both within and across issue areas (Kantola 2006; Weldon 2002).

A related line of research concerns the development of gender equality policies, also known as "women-friendly" or "gender-sensitive" public policy. Reflecting developments in feminist theory, policy approaches have evolved over time as policy makers have grappled with ongoing tensions between "equality" and "difference" (Bock and James 1992; Sarvasy 1992). Initial attempts to devise women-friendly public policy focused largely on equality as sameness, seeking to raise women to the standards of men. Dissatisfied with this approach, many advocates subsequently embraced the inverse strategy of difference, which entailed abandoning efforts to make women more like men toward focusing on women's needs as women (Bacchi 1996). However, concerned that such tactics might reify sexual difference, policy makers at both the national and international levels have now largely moved to a third stage known as "gender mainstreaming" (Booth and Bennett 2002; Squires 2005). This approach involves incorporating a gender perspective at all stages of the policy-making process, with the goal of (1) recognizing where policies might have a differential impact on women and men and (2) adjusting the policy in question such that it promotes gender equality. Although it entails domestic institutional change, international organizations and transnational activists have played a crucial role in the elaboration and spread of the mainstreaming approach (True and Mintrom 2001). Yet, its diffusion has led to a wide variety of national approaches to mainstreaming that have not always been transformative (Jahan 1995; Squires 2007). In fact, the adoption of mainstreaming has often served to marginalize women-specific policy concerns and, in some cases, to justify the end of women's policy agencies (Woodward 2003).

Scholars interested in questions of gender and public policy thus have a long history of self-critique, moving between theory and practice and back again. In line with this established pattern, recent work addresses new developments in political practice that have followed from increased recognition of multiple and intersecting facets of identity. A growing body of work offers theoretical—and, increasingly, methodological—insights into the ways in which it might be possible to study the intersectional needs and effects of public policy (Hancock 2007; Weldon 2006; Yuval-Davis 2006). At the same time, governments around the world have begun to move away from a sole focus on gender mainstreaming toward a model of "diversity mainstreaming," which aims to take into account multiple dimensions of marginalization when designing new public policies. In some countries, this shift has led to the amalgamation of state agencies based on gender, race, disability, and sexuality into a single policy unit. While this approach enables attention to multiple dimensions, it also complicates the policy-making process and raises further doubts about the ability of governments to design and implement such policies in a manner that is sensitive to the needs of all groups (Squires 2007; Verloo 2006).

Women, Gender, and the State

This discussion links to a sixth literature, on women, gender, and the state. Focusing on state-society interactions, feminists have been interested in understanding how states influence gender relations and, conversely, how gendered norms and practices shape state policies. One area of research concerns feminist theories of the state, which not only reflect different types of feminism but also distinct political strategies for engaging with state actors. Liberal feminists view the state in a relatively optimistic light, believing that while the state has been historically dominated by men, there is nothing inherent about this domination: with engagement, the state will become more open to women and their concerns. Radical feminists, in contrast, are more pessimistic about the transformative potential of the state, arguing that the state is patriarchal and thus can never be employed for feminist ends (MacKinnon 1989). Socialist and poststructuralist feminists, in turn, perceive the state as a mechanism of power and domination, asserting, albeit for different reasons, that political strategies centered on the state will not produce transformative change (Randall and Waylen 1998). To these some authors add Nordic feminism, which they argue combines faith in the ability of the state to change society in a positive direction, with awareness of the potential negative consequences of engaging with the state (Kantola 2006). This approach expresses concerns that state policies intended to reduce one set of inequalities may in fact serve to produce another set of inequalities, replacing women's dependence on men with women's dependence on the state (Hernes 1984).

A second set of questions relates to gender and the welfare state. This research compares the economic and social policies of various states to illustrate how they are shaped by particular normative views of gender relations (Orloff 1996; Sainsbury 1994). Many scholars have been influenced by mainstream welfare state typologies, exploring how different types of welfare state configurations create distinct opportunities for women to combine motherhood and care work with paid employment. They note that while social democratic welfare states enable women to combine motherhood and paid employment, conservative regimes tend to promote women's traditional status in the family, while liberal welfare states often adopt strict policies of nonintervention that reinforce existing inequalities (Esping-Andersen 1999; Sainsbury 1996). Yet, feminists also criticize the measures used to distinguish between welfare state models, arguing that a focus on state-market interactions should be extended to include the realm of the family, attention to stratification should be expanded to include a look at paid and unpaid labor, and concern for social rights and decommodification should be reconsidered in light of women's caring roles in the private sphere (Orloff 1993). These observations have led some to put forward the alternative "male breadwinner" family model (Lewis 1992), which over time has given way to a new 'adult worker' model, as women have joined the ranks of the employed, creating new challenges for combining care and wage labor (Lewis 2001).

In light of these dynamics, a third literature addresses how women's movements might interact with states to alter existing gender relations. Whereas earlier feminist activism debated the value of engaging with the state, more recent work has explored the ways in which the structure of political opportunities shapes the strategies of women's movements and the arenas—whether legislative, bureaucratic, or judicial—with which they choose to engage (Banaszak, Beckwith, and Rucht 2002; Chappell 2000). Their lobbying activities have not always met with success, but where women's groups have targeted state actors they have made some progress in gendering policy approaches and promoting women's rights (Chappell 2002). In some instances, women have entered the state apparatus as a means for achieving these ends. This has given

rise to a fourth area of study on women's policy agencies and the phenomenon of "state feminism." The basic feature of these feminist bureaucrats, also known as "femocrats," is that they seek to transform the state from within (Franzway, Court, and Connell 1989). Yet, as this concept has traveled around the world, it has taken on a range of distinct, and even contradictory, definitions. One emerges from work on gender and welfare states in Scandinavia, which argues that "women-friendly" policies in this region are the combined result of the political mobilization of women in civil society and the entry of increased numbers of women into political office and public administration (Hernes 1987). A second meaning of "state feminism" emerges from work on newly independent states, where modernizing—and sometimes authoritarian—regimes reform family and labor market policies to improve women's legal and economic status (Hatem 1992). The third and most common definition, however, refers to women's policy machineries and feminist bureaucrats in other parts of the state apparatus who seek to integrate a gender perspective in their own specialized policy fields (Stetson and Mazur 1995; Threlfall 1998).

The main challenges to traditional approaches for studying women, gender, and the state have revolved mainly around the nature and role of the state in an increasingly globalized world. While some scholars have begun to integrate questions of diversity and intersectionality into the study of the state in general, and the welfare state in particular (Josephson 2002), the main focus of research has been the impact of reduced state capacity on welfare state policies (Lewis 2002) and the emergence of new systems of multilevel governance (Outshoorn and Kantola 2007). A key concern has been to capture the effects of four processes of state reconfiguration (Banaszak, Beckwith, and Rucht 2003): uploading, or the shifting of power and responsibility to higher state levels; downloading, or the shifting of power and responsibility to lower state levels; lateral loading, or the shifting of power and responsibility to nonelected state bodies; and offloading, or the shifting of power and responsibility to nonstate actors. While some of these processes have been detrimental to women's organizing, others have created new opportunities for women's political engagement, in part by expanding the definition of "politics" to include a much wider range of issues, actors, and locations.

Conclusions

As mentioned at the outset, the main contribution of work on women, gender, and politics has been the introduction of the concept of "gender" and an expansion of traditional definitions of "politics." This literature has grown increasingly nuanced in recent years: challenges to the role of "gender" have appeared in studies pointing to the importance of multiple interacting identities, while new questions about "politics" have been raised in light of the perceived erosion of state capacities and the emergence of new patterns of multilevel governance. Aiming to capture these diverse developments, the goal of this volume is to acquaint readers with debates in six key areas of research: social movements, political parties, elections, political representation, public policy, and the state. Within each section, it becomes clear that feminist political scientists disagree in important ways with one another, in terms of (1) their relative emphases on "women" versus "gender," (2) their interpretations of women's status inside existing institutions, and (3) their preferred strategies for political change. Together, however, these contributions indicate what a feminist lens brings to the study of politics: awareness of the gendered nature of political concepts, attention to multiple types of power relations at work inside political structures and organizations, notice of the varied impact of outwardly neutral public policies, and deliberation over the most effective strategies for altering the status quo. In so doing, feminists have called attention not just to the role of formal institutions, but also to the more informal—and often more diffuse—dynamics sustaining patterns of inequality. Feminist research thus presents a profound challenge to existing political analysis by expanding the scope of "political science" itself.

Notes

1. Key authors include Mary Wollstonecraft, John Stuart Mill, and Betty Friedan (liberal feminism); Catharine MacKinnon, Mary Daly, Andrea Dworkin, and Shulamith Firestone (radical feminism); Gayle Rubin and Sheila Rowbotham (socialist feminism); and Judith Butler, Luce Irigaray, and Julia Kristeva (post-modern feminism).

2. It should be noted, however, that women's organizing has long had a global dimension, beginning with the early international suffrage campaigns in the late nineteenth century (Daley and Nolan 1994; Rupp 1997).

3. The only country where women do not have the right to vote today is Saudi Arabia, where men only gained the right to vote in 2005.

4. There are only a limited number of cases where women's numbers have been equal to or greater than men's, including some local councils in Norway in the 1970s and India in the 1990s, the National Assembly for Wales in 2003–2007, and most recently, the lower house of parliament in Rwanda, with 56 percent women elected in 2008.

References

Alvarez, Sonia E. 2000. "Translating the Global: Effects of Transnational Organizing on Latin American Feminist Discourses and Practices." *Meridians: A Journal of Feminisms, Race, Transnationalism* 1 (1): 29–67.

Archenti, Nélida, and Niki Johnson. 2006. "Engendering the Legislative Agenda with and without the Quota: A Comparative Study of Argentina and Uruguay." *Sociologia* 52: 133–153.

Bacchi, Carol Lee. 1996. *The Politics of Affirmative Action: "Women," Equality, and Category Politics.* Thousand Oaks, Calif.: Sage.

Bacchi, Carol Lee. 1999. *Women, Policy and Politics: The Construction of Policy Problems.* Thousand Oaks, Calif.: Sage.

Baldez, Lisa. 2002. *Why Women Protest: Women's Movements in Chile.* New York: Cambridge University Press.

Banaszak, Lee Ann. 1996. *Why Movements Succeed or Fail: Opportunity, Culture and the Struggle for Woman Suffrage.* Princeton, N.J.: Princeton University Press.

Banaszak, Lee Ann, Karen Beckwith, and Dieter Rucht. 2003. "When Power Relocates: Interactive Changes in Women's Movements and States." In *Women's Movements Facing the Reconfigured State.* New York: Cambridge University Press, 1–29.

Barrett, Edith J. 1995. "The Policy Priorities of African American Women in State Legislatures." *Legislative Studies Quarterly* 20 (2): 223–247.

Bashevkin, Sylvia. 1985. *Toeing the Line: Women and Party Politics in English Canada.* Toronto: University of Toronto Press.

Basu, Amrita, ed. 1995. *The Challenge of Local Feminisms: Women's Movements in Global Perspective.* Boulder, Colo.: Westview.

Bauer, Gretchen, and Hannah E. Britton, eds. 2006. *Women in African Parliaments.* Boulder, Colo.: Lynne Rienner.

Beckwith, Karen. 2000. "Beyond Compare? Women's Movements in Comparative Perspective." *European Journal of Political Research* 37: 431–468.

Beckwith, Karen. 2007. "Numbers and Newness: The Descriptive and Substantive Representation of Women." *Canadian Journal of Political Science* 40 (1): 27–49.

Black, Jerome H., and Lynda Erickson. 2003. "Women Candidates and Voter Bias: Do Women Politicians Need to Be Better?" *Electoral Studies* 22 (1): 81–100.

Bock, Gisela, and Susan James, eds. 1992. *Beyond Equality and Difference: Citizenship, Feminist Politics, and Female Subjectivity*. New York: Routledge.

Booth, Christine, and Cinnamon Bennett. 2002. "Gender Mainstreaming in the European Union: Towards a New Conception and Practice of Equal Opportunities?" *European Journal of Women's Studies* 9 (4): 430–446.

Braidotti, Rosi, et al. 1994. *Women, the Environment, and Sustainable Development: Towards a Theoretical Synthesis*. New York: Zed.

Britton, Hannah. 2005. *Women in the South African Parliament: From Resistance to Governance*. Boulder, Colo.: Lynne Rienner.

Bunch, Charlotte. 1990. "Women's Rights as Human Rights: Toward a Re-Vision of Human Rights." *Human Rights Quarterly* 12 (4): 486–498.

Butler, Judith. 1990. *Gender Trouble*. New York: Routledge.

Campbell, Rosie. 2006. *Gender and the Vote in Britain: Beyond the Gender Gap?* Oxford: ECPR Press.

Carroll, Susan J., ed. 2001. *The Impact of Women in Public Office*. Bloomington: Indiana University Press.

Carver, Terrell. 1996. *Gender Is Not a Synonym for Women*. Boulder, Colo.: Lynne Rienner.

Caul, Miki. 1999. "Women's Representation in Parliament: The Role of Political Parties." *Party Politics* 5 (1): 79–98.

Celis, Karen. 2006. "Substantive Representation of Women: The Representation of Women's Interests and the Impact of Descriptive Representation in the Belgian Parliament (1900–1979)." *Journal of Women, Politics and Policy* 28 (2): 85–114.

Celis, Karen, Sarah Childs, Johanna Kantola, and Mona Lena Krook. 2008. "Rethinking the Substantive Representation of Women." *Representation* 44 (2): 99–110.

Chaney, Paul. 2006. "Critical Mass, Deliberation and the Substantive Representation of Women." *Political Studies* 54 (4): 691–714.

Chappell, Louise. 2000. "Interacting with the State: Feminist Strategies and Political Opportunities." *International Feminist Journal of Politics* 2 (2): 244–275.

Chappell, Louise. 2002. "The 'Femocrat' Strategy: Expanding the Repertoire of Feminist Activists." *Parliamentary Affairs* 55 (1): 85–98.

Charrad, Mounira M. 2001. *States and Women's Rights: The Making of Postcolonial Tunisia, Algeria, and Morocco*. Berkeley: University of California Press.

Childs, Sarah. 2004. *New Labour's Women MP's: Women Representing Women*. New York: Routledge.

Childs, Sarah, and Mona Lena Krook. 2006. "Should Feminists Give Up on Critical Mass? A Contingent Yes." *Politics and Gender* 2 (4): 522–530.

Childs, Sarah, and Julie Withey. 2006. "The Substantive Representation of Women: The Case of the Reduction of VAT on Sanitary Products." *Parliamentary Affairs* 59 (1): 10–23.

Clark, Janine Astrid, and Jillian Schwedler. 2003. "Who Opened the Window? Women's Activism in Islamist Parties." *Comparative Politics* 35 (3): 293–312.

Conover, Pamela Johnston. 1988. "Feminists and the Gender Gap." *Journal of Politics* 50 (4): 985–1010.

Cowell-Meyers, Kimberly. 2001. "Gender, Power, and Peace: A Preliminary Look at Women in the Northern Ireland Assembly." *Women and Politics* 23 (3): 55–88.

Crowley, Jocelyn Elise. 2004. "When Tokens Matter." *Legislative Studies Quarterly* 29 (1): 109–136.

Cunningham, Karla J. 2003. "Cross-Regional Trends in Female Terrorism." *Studies in Conflict and Terrorism* 26 (3): 171–195.

Dahlerup, Drude. 1988. "From a Small to a Large Minority: Women in Scandinavian Politics." *Scandinavian Political Studies* 11 (4): 275–297.

Dahlerup, Drude, ed. 2006. *Women, Quotas, and Politics*. New York: Routledge.

Daley, Caroline, and Melanie Nolan, eds. 1994. *Suffrage and Beyond: International Feminist Perspectives*. Auckland: Auckland University Press.

Darcy, R., Susan Welch, and Janet Clark. 1994. *Women, Elections, and Representation*. 2nd ed. Lincoln: University of Nebraska Press.

Davis, Rebecca Howard. 1997. *Women and Power in Parliamentary Democracies: Cabinet Appointments in Western Europe, 1968–1992*. Lincoln: University of Nebraska Press.

Dominelli, Lena, and Gudrun Jonsdottir. 1988. "Feminist Political Organization in Iceland: Some Reflections on the Experience of Kwenna Frambothid." *Feminist Review* 30: 36–60.

Dovi, Suzanne. 2002. "Preferable Descriptive Representatives: Will Just Any Woman, Black, or Latino Do?" *American Political Science Review* 96 (4): 729–743.

Duverger, Maurice. 1955. *The Political Role of Women*. Paris: UNESCO.

Elman, R. Amy. 2007. *Sexual Equality in an Integrated Europe: Virtual Equality*. New York: Palgrave.

Esping-Andersen, Gøsta. 1999. *Social Foundations of Post-industrial Economies*. New York: Oxford University Press.

Evans, Sara. 1979. *Personal Politics: The Roots of Women's Liberation in the Civil Rights Movement and the New Left*. New York: Knopf.

Foucault, Michel. 1995. *Discipline and Punish: The Birth of the Prison*. New York: Vintage.

Franceschet, Susan. 2005. *Women and Politics in Chile*. Boulder, Colo.: Lynne Rienner.

Franceschet, Susan, and Jennifer M. Piscopo. 2008. "Gender Quotas and Women's Substantive Representation: Lessons from Argentina." *Politics and Gender* 4 (3): 393–425.

Franzway, Suzanne, Dianne Court, and R. W. Connell. 1989. *Staking a Claim: Feminism, Bureaucracy and the State*. Cambridge: Polity.

Freeman, Jo. 2000. "Building a Base: Women in Local Party Politics." In *A Room at a Time: How Women Entered Party Politics*. Lanham, Md.: Rowman and Littlefield, 149–178.

Fuss, Diana. 1989. *Essentially Speaking: Feminism, Nature and Difference*. New York: Routledge.

Gay, Claudine, and Katherine Tate. 1998. "Doubly Bound: The Impact of Gender and Race on the Politics of Black Women." *Political Psychology* 19 (1): 169–184.

Gelb, Joyce. 1989. *Feminism and Politics: A Comparative Perspective*. Berkeley: University of California Press.

Goetz, Anne Marie, and Shireen Hassim, eds. 2003. *No Shortcuts to Power: African Women in Politics and Policy Making*. New York: Zed.

Grey, Sandra. 2002. "Does Size Matter? Critical Mass and New Zealand's Women MPs." *Parliamentary Affairs* 55 (1): 19–29.

Hancock, Ange-Marie. 2007. "When Multiplication Doesn't Equal Quick Addition: Examining Intersectionality as a Research Paradigm." *Perspectives on Politics* 5 (1): 63–79.

Harvey, Anna. 1998. *Votes without Leverage: Women in American Electoral Politics, 1920–1970*. New York: Cambridge University Press.

Hatem, Mervat F. 1992. "Economic and Political Liberalization in Egypt and the Demise of State Feminism." *International Journal of Middle East Studies* 24 (2): 231–251.

Hawkesworth, Mary. 2003. "Congressional Enactments of Race-Gender: Toward a Theory of Raced-Gendered Institutions." *American Political Science Review* 97 (4): 529–550.

Hernes, Helga. 1984. "Women and the Welfare State: The Transition from Private to Public Dependence." In *Patriarchy in a Welfare Society*, ed. Harriet Holter. Oslo: Universitetsforlaget.

Hernes, Helga. 1987. *Welfare State and Women Power*. Oslo: Norwegian University Press.

Htun, Mala. 2003. *Sex and the State: Abortion, Divorce, and the Family under Latin American Dictatorships and Democracies*. New York: Cambridge University Press.

Hughes, Melanie M. 2008. *Politics at the Intersection: A Cross-National Analysis of Minority Women's Legislative Representation*. Ph.D. Diss., Ohio State University.

Inglehart, Ronald, and Pippa Norris. 2000. "The Developmental Theory of the Gender Gap: Women's and Men's Voting Behavior in Global Perspective." *International Political Science Review* 21 (4): 441–463.

Inglehart, Ronald, and Pippa Norris. 2003. *Rising Tide: Gender Equality and Cultural Change around the World*. New York: Cambridge University Press.

Jahan, Rounaq. 1995. *The Elusive Agenda: Mainstreaming Women in Development*. London: Zed.

Jalalzai, Farida. 2008. "Women Rule: Shattering the Executive Glass Ceiling." *Politics and Gender* 4 (2): 205–231.

Josephson, Jyl. 2002. "The Intersectionality of Domestic Violence and Welfare in the Lives of Poor Women." *Journal on Poverty* 6 (1): 1–20.

Kantola, Johanna. 2006. *Feminists Theorize the State*. New York: Palgrave.

Kathlene, Lyn. 1995. "Position Power versus Gender Power: Who Holds the Floor?" In *Gender Power, Leadership, and Governance*, ed. Georgia Duerst-Lahti and Rita Mae Kelly. Ann Arbor: University of Michigan Press, 167–194.

Katzenstein, Mary Fainsod. 1998. "Protest Moves inside Institutions." In *Faithful and Fearless: Moving Feminist Protest inside the Church and Military*. Princeton, N.J.: Princeton University Press, 3–22.

Kaufmann, Karen M., and John R. Petrocik. 1999. "The Changing Politics of American Men: Understanding the Sources of the Gender Gap. *American Journal of Political Science* 43 (3): 864–887.

Kittilson, Miki Caul. 2006. *Challenging Parties, Changing Parliaments: Women and Elected Office in Contemporary Western Europe*. Columbus: Ohio State University Press.

Krook, Mona Lena. 2006. "Reforming Representation: The Diffusion of Candidate Gender Quotas Worldwide." *Politics and Gender* 2 (3): 303–327.

Krook, Mona Lena. 2009. *Quotas for Women in Politics: Gender and Candidate Selection Reform Worldwide*. New York: Oxford University Press.

Lawless, Jennifer L., and Richard L. Fox. 2005. *It Takes a Candidate: Why Women Don't Run for Office*. New York: Cambridge University Press.

Lewis, Jane. 1992. "Gender and the Development of Welfare Regimes." *Journal of European Social Policy* 2 (3): 159–173.

Lewis, Jane. 2001. "The Decline of the Male Breadwinner Model: Implications for Work and Care." *Social Politics* 8 (2): 152–169.

Lewis, Jane. 2002. "Gender and Welfare State Change." *European Societies* 4 (4): 331–357.

Lovenduski, Joni. 1986. *Women and European Politics: Contemporary Feminism and Public Policy*. Amherst: University of Massachusetts Press.

Lovenduski, Joni. 1993. "Introduction: The Dynamics of Gender and Party." In *Gender and Party Politics*, ed. Joni Lovenduski and Pippa Norris. Thousand Oaks, Calif.: Sage, 1–15.

Lovenduski, Joni, and Pippa Norris, eds. 1993. *Gender and Party Politics*. Thousand Oaks, Calif.: Sage.

Luciak, Ilja A. 2001. *After the Revolution: Gender and Democracy in El Salvador, Nicaragua, and Guatemala*. Baltimore: Johns Hopkins University Press.

Mackay, Fiona. 2001. *Love and Politics: Women Politicians and the Ethics of Care*. London: Continuum.

Mackay, Fiona. 2008. "'Thick' Conceptions of Substantive Representation: Women, Gender, and Political Institutions." *Representation* 44 (2): 125–139.

MacKinnon, Catharine A. 1989. *Toward a Feminist Theory of the State*. Cambridge, Mass.: Harvard University Press.

Mansbridge, Jane. 1999. "Should Blacks Represent Blacks and Women Represent Women? A Contingent 'Yes.'" *Journal of Politics* 61 (3): 628–657.

Matland, Richard E. 1998. "Women's Representation in National Legislatures: Developed and Developing Countries." *Legislative Studies Quarterly* 23 (1): 109–125.

McDonagh, Eileen. 2002. "Political Citizenship and Democratization: The Gender Paradox." *American Political Science Review* 96 (3): 535–552.

Mohanty, Chandra Talpade. 1988. "Under Western Eyes: Feminist Scholarship and Colonial Discourses." *Feminist Review* 30 (1): 61–88.

Molyneux, Maxine. 1985. "Mobilization without Emancipation? Women's Interests, the State and Revolution in Nicaragua." *Feminist Studies* 11 (2): 227–254.

Molyneux, Maxine. 1998. "Analysing Women's Movements." *Development and Change* 29 (2): 219–245.

Mondak, Jeffrey J., and Mary R. Anderson. 2004. "The Knowledge Gap: A Reexamination of Gender-Based Differences in Political Knowledge." *Journal of Politics* 66 (2): 492–512.

Morgan, Kimberly J. 2003. "The Politics of Mother's Employment: France in Comparative Perspective." *World Politics* 55 (2): 259–289.

Mueller, Carol M., ed. 1988. *The Politics of the Gender Gap: The Social Construction of Political Influence.* Thousand Oaks, Calif.: Sage.

Niven, David. 1998. "Party Elites and Women Candidates: The Shape of Bias." *Women and Politics* 19 (2): 57–80.

Norgren, Tiana. 2001. *Abortion before Birth Control: The Politics of Reproduction in Postwar Japan.* Princeton, N.J.: Princeton University Press.

Norris, Pippa. 1996. "Mobilising the 'Women's Vote': The Gender-Generation Gap in Voting Behaviour." *Parliamentary Affairs* 49 (2): 333–342.

Norris, Pippa, and Joni Lovenduski. 1995. *Political Recruitment: Gender, Race, and Class in the British Parliament.* New York: Cambridge University Press.

Norton, Noelle. 1995. "Women, It's Not Enough to Be Elected: Committee Position Makes a Difference." In *Gender Power, Leadership, and Governance,* ed. Georgia Duerst-Lahti and Rita Mae Kelly. Ann Arbor: University of Michigan Press, 115–140.

Okin, Susan Moller. 1979. *Women in Western Political Thought.* Princeton, N.J.: Princeton University Press.

Orloff, Ann Shola. 1993. "Gender and the Social Rights of Citizenship: The Comparative Analysis of Gender Relations and Welfare States." *American Sociological Review* 58 (3): 303–328.

Orloff, Ann Shola. 1996. "Gender in the Welfare State." *Annual Review of Sociology* 22: 51–78.

Outshoorn, Joyce, and Johanna Kantola, eds. 2007. *Changing State Feminism.* New York: Palgrave.

Pateman, Carole. 1994. "Three Questions about Womanhood Suffrage." In *Suffrage and Beyond: International Feminist Perspectives,* ed. Caroline Daley and Melanie Nolan. New York: New York University Press, 331–348.

Paxton, Pamela. 1997. "Women in National Legislatures: A Cross-National Analysis." *Social Science Research* 26: 442–464.

Paxton, Pamela, Melanie M. Hughes, and Jennifer L. Green. 2006. "The International Women's Movement and Women's Political Representation, 1893–2003." *American Sociological Review* 71 (6): 898–920.

Phillips, Anne. 1995. *The Politics of Presence: The Political Representation of Gender, Ethnicity, and Race.* New York: Oxford University Press.

Pitkin, Hanna Fenichel. 1967. *The Concept of Representation.* Berkeley: University of California Press.

Randall, Vicky, and Georgina Waylen, eds. 1998. *Gender, Politics, and the State.* New York: Routledge.

Reif, Linda L. 1986. "Women in Latin American Guerrilla Movements: A Comparative Perspective." *Comparative Politics* 18 (2): 147–169.

Reingold, Beth. 2000. *Representing Women: Sex, Gender, and Legislative Behavior in Arizona and California.* Chapel Hill: University of North Carolina Press.

Reynolds, Andrew. 1999. "Women in the Legislatures and Executives of the World: Knocking at the Highest Glass Ceiling." *World Politics* 51 (4): 547–572.

Roseneil, Sasha. 1995. *Disarming Patriarchy: Feminism and Political Action at Greenham.* Buckingham: Open University Press.

Ruggie, Mary. 1984. *The State and Working Women: A Comparative Study of Britain and Sweden.* Princeton, N.J.: Princeton University Press.

Rupp, Leila C. 1997. *Worlds of Women: The Making of an International Women's Movement.* Princeton, N.J.: Princeton University Press.

Sainsbury, Diane. 1996. *Gender, Equality, and Welfare States.* New York: Cambridge University Press.

Sainsbury, Diane. 2004. "Women's Political Representation in Sweden: Discursive Politics and Institutional Presence." *Scandinavian Political Studies* 27 (1): 65–87.

Sainsbury, Diane, ed. 1994. *Gendering Welfare States.* London: Sage.

Salmond, Rob. 2006. "Proportional Representation and Female Parliamentarians." *Legislative Studies Quarterly* 31 (2): 175–204.

Sarvasy, Wendy. 1992. "Beyond the Difference versus Equality Policy Debate: Postsuffrage Feminism, Citizenship, and the Quest for a Feminist Welfare State." *Signs* 17 (2): 329–362.

Schwartz, Helle. 2004. *Women's Representation in the Rwandan Parliament.* M.A. Thesis, University of Gothenburg.

Schwindt-Bayer, Leslie. 2006. "Still Supermadres? Gender and the Policy Priorities of Latin American Legislators." *American Journal of Political Science* 50 (3): 570–585.

Squires, Judith. 1999. *Gender and Political Theory.* Cambridge: Polity.

Squires, Judith. 2005. "Is Mainstreaming Transformative? Theorizing Mainstreaming in the Context of Diversity and Deliberation." *Social Politics* 12 (3): 366–388.

Squires, Judith. 2007. *The New Politics of Gender Equality.* London: Palgrave.

Stetson, Dorothy McBride, and Amy G. Mazur, eds. 1995. *Comparative State Feminism.* Thousand Oaks, Calif.: Sage.

Stokes, Wendy. 2005. *Women in Contemporary Politics.* Cambridge: Polity.

Strolovitch, Dara Z. 2006. "Do Interest Groups Represent the Disadvantaged? Advocacy at the Intersections of Race, Class, and Gender." *Journal of Politics* 68 (4): 894–910.

Studlar, Donley T., Ian McAllister, and Bernadette C. Hayes. 1998. "Explaining the Gender Gap in Voting: A Cross-National Analysis." *Social Science Quarterly* 79 (4): 779–798.

Swers, Michele L. 1998. "Are Women More Likely to Vote for Women's Issue Bills Than Their Male Colleagues?" *Legislative Studies Quarterly* 23 (3): 435–448.

Swers, Michelle L. 2002. *The Difference Women Make: The Policy Impact of Women in Congress*. Chicago: University of Chicago Press.

Swers, Michelle. 2005. "Connecting Descriptive and Substantive Representation: An Analysis of Sex Differences in Cosponsorship Activity." *Legislative Studies Quarterly* 30 (3): 407–433.

Tamerius, Karen L. 1995. "Sex, Gender, and Leadership in the Representation of Women." In *Gender Power, Leadership, and Governance,* ed. Georgia Duerst-Lahti and Rita Mae Kelly. Ann Arbor: University of Michigan Press.

Tarrow, Sidney. 1998. *Power in Movement: Social Movements and Contentious Politics.* 2nd ed. New York: Cambridge University Press.

Thomas, Sue. 1994. *How Women Legislate.* New York: Oxford University Press.

Threlfall, Monica. 1998. "State Feminism or Party Feminism? Feminist Politics and the Spanish Institute of Women." *European Journal of Women's Studies* 5 (1): 69–93.

Tremblay, Manon. 2003. "Women's Representational Role in Australia and Canada: The Impact of Political Context." *Australian Journal of Political Science* 38 (2): 215–238.

Tripp, Aili Mari. 2001. "The New Political Activism in Africa." *Journal of Democracy* 12 (3): 141–155.

Tripp, Aili Mari. 2003. "Women's Movements, Customary Law, and Land Rights in Africa: The Case of Uganda." *African Studies Quarterly* 7 (4): 1–19.

Tripp, Aili Mari, and Alice Kang. 2008. "The Global Impact of Quotas: The Fast Track to Female Representation." *Comparative Political Studies* 41 (3): 338–361.

True, Jacqui, and Michael Mintrom. 2001. "Transnational Networks and Policy Diffusion: The Case of Gender Mainstreaming." *International Studies Quarterly* 45: 27–57.

Verloo, Mieke. 2006. "Multiple Inequalities, Intersectionality, and the European Union." *European Journal of Women's Studies* 13 (3): 211–229.

Verloo, Mieke, ed. 2007. *Multiple Meanings of Gender Equality: A Critical Frame Analysis of Gender Policies in Europe.* Budapest: Central European University Press.

Weldon, S. Laurel. 2002. "Beyond Bodies: Institutional Sources of Representation for Women in Democratic Policymaking." *Journal of Politics* 64 (4): 1153–1174.

Weldon, S. Laurel. 2006. "The Structure of Intersectionality: A Comparative Politics of Gender." *Politics and Gender* 2 (2): 235–248.

Wiliarty, Sarah Elise. 2001. *Bringing Women to the Party: The Christian Democratic Union (CDU) as a Corporatist Catch-All Party.* Ph.D. Diss., University of California, Berkeley.

Williams, Melissa. 1998. *Voice, Trust, and Memory: Marginalized Groups and the Failure of Liberal Representation.* Princeton, N.J.: Princeton University Press.

Wolbrecht, Christina. 2000. *The Politics of Women's Rights: Parties, Positions, and Change.* Princeton, N.J.: Princeton University Press.

Woodward, Alison. 2003. "European Gender Mainstreaming: Promises and Pitfalls of Transformative Policy." *Review of Policy Research* 20 (1): 65–88.

Yoon, Mi Yung. 2004. "Explaining Women's Legislative Representation in Sub-Saharan Africa." *Legislative Studies Quarterly* 29 (3): 447–466.

Young, Iris Marion. 2000. *Inclusion and Democracy.* New York: Oxford University Press.

Young, Lisa. 2000. *Feminists and Party Politics.* Vancouver: UBC Press.

Yuval-Davis, Nira. 2006. "Intersectionality and Feminist Politics." *European Journal of Women's Studies* 13 (3): 193–209.

Part I

WOMEN AND SOCIAL MOVEMENTS

This section contains readings on women and social movements, focusing on women's participation in women's and feminist movements, as well as women's involvement in other kinds of social movements. The section begins with a classic article on "women's interests" in social movement organizing (Molyneux 1985). It is followed by six other readings that map how the study of women and social movements has subsequently developed, focusing on broad patterns and variations in women's mobilization (Beckwith 2000), the moments when women organize as women in times of democratic transition (Baldez 2003), women's presence and struggles inside male-dominated institutions as a type of social movement activity (Katzenstein 1998), inequalities among advantaged and disadvantaged subgroups of women in interest group organizing (Strolovitch 2006), shifts in women's movement discourses and practices as a result of globalization and increasing contacts among women's groups across national borders (Alvarez 2000), and innovations in the repertoires of women's social movement participation to include terrorist groups (Cunningham 2003).

Maxine Molyneux studies women's mobilization in the Nicaraguan revolution that brought socialists to power in the 1970s. To understand why women would get involved in struggles that do not appear to further their "emancipation," she distinguishes between women's "practical" and "strategic" interests. She argues that practical interests arise inductively from the concrete conditions of women's positioning within the sexual division of labor, while strategic interests are derived deductively from the analysis of women's subordination and the formulation of an alternative set of arrangements to those which exist. Practical interests tend to emerge in response to immediate needs in women's daily lives, like access to food, shelter, and water; as such, they will vary significantly across countries and over time. Strategic interests, in contrast, require a level of feminist or gendered consciousness in order to be formulated, like demands for day care, reproductive choice, and freedom from wage discrimination. This distinction constitutes an initial attempt to understand why women mobilize as women and when and where they do. It has subsequently been used as a jumping off point for scholars who study women and social movements, as well as those concerned with theorizing the concept of "women's interests."

In a wide-ranging review of comparative research on women's movements, *Karen Beckwith* argues against conflating women's movements, feminist movements, and women in social movements. She then identifies four crucial issues to consider when analyzing individual movements: relationships between women's movements and political parties, "double militancy" as a potentially distinctive collective identity problem for women's movement activists, the extent to which political opportunities for women's movements are or can be gendered, and relationships between women's movements and the state. To better understand how and why women engage in protest, *Lisa Baldez* analyzes women's mobilization in the context of democratic transition in Chile, Brazil, East Germany, and Poland. She argues that in the first three cases, but not the fourth, women perceived moments of political realignment as uniquely gendered opportunities: building on existing formal and informal networks among women, as well as inspired by women's groups abroad, they came together across other dividing lines to organize as women against the regime in power. However, once opposition parties incorporated women's movement demands into their agendas, women often ceased to mobilize on this basis.

Critical of tendencies to associate social movements exclusively with civil society groups, *Mary Fainsod Katzenstein* observes that a great deal of movement activity has now moved inside institutions. Focusing on women in two very male-dominated institutions, the U.S. military and the Catholic church, she explores how feminists have pursued different political objectives and used various political strategies to effect changes within institutions, for example by spurring debates over hiring and promotion, rape and harassment, child care, and workplace benefits. Their participation in formal and informal networks of support, she argues, has previously not been associated but could be reframed in line with women's movement activity. Offering a different line of critique, *Dara Z. Strolovitch* seeks to establish whether interest group claims to speak for "all women" in fact reflect a diversity of women's views and experiences. She examines the policy advocacy of national organizations that represent marginalized groups to explore the degree to which they advocate on behalf of advantaged versus disadvantaged subgroups of their membership. Among women's groups, she finds that organizations are substantially less active on issues affecting disadvantaged subgroups than they are when it comes to issues affecting the advantaged subgroups. The analysis reveals how gender interacts with race and class to structure and perpetuate inequalities among female activists who are otherwise committed to improving the status of women as a group.

Calling attention to recent innovations in women's social movement activities, *Sonia E. Alvarez* examines links between transnational organizing and local women's movements in Latin America. She notes that through transnational contacts two new logics of women's movement organizing have emerged: an internationalist identity-solidarity logic, which provides a means for (re)constructing subaltern or marginalized identities and establishing personal and strategic bonds of solidarity with others who share locally stigmatized values, and a transnational nongovernmental organization advocacy logic, which involves organizing across borders in an effort to expand formal rights or affect public policy. *Karla J. Cunningham,* in turn, surveys women's involvement in terrorist groups, observing that while women have historically participated in terrorist groups in low numbers, female involvement is widening ideologically, logically, and regionally. She attributes these changes to several trends: new contextual pressures that drive terrorist organizations to recruit women while intensifying women's motivations for joining these groups, changes in societal controls over women that may make them more willing to engage in political violence, and operational imperatives for gaining strategic advantages over adversaries through "strategic innovation." Together, these readings reveal that women's social movement participation is diverse in terms of motivations, contexts, and tactics, with ongoing debates over the identities and needs of women as a group.

Chapter 2

MOBILIZATION WITHOUT EMANCIPATION? WOMEN'S INTERESTS, THE STATE, AND REVOLUTION IN NICARAGUA

Maxine Molyneux

. . . This [chapter] focuses on the Nicaraguan revolution and its progress since the seizure of state power by the Sandinistas in July 1979, in order to consider the proposition that women's interests are not served by socialist revolutions. The [chapter] examines how women are affected by government policies in the aftermath of a successful revolutionary seizure of power in which they participated on a mass scale. The first part of the discussion reviews some of the theoretical questions raised by this debate, particularly the matter of "women's interests." The second section describes and interprets the policies that the Sandinista state has adopted in relation to women in order to determine how women's interests are represented within the Sandinista state.[1] Women in Nicaragua have certainly not achieved full equality, let alone emancipation. But the argument set forth here takes issue with the view that women's interests have been denied representation or have been deliberately marginalized through the operations of "patriarchy."[2]

Women's Interests

The concept of women's interests is central to feminist evaluations of socialist societies and indeed social policies in general. Most feminist critiques of socialist regimes rest on an implicit or explicit assumption that there is a given entity, women's interests, that is ignored or overridden by policymakers. However, the question of these interests is far more complex than is frequently assumed. . . .

The political pertinence of the issue of whether states, revolutionary or otherwise, are successful in securing the interests of social groups and classes is generally considered to be twofold. First, it is supposed to enable prediction or at least political calculation about a given government's capacity to maintain the support of the groups it claims to represent. Second, it is assumed that the nature of the state can be deduced from the interests it is seen to be advancing.[3] Thus the proposition that a state is a "worker's state," a capitalist state, or even a "patriarchal state" is commonly tested by investigating how a particular class or group has fared under the government in question.

However, when we try to deploy similar criteria in the case of women a number of problems arise. If, for example, we conclude that because the Sandinistas seem to have done relatively little to remove the means by which gender subordination is reproduced, that women's interests have not been represented in the state and hence women are likely to turn against it, we are making a number of assumptions: that gender interests are the equivalent of women's interests, that gender is the principal determinant of women's interests, and that women's subjectivity, real or potential, is structured uniquely through gender effects. It is, by extension, also supposed that women have certain common interests by virtue of their gender, and that these interests are primary for women. It follows then that transclass unity among women is to some degree given by this commonality of interests.[4]

Although it is true that at a certain level of abstraction women can be said to have some interests in common, there is no consensus over what these interests are or how they are to be formulated. This is in part because there is no theoretically adequate and universally applicable causal explanation of women's subordination from which a general account of women's interests can be derived. Women's oppression is recognized as being multicausal in origin and mediated through a variety of different structures, mechanisms, and levels which may vary considerably across space and time. There is therefore continuing debate over the appropriate site of feminist struggle and over whether it is more important to focus attempts at change on objective or subjective elements, "men" or "structures"; laws, institutions, or interpersonal power relations—or all of them simultaneously. Because a general conception of interests (one which has political validity) must be derived from a theory of how the subordination of a determinate social category is secured, it is difficult to see how it would overcome the two most salient and intractable features of women's oppression—its multicausal nature, and the extreme variability of its forms of existence across class and nation. These factors vitiate attempts to speak *without qualification* of a unitary category "women" with a set of already constituted interests common to it. A theory of interests that has an application to the debate about women's capacity to struggle for and benefit from social change must begin by recognizing difference rather than by assuming homogeneity.

It is clear from the extensive feminist literature on women's oppression that a number of different conceptions prevail of what women's interests are, and that these in turn rest implicitly or explicitly upon different theories of the causes of gender inequality. For the purpose of clarifying the issues discussed here, three conceptions of women's interests, which are frequently conflated, will be delineated. These are women's interests, strategic gender interests, and practical gender interests.

Women's Interests

Although present in much political and theoretical discourse, the concept of women's interests is, for the reasons given earlier, a highly contentious one. Because women are positioned within their societies through a variety of different means—among them, class, ethnicity, and gender—the interests they have as a group are similarly shaped in complex and sometimes conflicting ways. It is therefore difficult, if not impossible, to generalize about the interests of women. Instead, we need to specify how the various categories of women might be affected differently, and act differently on account of the particularities of their social positioning and their chosen identities. However, this is not to deny that women may have certain general interests in common. These can be called gender interests to differentiate them from the false homogeneity imposed by the notion of women's interests.

Strategic Gender Interests

Gender interests are those that women (or men, for that matter) may develop by virtue of their social positioning through gender attributes. Gender interests can be either strategic or practical, each being derived in a different way and each involving differing implications for women's subjectivity. Strategic interests are derived in the first instance deductively, that is, from the analysis of women's subordination and from the formulation of an alternative, more satisfactory set of arrangements to those which exist. These ethical and theoretical criteria assist in the formulation of strategic objectives to overcome women's subordination, such as the abolition of the sexual division of labor, the alleviation of the burden of domestic labor and childcare, the removal of institutionalized forms of discrimination, the attainment of political equality, the establishment of freedom of choice over childbearing, and the adoption of adequate measures against male violence and control over women. These constitute what might be called strategic gender interests, and they are the ones most frequently considered by feminists to be women's "real" interests. The demands that are formulated on this basis are usually termed "feminist" as is the level of consciousness required to struggle effectively for them.[5]

Practical Gender Interests

Practical gender interests are given inductively and arise from the concrete conditions of women's positioning within the gender division of labor. In contrast to strategic gender interests, these are formulated by the women who are themselves within these positions rather than through external interventions. Practical interests are usually a response to an immediate perceived need, and they do not generally entail a strategic goal such as women's emancipation or gender equality. Analyses of female collective action frequently deploy this conception of interests to explain the dynamic and goals of women's participation in social action. For example, it has been argued that by virtue of their place within the sexual division of labor as those primarily responsible for their household's daily welfare, women have a special interest in domestic provision and public welfare.[6] When governments fail to provide these basic needs, women withdraw their support; when the livelihood of their families—especially their children—is threatened, it is women who form the phalanxes of bread rioters, demonstrators, and petitioners. It is clear, however, from this example that gender and class are closely intertwined; it is, for obvious reasons, usually poor women who are so readily mobilized by economic necessity. Practical interests, therefore, cannot be assumed to be innocent of class effects. Moreover, these practical interests do not in themselves challenge the prevailing forms of gender subordination, even though they arise directly out of them. An understanding of this is vital in understanding the capacity or failure of states or organizations to win the loyalty and support of women.

The pertinence of these ways of conceptualizing interests for an understanding of women's consciousness is a complex matter, but three initial points can be made. First, the relationship between what we have called strategic gender interests and women's recognition of them and desire to realize them cannot be assumed. Even the lowest common denominator of interests which might seem uncontentious and of universal applicability (such as complete equality with men, control over reproduction, and greater personal autonomy and independence from men) are not readily accepted by all women. This is not just because of "false consciousness" as is frequently supposed—although this can be a factor—but because such changes realized in a piecemeal fashion could threaten the short-term practical interests of some women, or entail a cost in the loss of forms of protection which are not then compensated for in some way. Thus the formulation of strategic interests can only be effective as a form of intervention when full account is taken of these practical interests. Indeed, it is the politicization of these practical interests and their transformation into strategic interests that women can identify with and support which constitutes a central aspect of feminist political practice.

Second, the way in which interests are formulated—whether by women or political organizations—will vary considerably across space and time and may be shaped in different ways by prevailing political and discursive influences. This is important to bear in mind when considering the problem of internationalism and the limits and possibilities of cross-cultural solidarity. Finally, because women's interests are significantly broader than gender interests, and are shaped to a considerable degree by class factors, women's unity and cohesion on gender issues cannot be assumed. Although they can form the basis of unity around a common program, such unity has to be constructed—it is never given. Moreover, even when unity exists it is always conditional, and the historical record suggests that it tends to collapse under the pressure of acute class conflict. It is also threatened by differences of race, ethnicity, and nationality. It is therefore difficult to argue, as some feminists have done, that gender issues are primary for women, at all times.[7]

This general problem of the conditionality of women's unity and the fact that gender issues are not necessarily primary is nowhere more clearly illustrated than by the example of revolutionary upheaval. In such situations, gender issues are frequently displaced by class conflict, principally because although women may suffer discrimination on the basis of gender and may be aware that they do, they nonetheless suffer differentially according to their social class. These differences crucially affect attitudes toward revolutionary change, especially if this is in the direction of socialism. This does not mean that, because gender interests are an insufficient basis for unity among women in the context of class polarization, they disappear. Rather, they become more specifically attached to and defined by social class.

An awareness of the complex issues involved serves to guard against any simple treatment of the question of whether a state is or is not acting in the interests of women, that is, whether all or any of these interests are represented within the state. Before any analysis can be attempted it is necessary to specify in what sense the term "interest" is being deployed. A state may gain the support of women by satisfying either their immediate practical demands or certain class interests, or both. It may do this without advancing their strategic objective interests at all. However, the claims of such a state to be supporting women's *emancipation* could not be substantiated merely on the evidence that it maintained women's support on the basis of representing some of their more practical or class interests. With these distinctions in mind, I shall turn now to the Nicaraguan revolution, and consider how the Sandinistas have formulated women's interests, and how women have fared under their rule.

The Nicaraguan Revolution

The Nicaraguan revolution represents an extreme case of the problems of constructing a socialist society in the face of poverty and underdevelopment, counterrevolution, and external intervention. . . . The forces which overthrew Anastasio Somoza in July 1979 distinguished themselves by their commitment to a socialism based on the principles of mixed economy, nonalignment, and political pluralism. An opposition was allowed to operate within certain clearly defined limits, and more than 60 percent of the economy remained in private hands, despite the nationalization of Somocista assets. "Sandinismo" promised to produce a different kind of socialism, one that consolidated the revolutionary overthrow of the old regime through the creation of a new army and its control of other organs of state power, but was more democratic, independent, and "moderate" than many other Third World socialisms had been. Through its triumph and its commitment to socialist pluralism, Nicaragua became a symbol of hope to socialists, not only in Latin America, but around the world as well. . . .

The Nicaraguan revolution also gave hope to those who supported women's liberation, for here too, the Sandinistas were full of promise. The revolution occurred in the period after the upsurge of the "new feminism" of the late sixties, at a time when Latin American women were mobilizing around feminist demands in countries like Mexico, Peru, and Brazil. The Sandinistas' awareness of the limitations of orthodox Marxism encouraged some to believe that a space would be allowed for the development of new social movements such as feminism. Some members of the leadership seemed aware of the importance of women's liberation and of the need for it in Nicaragua. The early issues of *Somos AMNLAE*, one of two newspapers of the women's organization, contained articles about feminist issues and addressed some of the ongoing debates within Western feminism. Unlike many of its counterparts elsewhere, the FSLN, the revolutionary party, did not denounce feminism as a "counterrevolutionary diversion," and some women officials had even gone on record expressing enthusiasm for its ideals. . . .

Once they were in power, these hopes were not disappointed. Only weeks after the triumph, article 30 of decree number 48 banned the media's exploitation of women as sex objects, and women FSLN cadres found themselves in senior positions in the newly established state as ministers, vice-ministers, and regional coordinators of the party. In September, AMPRONAC was transformed into the Luisa Amanda Espinosa Association of Nicaraguan Women (AMNLAE) to advance the cause of women's emancipation and carry through the program of revolutionary transformation. Public meetings were adorned with the slogan "No revolution without women's emancipation: no emancipation without revolution." The scene seemed to be set for an imaginative and distinctive strategy for women's emancipation in Nicaragua.

But after the first few years in power, the FSLN's image abroad began to lose some of its distinctive appeal. The combined pressures of economic scarcity, counterrevolution, and military threat were taking their toll on the Sandinista experiment in economic and political pluralism, placing at risk the ideals it sought to defend. In the face of mounting pressure from U.S.-backed counterrevolutionaries in 1982, a further casualty of these difficulties appeared to be the Sandinista commitment to the emancipation of women.

AMNLAE, the women's union, reduced its public identification with "feminism" and spoke increasingly of the need to promote women's interests in the context of the wider struggle. Already, at its constitutive assembly at the end of 1981, it had defined its role as enabling women to integrate themselves as a decisive force in the revolution. AMNLAE's first priority was given as "defense of the revolution." But it was only in 1982, as the crisis deepened and the country went onto a war footing that the priority really did become (as it had to) the revolution's survival, with all efforts directed to military defense. AMNLAE became actively involved in recruiting women to the army and militia. Under such circumstances it is hardly surprising that the efforts to promote women's emancipation were scaled down or redefined. Emancipation was to come about as a by-product of making and defending the revolution. Yet, even before the crisis deepened, little had been achieved to tangibly improve the position of women, and FSLN cadres considered that progress in this area was necessarily limited. . . .

Sandinista Policy with Regard to Women

. . . Most contemporary states have enshrined within their constitutions, or equivalents, some phrase which opposes discrimination on the grounds of race, sex, or creed. What distinguishes socialist states such as Nicaragua is their recognition of the specificity of women's oppression and their support for measures that combine a concern to promote equality with a desire to remove some of the obstacles to achieving it. Some of the strategic interests of women are therefore recognized and, in theory, are advanced as part of the process of socialist transformation. In its essentials, the FSLN's theoretical and practical approach to women's emancipation bears some resemblance to that found in those state socialist countries that espouse Marxist theory. They share an approach that links gender oppression to class oppression and believe women's emancipation can only be achieved with the creation of a new, socialist society and with the further development of the productive capacity of the economy. . . .

According to official views and party documents, this involves implementing the principles of the classic socialist guidelines for the emancipation of women. . . . Some of these guidelines have been incorporated into AMNLAE's official program which lists its main goals as (1) defending the revolution; (2) promoting women's political and ideological awareness and advancing their social, political, and economic participation in the revolution; (3) combating legal and other institutional inequalities; (4) encouraging women's cultural and technical advancement and entry into areas of employment traditionally reserved for men, combined with opposing discrimination in employment; (5) fostering respect for domestic labor and organizing childcare services for working women; and (6) creating and sustaining links of international solidarity. The 1969 program of the FSLN also made special mention of eliminating prostitution and other "social vices," helping the abandoned working mother, and protecting the illegitimate child. Each of these issues has been addressed in subsequent legislation and social policy. There is also official concern for allowing greater freedom of choice to women in the matter of childbearing, by making contraceptives more widely available and by not prosecuting those who carry out abortions, except in a few cases.[8]

Although these goals, if realized, would be insufficient to achieve the complete emancipation of women, based as they are on a somewhat narrow definition of gender interests, they do embody some strategic concerns, in that they are directed toward eliminating some of the fundamental inequalities between the sexes. However, progress in Nicaragua has so far been uneven. There is official support for the implementation of the full program, but only some of the guidelines have been translated into policy and then only with limited effect. . . . The greatest benefits that women received were from the welfare programs and from certain areas of legal reform. Women also felt the impact of change in the realm of political mobilization in which they played an increasingly active part. Despite these advances it was evident that the gap between intention and realization was considerable.

. . . It is clear that the FSLN was able to implement only those parts of the program for women's emancipation that coincided with its general goals, enjoyed popular support, and were realizable without arousing strong opposition. The policies from which women derived some benefit were pursued principally because they fulfilled some wider goal or goals, whether these were social welfare, development, social equality, or political mobilization in defense of the revolution. This is, in effect, what the Sandinistas meant by the need to locate women's emancipation within the overall struggle for social reform and survival against intensifying external pressure.

This kind of qualified support for women's emancipation is found in most of the states that have pursued socialist development policies. Indeed, the guidelines that form the basis of their program for women's emancipation (discussed earlier) all have universalistic as well as particularistic goals, in which the former is the justification for the latter. Thus, women's emancipation is not just dependent on the realization of the wider goals, but it is pursued insofar as it *contributes to* the realization of those goals. There is therefore a unity of purpose between the goals of women's emancipation and the developmental and social goals of revolutionary states.[9]

Revolutionary governments tend to see the importance of reforming the position of women in the first period of social and economic transformation in terms of helping to accomplish at least three goals: to extend the base of the government's political support, to increase the size or quality of the active labor force, and to help harness the family more securely to the process of social reproduction. The first aim, of expanding or maintaining the power base of the state, is pursued by attempting to draw women into the new political organizations such as the women's, youth, and labor unions; the party; and neighborhood associations. There is a frequently expressed fear that unless women are politicized they may not cooperate with the process of social transformation. Women are seen as potentially and actually more conservative than men by virtue of their place within the social division of labor, that is, as primarily located outside the sphere of production. More positively, women are also regarded as crucial agents of revolutionary change whose radicalization challenges ancient customs and privileges within the family, and has important effects on the next generation, through the impact on their children. The political mobilization of women supposes some attempt to persuade them that their interests as well as more universal concerns (national, humanitarian, and so forth) are represented by the state.[10]

The second way in which the mobilization of women is regarded as a necessary part of the overall strategy is more directly relevant to the economy. The education of women and their entry into employment increases and improves the available labor supply, which is a necessary concomitant of any successful development program. In most underdeveloped countries, women form only a small percentage of the economically active population (usually less than 20 percent), and although the figures tend to conceal the real extent of women's involvement, by registering mainly formal rather than informal activities, the work they do is frequently unpaid and underproductive, confined to family concerns in workshops or in the fields, and subject to the authority of male kin. Government policies have therefore emphasized the need for both education and a restructuring of employment to make better use of the work capacities of the female population.

The third aim is to bring the family more into line with planning objectives and to place it at the center of initiatives aimed at social reconstruction. Postrevolutionary governments regard women as key levers in harnessing the family more securely to state goals, whether these be of an economic or an ideological kind. The prerevolutionary family has to be restructured to make it more compatible with the developmental goals of revolutionary governments. Once this has been accomplished, the reformed family is expected to function as an important agent of socialization, inculcating the new revolutionary values into the next generation. Women are seen as crucial in both of these processes. . . .

If we disaggregate women's interests and consider how different categories of women fared since 1979, it is clear that the majority of women in Nicaragua were positively affected by the government's redistribution policies. This is so even though fundamental structures of gender inequality were not dismantled. In keeping with the socialist character of the government, policies were targeted in favor of the poorest sections of the population and focused on basic needs provision in the areas of health, housing, education, and food subsidies. In the short span of only five years, the Sandinistas reduced the illiteracy rate from over 50 percent to 13 percent; doubled the number of educational establishments; increased school enrollment; eradicated a number of mortal diseases; provided the population with basic healthcare services; and achieved more in their housing program than Somoza had in his entire period of rule.[11] In addition, the land reform canceled peasants' debts and gave thousands of rural workers their own parcels of land or secured them stable jobs on the state farms and cooperatives.[12]

These policies have been of vital importance in gaining the support of poor women. According to government statistics, women form more than 60 percent of the poorest Nicaraguans; in the poorest category in Managua (incomes of less than 600 cordobas per month), there are 354 women for each 100 men.[13] It is these women, by virtue of their *class* position, who have been the direct beneficiaries of Sandinista redistributive efforts, as have their male counterparts. Of course not all women were to benefit from these programs; women whose economic interests lay in areas adversely affected by Sandinista economic policies (imports, luxury goods, and so forth) have suffered some financial loss, as have most women from the privileged classes as a result of higher taxation. It is also the case that while poor women benefited from the welfare provisions, they were also the most vulnerable to the pressures of economic constraints and especially to shortages in basic provisions.[14]

In terms of *practical* gender interests, these redistributive policies have also had gender as well as class effects. By virtue of their place within the sexual division of labor, women are disproportionately responsible for childcare and family health, and they are particularly concerned with housing and food provision. The policy measures directed at alleviating the situation in these areas have, not surprisingly, elicited a positive response from the women affected by them as borne out by the available research into the popularity of the government. Many of the campaigns mounted by AMNLAE have been directed at resolving some of the practical problems women face, as is exemplified by its mother and child healthcare program, or by its campaign aimed at encouraging women to conserve domestic resources to

make the family income stretch further and thus avoid pressure building up over wage demands or shortages.[15] A feature of this kind of campaign is its recognition of women's practical interests, but in accepting the division of labor and women's subordination within it, it may entail a denial of their strategic interests.

With respect to strategic interests, the acid test of whether women's emancipation is on the political agenda or not, the progress which was made is modest but significant. Legal reform, especially in the area of the family, has confronted the issue of relations between the sexes and of male privilege, by attempting to end a situation in which most men are able to evade responsibility for the welfare of their families, and become liable for a contribution paid in cash, in-kind, or in the form of services. This also enabled the issue of domestic labor to be politicized in the discussions of the need to share this work equally among all members of the family. The land reform encouraged women's participation and leadership in cooperatives and gave women work for their wages and titles to land. There has also been an effort to establish childcare agencies such as nurseries, and preschool services. Some attempts have been made to challenge female stereotypes not just by outlawing the exploitation of women in the media, but also by promoting some women to positions of responsibility and emphasizing the importance of women in the militia and reserve battalions.[16] And finally there has been a sustained effort to mobilize women around their own needs through the women's union, and there has been discussion of some of the questions of strategic interest, although this has been sporadic and controversial.

To sum up, it is difficult to discuss socialist revolutions in terms of an undifferentiated conception of women's interests and even more difficult to conclude that these interests have not been represented in state policymaking. The Sandinista record on women is certainly uneven, and it is as yet too early to make any comprehensive assessment of it, especially while it confronts increasing political, economic, and military pressures. Nonetheless, it is clear that the Sandinistas have gone further than most Latin American governments (except Cuba) in recognizing both the strategic and practical interests of women and have brought about substantial improvements in the lives of many of the most deprived. . . .

Notes

1. This discussion necessarily leaves out the specific situation of women in Nicaragua's ethnic minorities. The Miskito Indian communities in particular require separate consideration because they have, and have had historically, a very different relationship to central government than that which is described here.

2. Male power—whether institutionalized or interpersonal—and the essentialist or naturalist arguments which legitimate it do play a part in the explanation of women's continuing subordination after revolutionary upheavals; but the importance of such factors should not be exaggerated. There are differing definitions of patriarchy, but most of them agree that patriarchy describes a power relation existing between the sexes, exercised by men over women and institutionalized within various social relations and practices, including law, family, and education.

3. There is a third usage of the term "interest" found in Marxism which explains collective action in terms of some intrinsic property of the actors and/or the relations within which they are inscribed. Thus, class struggle is ultimately explained as an effect of the relations of production. This conception has been shown to rest on essentialist assumptions and provides an inadequate account of social action. For a critique of this notion, see Edward Benton, *Realism, Power, and Objective Philosophy* (Cambridge: Cambridge University Press, 1982); and Barry Hindess, "Power, Interests, and the Outcome of Struggles," *Sociology* 16 (1982): 498–511.

4. Zillah Eisenstein, editor of *Capitalist Patriarchy and the Case for Socialist Feminism* (New York: Monthly Review Press, 1978), has produced a sophisticated version of the argument that women constitute a "sexual class" and that for women, gender issues are primary. See her "Women as a Sexual Class" (paper presented at "A Marx Centenary Conference," Winnipeg, Canada, 1983).

5. It is precisely around these issues, which also have an ethical significance, that the theoretical and political debate must focus. The list of strategic gender interests noted here is not exhaustive, but is merely exemplary.

6. See, for example, Temma Kaplan, "Female Consciousness and Collective Action: The Case of Barcelona, 1910–1918," *Signs* 7 (Spring 1982): 546–66; and Olwen Hufton, "Women in Revolution, 1789–1796," *Past and Present*, no. 53 (1971): 90–108.

7. This is the position of some radical feminist groups in Europe.

8. In the first three years, only one case had been tried and this was of an abortionist accused of gross malpractice.

9. For a fuller discussion of socialist policies with regard to women and the family, see my "Women's Emancipation under Socialism: A Model for the Third World?" *World Development* 9 (1981): 1019–37. Also published in *Monthly Review* 34 (July 1982): 56–100; and in Magdalena Leon, ed., *Sociedad, Subordinación y Feminismo* (Colombia: ACEP, 1982).

10. This viewpoint has to be compared and contrasted with many nationalist movements that call for the sacrifice of women's interests (and those of other oppressed groups) in the interests of the nation.

11. See Walker, ed., *Nicaragua Five Years On* (New York: Praeger, 1985).

12. For a discussion of the agrarian reform and its effects on women, see Carmen Diana Deere, "Co-operative Development and Women's Participation in Nicaragua's Agrarian Reform," *American Journal of Agrarian Economics* (December 1983).

13. Data are from the Instituto Nacional de Estadisticas y Censos, December 1981.

14. Basic provisions were rationed and heavily subsidized until 1983 when it became increasingly difficult to peg prices due to mounting economic pressures.

15. AMNLAE argued that the implications of women conserving resources under a socialist government were radically different from those under capitalism because in the first case the beneficiaries were the people, and in the second, private interests.

16. Although there are no women in the nine-member junta that constitutes the FSLN leadership, the vice-president of the council of state (until the elections of November 1984) was a woman, and women assumed many key positions in the party at the regional level. On three occasions after 1979, women filled ministerial posts.

Chapter 3

BEYOND COMPARE?
WOMEN'S MOVEMENTS IN
COMPARATIVE PERSPECTIVE

Karen Beckwith

. . . A major conceptual problem for the study of women's movements is that the literature has not yet produced a definition of women's movements that can be employed for comparative political purposes. In part this is the result of how quickly and with what magnitude an international body of comparative women's movement literature, case-specific and based on field research, has emerged; initial working definitions guided research in progress and have produced a range of competing definitions that have yet to be assessed and culled. The lack of definitional agreement and clarity is most evident in the research on nations where women's movements, and particularly feminist movements, have most recently emerged. . . .

This range of definitions of women's movements encompasses individual actions as well as collective actions, collective endeavor with diffuse and generally human rights content or with specifically feminist content, a sense of accountability, use of women's social service agencies, and women's rights organizations. The collective range of this definitional continuum, although admirably inclusive, marks a difficulty in the broader range of definitional attempts: the impulse to identify (any) women's activism as part of a women's movement and an eagerness to recuperate (almost any) women's activism as feminist. In definitional terms alone, overly inclusive conceptualizations of women's movements obscure the general, persistent, enduring activism of women of different classes and races across the past 100 years, much of which has not been located in what might technically be referred to as women's

movements but was instead women's activism in other political movements more accurately identified, for example, as class-based movements or nationalist movements.

. . . The specific content of women's issues and women's gendered experiences will, of course, vary across national and state structures, cultural contexts, and women's intersecting classed, racialized, and other experiences and identities. In definitional terms, "women's movements" can encompass right-wing or antifeminist women's movements as well as progressive, left-wing, or feminist women's movements, but exclude women's activism in other social movements (e.g., women in nationalist movements that lack gender content and where men predominate in leadership roles and decision making). In this regard, "women's movements" are distinguished from "women in movement."

Feminist movements are distinguished by their challenge of patriarchy. Feminist movements share a gendered power analysis of women's subordination and contest political, social, and other power arrangements of domination and subordination on the basis of gender. Note that this definition is silent on other power inequalities, leaving open the conceptual possibility of feminist movements that are highly class-constrained, racist, or nationalist. The extent to which feminist movements challenge inequalities and powerlessness of other subordinated groups is an empirical question. Our capacity to understand how feminist movements emerge, how feminists mobilize, their strategic decisions, their coalition possibilities, and their relationship to the state will be strengthened to the extent that we do not privilege feminist movements, at least in definitional terms, as distinctively inclusive, just, antiracist, or typical of all women's movements. . . .

Comparative Women's Movement Research: Advances and Opportunities

. . . The arenas of well-developed research on women's movements include: (1) the relationship between women's movements and political parties; (2) "double militancy" for women's movement activists; (3) women's movements' agency and opportunities, including the extent to which political opportunities for women's movements are (or can be) gendered; and (4) the relationship between women's movements and the state. . . .

Women's Movements and Political Parties

One of the key issues for feminist movements, and for comparative women's movements scholarship, is the conditions under which political parties as institutional carrying agents for advancing women's issues and improving women's status. . . .

A substantial body of scholarly literature focuses on women's movements across multiple political party types, party systems, and government v. opposition parties. The relationship of feminist movements to political parties of the left is well-documented for late 20th-century Western nations. Where women's movements have made alliances with political parties, they have done so overwhelmingly with parties of the left.[1] Women's movements have been more successful in pursuing policy goals through socialist, communist, social democratic, and labor parties than through other types of parties; similarly, parties of the left have generally evidenced higher numbers and percentages of female nominees for national legislatures.[2] This is not to say, however, that these alliances have been more successful for feminist movements than have other political strategies; indeed, the evidence concerning the success of feminist movements working through left-wing parties is mixed. Political parties of the left have served to advance feminist policy issues (Beckwith

1987; della Porta 2000; Threlfall 1996; Valiente 2000) but have also failed to do so, containing and controlling feminist movement activists (Jenson 1980, 1996; Jenson & Ross 1984; Lovenduski & Randall 1993; Mazur 1995; Rowbotham 1996).

The position of left-wing parties may shape feminist movement opportunities for policy influence, by advancing movement interests (even while in opposition) or, in some cases, by failing to protect feminist interests against attack. For example, in Britain, the nearly two decades during which the Labour Party was in opposition served to exclude the British feminist movement from political influence (Bashevkin 1998; Lovenduski & Randall 1993; Rowbotham 1996; Ruggie 1987). Evidence from West Europe and North America suggests that while left-wing parties may not always serve to advance feminist (or even women's) interests, or may extract a high price from the movement while doing so, feminist movements may be even less protected in the absence of governing left-wing parties (Bashevkin 1996; Rowbotham 1996: 8). . . .

The West European cases may be distinctive in the configuration of left party-feminist movement relationships. . . . Nonetheless, . . . there are circumstances where feminists, allied with progressive opposition parties, dramatically increase their policy influence under conditions where the political opportunity structure shifts. Brazilian feminists and Spanish feminists, under authoritarian military regimes, positioned themselves in alliance with (and directly within) left opposition parties. As the Brazilian and Spanish regimes fell, and socialist parties came to governing power, feminist movements were advantageously positioned to institute major constitutional and policy changes (Alvarez 1990; Threlfall 1996: 118–120). . . . These cases . . . suggest that shifts in electoral balance or unanticipated changes in government and opposition of large magnitude open major opportunities for women's movements and that feminist movements, allied in advance with left-wing opposition parties, can achieve rapid and large-scale policy changes.

Despite these cases, however, the relationship between feminist movements and political parties, even left-wing parties, is not always amicable. The tension between the need to ally with a formally organized, electorally experienced political party and the (perceived) benefits of a nonallied, independent political position is evidenced in comparative women's movement scholarship. Feminist movements in multiple nations have undertaken debates concerning autonomy versus coalition as political strategies. Many women's movements have struggled to maintain autonomy from political parties and have succeeded in policy terms and in goal achievement when they have remained autonomous (Hellman 1987; Hubbard & Solomon 1995: 174; Kemp et al. 1995: 132–133; Quindoza Santiago 1995: 124–125). . . .

Despite these tensions, the strategic solution of establishing a feminist political party, or a women's party, is rare.[3] The paucity of women's political parties, across political and electoral systems, has yet to find adequate theoretical or explanatory grounding. . . .

Double Militancy: Identity and Location

Because women's movements have not given rise to women's political parties, the relationship of the women's movement to linkage organizations (such as political parties) and to formal political institutions and state structures involves unresolved tensions and conflicts. Within feminist and women's movements, debates concerning the utility of an "inside" strategy of working within institutions and of the value of an autonomous "outside" position independent of political parties concern more than simply structural concerns. They also involve issues of competing collective identities, characterized across nation-states and regions, in the 1970s and the 1980s, by the dilemma of "double militancy."

The "double militancy" of its activists may be a distinctive characteristic of women's movements. By double militancy, I mean the location of activist women in two political venues, with participatory, collective identity and ideological commitments to both. For example, double militancy was evidenced in feminist movement activists within the Italian Communist Party (PCI) in the 1970s and 1980s (Beckwith 1985; della Porta 2000; Hellman 1987: 60). . . . With political commitments to feminism and to the left, Italian activist women confronted intersecting collective identities as feminists and as socialists that were

problematized by the strong organizational presence of the PCI, with a highly "workerist" political culture (Hellman 1987), and by the developing presence and organizational innovations of the autonomous feminist movement. . . .

Double militancy is related to but distinguishable from the multiplicity of women's intersecting identities of gender, race, ethnicity, sexuality, and nationality, for example. Arising from structural locations of collective political action, double militancy both emerges from and influences the organization and tactical forms of women's movement activism. Given the complex collective gender identities that emerge from intersections with class, race, and other collective identities, collective action commitments may be elicited simultaneously in more than one organizational venue; that is, double militancy, a potentially distinctive feature of women's movements, has organizational and tactical implications.

One implication is that feminist activists have to negotiate their feminism within nonfeminist organizations that nonetheless provide resources, contacts, and scope for feminist activist goals. . . . Such identity crises may be resolved when the state refuses to fund feminist NGOs, closing a venue within which feminist activists work from multiple political commitments. Alternatively, feminists may reconcile identity tensions by relinquishing involvement in one set of issues, choosing to focus on campaigns and struggles where double militancy tensions are less acute.

Under other circumstances, depending upon political culture and the presence of a strong left party, feminists may maintain and extend their activism, accommodating if not resolving tensions of double militancy. In other cases, feminist activists may be purged from local party organizations; they may seek other venues for action; or they may dissolve their own organizations and rely on "spontaneous," autonomous local organizing campaigns around specific issues. . . .

For feminists who persist in double militancy, recourse to discursive struggle may clarify, if not resolve, competing allegiances and demands. . . . To the extent that feminist activists can shape and control political discourse concerning women, they may be able to employ feminist discourse as a resource for shaping and influencing public policy.

Another implication of double militancy concerns the internal transformations of nonfeminist organizations in response to feminist activism and the empowering of feminists within those organizations for feminist purposes. Double militancy can emerge within women's movements even where the state organizes the movement (e.g., China). In these cases, women's activism may be coopted and controlled by the state but, at the same time, female activists can employ these organizations for their own purposes and as a staging ground for feminism. Zhang and Wu observe that the All-China Women's Federation (ACWF), established by the Chinese Communist Party in the 1940s, emerged (if in limited form) as a location for women's progressive policy initiatives and leadership development, even as its programs "were all state induced" (Zhang & Wu 1995: 30–31). . . .

This transformative capacity of double militancy may be matched by the empowering possibilities for feminist activists in nonfeminist institutions and organizations. Double militancy may position feminists within state structures, government and political party systems more powerfully, more influentially, and with more protection and support than they would otherwise be able to provide for themselves independently. Funding for feminist ventures and campaigns is in many cases more easily raised where feminists are also located in nonfeminist organizations willing to provide financial support for feminist publications (Beckwith 1985; Hellman 1987), feminist meetings and conferences (Sternback, Navarro-Aranguren, Chuckryk & Alvarez 1992), and feminist offices and research centres (Lovenduski & Randall 1993). . . .

The relationship of women's movements to linkage organizations such as political parties, and a resulting emergence of double militancy, have implications for women's strategic collection action. Dieter Rucht, comparing multiple social movements across time (1970s to 1990s) and nations (France, Germany, the Netherlands, and Switzerland), finds that women's movements[4] are distinctive, even within a "family" of left-libertarian movements, in that they rely very little, in comparative movement terms, upon protest as a tactic for achieving their ends. . . . The use of protest, rarely violent, when focusing on national issues, and national mobilization targeted toward the state, rather than toward parties, other interest groups, or employers or business firms, suggest that women's movements are positioned differently from other movements (e.g., labor, peace) to achieve their ends.

Gendered Political Opportunities: Response and Creation

. . . Research on women's movements suggest[s] that political opportunities are gendered in ways both advantageous and deleterious to women's movements. . . . Women are located both externally to institutions whose actions they aim to influence (e.g., government agencies) and internally within institutions where institutional membership and participation are the goals (e.g., labor unions, universities). As a result, political opportunity for women's movements is structured differently, even within the same institution, depending upon the movement's goals and its internal or external position vis-à-vis the institution. Most research on women's movements and feminist movements has focused on women's movements positioned externally to institutions and the movements' attempts to exact policy changes.

. . . Although no systematic classification of political opportunities for women's movements has yet been devised, the literature suggests that political opportunities may be gendered in ways that advantage female actors rather than male actors, and that privilege movements that employ specifically gendered discourses (Beckwith 1998b; Berkovitch & Moghadam 1999: 278–287; Katzenstein 1995, 1998).

First, political opportunities are structurally gendered in cases where male actors are precluded, by law or by threats of coercion or retribution by states or other groups, from engaging in movement actions or campaigns. In the United States, for example, labor union members in predominantly male workforces may be precluded by labor law, court injunctions, or threat of job loss from engaging in picketing or mass demonstrations; in these cases, organized women in the community, often specifically identifying themselves as activist women, mothers, wives, or daughters, may initiate challenging actions designed to further the interests of striking workers where they themselves are not subject to legal punishment (Beckwith 1998a; Fonow 1998; Maggard 1990). . . . The range of available responses by the state and other actors may also be gendered insofar as they may feel constrained in using their full capacity to repress women's collective action.

Second, political opportunity structures may be gendered insofar as increases in particular types of political opportunity structures are commonly favored by women's movements to advance their interests. . . . It is notable that women's movements, and feminist movements specifically, employ their position within, and alliances with, left-wing parties to advance their policy concerns when: (1) new constitutional arrangements seem likely or are formally under consideration; (2) an alternation in power between governing and opposition parties is likely, or when a party realignment is anticipated;[5] and (3) in revolutionary periods.

Constitutional redrafting offers mobilization opportunities for women's movements to engage not only in the direct campaign to shape a new or revised constitution but, in doing so, to craft changes that shift the political opportunity structure for future campaign purposes. Women's movements mobilized to influence the writing of new (or revised) constitutions (or other state arrangements) in Canada, South Africa, Namibia, Scotland, Germany, and other nations across the past decade. . . .

In these cases, women's movements are commonly organized within and active across a range of venues. Dobrowolski characterizes the Canadian women's movement as employing a "wide and adaptable" strategic repertoire, arguing that "women's movements transcend the representational confines of parties, interest groups and social movements to promote a more expansive political outlook and more diverse political practices" (Dobrowolski 2000: 39–40). In the context of Canadian constitutional reform, women's movements mobilized for specific reforms, placing themselves to create and to shape political opportunities and actual politics (Dobrowolski 2000; Meyer 2000). . . .

Women's movements may miss opportunities to bring about change or to restructure the political opportunity context to their advantage if they do not organize across multiple political venues. . . . An unwillingness on the part of East German feminists to change their understanding of the state and an inability to recognize the potential of increasingly open access in the new German state, feminists in the East missed an opportunity to engage the state. East German feminists' historic resistance to the state and their focus on the "private" sphere isolated and disempowered them. . . .

Autonomy, Involvement, and the State

The range of political opportunities available to women's movements varies across nation and time, and presents activist women with strategic choices between autonomy and involvement (Berkovitch & Moghadam 1999: 283; Randall 1998; Randall & Waylen 1998), not only in regard to political parties but in terms of the state. The increasing centrality of the state in feminist theory and in feminist movement scholarship underscores the state as an important structural, legal, and discursive venue for women's movements. Amrita Basu identifies the level of state control as a crucial variable for understanding women's movements, hypothesizing that "women's movements tend to be weak where state control permeates civil society and strong where state control is or has been relaxed" (Basu 1995: 2). . . . The comparative women's movement scholarship has yet to identify the conditions under which women's movements position themselves vis-à-vis the state; the literature is clear, however, that the strategic divide between autonomy and involvement presents a dilemma to women's movements cross-nationally.

. . . In facing the strategic divide of movement autonomy or state involvement, women's movements often fracture. . . . Where splits occur and women's movements choose to disengage from the state, however, they may be foreclosed from policy influence (Rowbotham 1996: 14, although see also Bashevkin 1998, 1994a, 1994b). Rowbotham sees a major failure for West European feminist movements, for example, in their inability "to reorient their strategies to new circumstances in the economy and in the role of the state" (Rowbotham 1996: 13). . . .

In other cases, splits over the strategic divide may serve to benefit one segment of the movement, leaving the others disempowered and unprotected.

Rowbotham concludes that most successful feminist movements in the 1990s have been liberal feminist movements, which have "been adept at negotiating the disintegratory modernizing impulse in capitalism and securing a piece of the cake. . . . Liberal feminism has secured real gains particularly in the US, though its major weakness is that it has had little to offer the American poor, many of whom are women of color" (Katzenstein 2000; Mink 1998; Rowbotham 1996: 15).

Women's movements' relationship to the state can shift with regime changes as well, changing the context within which movements act and, in some cases, resulting in the movement's rapid exclusion from state influence. Research on women's movements in East and Central Europe, and in Latin America, suggests that regime changes concurrent with democratic transitions serve to transform the context of political opportunity for women's movements, and scholars have specified conditions under which movements may sustain their activism and influence (Alvarez 1994; Behrend 1995; Dodds 1998; Miethe 1999; Saint-Germain 1997; Schild 1998; Tong 1999; Waylen 1994; Young 1996). These include fluidity of electoral politics; alliance with a progressive or left party; feminist or woman-centered discourse as part of party discourse; a unified women's movement with multiple women's groups and organizations; mobilization and presence within multiple political venues; a willingness or ability to persist in party politics in the post-transition period; and capacity to negotiate women's policy concerns as a condition of movement support for a party or the state.

Regime changes also serve to shift the opportunity context within stable states (e.g., Britain). A change of governing regime, within a single state, may transform the context within which women's movements mobilize and act collectively. In Britain, for example, the Thatcher governments constituted a regime shift sufficient to marginalize the British feminist movement and to encourage its abeyance in the 1980s (Bashevkin 1998, 1996, 1994a). In other cases, regime change facilitates feminist movement activism and development. Della Porta argues that, for the Italian case, the combination of a Christian Democratic regime and *partitocrazia* (governance and influence possible only through political parties) "reduced

the space of an autonomous movement, in part 'absorbing' the political demands of feminism" (della Porta 2000: 18). . . .

Conclusion: Beyond Compare?

Women's movements, however problematically defined, are not beyond compare in studies that clearly identify their research questions, specify the frameworks of analysis they employ, and explicate the concepts they seek to investigate. The best comparative women's movements research is clear about the limitations of its evidence and cautious about generalizing from the case foci to other politically relevant contexts (e.g., nation-states, regions, class identities). The potential benefits, in terms of building a body of knowledge, of developing new indicators and perspectives and of honing existing ones, and of increasing our confidence about strategic and policy recommendations for women's movements, are substantial.[6] . . .

Notes

1. This seems not to be an artifact of case selection, although it is nonetheless true that little research focuses on links between women's movements (or simply rightwing women) and parties of the right.
2. Note that this is not to suggest that the nomination of women is necessarily feminist.
3. Such few parties include, for example, the Filippina feminist party Women for the Motherland; the French group Choisir (which competed in French National Assembly elections in 1978 and 1989); and women's parties in Iceland and Russia.
4. Here Rucht uses the term "women's movements" as synonymous with feminist movements (Rucht 2000).
5. Note that women's movements can help to *create* these opportunities as well.
6. For an earlier articulation of this position, see Beckwith 1980.

References

Alvarez, S. (1994). The (trans)formation of feminism(s) and gender politics in democratizing Brazil. In J. S. Jaquette (ed.), *The women's movement in Latin America: Participation and democracy* (2nd ed., pp. 13–63). Boulder: Westview.

Alvarez, S. (1990). *Engendering democracy in Brazil: Women's movements in transition politics.* Princeton, N.J.: Princeton University Press.

Banaszak, L. A. (1996). *Why movements succeed or fail: Opportunity, culture, and the struggle for woman suffrage.* Princeton: Princeton University Press.

Bashevkin, S. (1998). *Women on the defensive: Living through conservative times.* Chicago and London: University of Chicago Press.

Bashevkin, S. (1996). Tough times in review: The British women's movement during the Thatcher years. *Comparative Political Studies* 28: 525–552.

Bashevkin, S. (1994a). Confronting neo-conservatism: Anglo-American women's movements under Thatcher, Reagan and Mulroney. *International Political Science Review* 15: 275–296.

Bashevkin, S. (1994b). Facing a renewed right: American feminism and the Reagan/Bush challenge. *Canadian Journal of Political Science* 27: 669–698.

Basu, A. (1995). Introduction. In A. Basu (ed.), *The challenge of local feminisms: Women's movements in global perspective* (pp. 1–21). Boulder: Westview.

Beckwith, K. (1998a). Collective identities of class and gender: Working-class women in the Pittston coal strike. *Political Psychology* 19(1): 147–167.

Beckwith, K. (1998b). Gender frames and collective action. Paper presented to the Department of Political Science, Labor Studies Program, and Women's Studies Program at the Pennsylvania State University, April 30.

Beckwith, K. (1987). Response to feminism in the Italian parliament: Divorce, abortion, and sexual violence legislation. In M. F. Katzenstein & C. M. Mueller (eds.), *The women's movements of the United States and Western Europe* (pp. 153–171). Philadelphia: Temple University Press.

Beckwith, K. (1985). Feminism and leftist politics in Italy: The case of UDI-PCI relations. *West European Politics* 8(4).

Beckwith, K. (1980). The cross-cultural study of women and politics: Methodological problems. *Women & Politics* 1(2): 7–28.

Behrend, H. (1995). East German women and the *Wende, European Journal of Women's Studies* 2(2): 237–255.

Berkovitch, N. & Moghadam, V. (1999). Middle East politics and women's collective action: Challenging the status quo, *Social Politics* 6 (3): 273–291.

della Porta, D. (2000). The women's movement, the left, and state: Continuities and changes in the Italian case. In L. A. Banaszak, K. Beckwith & D. Rucht (eds.). *Women's movements facing the reconfigured state.* Unpublished collection.

Dobrowolski, A. (2000). Shifting "states": States, strategies and identities: Women's constitutional organizing across time and space. In L. A. Banaszak, K. Beckwith & D. Rucht (eds.). *Women's movements facing the reconfigured state.* Unpublished collection.

Dodds, D. (1998). Five years after unification: East German women in transition, *Women's Studies International Forum* 21(2): 175–182.

Fonow, M. M. (1998). Protest engendered: The participation of women steelworkers in the Wheeling–Pittsburgh Steel strike of 1985. *Gender & Society* 12(6): 710–728.

Hellman, J. A. (1987). *Journeys among women.* New York: Oxford University Press.

Hubbard, D. & Solomon, C. (1995). The many faces of feminism in Namibia. In Amrita Basu (ed.), *The challenge of local feminisms* (pp. 163–186). Boulder: Westview.

Jenson, J. (1996). Representations of difference: The varieties of French feminism. In M. Threlfall (ed.), *Mapping the women's movement: Feminist politics and social transformation in the north* (pp. 73–114). London and New York: Verso.

Jenson, J. (1980). The French Communist Party and feminism. *The Socialist Register* 121–148.

Jenson, J. & Ross, G. (1984). *The view from inside.* Berkeley: University of California Press.

Katzenstein, M. F. (2000). Dividing citizens, divided feminisms: The reconfigured U.S. state and women's citizenship. In L. A. Banaszak, K. Beckwith & R. Rucht (eds.), *Women's movements facing the reconfigured state.* Unpublished collection.

Katzenstein, M. F. (1998). *Faithful and fearless: Moving feminist protest inside the church and military.* Princeton, N.J.: Princeton University Press.

Katzenstein, M. F. (1995). Discursive politics and feminist activism in the Catholic church. In Myra Marx Ferree and Patricia Yancey Martin (eds.), *Feminist organizations: Harvest of the new women's movement* (pp. 35–53). Philadelphia: Temple University Press.

Kemp, A., Madlala, N., Moodley, A. & Salo, E. (1995). The dawn of a new day: Redefining South African feminism. In A. Basu (ed.), *The challenge of local feminisms* (pp. 131–162). Boulder: Westview.

Lovenduski, J. & Randall, V. (1993). *Contemporary feminist politics: Women and power in Britain.* Oxford: Oxford University Press.

Maggard, S. W. (1990). Gender contested: Women's participation in the Brookside Coal strike. In G. West & R. L. Blumberg (eds.), *Women and social protest* (pp. 75–98). New York: Oxford University Press.

Mazur, A. G. (1995). *Gender bias and the state: Symbolic reform at work in Fifth Republic France.* Pittsburgh: University of Pittsburgh Press.

Meyer, D. S. (2000). Restating the woman question: Women's movements and state changes. In L. Banaszak, K. Beckwith & D. Rucht (eds.), *Women's movements facing the reconfigured state.* Unpublished collection.

Miethe, I. (1999). From "mother of the revolution" to "fathers of unification": Concepts of politics among women activists following German unification, *Social Politics* 6(1): 1–22.

Mink, G. (1998). *Welfare's end.* Ithaca and London: Cornell University Press.

Quindoza Santiago, L. (1995). Rebirthing *Babaye*: The women's movement in the Philippines. In A. Basu (ed.), *The challenge of local feminisms: Women's movements in global perspective* (pp. 110–128). Boulder: Westview.

Randall, V. (1998). Gender and power: Women engage the state. In V. Randall & G. Waylen (eds.), *Gender, politics and the state* (pp. 185–205). London and New York: Routledge.

Randall, V. & Waylen, G. (eds.) (1998). *Gender, politics and the state*. London and New York: Routledge.

Rowbotham, S. (1996). Introduction: Mapping the women's movement. In M. Threlfall (ed.), *Mapping the women's movement: Feminist politics and social transformation in the north* (pp. 1–16). London and New York: Verso.

Rucht, D. (2000). Interactions between social movements and states in a comparative perspective. In L. A. Banaszak, K. Beckwith & D. Rucht (eds.), *Women's movements facing the reconfigured state*. Unpublished collection.

Ruggie, M. (1987). Workers' movements and women's interests: The impact of labor-state relations in Britain and Sweden. In M. F. Katzenstein & C. M. Mueller (eds.), *The women's movements of the United States and Western Europe* (pp. 247–266). Philadelphia: Temple University Press.

Saint-Germain, M. A. (1997). *Mujeres '94*: Democratic transition and the women's movement in El Salvador, *Women & Politics* 18(2): 75–99.

Schild, V. (1998). Market citizenship and the "new democracies": The ambiguous legacies of contemporary Chilean women's movements, *Social Politics* 5(2): 232–249.

Sternback, N. S., Navarro-Aranguren, M., Chuckryk, P. & Alvarez, S. E. (1992). Feminisms in Latin America: From Bogotá to San Bernardo, *Signs* 17(2): 393–434.

Threlfall, M. (1996). Feminist politics and social change in Spain. In M. Threlfall (ed.), *Mapping the women's movement: Feminist politics and social transformation in the north* (pp. 115–151). London and New York: Verso.

Tong, I. L. K. (1999). Reinheriting women in decolonializing Hong Kong. In J. M. Bystyzienski & J. Sekhon (eds.), *Democratization and women's grassroots movements* (pp. 49–66). Bloomington: Indiana University Press.

Valiente, C. (2000). The feminist movement and the reconfigured state in Spain (1970s–1990s). In L. A. Banaszak, K. Beckwith and D. Rucht (eds.), *Women's movements facing the reconfigured state*. Unpublished collection.

Waylen, G. (1994). Women and democratization: Conceptualising gender relations in transition politics. *World Politics* 46(3): 327–354.

Young, B. (1996). The German state feminist politics: A double gender marginalization, *Social Politics* 3(2/3): 159–184.

Zhang, N., with Wu, X. (1995). Discovering the positive within the negative: The women's movement within a changing China. In A. Basu (ed.), *The challenge of local feminisms: Women's movements in global perspective* (pp. 25–57). Boulder: Westview.

Chapter 4

WOMEN'S MOVEMENTS AND DEMOCRATIC TRANSITION IN CHILE, BRAZIL, EAST GERMANY, AND POLAND

Lisa Baldez

In many countries women have responded to transitions to democracy by mobilizing along gender lines to advance their own agendas. In countries as diverse as Argentina, Korea, Spain, and South Africa, women saw popular demands for democracy as an opportunity to press for the democratization of everyday life and the extension of women's rights. They mobilized across class and party lines to demand that incoming democratic governments ensured women's equal participation in politics. Yet not all transitions to democracy have been accompanied by the mobilization of women as women. In most of the transitions in Central and East Europe women who participated in dissident movements did not organize on the basis of their status as women. Within democratic transitions, when will women mobilize on the basis of their gender identity? . . .

Women's movements represent many different identities, interests, and issues.[1] Despite important differences, however, many women's movements experience a particular moment at which women unite on the basis of their gender identity. At this moment, the peak of mobilization in women's movements, a diverse array of women's organizations comes together to form a coalition that transcends cleavages along class, race, or partisan lines. These peak moments typically occur at a rally, a demonstration, or a conference. They differ from other points in the evolution of a movement in terms of their size, breadth, and significance. They frequently constitute the largest convocation of organizations in the history of a movement. They represent the acme of unity and the ideal expression of the goals of the movement, while at the same time encompassing a wide array of interests and issues. They typically inaugurate a movement in the public eye and introduce women's demands into the public arena.

Peaks of protest consolidate women's political clout. They attract the attention of (primarily) male political actors, who seek to harness women's capacity to mobilize for their own electoral goals. Interest from political parties leads to the incorporation of women's demands in the political agenda and further fuels popular support for the movement. The coalitions that emerge out of such moments often come to serve as the institutional representatives of the women's movement in the political arena. Scholars and activists alike uniformly acknowledge the importance of these moments in the history of a movement; they take on mythic proportions in histories of movements and in the memories of activists.

The formation of such coalitions is not inevitable, as women's movements typically include groups with diverse and conflicting agendas. What prompts women's groups to coalesce is their exclusion from the process of realignment, the point at which actors within the democratic opposition form new alliances with one another. The exclusion of women and women's concerns from the agendas articulated by primarily male opposition leaders heightens the political salience of gender relative to other cleavages and triggers the formation of a united front among women's organizations.

At the same time, these peak moments prove difficult to sustain. Conflict seems to break out among groups within the women's movement almost as soon as the peak of unity occurs. But the ephemeral nature of these moments does not undermine their significance. Peaks of protest demonstrate women's capacity for mobilization, which attracts the attention of party elites. Once male politicians see women as a constituency worth coopting, they begin to compete for women's support. The advent of electoral competition fragments the movement.

This argument will be examined with regard to three countries in which women mobilized during democratic transition—Brazil, Chile, and East Germany—and one in which women did not—Poland. These cases provide variation on the dependent variable and enhance the validity of the inferences that can be drawn from them.[2] The women's movements that emerged in Chile and Brazil were two of the largest and most vibrant in Latin America; they joined human rights groups, feminist organizations, and shantytown groups organized around issues of economic subsistence. In East Germany the movement included women's peace organizations, lesbian collectives, radical feminists, socialists, and neighborhood groups. In Poland the level of autonomous organizing among women remained minuscule in comparison. . . .

Women's Movements and Democratization

. . . Systematic comparison across cases and regions reveals three factors as critical to the mobilization of women in democratic transitions: organizational networks, direct contact with international feminism, and exclusion from the process of decision making within the opposition.

Resource Mobilization

According to this perspective, movements emerge as a function of individual decisions about the costs and benefits of collective action or as a function of material resources that can be brought to bear on organizing.[3] Factors such as money, leadership, and (especially) existing organizational networks facilitate mobilization. People who already participate in groups can be mobilized around other issues more easily than isolated individuals.

Organizational networks constitute a necessary but not sufficient cause for the emergence of women's movements. In all four cases discussed here, significant numbers of women participated in both formal and informal groups that could have formed the organizational infrastructure of an autonomous women's movement. Many kinds of networks can serve as crucibles for women's organizing. In these four cases households, churches, and unions generally provided the foundation on which women's movements could be built. In Latin America political parties and international organizations also provided mobilizational resources for women.

In some cases the demands of domestic work forced women to organize collectively. The most explosive rates of mobilization in Latin America took place in poor and working-class neighborhoods, where deep economic crisis prompted women to organize around household activities, forming soup kitchens, shopping collectives, and craft workshops. Many poor and working-class women became politicized as a result of these informal neighborhood groups.[4] . . .

In the socialist countries, performing household tasks in conditions of scarcity also fostered informal networks among extended family members, trusted friends, and neighbors. Accounts of the status of women in Communist countries consistently point to the "double burden" of formal employment and housework as an obstacle to autonomous organizing among women, yet in many cases it promoted social ties.[5] . . .

Churches provided dissident groups with space to meet, funding, and, most important, protection from repression. In Latin American countries the Catholic church fostered women's participation at the grass-roots level through ecclesiastical base communities and human rights work.[6] In Poland the Catholic church supported dissident activity through the Solidarity movement. In East Germany Protestant churches played a similar role; their neutrality with regard to the Communist regime allowed them to shelter the opposition.

In Latin America participation in political parties facilitated women's mobilization in two ways. First, it provided women with valuable organizational skills. Second, it often brought them face to face with sexist attitudes of their male colleagues, which fueled awareness of feminist concerns.

Aid from international organizations and foreign governments helped incipient women's groups build support and become institutionalized. In the former Soviet Union and East and Central Europe dissident groups received far less support from international organizations until after 1989. . . .

Cultural Framing

. . . Frame analysis highlights the role that ideas, beliefs, culture, and discourse play in shaping collective action. This approach focuses on the way in which activists perceive their status and convey their concerns to the public.[7] The concept of framing suggests that movement discourse is contingent and strategic. The decision to mobilize as women, for example, represents a decision about how to frame collective action. Women can participate in social movements on the basis of many identities—as workers, students, poor people, or environmentalists—but they will frame their actions in terms of gender identity only if they believe that their concerns stem from their status as women and if they perceive some advantage to be gained by presenting themselves as women to the outside world.

Many have pointed to the diffusion of international feminist discourse as a key factor in mobilizing women in Latin American transitions. . . . Nonetheless, while the discourse articulated at international women's conferences was ostensibly available to women from all countries, it did not foster mobilization in all countries. Many women in the former Communist countries explicitly rejected international feminist perspectives. . . . Communist governments consistently claimed to have emancipated women and to have solved the "woman question" by instituting full employment for women. But these claims rang hollow when participation in the work force did not result in gender equality and did not improve the quality of women's lives.

Thus, international feminism fostered women's movements in Latin America but impeded them in the former Communist countries. However, not all women in Communist countries rejected feminist discourse. In East Germany women embraced international feminism; geographic and linguistic proximity to West Germany gave East German women access to information that allowed them to challenge prevailing views. Moreover,

while international feminism inspired women to take action in Latin America, its impact was not automatic or unequivocal. Resistance to feminism has proven strong in Latin America, a region also characterized by a traditional culture that venerates the image of women as mothers. . . .

Political Opportunities

. . . Movements rise and fall in part in response to changes within the political arena, known as changes in political opportunities.[8] . . .

Within cases of transition in Latin America, scholars generally concur that the suppression of conventional forms of political activity under military rule provided a space for nontraditional actors and nontraditional forms of participation to emerge. More precisely, repression directed primarily against male-dominated political parties and trade unions allowed women to develop new styles of political engagement. These spaces expanded as military regimes liberalized but shrank when political parties (re)gained control within the political arena.[9]

. . . The pervasive power of Communist parties clearly limited the space for independent mobilizing, yet the breakdown of these regimes in the 1980s did not always foster the emergence of women's movements. The reason has to do with the dynamics within the opposition itself. . . . The absence of women and women's concerns from the agendas articulated by primarily male opposition leaders prompted women's organizations representing diverse interests to unite on the basis of gender identity.

To a certain extent, periods of realignment provided an opportunity for all organized groups within civil society to press for the incorporation of their concerns in the political agenda. Yet in most cases the vast majority of people involved in these discussions were men. Despite whatever role they may have played in opposition activities up to this point, women suddenly found themselves frozen out of the process of negotiating the terms of transition. . . . The common experience of exclusion prompted diverse groups to join together to demand a role in setting the agenda. Where women were included in the process, there was no catalyst for the formation of a women's movement.

Brazil

When the Brazilian military seized power in 1964, it sought to restructure Brazilian society fundamentally, in economic, political, and social terms. The military regime's policies created three sets of issues around which women mobilized: human rights violations, economic subsistence, and women's rights.[10] Women made up a majority of the participants in approximately 100,000 Christian base communities organized by the Catholic church.[11] Many of these women went on to organize in neighborhoods to demand "adequate schools, health centers, running water, transportation, electricity, housing and other necessities of urban infrastructure."[12] The government did not suppress these groups, but the government's lack of responsiveness and refusal to take women's concerns seriously was a radicalizing experience.

Feminist framing did not automatically take in Brazil. . . . Things began to change during the period of liberalization in the late 1970s as women who had been exiled began to return home. . . . Returning exiles brought feminist ideas back with them. They had a tremendous impact on women's organizing in Brazil, particularly in regard to the issue of movement autonomy. . . . Women who had been in exile in Italy and France, for example, persuaded others that it was possible to create a feminist movement in a predominantly Catholic culture.[13] International organizations provided resources to bolster these efforts. A 1975 meeting organized to mark the United Nations International Year of the Woman led to the creation of several groups dedicated to promoting awareness of the status of women. . . .

The peak of protest for the Brazilian women's movement occurred in 1979, in the midst of conflicts among the opposition political leaders that ended in a major realignment of the party system. . . . Women's groups campaigned to put women's issues on the opposition agenda for the November 1978 elections, but with little success. . . . Exclusion from the process of realignment provided the conditions for women to unite. Women's mobilization reached a peak during this period. On March 8, 1979, International Women's Day, close to one thousand women gathered for a two-day Women's Congress in São Paulo that included women from trade unions, neighborhood groups, feminist organizations, professional associations, mothers' clubs, black feminist groups, and academic research centers.[14] The First National Women's Conference took place in Rio de Janeiro a month later. . . . Thus, while Brazilian women began to organize against authoritarianism in the early 1970s, the movement did not peak until the beginning of 1979. Its peak coincided with the emergence of competing coalitions within the opposition.

Women's organizations continued to proliferate in the 1980s, but the unity evident at the First Women's Congress soon dissolved. The anticipated reform of the party system came in November 1979, when President General João Batista Figueiredo dissolved the two-party system and decreed a law that permitted the formation of new parties. . . . The military government hoped that the various factions would compete against one another and weaken support for the opposition, but its strategy strengthened the links between politicians and the grass roots.[15] All of the opposition parties began to compete for the support of women's organizations. Realignment thus further spurred popular support for the women's movement because of a convergence of interests between the new parties and women's organizations. . . . All the new parties included at least some women's demands on their agendas.[16] Yet the realities of electoral competition also fragmented the movement, as different groups aligned themselves with particular parties.

Chile

The military government that seized power on September 11, 1973, employed draconian measures in its efforts to achieve economic stability and political order. It banned political parties, shut down congress, and engaged in a systematic campaign of terror and repression that resulted in the torture, death, and disappearance of thousands of people. During the first ten years of military rule under General Augusto Pinochet fierce repression curtailed overt expressions of opposition to the regime. Scores of organizations formed clandestinely. Chilean women played a prominent role in this underground opposition. They organized along three lines, in a pattern similar to

Brazil. Human rights groups grew out of women's efforts to support political prisoners and locate relatives who had been detained. Women in poor and working-class urban neighborhoods organized economic subsistence groups to deal with economic crisis and cuts in social spending. In the late 1970s university-educated women, many of whom had been active in Salvador Allende's Popular Unity government, organized small, informal feminist discussion groups to reflect on the changes that living in a dictatorship had wrought on their lives.[17] International support proved critical in the emergence and survival of all of these groups. The Catholic church provided safe places to meet for many of them. Religious men and women helped to organize soup kitchens and women's centers in the shantytowns around Santiago. By the early 1980s Chilean women had created a dense organizational network.

Women who returned to Chile after spending time in exile brought back ideas about feminism with them, particularly from countries with active feminist movements, such as Sweden, Canada, Austria, West Germany, and the U.S. . . .

Ideas about feminism were not new to Chile. Media sources from the period indicate awareness of women's liberation movements in other countries. Prior to the 1980s, however, Chileans tended to view feminism either as radical man hating that violated traditional gender norms or bourgeois false consciousness that betrayed the prospects for socialist revolution. Living in exile provided some Chilean women with a different context in which to interpret feminist ideas. Feminism gave these women a language to make sense of their experiences and showed them the value of identifying with women as women in a way that transcended national boundaries and national identity.

As in Brazil, funding from international organizations, particularly the Ford Foundation, allowed women academics to conduct research on the status of women. . . . Participation in regional and international conferences strengthened the incipient movement and provided a space for the further articulation of autochthonous understandings of feminism.

Protest in the Chilean women's movement peaked in 1983. In May 1983 Chileans opposed to the regime organized a mass demonstration in Santiago. Organizations representing labor, students, human rights groups, the poor, and white-collar professionals took to the streets to denounce the regime. The surprising success of this demonstration triggered a series of general protests that took place every month for the next three years, until 1986. The opposition political parties moved quickly to assume leadership of the protests. Defying the regime's ban on party activity, opposition politicians formed two separate alliances. . . .

Conflicts over strategy between these two coalitions galvanized women in the opposition. In November 1983 a group called Women for Life (*Mujeres por la Vida*, MPLV) unified women across party lines. The sixteen women who formed the group represented the full spectrum of political parties within the opposition. They served as referents of various positions but did not represent their parties in an official capacity. Even though they were party leaders, they framed their actions in terms of women's status as political outsiders in order to highlight their exclusion from the decision-making process. Women for Life saw the task of inspiring unity within the opposition as one that women were uniquely qualified to carry out. . . .

On December 29, 1983, Women for Life held a massive rally in the Caupolicán Theater in downtown Santiago. This event drew 10,000 women representing a diverse array of issues and interests from all the factions within the opposition, the Democratic Alliance and the Popular Democratic Movement, and activists from human rights groups, subsistence organizations, and feminist collectives. The rally catalyzed the formation of a broad-based, multisector women's movement. Women had formed separate organizations prior to this point, and many of them had participated in the general protests, but not in a coordinated way under a single banner.[18] . . .

But the unity expressed at the Caupolicán rally did not last long. Soon afterward, the movement split along partisan lines. Ultimately, women in the opposition overcame these divisions enough to create another umbrella group, the Coalition of Women for Democracy, to force the incoming democratic government to adopt some of their demands, but they were never able to recapture the Caupolicán moment.[19]

East Germany

The Socialist Unity Party of Germany (SED) exercised a remarkable degree of control over the lives of East German citizens. It forbade any groups that did not support the party. Yet dissident activity among women emerged in the 1980s, primarily in the universities and under the protection of the Protestant church.[20] The church sheltered peace, environmental, gay and lesbian, and women's groups. It provided physical space for them to meet, publicized their events in the church press, and held annual rallies that facilitated regular contact among dissidents.[21] The church sponsored informal discussion groups for women during their "baby year," mandatory one-year maternity leave, which helped to raise their consciousness about gender inequality.[22]

The most prominent of the East German peace groups was Women for Peace, which mobilized in opposition to a 1982 law that allowed women to be drafted into military service. Women for Peace actively sought out contacts in the West, particularly in West Germany where shared language facilitated communication. . . . The ruling party permitted the publication of foreign feminist writings, although it prohibited them from being discussed.[23] Regular contact with western feminists and awareness of feminist ideas changed East German women's perceptions about their role in the dissident peace movement and convinced them of the advantages of women-only peace groups. The Communist regime's increasingly conservative policies toward women, known as "mommy politics," further enhanced the appeal of feminism.

International attention shielded women's groups from repression. Amazingly, despite its notoriously pervasive surveillance, the East German security forces (the Stasi) proved unable to stop Women for Peace from holding demonstrations. Women's structureless and leaderless protests stymied the Stasi's customary strategy of "rounding up the ringleaders" of dissident groups, at least initially.[24] When the Stasi arrested the core leaders of the group in December 1983, the women called upon their foreign contacts to pressure the regime for their release. . . . Nonetheless, the Stasi prevented the growth of popular support for the group.[25]

Women's mobilization in East Germany peaked in the climate of political realignment. In the first few weeks of September 1989 four distinct citizens' movements emerged, each offering a different set of proposals for constructing a new state. . . . September 1989 was thus a ripe moment for women's organizations to coalesce. Female political entrepreneurs responded publicly to the absence of women's issues on the agendas of the new coalitions just a few weeks later and "organized in virtually every city in the former GDR" around the goal of participating in the political process as women. The movement quickly gained momentum. On October 11, 1989, a group called Lila Offensive staged a protest during a government-sponsored rally in which they called for women to participate as equals in society and politics. . . . On December 3, a month after the collapse of the Berlin Wall, women's groups came together to form the Independent Women's League (UFV), a coalition that represented a wide array of organizations, including radical feminist groups, lesbians, socialists, groups with national visibility, and local grassroots organizations.[26] Twelve hundred women attended this initial gathering, which took place at the People's Theater in East Berlin. . . .

The UFV rally represented the peak of women's mobilization in East Germany. . . . The UFV won concessions from the opposition in the short term. Members of the group represented women's issues at the National Roundtable in 1989–90 and fielded candidates in the 1990 parliamentary election. Yet none of the UFV candidates won, and women's influence waned as the issue of reunification monopolized the agenda.

Poland

From the Communist takeover of 1945 to the emergence of Solidarity in 1980, dissident women's organizations were extremely rare in Poland. Their rarity cannot be explained as a function of limited mobilizational resources.[27] Women participated in dissident unions; they made up half the members of Solidarity, for example. Many women worked in primarily female fields, such as textiles and nursing, but only on a handful of occasions did female-dominated unions engage in opposition activities that emphasized their status as women.[28] The high level of mobilization in Poland in the late 1970s and early 1980s begs the question of why a women's movement did not emerge in Poland during this period.[29]

Awareness of international feminism inhibited women's independent mobilizing in Poland, exactly the opposite effect that it had in Brazil, Chile, and East Germany. Poles were aware of international feminist ideas, but they associated them with the Women's League, the official women's organization, and thus discredited them. The state both mediated and monopolized information from abroad, rendering foreign ideas suspect among ordinary Poles. . . . For dissidents, direct contact with the western world remained very limited. . . . In this context, women were likely to have associated western feminist ideas with the party and thus to have seen them as (another) source of oppression, rather than as a potential source of liberation.[30] . . .

The absence of autonomous organizing by women in Poland stands out in relief against a cycle of antiregime protests that broke out in the late 1970s. The cycle began in June 1976 when workers staged a protest against recently announced price increases. The government responded to these strikes promptly—it eliminated the price increases and brutally suppressed the workers—but its actions set off explosive levels of popular mobilization that lasted several years.[31] . . . By 1980 the economic situation had deteriorated, resulting in widespread food shortages. Another attempt to impose price increases in June 1980 prompted the Gdansk shipyard workers to go on strike, triggering a wave of strikes that quickly spread throughout the country. Their efforts brought the government to the negotiating table in August 1980 and resulted in a series of concessions to workers known as the Gdansk Agreements. The emergence of Solidarity constitutes a realignment: the formation of a new coalition within the antiauthoritarian opposition. . . . Dissidents took over unions and other party-dominated groups, but the Women's League remained immune to pressures to democratize.[32] Why did women's groups not form during this period of realignment?

The main reason is that women did not consider themselves to be excluded from this process. The strike leaders explicitly addressed women's issues during the roundtable discussions between Solidarity and the Gierek regime. The Interfactory Strike Committee won several concessions that women strongly supported: a three-year paid maternity leave, guaranteed day care slots for working women, and, for nurses, higher wages and housing.[33] Women made up a minority of the delegates to the 1981 Solidarity Congress (only 8 percent), and many women were conscious of the degree to which men dominated the Solidarity leadership.[34] But the vast majority of women raised little objection.[35] . . .

The climate for women's organizing in Poland changed in 1989, when the proposal of an antiabortion law in the Sejm in June 1989 "activated" the women's movement.[36] Thirty women's groups emerged during the abortion debate, but they were "dramatically fragmented and reluctant to enter alliances or to create a united front, in part for fear of being associated with the communists."[37] Women created a formal separate division within Solidarity in fall 1989, but demands for the inclusion of women did not enjoy popular support. Opportunities and issues around which women could mobilize exist, but feminist organizations remain "tiny minority groups," a far cry from the explosive levels of mobilization that occurred in Brazil, Chile, and East Germany.[38]

Conclusion

Three variables are significant in explaining women's mobilization during democratization. Formal and informal networks in which women were involved constituted the organizational infrastructure to build women's movements. Direct contact with the international feminist community prompted women to frame their situation in terms of their status as women and to organize separately from men. Finally, exclusion from the process of realignment within the democratic opposition catalyzed the formation of a formal coalition among diverse women's organizations. . . .

Notes

1. Amrita Basu, ed., *The Challenge of Local Feminisms* (Boulder: Westview Press, 1995).

2. Gary King, Robert Keohane, and Sidney Verba, *Designing Social Inquiry* (Princeton: Princeton University Press, 1994).

3. John D. McCarthy and Mayer N. Zald, *The Trend of Social Movements in America* (Morristown: General Learning Press, 1973).

4. Philip Oxhorn, *Organizing Civil Society* (University Park: Pennsylvania State University Press, 1995); Cathy Lisa Schneider, *Shantytown Protest in Pinochet's Chile* (Philadelphia: Temple University Press, 1995).

5. Katherine Verdery, *What Was Socialism, and What Comes Next?* (Princeton: Princeton University Press, 1996).

6. Pamela Lowden, *Moral Opposition to Authoritarian Rule in Chile, 1973–90* (New York: Macmillan, 1996). In Argentina the church played a more ambiguous role. See Alison Brysk, *The Politics of Human Rights in Argentina* (Stanford: Stanford University Press, 1994); Rita Arditti, *Searching for Life: The Grandmothers of the Plaza de Mayo and the Disappeared Children of Argentina* (Berkeley: University of California Press, 1999); Marysa Navarro, "The Personal Is Political: Las Madres de la Plaza de Mayo," in Susan Eckstein, ed., *Power and Popular Protest* (Berkeley: University of California Press, 1989); Anthony James Gill, *Rendering unto Caesar* (Chicago: University of Chicago Press, 1998).

7. Lee Ann Banaszak, *Why Movements Succeed or Fail* (Princeton: Princeton University Press, 1996); David E. Snow, "Master Frames and Cycles of Protest," in Aldon D. Morris and Carol McClurg Mueller, eds., *Frontiers in Social Movement Theory* (New Haven: Yale University Press, 1992); David E. Snow and Robert Benford, "Ideology, Frame Resonance, and Participant Mobilization," in Bert Klandermans et al., eds., *From Structure to Action* (Greenwich: JAI Press, 1988); Ann Swidler, "Culture in Action: Symbols and Strategies," *American Sociological Review*, 51 (1986).

8. Mary Fainsod Katzenstein and Carol Mueller, eds., *The Women's Movements of the United States and Western Europe* (Philadelphia: Temple University Press, 1987); Doug McAdam, *Political Process and the Development of Black Insurgency, 1930–1970* (Chicago: University of Chicago Press, 1982); Herbert Kitschelt, "Political Opportunity Structures and Political Protest," *British Journal of Political Science*, 16 (1986); Joyce Gelb, *Feminism and Politics* (Berkeley: University of California Press, 1989); Anne N. Costain, *Inviting Women's Rebellion* (Baltimore: Johns Hopkins University Press, 1992); Charles Tilly, *From Mobilization to Revolution* (Reading: Addison-Wesley, 1978); Sidney G. Tarrow, *Power in Movement* (New York: Cambridge University Press, 1994).

9. Elisabeth J. Friedman, *Unfinished Transitions: Women and the Gendered Development of Democracy in Venezuela, 1936–1996* (University Park: Pennsylvania State University Press, 2000).

10. See Sonia E. Alvarez, *Engendering Democracy in Brazil* (Princeton: Princeton University Press, 1990); Marianne Schmink, "Women in Brazilian 'Abertura' Politics," *Signs*, 7 (1981); Vera Soares et al., "Brazilian Feminism and Women's Movements," in Basu, ed.; June Edith Hahner, *Emancipating the Female Sex* (Durham: Duke University Press, 1990); Fanny Tabak, "Women in the Struggle for Democracy and Equal Rights in Brazil," in Barbara Nelson and Najma Chowdhury, eds, *Women and Politics Worldwide* (New Haven: Yale University Press, 1994).

11. Alvarez, p. 70.

12. Soares et al., p. 311.

13. Sonia Alvarez, "The Politics of Gender in Latin America" (Ph.D. diss., Yale University, 1988), p. 355.

14. Alvarez, *Engendering Democracy in Brazil*, p. 113.

15. Scott Mainwaring, *Rethinking Party Systems in the Third Wave of Democratization* (Stanford: Stanford University Press, 1999).

16. Alvarez, *Engendering Democracy in Brazil*, p. 161.

17. See Ann Matear, "Desde la Protesta a la Propuesta," *Democratization*, 3 (1996); Veronica Schild, "New Subjects of Rights?" in Sonia Alvarez et al., eds., *Politics of Culture, Cultures of Politics* (Boulder: Westview Press, 1998); Maria Elena Valenzuela, "The Evolving Roles of Women under Military Rule," in Paul W. Drake and Ivan Jaksic, eds., *The Struggle for Democracy in Chile* (Lincoln: University of Nebraska Press, 1995); Maria Elena Valenzuela, "Women and the Democratization Process in Chile," in Jane S. Jaquette and Sharon L. Wolchik, eds., *Women and Democracy* (Baltimore: Johns Hopkins University Press, 1998); Marjorie Agosin, *Tapestries of Hope, Threads of Love* (Albuquerque: University of New Mexico Press, 1996); Patricia Chuchryk, "From Dictatorship to Democracy," in Jane S. Jaquette, ed., *The Women's Movement in Latin America* (Boulder: Westview Press, 1994); Alicia Frohmann and Teresa Valdés, "Democracy in the Country and in the Home," in Basu, ed.; Julieta Kirkwood, *Ser politica en Chile* (Santiago: FLACSO, 1986); Teresa Valdés and Marisa Weinstein, *Mujeres que sueñan* (Santiago: FLACSO, 1993).

18. Chuchryk.

19. Lisa Baldez, "Coalition Politics and the Limits of State Feminism," *Women and Politics*, 22 (2001).

20. See Hildegard Maria Nickel, "Women in the German Democratic Republic and in the New Federal States," in Nanette Funk and Magda Mueller, eds., *Gender Politics and Post-Communism* (New York: Routledge, 1993), p. 144; Brigitte Young, *Triumph of the Fatherland* (Ann Arbor: University of Michigan Press, 1999); Myra Marx Ferree, "The Rise and Fall of 'Mommy Politics,'" *Feminist Studies*, 19 (1993); Lynn Kameitsa, "East German Feminists in the New Democracy," *Women and Politics*, 17 (1997); Eva Maleck-Lewy, "The East German Women's Movement after Unification," in Joan Wallach Scott et al., eds., *Transitions, Environments, Translations* (New York: Routledge, 1997).

21. Christina Schenk, "Lesbians and Their Emancipation in the Former German Democratic Republic," in Funk and Mueller, eds.; Christian Joppke, *East German Dissidents and the Revolution of 1989* (New York: New York University Press, 1995).

22. Anne Hampele, "The Organized Women's Movement in the Collapse of the GDR," in Funk and Mueller, eds., p. 181.

23. Young, p. 72.

24. Barbara Einhorn, "Where Have All the Women Gone? Women and the Women's Movement in East Central Europe," *Feminist Review* (1991), 26.

25. Barbara Einhorn, *Cinderella Goes to Market* (London: Verso, 1993), pp. 207–8.

26. Young, p. 84.

27. Grzegorz Ekiert and Jan Kubik, "Contentious Politics in New Democracies: East Germany, Hungary, Poland, and Slovakia," *World Politics*, 50 (1998), argue that Poland was resource rich in this regard.

28. Padraic Kenney, "The Gender of Resistance in Communist Poland," *American Historical Review*, 104 (1999).

29. See Ewa Hauser et al., "Feminism in the Interstices of Politics and Culture," in Nanette Funk and Magda Mueller, eds., *Political Change in Poland* (New York: Routledge, 1993); Kenny; Renata Siemienska, "Consequences of Economic and Political Changes for Women in Poland," in Jaquette and Wolchik, eds.; Anna Titkow, "Political Change in Poland: Cause, Modifier or Barrier to Gender Equality?" in Funk and Mueller, eds., *Gender Politics and Post-Communism*; Joanna Regulska, "Transition to Local Democracy: Do Polish Women Have a Change?" in Marilyn Rueschemeyer, ed., *Women in the Politics of Postcommunist Eastern Europe* (Armonk: M. E. Sharpe, 1998); Judy Root Aulette, "New Roads to Resistance," in Jill M. Bystydzienski and Joti Sekhon, eds., *Democratization and Women's Grassroots Movements* (Bloomington: Indiana University Press, 1999).

30. Members of the Greenham Common Women eventually visited Poland as well, but not until later, in 1983. Padraic Kenney, *A Carnival of Revolution* (Princeton: Princeton University Press, 2002), p. 100.

31. Grzegorz Ekiert, *The State against Society* (Princeton: Princeton University Press, 1996), p. 232.

32. Jean Robinson, "The Liga Kobiet in Poland," in Dorothy McBride Stetson and Amy Mazur, eds., *Comparative State Feminism* (Thousand Oaks: Sage, 1995), p. 204.

33. Renata Siemienska, "Dialogue: Polish Women and Polish Politics since World War II," *Journal of Women's History*, 3 (1991).

34. Kristi S. Long, *We All Fought for Freedom* (Boulder: Westview Press, 1996), p. 168.

35. Hauser et al., p. 263.

36. Malgorzata Fuszara, "Women's Movements in Poland," in Scott et al., eds., p. 134.

37. Hauser et al., p. 258.

38. Einhorn, *Cinderella Goes to Market*.

Chapter 5

PROTEST MOVES INSIDE INSTITUTIONS

Mary Fainsod Katzenstein

Protest in American society has moved inside institutions. In recent years, there have been only sporadic instances of marches, strikes, and demonstrations; yet the common image of protest continues to be one of placard-bearing activists whose job actions, pickets, sit-ins, and processions made lively television and news copy in decades past. What this [chapter] sets out to do is to convince those schooled to believe that protest happens only on the streets of an additional and newer institutional reality: that understanding the emergence of gender, race, and sexual politics in contemporary American society means recognizing the importance of protest inside institutions.[1] To limit the definitional purview of protest . . . is to be oblivious to a territory where major struggles over power, resources, and status in American society presently occur. . . .

The Meaning of Protest

This [chapter] is about contemporary feminist protest located inside the core institutions of both state and society. Since the 1970s, feminists have voiced demands for equal roles within the U.S. armed forces, within the institutional spaces of most religious denominations, within prison management, the health sector, universities, police forces, the professions, unions. Indeed, no major institution has been untouched. Feminist groups inside these institutions have pressed for equity in pay, hiring, and promotion, for the end to harassment and sexual abuse, for greater attention to everyday needs as defined by the realities of women's lives (day care, flexible work times, a more nurturant work environment).

In calling this demand making the politics of protest, I wish to highlight the way in which its purpose is often disruptive. Feminist organizing in institutional contexts may not press for the instant cessation of daily business sought by the earlier sit-ins or the demonstrations that led to the destruction of property of clashes with police. But feminist organizing (in its most adversarial and even sometimes in its more accommodative forms) does seek to transform the world. Even some of the most narrow versions of feminist politics that decline to embrace antiracist, antiheterosexist, and antipoverty agendas intend through their focus on equal jobs, promotions, harassment, rape, and other forms of sexual violence to fundamentally change the way American institutions function. In the 1990s, protest pursued in the byways of institutional life can be as disturbance-making as that orchestrated on the public staging grounds of earlier social movements.

I use the term *protest* despite the fact that the women whose activism I describe are far from lawless, rarely use civil disobedience, and never resort to violence. Less lawbreaking than norm-breaking, these feminists have challenged, discomfited, and provoked, unleashing a wholesale disturbance of long-settled assumptions, rules, and practices. Mostly this is intentional or at least, as many advocates of equality would say, inevitable. Sometimes by their mere presence, but more often by claiming specific rights, and by demanding in certain facets the transformation of the institutions of which they are a part, feminists have reinvented the protests of the 1960s inside the institutional mainstream of the 1990s. . . .

When advocates of gender equality in the military proclaim that gender alone should not bar women from flying bomber missions, when feminists in the Catholic Church write that the words of the gospel provide for a church that would include women in all its ministries, they are violating firmly established institutional norms and participating in role-shattering behavior. This too is protest. This is not mere "resistance" to the power of dominant elites; it is proactive, assertive, demand-making political activism. If groups inside institutions were not in organized ways making these kinds of demands, if these forms of institutional activism were not deeply unsettling, the fear-laden conservative backlash of the last twenty years might well have been, one can only speculate, less virulent.

It is limiting, I think, to define protest in terms of any preestablished, particular set of political tactics or events.[2] What constitutes nonnormative behavior, disrupts existing understandings, and challenges established roles is context-specific. To fail to see disruption as situation-specific can be to misrepresent the course of social movements themselves. Marking the beginning or ending of social movements by the rise and decline of media-covered protest "events" or by the requisite use of particular demonstrative actions (sit-ins, demonstrations, marches) may leave much convention-breaking speech and action unremarked.[3] To recognize protest requires knowing as much about the "who, when, what, and where" as it does about the "how." . . .

Unobtrusive Mobilization and Civic Associationalism

What I have called protest inside institutions is only part of the repertoire of American feminism. Institutional protest exists alongside and would not exist without the rich associational activity that has constituted feminist activism in the 1980s and 1990s. This associationalism has outlived the marches, the litigation, the cascade of legislative activity that marked the first decades of the contemporary women's movement and won much media attention. Even as these dramatic days of demonstrations, court cases, and legislative battles have mostly faded, there continue to be vast numbers of organizations operating in the interstices of society, doing the important work of what I call unobtrusive mobilization.[4]

Protest inside institutions is different from unobtrusive mobilization. When activism inside institutions turns into protest, it is almost never, in the sense of escaping public notice, unobtrusive. When institutional routines are disrupted and the norms of an organization contested, it is almost always because the public gaze has been focused on these institutions and institutional elites feel exposed.

What I am calling unobtrusive mobilization occurs both inside institutions and in the space outside institutions, in what Susan Hartmann has elsewhere designated as the work of autonomous feminism.[5] What is specific to *institutional* mobilization is its connection to a parent organization. Formed or re-formed with the intention of holding a parent-institution accountable to feminist concerns, activism inside institutions ranges across different sectors of the workforce from women's studies programs in universities to women's groups located in the larger professional associations of lawyers, engineers, doctors, and scientists, to the Congressional Caucus for Women's Issues of the U.S. Congress, to the Coalition of Labor Union Women in the union movement.

These institution-based organizations are different from more autonomous women's organizations. Autonomous organizations (although they may receive governmental or foundation funding) think of themselves as more free-floating, situated outside government and less directly beholden to institutional supervision. Institution-based organizations are more connected administratively or financially to the political institutions they intend to influence. They may receive funds, may have overlapping memberships or meeting spaces, and may share a common normative or ideological purpose with the larger, male-dominated institutional body of which they are a part. They must also on a more daily basis than autonomous feminist groups negotiate the often hazardous terrain where influence and access are traded against independence and critical distance. . . .

Associational activism in American politics organized with the purpose of reshaping some facet of gender relations is nothing new. It is unclear, given the widely dispersed and often inconspicuous character of much of women's organizing, whether the degree of associational activism that has accompanied second-wave feminism is much the same as in earlier times, greater than before, or whether (as seems unlikely) it has declined over time as Robert Putnam claims is the case with civic associationalism in the United States more generally.[6] What I call unobtrusive mobilization by women has always existed in profusion in American society. What is clearly new is its development inside male-dominant organizational environments—the media, law enforcement, the churches, universities, business, prisons, unions, and engineering, to name just a few of these institutional locales. In these new environments, feminists have spurred debates over hiring and promotion, rape and harassment, child care, and workplace benefits (including coverage for lesbian and gay partners); they have sometimes enagaged in intense contestation over how the quality of work and the fairness and worth of what men and women do should be assessed. If the profusion of unobtrusive feminist networks, caucuses, associations, coffeehouses, bookstores, Internet lists, informal and formal organizations, both inside and outside institutions, is any indication, civic associationalism not only is present but can provide a breeding ground for a form of protest politics that operates within both arterial and capillary corridors of society and of the state.

Feminist Protest in the U.S. Military and the Catholic Church

Why the U.S. military and the Catholic Church? What makes these institutions important to an analysis of protest inside institutions? . . .

Sex discrimination in many other sectors of society is as much de facto as de jure, and the practices against which women must rail are sometimes subtle and indirect, often part of institutional cultures rather than matters of rules or law. In the case of the U.S. military and the Catholic Church, by contrast, discrimination is not subtle. Much prejudice takes the form, to mistrans-

late the Latin expression *prima facie*, of "in your face" discrimination. Because you are a woman and cannot be ordained, you are barred from the deaconate, priesthood, and all higher offices of the Catholic Church. Similarly, in the military, even with the policy changes of the early 1990s that permitted women to fly combat missions and serve on surface warfare ships, there are still combat roles from which women are explicitly barred. For lesbians, of course, there is legalized exclusion from the armed services in its entirety. But provocation is one thing and activism is another. What needed making sense of was why feminists, women and men, did speak out when to do so could invite the negative sanctions of institutions whose capacity for repression is greater than that of many others in contemporary times. In the church, the powers of excommunication can and have been used against those who espouse feminist ideas, specifically support for women's reproductive choice. For other expressions of dissent from institutional teachings, feminists have been fired from their jobs in church institutions or officially silenced; scheduled speeches have been canceled, and pressures have been put on religious communities to rein in aberrant members. In the military, the risk to promotion and job security is no less real. The military lawyer who refuses to prosecute a suspected gay or lesbian servicemember risks possible court-martial for disobeying an order, or the necessity of resigning his or her commission; the whistle-blower or complainant who reports illegal harassment risks retaliation in the form of a blocked promotion or unwelcome job assignment. Distinct to the military, specifically, is the widespread experience of feminists and women in general who face daily harassment from male peers in the form of comments, jeers, gossip, rumor—all amounting to accusations about their sexuality or their alleged incompetence at their job.[7] The puzzle is, in the face of the pressures and institutional penalties that exist in *both* the military and the church, why speak out as a feminist?

Despite the strong similarities between the military and the church—the deeply gendered assumptions embodied within institutional doctrine, the hierarchical structures, and the coercive measures that can be deployed against internal criticism—feminists in the two institutions pursue very different political objectives and use different political strategies. For most feminists in the military a gender-equal society is one in which qualified women have the same opportunities as qualified men. What this reformist vision requires, many military women would say, are better laws, policies, and education. For many activists in the Catholic Church, by contrast, feminism is inseparable from the all-encompassing goal of antimilitarism, class equality, race and gender equity, a homophobia-free society, and social justice on a comprehensive scale. This is a radical vision that demands, many Catholic feminists believe, nothing less than a reconstructed world achieved through an entire restructuring of societal institutions. No doubt both institutions have been unsettled by feminists in their midst. And yet feminists in each of these institutions might be just as unsettled by the version espoused by their counterparts in the other of what it means to undertake activism on behalf of gender equality. . . .

It might be easy . . . to cite the different institutional traditions in the military and the church as explanations of the different political visions to which feminists have turned, although the church in America does have a history of radical politics. . . . It might also be plausible to attribute the difference in institutional feminisms to individual self-selection. . . . But numerous interviews suggested otherwise. Many of those I spoke with emphasized that their political ideas were not at all fully formed at the time they became nuns or joined the military, or that their politics had little to do with why they chose to become what they became. . . .

What convinces me that we must look beyond the "different institutional traditions" or the "self-selection" explanations of feminism's differing manifestations in the military and the church is the fact that women's attitudes have not always *been* as different in the two institutions as they are now. Until the mid-1970s, what was striking about the attitudes and practices of military and church women was their similarity, *not* their differences. In the first half of the twentieth century, the organizational affinity of the two institutions seemed to correspond to a similarity in women's understandings of their roles within the two institutions. In neither the military nor the church did women expect to exercise an equal voice in governance, and in neither institution did women expect to be considered equal partners with men in daily affairs. Rather, women in both the military and the church saw themselves in relation to men as fulfilling a different but complementary role. Why is it that in the last two and a half decades when women in the military and in the church turned to feminism, they did so in very different ways—to an interest-group (influence-seeking) liberal feminism in one case and to a radical, discursive politics in the other?

Institutional Protest in Its Different Forms: Interest-Group and Discursive Politics

It is important to understand the differences between feminism in the military and in the church as part of a larger universe of protest that exists inside institutions. What bears emphasizing is that protest inside institutions is not monolithic. The objectives and forms may vary hugely. Some protest internal to institutions aims at moderate change, some at the radical restructuring of the institution. Some protest emphasizes influence seeking in order to shape policy; other instances emphasize the crafting of language and the formulation of meanings in print and speech. I have called feminist protest inside the military "moderate, interest-group, influence-seeking" politics and that within the church "discursive radicalism." . . .

It is not difficult to envision what feminists do when they engage in *interest-group* politics. We can readily visualize feminist lobbyists walking the corridors on the Hill. . . . In the United States, interest-group activism is the way many feminists do politics. Not that this form of feminist politics necessarily elicits public acclaim. The selection of Geraldine Ferraro as a Democratic vice presidential candidate provoked accusations that feminists had acted as an interest group, "biasing" the selection of Walter Mondale's running mate. Some feminists, too, are disquieted, albeit differently. When feminists do interest-group politics, some suspect, they have bought into a world of political compromise. But on the whole, interest-group politics is seen as politics-as-usual.

Discursive politics requires greater elucidation. Most succinctly, it is the politics of meaning making.[8] By discursive, I mean the effort to reinterpret,

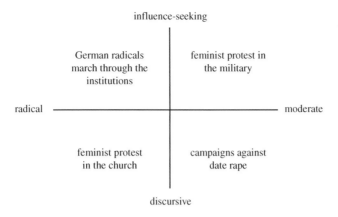

Figure 5.1: Four Types of Institutional Protest.

reformulate, rethink, and rewrite the norms and practices of society and the state. Discursive politics relies heavily but not exclusively on language. It is about cognition. Its premise is that conceptual changes directly bear on material ones. Its vehicle is both speech and print—conversations, debate, conferences, essays, stories, newsletters, books. . . .

I do not mean to draw too neat a line between interest-group and discursive politics. All political activism does interpretive work using language and symbols, so in this sense all politics is discursive. Similarly, all political activism is, in some ways, about advancing the interests of some sectors of society over others. I am suggesting, however, that political activism is at any point in time (whether by choice or by default) more fully absorbed by one kind of political project than by the other—by the intention to influence policy and shape immediate outcomes or by the effort to deploy language and symbols to convince others of new possibilities.

Feminism in the military engages in an influence-seeking *interest-group* form of politics. It is grounded in norms of equal opportunity and a belief in social change through adherence to institutional rules. It is common to hear women activists in the military speak of the need to be mission-oriented team players, to work for change from within, to follow the chain of command (phrases distinctly absent from the vocabulary of women in the church). Military activists often welcome the attention of the press and have on occasion looked the other way when information was leaked to the

news media, but going public with a *New York Times* advertisement, or undertaking the kind of public protest that armband-bearing sisters presented during the pope's visit, would be unthinkable for women who intend to pursue a military career. . . . Women activists in the military pay attention to who wields influence in the military hierarchy and in positions of political importance outside the military, and they endeavor to build connections to those who can make change happen. At the same time, what they aim to do is to play by the rules and change the gendered assumptions embedded in the norms of the institution.

Feminism in the Catholic Church relies heavily on a discursive politics that self-consciously invokes the language of "radical equality."[9] I emphasize the discursive aspects of radical politics in the church to call attention to the energy that feminists in the church devote to language and interpretation—to seeing the meaning of God, of church, of ritual, of justice through a feminist, antiracist, globalist, nonelitist, and nonheterosexist politics. Most feminists in the church (both sisters and lay activists) work for a living in paid jobs not unlike those of women generally. They spend significant amounts of time, however, and most would spend far more if they could, reading, writing, attending (and planning) conferences, engaged in creating a new vision of church and society in prose.

In both the U.S. military and the American Catholic Church over the last twenty years women activists have worked to create a consciousness that challenges discriminatory institutional practices. In both institutions, feminists have created organizational habitats (formal groups and informal networks) within which feminists (mostly women) share stories, develop strategies, and find mutual support. In both institutions, numerous initial- and acronym-denoted organizations carry the burden of keeping gender equality on the institutional agenda. . . .

Despite this common project of institutional change, and despite the existence in both institutions of woman-made organizational spaces within which those at odds with institutional practices gather energy and devise plans of action, there are profound differences in their agendas.

In describing interest-group feminism in the military and feminist discursive radicalism in the church, I wish to defend the usage of two words. The first is military *feminism*. Only about half of those I interviewed described themselves as feminists. Those who did often laced their self-description with humor, irony, or a touch of bravado. . . . Others eschewed the feminist label, occasionally expressing impatience with my question. . . .

Second, I believe it is no less important to explain the term "radical" as I use it to describe feminism in the church. By the term, I mean that feminist activists in the church seek an understanding of the *structural* or *systemic* bases of inequality in the church and in society. . . . It was not enough merely to ordain women; a true "radical" equality demands a reenvisioning of church hierarchy itself, including ritual and prayer and all elitist structures of church and society. When feminists in the church describe their dedication to radical equality, they do not mean the kind of commitment to the poor evinced by a Mother Teresa with her ministries to the sick and dying. What feminists mean is the identifying and rooting out of the very *systems* that cause the poor to be poor, the homeless to be homeless, and that cause people to die of poverty or oppression.[10] . . .

The advent of feminist protest inside institutions is part of a larger story about the last half-century in American society. Prior to the 1950s, the political rights (the vote, specifically) granted to Blacks, to immigrants, and to women were unaccompanied by privileges of citizenship in the reigning social institutions of the time. . . . By midcentury, sections of each of these groups had become middle-class, had gained in some cases a foothold, in some cases substantial representation in the educational, occupational, and cultural institutions of mainstream society. At the same time, beginning in the 1950s, laws and court decisions recognizing this right of entry provided these diverse groups with authoritative language through which to make claims within their institutions. The conjunction of these patterns of mobility with the legislative and judicial affirmation of equal rights has given rise to the proliferation of claims making within institutions. Feminist protest inside the U.S. military and the Catholic Church is party to this history. . . .

Notes

1. The importance of dramatic, on-the-streets, political protest is largely associated with the writings of Richard A. Cloward and Frances Fox Piven (Piven and Cloward 1971 and 1977). In a more recent essay, Piven and Cloward observe that the "continuities between conventional social life and collective protest" that the literature on resource mobilization has described have been useful. The essay, however, warns against "blurring the distinction between normative and nonnormative forms of collective action" (Piven and Cloward 1992, 301). The large literature on protest politics is usefully synthesized in Tarrow 1994.

2. Piven and Cloward, as a careful reading of their work will show, do not do this. But their focus on movements that have relied heavily on strikes, demonstrations, riots, and so on makes it easy to interpret them as saying that protest is synonymous with a particular set of movement tactics, e.g., marches, rent strikes, boycotts, and riots.

3. So-called political process studies of social movements have used protest events as the "staple" signifier of movement stages. I am grateful to David Meyer for helping me to see this point.

4. In an earlier *Signs* article, in which I used the term "unobtrusive mobilization," I grouped together rather than attempting as I do here to make a distinction between groups inside institutions (owing accountability primarily to their parent institution) involved in very visible and disruptive protest and those groups that are much less noticed and, I would argue, much less likely therefore to be disruptive. Katzenstein 1990, 27–52.

5. Hartmann 1998.

6. Putnam 1995.

7. In the course of my interviewing, I heard of no lawyer who was actually court-martialed for failure to participate in a prosecution of a gay or lesbian servicemember, but I was told of a male JAG (judge advocate general) member who resigned.

8. I owe this phrase to a discussion with Martha Minow. For a definition of discursive politics and the role, particularly, of feminist publishing and autotheoretical texts, see Young 1997. See also Fraser 1990, 56–79.

9. This phrase is widely utilized by feminists in the church. See, for example, the conference materials from the Women's Ordination Conference 1995, in Crystal City, Virginia.

10. The words of one Sister of Mercy who was asked by the *New York Daily News* to comment on the work of Mother Teresa help to illuminate the ways that an understanding of structural inequality is central to this vision:

Before I opened my mouth I knew I was about to get myself in trouble.

I had no idea how much.

Carefully, I began:

"I think Mother Teresa is a holy and compassionate woman. There is no minimizing the good that she does for Calcutta's abandoned poor and dying. But I think she does many sisters a disservice by allowing the media and ecclesiastical authorities to promote her as the role model for all religious throughout the world, especially in the United States."

The reporter pressed her to explain herself. She continued,

We confront different needs, a variety of injustices. . . . Sisters here—as in other place—must discover corporately and by themselves what needs exist and how to address them. And even in Calcutta, someone ought to be figuring out who or what it is that causes so many people to perish in the streets. There have got to be direct ministers in the streets, but there must also be people who invade high places to learn why people die in the streets. There must also be sisters who find ways to change the killing systems wherever they are.

There have got to be yet others who expose the evil. (D'Arienzo 1985, 33)

References

D'Arienzo, Camille. 1985. "My Pact with Camillus." In *Midwives of the Future: American Sisters Tell Their Story*, ed. Ann Patrick Ware, 22–36. Kansas City, MO: Leavan Press.

Fraser, Nancy. 1990. "Rethinking the Public Sphere: Contribution to the Critique of Actually Existing Democracy." *Social Text* 8, no. 3; 9, no. 1: 56–79.

Hartmann, Susan. 1998. *Feminist Footholds Everywhere: Capturing the Liberal Establishment in the 1960s and 1970s*. New Haven: Yale University Press.

Katzenstein, Mary Fainsod. 1990. "Feminism within American Institutions: Unobtrusive Mobilization in the 1980's." *Signs* 16, no. 11 (Autumn): 27–52.

Piven, Frances Fox, and Richard A. Cloward. 1971. *Regulating the Poor: The Functions of Public Welfare*. New York: Pantheon Books.

Piven, Frances Fox, and Richard A. Cloward. 1977. *Poor People's Movements: Why They Succeed, How They Fail*. New York: Pantheon Books.

Piven, Frances Fox, and Richard A. Cloward. 1992. "Normalizing Collective Protest." In *Frontiers in Social Movement Theory*, ed. Aldon D. Morris and Carol McClurg Mueller, 301–26. New Haven: Yale University Press.

Putnam, Robert D. 1995. "Bowling Alone: America's Declining Social Capital." *Journal of Democracy* 6, no. 1 (January): 65–78.

Tarrow, Sidney. 1994. *Power in Movement: Social Movements, Collective Action, and Politics*. Cambridge: Cambridge University Press.

Young, Stacey. 1997. *Changing the Wor(l)d: Discourse, Politics, and the Feminist Movement*. New York: Routledge.

Chapter 6

Do Interest Groups Represent the Disadvantaged? Advocacy at the Intersections of Race, Class, and Gender

Dara Z. Strolovitch

Interest groups have a long history in American politics as advocates of corporate and professional interests. Since the explosion in the ranks of organizations representing marginalized groups such as women, racial minorities, and low-income people in the 1960s, these organizations have also become a crucial conduit for the articulation and representation of disadvantaged interests (Berry 1989, 1999; Pinderhughes 1995; Schlozman 1984). While they comprise a small part of the broader interest group universe, organizations such as the National Association for the Advancement of Colored People (NAACP), the National Organization for Women (NOW), and the Center for Law and Social Policy (CLASP) are a significant and visible presence in Washington politics.

Organizations such as these provide an institutionalized voice for the concerns of groups that continue to lack sufficient formal representation in national politics and that are ill-served by the two major political parties (Frymer 1999). Decades after the explosion in the number of these organizations, however, important questions remain about how well they live up to their promise to represent their members. There are many ways to assess the effectiveness of representation for these marginalized groups, such as asking how well such organizations empower those members of marginalized groups who will be in the best position to uplift less powerful members of their communities (DuBois 1903). This [chapter] assesses their efficacy by examining the degree to which organizations claiming to speak for these groups attend to the particular challenges of advocating on behalf of disadvantaged subgroups of their own marginalized constituencies. To do so, I collected new data using a survey of 286 national advocacy organizations. Supplemented with information from face-to-face interviews that I conducted with 40 organization officers and analyzed in light of insights based in theories of intersectionality, these data allow for the first generalizable examination of the extent to which women's, racial minority, and economic justice organizations represent disadvantaged subgroups of their members.

Using these data, I find that while advocacy groups provide some representation for their disadvantaged members, they are *substantially less active when it comes to issues affecting disadvantaged subgroups* than they are when it comes to issues affecting more advantaged subgroups. Organization officers are concerned about representing disadvantaged subgroups, and most feel a responsibility to represent many subgroups. However, attention to these concerns is overridden by the fact that officers at these organizations marginalize and downplay the impact of such issues, framing them as narrow and particularistic in their effect, while framing issues affecting advantaged groups *as if they affect a majority* of their members and have a broad and generalized impact. . . .

The New Mobilization of Bias

Like their corporate and professional analogues, organizations representing groups such as women, racial minorities, and low-income people exist to represent their members and to advocate on their behalf. Unlike these other groups, however, they do so in a political world in which their constituents, while formally enfranchised, continue to be marginalized and underrepresented. As such, most of these groups claim that they are advocates for the weak and marginalized and that they are motivated by a desire to advance social justice and equality (Berry 1999). Indeed, their political legitimacy derives from these claims.

Because of their mandate to give voice to the voiceless, the explosion in the number of these organizations in the 1960s and 1970s brought with it the promise of a new era in which the interest-group system ensures representation for everyone, even those underserved by electoral politics. . . . The extent to which this promise has been fulfilled has been the source of much debate. Although there is broad agreement that the increase in the number of these organizations has helped marginalized groups, crucial concerns remain about how well these organizations represent their constituents. The growth in the number of these groups has been outpaced by the growth in the number of trade, business, and professional organizations that had previously dominated the interest group universe (Baumgartner and Leech 1998; Berry 1989; Schlozman 1984; Schlozman and Burch 2009; Tichenor and Harris 2002–2003; Walker 1991). Consequently, their relative power remains outflanked by the host of organizations representing more advantaged interests.

Moreover, many argue that in spite of their potential, organizations that represent marginalized groups replicate the mobilization of bias lamented by Schattschneider (1975), in which the concerns of weak groups are "organized out" of politics by elites who manipulate the agenda toward their own interests. While Schattschneider critiqued biases toward powerful interests within the broader pressure-group system, new scholarship identifies biases within the organizations that claim to remedy these inequities. I focus here on four main concerns about such biases. The first cluster critiques a middle-class bias in the agendas of organizations representing formerly excluded groups. Berry (1999) argues that liberal advocacy groups have abandoned economic justice issues and are instead dominated by "post-materialist" issues such as the environment, which, he argues, are of interest mainly to the middle class. . . . A second set of concerns is the mirror image of this first cluster and alleges that organizations concerned with economic issues marginalize issues of race, gender, and sexuality (Frymer 1999).

Although not directly concerned with representation for disadvantaged subgroups, other scholars suggest a third set of mainly strategic reasons to be concerned that organizations will not be active when it comes to issues affecting disadvantaged subgroups. . . . Interest groups will likely ignore targeted issues affecting numerically small subgroups—whether weak or strong—in favor of issues that have a wide impact and that affect their median member. Concerns about organizational maintenance also lead organizations to try to avoid alienating allies, members, and potential members (Wilson [1974] 1995), and so they will also avoid issues that are unpopular or controversial among their members or the public, as are many of the issues affecting disadvantaged groups (Kollman 1998; Rothenberg 1992). They will also prefer to exploit political opportunities and policy windows by pursuing issues that are politically salient and likely to "win" (Kingdon 1995). Attention to issues affecting disadvantaged groups is rendered even less likely due to socioeconomic biases that lead to low levels of organizational membership among women, African Americans, Latinos, and people with lower levels of income and education (Verba, Schlozman, and Brady 1995). . . .

Intersectional Marginalization

[An alternative] approach to understanding how well organizations represent their disadvantaged members contends that the quandary cannot be understood as the outcome of rational strategic choices, nor as a zero-sum trade-off between economic and social issues. Instead, adherents of this approach assert, organizations fail to address issues that affect subgroups of their constituencies whose marginalized positions are constituted by the *intersections* of different forms of disadvantage (Cohen

1999; Crenshaw 1989). . . . An example is African-American gay men, who face discrimination based on both race and sexuality. Recognizing that inequities persist *between* marginalized and dominant groups, intersectional approaches stress the overlapping inequalities *within* groups and the resulting unevenness in the gains they have made.

Groups can be marginalized or lack power in many ways: they might lack financial resources, they might be the objects of *de jure* or *de facto* discrimination, they might lack electoral power and have few elected representatives, or they might be stigmatized by the broader society or the dominant culture (Williams 1998, 15). They may also be few in number (i.e., a minority), though as illustrated by the example of billionaires, who are a minority of all Americans, and by women, who constitute a majority of the population, minority status on its own is not necessary or sufficient to qualify a group as marginalized (Williams 1998). Theories of intersectionality tell us that these many disadvantages are not static or rankable and that they do not operate along single axes in additive ways. Instead, these systems are dynamic and create inequalities that define, shape, and reinforce one other in ways that constitute the relative opportunities and positions of different members of marginalized groups. . . .

While marginalization occurs along multiple intersecting and overlapping axes such as gender *and* race *and* poverty, the typical *political response* to oppression and disadvantage in the United States, with few exceptions, has been to organize interest groups and to pursue policies that are dedicated to addressing *single* axes of oppression—gender *or* race *or* poverty. . . . [Yet,] the single-axis interest groups that dominate advocacy politics do not represent unitary constituencies with clearly defined and bounded interests. Instead, the broad constituencies represented by these organizations are coalitions of intersecting and overlapping groups that are organized around one particular axis that is *constructed* or framed as what they have in common. Organizing around one axis, however, means that so-called common interests are actually those that affect or are "rooted in the experiences of" the more privileged members of a group, and the policy issues addressed by these organizations are likely to be those that affect these more privileged members as well (Cohen

1999, 23). The claims and needs of intersectionally disadvantaged groups, on the other hand, are constructed and framed as being *outside* the purview of these single-axis organizations, and therefore "fall through the cracks" between the axes of existing organizations. . . .

Policy Typology

Despite widespread interest in intersectionality, it has proven difficult to assess empirically and to measure its effects, particularly in a systematic way (Hancock 2007). In addition, while helpful for understanding representation for disadvantaged subgroups, extant intersectional frameworks are limited, relying as they do on dichotomous distinctions that differentiate only between, on the one hand, *single-axis issues* (or, in Cohen's terminology, consensus issues) that affect the whole group, and, on the other hand, *intersectional issues* (or, in Cohen's terminology, cross-cutting issues) that affect disadvantaged members. . . .

To operationalize the concepts underlying theories of intersectionality and assess their explanatory power relative to other theories of interest group behavior, I designed a four-part policy typology. . . . The four categories in this typology are: (1) *universal issues*, which theoretically affect the population as a whole (i.e., not only the marginalized members of the organizations being examined here), regardless of race, gender, sexual orientation, disability, class, or other identity; (2) *majority issues*, which affect an organization's members relatively equally; (3) *disadvantaged-subgroup issues*, which affect a subgroup of an organization's members who are *disadvantaged* economically, socially, or politically compared to the broader membership; and (4) *advantaged-subgroup issues*, which also affect a subgroup of an organization's members, but one that is relatively strong or advantaged compared to the broader membership.

For example, universal issues are policy issues such as Social Security. Though not everyone is affected in precisely the same way by such issues, issues such as these, as their name implies, are relatively "equal opportunity" in their potential impact, both among members of constituencies of the organizations in this study but also outside of these constituencies. *Majority* issues, in contrast, have particular effects on the members of the organization in question. However, among these members, a majority issue is also an "equal opportunity" issue, equally likely to affect any member of an advocacy organization's membership even if it does not affect a numerical majority. An example is violence against women as an issue for women's organizations. This issue is of concern to all women, who are relatively equally likely to be victims, even if not every woman is a victim in her lifetime.

While both universal and majority issues are, in different ways, equal opportunity issues, neither disadvantaged- nor advantaged-subgroup issues can be characterized in this way. When it comes to these issues, different subgroups of an organization's members are *unequally* likely to benefit or to be harmed. In the case of disadvantaged-subgroup issues, they are more likely to benefit or harm a subgroup of an organization's members that is *disadvantaged* relative to other members. For example, welfare reform is a disadvantaged-subgroup issue in the case of women's organizations. That is, the majority of people directly affected by this policy are women (and their children), but the majority of women are not affected by it, nor are all women equally likely to be affected by it. Instead, welfare reform has a disproportionately high chance of affecting particular subgroups of women—in particular low-income women and women of color, i.e., intersectionally disadvantaged subgroups of women.

In contrast to disadvantaged-subgroup issues, advantaged-subgroup issues, while also unequal in their potential impact, are more likely to benefit or harm a subgroup of an organization's members that is *advantaged* relative to other members. So, while issues falling into this category affect a subgroup of the broader group or involve multiple axes of identity, many of those axes may be associated with advantage or privilege (e.g., middle-class, male, white, heterosexual) rather than with disadvantage or marginalization. Although they affect a subgroup of an organization's members, issues falling into the advantaged-subgroup category are also more likely than disadvantaged-subgroup issues to be constructed or framed as majority issues. An example of an advantage-subgroup issue is affirmative action in higher education as an issue for women's organizations. While this policy benefits women, women are not all equally

likely to benefit from it. Such programs are more likely to help middle-class and affluent women, who are more able than low-income women to attend college and graduate school.

It might not be reasonable to expect organizations to represent intersectionally disadvantaged subgroups of their members if they made no claims to represent broadly defined constituencies. Few organizations construe their constituencies so narrowly. Instead, key to the mission statements of many organizations is a claim to represent *all* members of the group. . . . Evidence from the survey also demonstrates that officers at most organizations approach their role as representatives with very broad mandates. To gauge their ideas about the scope and content of their representational obligations, respondents were asked to assess to what degree their organization addresses the policy concerns of ten groups: Asian Pacific Americans, African Americans, Latinos, Native Americans, elderly people, LGBT (lesbian, gay, bisexual, and transgender) people, immigrants, poor or low-income people, women, and workers. Most of the organizations in the study claim that they address the concerns of many of these groups—on average, eight of the ten groups about which they were asked. Just under half (43%) claim to address the policy concerns of *all ten* groups. These responses reveal that most organizations see themselves as representatives of many subgroups of their constituencies.

As representatives of these broad constituencies, organizations representing marginalized groups also embrace broad policy mandates. To assess the scope of their policy mandates, survey respondents were asked about their organizations' interest in eight broad policy areas: antipoverty policy; civil rights and civil liberties; criminal justice; health and human services; immigration; labor policy; urban policy and development; and women's equality. Responses to these questions reveal that the organizations in this study are at least minimally interested in an average of 6.9 out of these 8 policy areas, and that they are, on average, "very interested" in 3.

By announcing broad policy agendas and a determination to speak for all members of a given constituency, advocacy organizations claim implicitly to speak for less privileged members of these groups. Many ask why we should expect these organizations to act altruistically rather than strategically. Indeed, organizations cannot represent every member at all times, nor can they focus exclusively on disadvantaged subgroups to the exclusion of majorities. Nonetheless, characterizing representation for disadvantaged subgroups as an act of altruism underscores one of the main points about intersectionality. The notion that it is altruistic to work on behalf of disadvantaged subgroups of a constituency rests on the assumption that these members are *not a part of* the group and that it is an act of charity rather than one of responsibility and common interests to advocate for them. Unless organizations qualify their claims and say, for example, "we speak for white, heterosexual, middle-class women," their claims to represent groups such as women, Latinos, and low-income people *include* disadvantaged subgroups of these populations. . . .

Hypothesis and Model

Using the survey data, I adjudicate between the various possibilities suggested by extant research about the levels of advocacy that organizations devote to issues affecting disadvantaged subgroups by testing the hypothesis that the level of activity that organizations devote to an issue depends more on the relative *advantage* of the subgroup affected by the issue than it does on the relative *size* of the affected group. If true, we should find that organizations are less active when it comes to disadvantaged-subgroup issues that they are on majority and advantaged-subgroup issues. . . .

Policy Type and Proportion of Members Affected

The most striking finding is that organizations do not allocate their advocacy in ways that benefit the greatest number of members. In fact, quite the opposite is true. The coefficient for the variable that tests how the size of the constituency affected by an issue influences the level of advocacy devoted to that issue (*members affected*) is significantly *negative*. This indicates that activity does *not* increase as the proportion of members affected by an issue increases. Instead, the broader

the impact, the *less* attention an issue receives. The coefficient for the main effect of the measure of advantaged-subgroup issues is the largest, and it is also the only significant measure for the main effects of policy type. Controlling for all other effects in the model, then, issues affecting advantaged subgroups receive more attention than all other issue types.

Examining the interaction of these measures with the measure of the proportion of members affected provides a great deal of support for an intersectional approach. Specifically, the effects of the interaction between the proportion of members affected and both the majority issue and the disadvantaged-subgroup issue are positive and significant, while the interaction between the proportion affected and the advantaged-subgroup issue is not significant. Breadth of impact, it seems, is a crucial determinant of the level of advocacy when it comes to majority and disadvantaged-subgroup issues, but has no effect in the case of advantaged-subgroup issues. These results reveal a double standard applied by organizations that helps to determine the level of advocacy that they devote to issues, a double standard that benefits privileged subgroups at the expense of other members. Specifically, the existence of interaction effects for both majority and disadvantaged-subgroup issues and their absence for advantaged-subgroup issues demonstrates that when it comes to issues that affect advantaged subgroups, advocacy is high regardless of the proportion of members affected. However, when it comes to the other two issue types—majority issues and disadvantaged-subgroup issues—organizations are more active when they perceive that more members are affected.

. . . If the driving concern were to have a "broad" impact, we should see low levels of activity on issues affecting advantaged *as well as* disadvantaged subgroups. However, organizations do not increase their efforts in response to an increase in the proportion of members affected. Instead, this is true only for disadvantaged-subgroup issues; issues affecting privileged subgroups receive high levels of attention regardless of the proportion of an organization's members that are affected. Indeed, controlling for all other effects, issues affecting advantaged subgroups receive more attention than majority issues.

The face-to-face interviews provide additional support for an intersectional understanding of policy advocacy and suggest further that the distribution of activity across issues and subgroups is due to the ways in which advocacy groups frame issues. Whereas survey respondents generally recognized that majority issues affect more members than do the advantaged-subgroup issues, in face-to-face interviews respondents framed advantaged-subgroup issues *as if* they were majority issues that affect many more members than they actually do. In contrast, they framed issues affecting *disadvantaged* subgroups as affecting a narrow portion of their membership.

For example, among the women's organizations in the Survey of National Economic and Social Justice Organizations (SNESJO), 38% of those surveyed said that the majority issue, violence against women, affects "almost all" of their members. Far fewer, 13.6%, said that the disadvantaged-subgroup issue, welfare reform, affects almost all members, and only 9.8% said that the advantaged-subgroup issue, affirmative action in higher education, affects almost all members. Levels of activity, however, do not reflect these assessments. Whereas 86% of women's organizations are active on violence against women, the majority issue, almost as many—80%—are active on affirmative action in higher education, even though respondents recognize that this issue affects fewer members. A far smaller proportion of women's organizations—only 62%—are active on welfare reform, although they recognize that this issue has almost the same impact on their members as affirmative action in higher education. However, as I will show below, respondents in the face-to-face interviews framed both violence against women and affirmative action in higher education as affecting *all* women. In contrast, they framed welfare reform as having a very *narrow* impact even though, like affirmative action in higher education, it affects a subgroup of all women. Notably, welfare reform affects a *disadvantaged* subgroup of women, rather than a relatively advantaged subgroup, as is the case with affirmative action in higher education. In reality, the proportion of women affected by each of these issues is quite similar. For example, according to the 2002 Current Population Survey, approximately 17.5% of women over the age of 25 have college degrees, while approximately 12.6% of all women live below the poverty line, as do 26.5% of female-headed households, and 22.9% of women living alone.

Consider this typical judgment by the field organizer at a women's organization. Asked why her organization is so active on the majority issue of violence against women, she framed the issue as one that affects most women: "It's so prevalent," she said. "It really prevents so many women's freedom and success and equality." When asked about the advantaged-subgroup issue of affirmative action in higher education, the vice president of another women's group also framed this issue as one that affects *all* women, not just the relatively advantaged subset who attend college or graduate school. She said, "I think it's a priority because . . . affirmative action is one of the reasons that women and minorities have made so much progress. . . . It has a huge impact and . . . [it affects] *all* women who are in the workforce or go to college or start their own business and are competing for government contracts—that's a lot of women." She went on to say that women on welfare "don't go to college, but that's a smaller and smaller set of people," thus downplaying the number of women who cannot avail themselves of affirmative action in higher education and retaining the framing of it as a benefit to "all women." Finally, when asked about her organization's activity on welfare reform, a disadvantaged-subgroup issue, this organizer's comments were particularly revealing, capturing the tenor of many comments. "[We are] not as active [on that as we are on] some of the other projects," she said. "We work in coalition with organizations that do work on welfare reform, but it's really just not our cup of tea. . . . We definitely see welfare reform as [a] gendered issue. It's definitely something that we're concerned with and have been involved in but just not on the same level."

These statements about welfare reform, affirmative action, and violence against women are typical of general trends in the connections drawn by respondents between the effects of various policy issues as they influence their levels of advocacy on those issues. As such, these statements help to explain the patterns of involvement in public policy issues reflected in the data from the SNESJO and help to illuminate how the respondents frame and justify their reasons for being involved in some issues and not in others. Specifically, they play *up* the impact of majority and advantaged-subgroup issues, and play *down* the impact or relevance of disadvantaged-subgroup issues. Essentially, no interaction effect exists for advantaged-subgroup issues because organization leaders strategically conflate status and impact, using the high status of advantaged groups to supplement the relatively narrow impact of the issues that affect them. As such, officers justify prioritizing majority and advantaged-subgroup issues by framing them both as having a broad impact. Issues affecting disadvantaged subgroups, on the other hand, are framed in a manner that is both narrow and particularistic, justifying low levels of attention. Since the survey data show that advocacy on disadvantaged-subgroup issues depends on the proportion of members affected, framing them narrowly exacerbates biases against them. . . .

Exacerbating the Bias: Member Concern and Support

Low levels of advocacy on disadvantaged-subgroup issues are due in part to the tendency on the part of organizations to downplay the effects that these issues have on the members affected by these issues. Nevertheless, other factors also exacerbate the biases against disadvantaged subgroups discussed above. For example, member concern about an issue leads to increased advocacy on that issue. The interviews confirm that organizations are more active on issues that they perceive as being important to their members. Several respondents said, for example, that they make the decision to address an issue when they begin "getting lots of phone calls" about it. Conversely, the executive director of an economic justice organization told me that his organization has never done anything regarding public funding for abortion (which affects low-income women, a disadvantaged subgroup of low-income people) because, he said, they do not "get a lot of pressure from" their members about it.

In addition to responding to member *concerns*, the data show that the higher the proportion of constituents that *agrees* with an organization's position on an issue, the more active the organization

is likely to be on that issue. Many interview respondents concurred that they are unlikely to take action on issues unless their members agree with their position. The executive director of an Asian-American organization commented, for example, "We don't want to turn off or upset our community. . . . What's the point of having an advocacy organization if you're turning them off?" Her organization therefore avoids addressing violence against women because, she argued, it is "not a topic that is openly discussed in our community."

Paying attention to member interest and support certainly makes sense: organizations that depend on member support are understandably concerned not to alienate these members. While understandable, however, pegging levels of activity to member concern and agreement depresses advocacy on issues that affect disadvantaged subgroups because concern about these issues is, on average, lower than it is for majority and advantaged-subgroup issues. For example, while 58% of respondents reported that "almost all" of their members are concerned about the majority issues, and 45% gave this answer regarding the advantaged-subgroup issues, only 30% believed that almost all of their members are concerned about the disadvantaged-subgroup issues. The effect of these uneven levels of concern is compounded further by the fact that interest groups, like members of Congress, are more likely to address issues that are important to those "passionate minorities" of their constituencies who have the motivation and the resources to make themselves heard (Kollman 1998). Because advantaged subgroups are likely to have the resources necessary to make organizations aware of their concerns, organizations perceive more interest in the issues of concern to those groups, which contributes to the disproportionately high levels of attention devoted to advantaged-subgroup issues. Member *dissent* is also more likely to prevent advocacy when it comes to issues affecting disadvantaged subgroups—in the case of violence against women discussed above, for example, dissent prevents the Asian-American organization from working on an issue affecting its women members. It is part of an organization's mandate to respond to its members' preferences, but responding to objections to disadvantaged-subgroup issues by avoiding such issues reinforces the marginaliza-tion of intersectionally disadvantaged groups by validating the idea that disadvantaged subgroup issues and the people that they affect are not wor-thy of attention. Thus, the patterns of response and nonresponse to member preferences exacer-bate biases against disadvantaged subgroups. . . .

Discussion and Conclusion: Closer to a Pluralist Heaven?

Advocacy organizations provide a crucial form of political representation for marginalized groups such as women, racial minorities, and low-income people by supplementing their political voice, offsetting some of the bias against them in politics and public opinion, and playing a cru-cial role in improving their status and expand-ing the resources available to them. However, the data reveal persistent and widespread barriers to representation for disadvantaged subgroups of these marginalized groups. As an intersectional approach would predict, levels of advocacy are closely related to the relative status of the sub-group that is affected, and issues are framed in ways that tend to overestimate the breadth of the impact of advantaged-subgroup issues while underestimating the impact of disadvantaged-subgroup issues. Organizations therefore devote much energy and resources to issues that they perceive as having the broadest impact, but also to those that they *define* as broad, whether or not they really are. While levels of advocacy do respond to political opportunities, other strate-gic influences, such as members' concerns and the desire to carve out policy niches, are applied selectively in ways that reinforce the biases against disadvantaged subgroups. When it comes to issues affecting subgroups of their member-ship, organizations employ a double standard: Issues affecting advantaged subgroups are given considerable attention regadless of their breadth of impact, whereas issues affecting disadvantaged subgroups, with rare exceptions, are not. . . .

References

Baumgartner, Frank R., and Beth Leech. 1998. *Basic Interests*. Princeton: Princeton University Press.

Berry, Jeffrey M. 1989. *The Interest Group Society*. 2nd ed. New York: Harper Collins.

Berry, Jeffrey M. 1999. *The New Liberalism*. Washington, DC: Brookings Institution Press.

Cohen, Cathy. 1999. *The Boundaries of Blackness*. Chicago: University of Chicago Press.

Crenshaw, Kimberlé. 1989. "Demarginalizing the Inter-section of Race and Sex." *University of Chicago Legal Forum* 39: 139–67.

DuBois, W. E. B. 1903. *The Souls of Black Folk*. Chicago: A. C. McClurg & Co.

Frymer, Paul. 1999. *Uneasy Alliances*. Princeton: Princeton University Press.

Hancock, Ange-Marie. 2007. "When Multiplication Doesn't Equal Quick Addition: Examining Inter-sectionality as a Research Paradigm." *Perspectives on Politics*.

Kingdon, John W. 1995. *Agendas, Alternatives, and Public Policies*. New York: Harper Collins.

Kollman, Ken. 1998. *Outside Lobbying*. Princeton: Princeton University Press.

Pinderhughes, Dianne M. 1995, "Black Interest Groups and the 1982 Extension of the Voting Rights Act." In *Blacks and the American Political System*, ed. Huey L. Perry. Gainesville: University of Florida Press, pp. 203–24.

Rothenberg, Lawrence S. 1992. *Linking Citizens to Government*. New York: Cambridge University Press.

Schattschneider, E. E. 1975. *The Semisovereign People*. New York: Harcourt Brace Jovanovich.

Schlozman, Kay Lehman. 1984. "What Accent the Heavenly Chorus? Political Equality and the American Pressure System." *Journal of Politics* 46 (4): 1006–32.

Schlozman, Kay Lehman, and Traci Burch. 2009. "Political Voice in an Age of Inequality." In *America at Risk: The Great Dangers*, eds. Robert F. Faulkner and Susan Shell.

Tichenor, Daniel, and Richard Harris. 2002–2003. "Organized Interests and American Political Development." *Political Science Quarterly* 117 (4): 587–612.

Verba, Sidney, Kay Lehman Schlozman, and Henry Brady. 1995. *Voice and Equality: Civic Voluntarism in American Politics*. Cambridge, MA: Harvard University Press.

Walker, Jack. 1991. *Mobilizing Interest Groups in America*. Ann Arbor: University of Michigan Press.

Williams, Melissa S. 1998. Voice, *Trust, and Memory*. Princeton: Princeton University Press.

Wilson, James Q. [1974] 1995. *Political Organizations*. Princeton: Princeton University Press.

Chapter 7

TRANSLATING THE GLOBAL: EFFECTS OF TRANSNATIONAL ORGANIZING ON LOCAL FEMINIST DISCOURSES AND PRACTICES IN LATIN AMERICA

Sonia E. Alvarez

International activism has been a defining feature of both first- and second-wave feminisms in Latin America and most other world regions.[1] From the onset of the contemporary wave, periodic Latin American and Caribbean feminist *encuentros* (region-wide feminist meetings; literally, "encounters") helped forge a self-consciously regional feminist political identity, affirming a feminism distinct from its putatively bourgeois, imperialist North American and European variants.[2] By the early 1990s, the bonds of solidarity created and strategic issues debated at these periodic gatherings had facilitated the emergence of dozens of region-wide issue- or identity-based feminist networks—such as the Latin American and Caribbean Network against Violence against Women and the Afro-Latin American and Afro-Caribbean Women's Network.

The 1990s witnessed the ascendance of a new form of international activism among growing numbers of feminists in the region—one targeting intergovernmental organization (IGO) and international policy arenas and thereby hoping to gain global leverage in pressuring for changes in gender policy on the home front. The UN summits held during the first half of the 1990s—culminating with the Fourth World Conference on Women (FWCW) in Beijing in 1995—prompted thousands of women's rights advocates in Latin America and around the globe to intensify their transnational organizing efforts and catapulted

feminism onto the regional and world policy stages. Seeking to influence the international norms and accords forged at these intergovernmental meetings, feminist activists fashioned new transnational advocacy networks and fortified pre-existing linkages with their counterparts across national borders. . . .

Few studies have explored the critical question of how feminist activists' engagement with policy advocacy on a supranational plane *translates* locally in terms of movement dynamics, discourses, and practices. By analyzing some of the local impacts of a wide array of transborder activities undertaken by Latin American feminists over the past two decades, I want to draw attention to three oft-neglected dimensions of the *transnationalization of local feminist discourses and practices*.

The local and transnational forces shaping feminist movement dynamics are, of course, mutually constitutive and therefore difficult to disentangle analytically. In the sense used here, transnationalization refers to local movement actors' deployment of discursive frames and organizational and political practices that are inspired, (re)affirmed, or reinforced—though not necessarily caused—by their engagement with other actors beyond national borders through a wide range of transnational contacts, discussions, transactions, and networks, both virtual and "real."[3]

First, whereas many recent studies suggest that contemporary international feminist activism largely has been propelled by a top-down process or is the outgrowth of the UN Women's Decade (1976–85) and the World Summits of the 1990s, I want to stress that, *in the case of Latin America, the particularities of the regional and national political contexts in which feminisms unfolded also impelled local movement actors to build transborder connections from the bottom up.*[4] Feminists throughout the region have been involved in a variety of dense "transnational civil society exchanges" (Fox 1999)—such as the periodic Latin American and Caribbean feminist encuentros and the vast array of region-wide *redes*, or networks—since at least the early 1980s.

Second, I will suggest that the logic informing such transnational exchanges differed significantly from that driving an increasing number of international and intraregional feminist advocacy efforts in Latin America in the 1990s. *Among Latin American feminisms, I will argue, an internationalist identity-solidarity logic prevailed in the "encuentro-like" intraregional feminist activism of the 1980s and 1990s, whereas a transnational IGO-advocacy logic came to predominate in region-wide feminist organizing around the Rio, Vienna, Cairo, and Beijing Summits of the 1990s. . . .*

I will suggest that local movement actors pursue transnational linkages with their counterparts beyond the boundaries of the nation-state for (at least) two distinct reasons. First, local movement actors use transnational contacts as a means to (re)construct or reaffirm subaltern or politically marginalized identities and to establish personal and strategic bonds of solidarity with others who share locally stigmatized values (for example, feminist ideals) or identities (for example, as Afro–Latin Americans or as lesbians). Second, activists also organize across borders in an effort to expand formal rights or affect public policy, seeking to enhance their local political leverage via what Margaret Keck and Kathryn Sikkink (1998a, 12–13) call the "boomerang pattern" of influence. By this means, transnational coalitions of nongovernmental, governmental, and intergovernmental actors exert pressure on more powerful states and on IGOs to in turn bring pressure to bear on a particular government that violates rights or resists a desired policy change.[5] . . .

Finally, I will maintain that these *distinctive transnational activist logics nonetheless can have different effects on local movement organizational dynamics and power relations and can sometimes clash in local movement arenas.* Whereas the existing literature typically lumps all cross-border organizing efforts under a single analytical rubric (for instance, "global civil society" or transnational social movements), I want to suggest that different modalities of transborder activism not only can have differential impacts on promoting desired policy changes, but also can have distinct political consequences for activist discourses and practices and for intramovement power relations on the home front.[6] In conclusion, I will argue that while the interplay of these two transnational activist logics has brought numerous benefits to local movements, the predominance of IGO-advocacy activities among growing sectors of Latin American feminist movements in recent years has had more ambiguous and sometimes contradictory local consequences.

Encountering Feminism: Intraregional Solidarity and the Configuration of Latin American Feminist Identities

. . . Building on internationalist solidarities, the regional *encuentros* helped fashion an "imagined" Latin American feminist community whose proper boundaries have been continually renegotiated and redrawn. Who rightfully "belongs" to that community has been a subject of considerable contention locally, and those contests often have been reenacted and redefined in critical transnational sites, such as the periodic regional meetings. Whether or not women who continued to identify primarily with the Left and to privilege the "general" struggle for revolutionary transformation should be included in that imagined feminist community, for instance, has been a key axis of regional and local debate since the First Encuentro. . . .

The sense of "group-ness" (Stein 1995, 135) and the transnational feminist community imagined at the *encuentros*, of course, sometimes drew less-than-inclusive boundaries, actively contested by those excluded. At the Mexico meeting, for instance, hundreds of poor and working-class women active in community struggles, human rights organizations, and other sectors of the grassroots women's movement in the region who had come to identify as "popular feminists" insisted that they too "belonged." Black women and lesbians—whose needs and concerns often were excluded, as a consequence of the racism and heterosexism prevalent among many feminists locally—also sought out transnational linkages. They endeavored by this means to reaffirm their distinctive identities, to exchange strategies for advancing their race- and sexuality-specific claims, and to imagine alternative feminist communities of their own. Indeed, the transactions made possible by the periodic *encuentros* and other regional or subregional workshops, meetings, and events facilitated the configuration of a number of "identity-based" transborder networks. A network of Latin American lesbian feminists was established in 1987 at a regionwide meeting held in Mexico in tandem with the Fourth Encuentro. The Afro–Latin American and Afro-Caribbean Women's Network was founded during the Fifth Encuentro in Argentina and has held two regional meetings (1993 and 1996) of its own since then. . . .

The kinds of internationalist identity-solidarity exchanges of which the *encuentros* are emblematic, as Peruvian feminist Virginia Vargas suggests, were "fundamentally oriented toward recreating collective practices, deploying new categories of analysis, new visibilities, and even new languages which feminisms at the national level were outlining, to name that which heretofore had no name: sexuality, domestic violence, sexual harassment, marital rape, the feminization of poverty [and so on]. These were some of the new signifiers that feminism placed at the center of democratic debates" (1998, 3). A Latin American feminist cultural politics . . . thus was fostered in such transnational spaces, in interaction with local movement arenas. These transborder exchanges furnished local feminist activists with new discursive repertoires, . . . which accompanied the practices of the movement, "creating dates, recovering leaders, histories, symbols" (Vargas 1998, 3).

Regionwide "days of protest" or feminist action proposed by participants in the *encuentros*, for example, not only helped draw public attention to particular feminist issues but also contributed to a sense that activists—most often a relatively small minority in their own national context—were "not alone" in their local struggles for gender(ed) justice. At the First Encuentro, for instance, participants decided to proclaim November 25 the Day against Violence against Women, in honor of three sisters from the Dominican Republic who were murdered by security forces of the Trujillo dictatorship on that day in 1960. Since the Bogotá meeting, feminists throughout the region have commemorated that occasion simultaneously by whatever means appeared most appropriate to local conditions—including mounting demonstrations and other protest actions, holding workshops, lobbying legislators, staging dramatic performances, or launching public education campaigns on sexual and domestic violence (Keck and Sikkink 1998a, 178). Many other dates have come to mark the feminist calendar regionwide, such as September 28, the Day of Struggle for the Decriminalization of Abortion, and October 11, Indigenous Women's Day.

These simultaneous commemorative occasions, along with the many theoretical and strategic exchanges facilitated by the *encuentros* and innumerable other intraregional meetings, publications, electronic communications, and websites often have fueled deeper feminist reflection among local activists and introduced new ways of discursively framing local feminist struggles. . . .

The UN Is Knocking at Your Door: The "Globalization" of Local Latin American Feminist Policy Advocacy in the 1990s

In the early 1990s, a very different activist logic began propelling increasing numbers of Latin American feminist NGOs to pursue transnational linkages with their counterparts throughout the region and across the globe. Largely inspired by the UN's declared intention to promote greater NGO participation in the "megaconferences" or world summits it sponsored during the first half of that decade (Clark, Friedman, and Hochstetler 1998, 6; Otto 1996; Weiss and Gordenker 1996), many feminists in Latin America for the first time came to view IGOs and the intergovernmental arena as potential venues for advancing women's rights locally.[7]

The organized, regionally coordinated participation of Latin American feminists in "official" international publics such as the UN or ECLAC (the Economic Commission on Latin America and the Caribbean)—as compared to the many "alternative" transnational arenas discussed above—was a novelty. As Marysa Navarro recounts, "For

Latin American and Caribbean feminists, the first world conferences on women did not have great relevance (with the exception of the Brazilians and Mexicans who did see themselves affected by the beginning of the Women's Decade). [At the world conference of the International Women's Year] in Mexico, the presence of Latin American feminism was minimal since, though groups had emerged in some countries, there still were no movements [as such]" (1998, 108).

By the time of the Beijing conference, in contrast, "the [regional] women's movement (and its feminist expression) took part in the official conference process, with its many currents, issues, and forces" in expressive numbers, whereas "at previous conferences on women . . . it participated only in the World [NGO] Forum and barely managed to establish relations with official circles" (Vargas and Olea Mauleón 1998a, 16). Though most were inexperienced in "global policy advocacy," a specialized skill perfected by feminist international NGOs (INGOs) based mostly in the North, many local activists were by then persuaded that influencing their government's reports to the UN and lobbying for changes in international legal norms might provide them with additional political leverage on the home front.

The difference between Latin American feminists' scant presence in Mexico and their significant participation in the Beijing process was not due only to the impressive expansion of feminist movements in the region in the two intervening decades, however.[8] It is also attributable to changes in the national political contexts in which the movements unfolded. With the return of electoral democracy (however flawed and restricted) and liberal rights discourses (however hollow and "neo") to much of the region by the end of the 1980s, many governments in the mid-1990s claimed to be more receptive to selected feminist claims. Whereas during the 1970s and much of the 1980s feminists for the most part turned their backs on the state and eschewed the conventional political arena—then (rightly) viewed as exclusionary, oppressive, and self-evidently inimical to any and all claims for social justice, let alone gender justice—by the 1990s growing numbers of feminists were directing their organizing efforts at influencing gender policies (Alvarez 1998, 1999). The possibility of pursuing local policy changes

through intergovernmental venues such as the UN conferences, then, appealed particularly to that sizable subset of Latin American feminist activists who had become most directly involved in local gender policy matters during the previous decade. . . .

The Complementarity of Transnational Activist Logics in Latin America

The new transnational activist logic spurred particularly by the Beijing preparatory process built upon and sometimes reinforced the internationalist solidarity exchanges of the 1980s and early 1990s. That is, the two transnational activist logics outlined in the introduction, though sometimes running on parallel or seldom-intersecting tracks, at other times proved to be complementary, with largely positive consequences for local movement dynamics, discourses, and practices.

The NGO forums at the Mexico, Copenhagen, and Nairobi UN women's conferences, for instance, were "important for the development of a regional feminist movement. They played a significant role in fostering bonds of solidarity . . . [and] provided the foundations for an intense and informal network of relationships and exchange" (Vargas and Olea Mauleón 1998a, 16, 2n). Indeed, it was at the mid-decade of the Woman Conference in Copenhagen (1980) that some Venezuelan feminists decided to promote the first regional *encuentro*, which Colombian feminists organized the following year (Navarro 1998, 108; Navarro 1982).

The *encuentros* and other intraregional feminist gatherings and exchanges in turn facilitated the formation of transnational social networks and nurtured intense personal and political bonds and affinities among feminists in far-flung reaches of Latin America which provided a crucial backdrop for the creation of policy-focused networks and regional advocacy coalitions.[9] The variety of internationalist identity-solidarity exchanges gave impetus to the more formalized, policy-centered feminist networks, such as the Network of Women in Politics (established at the Argentine *encuentro*) and others which combined an identity-solidarity logic with an emphasis on promoting policy change, such as the Latin American and Caribbean Network against Violence against

Women and the regional women's health and reproductive rights network. . . .

The transnational IGO-advocacy of the 1990s sometimes built on, reinforced, or extended the affinities and complementarities fostered by earlier identity-solidarity exchanges. This was particularly evident in the case of black and indigenous women, lesbians, and others whose voices were often muted in local movement arenas despite their considerable prior local and cross-border organizing efforts. Those efforts contributed to the "globalization" of feminist discourses about difference and diversity among women, and fostered the incorporation of elements of those discourses by IGOs and the liberal Northern states that are hegemonic in international policy arenas. As a consequence, UN agencies and Northern-based private foundations and INGOs often conditioned funding for participation in international forums on local movements' ability to "incorporate diversity." The Beijing process thus furnished a new "top-down" incentive for Afro–Latin American women, lesbians, disabled women, young women, and indigenous women to engage in transnationalized rights advocacy around their specific needs and concerns. This participation, in turn, emboldened them to assert a more vocal presence in local, national, and regional women's movement arenas. . . .

The heightened visibility of Latin American feminist NGOs in official international policy arenas also appears to have helped legitimate feminist claims vis-à-vis nonfeminist parallel sectors of national and international civil society, prompting both INGOs, such as Human Rights Watch, as well as local human rights groups to be more attentive to women's rights and to seek out alliances with local and transnational feminist NGOs. As Peruvian activist and former regional coordinator of the Comité Latinoamericano de Defensa de los Derechos de las Mujeres (the Latin American Committee for the Defense of Women's Rights, or CLADEM) Roxana Vasquez told me, "Vienna forced the National Coordination of Human Rights Organizations to seat us at the table. Vienna legitimated the topic of women's human rights and obliged them to pay attention to violence against women," a rights violation until then seldom addressed by national and regional mainstream human rights organizations.[10] . . .

Engagement with transnationalized gender policy advocacy has provided advocates with new, internationally sanctioned political scripts they can deploy locally, which, unlike the shared feminist movement signifiers diffused through inward-oriented identity-solidarity exchanges, have greater potential political resonance vis-à-vis local policy makers. Latin American rights advocates now more regularly invoke international human rights law to press for local compliance with new global gender equity norms, and they appeal to UN and OAS (Organization of American States) conventions in promoting women's rights locally. In late 1996, for instance, Brazilian members of CLADEM brought two local cases of violence against women before the Inter-American Commission on Human Rights.[11] Invoking the Inter-American Convention on Violence against Women—ratified by Brazil in 1995 and promulgated by Decree 149 in 1996—local feminists argued that the Brazilian government had failed to investigate and prosecute the deaths of two São Paulo women killed by their male lovers, thereby violating the fundamental rights assured to women by the convention. "The simple fact of bringing these women's rights violations to the attention of the international community," local CLADEM members argued, "imposes a political and moral condemnation on the Brazilian State."[12] . . .

Contradictory Consequences of "Transnationalized" Feminist Policy Advocacy for Local Movement Discourses, Practices, and Power Dynamics

The new transnationalized advocacy repertoires developed by those sectors of the Latin American women's movements most centrally involved in the UN conference processes of the 1990s did not always translate smoothly in local policy and movement arenas. First, though analysts of transnational advocacy networks and local social movements alike have stressed the centrality of frame resonance—defined as "the relationship between a movement organization's interpretive work and its ability to influence broader public understanding" (Keck and Sikkink 1998, 17)—to advocates' success in promoting desired policy changes (see also Tarrow 1998; McAdam, Mc-Carthy, and Zald 1996), I want to suggest that the framing processes appropriate when persuading state or IGO public officials are sometimes more problematic when what is desired is also broad cultural change. This is a particularly tricky issue for feminist rights advocates, since framing their claims in ways that will have cultural resonance in local policy arenas may clash with their principled quest to transform larger publics' cultural understandings of gender power relations. . . .

Though political give-and-take, cautious language, and a willingness to make discursive concessions may well be essential to effective policy advocacy, public policies, of course, have cultural effects. That is, policies help (re)shape cultural understandings of particular social problems. Thus, if the feminist framing process is reduced to discursive accommodation and spills over the negotiating table and onto the streets, into the larger public debate about women's rights or gender justice, it can have troubling implications.

For example, in Chile, as in several other Latin American nations, the Congress—at the urging of local feminist policy advocates and under pressure from new international women's rights norms—enacted legislation on intrafamilial violence (*violencia intra-familiar*). Local feminist rights advocates engaged in protracted negotiations to persuade policy makers of the urgency of legislating on this issue, and the law unquestionably represents an important step in combating violence against women. However, the watered-down law that ultimately prevailed centered on "strengthening the family," prescribed efforts at "family reconciliation," recommended "couples' therapy," and largely ignored the gendered power relations so central to feminist understandings of the causes and remedies for this dramatic and systematic violation of women's human rights. . . .

Though sometimes complementary or mutually reinforcing, then, the two transnational activist logics can clash in local movement arenas. . . . The clash between the two transnational logics, moreover, seems to have further fueled the growing local schism between the so-called *institucionalizadas*, or "institutionalized feminists"—as their critics have dubbed those activists who in recent years have gone to work in government institutions or who focus their activism on lobbying those official

arenas—and the self-proclaimed "pure" and radical *autónomas*, or "autonomous" feminists, who view any involvement with local or international policy arenas as an automatic capitulation to the forces of "global, neoliberal patriarchy."

This clash, appropriately enough, came to a head precisely in one of those alternative international public spaces so central to fomenting the bonds of solidarity which made the formation of transnational advocacy coalitions possible—the Seventh Latin American and Caribbean Feminist Encuentro, held in Cartagena, Chile, in November 1996. During the often-acrimonious debates at that *encuentro*, the *autónomas*—a recent, relatively small, but highly vocal political current within the Latin American feminist field—accused transnationalized, policy-centered NGOs of having "sold out" the women's movement to IGOs and local states.[13] . . .

Notes

1. On first-wave feminist international activism, see especially Miller 1990 and 1991; Rupp 1997; Waterman 1998; and Keck and Sikkink 1998a, chap. 2.
2. On the *encuentros*, see Navarro 1982; Sternbach et al. 1992; Fischer 1993; Stephen 1997; Beckman 1998; Craske 1999; and Olea Mauleón 1998.
3. I am grateful to my colleague Jonathan Fox for calling my attention to the variety of possible types of transborder civil society exchanges. See Fox 1999.
4. Most analyses stress the centrality of UN processes in the formation of global women's networks, suggesting that "any chronology of the international women's movement reads like a litany of UN meetings: Mexico, Copenhagen, Nairobi, Vienna, Cairo, Beijing" (Sikkink 1995, 9). The contemporary wave of transnational feminist organizing is said to have "gained momentum during International Women's Year (IWY) and the UN Decade for Women (1976–85), which in turn catalyzed networks around women's rights" (Keck and Sikkink 1998a, 169). See also Chen 1996; Kardam 1997; Prugl and Meyer 1999; West 1999; and Tinker 1999.
5. These two categories are not in any way intended to be exhaustive. For instance, a third and distinct motive force not discussed here is implicated in transnational organizing among activists who share concrete material interests or a common legal or cultural fate despite their location in different national settings. Examples of this kind of "logic" might include cross-border organizing efforts by employees of the same transnational corporation, such as the 1997 "Eurostrike" staged by Renault workers in Belgium and France (Tarrow 1998, 176–77).

6. For a sampling of recent analyses of "global civil society, "see Clark, Friedman, and Hochstetler 1998; Lipschutz and Mayer 1996; Otto 1996; and Shaw 1994. On transnational social movements, see Smith 1998; Smith, Chatfield, and Pagnucco 1997; and McCarthy 1997.

7. These world summits included the UN Conference on Environment and Development held in Rio de Janeiro in 1992, the UN World Conference on Human Rights held in Vienna in 1993, the International Conference on Population and Development held in Cairo in 1994, the Social Development Summit held in Copenhagen in 1995, and the Fourth World Conference on Women held in Beijing in 1995.

8. More than 1,800 women from the Latin American and Caribbean region participated in the NGO Forum at Huairou, with some two to three hundred staying on to lobby at the official Beijing conference (Alvarez 1998). Local Beijing "initiative" coalitions and articulations were established in most countries or subregions, involving thousands of women who were unable to travel to the summit to participate locally in this transnational process.

On the development of feminist movements in the Latin American region, see Jaquette 1994; León 1994; Jaquette and Wolchik 1998; Craske 1999; Sternbach et al. 1992; and Alvarez 1998.

9. As Keck and Sikkink note, "Social movement theorists have repeatedly stressed the importance of social networks—concrete linkages that derive from locality, shared experience, kinship, and the like—as foundations on which movements are built. . . . [M]any social networks that nourish the creation of transnational advocacy networks and support their work reveal histories of personal relationships and shared experiences that parallel those found in domestic movements" (1998b, 219).

10. Formal interview with Roxana Vásquez, CLADEM, and Guilia Tamayo, Centro Flora Tristán, Lima, Peru, 16 August 1997. A recent survey of 155 international nongovernmental human rights organizations based in both the North and South revealed that fully 51 percent claimed that "promoting or protecting women's rights" was among their primary organizational goals (Smith, Pagnucco, and Lopez 1998, 388) and that 58 percent had sent participants to the Fourth World Conference on Women in Beijing.

11. Interview with Maria Amélia de Almeida Teles, União de Mulheres de São Paulo, and Flávia Piovesan, Procuradora do Estado de São Paulo and member of CLADEM/Brasil, São Paulo, 31 August 1998.

12. Flávia Piovesan, Maria Amélia de Almeida Teles, and Silvia Pimental, "Estrategias para a Proteção Internacional dos Direitos Humanos das Mulheres," *Fêmea* 6 (April 1997): 8.

13. On that debate and its local and regional aftermaths, see especially Olea Mauleón 1998. See also special issues of *Cotidiano Mujer* (Uruguay), nos. 22 (May 1996) and 23 (March 1997); *Enfoque Feminista* (Brazil) 6 (May 1997): *Brujas* (Argentina), March 1997; and *Femindria* (Argentina), June 1997.

Works Cited

Alvarez, Sonia E. 1998. "Latin American Feminisms 'Go Global': Trends of the 1990s and Challenges for the New Millennium." In *Cultures of Politics/Politics of Cultures: Re-visioning Latin American Social Movements*, edited by Sonia E. Alvarez, Evelina Dagnino, and Arturo Escobar. Boulder, Colo.: Westview Press.

Alvarez, Sonia E. 1999. "Advocating Feminism: The Latin American Feminist NGO 'Boom.'" *International Feminist Journal of Politics* 1, 2.

Beckman, Ericka. 1998. "Debating Feminisms: The Latin American and Caribbean Feminist *Encuentros* (1981–1996)." M.A. thesis, Stanford University.

Chen, Martha Alter. 1996. "Engendering World Conferences: The International Women's Movement and the UN." In *NGOs, the UN, and Global Governance*, edited by Thomas G. Weiss and Leon Gordenker. Boulder, Colo.: Lynne Rienner.

Clark, Ann Marie, Elisabeth J. Friedman, and Kathryn Hochstetler. 1998. "The Sovereign Limits of Global Civil Society: A Comparison of NGO Participation in UN World Conferences on the Environment, Human Rights, and Women." *World Politics* 51 (October): 1–35.

Craske, Nikki. 1999. *Women and Politics in Latin America.* New Brunswick, N.J.: Rutgers University Press.

Fischer, Amalia. 1993. "Feministas Latinoamericanas: Las Nuevas Brujas y sus Aquelarres." Draft manuscript.

Fox, Jonathan A. 1999. "Assessing Binational Civil Society Coalitions." Paper presented at the Conference on the "Dilemmas of Change in Mexican Politics," Center for U.S.–Mexican Studies, University of California, San Diego, La Jolla, October 8–9.

Jaquette, Jane S., ed. 1994. *The Women's Movement in Latin America: Participation and Democracy.* Boulder, Colo.: Westview Press.

Jaquette, Jane S., and Sharon L. Wolchik, eds. 1998. *Women and Democracy: Latin America and Eastern Europe.* Baltimore: Johns Hopkins University Press.

Kardam, Nuket. 1997. "The Emerging International Women's Regime." Unpublished manuscript.

Keck, Margaret E., and Kathryn Sikkink. 1998a. *Activists beyond Borders: Advocacy Networks in International Politics.* Ithaca, N.Y.: Cornell University Press.

———. 1998b. "Transnational Advocacy Networks in the Movement Society." In *The Social Movement Society: Contentious Politics for a New Century*, edited by David S. Meyer and Sidney Tarrow. New York: Rowman & Littlefield.

León, Magdalena, ed. 1994. *Mujeres y Participación Política: Avances y Desafíos en América Latina.* Bogotá: Tercer Mundo Editores.

Lipschutz, Ronnie D., with Judith Mayer. 1996. *Global Civil Society and Global Environmental Governance.* Albany, N.Y.: State University of New York Press.

McAdam, Doug, John D. McCarthy, and Mayer N. Zald, eds. 1996. *Comparative Perspectives on Social Movements: Political Opportunities, Mobilizing Structures, and Cultural*

Framings. New York: Cambridge University Press.

McCarthy, John D. 1997. "The Globalization of Social Movement Theory." In *Transnational Social Movements and Global Politics: Solidarity beyond the State*, edited by Jackie Smith, Charles Chatfield, and Ron Pagnucco. Syracuse, N.Y.: Syracuse University Press.

Miller, Francesca. 1990. "Latin American Feminism and the Transnational Arena." In *Women, Culture, and Politics in Latin America*, edited by the Seminar on Feminism and Culture in Latin America. Berkeley: University of California Press.

———. 1991. *Latin American Women and the Search for Social Justice*. Hanover, N.H.: University of New England Press.

Navarro, Marysa. 1982. "First Feminist Meeting of Latin America and the Caribbean." *Signs* 8, 1: 154–57.

———. 1998. "Una Reflexión: Notas sobre Uno de los Posibles Mapas del Feminismo Latinoamericano para Ir Creando Futuras Cartografías." In *Encuentros, (Des) Encuentros y Búsquendas: El Movimiento Feminista en América Latina*, edited by Cecilia Olea Mauléon. Lima: Ediciones Flora Tristán.

Olea Mauléon, Cecilia, ed. 1998. *Encuentros, (Des) Encuentros y Búsquedas: El Movimiento Feminista en América Latina*. Lima: Ediciones Flora Tristán.

Otto, Diane. 1996. "Nongovernmental Organizations in the United Nations System: The Emerging Role of International Civil Society." *Human Rights Quarterly* 18: 107–41.

Prugl, Elisabeth, and Mary K. Meyer. 1999. "Gender Politics in Global Governance." In *Gender Politics in Global Governance*, edited by Mary K. Meyer and Elisabeth Prugl. New York: Rowman & Littlefield.

Rupp, Leila J. 1997. *Worlds of Women: The Making of an International Women's Movement*. Princeton, N.J.: Princeton University Press.

Shaw, Martin. 1994. "Civil Society and Global Politics: Beyond a Social Movements Approach." *Millienium: Journal of International Studies* 23, 3: 647–67.

Sikkink, Kathryn. 1995. "Transnational Networks on Violence against women." Paper presented at the Nineteenth International Congress of the Latin American Studies Association, Washington, D.C., September 28–30.

Smith, Jackie. 1998. "Global Civil Society? Transnational Social Movement Organizations and Social Capital." *American Behaviorist Scientist* 42 (September): 93–107.

Smith, Jackie, Charles Chatfield, and Ron Pagnucco. 1997. "Social Movements and World Politics: A Theoretical Framework." In *Transnational Social Movements and Global Politics: Solidarity beyond the State*, edited by Jackie Smith, Charles Chatfield, and Ron Pagnucco. Syracuse, N.Y.: Syracuse University Press.

Smith, Jackie, and Ron Pagnucco, with George A. Lopez. 1998. "Globalizing Human Rights: The Work of Transnational Human Rights NGOs." *Human Rights Quarterly* 20: 379–412.

Stein, Arlene. 1995. "Sisters and Queers: The Decentering of Lesbian Feminism." In *Cultural Politics and Social Movements*, edited by Marcy Darnovsky, Barbara Epstein, and Richard Flacks. Philadelphia: Temple University Press.

Stephen, Lynn. 1997. *Women and Social Movements in Latin America: Power from Below*. Austin: University of Texas Press.

Sternbach, Nancy Saporta, Marysa Navarro-Aranguren, Patricia Chuchryk, and Sonia E. Alvarez. 1992. "Feminisms in Latin America: From Bogota to San Bernardo." In *The Making of Social Movements in Latin America: Identity, Strategy, and Democracy*, edited by Arturo Escobar and Sonia E. Alvarez. Boulder, Colo.: Westview Press.

Tarrow, Sidney. 1998. *Power in Movement: Social Movements and Contentious Politics*. 2d ed. New York: Cambridge University Press.

Tinker, Irene. 1999. "Nongovernmental Organizations: An Alternative Power Base for Women?" In *Gender Politics in Global Governance*, edited by Mary K. Meyer and Elisabeth Prugl. New York: Rowman & Littlefield.

Vargas, Virginia. 1998. "Los Feminismos Latinoamericanos Construyendo los Espacios Transnacionales: La Experiencia de Beijing." Paper presented at the Conference on Transnational Organizing in the Americas, University of California at Santa Cruz, December 4–7, 1998.

Vargas, Virginia, and Cecilia Olea Mauléon. 1998a. "Roads to Beijing: Reflections from Inside the Process." In *Roads to Beijing: Fourth World Conference on Women in Latin America and the Caribbean*. Lima; Santafé de Bogotá; Quito: Ediciones Flora Tristán; UNICEF; UNIFEM.

———. 1998b. "Knots in the Region." In *Roads to Beijing: Fourth World Conference on Women in Latin America and Caribbean*. Lima: Santafe de Bogotá: Quito: Ediciones Flora Tristán: UNICEF; UNIFEM.

Waterman, Peter. 1998. *Globalization, Social Movements and the New Internationalisms*. London: Mansell.

Weiss, Thomas G., and Leon Gordenker, eds. 1996. *NGOs, the UN & Global Governance*. Boulder, Colo.: Lynne Rienner.

West, Lois A. 1999. "The United Nations Women's Conferences and Feminist Politics." In *Gender Politics in Global Governance*, edited by Mary K. Meyer and Elisabeth Prugl. New York: Rowman & Littlefield.

Chapter 8

CROSS-REGIONAL TRENDS IN FEMALE TERRORISM

Karla J. Cunningham

Although women have historically been participants in terrorist groups[1] in Sri Lanka, Iran, West Germany, Italy, and Japan, to name a few cases, very little scholarly attention has been directed toward the following questions: first, why women join these groups and the types of roles they play; and second, why terrorist organizations recruit and operationalize women and how this process proceeds within societies that are usually highly restrictive of women's public roles. . . . Regardless of region, women's involvement with politically violent organizations and movements highlights several generalizable themes. First, there is a general assumption that most women who become involved with terrorist organizations do so for personal reasons, whether a personal relationship with a man or because of a personal tragedy (e.g., death of a family member, rape). This assumption mirrors theories about female criminal activity in the domestic realm, as well as legitimate political activity by women,[2] and diminishes women's credibility and influence both within and outside organizations.

Second, because women are not considered credible or likely perpetrators of terrorist violence, they can more easily carry out attacks and assist their organizations. Women are able to use their gender to avoid detection on several fronts: first, their "non-threatening" nature may prevent in-depth scrutiny at the most basic level as they are simply not considered important enough to warrant investigation; second, sensitivities regarding more thorough searches, particularly of women's bodies, may hamper stricter scrutiny; and third,

a woman's ability to get pregnant and the attendant changes to her body facilitate concealment of weapons and bombs using maternity clothing, as well as further impeding inspection because of impropriety issues. Finally, popular opinion typically considers women as victims of violence, including terrorism, rather than perpetrators, a perspective that is even more entrenched when considering women from states and societies that are believed to be extremely "oppressed" such as those in the Middle East and North Africa (MENA). Such a perspective is frequently translated into official and operational policy, wherein women are not seriously scrutinized as operational elements within terrorist and guerilla organizations because of limited resources and threat perception.

This analysis contends that female involvement with terrorist activity is widening ideologically, logistically, and regionally for several reasons: first, increasing contextual pressures (e.g., domestic/international enforcement, conflict, social dislocation) create a mutually reinforcing process driving terrorist organizations to recruit women at the same time women's motivations to join these groups increases; contextual pressures impact societal controls over women, thereby facilitating, if not necessitating, more overt political participation up to, and including, political violence; and operational imperatives often make female members highly effective actors for their organizations, inducing leaders toward "actor innovation" to gain strategic advantage against their adversary.[3]

Contextual Pressures and Innovation

Since 11 September 2001 United States law enforcement and national security efforts have been aggressively targeted at identifying current and potential terrorist actors who threaten the country's interests. This activity has largely centered on Muslim males because of the types of terrorist attacks that have threatened the United States over the past decade (e.g., the World Trade Center [1993], the African Embassy bombings [1998], and the USS *Cole* bombing [2000] to name a few). All of the incidents were planned and implemented by Muslim, and predominantly Arab, males residing within the United States or abroad.

Terrorist organizations tend to be highly adaptive, and although there are fundamental differences among terrorist groups along ideological lines (e.g., ethnonationalist, religious, Marxist-Leninist) that influence the types of ends these organizations seek, they are typically unified in terms of the means (e.g., political violence) they are willing to employ to achieve their goals. The means/goals dichotomy is reflected by the absence of a single definition of terrorism with which all can agree.[4] Nevertheless, an ancient Chinese proverb quickly gets to the heart of terrorism, noting that its purpose is "to kill one and frighten 10,000 others."[5]

Problematic, and evidenced by the evolving nature of campaigns in Sri Lanka and Israel/Palestine, as well as historical examples from Ireland and Lebanon, is that terrorist organizations tend to adapt to high levels of external pressure by altering their techniques and targets. Terrorist organizations learn from each other, and "[t]he history of terrorism reveals a series of innovations, as terrorists deliberately selected targets considered taboo and locales where violence was unexpected. These innovations were then rapidly diffused, especially in the modern era of instantaneous and global communications."[6] Corresponding to existing terrorism theory, the use of suicide campaigns is an example of one type of tactical adaptation utilized by terrorist organizations, especially in the Arab-Israeli conflict and Sri Lanka, and both cases have also witnessed an evolution in targets (e.g., combatant to civilian).

This analysis suggests that terrorist organizations "innovate" on an additional level, particularly under heavy government pressure or to exploit external conditions, to include new actors or perpetrators.[7] In both Sri Lanka[8] and Palestine, female participation within politically violent organizations has increased and women's roles have expanded to include suicide terrorism. Sri Lanka's "Black Tigers," composed of roughly 50 percent women, is symbolic of this adaptation. In 2002, the Al-Aqsa Martyrs Brigade in the Occupied Territories began actively recruiting women to act as suicide bombers in its campaign against Israeli targets. Other organizations have demonstrated efforts to recruit and employ women. For example, the Algerian-based Islamic Action Group (GIA) operation planned for the Millennium celebration in 1999 reportedly had a woman, Lucia Garofalo, as a central character. The Revolutionary Armed Forces of Colombia (FARC) and Peru's Shining Path have growing levels of female operatives, and even right-wing extremist groups in the United States, such as the World Church of the Creator (WCOTC), are reportedly witnessing high female recruitment levels, and one woman associated with the rightist movement, Erica Chase, went on trial in summer 2002 with her boyfriend in an alleged plot to bomb symbolic African-American and Jewish targets. . . .

Patterns of Operational Female Terrorism

Not only have women historically been active in politically violent organizations, the regional and ideological scope of this activity has been equally broad. Women have been operational (e.g., regulars) in virtually every region, and there are clear trends toward women becoming more fully incorporated into numerous terrorist organizations. Cases from Colombia, Italy, Sri Lanka, Pakistan, Turkey, Iran, Norway, and the United States suggest that women have not only functioned in support capacities, but have also been leaders in organization, recruitment, and fund-raising, as well as tasked with carrying out the most deadly missions undertaken by terrorist organizations—suicide bombings. Regardless of the region, it is clear that women are choosing to participate in politically violent organizations irrespective of their respective organizational leaders' motives for recruiting them.[9]

European Female Terrorism

European terrorist organizations are among the oldest groups to examine and offer the first insights into women's roles in these organizations. Women have been drawn to leftist and rightist organizations in Europe, and have thus been involved in groups with goals ranging from separatism to Marxist-Leninism. Women have been, and in certain cases continue to be, active members of several terrorist organizations within Europe including the Euskadi Ta Askatasuna (ETA, Basque Homeland and Unity), the Irish Republican Army (IRA), and the Italian Red Brigades (RD), to name a few. Mirroring the Palestinian conflict, which will be discussed later, Irish women, particularly mothers, have been widely active in their conflict with the British, which was waged close to home in their neighborhoods and communities.

One examination of the operational role of women in Italy's various terrorist factions during the 1960s and 1970s identifies several important tendencies. Although women generally accounted for no more than 20 percent of terrorist membership during this period, Italian women who participated in terrorist organizations were overwhelmingly drawn to leftist and nationalist organizations. . . .

The Italian experience correlates with a general trend[10] in which leftist organizations tend to attract more female recruits not only because their ideological message for political and social change (e.g., equality) resonates with women, but also because those ideas influence leadership structures within the groups. As a result, "[w]omen tend to be overrepresented in positions of leadership in left-wing groups and to be underrepresented in right-wing groups."[11] Conversely, rightist organizations have more limited recruitment of women, and they have historically been characterized by an almost uniform absence of female leaders. . . .

Latin American Female Terrorism

Women have historically been involved in numerous revolutionary movements in Latin America (e.g., Cuba, El Salvador, Nicaragua, Mexico) so their more visible role in groups like the FARC and Shining Path is not surprising.[12] Within Latin America, two of the most notable terrorist organizations designated by the U.S. Department of State, Colombia's FARC and the Shining Path of Peru, have increasingly incorporated women into their organizations. Figures on total female membership within the FARC vary from 20 to 40 percent, with a general average of 30 percent.[13] Although the FARC's senior leadership structure, particularly the Secretariat, remains all male, women have been ascending throughout the group's ranks, with women now reportedly bearing the title "Commandante." Like Shining Path, the FARC has recruited and retained women for more than a dozen years. Unlike the FARC, the Shining Path's senior leadership structure, the Central Committee, is composed of eight women (out of 19).[14] The Latin American phenomenon of "machismo" is noted as responsible for the continuation of senior male leadership for the FARC and the "cult of personality" that is said to surround the Shining Path's former leader, Abimael Guzman. As with the Liberation Tigers for Tamil Eelam (LTTE), women of both groups experience the same types of training and expectations as their male counterparts and women have been increasingly used in intelligence roles by the FARC.[15]

In Latin America, female activism in politically violent organizations remains concentrated within leftist movements, corresponding to themes seen in Europe and North America. In both Colombia and Peru, the revolutionary features of the respective movements are significant, mirroring processes in Palestine and Sri Lanka, as well as Iran, South Africa, and Eritrea. For the most part, women join the FARC and Shining Path while young, engage in all facets of the organization, and often remain members for life, although activism rates may alter with age, as is true with their male counterparts. . . . The fact that poor, young individuals are frequently drawn to terrorist organizations and politically violent groups is neither regionally limited nor gendered.

South Asian Female Terrorism

The Sri Lankan case shares some parallels with MENA terrorist organizations, including the structural imperatives that favor the use of women as suicide bombers, the intersection of political and sociocultural goals of liberation, and sociocultural norms that idealize sacrifice.[16] As of 2000, roughly half of the LTTE's membership[17] were females, who are frequently recruited as children into the Black Tigers, an elite bomb squad composed of women and men.[18] Women enjoy equivalent training and combat experience with their male counterparts and are fully incorporated into the extant structure of the LTTE. Women's utility as suicide bombers derives from their general exclusion from the established "profile" of such actors employed by many police and security forces (e.g., young males), allowing them to better avoid scrutiny and reach their targets. The 1991 assassination of Rajiv Gandhi, then leader of India, by a young Tamil woman who garlanded him, bowed at his feet, and then detonated a bomb that killed them both, provides proof of the power of this terrorist weapon. However, that woman, identified as Dhanu (a.k.a Tanu), suggests some of the contradictory themes that arise when considering women's roles in the LTTE.

Reportedly prompted to join the LTTE because she was gang-raped by Indian peacekeeping forces who also killed her brothers,[19] Dhanu has become an important mythical force utilized for further recruitment as rape has been identified as one of the primary reasons motivating young women to join the LTTE. The goal of *eelam* (freedom) pursued by the LTTE is said to be conjoined with the pursuit of similar personal, and perhaps even societal, freedom for female recruits as "[f]ighting for Tamil freedom is often the only way a woman has to redeem herself."[20] Also inherent in the struggle is the ideal of sacrifice, particularly for Tamil rape victims who are said to be socially prohibited from marriage and childbearing. Equating the sacrifice of the female bomber as an extension of motherhood, suicide bombings become an acceptable "offering" for women who can never be mothers, a process that is reportedly encouraged by their families.[21] "As a rule, women are represented as the core symbols of the nation's identity" and the "Tamil political movements have used women's identity as a core element in their nationalism."[22] . . .

Sri Lanka is not the only place in South Asia, however, where women are, or have been, allegedly involved with terrorism. Among Sikh militants, women have participated in an array of roles including armed combat. Importantly, Sikh-ism does not distinguish between male and female equality forming a religio-societal grounding that neither precludes female combat nor categorizes that role as uniquely masculine (or "unfeminine"). Rather, societal resistance to female combat roles is fostered by well-founded fears of sexual abuse, rape, and sexual torture of women if captured. Within the Sikh case, women's "support" roles are not viewed as peripheralized or indicative of women's marginalization within the political sphere. Instead, women's support of their husbands and sons is seen to critically enable their ability to fight and die for the nation, and women's roles as mothers producing future fighters for that nation is also recognized. As a result, "[w]hile it is obvious that the celebrated virtues of courage, bold action, and strong speech are consonant with masculinity as understood in the West, among Sikhs these qualities are treated as neither masculine nor feminine, but simply as Sikh, values. Women may be bound to the kitchen and may have babies in their arms, but they are still fully *expected* to behave as soldiers, if necessary."[23] . . .

Several themes arise from the South Asian context that provide additional insight into female terrorists, particularly suicide terrorism. First, personal motives (e.g., family, rape, financial) are argued to greatly influence women to join organizations like the LTTE and, even more importantly, into becoming suicide bombers (e.g., rape). Second, freedom and liberation are key themes at both the collective and individualistic levels. . . . However, this has led to accusations that women are less committed to *eelam* as their primary motivation for participating in the LTTE, joining instead for personal vengeance.[24] The idea of sacrifice as an ideal is the third theme, and it centers both on the role of women within society as a whole (e.g., motherhood) as well as for suicide bombers more particularly. Female sacrifice for her family, and particularly for her male children, is seen as a generalized cultural norm that is usefully extended to female self-sacrifice for her community and family, particularly if she is unable (e.g., because of rape) to undertake her role as wife and mother within the society. In both the Sikh and Sri Lankan examples, female martyrdom is viewed as necessary to overcome the individual and—more importantly—collective shame of dishonor caused by rape. Fourth, the personalism of women's motives that arguably drive them to join organizations like the LTTE is both responsible for somehow diminishing the overall "authenticness" of women's roles in these organizations, particularly for outside observers. . . .

Middle East and North African Female Terrorism

From the earliest days of the Palestinian resistance, women have been involved in both the leftist and rightist sides of the Palestinian struggle against Israel.[25] . . . One of the most well-known female terrorists is Leila Khaled, affiliated with the Popular Front for the Liberation of Palestine (PFLP), who hijacked a plane in 1969. Although there has been a low probability that women will be used by Islamist terrorist groups, continuing the trend of lower female representation among rightist organizations, there is precedent for such inclusion in Palestine. Etaf Aliyan, a Palestinian woman who is also a member of Islamic Jihad, was scheduled to drive a car loaded with explosives into a Jerusalem police station in 1987 but was apprehended before the attack could take place. If the attack had occurred, it would have represented "the first suicide vehicle bombing in Israel,"[26] and significantly, it would have been implemented by a woman.

Women's roles were increasing among secular and Islamist Palestinian organizations before 2002, suggesting a warning sign of the impending escalation of Palestinian violence against Israeli targets. . . . In hindsight suicide bombing by women appeared to be a logical progression in women's operations within various organizations, and suggests that women may be tasked with tandem suicide bombing and other operations in the future. . . .

However, despite the escalating role of women in the *intifada*, the prospect of a female suicide bomber remained remote through the first weeks of 2002 because "[t]here have been very few cases of Arab women found infiltrating Israel on a mission to murder civilians."[27]

That perception changed dramatically in the wake of 28 January 2002 when Wafa Idris (a.k.a. Wafa Idrees, Shahanaz Al Amouri)[28] detonated a 22-pound bomb in Jerusalem that killed her, an 81-year-old Israeli man, and injured more than 100 others. Confusion punctuated the immedi-

ate aftermath of the attack given that heretofore women had only helped plant bombs and it was not clear whether Idris had intended to detonate the explosive or whether the explosion was accidental. Equally unclear was whether she was acting on behalf of some group or how she had obtained the explosives. This confusion made the Israelis reticent to confirm that the attack constituted the first "official" case of a female suicide bomber related to the Arab–Israeli conflict and, therefore, a significant shift in the security framework within which the Israelis would have to operate. . . .

Idris's motivation to commit a suicide operation was arguably prompted by a sense of hopelessness under occupation and rage, not heaven as promised to her male counterparts.[29] As a result, her action is seen "to have been motivated more by nationalist than religious fervor,"[30] a motivation that is frequently attributed to her male counterparts. In addition to not being a "known" member of a terrorist organization, and therefore more likely to be identified as a potential suicide bomber, Idris did not carry out the attack in the "normal" fashion. She carried the bomb in a backpack, rather than strapped to her waist, raising widespread speculation that she did not intend to detonate the bomb and the explosion was accidental.[31] Another cause for skepticism about Idris's role in the attack arose from the lack of a note and martyr's video, which are typically left behind by one engaging in a "martyr's operation."

The response by secular and Islamist Palestinian leaders to the attack is important. Although the Al-Aqsa Martyrs Brigade claimed responsibility for the attack, it did not do so immediately. The strong reaction by the "Arab street" to the attack, and the heightened sense of insecurity noted by Israeli officials, provide two excellent reasons why women's operational utility increased for Al-Aqsa's leaders. First, Idris's action resonated strongly throughout the Arab world. Egypt's weekly *Al-Sha'ab* published an editorial on 1 February 2002 entitled "It's a Woman!" that is reflective of the general tone that emanated throughout the Arab press regarding the attack. The editorial stated, in part, "It is a woman who teaches you today a lesson in heroism, who teaches you the meaning of Jihad, and the way to die a martyr's death. . . . It is a woman who has shocked the enemy, with her thin, meager, and weak body. . . . It is a woman who blew herself up, and with her exploded all the myths about women's weakness, submissiveness, and enslavement."[32] . . .

Historical and recent cases of female Palestinian terrorism suggest several trends. First, female activism has tended to be more active within the secularist context (e.g., leftist) rather than among Islamists (e.g., rightist), reflecting a general global trend. However, although women have been more active with the nationalist/secular side of the Palestinian movement, women have been linked to Islamist groups either directly or in terms of their overall support. Second, as the conflict with Israel deepened, the scope of activism widened to include women in an increasing array of activities, up to and including suicide bombing, and women pushed for these expanded roles. Third, women activists have tended to be young, with one or more politically active family members (male), and exposed to some form of loss (e.g., within their family or immediate community) that arguably contributed to their mobilization. Importantly, marital, educational, and maternal status were not uniform factors. Also, these factors are not radically divergent from males who undertake suicide operations within this context. Fourth, Palestinian secular leaders' willingness to include women in martyr operations was influenced by security assessments (e.g., an ability to evade security scrutiny and travel more deeply into Israel), operational constraints (e.g., growing Israeli pressure on male operatives), and publicity. Female suicide bombers represent one way to overcome Israeli security pressures, heighten Israeli insecurity, and exhaust Israeli security resources by significantly increasing the operational range and available pool for suicide operations. . . .

Conclusion: Preliminary Trends and Themes

Although there is a tendency to dismiss the overall threat of women suicide bombers, or female terrorists more broadly, because they have historically engaged in such a small percentage of terrorist activities, contextual pressures are creating a convergence between individual women, terrorist organization leaders, and society that is not only increasing the rate of female activity within terrorist and politically violent organizations, but is also expanding their operational range. The tactical advantage of this convergence is apparent particularly with respect to female suicide bombers, a tactic designed to attract attention and instill widespread fear in the target audience, because as one observer noted in the wake of Idris's attack, "it's the women we remember."[33] Because suicide terrorism is designed to attract attention and precipitate fear, in an increasingly charged atmosphere it takes more and more to attract attention, increasing the utility of female suicide bombers. Female suicide bombers also fundamentally challenge existing security assessments and socially derived norms regarding women's behavior, heightening the fear factor. Finally, and more significantly, the small number of women who have, to date, been used in such operations suggests that they will be able to better evade detection than their male counterparts. . . .

Notes

1. Organizations labeled as "terrorist" are derived from the United States Department of State listing of designated terrorist organizations through either support or operational activities (see *Patterns of Global Terrorism 2000*, available at http://www.state.gov/s/ct/rls/pgtrpt/2000/2450.htm). This analysis will utilize this designation for the sake of simplicity.
2. Because a woman's place is "naturally" private her motivation to become "public" would have to be personal. This suggests as well that once this personal reason has been resolved she will willingly and naturally return to her normal, private, role.
3. The common belief that women's participation in political violence is quite limited is not supported by even a cursory examination of history. However, what is clear from that cursory look is that women's experiences with political violence have not received sustained attention, and what examination has occurred has often been heavily influenced by established Western norms of appropriate female behavior. Given the constraints of any article-length analysis, certain limitations were necessary in approaching the subject matter. As a result, this work should not be construed as an exhaustive inventory of women's participation in politically violent or terrorist organizations, past or present, but rather a selective examination of primarily current critical cases.
4. Several of the most oft-quoted terrorism definitions include those used by the United States Federal Bureau of Investigation (FBI), the United States

Department of State, and the United States Department of Defense (DoD). The FBI defines terrorism as "the unlawful use of force and violence against persons or property to intimidate or coerce a government, the civilian population, or any segment thereof, in furtherance of political or social objectives" (28 Code of Federal Regulations Section 0.85). The State Department defines terrorism as "premeditated, politically motivated violence perpetrated against noncombatant targets by subnational groups or clandestine agents, usually intended to influence an audience" (United States Department of State, *Patterns of Global Terrorism 2000*, available at http://www.state. gov/s/ct/rls/pgtrpt/2000/, 13 April 2001). Problematic with both definitions, however, is that they fail to capture organizations motivated by religious or economic motives, such as Islamist organizations in the Middle East and North Africa (MENA) or narcoterrorist organizations such as the Revolutionary Armed Forces of Columbia (FARC) and National Liberation Army (ELN) in Colombia. The DoD partially overcomes this deficiency by widening the goal orientation of terrorist organizations as it defines terrorism as "the calculated use of violence or the threat of violence to inculcate fear; intended to coerce or to intimidate government or societies in the pursuit of goals that are generally political, religious, or ideological" (Department of Defense, "DoD Combating Terrorism Program," Directive Number 2000, 12, available at http://www. defenselink.mil/pubs/downing_rpt/annx_e.html, 15 September 1996).

5. Jamie L. Rhee, "Comment: Rational and Constitutional Approaches to Airline Safety in the Face of Terrorist Threats," *DePaul Law Review* 49(847) Lexis/Nexis (Spring 2000).

6. Martha Crenshaw, "The Logic of Terrorism: Terrorist Behavior as a Product of Strategic Choice," in Walter Reich, ed., *Origins of Terrorism: Psychologies, Ideologies, Theologies, States of Mind* (Washington, DC: Woodrow Wilson Center Press, 1998), p. 15.

7. If we examine state behavior with respect to military recruitment, we see a similar process. Samarasinghe notes "most nations have increased women's military roles only when there has been a shortage of qualified men and a pressing need for more warriors. . . . The decision to permit women into combat is made by men. . . . [And] the allowable space within which women could operate in military units is also determined by them" (Vidyamali Samarasinghe, "Soldiers, Housewives and Peace Makers: Ethnic Conflict and Gender in Sri Lanka," *Ethnic Studies Report* 14[2] [July 1996], p. 213).

8. As of early 2002, a cease-fire deal was secured between the Tamil Tigers and the government of Sri Lanka, halting the type of violence that will be discussed in this article. However, even if this activity is now a matter of historical record, rather than a current phenomenon, it offers important insights into how women were (are) mobilized into a politically violent movement.

9. The regional cases that are discussed later are utilized to demonstrate these developments given the constraints of an article. However, it should be understood that it is not, and is not intended to be, an exhaustive inventory of cases in which women have engaged in political violence or terrorism. Cases from Africa (Eritrea, South Africa) and East Asia (Japan, Korea, Vietnam) are also worth investigating.

10. For a good analysis of female participation in left- and right-wing organizations within the United States during the 1960s and 1970s please see Jeffrey S. Handler. "Socioeconomic Profile of an American Terrorist: 1960s and 1970s," *Terrorism* 13(3) (May–June 1990), pp. 195–213.

11. Ibid., 1990, p. 204.

12. For a useful examination of women's roles in Latin American guerilla movements please see Linda M. Lobao, "Women in Revolutionary Movements: Changing Patterns of Latin American Guerilla Struggle," *Dialectical Anthropology* 15 (1999), pp. 211–232.

13. For varying figures see Jeremy McDermott, "Girl Guerillas Fight Their Way to the Top of Revolutionary Ranks," *Scotland on Sunday*, 23 December 2001, Lexis/Nexis, 2 April 2002; Karl Penhaul, "Battle of the Sexes: Female Rebels Battle Colombian Troops in the Field and Machismo in Guerilla Ranks," *San Francisco Chronicle*, 11 January 2001, Lexis/Nexis, 2 April 2002; and Martin Hodgson, "Girls Swap Diapers for Rebel Life," *Christian Science Monitor*, 6 October 2000, available at http://www.csmonitor.com/durable/2000/10/06/p6s1.htm, 2 April 2002. Aside from a fascination with the makeup habits of the female FARC members, these articles offer some insights into the motivations of women in the FARC's ranks.

14. M. Elaine Mar, "Shining Path Women," n.d., *Harvard Magazine*, available at http://www.harvardmagazine. com/issues/mj96/right.violence.html, 2 April 2002. During the late 1980s, "approximately 35 percent of the military leaders of . . . [the shining Path], primarily at the level of underground cells . . . [were] also women" (Juan Lazaro, "Women and Political Violence in Contemporary Peru," *Dialectical Anthropology* 15[2–3] [1990], p.234). Additionally, by 1987 roughly 1,000 women had been arrested on suspicion of terrorism in Peru including four senior Shining Path female leaders: Laura Zambrano ("Camarada Meche"), Fiorella Montano ("Lucia"), Margie Clavo Peralta, and Edith Lagos (ibid., p. 243).

15. This position is advanced by McDermott, "Girl Guerillas Fight Their Way to the Top."

16. Interestingly, the LTTE's creation of an organized squad of female suicide bombers is said to be mirrored after the Indian National Army's (INA) activities against the British during the early to mid-1940s (see Peter Schalk, "Women Fighters of the Liberation Tigers in Tamil Ilam: The Martial Feminism of Atel Palacinkam," *South Asia Research* 14 [2] [Autumn 1994], p. 174).

17. United States Department of State, *Patterns of Global Terrorism 2000*, "Asia Overview," 30 April 2001,

available at http://www.state.gov/s/ct/rls/pgtrpt/ 2000/2432.htm, 2 April 2002.

18. Some observers further identify the female cadre of the Black Tigers as the "Birds of Freedom." See, for example, Charu Lata Joshi, "Sri Lanka: Suicide Bombers," *Far Eastern Economic Review*, 1 June 2000, available at http://www.feer.com/_0006_01/p64 currents.html, 11 March 2002. The idea of a bird carrying the soul of the martyr to paradise is a theme seen in Islamist discourse on martyr operations.

19. Ana Cutter, "Tamil Tigresses: Hindu Martyrs," n.d., available at http://www.columbia.edu/cu/sipa/ PUBS/SLANT/SPRING98/article5.html, 11 March 2002. Also see Frederica Jansz, "Why Do They Blow Themselves Up?" *Sunday Times*, 15 March 1998, available at http://www.lacnet.org/suntimes/980315/ plus4.html, 3 April 2002.

20. Cutter, "Tamil Tigresses," 55. Ibid.

21. Ibid.

22. Joke Schrijvers, "Fighters, Victims and Surviors: Constructions of Ethnicity, Gender and Refugeeness among Tamils in Sri Lanka," *Journal of Refugee Studies* 12 (3 September 1999). The quotation on women as core national symbols is on p. 308; the quote on Tamil use of women's identity is on p. 311; and the quote on purity and suicide bombing is on p. 319 with emphasis in the original.

23. The discussion of the role of Sikh women was drawn from Cynthia Keppley Mahmood. *Fighting for Faith and Nation: Dialogues with Sikh Militants* (Philadelphia: University of Pennsylvania Press, 1996), pp. 213–234. The quotation is located on pp. 230–231, emphasis added.

24. Jansz, "Why Do They Blow Themselves Up?"

25. For two good studies on the role of women in Palestinian resistance both before and during the first *intifada* see Soraya Antonius, "Fighting on Two Fronts: Conversations with Palestinian Women," *Journal of Palestine Studies* 5 (October 1979), pp. 26–45, and Graham Usher, "Palestinian Women, the Intifada and the State of Independence," *Race & Class* 34(3) (January– March 1993), pp. 31–43.

26. David Sharrock, "Women: The Suicide Bomber's Story," *Guardian*, 5 May 1998, Lexis/Nexis, 30 March 2002.

27. Phil Reeves, "The Paramedic Who Became Another 'Martyr' for Palestine," *Independent*, 31 January 2002, available at http://www.ccmep.org/hotnews/ parameic013102.html, 6 March 2002.

28. Hizbollah television identified the bomber as Shahanaz Al Amouri following the attack. See Imigo Gilmore, "Woman Suicide Bomber Shakes Israelis," *Daily Telegraph* (London), 28 January 2002, Lexis/Nexis, 6 March 2002.

29. Lamis Andoni, "Wafa Idrees: A Symbol of a Generation," *Arabic Media Internet Network* (AMIN), 23 February 2002, available at http://www.amin.org/eng/ uncat/2002/feb/feb23.html, 6 March 2002.

30. Reeves, "The Paramedic Who Became Another 'Martyr'"; James Bennet, "Filling in the Blanks on Palestinian Bomber," *New York Times*, 31 January 2002, Lexis/Nexis, 6 March 2002; and Wafa Amr, "Palestinian Woman Bomber Yearned for Martyrdom," *Jordan Times*, 31 January 2002, available at http://www.jordantimes.com, 31 January 2002.

31. Peter Beaumont, "From an Angel of Mercy to Angel of Death," *Guardian*, 31 January 2002, available at http:// www.guardian.co.uk/Print/0,3858,4346503,00.html, 6 March 2002.

32. Quoted in "Inquiry and Analysis No. 84: Jihad and Terrorism Studies Wafa Idris: The Celebration of the First Female Palestinian Suicide Bomber—Part II," *Middle East Media and Research Institute*, 13 February 2002, available at http://www.memri.org, 6 March 2002. Also see James Bennet, "Arab Press Glorifies Bomber as Heroine," *New York Times*, 11 February 2002, Lexis/Nexis, 6 March 2002.

33. Melanie Reid, "Myth That Women Are the Most Deadly Killers of All," *Herald* (Glasgow), 29 January 2002, Lexis/Nexis, 6 February 2002.

Part II
Women and Political Parties

This section collects together readings on women and political parties, exploring interactions between women's movements and political parties, the activities of women inside established political parties, and some of the conflicts between feminism and party politics as illustrated by attempts to form women's parties. The first selection offers a general introduction to the dynamics of gender and party (Lovenduski 1993). It is followed by contributions that discuss typologies for thinking about feminist strategies and party responses (Young 2000), the traditional roles that women have played inside political parties (Freeman 2000), the ways that women and feminists have transformed political parties from within (Sainsbury 2004), the limits for women and feminists in working with political parties (Goetz 2003), and some of the tensions and challenges inherent in trying to experiment with new feminist ways of "doing party politics" (Dominelli and Jonsdottir 1988).

Joni Lovenduski presents an overview of women's activities inside political parties in Western countries to illustrate how gender has affected party politics and how party politics has shaped gendered patterns of political representation. She observes that women have largely mobilized from within political parties—rather than through social movements outside the parties—for greater presence in political decision making and greater attention to women's concerns in public policy. She also discusses some of the ways that parties have responded to these demands through programmatic and organizational change. Taking up but extending some of these themes, *Lisa Young* analyzes contacts between feminists and political parties in Canada and the United States. Based on her comparison, she theorizes feminist strategies according to decisions, first, to engage or not engage in electoral politics and, second, to adopt partisan, crosspartisan, or apartisan stances vis-à-vis political parties. She then discerns two broad types of party responses: representational responsiveness, which entails recruitment of more women to positions of power, and policy responsiveness, which involves greater attention to issues of concern to women. On this basis, she develops a typology of party responsiveness to feminist demands, which she describes as responsive, co-optive, nonresponsive, and oppositional.

Turning to the internal life of political parties, *Jo Freeman* documents some of the traditional roles that women have played inside political parties, even before women gained the right to vote. In the United States, this included giving speeches, cooking and cleaning at political rallies, organizing partisan meetings with female voters, mobilizing male and female voters, and writing campaign literature. Despite these important roles, however, women were usually discriminated against within the parties and often not seen as full political actors in their own right. Examining a different case, *Diane Sainsbury* studies the evolution of ideas on gender equality within Swedish political parties, focusing on the roles of women's groups inside and outside the parties. She emphasizes the importance of women's agency in explaining why Sweden has long had among the highest levels of female parliamentary representation in the world. These transformations were due in large part, she argues, to various discursive strategies to reframe women as a minority within the parties to a majority of the citizenry. Similar to the arguments made by Katzenstein (see previous section), Sainsbury contends that these women form a crucial part of the women's movement in Sweden, even if women's movements are usually seen as operating outside political parties.

Adopting a more skeptical approach, *Anne Marie Goetz* addresses women's participation in the 'no-party' system in Uganda, where women have been integrated into the political regime through an extensive system of reserved seats. In contrast to Sainsbury, who identifies some of the resources available to women's movement actors who work inside the parties, Goetz argues that, in the case of Uganda, women's presence in politics is part of a strategy to legitimize what is in fact a one-party regime. As such, their inclusion comes at the important cost of women not being able to organize more autonomously. Women's increased access to political office may thus have negative consequences for women's political effectiveness, revealing the costs and benefits of this particular system of political patronage. On the other end of the political scale, *Lena Dominelli and Gudrun Jonsdottir* study the emergence and experiences of women's lists for local elections in Iceland, exploring how these lists navigate the tensions between being a social movement and a political party. They document how a particular women's list sought to implement new "feminist" ways of doing "politics" through flattened hierarchies, unanimous voting, consensus decision making, group consultation, and rotation of representatives. As a group, these readings offer insights into the possibilities and limits for women as a group to transform party politics by mobilizing within and outside the party system.

Chapter 9

THE DYNAMICS OF GENDER AND PARTY

Joni Lovenduski

The issue of the political representation of women has changed substantially since women first secured the franchise. When nineteenth-century feminists sought the right to vote they also wanted the right to stand in elections because they were convinced that changes in women's condition would come about only when women themselves became members of elected legislatures. In contrast, during the 1960s and 1970s many second-wave feminists were cynical about political institutions and electoral politics, preferring the political autonomy they found in new social movement organizations. By the early 1980s, however, there had been a reconsideration of the importance of mainstream politics and feminists became active members of political parties. Meanwhile some of the women who were already established in their parties began to claim parity of political representation. The struggle for equal pay was a watershed. Once parties became committed to the policy of equality at work it was only a matter of time before more substantial demands for equal political representation than "one person, one vote" were made. During the 1980s support for getting more women into politics grew in each of the countries discussed in this chapter. There was a shift in the agendas of both the parties and their women members.

Over the same period political parties were a major site of women's activity. There was a clear challenge to parties by women who claimed a voice in decision-making and pressed for changes in the political agenda. Women demanded and secured party reforms with varying degrees of success. In some countries this led to the appearance of new issues in party programs, new systems of candidate selection, new means of policy-making, and the establishment of new structures of government such as ministries for women, equal opportunities ombudspersons, and publicly funded women's committees. In response to pressure from women activists, members, and voters, gender became an explicit issue for many political parties. This took place in contexts affected by different kinds of party politics. The extent and the manner of party accommodation of gender has been influenced by increased party competition via the entry of new parties and/or the decline of established parties, the erosion of established coalitions, modernization strategies devised to replace or renew declining constituencies, system-level constitutional change, and altered party-state relationships.

Demands for women's representation have had the most dramatic success in Scandinavia. Norwegian feminists were early in advocating the integration of women into the existing party structure as a strategy of empowerment. It has now been more than twenty years since the "women's coup" overturned agreed party preferences on candidates lists for local authority elections and returned three local councils with a majority of women. The implications of this initial display of women's solidarity were understood rapidly by parties and the progress that Norwegian women have made since then is remarkable. . . .

Near the other end of the scale is Britain, where demands for equality in women's representation came later, gathering force in the opposition parties only in the early 1980s and becoming a feature of the ruling Conservatives' strategies of representation as late as the early 1990s. By then women comprised fewer than 10 percent of members of the House of Commons. Of course, the timing of demands for representation is only part of the story. The Norwegian and British political systems present different possibilities for women. In general the rules of the game in Norway favor the representation of women while in Britain they do not.

This raises the question of what we mean by political representation. In democratic societies, the representation of a group's interests has two dimensions: the presence of its members in decision-making arenas and the consideration of its interests in the decision-making process. An implication of the first dimension is that, to be democratic, the composition of the elected assemblies should mirror the composition of the society it serves. But the second dimension implies that it is enough that an assembly takes into account the interests of all its electors. There have been intense theoretical arguments about which of the two formulations should prevail and these arguments have been reflected in debates amongst feminists who have disagreed sharply about the nature of women's interests and the political strategies required to press them. In practice the demands women have made to be represented in party politics reflect both programmatic and organizational concerns. Thus parties have been under pressure to promote policies to attract women voters, to undertake campaigns to recruit women members, to promote women into key positions in the party organization, and to nominate women candidates. Party programs have been expanded to include policies on equal opportunities and reproductive rights, as well as to revise traditional party positions on family policy to take into account new understandings of gender and power. . . .

We argue that liberal democracies offer women the means to claim equality of representation by utilizing the political opportunities offered by the party system. Party systems have responded to women's demands, but to varying degrees. . . . These contrasts indicate changes in party politics to accommodate women's demands for political representation but they also reflect different social, cultural, and historical circumstances. And

there are common patterns here as well. Women's demands for political representation inevitably affect party politics; party politics inevitably affects the strategies that women employ to press their claims. A continuous process of adjustment and accommodation takes place on both sides. We need to look beyond the particular and specific cultures in which that adjustment takes place if we are to gain a good overview of women in contemporary party politics. . . .

The Development of Women's Claims

Women have made demands on political parties since the issue of female suffrage was first raised. In this discussion I consider three aspects of their development:

1. How women have made their claims.
2. How they intervened in party politics.
3. The mutual accommodation between parties and women claiming increased political rights.

The development of party gender politics in recent years is an effect both of the infiltration of feminist ideas and the attention women influenced by those ideas have paid to the imperatives of party politics. There are four identifiable components to the strategies such women devised. First, women's issues were brought to the political agenda. Prominent party women, supported by women's organizations and networks, raised issues of sex equality in the parties. Often they began with demands for policies to secure sex equality in employment, but the implications of equality for childcare, reproductive rights, and family policies were also issues. Secondly, seeking to avoid accusations of sectionalism, they sought to transform women's issues into universal issues. Thirdly, women used a dual strategy of working within women's networks and in male-dominated areas of the party. Finally, women paid close attention to the rules of the game. They sought to transform gender relations in politics from within, hence they were careful to affirm their commitment to their parties.

The gains made during the 1970s and 1980s must be considered in the light of a large mobilization of women. This background gave credence to efforts to get women's issues on the political agenda. The emergence of the second wave of feminism after the end of the 1960s had important effects. Even in countries in which a widespread and radical women's liberation movement did not appear, ideas about sex equality were in the air and women began to seek inclusion in a variety of areas of social life. Gradually campaigns for equality gained support and parties began to respond. But the momentum built up by wide-ranging movements in support of equal rights would not have been enough to secure changes in party policies. Political parties moved on women's issues when they were pressed to do so. . . .

Once a party committed itself formally to the principle of gender equality in one sphere, then party women were able to use this commitment in their arguments for increased representation. . . . An implicit goal of feminist infiltration of parties is to secure changes in attitudes about gender, mainly by increases in understanding and awareness of gender differences and their implications for power relations. . . .

In almost all parties, women kept to the rules of the political game. Party divisions outweighed gender divisions. Cross-party alliances are exceptional within and outside legislatures. Party women have primarily sought change from within the parties except in the United States where party loyalties are exceptionally weak and the rules of the game allow greater flexibility in making coalitions.

Attention to party imperatives presents a dilemma for feminists who seek to transform parties into more women-friendly entities, but risk incorporation as they adapt to the rules of the game. A great dilemma for second-wave feminism has been whether women will change institutions before institutions change women. Originally, some feminists were dismissive of party structures with their hierarchies and rituals, preferring separate autonomous organizations that sought political change from outside the established political structures and institutions. However, the cost of such separatism was low effectiveness. Understanding this, many feminists acknowledged the necessity of party politics, implicitly by their activism and explicitly in their publications and debates.

Party Change

The justification for such a strategy is that parties will adapt to accommodate the new demands, and in so doing will become carriers of feminist ideas. This raises a number of questions, the most obvious of which is whether parties do adapt. To answer we need to look at the main sites of women's interventions in the parties. This requires us to examine the ways that parties differ in their policies to represent women. Here we must consider both the programmatic and the organizational dimensions of representation: how parties differ in their treatment of women's issues and in their strategies to promote women's representation.

Programmatic Change

Parties devised gender policies to respond to the claims of women voters, members, and activists. Over the past twenty years the sort of sex equality policies women demand has developed from a set of fairly straightforward employment laws to a wide-ranging program affecting the whole of society. Most political parties have accommodated these demands in ways that are congruent with their ideologies. There was a tendency for parties to converge in the sense that, eventually, they all adopted particular policies to satisfy women voters and members, for example by making laws about equal pay or childcare, but the policies themselves reflect the ideology of the party. . . .

The activity of party women is vital if such changes are to be secured. There is considerable evidence now that, within political life, women take an active part in creating definitions of reality that support efforts to make new policies. . . . Parallel to women's integration into party politics, new agendas were established including strategies to get more women into political office.

Organizational Change

Parties have developed strategies to promote women internally into decision-making positions in the party organization and externally into elected assemblies and public appointments. Generally they have been more radical, determined, and imaginative in devising policies to bring women into internal positions than to nominate women as candidates for elected office. There appear to be three party strategies for increasing the proportion of women in decision-making positions. These are:

1. *Rhetorical* strategies whereby women's claims are accepted in campaign platforms and party spokespersons make frequent reference to the importance of getting more women into office.
2. Strategies of *positive* or *affirmative action* in which special training is offered to aspirant women, targets are set for the inclusion of women, and considerable encouragement, including sometimes financial assistance, is given to enable women to put themselves forward to be considered.
3. Strategies of *positive discrimination* in which places are reserved for women on decision-making bodies, on candidate slates, on shortlists. In addition, special women's committees with significant powers may be set up parallel to or within existing party decision-making structures and institutions. All three strategies may be controversial, but most parties now have rhetorical strategies to promote women and many have adopted strategies of positive action. Positive discrimination, however, is much less common and tends to be restricted to women's access to internal party structures. . . .

The Rules of the Game: Ideology, Organization, Political Careers, and Gender

The claims that women make and the strategies they employ are considerably affected by the kind of party they seek to influence. All political parties have decision-making procedures consisting of formal rules, informal practices, and customs. These reflect the party's political environment and patterns of internal conflict as well as expressing its ideology and goals. They also structure the party's organization. When women become political claimants, when they seek political representation, they must take the rules into account and pay attention to the ideology and organization of their party. All their claims will

be contested in the party, but the most intense opposition will occur when the inevitable claim for an increased women's presence in the national legislature is made. Seats in the legislature are the political prize toward which much of party politics is directed, hence access to them is usually carefully guarded.

The pattern of the political careers of party parliamentarians tells us a great deal about the rules of the game. In the past, in many systems, women's political careers have differed from those of men, and in many systems women have not been nominated because they do not have appropriate "qualifications." Inhibitions about the appropriateness of their qualifications may stop women from seeking candidacy. The qualifications a party requires of its candidates are, of course, a function both of ideology and organization. This is an area of some variation. Different countries and parties have developed different political apprenticeships and it is clear that some are more accessible to women than others. In Ireland the traditional route for women to elected office was kinship with the previous incumbent. This used to be termed the "widow factor" in the United States and Australia. In the Netherlands and in the Italian PCI and its successors, the long party career is the main qualification for candidacy to the legislature. Requirements for continuous and lengthy apprenticeships in firms are thought by equal opportunities experts to favor men as employees. In politics the effect appears to be similar.

But requirements for *local* experience need not have a negative effect on women. It has long been argued that women's political concerns tend to be centered on the locality and the community, hence an emphasis on local experience should benefit them. In Sweden, which has the highest proportion of women legislators in the liberal democratic world, this is borne out. The political qualification for the Riksdag is local elected office. This is the case across the political parties and men's and women's career paths do not diverge. A similar tendency is becoming apparent in the British Labour party. In Italy, where pre-parliamentary careers are important, candidates in good positions tend to have held local or party elected office simultaneously. Italian women's political careers are coming to resemble men's. By contrast, in France, the absence of women in elected office may in part be explained by their exclusion from local politics. Local political bases are essential to the careers of French politicians and there is great competition amongst men for likely offices. Women have been largely excluded from these competitions and have not therefore been able to make the first steps of a standard French political career.

When party rules alter to facilitate women's candidacy they may well upset normal career paths. Eva Kolinsky notes that the adoption of quotas of candidates in the German SDP has changed the nature of the political apprenticeship there. It has sharply reduced the *Oschentour* (slaving like an ox), the long haul necessary to become qualified as a candidate. The backlog of "qualified" women who sought careers was very quickly cleared after which novices became candidates. Quotas broadened access routes and increased the pool of women who were "eligible."

Parties of the left have traditionally been more willing than parties of the center and the right to make agreements to nominate women and they also appear to be more able to deliver on such agreements. But ideology is a less reliable indicator of party support for women's representation than it once was. Today the trend is for parties across the ideological spectrum to seek ways of promoting women.

Party organization is another variable that we must take into account. As we have seen, weak or decentralized party organization means that party centers are less able to implement policies to promote women because they have low levels of control over their local branches and constituency organizations. Federal party organizations embracing affiliates of various kinds are similarly impeded. In the British Labour party, it is difficult to exercise effective control over the way that affiliated trade unions exercise their considerable selection powers. . . . [In Italy,] the way a party is structured has considerable impact on the capacity of its leadership to influence the composition of the candidates list. This is both because of the power that the center has over the localities and because centralized parties with relatively large bureaucracies are able to recruit, develop, and support officials who constitute a corps of professional politicians. The bureaucracy also offers the security of paid employment for politicians who lose their seats. But in Italy's factionalized parties with weak bargaining structures (notably the Christian Democrats), it is still the core elite who are in control; the difference between the two types is that the elite is fragmented rather than cohesive. In practice the localities in almost all parties have some bargaining power in the candidate selection process, but the amount of local power will vary considerably by the type of electoral system and by the strength of the party. The level of competition for candidacy also varies considerably by party and is closely associated with party fortunes. But other factors are also important. In Italy, high levels of political competition for candidacy impede women's chances of securing nominations. In Canada, where levels of turnover are high and there are comparatively few safe seats, women have relatively high rates of entry. In most countries minor parties with lower chances of electoral success are more likely to nominate women, but this is not a reliable indicator that they wish to see more women in power. Such parties are generally more likely to nominate atypical candidates because they have a limited choice of applicants.

The disadvantages that women candidates may experience are sometimes transformed by political circumstances. In the United States in the 1990s women have the advantage of being perceived as outsiders by the public at a time when it is a "plus" to be outsiders. Similarly in Italy, the contemporary crisis is essentially about political representation, hence the issue of women's representation is readily incorporated into the current debates about restructuring the party system.

There is no party in which efforts to nominate more women have occurred without an intervention by women making claims. In Sweden, organized women pressed their parties to nominate women candidates and place them in favorable positions on party lists by several means. At first, they simply put women's names forward, a tactic that was very important in the early stages. They also conducted campaigns to promote women candidates and made proposals to get women into better positions on party lists. Finally they acted as watchdogs and protested whenever reversals occurred. The task of securing substantial increases in women's electoral fortunes has been achieved without recourse to formal quotas. Recommendation, arguments, and the threat to work for quotas achieved agreements to set targets of 40 percent of nominations going to women. Once these targets were set, considerable progress was made.

The Dynamic of Gender and Party Politics

In conclusion, it is evident that there is a dynamic between women's claims and party responses whereby initiatives on women's representation lead to more radical such initiatives by both sides.

When parties fail to respond or, as is the case when they adopt rhetorical strategies, they respond only minimally, women increase their demands. As a result rhetoric leads to positive action strategies which by the same dynamic become more comprehensive as time passes. When positive action strategies lead to good results women become more integrated into their parties and thus better positioned to secure and maintain adequate levels of representation. When insufficient change results from positive action, demands for positive discrimination are made and these have been adopted in many countries. . . .

Chapter 10

THEORIZING FEMINIST STRATEGY AND PARTY RESPONSIVENESS

Lisa Young

The focus of this [chapter] is on the responses of political parties to the contemporary women's movement. Not all women are feminists, and many women involved in partisan politics would object to the idea that their political involvement is best understood as related to feminist efforts to reform political parties. Nonetheless, changes in the role of women inside political parties coincided with the rise of modern feminism, so it is reasonable to frame this discussion in that context.

This raises a crucial question: to what extent have feminist organizations in the United States and Canada engaged with political parties? If we are to understand parties' responses to feminism, we must first come to grips with the stimulus to which they are responding. The emphasis that women's movement organizations place on electoral politics, the movement's partisan orientation, and the character and intensity of ties between movement and party organizations may all affect partisan responses to feminism. . . .

Categorizing Movement Strategy

When characterizing the orientation of a movement toward political parties and the electoral system, two dimensions require examination: the importance of electoral or partisan activities relative to other movement undertakings, and the movement's choice among partisan, multipartisan, and apartisan orientations.

Social movements vary in the emphasis they place on political parties and electoral politics relative to other priorities. If partisan and electoral strategies are a regular element of movement activity over an extended period, and consume significant financial and human resources, then they can be considered core activities of the movement. If, however, the movement only expends effort and resources on these activities sporadically, and if the resources expended are minimal, then these activities can be considered peripheral activities of the movement.

The second dimension of a movement's orientation involves its stance toward the political party system. A movement that adopts a *partisan* stance enters into some form of exclusive relationship with one established political party. In its most regularized form this would entail a formal relationship between one or more major movement organizations and a particular political party such as that between unions and the British Labour party. Less institutionalized manifestations of a partisan stance would include movement organizations endorsing a party in elections, significant informal contact between movement leaders and party officials, financial support exclusively for the party and/or its candidates, movement involvement in internal party affairs, and organized efforts for movement adherents to become active in the party. To say that the movement has become partisan, it would be necessary to see evidence of several of these indicators over time.

A movement that is *multipartisan* in orientation engages with more than one political party. In this case, movement organizations avoid endorsing a single party and their leaders have meaningful

Table 10.1. Models of Party Responsiveness

	Responsive	*Co-optive*	*Nonresponsive*	*Oppositional*
Representational	High or moderate	High or moderate	Low	Low
Policy	Positive	Negative	Neutral	Negative

contact with more than one party. If financial support is offered, it is divided among the parties. Movement organizations that are multipartisan may act like interest groups during elections, engaging in such activities as rating party platforms and staging debates on key issues.

A movement that is not engaged with political parties in any way can be termed *apartisan*. A distinction must be made, however, between movements or groups that are apartisan because they are apolitical, and politicized movements that have chosen not to engage with parties. Politicized apartisan movements may choose to form their own political parties to compete with other parties, or they may choose to work outside the electoral arena to achieve social change. Clearly, these are very different kinds of behaviors, yet they share an aversion to working within the confines of the existing political parties. . . .

Party Responsiveness to Feminism

Party responsiveness to feminism is a two-dimensional concept. The first dimension, representational responsiveness, refers to both the numerical representation of women in partisan elites and the extent to which the party employs quotas or other representational guarantees for women. The second dimension is policy responsiveness, which includes the extent to which the party adopts or opposes the movement's policy agenda, as well as the attitudinal support for this agenda among partisan elites. . . .

Representational and policy responsiveness do not necessarily work in tandem. It is, for example, possible to conceive of a situation in which the political party is highly responsive in representational terms, but opposed to the women's movement's policy agenda. The pattern of possible responses is outlined in Table 10.1. A political party that is responsive to feminism will include women in partisan elites in significant numbers, may employ quotas or other measures guaranteeing women such representation, and will include significant elements of the movement's policy agenda in its platform. Conversely, a political party that makes little effort to include women in partisan elites and adopts stances in opposition to the women's movement can be understood to have an oppositional orientation. A low degree of representational responsiveness, when combined with a failure to respond to the movement's policy agenda in either a negative or positive manner, would suggest a nonresponsive stance. If, however, a high degree of representational responsiveness is mixed with policy stances in direct opposition to those of the movement, then the pattern of party responsiveness is best understood as co-optation, as women are probably being included in partisan elites in an effort to mask or soften the party's stance on these issues.[1] . . .

Note

1. For a discussion of the co-optation model as applied to Canadian political parties, see Lise Gotell and Janine Brody, "Women and Parties: More Than an Issue of Numbers," in *Party Politics in Canada*, 6th ed., ed. Hugh Thorburn, 53–67 (Toronto: Prentice-Hall, 1991).

Chapter 11

BUILDING A BASE:
WOMEN IN LOCAL PARTY POLITICS

Jo Freeman

As suffrage became a reality, the ranks of party women mushroomed. Women rushed into the realm of practical politics with enthusiasm, eager to learn and do everything. . . . By 1930 women had been absorbed and co-opted; the parties digested women with only a few burps.

When women opened the door of the political house, the edifice they entered was not empty. It was a labyrinthine complex of many rooms, built largely by men for their comfort and convenience, full of the furniture brought there by past and present occupants, permeated by smoke, reeking with the fumes of alcohol, and rather messy. On every level, national, state, and local, women had to operate within existing political arrangements, most of which were unfamiliar to them, and had to deal with men far more knowledgeable of these arrangements than they were and with little inclination to share that knowledge. Women learned that despite their formal admission to the official party bodies, the actual decisions were made at times and places of which they were not even told, let alone invited to. The most important rooms of the political house were closed to them, often hidden from sight, and their ability to rearrange the furniture in the rooms they could occupy was not great. Party women set about educating themselves and other women in party and public affairs. They soon learned that they could make a place for themselves in the political house, but mostly as servants to party men. While they made the beds, tended the plants, and served the coffee, they also created their own spaces, infiltrated many interior rooms, and took over the basement.

Although the strength and organization of the major political parties varied from state to state, party leadership everywhere had the same attitude: They wanted women as voters and workers but not as leaders or decision makers. The few exceptions were women who demonstrated their loyalty to party men, usually to one man who acted as their sponsor and protector. Beyond this, few generalizations can be made because politics differed from state to state, and within each state. Some states and cities had strong party organizations, others relied on "friends and neighbors" politics, or were dominated by traditional elites whose economic interests were sustained through political control. Still others had a populist tradition, or had been suffused by progressive ideals that preferred weak parties. The limited evidence available does not show that women more quickly entered politics in visible positions in one type than in another. But it does indicate that where a party was strong, party leaders chose the women to organize and educate other women, and the women they chose were ones without competing claims on their loyalties. Where parties were weak, party men accepted help from their national committees, or asked suffragists and reformers to organize women for their party, or let women organize on their own. After these women succeeded enough to make demands, they were squeezed out of the party.[1]

Bringing Women into the Parties

Party men in the states where women were not already organized invited well-known women with organizational experience to be their women leaders. Some Republican state leaders sought out prominent suffragists such as Harriet Taylor Upton of Ohio, Louise Dodson of Iowa, Lillian Feickert of New Jersey, and Nina Otero-Warren of New Mexico.[2] Quite a few Republican state party leaders drafted leaders of women's clubs. . . .

Locales with strong parties were less concerned with organizational experience than with loyalty. Party bosses recruited women like themselves—ethnically and politically—to head their women's organizations. . . . Where parties were weak, women often organized themselves. In Maryland, a Democratic state whose governor had opposed suffrage, six suffragists decided to organize Republican women in November 1920. . . . Despite only token help from party men some of whom "were leery of women in 'a man's sphere' and others who looked with suspicion upon those women who were ardent members of the Women's Christian Temperance Union" they convened the first meeting of the Maryland Federation of Republican Women's Clubs in June of 1921.[3]

Political Clubs

The women's party club was modeled on the women's club, not on men's party clubs. The latter generally started as social clubs in the nineteenth-century saloon. Indeed Tammany Hall, the first grand Democratic organization, was "practically conceived in a tavern; and ever since the eating-house and the saloon have been its chief supports." . . . Women had organized campaign clubs since the 1840s and these flourished in the 1880s, but when J. Ellen Foster encouraged Republican women to form permanent organizations, she knew that alcohol would not be the glue that held them together. Women had already organized themselves into numerous clubs, largely for study and self-improvement. The study of issues and the education of women about politics would be the task of women's Republican clubs between campaigns. . . .

As Republican women organized, they debated whether to be independent or auxiliaries to men's clubs. Foster suggested that women should form separate clubs to study politics, but cooperate with men in campaigns; by and large that is what they did. Nonetheless the conflict between independence versus cooperation (or subservience) would continue for many decades, with local politics and individual personalities usually being the determining factor.[4]

Lacking support from their national committee, and seldom favored by their state committees, Democratic women took longer to form ongoing organizations. Since the social base of the Democratic Party outside the South was urban, ethnic, and working class, the saloon played a much greater role in party organization than in that of the Republican Party. Outside the four full suffrage states, there appear to be few Democratic women's clubs, other than temporary campaign clubs, prior to 1912. There were at least one, maybe two, Democratic women's clubs in New York City and a couple in Illinois that continued to work between campaigns, but most Democratic women did other things.

In the suffrage states it was largely on the coattails of populism that women gained a voice in the Democratic Party. Democratic women were strongest in Colorado, founding the Colorado Women's Democratic Club on May 24, 1894. . . . The 1896 fusion brought many into the Democratic Party. After the 1896 election, many clubs fell apart as the parties realigned, but by 1900 they were on the rise again. . . .

While campaign clubs of women flourished at every election, ongoing clubs and statewide federations were harder to sustain in the states where women did not have full suffrage. . . . Only in the 1920s, when the Republican National Committee (RNC), Democratic National Committee (DNC), National American Woman Suffrage Association (NAWSA), and its successor the League of Women Voters (LWV) all encouraged women to join political parties, did club organization increase exponentially. Encouraged by the national parties, and sometimes by the state parties, women in many states turned their 1920 campaign organizations into permanent ones.

Not all clubs were begun by the regular party organizations; indeed competing clubs were sometimes created by local factions, or even by women who wished to remain independent of partisan infighting. . . . This kind of independence was exactly what party men feared the most. They wanted women to work loyally for party nominees in the general election, but not to take sides in primaries. An April 1924 article on "Women's Party Clubs" in the *National Republican* said there was "great variety" in their organization, describing some of the patterns. Clubs were more common in cities, "while rural districts keep to the regular party organizations." And "in some states there is rivalry between what is called the women's division and the women's clubs." In some states, the state committee divided the territory up among the women vice chairmen; in others they sent out their own organizers. Independence from the state party was discouraged as leading to disharmony. Indeed clubs which "try to . . . map out a program of their own . . . may be a menace. It has happened, in some cases, that women have organized so effectively that they became a great power, . . . demanding this and that regardless of party decisions. . . . Some . . . have operated as a belligerent anti-man league, a female bloc, whose chief function was to grasp for the sex offices and power in the party and in the government." Women's clubs were urged to be "helpful" to the party; they were not to be a "machine."[5] . . .

Keeping Women in Their Place

After a few years the party men who had appointed suffragists to be their women leaders realized that they had made a mistake. The best party women were not those who had learned their craft in service to a great cause, whether suffrage or reform. Such women were just not party loyalists. Party men replaced them with their own women, frequently wives of party men or major contributors, whom they could control. The Republican Party of New Jersey concluded that Lillian Feickert was too independent because she demanded that the party support certain legislation, insisted on planks in the party platform, and refused to submit to party discipline. In 1924 she and other suffragists were targeted for removal from the party state committee. Despite her defeat, she continued as president of the New Jersey

Women's Republican Clubs (NJWRC). However her successor as vice chairman of the state committee organized women into "official" Republican women's clubs. By 1925 women's planks had disappeared from the state party platform. The last suffragist was removed from the state committee in 1928. And in 1929, the official Women's State Republican Club of New Jersey was created; the NJWRC disbanded in 1930. Loyal party women had eclipsed suffragists in the New Jersey Republican Party.[6]

Republican women in New York had a similar experience. Party men had been quite horrified by suffragists when Mary Garrett Hay spoke against the reelection of Senator James W. Wadsworth in 1920. They much preferred party women like Helen Varick Boswell and Sarah Schuyler Butler who never questioned the qualifications of *any* Republican. Being a suffragist practically became a disqualification for high party office, even after years of party work. On September 6, 1929, the Republican State Committee met to pick a successor to Pauline Sabin, who had resigned as national committeewoman to organize the Women's Organization for National Prohibition Reform (WONPR). Henrietta Wells Livermore, founder of the Women's National Republican Club (WNRC), had "strong backing among the women."[7] But newly elected Congresswoman Ruth B. Pratt was chosen, even though she had not sought the office. She had worked in the trenches of the Republican Party for ten years, without a background in suffrage or reform. . . .

Political Machines

During the first half of the twentieth century there were at least a dozen states with party organizations strong enough to be called machines by political analysts.[8] Although political parties were hierarchically organized, with the state central committee being the highest official body, machines were generally organized at the county level and the party county leader was the machine boss. Sometimes there would be bosses at other levels, such as the assembly district, or ward, even the city, but it was usually as head of a county committee that a boss ruled. . . . But only a few state machines survived well into the twentieth century. . . . In some of these machines individual women made their mark. Many worked with their husbands, to whom the material reward usually went. . . .

Most precinct captains, leaders, and bosses were men. Gosnell estimated that women were 5.1 percent of the Chicago precinct captains in 1928 and 11 percent in 1936, though they were as much as 25 percent in the "colored wards." He did not count those women who ran a precinct with their husbands, or in their husbands' name.[9] No one else counted the women, individually or in clubs, so there is no way of knowing if women did better in one area, or party, or machine, than in another. Blair felt that "generally speaking, the boss-controlled machines have been more hospitable to women than those led by more idealistic politicians." But Helen V. Boswell observed that male captains were still given twice the money to get out their vote that women got.[10] Beyond this there is little evidence that strong party machines had different attitudes toward women than weak party organizations. Some women were chosen for positions by bosses, some achieved recognition through their work, a few were elected to office, and many more got patronage jobs. More important to the male bosses than sex was loyalty. If women had to be given a place, then so be it, as long as they were loyal women.

Although women did work in and for political machines, they also organized against machines. This was particularly true of elite women, for whom machines represented everything that was bad about politics. The municipal reform movements of the 1890s and early 1900s saw the formation of separate women's organizations through which women worked to elect candidates as good-government reformers alongside the men's organizations. . . . Sometimes party women organized against the machines in their states. . . . More commonly, nonpartisan political clubs . . . provided a way for women to be involved in politics who did not want to be party women, or who lived in times and locales where parties did not offer suitable opportunities for female participation.[11]

In the 1930s, 1940s, and 1950s, elite women in New Orleans worked through a succession of organizations to defeat politicians they thought were corrupt. The political machine created by Huey Long, elected governor of Louisiana in 1928, and his successors effectively bifurcated state politics into Longs and anti-Longs for several decades. In 1933 Hilda Phelps Hammond formed the Women's Committee for Louisiana to protest the election of a Long machine senator with stuffed ballot boxes. Active until Long was assassinated in 1935, the committee provided a basic education in practical politics for New Orleans women "of brains and standing." One of these was Martha Robinson, who turned the Women's Division of the Honest Election League into the independent Woman Citizens' Union (WCU) in June of 1934. As women, the WCU lobbied for clean election laws, registered voters, removed false names from the registration lists, and monitored the polls on election day. . . .

Illusion and Disillusion

By the end of the 1920s many women were disillusioned with the major political parties. While some were disappointed that they got work but no "plums," the most unhappy were those who had cut their political teeth in reform or suffrage movements but heeded the call to join a political party rather than remain nonpartisan or work through women's organizations. They had believed that women could make a difference, and mostly found that they were used. Winifred Starr Dobyns, a progressive Chicago Republican, resigned after several years as the woman state vice chairman, quoting the famous limerick about "The Lady and the Tiger." In a January 1927 article with that title, she explained that she now knew that "the aim of the political organizations is not good government, patriotic service, [or] public welfare. . . .[M]achines are . . . highly efficient business organizations" operating in the self-interest of their leaders. Women were welcomed because "once in the organization we could be controlled. Our nuisance value was gone." She concluded that "the political machine is the greatest menace to democracy that exists today," and that it could not be reformed from within.[12]

She was answered a few months later by Emily Newell Blair, who was still the vice chairman of the DNC. She wrote that women needed to fight longer and harder, or not fight at all. Power could only be won through fear. If women wanted recognition, they must organize a following, and try, try again. In December of 1927 New York Republican leader Henrietta Wells Livermore told Republican women: *Don't Resign—Fight!* "Until politicians treat women fairly and do not discriminate against them because they are women, women must go into politics with the backing of women. . . . [They]. . . must learn solidarity in order to overcome these special temporary handicaps." In April of 1928, Eleanor Roosevelt, experienced party woman and prominent political wife, combined cynicism and hope. Summarizing the complaints of women from both parties who worked hard but were ignored when important decisions were made, she confirmed that "Politically, as a sex, women are generally 'frozen out' from any intrinsic share of influence in their parties." She acknowledged that an occasional woman was elected to public office, but for the most part, party men were recognized and taken care of, while women "are generally expected to find in their labor its own reward." Her solution was for women to organize as women, select competent women as "bosses," and follow their lead as they bargained and dickered in "the hard game of politics with men." But, she cautioned, women should do this within the parties and should not organize a "Woman's Party."[13] . . .

Female Infiltration

During World War II "much of the hard, gruelling work of Party organization fell upon women." After the war, women kept their stake in the "bottom rung of the political ladder" as election clerks and inspectors, poll watchers, and vote pullers. By the 1950s women had taken over most of the grunt work of canvassing, telephoning, and mailing. One reason for this was that they were good at it. Party leaders constantly commented on women's superior "people" skills. Another was that they were cheap. As Jim Farley found in the 1930s, women worked for "the cause" more than for jobs. By the postwar period the continual assault on patronage and party prerogatives begun by Progressives had significantly reduced the available jobs for party service and consequently the number of available men. Postwar

prosperity made it easy for men to get jobs without party help. Women, on the other hand, were told to go home and give up their paid jobs to men. For ten to twenty years, until women regained their place in the labor force, many more women than men were available for volunteer work of all types.[14]

Among younger women, decades of exhortation to participate in the political process saw fruit; as party work lost its image as a male domain, it became less of a male domain. Women in the 1950s, like the educated, middle-class women of the 1890s, found party work to be a pleasant way to spend their discretionary time. It was mildly challenging, provided social contact, and since it was unpaid with flexible hours, did not conflict with family obligations or incur the social disapproval that came with paid employment. Housewives flowed into the vacuum created by the departure of men. By the 1950s they were doing most of the campaign work and were often the only workers sustaining the parties between campaigns. This was just as true of black women as of white, even though the former were more likely to be in the paid labor force. Clare Williams said three million Republican women were active in the 1958 campaign. Six million women volunteers was the estimate for the 1960 presidential campaign. By 1962 even Attorney General Robert Kennedy, who admitted he had no great love for women, agreed "that men do ninety percent of the talking in the campaign and women do ninety percent of the work." In 1971, RNC Chairman Robert Dole told the RNC that "women do 90 percent of the work, they should get 50 percent of the delegates."[15]

Unlike earlier decades, the new party women were just as likely to be Democrats as Republicans. After losing the presidency in 1952, a reform movement swept the Democratic party. Adlai Stevenson's wry humor, elegant speeches, and image of intelligence and integrity reinvigorated the Democratic Party. During his campaign thousands of political clubs were founded throughout the country. The Stevenson campaign and the subsequent reform movement brought into Democratic Party politics a new breed, the amateur Democrat, who was educated, middle-class, professionally employed (and/or married to a professional), and motivated by ideals more than patronage. These "ardent amateurs" set up their own organizations to combat the regulars for control of the Democratic Party. In New York City, reform clubs admitted both men and women members, but elsewhere separate clubs were often founded. Elizabeth Snyder, southern chairman of the California Democratic Women's Division from 1952 to 1954, said in 1977 that the Stevenson campaign was "when we formed many of the women's clubs that are still in existence today."[16] . . .

Notes

1. Mayhew 1986, reviews party organization in the fifty states as of the late 1960s, supplemented by historical material. Based on his estimates, roughly two-fifths of the American population lived in states with the strong parties in the 1920s, with a small but steady decline thereafter.

2. Upton 1926, XXV: 1. On New Jersey, see Gordon 1986, 78–79. On Dodson, "To Direct Women's Campaigning," *New York Sun*, Jan. 23, 1930, 10:1. Upton and Dodson soon left their states to work for the RNC, though Dodson returned. On Otero-Warren, see Salas 1999, 165.

3. Helmes 1983, 1–2.

4. *New York Trib*, July 28, 1900, 7:2, "California Women in Politics" reported that "the Women's Republican State Central Committee of California, which was organized six years ago in San Francisco." On Wyoming, see *Chicago Trib,* July 10, 1892, 10. On Kansas, see state report in *WJ,* Nov. 10, 1894, second quote 354. On Ohio see *WJ,* June 29, 1895, 201, "Republican Women Organizing." On Illinois see *WJ,* Nov. 10, 1894, 358, "Republican Women at Work." On Colorado see Sumner 1909, first quote 67, 69. "Leaders in Colorado's Republican Woman's Club," *Denver Times,* Oct. 7, 1900. Third quote and photos of clubhouse in Wixon 1902, 414. IV *HWS* 1902, 520, 522, credits Mrs. Frank Hall, vice chairman of the Republican State Committee, for organizing women in Colorado, and the silver issue for recombining women's party clubs in ways too complex to go into. Yost wrote in 1931 that Utah, "organized in 1899 and incorporated in 1901," had the oldest Republican Club still in existence.

5. "Women's Party Clubs," *National Republican*, April 12, 1924, 17-18.

6. Gordon 1986, 90-91, 93, 96. *New York Times:* July 3, 1925, 5:1; April 15, 1928, X:6:1; Nov. 9, 1929, 9:6; Feb. 15, 1930, 9:8; obit, Jan. 22, 1945, 17:5, *New York Herald Tribune*: July 13, 1929, July 21, 1929.

7. *BDE,* July 9, 1929, 7:3; Aug. 19, 1929, 3:1.

8. Mayhew's extensive review of the structure of state and local parties as of the mid-sixties restricts the term "machine" to "a party organization that exercised overall control over government at a city or county level," 1986, 21. The popular view used the term

much more liberally, probably including all of those organizations which he labeled strong "traditional party organizations." He summed up his assessment in 1991, 762, "thirteen states supported arrays of strong 'traditional party organizations' as late as the 1960s; Rhode Island and Connecticut in southern New England; New York, New Jersey, Pennsylvania, Maryland and Delaware (for which the evidence is notably scanty) in the Middle Atlantic area; Ohio, Indiana, and Illinois in the southern Midwest; and the noncoastal border States of West Virginia, Kentucky, and Missouri. The pattern is substantially specific to each state." While he didn't describe the pre-1960s pattern, Mayhew also said "a geographic pattern of party organization had coalesced by 1900, one that resembled the later 'traditional party organization' map of the 1960s"; 766. A few states had strong party organizations in at least part of the state for some of the decades between 1900 and 1960. These include Tennessee, Louisiana, New Mexico, and to a lesser extent, Arkansas, Texas, Virginia, and Georgia.

9. Gosnell 1937, 61–62. Although Forthal 1946 also found only 5 percent of the precinct captains were women in 1927, her inclusion of the work of wives makes it clear that more women were active party workers than those who were official captains.

10. Blair 1937, 182. Boswell's observation was made at a meeting of the National Council of the Women's National Republican Club, Jan. 10, 1931; reporter's minutes, 7, WNRC. It's unclear whether she is referring to Tammany or Republican politicians, or both.

11. Monoson 1990. *SFCall* 1908: March 21, 8:2; March 29, 27:1; April 12, 30:3; Oct. 17, 7:2. Pinchot wrote about "The Influence of Women in Politics" as a result of his victory, 1922, quote on 12; "What Women Did in Gary," *Ladies Home Journal*, October 1951, 51.

12. Egan 1920, 185. Dobyns 1927. The poem goes: "There once was a lady from Niger, who smiled as she rode on a tiger. They came back from the ride, with the lady inside, and the smile on the face of the tiger."

13. Livermore 1927, 4. Blair 1937. Roosevelt 1928. There were attempts to organize women outside the parties for electoral work, but none lasted. See "Women, Go into Politics!" about the "Multi-Party Committee of Women, a non-partisan organization formed to encourage the participation of women in politics." Its founder, Edesse Dahlgren, explained that "It is not a feminist organization" but wanted to see that "women candidates get the recognition and support they deserve": *New York Sun*, Feb. 5, 1947.

14. First quote, DD [Democratic Digest], "Fifty-Fifty," June, 1946, 12. Second quote in Fisher 1947, 87. Farley 1938, 55. Young 1950, 81. Dougherrty 1946, 17. Salisbury 1956–66. Ducas 1936, describes the experiences and motivations of three types of party women as they took over the work of party drones. Early in 1941, DNC Chairman Edward J. "Flynn Advises Women to Assume Heavier Role in Party Work" in a talk before the WNDC [Women's National Democractic Club]: WES [Washington, DC *Evening Star* or *Sunday Star*,

Jan. 19, 1941. Baker 1999 makes similar observations on the change in the party work force.

15. Those who commented on women's takeover of campaign and party work include: Dougherty 1946, 17: Sanders 1956, 31; Grafton 1962, 156, 120; Gruberg 1968, 52–53; Smith 1992, 148. Bone found in 1951 that "both Republican and Democractic headquarters during elections appear to be staffed, in the main, by middle-aged and elderly women, and women play a most active part in the organizations." Eighty percent of these were housewives; 1952, 10–11, 18. Louchheim said that women campaign workers "outnumber the men by two or three to one"; in Shelton, "Women, Once Ignored, Play Vital Role in Politics Today," WES, Oct. 3, 1954. On black women, see, Clayton 1964, Chapter 7, especially quote from Cong. William Dawon (D. Ill.), 122: "the Negro woman has been the salvation of Negroes politically." 1958 estimate in "What Women Do in Politics," Dec. 1958. 1960 estimate in Sanders 1963, who divided the volunteers into three: "Issues Girls, Club Ladies, [and] Camp Followers." Kennedy quote from "Comments . . . Before the CONFERENCE ON EMPLOYMENT OPPORTUNITIES FOR WOMEN," Sept. 24, 1962; Box 58, Louchheim Papers, LoC. Jackie Kennedy repeatedly told women's groups that President Kennedy thought "One woman is worth ten men in a campaign": WES, Nov. 30, 1960, C:4:1. Dole quote in WES, "More Women, Dole Says," Dec. 10, 1971, and "'Distinction' for Women," Feb. 3, 1972.

16. The term is in Sanders 1955, 29–32. Quote in Snyder, who gives a first-person account of Stevenson's magnetism, 1977, 80. Synder thought women did more campaign work in 1952 than in 1977; 83.

References

Baker, Paula, "She Is the Best Man on the Ward Committee": Women in Grassroots Party Organizations, 1930s–1950s," in Gustafson, Miller, and Perry, 1999, 151–60.

Blair, Emily Newell, *Gamma's Story*, unpublished autobiography, Books I and II, Schlesinger Library, Cambridge, MA, and Case Western Reserve Library, Cleveland, OH, 1937.

Bone Hugh A., *Grass Roots Party Leadership (A Case Study of King County, Washington)*, Seattle: University of Washington Bureau of Governmental Research and Services, October 1952; 40-page pamphlet.

Clayton, Edward T., "The Woman in Politics," in *The Negro Politician: His Success and Failure*, Chicago: Johnson Publishing Company, 1964, 122-48.

Dobyns, Winifred Starr, "The Lady and the Tiger, or, the Woman Voter and the Political Machine," *Woman Citizen,* January 1927, 20–21, 44–45.

Dougherty, Page H., "It's a Man's Game, but Woman Is Learning," *New York Times Magazine*, Nov. 3, 1946, VI:17, 54, 56.

Ducas, Dorothy, "All for the Party," 129 *Delineator*, Oct. 1936, 10–11, 50.

Egan, Eleanor Franklin, "Women in Politics to the Aid of Their Party," 192 *Saturday Evening Post*, May 22, 1920, 12–13, 185–86, 189–90.

Farley, James A., *Behind the Ballots: The Personal History of a Politician,* New York: Harcourt, Brace and Co., 1938.

Fisher, Marguerite J., "Women in the Political Parties," 251 *Annals of the American Academy of Political and Social Science*, May 1947, 87–93.

Forthal, Sonya, *Cogwheels of Democracy: A Study of the Precinct Captain*, New York: William-Frederick Press, 1946.

Gordon, Felice D., *After Winning: The Legacy of the New Jersey Suffragists, 1920–1947*, New Brunswick, N.J.: Rutgers University Press, 1986.

Gosnell, Harold F., *Machine Politics: Chicago Model*, Chicago: University of Chicago Press, 1937, 1968.

Grafton, Samuel, "Women in Politics: The Coming Breakthrough," 89 *McCalls,* September 1962, 102–3, 156, 158, 160.

Gruberg, Martin, *Women in American Politics: An Assessment and Sourcebook*, Oshkosh, Wisc.: Academia Press, 1968.

Gustafson, Melanie, Kristie Miller, and Elisabeth I. Perry, eds., *We Have Come to Stay: American Women and Political Parties, 1880–1960*, Albuquerque: University of New Mexico Press, 1999.

Helmes, Winifred G., *Republican Women of Maryland, 1920–1980*; 39-page pamphlet, no publisher, 1983.

Livermore, Henrietta W., "Women's Place in Political Parties," 5:5 *Republican Woman* (of Illinois), December 1927, 4–5.

Louchheim, Katie, *By the Political Sea*, Garden City, N.Y.: Doubleday, 1970.

Mayhew, David R., *Placing Parties in American Politics*, Princeton: Princeton University Press, 1986.

Monoson, S. Sara, "The Lady and the Tiger: Women's Electoral Activism in New York City before Suffrage," 2:2 *Journal of Women's History,* Fall 1990, 100–35.

Roosevelt, Eleanor, "Women Must Learn to Play the Game as Men Do," *Redbook*, April 1928, 78–79, 141–42.

Salas, Elizabeth, "Soledad Chavez Chacon, Adeline Otero-Warren, and Concha Ortiz Y Pino: Three Hispana Politicians in New Mexico Politics, 1920-1940," in Gustafson, Miller, and Perry, 1999, 151–60.

Salisbury, Robert H. "The Urban Party Organization Member," 29 *Public Opinions Quarterly*, Winter 1965–66, 550–64.

Sanders, Marion K. *The Lady and the Vote*. Cambridge: Houghton Mifflin, 1956.

Sanders, Marion K. "Issues Girls, Club Ladies, Camp Followers." *New York Times Magazine*, December 1, 1963.

Smith, Mary Louise. Interview with Louise R. Noun, in *MORE Strong-Minded Women: Iowa Feminists Tell Their Stories*. Ames, Iowa: Iowa University Press, 1992, 146–57.

Sumner, Helen L. *Equal Suffrage: The Results of an Investigation in Colorado Made for the Collegiate Equal Suffrage League of New York State.* Harper and Brothers, 1909. Reprinted New York: Arno Press, 1972.

Upton, Harriet Taylor, *Random Recollections*, unpublished memoir presented to the Martha Kinney Cooper Ohioana Library Association by the Committee for Preservation of Ohio Woman Suffrage Records, n.d. (1926).

Young, Louise M. *Understanding Politics: A Practical Guide for Women.* New York: Pellegrini & Cudahy, 1950.

Chapter 12

WOMEN'S POLITICAL REPRESENTATION
IN SWEDEN:
DISCURSIVE POLITICS AND INSTITUTIONAL
PRESENCE

Diane Sainsbury

. . . This [chapter] addresses the following questions: What were the patterns of interaction between the women's movement, the state, and political parties in altering women's representation? Why did women experience much more success in gaining office during recent decades in contrast to their earlier attempts? Finally, how is women's descriptive representation related to their substantive representation?

To understand the process of improving representation I analyze three crucial debates spanning several decades. The first debate on more women in politics (1967–1972) put the issue of women's representation on the agenda. The second debate (1985–1987) dealt with quotas for appointed positions. The third debate concerned the decline of women's parliamentary representation and the establishment of a women's party (1991–1994). . . .

The Women's Movement

. . . Probably three features largely account for the picture of a weak women's movement in Sweden during the 1970s and 1980s. The first is that radical feminism was not the major ideological inspiration of the Swedish movement. Instead, varieties of socialist feminism growing out of the new left and especially a distinctive brand of reformist feminism dominated. Reformist feminism encompasses liberal feminism's concerns about equal rights and equal status of women and men

and its strategy of legislated reforms. However, it moves beyond liberal feminism by virtue of its emphasis on equality of result—not solely equal opportunities or formal equality. This emphasis allows for reforms that conflict with certain liberal principles, e.g., a cautionary or critical attitude toward the state and government intervention. It also sanctions positive discrimination to reach equality of outcomes and a redefinition of the private and public spheres. . . .

The second feature contributing to the picture of a weak women's movement was the paucity of newly formed organizations in the 1970s. . . . Equally important, the new women's movement invigorated the established women's organizations of the political parties and the Fredrika Bremer Association. It also led to an intensification of women's activity in the political parties and other mainstream organizations. . . .

A third feature is the embeddedness of feminists in institutions, which reduces their visibility. . . . Among the waves of mobilization in Sweden, the first wave produced organizations, such as the Fredrika Bremer Association and the women's sections of four of the political parties: the Conservatives, the Liberals, the Centre Party (formerly the Agrarians), and the Social Democrats. The establishment of these first-wave organizations, mostly in connection with the suffrage struggle, resulted in the institutionalized presence and influence of women. The lack of attention to how the variable of institutional participation differentially empowers social movements has been nurtured by a variety of assumptions. Perhaps the most pervasive is that institutionalization inevitably leads to deradicalization.

Discursive Opportunity Structures and a Discursive Turn

. . . Until recently, a neglected aspect of political opportunities has been their discursive component, and it is precisely this aspect that helps us understand the difference before and after 1970. . . . In Sweden the shift in the political discourse during the 1960s away from freedom of choice to equality and greater democracy altered the discursive opportunity structure, privileging groups that could and did frame their claims in the current terms of the debate. Moreover, demands for gender equality were integrated into the larger debate on equality. The push to get gender equality on the agenda came from two sources: (1) a network of academics who launched a debate on sex roles in the early 1960s and (2) women's sections of the political parties. Getting gender equality on the agenda was of crucial importance because it transformed perceptions of women's demands. They were no longer issues of a special minority within the parties; they were now major party issues. . . .

Of the women's sections of the parties, the efforts of Social Democratic women to get gender equality onto the public agenda were the most important. In the mid-1960s they published "Women's Equality" (Kvinnans jämlikhet 1964), an ambitious program of reform.[1] Its proposals dealing with taxation, labor market policy, family law, education, social security, and public services were eventually incorporated in the "Towards Equality" program adopted by the 1969 party congress. Ironically, the demand for women's political representation was not voiced in the 1964 women's program, and the problem of under-representation of women in public office was only briefly mentioned in the Towards Equality program (Jämlikhet 1969, 24, 94). The issue of women's representation was eclipsed by emphasis on other reforms to achieve equality of women and men. Nonetheless, the Towards Equality program put the aspiration of equality at the top of the party agenda and made gender equality an integral part of the aspiration. . . .

In short, framing women's issues as demands for gender equality and gendering the debate on democracy formed a discursive turn that had implications for both substantive and descriptive representation. Redefining women's issues as demands for gender equality recast the conditions for substantive representation—the incorporation of women's preferences in policies. Gendering the debate on greater democracy altered the meaning of democratic representation and made certain understandings impossible or untenable—improving the potential for descriptive representation.

"More Women in Politics," 1967–1972

By 1968 the demand for increased political representation for women had begun to gain momentum, and it was voiced in many quarters and across the political spectrum. Those calling for more women in politics included the women's sections of the political parties, the Fredrika Bremer Association, and the reform communist party. Party leaders endorsed the demand, it was written into party documents, and it eventually became an integral part of the official gender equality policy.

The initial demands preceded the emergence of the new women's movement, but their gain in momentum paralleled the early growth of the movement and the political mobilization of women. . . . Among the first to voice the demand were the reform communists. The 1967 program of the Left Party Communists (VPK), "Socialist Alternative," contained a strong plank calling for the equality of the sexes. It proclaimed that "women are also under-represented in the leadership of the Labour Movement organisations. It is a blatant injustice and a threat to democracy that half of the population of Sweden is poorly represented on boards and executive committees" (p. 13). The Centre Party women, who had the poorest representation in parliament in the 1960s, were also very early in pointing to women's under-representation as a contradiction in democratic principles (Larsson 1973).

Across the political spectrum, the demand was framed in surprisingly similar terms: The problem was the deficient functioning of Swedish democracy, manifested in gross under-representation.

Women were half the citizenry, but only a small proportion held political office. Women made their claims as voters and citizens—not as women. As citizens they demanded that the principle of equal rights to political office be translated into reality. . . .

Framing the issue of women's representation as citizens' rights had strategic implications. First, it enhanced unity among women. Women as a special minority within the parties were fragmented along partisan lines. As citizens they had equal rights and were joined together in redressing the denial of their rights. Second, as half the citizenry, women were entitled to a corresponding share of the seats. Third, framing women's under-representation as a contradiction of democratic principles made it hard to argue against the demand for increased representation of women. In fact, a consensus emerged. All the party leaders expressed their support of more women in office, but they were quick to point out that it was up to local constituencies, which were responsible for the nomination of candidates, to rectify the situation (see, e.g., Rapport FN 1968, 81).

. . . Within and outside the parties, women pursued a debate on what constituted a fair distribution, developing two types of solutions. The first was to get women into positions high enough on the party list to be elected. After pressure from women, the local Stockholm party branch of the Social Democrats decided that every third place on the ballot was to be occupied by a woman (Karlsson 1996). Järfälla, a suburb of Stockholm, was the first municipality where the Social Democratic party list nominated a woman for every other seat on the local government council. This was achieved only gradually. The initial step was to alternate female and male candidates from the 11th to the 35th seat on the party list in 1970; candidates were alternated from the fifth seat in 1973, and then through the entire list in 1976 (SOU 1987:19, 85; cf. Leijon 1991, 108).

The other tactic was to persuade the party congress/conference to adopt guidelines for women's representation in party and elected office. The Liberals were the first party to do so. In 1972 they recommended that at least 40 percent of the posts in all party bodies be held by women (Sandberg 1975, 80). Eventually the Social Democrats also adopted such guidelines. . . . The Social Democratic

Women's Federation (SSKF) had proposed that neither sex should have more than 60 percent of the positions and that quotas should be introduced if a fair distribution of positions could not be reached through agreement between the sexes (Karlsson 1996, 160). . . .

As part of the campaign, the SSKF congress in 1972 produced a six-point resolution on gender equality. One point was to appoint a special task force at the cabinet level to monitor and promote issues related to women's equality (Fagerström 1974, 45). Subsequently the party congress adopted a decision supporting the establishment of a working group on gender equality at the cabinet level. This decision seems to have placated Social Democratic women, whose officers adopted a wait-and-see stance on the issue of women's representation (Karlsson 1996, 158). Following the congress decision, the Advisory Council to the Prime Minister on Equality between Men and Women was established in late 1972.

Many accounts of the formation of the Council fail to note the role of the SSKF. Instead Olof Palme's speech at the 1972 party congress has been hailed as a turning point, and he is assigned credit for the Council's establishment (e.g., Elman 1995, 241). On the basis of these accounts, the outcome would be classified as preemption. The acknowledgment of the actions of the SSKF calls for a revision, however. The creation of the Council corresponded to the demands of the SSKF and therefore should be categorized as a dual response in the sense that it both corresponded to the goals of the women's movement and incorporated women in the decision-making process. The Advisory Council to the Prime Minister on Equality between Men and Women was set up to appease party women who were angered by their continued under-representation in elected and party office. Party women proposed the Council, and it was eventually staffed almost entirely by women.

In short, ideological and strategic imperatives conjoined, offering a window of opportunity. The radicalization of the Social Democrats, emphasizing equality and greater democracy, offered a discursive opportunity. How could the party present itself as a proponent of greater democracy and at the same time not improve its own record on women's representation? Moreover, the party incorporated gender equality in the Towards Equality program. All this made it difficult for the party to deny the legitimacy of women's demands for equal representation.

Strategically the Social Democrats were under pressure as both the right and the left outflanked them. The pressure was keenly felt because the party wanted to lay claim to the issue of gender equality. On the right, the Fredrika Bremer Association brought up the issue of quotas and mounted a campaign "More Women in Politics" in 1972–1973. The Liberals were first to adopt guidelines for party office—setting 40 percent as a goal for women's representation. The transformation of the Communist Party into a leftist alternative emphasizing women's issues and the emergence of Group 8 as an independent socialist women's organization also gave Social Democratic women extra leverage (Karlsson 1996). Moreover, all parties were vying for the support of women, especially those whose interest in politics had been fired by a growing women's movement.

"Every Other Seat for a Woman," 1985–1987

Once established, the Council to the Prime Minister on Equality between Men and Women put new areas of increased women's representation on the agenda. Because nominations to public office are the prerogative of the political parties and state intervention in party activities has been minimal, this area was largely out of reach for the Advisory Council but posts within the state were not. During the first year of its existence (1973) the Advisory Council wrote to the government, pointing out that few women were members of inquiry commissions or on the boards of national administrative agencies. In 1975 the Council went on to criticize the low representation of women in regional administrative bodies (Sandberg 1975, 81).

Reports to the UN offered opportunities for agenda setting and moving positions for negotiations forward. "Step by Step" (Steg på väg), a national plan for gender equality, also served as the report to the 1980 United Nations Women's Conference. . . . As in the first debate, the master frame was democracy, and women's underrepresentation was the problem. . . .

The commission also gendered decision making in the state bureaucracy and political power. Administrative bodies make decisions that distribute resources, but women and men have different concerns. Without women representatives in these bodies, decisions would fail to take into account their interests and priorities. Examples of conflicts of interest between the sexes, mentioned by the commission, were different priorities concerning investments in road construction vis-à-vis public transport, social services, and work time (SOU 1987:19, 54–55). . . .

The corrective action centered on the recruitment process and the special barriers it posed to women. The most controversial proposal of the commission was the introduction of quotas. The commission recommended quotas and drafted a bill to this effect. In addition to legislated quotas and formulating targets and deadlines to increase women's representation, the commission proposed the following changes in the recruitment process: making the process more visible and transparent, specifying and formalizing recruitment criteria, and broadening the recruitment base. To make the process more visible and open, the commission recommended annual statistics. The annual reports would identify the laggards and put them to shame.

The commission mixed strong words and recommendations with a conciliatory stance. The commission stated it was firmly convinced that only quotas would achieve quick results. However, as a concession, it had chosen a "softer" approach as a sign of its confidence in the nominating organizations' assurances that they only needed more time. Accordingly, the commission recommended that the government give the organizations a chance to show their good intentions by nominating more women. The commission laid down the following targets for women's representation on administrative bodies and inquiry commissions: 30 percent by 1992, 40 percent by 1995, and 50 percent by 1998. If the goal of 30 percent was not reached by 1992, the commission proposed the introduction of legislated quotas.

In strategic terms, the commission's concession put the onus on the nominating organizations. Quotas could be avoided if they nominated women. The conciliatory move also prevented an open division among women over the issue of quotas. Its final recommendations met with the approval of the women's sections of the political parties. . . .

In summary, the drive to increase women's representation in appointed positions in the state administration has been a project of femocrats involved in women's policy machinery. The Advisory Council to the Prime Minister first brought up the issue. Women worked to get it onto the policy agenda and to keep it there, using the reports to the UN women's conferences as a vehicle. Femocrats were not only involved in agenda setting, they also framed the debate, gendering the decisions of the state bureaucracy by emphasizing their relevance for women. Feminists were also in charge of the inquiry commission leading to legislation, the government bill, and the eventual evaluation to see if the targets for women's representation were fulfilled (cf. Bergqvist 1994, 104–5). It was a case of dual response *par excellence*—women were central in the debate as well as the policy process, and the outcome corresponded to the goals of the women's movement. A swift feminization of key positions in the state bureaucracy occurred during the next decade, and in 1998 women's representation in appointed positions in the national administrative agencies and inquiry commissions approached the proportion of women in elected office.

Why was there a take-off in the late 1980s—and not one in the late 1970s? Women's policy machinery had already put the issue of appointed positions on the agenda, and it was strongly supported by the women's movement, feminist activists, and supposedly by the major interest organizations. Perhaps most important were changes in the policy environment. The organization of women's policy machinery was a bone of contention among the political parties. Upon forming a government after the 1976 election, the nonsocialists replaced the Advisory Council to the Prime Minister with a parliamentary commission assigned the task of formulating a national plan for gender equality. The nonsocialists complained that the Council was an exclusive body monopolized by the Social Democrats; a merit of a parliamentary commission was that it would include all the political parties.

In retrospect, a tighter organization may have been more effective than the more inclusive organization of the parliamentary commission. For one thing, it is doubtful that the all-party commission could have forcefully advocated quotas, since the parties disagreed over the matter. Not only was the parliamentary commission politically unwieldy, the national plan it produced was a comprehensive catalog of recommendations covering a wide range of policy areas. Nor was much attention paid to implementation. The national plan's philosophy was one of voluntarism: for change to be lasting it had come from the organizations and their members themselves (SOU 1979:56). In other words, implementation was the responsibility of the organizations.

By contrast, the 1985 commission was an expert commission, and it concentrated on a single issue. Its final report spelled out concrete targets to be implemented, and members of the commission attempted to persuade key persons involved in the recruitment process of the need for change. Voluntarism was now combined with potential sanctions. . . . Finally, the positive responses of the nominating organizations, especially the trade unions, may have been spurred by the mounting criticisms of the corporatist system, and labor's desire to keep the system in place. Simultaneously, women within the unions mobilized and from the late 1980s onwards women were elected to top positions of union leadership.[2]

"Half the Power, Full Pay," 1991–1994

Women's representation in parliament fell from 38 to 34 percent in the 1991 election; it was the first time since 1928 that there was a major setback. Women were both angered by their weakened position in parliament and fearful of the consequences. Immediately after the election, women formed a network, the "Support Stockings" (*Stödstrumporna*), whose rally cry was "Half the power, full pay." Their goals included improving women's representation in parliament and preventing a dismantling of the public sector and women-friendly policies by the new coalition government headed by the Conservatives (Stark 1998). Together with the New Democrats, the Conservatives had won sizeable gains and interpreted their victory and the rightward shift in the electorate as a mandate for change.

In a more pronounced fashion than previously the issue of women's representation was framed in terms of power, as evident in the demand for 50 percent of the power. The problem was the failure of parties to nominate women. The solution proposed by the Support Stockings was to start a women's party that would put up its own list of candidates in the 1994 election. The establishment of the party depended upon whether the major parties selected sufficient female candidates to reinstate and even improve women's parliamentary representation so that they would hold half the power. . . . In short, the Support Stockings gendered both the problem and the solution of the debate. The problem was male power in the parties and the solution was a women's party.

. . . In addition to pointing to the threat of a women's party during nominations, Social Democratic women used the threat in a different way. In the words of Margareta Winberg, president of the SSKF, "Let us demonstrate that the Social Democrats are the women's party in Sweden" (SD 1993b, 35). . . . To become a women's party, [they] concluded, women must have the same opportunities to influence society as men. This demand encompassed all elected positions, chairpersons, and party functionaries (SD 1993a). Simultaneously, as an alternative to this demand, SSKF women proposed special women's lists (Eduards 1992; SD-motioner 1993). In effect, SSKF women pursued the same tactics as the Support Stockings but inside the party. If the party did not act to improve women's representation, women would introduce their own lists.

Social Democratic women also pointed to the male political culture of the party. . . . It concluded that if women were not represented, male interests and knowledge would govern decisions, and that under-representation meant that democracy was incomplete (SD 1993a, 3, 16). . . .

Women's parliamentary representation rebounded, reaching a new high of 40 percent in the 1994 election. The Social Democratic government that came into office after the 1994 election was the first cabinet in which women and men were equally represented. The government launched gender mainstreaming under the auspices of the deputy prime minister, Mona Sahlin, who was also minister of gender equality.

The Social Democrats also changed their by-laws to stipulate that the party lists provided an equal distribution of sexes at the 1993 party congress. The change gave new legitimacy to the existing praxis of alternating lists, pushing Social Democratic women's parliamentary representation closer to 50 percent. Their share rose from 41 to 48 percent in the 1994 election.

These outcomes were the product of the combined pressures of women inside the parties and the external women's movement. In this debate the external movement, and especially the network, figured much more prominently than previously. Obviously, the threat to start a women's party was critical, and party women utilized the threat during the candidate selection process or pointed to the gains of women during the nominations of other parties. Furthermore, the 1990s witnessed resurgence and a generational renewal of the women's movement as younger women became involved. . . . The main organizers of the network were women academics and publicists on the left, who were not party members. . . .

The Support Stockings practiced the tactics of disruption by creating uncertainty—first about the network's existence and then through their threat to start a women's party. They kept threatening to form a party but always at the last minute postponed the decision. If they had acted upon their threat, it is likely that the new party would have thrown the party system into a state of disarray. Opinion polls indicated that a women's party led by Maria-Pia Boëthuis could have attracted 25 percent of the vote—some reports claimed as much as 40 percent (Stark 1998, 235). Furthermore, the media were a major player in the debate, showering attention on the Support Stockings and booming up the prospects of a women's party.

The constellation of party strength also altered the political opportunity structure. Not only did the 1991 election remove the Social Democrats from office; it was their worst election since 1928. The disaster at the polls caused much soul searching within the party, opening up space for new ideas and the acceptance of previously controversial proposals. Moreover, opinion polls showed that supporters of the left parties were most prone to vote for the party proposed by the Support Stockings. Finally, the votes of women were especially important to the left parties. In recent elections, a larger proportion of women than men had voted for the Social Democrats and the Left Party, and party women noted the importance of the women's vote.

Conclusion

Why Did Women's Political Representation Experience a Take-Off in the Early 1970s in Contrast to the First Decades of the Postwar Period?

The timing of the take-off was related to two aspects of a discursive turn. First, the leaders and the rank and file of the political parties had regarded women's issues as particular to women who were a special minority. Women's issues were neither their issues nor the major issues of the parties. Transforming women's issues into demands for gender equality was one of the crucial aspects of the discursive turn that altered this perception. . . . Putting gender equality on the political agenda definitely aided the cause of women's representation. It proved more advantageous than the more general aspiration of social equality, because it changed the basis of coalition building, making possible an alliance across class and gender.

The second aspect of the discursive turn was gendering the demand for greater democracy. Initially framing the issue in terms of the equal rights of all citizens rather than the representation of women's interests emphasized an understanding of political women as citizens rather than party activists, strategically converting political women from a minority within each of the parties into a majority of the electorate. As a majority of the electorate, women laid claim to at least half of the seats. Furthermore, the emphasis on women's under-representation as a glaring contradiction of democratic principles had great resonance—all the more so because greater democracy was on the political agenda. Its resonance, however, continued into the 1980s and 1990s; extending democracy constituted the master frame in all three debates.

. . . The ascendancy of the left from the mid-1960s to the mid-1970s promoted a public discourse on equality and greater democracy, and the new terms of the debate altered the discursive opportunity structure. The key activists and speakers shaping the debate were women and men on the left, ranging from the Liberals to the far left. In other words, this was more than a discourse fit or taking advantage of a shift in discourse; it was an instance of making a discursive opportunity.

By contrast, the timing of women's gains in appointed offices underlines the significance of organizational resources and strategies. Women's institutional presence was both necessary and effective in triggering the increases in appointed positions. In short, the preceding analysis reveals the importance of coupling discursive resources to strategic and organizational resources—especially institutional influence. It has been their co-occurrence that has shaped outcomes. . . . As already noted, the first wave of women's mobilization in Sweden led to institutionalized participation that was a resource during the next wave of mobilization. The preceding analysis of the second wave points to the importance of an institutional presence in promoting women's political representation. Party women as inside agitators continually pressed the issue and they came up with the practical solution of granting women every other seat on the ballot. The second wave also consolidated the institutional influence of women within the state itself.

What Was the Relationship between Substantive and Descriptive Representation in the Three Debates?

In the period leading up to the first debate, the reframing of women's issues as issues of gender equality and getting them on the agenda put a premium on women's substantive representation. The first debate entailed a shift from substantive to descriptive representation and a broadening of the advocates of women's representation; there was no attempt to link the two types of representation in the debate. However, getting women's issues on the agenda favorably altered the preconditions for descriptive representation. Women's issues were politicized and became a source of political activism, mobilizing new women. On these issues women could also claim special competence. In the second and third debates, the interrelationship between the two forms of representation was emphasized but in different ways. The inquiry commission on improving women's representation in appointed positions maintained that women representatives were necessary in order to guarantee that certain preferences held by women were represented and incorporated in the policy process—especially when there was a conflict between the interests of women and men. The third debate and its aftermath raise the issue of whether "half the power" is a prerequisite for gender mainstreaming to function according to feminist intentions.

What Were the Patterns of Interaction between the Women's Movement, the State, and the Political Parties in Altering Women's Representation?

The Swedish experience discloses an interesting dynamic between the demands for more women in political office and the rise of state feminism in a narrow sense, and the feminization of the state bureaucracy more generally. The first state body charged with the task of promoting gender equality, the Council to the Prime Minister on Equality between Men and Women, was established as a response to women's demands for greater political representation. Subsequently the Council and its successors put women's representation in administrative positions on the agenda, and women's policy machinery was eventually instrumental in bringing women into appointed office and in staffing many positions in the state bureaucracy with femocrats.

These developments suggest the need to complement the prevalent narrow definition of state feminism with a broader conceptualization. More narrowly, state feminism has been strictly associated with women's policy agencies that are formally charged with promoting women's status and gender equality (Stetson & Mazur 1995). A broader form of state feminism consists of women holding bureaucratic office who bring a feminist perspective to their positions. The narrow conceptualization is problematic because it obscures the fact that femocrats are not confined to agencies devoted to women's policies and can be located in other sites of the state bureaucracy, and their location is a major variation across countries which requires investigation.

The constellation of party strength, the uncertainty of the parliamentary situation, and intense party competition were important in both the 1970s and the 1990s. The parties—although there was some reluctance on the part of the Conservatives—vied to make gender equality an issue of their own. Party competition produced a virtuous circle in two respects. After the Liberals adopted guidelines on women's representation, the other parties eventually followed suit (Wängnerud 2002, 139), and over time there has been a tendency to improve the targets for women's representation. Second, with each alternation in power between the Social Democrats and the nonsocialists, the incoming government matched or increased the proportion of women on the cabinet in relation to its predecessor (Bergqvist et al. 1999, 310). . . .

In the Swedish case, the increase in women's political representation and the fact that the goal of gender equality is still on the agenda while equality and greater democracy have long since faded from the public discourse attest to the vitality of the women's movement and the achievements of feminists. These accomplishments run counter to conclusions of decline and that institutionalization necessarily saps the vitality of a social movement. They challenge the image of the Swedish experience as "state feminism without feminists" (Gelb 1989) and call attention to subtle forms of activism and mobilization within central political institutions.

Notes

1. Members of the drafting committee were also part of the sex roles debate network.
2. Among the top positions secured by women were: the president of the municipal workers' union, the largest blue-collar union (1989); the president of the confederation of white-collar workers (TCO) (1994); the president of the confederation of trade unions (LO) (2000); and most recently the peak organization of professionals and academics (SACO) (2001).

References

Bergqvist, C. 1994. *Mäns makt och kvinnors intresse, skrifter utgivna av* Statsvetenskaplig föreningen i Uppsala, 121. Uppsala: Acta Universitatis Upsaliensis.

Bergqvist, C., Borchorst, A., Christensen, A.-D., Ramstedt-Silén, V., Raaum, N. & Styrkársdóttir, A., eds. 1999. *Equal Democracies? Gender and Politics in the Nordic Countries.* Oslo: Scandinavian University Press.

Eduards, M. 1992. "Against the Rules of the Game: On the Importance of Women's Collective Actions," in Eduards, M. et al., eds., *Rethinking Change: Current Swedish Feminist Research.* Stockholm: Swedish Council for Research in the Humanities and Social Sciences.

Elman, A. 1995. "The State's Equality for Women: The Equality Ombudsman," in Stetson, D. & Mazur, A., eds., *Comparative State Feminism.* Thousand Oaks, CA: Sage.

Fagerström, E. 1974. "Fler Kvinnor i politiken—en studie av det socialdemokratiska partiets and kvinnoförbundets åtgärder för att nå detta mål mellan valen 1970 och 1973." Unpublished paper. Stockholm: Department of Political Science, University of Stockholm.

Gelb, J. 1989. *Feminism and Politics. A Comparative Perspective.* Berkeley: University of California Press.

Jämlikhet 1969. *Jämlikhet. Första rapport från SAP-LO: s arbetsgrupp för jämlikhetsfrågor.* Stockholm: Prisma.

Karlsson, G. 1996. *Från broderskap till systerskap. Det socialdemokratiska Kvinnoförbundets kamp för inflytande och makt i SAP.* Lund: Arkiv.

Kvinnans jämlikhet 1964. Stockholm: Tiden.

Larsson, M. 1973. *Kvinnor i tidsspegel. En bok om Centerns Kvinnoförbund.* Stockholm: LTs förlag.

Leijon, A.-G. 1991. *Alla rosor ska inte tuktas!* Stockholm: Tiden.

Rapport FN 1968. *Rapport till Förenta Nationerna över kvinnornas status i Sverige.* Stockholm: Ministry of Foreign Affairs.

Sandberg, E. 1975. *Målet är jämställdhet,* SOU 1975:58. Stockholm: Ministry of Labour.

SD 1993a. *Är socialdemokraterna ett kvinnoparti?* Stockholm: Socialdemokraterna.

SD 1993b. Kongressprotokoll, B. *Protokoll. Socialdemokraternas 32: a kongress 15–21 september 1993.* Stockholm: Socialdemokraterna.

SD-motioner 1993. *Motioner. Socialdemokraternas 32:a kongress 15–21 september 1993.* Stockholm: Socialdemokraterna.

SOU 1979:56. *Steg på väg. Nationell handlingsplan för jämställdhet utarbetad av Jämställdhetskommittén.* Stockholm: Ministry of Labour.

SOU 1987:19. *Varannan damernas.* Stockholm: Ministry of Labour.

Stark, A. 1998. "Combating the Backlash: How Swedish Women Won the War," in Oakley, A. & Mitchell, J., eds., *Who's Afraid of Feminism: Seeing through the Backlash.* London: Penguin.

Stetson, D. & Mazur, A., eds. 1995. *Comparative State Feminism.* Thousand Oaks, CA: Sage.

Wängnerud, L. 2002. "Kvinnors röst: En kamp mellan partier," in Jönsson, C., ed., *Rösträtt 80 år.* Stockholm: Bank of Sweden Tercentenary Foundation and Ministry of Justice.

Chapter 13

THE PROBLEM WITH PATRONAGE: CONSTRAINTS ON WOMEN'S POLITICAL EFFECTIVENESS IN UGANDA

Anne Marie Goetz

One of the many achievements for which Yoweri Kaguta Museveni's government in Uganda has been applauded internationally is the increase in the numbers of women in representative politics from the national legislature (25 percent of MPs are women as of the June 2001 parliamentary elections) down through all five tiers of local government (where women average 30 percent of local councillors). High-profile appointments of women to senior civil service positions have also significantly enhanced women's presence in the administration. These increases in women's public presence have been accomplished through the creation and reservation of new seats in national and local government for women, and through a principle of affirmative action in administrative appointments. This chapter considers how the means of women's access to politics has affected their legitimacy and effectiveness in policy making. Particular attention is paid to the extent to which women have benefited or lost from the suspension of party competition in Uganda's "no-party" democracy. The relatively nondemocratic means of women's access to power through reservations and affirmative action has been effective in ensuring their rapid promotion through the "benevolent autocracy" (Norris 1993: 329) that Museveni's government represents (at least as far as women are concerned). But this has been at the cost of politically internalized safeguards on these gains. Without institutionalized parties, and without a democratic decision-making structure within Museveni's "Movement," women have no means of asserting their rights to be fronted as candidates in open elections, of bringing membership pressure to bear on party executives to introduce gender sensitivity in the staffing of party posts, or of using the dynamic of multiparty competition to develop political clout around a gendered voting gap. Instead, they have been recruited to the project of legitimizing the Movement's no-party state, risking the discrediting of the entire project of representing women's interests in the political arena should the present system collapse. . . .

The "No-Party" System

The very first official act of the National Resistance Movement (NRM) government after the military triumph of the National Resistance Army (NRA) was the suspension of party politics.[1] From the start, Museveni promoted an alternative and, he argues, particularly Uganda-appropriate version of democratic politics. It is based on the notion that all Ugandans can compete for office without party backing, but on the basis of their "individual merit." The democratic content of this "no-party" system is grounded in the multiplication of opportunities for ordinary people to participate in decision making through the local government Resistance Council (RC) system. Museveni justifies the continued suppression of party competition on the grounds that parties exacerbate ethnic conflict in Uganda (Museveni 1997: 187; Kasfir 1998: 60).

The system has evolved through various self-imposed moments of reckoning, each of which has stiffened the executive's resistance to political competition, and provided occasions for winnowing out more democratically minded members of the NRM. . . . Since the passing of the Movement Act in 1997, the "no-party" system has been known as the "Movement" system. This Act gives the "Movement" privileged constitutional status, where it is described as the country's political system, a system which prohibits parties from functioning through elections (though they are not formally banned), and will do so until a national majority recalls the system through a referendum. The 1997 Movement Act creates a new set of local council structures paralleling the existing system, and culminating in a National Movement Conference and a permanent secretariat. Membership in the local Movement Councils is mandatory for all Ugandans, and all members of Parliament are obliged to be members of the National Conference. . . .

The first and highly successful demonstration of this consultative spirit was the way the Uganda Constitutional Commission (1988–93) conducted seminars in all of Uganda's 870 subcounties, specifically consulting socially excluded groups such as women, and collected over 25,000 submissions. Another expression of this consultative mode was the introduction, after 1989, of a range of affirmative action measures to institutionalize a voice in politics for certain social groups: women, the disabled, youth, and workers. Women have been the most spectacular beneficiaries of these measures, which began in 1989 with the reservation of one seat for a secretary of women's affairs on each RC council, and the selection, through an electoral college composed of RC leaders, of one woman from each district to sit on the National Resistance Council (NRC).

Reconciliation of social differences and moderation of ethnic tensions have also been approached through the restoration of some of the traditional kingdoms, most notably the powerful Buganda kingdom in 1995. . . . The restoration of traditional leaders and the revived cultural rights enjoyed by tribes can conflict, however, with the equal rights granted to women in the constitution, since customary laws tend to subordinate women's property and personal rights to men's. . . .

The "Movement" continues to resist definition as a political party, because of course otherwise it would be in violation of Article 269 of the constitution which controls party activities. Critics, however, are at pains to advertise the many ways in which it does nevertheless act as a party: actively campaigning for its candidates during elections, with a distinct active membership composed of the "historicals" involved in the guerrilla war and newer members, and with its caucus in Parliament (Human Rights Watch 1999: 59). Its rural structures (the local Movement Councils paralleling the local government system) were used in the June 2000 referendum to mobilize support for the government's position, just as a political party's branch structures might have been employed to support a political campaign.

Women's Engagement with the National Resistance Movement

Women's professional organizations, religious associations, nongovernmental development organizations, rural self-help groups, and feminist policy advocacy groups have thrived under the NRM, constituting, according to Aili Mari Tripp's detailed study of the Ugandan women's movement, "one of the strongest mobilized societal forces in Uganda" (Tripp 2000: 23), and indeed, "one of the strongest women's movements in Africa" (Tripp 2000: 25). This was not the case at the moment of the NRA's victory in 1986, when what remained of autonomous women's associations had been driven underground by the efforts of Uganda's authoritarian rulers to co-opt and control the country's female constituency. . . .

Though the Ugandan women's movement had atrophied by the mid-1980s, . . . it is testimony to the resilience and energy of women in civil society in Uganda that a small group of urban women's organizations mobilized to lobby Museveni soon after his takeover. They demanded that women be appointed to leadership positions, arguing that women's support for the NRA during the 1981–86 guerrilla war justified this. Later that year, one new urban feminist association, Action for Development (ACFODE), a small group of professional women, conferred with other women's organizations to generate a list of demands to present to the new government (Tripp 2000: 70). This hastily compiled women's manifesto called for the creation of a Women's Ministry, for every ministry to have a women's desk, for women's representation in local government at all levels, and for the repeal of the 1978 law linking the National Council of Women (NCW) to the government.

Museveni made quick political capital out of urban women. In response to their initial submission, he appointed women who were strong NRM supporters to very prominent positions. . . . Two years later, Museveni appointed two women lawyers to the Constitutional Commission . . . and also created a Ministry of Women in Development. He acceded to the demand to create a seat for a woman at all levels of the now five-tier (village to district level) Resistance Council system. . . . And, in a gesture which laid the foundation for the pattern of patronage appointments which was to follow, Museveni went one step beyond women's demands for political representation. They had asked for seats for women in local councils, but he added 34 dedicated seats for women in the national assembly (the National Resistance Council), one for each of the country's districts. Election to this position was to be determined not by popular suffrage, but by an electoral college composed of leaders (mostly male) of the five levels of the RC system.

A critical opportunity for the women's movement to embed its concerns in the institutions and politics of the country was presented by the extended period of preparing a new (the fourth) constitution for the country between 1989 and 1995. The two women lawyers on the Constitutional Commission (which prepared drafts between 1989 and 1993) introduced clauses on matters of importance to women, and the Women's Ministry organized a nation-wide consultation exercise to compile a memorandum for the Commission which set out women's interest in seeking the repeal of legislation which discriminates on the basis of sex, particularly in relation to marriage, divorce, and property ownership.

Fifty-two women, or 18 percent of delegates, participated in the Constituent Assembly (CA) constitutional debates of 1994–95. Most of them were occupying the seats reserved for women representatives from the districts, but nine had won in open contests, this time on the basis of universal adult suffrage, to be county representatives. The large number of women in the CA

enabled women to act as a distinct negotiating and voting bloc. Most of them joined a non-partisan Women's Caucus. . . . The Women's Caucus was instrumental in ensuring that a number of key provisions were included in the constitution: a principle of nondiscrimination on the basis of sex; equal opportunities for women; preferential treatment or affirmative action to redress past inequalities; provision for the establishment of an Equal Opportunities Commission; as well as rights in relation to employment, property, and the family. . . .

One of the most contentious issues defended by the Women's Caucus at that time was the use of the principle of affirmative action to reserve one-third of local government seats for women. Many male CA members objected to this on the grounds that it violated the principle of equal rights in the constitution. Women delegates countered that participatory democracy did not deliver equal participation of women without specific instruments to enable women to attain representative office, particularly at the local level (Ahikire 2001: 13).

Implications of Reserved Seats for Women's Legitimacy as Politicians

The way the one-third reservation for women was implemented in the 1997 Local Government Act raises ambiguities about the constituencies they are supposed to represent. The one-third reservation has not been applied to existing seats in local government councils. Rather, the number of seats on all Local Councils (LCs—previously Resistance Councils) save at the village level have been expanded by a third to accommodate women. The "women's seats" therefore do not disturb established competitions for ward seats. Instead, new "women's seats" are cobbled together out of clusters of two to three wards, in effect at least doubling the constituency which women are meant to represent, compared to regular ward representatives. The "afterthought" nature of these seats is emphasized by the fact that elections for the women's seats are held separately, a good two weeks after the ward elections. And the mechanics of voting are different: instead of a secret ballot, voters indicate their choice through the old bush war system of physically queuing up behind the candidate in question (this was changed to a secret ballot for district-level women's councillor seats in 2001). . . . Women now in these seats express confusion over who or what they are supposed to represent: women in their wards, or all of the population in their wards. Either way, they are very often sidelined by the "real" ward representatives, to whom locals go first with their problems (Ahikire 2001).

Similar ambiguities and constraints afflict the women in the 53 reserved district-level parliamentary seats. As detailed by Sylvia Tamale in her book on women parliamentarians in Uganda, it has never been clear that these women district representatives are supposed to represent women's interests. The constitution makes a subtle distinction between these women representatives and other categories of special representatives (for whom there are simply a few national seats, not district seats), such as youth, workers, and disabled people. Representatives of other special interest groups are elected directly by their national organizations, but women are elected primarily by district local government politicians. Affirmative action seats for youth, the disabled, the army, and workers are described as being for people who will be "representatives *of*" these special interests. Women district representatives, in contrast, are not described in the constitution as representatives *of women*, but as representatives *for* each district (Tamale 1999: 74). Women running for these seats must therefore appeal to a narrow electorate of mostly male district elites, not a broader electorate, and inevitably this favors elite and socially conservative candidates. The women MPs in affirmative action seats are not necessarily people who may appeal to a wider women's constituency. Indeed, in many districts, professing a commitment to women's rights might well constitute a disqualification in the eyes of the electoral college. . . .

The "add-on" mechanism of incorporating women into politics has been based on a principle of extending patronage to a new clientele, and indeed of "extending the state"—creating new representative seats, new political offices, and where possible, new political resources. . . . The "add-on" method influences the relationship between women in office and those in the women's movement. The reservations for women-only competition mean that women are treated as a social group whose disadvantage justifies protected access to the state. But this recognition is not accompanied by an acknowledgment that women as a group may have specific interests which need to be identified through a process of public debate involving women in civil society. Thus it is their gender, not their politics, that is their admission ticket. . . . Moreover, it is assumed that these values are shared by all women. There are no further screening processes beyond ascertaining the candidate's gender, no process of winnowing out likely candidates according to their effectiveness in promoting any particular party platform or social program, and no process to enable the women's movement to review candidates. The efforts to include women do not threaten the position of incumbent politicians or entrenched interests. They do not challenge these interests by suggesting that women as a group may have a set of interests to represent which may change the orientation and beneficiaries of these institutions.

Women's Resistance to Patronage

The payoff for the NRM of this patronage of women is a large vote bank. Moreover, the NRM has made efforts to construct women as a non-sectarian political constituency, a model of the non-ethnic vision of citizenship and political participation promoted in the "no-party" political system, and therefore key to Museveni's legitimation project. . . .

The women's movement . . . has not been uncritical of the NRM's instrumental interest in women as a constituency. But it has often been in a reactive rather than proactive position in the competition to establish the authoritative discourse on the purpose and means of women's inclusion in politics. Up to the June 2001 elections, the domestic women's movement had not put pressure on the NRM to institutionalize women's political gains and secure them from a future loss of patronage. Such institutionalization would involve revising the electoral system to enable women to compete more effectively against men for "mainstream" seats. This would require a review of means of articulating and promoting women's interests in politics, which would include a review of the regulations on political parties, starting with the NRM itself. . . .

During the 1994–95 Constituent Assembly debates, the Women's Caucus did not take a stand on the debate over the country's political system. . . . The Women's Caucus's positions on key debates in the CA were in part informed by the nation-wide consultation process which the Women's Ministry had conducted in the preceding years in order to collect women's perspectives on important areas for legal change. . . . In the Women's Ministry summary of the advantages of the new constitution for women, no mention is made of the constraints on political parties. . . . There was a similar lack of discussion of the implications of a lack of pluralism for women's policy ambitions, and for their prospects as politicians, on the occasion of the June 2000 referendum. . . .

The restraint shown by the women's movement in engaging in debates on pluralism should not be taken as collusion with the deepening authoritarianism of the Movement. It is testimony, instead, to the growing risks associated with opposing the Movement, the lack of credible alternative arenas for political activism in the malingering old parties, and skepticism about the value of engaging with the state. . . . The failure to keep a critical eye on the undermining of democracy in the country—risky as it is to challenge the NRM—has contributed not only to a deepening stagnation and paralysis in the old political parties, but also to an erosion of democracy within the NRM itself. By neglecting questions of party development, the women's movement has failed to scrutinize the position of women within the NRM, and, as will be shown below, has done little to promote the institutionalization of gender equity concerns within the party—in its recruitment, candidate promotion, policies, or leadership.

There is an exception to this. In the run-up to the 2001 parliamentary elections one umbrella women's organization, the Uganda Women's Network (UWONET), spearheaded an initiative which took public steps towards challenging the lack of internal democracy in the Movement. UWONET's "People's Manifesto," backed by like-minded NGOs, broached the issue of internal reform in the Movement, raising the need to bring gender-equity concerns to the attention of the National Executive Committee and the Movement Secretariat.[2] . . .

One area in which women's resistance to the NRM's patronage has been most marked and successful, though least coordinated and overt, is in relation to the NRM's admittedly muddled efforts to create a female party organ along the lines of an "old-style" women's wing. Early in the NRM's tenure, when Museveni responded quickly to many of the women's movement's initial demands for the representation of women, he held back on one key demand: the repeal of legislation linking the National Council of Women to the state. This body maintained a register of women's associations, and its formal connection to the government was a reminder of the tradition of ruling parties controlling women's association in Uganda. In 1993 Museveni abolished the link between the NCW and the state, but instead established a much more comprehensive and complex system of supervision of women's association activities in the country, confusingly titled "National Women's Councils." Designed by the Directorate of Women's Affairs in the NRM Secretariat, the National Women's Councils parallel the country's five-tier local government councils. They are designed to mobilize rural women into political and development work, and to channel development resources to rural women. In effect, they impose a double duty of political participation on women, as women are also enjoined to engage with the local government system. . . .

In the end, however, the new National Women's Council system failed to pose the expected threat to the autonomy of women's civil society activism. There are several reasons for this. One is because of a desperate shortage of resources for the National Women's Council system. . . . Another reason is the lack of enthusiasm of women in the country for these parallel councils, and for the political control of women's activism which they portend. Urban women's associations are highly suspicious of the potential of the NCWs to function as a women's wing of the NRM. Some rural women have taken advantage of the NCW system as an arena of political apprenticeship. . . . However, the fact that few development resources are accessible through the NCWs discourages the majority of rural women from taking them seriously. But though the NCW system is in many places near-moribund, it represents an institutional structure which could be revived to constitute a women's wing of the NRM if necessary.

Women in Politics and Gender-Friendly Legislation

One measure of the institutional security of women politicians, and of their relative autonomy from male or party interests which are hostile to a gender equity agenda, is their capacity to promote gender equity legislation. Women in Parliament started out well on this score, passing an amendment to the penal code in 1990 that made rape a capital offense. A few years later, women Constituent Assembly delegates were effective in writing gender equity provisions into the new constitution. But between the CA debates and the run-up to the 2001 parliamentary elections there was a notable flagging of energy around a gender equity agenda, or around efforts to act in concert on other issues. The Women's Caucus in Parliament was largely inactive between 1996 and 2001. Women politicians did not use their valuable positions on parliamentary committees to support each other or to push a united policy agenda. . . . A major stumbling block is that it is impossible to pass new legislation without the endorsement of the top leadership of the Movement. . . . At least two important recent efforts to promote women's rights have quite clearly lacked this essential Movement endorsement.

The most dramatic example of Movement hostility to women's concerns, and indeed, direct presidential sabotage, was the undermining of efforts to include a clause in the 1998 Land Bill to give women equal rights with men over joint property, such as the homestead. Women in civil society first took up this issue in 1997, joining the Uganda Land Alliance (a civil society coalition). . . . They demonstrated the prevalence of the tragedy of widows being forced off their homesteads by their husband's families. They also argued in favor of what became known as the "spousal co-ownership" amendment, that without wives' right to homestead land, husbands could sell family land without their wives either consenting or gaining any financial benefit from the transaction.[3]

Assiduous lobbying by women's groups generated support from many women MPs (but not three of the then five women in Cabinet, who remained strongly opposed). . . . But when the Land Act was published, . . . there was no trace of this amendment. It took months for women

MPs and women in civil society to trace this "lost amendment." They were told that there had been procedural irregularities in the way they had tabled the amendment which then disqualified it. In the end, the president admitted that he had intervened personally to delete the amendment (Tripp 2002). . . .

The president's suggestion of appending the co-ownership amendment to the Domestic Relations Bill (DRB) has as good as extinguished the amendment altogether, because of the political near-impossibility of passing the DRB. . . . The bill aims to protect women's rights in relation to polygamy, bridewealth, child custody, divorce, inheritance, consent in sexual relations, and property ownership. This kind of legislation, which challenges men's rights to control women and children in the family, is inevitably deeply controversial in a sexually conservative society. The item in the bill which has aroused the most ferocious objections from many men relates to criminalizing marital rape. In addition, the Muslim community has objected to the restrictions on polygamous unions in the bill. Already burdened with these "unpassable" clauses, the DRB can hardly act as a vehicle for pushing through the spousal co-ownership clause. The bill has no champion amongst women MPs, . . . [who have] not wanted to risk their political careers on such unpopular legislation. . . .

The Minister of Justice has done more than footdragging to hobble another important piece of legislation: the Sexual Offenses Bill. This draft legislation, which raises the age of consent to 18, is very popular among Ugandan women because of the deep outrage about what is called "defilement" of young girls, particularly in the context of the rapid spread of HIV/AIDS. However, when the Minister of Justice presented it to Cabinet in 1999, it was referred back to the Law Reform Commission because of the poorly prepared principles and missing background documentation justifying the law. The commission was mystified, given that the principles and documentation had been prepared in full. It transpired that the Minister of Justice, personally objecting to setting the age of consent at 18, had taken it upon himself to revise the draft legislation and lowered the age to 16, redrafting the legislation in great haste.[4] This cavalier disregard for the views of the women's movement as expressed in the commission's work shows contempt for the expression and pursuit of women's interest through political processes. . . .

There is, however, one noticeable contribution which women MPs have made: some of them are beginning to constitute an anticorruption lobby. . . . For women within the Movement, it may be that raising issues of corruption is the only way in which to make an implicit critique of the lack of internal democracy in the Movement. . . . Women MPs have concentrated more closely on corruption than any other group in Parliament, save for the group of new/young parliamentarians between 1996 and 1999, after which key leaders amongst them were neutralized by being absorbed into the Cabinet as ministers of state. . . .

The No-Party Movement—Problems of Institutionalization and Consequences for Women

. . . Though the government insists the Movement is not a party, there is little doubt that today the Movement system does function as a ruling party in the sense that it promotes the electoral prospects of its own members. . . . In the first half of the 1980s, no efforts were put into constituting the NRM into a political party—it was merely the public negotiator for the National Resistance Army (NRA). At the time of its coming to power in 1986, the NRM/A was primarily a guerrilla army, given coherence by its overwhelming loyalty to the person of Museveni and its one priority of getting rid of Milton Obote and seizing power. Aside from presiding over the Resistance Council system in liberated areas, the NRM/A had no formal internal structures for electing leaders or debating policies. . . . Between 1986 and 1997 the NRM set up shop in an office block in Kampala and established directorates to perform some functions associated with a party: political mobilization, organizing Resistance Council elections, supporting the NRM representatives in the districts, supporting a caucus of NRM MPs in government, and organizing political education and self-defense for villagers (*chaka muchaka*). Since 1997 the Movement Act, as shown earlier, has generalized the NRM's idea of no-party democracy into a national political system.

The women's movement, like most other sectors of civil society, was not centrally engaged in Museveni's liberation struggle. However, women in combat areas in the center and south of the country did give marked support to the bush war by acting as couriers, providing nursing skills, and caring for orphans. A few women were prominent as fighters in the NRA and activists in the NRM, but they had not formed themselves as a distinct constituency. There was no women's wing, and senior women . . . did not identify themselves with women's issues. . . . Women supporters and combatants had not had a chance to articulate a position on internal representation of women, or on gender equity in party policy. In the post-1986 period, senior women within the NRM have diverged according to their interest in gender equity in politics. . . . Some of these women appear to have been neutralized by inclusion in the Cabinet. . . .

There has been no structured approach to encourage women's engagement in setting policy priorities within the NRM. Senior women in the Movement appear to have focused upon the politics of national reconstruction in the post-1986 period, rather than upon internal democratization. . . . There are no measures to ensure parity in the participation of women in these Movement Councils, nor to ensure their representation in the leadership of these councils. In any case, the automatic leadership of these councils by the LC chairperson ensures almost completely male leadership, since most elected LC chairpersons at all levels are men.

One possible reason that little attention was paid to women's engagement in the Movement Councils is because a parallel structure exclusively for women was set up earlier: the National Women's Council system. No provision for a structured input of policy concerns from the Women's Councils to the Movement Councils (or even the Local Councils) exists. This underlines women's separateness, and strengthens the notion that women's participation in politics is constructed around notions of their difference from men, rather than equality.

There are other organs for policy making in the Movement: the National Executive Committee (NEC) of the Movement, elected at the Movement's National Conference, and the Movement's Parliamentary Caucus. More important still are the decision-making arenas in government: the Cabinet, and the informal and shifting collection of friends and advisers around the president. . . . There are 150 people on the NEC. This includes a few seats for representatives of special interest groups (5 are for women), while the rest are filled by the 45 district chairpersons (all men), and 1 MP chosen from each district (most of whom are men). According to one of the few women MPs on the NEC, there has been no discussion since 1998 about gender issues, no mention of any need for the Movement to offer women special support in elections, or to create a quota to ensure that a certain proportion of Movement candidates are women. The NEC has never functioned as an effective policy-setting body. . . .

The Movement Secretariat is legally charged with ensuring that legislative activity is in line with the Movement's policy. . . . The NEC is supposed to appoint these directors but, in practice, it is the president who personally nominates them, and expects the NEC to approve them. There are 16 directors in the Secretariat, 3 of whom are women. The head of the subdirectorate for Gender, Labor and Development . . . is not connected to the women's movement, and her directorate has made few efforts to ensure that the government is enacting the legislation previewed in the constitution to protect women's rights. . . .

There is no comprehensive statement of Movement policy, and it would be difficult to put a single label on the Movement's ideology. Its values are summarized in a thin 1999 document that updates the NRM's 1986 10-point program into a 15-point program. Gender is mentioned at point 14, which endorses affirmative action as a means to encourage political, social, and economic participation of marginalized groups (Movement Secretariat 1999: 46). . . . The terms "gender equity" or "equality" are never used, nor are any measurable goals mentioned, in terms of aiming for parity in women's and men's political or economic engagement. . . .

The Cabinet is an important forum for debating policy. But although there were six women ministers in the 1996–2001 Cabinet, none of them was close to real decision making. Research by the Forum for Women in Democracy (FOWODE) has shown that these women control small budgets in low-visibility ministries with few staff (FOWODE 2000:10). The vice-president has been sidelined, described by one woman MP as "just an errand girl for the President."[5] . . . In any case, the Cabinet is not the true locus of decision making for the Movement. Insiders say that most decisions are debated by a very tight circle of close army comrades of the president's: friends on the Army Council, the president's brother Salim Saleh, and a few senior Movement stalwarts in the Cabinet. This is popularly known as the "Movement Political High Command." There are no women in this inner circle.

Because membership in the Movement is mandatory and universal, it does not have policies on recruitment, and hence women have not had the opportunity to push for focused recruitment of women members. There has been no structured approach to improving women's chances as Movement candidates in open contests. . . . This means that there is no way for women to insist that the Movement provide backing to a quota of women candidates in the way that their South African sisters so successfully did in the African National Congress (ANC).

. . . Ever since the CA elections of 1994, the NRM Secretariat has unofficially sponsored district-level committees to recommend "NRM candidates" for support. At the time, the objective was mainly to eliminate candidates supportive of pluralism (Besigye 2000: 32). Nevertheless, most of the women politicians interviewed for this study who had come to Parliament through competition for an open county seat (as opposed to an affirmative action seat) claimed they had received no support from the NRM in the 1996 parliamentary elections. By keeping the candidate selection system unofficial and informal, personal preferences can be muscled through by local strongmen. . . . Women politicians who wish to receive Movement backing must buy into these local power structures. . . . There have occasionally been efforts to democratize the movement from within, but all the individuals who have dared to challenge abuses of power have lost their positions within the Movement. . . .[6]

Notes

A shorter version of this chapter was published in the *Journal of Modern African Studies*. This chapter is based on in-depth interviews conducted between 1998 and 2000 with ten MPs, ten local government councillors (both MPs and councillors were a mix of women and men from across the political spectrum), six activists from political parties, six women's rights activists, and six representatives of development organizations, as well as a number of academics. This chapter also draws on group discussions held with women local government councillors in December 2000 and organized by the Centre for Basic Research in Kampala.

1. Through Legal Notice No. 1 of 1986.
2. UWONET (2000), "The People's Manifesto," mimeo, Kampala.
3. UWONET, *Women and Land Rights in Uganda* (Kampala: Friedrich Ebert Stiftung, October, 1997): UWONET and the Association of Women Parliamentarians (AWOPA), *Proposed Amendments on the Land Bill 1998* (Kampala, UWONET, April 1998).
4. Interview with an ex-member of the Uganda Law Reform Commission (21 February 2000).
5. Interview with a woman MP (23 February 2000).
6. They include Sam Njuba, a government minister who objected to the NRM's pressure on the constitutional commission to write the no-party system into the draft constitution; Onyango Odongo, an early Director of Information and Mass Mobilization in the NRM Secretariat, who proposed procedures for electing the NRM's top leaders and limiting their terms of office (Onyango, 2000; 77–78); and Dr. Kiiza Besigye, who was threatened with court-martial for an open letter he published in the opposition paper in November 1999 discussing the Movement's lack of internal democracy and the corruption of high officials.

References

Ahikire, J. (2001) "Gender Equity and Local Democracy in Contemporary Uganda: Addressing the Challenge of Women's Political Effectiveness in Local Government." Working Paper 58, Centre for Basic Research, Kampala.

Besigye, K. (2000) "An Insider's View of How NRM Lost the Broad-base." *Sunday Monitor*, 5 November.

FOWODE (2000) *From Strength to Strength: Ugandan Women in Public Office*, Forum for Women in Democracy publication, Kampala, May.

Human Rights Watch (1999) *Hostile to Democracy: The Movement System and Political Repression in Uganda*, Human Rights Watch, London.

Kasfir, N. (1998) " 'No-Party Democracy' in Uganda." *Journal of Democracy*, 9. 2:49–63

Movement Secretariat (1999) *Movement Fifteen Point Programme*, Pamphlet, Movement Secretariat, Kampala.

Museveni, Y. K. (1997) *Sowing the Mustard Seed*, London: Macmillan.

Norris, P. (1993) "Conclusion: Comparing Legislative Recruitment." In J. Lovenduski and P. Noris (eds.), *Gender and Party Politics*, London: Sage.

Onyango, Odongo (2000) *A Political History of Uganda: The Origin of Yoweri Museveni's Referendum 2000*, Kampala. The Monitor Publications.

Tamale, S. (1999) *When Hens Begin to Crow: Gender and Parliamentary Politics in Uganda*, Kampala: Fountain Publishers.

Tripp, A. M. (1994) "Gender, Political Participation, and the Transformation of Association Life in Uganda and Tanzania," *African Studies Reveiw*, 37.1.

———. (2000) *Women and Politics in Uganda*, Oxford: James Currey.

Chapter 14

FEMINIST POLITICAL ORGANIZATION IN ICELAND: SOME REFLECTIONS ON THE EXPERIENCE OF KWENNA FRAMBOTHID

Lena Dominelli

Gudrun Jonsdottir

The Formation of a Feminist Political Party

. . . Kwenna Frambothid (KF) came about through the efforts of a group of ten to twenty women who were concerned about women's invisibility in Icelandic society, particularly their lack of voice and political power. These women had previously been active in the Red Stockings, but had grown disillusioned with its failure to secure significant changes in the position of women in Iceland and fed up with its factional in-fighting. Meeting regularly during the summer of 1981, they discussed the possibility of forming a women's party to take part in the forthcoming municipal elections. During these meetings they shared their understanding of women's position in Iceland and developed the ideological base which was subsequently adopted by KF. . . .

They found that like women in other parts of the world, Icelandic women neither owned nor controlled substantial proportions of the country's resources. Moreover, women's material poverty was reflected in and exacerbated by their low wages. . . . From their feminist perspective, the problem formed part of a vicious circle, in that women received low wages because they were women and were being used as a reserve army of labor because they were women whose experience of waged work was circumscribed by their familial commitments.

The KF founding group's analysis of women's position also revealed the poor representation women had in Iceland's social power base. In 1982, only three out of sixty parliamentary representatives were women. Their position in local authorities was equally deplorable; out of 1,076 councillors, only seventy-one were female. Although women's membership profile in the unions was high and 80 percent of women of working age were in paid employment, there were only two women on the central committee of Iceland's national trade union organization. Women's impact on employing bodies was even worse, for there were no women representatives in the national employers' associations.

The group became incensed by this state of affairs and was determined to do something about it. The realization that they were confronting a political problem of mammoth proportions at a time when city council elections were pending pushed these women into entering electoral politics as well as engaging in other feminist/pro-women activities such as establishing women's refuges and women's centers. . . .

The decision to put forward a Women's List in the pending local elections was taken that autumn. A problem which the group identified, but did not resolve, was that of finding ways to stand outside the political system and adhere to feminist principles and practice while still being part of the conventional political apparatus. . . .

KF was launched as a feminist political party at an open meeting attended by about 600 women of all ages and classes in November 1981. . . .

They agreed to form Kwenna Frambothid, a party of women for women, run on egalitarian feminist lines, and accepted a program aimed at eliminating gender oppression and transforming gender relations in ways which fostered collective, caring values. . . .

KF's attempts to secure power began with the placing of candidates on a Women's List for the May 1982 local authority elections in Reykjavik and Akureyri.[1] . . . KF's Women's List named fifty candidates. . . . In Reykjavik and Akureyri, KF received 11.7 percent and 18 percent of the vote, respectively. This resulted in two women being elected in Reykjavik, the first and second on the list.

The failure of the Akureyri elections to produce a majority ruling group led the KF candidates there to join a left of center coalition, a decision which was perplexing to a number of KF women in Reykjavik. . . . A year later, one of KF's breakaway factions, Kwenna Listin, was fighting national (parliamentary) elections. . . .

Ideological Ambiguities in Kwenna Frambothid's Position

. . . KF rejected those aspects of familial ideology which gave women an inferior status in society by arguing that women's work in the home was socially valuable and deserved public recognition. . . . The idea of a "feminine tradition" heralding a new social order appealed to all KF supporters. Its ambiguity from a feminist point of view gave it the scope to attract a broad cross-section of women following progressive persuasions. Moreover, the feminine tradition was capable of uniting women on a gender basis because it was predicated on a heritage of family-centerd domestic labor which all Icelandic women held in common. . . .

Working-class women were often just too physically exhausted after their daily exertions to participate in activities not essential for the survival of their family unit. . . . The tyranny of domestic commitments which bars working-class women from having time to consider their own liberation must be directly addressed by feminist political organizations if they expect to draw working-class women into their ambit. KF's record on this front has been mixed. The existence of the problem was acknowledged, but the practical steps taken

to eliminate it were limited largely to endorsing the establishment of SKV [Samtok Kwenna a Vinnumarkadnum, The Organization of Women in the Labor Market]. . . .

Contradictions of Feminist Participation in the Electoral Process

. . . Most of the women involved in these activities had never before participated in political work of this nature. But they, alongside the few women who had been engaged in previous campaigning activities, found the preparation for and the running of the election campaign a profound experience of sisterhood in action. About 100 women were actively involved in electoral work for the 1982 municipal elections. They attended election meetings held by other political organizations, making sure that they publicly addressed women's issues; wrote newspaper articles; spoke on radio; and appeared on television presenting their case for women. . . .

After this exuberant experience, the entry of the two successful candidates into city council work and the awesome display of power held by KF's opposition engendered a profound sense of shock. For the councillors, there was the realization that working in the system was a lonely affair. They were ostracized by the other political parties which, while feeling threatened by KF's exposure of their failure to advance the position of women, found it difficult to take them and their position seriously. Moreover, the very nature of council work and its reliance on formal membership of committees forced the KF councillors to tread a lonely path whereby they often had to make snap decisions on behalf of other women. This made them feel isolated from their power base and removed from the heady influence of sisterhood. For many KF women, the separation between them and their councillors was a new and frightening experience, and was difficult for both sides to handle. In addition, since many of their efforts bore no fruit, it was hard for KF councillors to point out to the membership the results of their struggles and use them to reassure women at the grassroots of the value of their work. . . .

KF's venture into electoral politics badly skewed its action program because city matters began to consume an inordinate amount of KF women's time and energies. KF's initial intention of limiting its involvement in city politics to a small part of its plan of action was frustrated by the sheer volume of work generated by trying to uphold the practice of collective mandating. This required KF councillors to meet weekly with its supporters to make and consider KF policy on issues coming up before the council. Their meetings were established as nonhierarchical forums to facilitate dialogue, mutual exchanges, and collective decision making, and to ensure that KF councillors remained accountable to the grassroots. For a short period the women were swept along by postelection euphoria, and the meetings operated successfully. But over the longer term, and as the weight of city council business increased, disillusionment set in.

. . . Women's reduced involvement occurred as the KF councillors were becoming familiar with local authority decision-making structures. This combination of reduced grassroots involvement and a greater familiarity with local authority procedures greatly enhanced the KF councillors' power and, despite their intentions, distorted the relationship between them and their supporters by eroding the nonhierarchical structures KF had worked hard to establish at its inception. For a time, the KF councillors resisted the encroachment of hierarchy with a modicum of success. However, their struggle to maintain the balance between non-authoritarian directional leadership and hierarchical leadership was precarious. . . .

This dissatisfying state of affairs did not creep upon KF activists unawares. They had foreseen some of these problems in the pre-election period and had taken measures such as engaging in regular critical reflection on their progress. KF women now attempted to reduce the rigidity of meetings and the power of hierarchy by deliberately introducing nonhierarchical techniques into meetings. . . .

Despite these innovations, KF women were anxious about drifting into apathy which would destroy their democratic and feminist impetus and institutionalize their creativity. This danger appeared very real to the KF women who were involved in giving evidence to various subcommittees of the council, where the rules and procedures established under the masculine tradition failed to change under the influence of feminism. The feminists who braved the groups of powerful men at these meetings to argue their case often felt disparaged and ridiculed by those whose minds and attitudes they sought to alter. Some KF women, disillusioned with KF's lack of progress in democratizing committee proceedings, felt that some gains had nonetheless been achieved. . . .

Actions by KF women have forced men politicians to acknowledge feminism and its demands, but in practice they did not alter their relationships with women or their perceptions of them. Moreover, many men responded to feminism's challenge in disturbing ways. Some used it to confirm their misogynist prejudices and insist more stridently that feminists "hate men." Labeling feminists as man-haters became a way of putting down KF's feminism and providing a diversionary tactic which encouraged people not to take either KF's challenges or the feminist movement seriously. . . .

Kwenna Frambothid Splits; Kwenna Listin Is Formed

Another issue which arose from KF women's frustration at their experience of electoral politics concerned the appropriateness of their entry into this arena. . . . A major crisis erupted while the question of increasing grassroots participation remained unresolved. . . . It revolved around the question of putting up KF candidates for the parliamentary election of 1983. After months of agonizing discussions, KF supporters voted by a majority of one not to have candidates stand in the elections. . . .

However, the narrowness of the vote against taking part in the parliamentary elections did not satisfactorily resolve the issue for the substantial number of women who remained committed to entering the parliamentary arena. Taking the matter into their own hands, they formed a breakaway group, Kwenna Listin (KL), and put up their own candidates for the 1983 parliamentary elections. These candidates were fielded in three areas—Akureyri and environs, Reykjavik city, and Reykjavik environs. The Akureyri region was the only area which did not return a KL candidate. The other two areas returned three of their women candidates to parliament.

The issue at stake in the breakaway action was not simply that of parliamentary politics, for the debate revealed further divisions amongst KF supporters—divisions about how they should conduct a parliamentary campaign, and ideological divisions between the pro-women faction and the feminist faction. Although their ideological differences were far from clear-cut, KL's commitment to increasing the number of women in parliament gave it a slightly different philosophy from KF and attracted to its membership women from all parts of the political spectrum, rather than primarily progressive or left-oriented women. This has produced tensions between the pro-woman group, which felt that being of the female gender was the only criterion for membership in KL, and the feminist group which wanted a feminist political orientation and commitment to transforming gender relations as the criteria for eligibility into KL's ranks.

As their philosophies and methods of working were different, relationships between KF and KL were somewhat strained. Even on policy issues which were of mutual interest, such as day-care provisions, KL and KF pursued their individual lines. . . . As the situation amongst its activists deteriorated following the split in the organization, the morale of both councillors and supporters reached an all-time low. Attendance at meetings dropped further as women with little interest in being an effective support group for councillors ceased attending. Work on other aspects of KF's program continued to slow down as council business consumed most of the active women's time and resources.

Kwenna Frambothid's Influence on Traditional Parties

Meanwhile, existing political parties responded to KF's challenge by increasing women's involvement in their own party structures, particularly at the lower levels. They hoped that this strategy would spike KF's electoral ambitions. The feminist challenge was greatest for left-oriented parties because KF was attracting women who would have normally given these parties their electoral support. By early 1983, left politicians were worried enough about the

threat posed by KF to make overtures to KF women and ask them to join them in fighting the 1983 parliamentary elections. . . . In other words, they waited until the women had proved themselves as politicians and chalked up an election victory in their own right before deeming them worthy of consideration. Arguing that the left should resist fragmentation because men and women had more interests in common than differences, and that they should avoid splitting the anti-conservative vote because it would decimate the left, leading left-wing male politicians asked KF women individually to stand as candidates in their own parties and to wind up KF as a party political entity. The KF women's rejection of such overtures turned these politicians against KF, and during the parliamentary campaign they used every possible opportunity to discredit KF's work on the city council and make the positions it adopted seem ridiculous. . . .

KF women felt justified in reacting skeptically to the male politicians' proposals. The Icelandic left historically had a poor record in furthering women's rights and interests. . . . For KF women, achieving equal power between men and women within traditional party structures was impossible.

KF feminists urged women not to resolve their problems within the context of a mixed left-wing political group. Although this position was an appropriate interim response, given the earlier failure of the left in promoting women's interests and women's need to develop their strengths and organizations, the old dilemma of the point at which feminism and socialism converged remained. . . .

The Significance of Women-Only Organizations in the Political Process

From KF feminists' perspective, at least in the short term, women needed to devote their energies to developing their own skills and talents and helping one another grow strong and confident so that they could tackle gender oppression. It was much easier to ensure that this happened if women worked within women-only organizations and formed their own independent power base. Moreover, as KF women discovered, organizing in women-only groups had a number of merits besides bolstering women's confidence and morale.

Various examples of women-only direct action demonstrated that acting in concert with other women renewed individual women's determination and conviction so that their actual struggle against gender oppression was maintained and their strength of purpose reinforced. They also found that working with other women had therapeutic spin-offs. Knowing that other women shared their view of the world and confronted similar problems recharged them psychologically. Moreover, women had lots of fun and derived great pleasure when working alongside other women, even when the objective situation they faced was grim. Such women-only organizations as SKV made women feel more comfortable and spontaneous in their reactions. This was amply revealed during the Supermarket Demonstration of March 1984. . . .

The Supermarket Demonstration was organized to highlight the problems women encountered as wage-laborers. . . . They argued that as women earned only 66 percent of the male average wage in Iceland, they should pay only 66 percent of the price being asked for commodities.

Having alerted the media that a demonstration was going to take place, KF activists went to the downtown supermarkets to buy the ingredients for making a rice pudding which the (male) Minister of State for Economic Affairs claimed all low-income families could afford. The KF women tendered 66 percent of the asking price, explaining their rationale to the perplexed (female) cashiers. Several cashiers, sympathizing with the protesting women's actions, accepted the sum of money offered. Others, worried about management's response and the possibility of losing their jobs, called for managerial intervention. Management asked the women to leave, but the women refused to go and began chanting and singing protest songs. Management called the police, who stood by helplessly watching a group of women singing and dancing in the supermarket. . . . The Supermarket Demonstration and other forms of direct action planned by KF on a woman-only basis forced people to think about old situations in novel ways. . . .

Kwenna Frambothid Fails to Resolve the Ideological Rifts

. . . The failure of the 1984 conference to attract large numbers of women resulted in KF's decision not to hold another conference in 1985. Instead, the women decided to organize several evening meetings aimed at deciding how to respond to the 1986 local elections. The attendance at these meetings continued to be low, with never more than twelve to sixteen women present. This exacerbated the feelings of disillusionment amongst the KF activists.

The two KF councillors found it difficult to agree between themselves either on the analysis of the situation or on how to handle the impending dissolution of KF. One councillor was convinced that KF had served its purpose and should be wound up. She interpreted the membership's poor participation rate as a statement of the return to traditional model politics. For her, the message from the majority of women who had participated in the 1982 campaign was that the grassroots were abdicating their electoral responsibilites to their elected representatives. . . .

During the period of declining participation, various forms of fund-raising and direct action continued, and received the support of large numbers of women. The most challenging of these was the response to the speech made by the mayor of Reykjavik while taking part in the selection of the beauty queen of Iceland at one of the town's leading restaurants. In the televised version of events, while he was crowning the victor, the Mayor was quoted as saying:

> If the candidates of KF were as nice looking and had as good measurements as the thirteen girls taking part in the competition, I would most certainly lose in that next election as they would sweep the electorate off their feet.

The KF women decided to retaliate with pointed humor at the next meeting of the Reykjavik City Council. . . . Dressed in either gala dresses or bikinis, and wearing makeup, jewelry, crowns of silver paper, and sashes depicting virtues men desired in women—Miss Patience, Miss Easy-to-Handle, and so on—the women took their places in the proceedings. . . . The KF councillor spoke at the beginning of the meeting and read a declaration

explaining the action. She stated that KF was protesting against the sexist manner in which women
had been described by the mayor and that during
the meeting they would . . . keep quiet and follow
the men's lead without expressing an opinion of
their own. . . . At the end of the meeting, the KF
councillor again read a statement describing how
difficult it had been for the KF women to play
the roles ascribed to them by men and that they
hoped the absurdity of that role had been made
clear. Having been given prior warning of the
event, media coverage of the meeting was intense.
Angry and embarrassed by the publicity, the mayor
accused KF of "being a disgrace to the city council." For the women who took part, however, the
action was extremely satisfying because it managed
to recapture the spirit of 1982. . . .

But this form of demonstration was not rep-
licated. It stands as KF's swansong. The wrangles
over the position they should adopt in relation
to the 1986 municipal elections continued with
acrimonious debates. In the end, the issue was
resolved by a vote not to become involved at all.
Those against participation in elections argued
that their current attempt at using the process to
acquire fundamental changes favoring women
had been futile. The arguments on the other side
were that KF was admitting defeat in not putting
up a list; that the women's voice in the system
would be lost without KF participation; that in
a situation in which women did not have equal
electoral representation with men at either parliamentary or city-council level a separate Women's
List was essential; and that a Women's List was
an appropriate form of feminist intervention. Following this meeting, held in January 1986, KF
issued a press statement lamenting the failure of
KF to have a fundamental impact on Iceland's
electoral system, announcing that KF would not
put forward a Women's List again and declar-
ing that the 1982 List was aimed at promoting
discussion about the status and life of women in
Iceland and at making it plain that women were
oppressed there. . . .

The final outcome of this split was that a
Women's List for the 1986 local elections came
out under the auspices of KL. Most of the women
at the top of the list had been on KF's list of 1982,
including, at the very top, the former number
two who had been a KF councillor.

The results acheived by KL in these elections
were less optimistic than those obtained by KF in
1982. KL lost ground, receiving 8.2 percent of
the vote compared to KF's 11.7 percent in 1982,
and it got only one representative on the city
council. . . . A Women's List was also put up in
two places outside of Reykjavik. In one of these,
no women candidates were elected; in the other,
one woman gained a place in the council chambers. Overall, out of 1,180 people sitting in local
government in Iceland as a whole, 226 were now
women. The picture had changed somewhat, tip-
ping slightly toward a greater representation of
women in these bodies, but it was not a feminist
gain, for most of the women had been put up
by the traditional parties. KL women also stood
for the parliamentary elections in the spring of
1987, with nine of their members elected. They
believe that it is important that the skills acquired
by women who had previously participated in the
electoral system should not be lost. . . .

Lessons Drawn from Kwenna Frambothid's Entry into the Party Political Arena

KF's entry into the electoral process has produced
mixed results. On the positive side, its activities
have raised public consciousness of feminism and
given a considerable boost to feminist work. . . .
Organizing a women-only political party and
the experience of working together collectively
through direct action boosted women's morale
and confidence, added to their storehouse of in-
ventiveness, and gave them considerable expertise
in the "male" way of handling politics.

On the negative side, KF's venture into electoral politics badly skewed its action program,
because city matters took up so much of KF
women's time and energies and tended to turn
them into servants of the electoral process. It also
raised problems about the connections between
policy and process, especially the contradiction
of trying to operate on a collaborative, nonhierarchical, democratic basis within the extremely
hierarchical structures of representative democracy in the local authority setting. As feminists, KF
women opted for democracy on an ongoing, par-
ticipative basis rather than the traditional basis of
voters endorsing a representative once every four

years. But this was extremely difficult to maintain in practice.

Ambiguity over what constituted a feminist position and whether it could be confined to gender issues bedevilled KF not just in its electoral politics but in its policy making more generally. The fear of exacerbating divisions and of causing further rifts in the organization prevented KF from having full debates on its parliamentary position as well as on other crucial matters such as its position vis-à-vis the family. But it was the division over electoral intervention which caused its demise.

Whether feminists should operate within or outside state structures is an important question for feminist political organizations. The experience of KF suggests that feminists must work effectively in both. They must tackle gender oppression wherever it is located and fight it simultaneously on a number of different levels. However, becoming part of the state hierarchy carries with it the grave risk of incorporation and of tokenism. The local state could use the fact of women's participation to argue that it was "doing" something to promote women's interests. Meantime, it could abdicate its responsibility for providing women with the additional material resources they needed and were demanding. On the other side of this coin, KF women worried that their own "self-help" efforts would make it easier for the state to withhold resources from women on the grounds that they could provide the services they needed for themselves. . . .

KF's commitment to electoral success meant that its feminist ideology was diluted to appeal to too broad a group of women—feminists and non-feminists alike. Rather than focusing on demands for the transformation of society, its main goal became that of rendering the hitherto invisible experience of women visible and getting it accepted as being equally valuable as men's. This made it easy for women who saw themselves primarily as mothers or housewives to identify with KF in that it highlighted their caring role. But it meant that the specific form of women's oppression and questions about who the oppressors are, and why, were never directly addressed. KF women avoided questions about the nature of the family, women's sexuality, lesbianism, and other controversial matters which might frighten the voters and cause a substantial number of women, particularly working-class women, to leave its ranks. Hence, discussions about women's family life and their sexuality occurred only amongst small groups of mainly middle-class women who were very close friends. . . .

Note

1. The observations on KF in this article deal with the Reykjavik group, unless otherwise specified. Akureyri KF had developed its own electoral response, and to do justice to its position would require another article which neither of us is in a position to write. Communication between the two groups was sporadic and they lacked a formal coordinating structure between them.

Part III

WOMEN, GENDER, AND ELECTIONS

This section brings together readings on women, gender, and elections, focusing on women's and men's distinct electoral preferences, opportunities and barriers to the selection of female candidates to political office, and explanations for cross-national variations in the election of women to national parliaments. The first article focuses on the "gender gap" by surveying and analyzing changes in patterns of male and female voting behavior across countries and over time (Inglehart and Norris 2001). The second outlines a basic model for understanding patterns of legislative recruitment (Norris and Lovenduski 1995), which is elaborated further in terms of supply-side (Fox and Lawless 2004) and demand-side (Niven 1998) explanations for women's under-representation in electoral politics. Addressing variations across countries, the next three selections present what is now largely seen as the conventional wisdom regarding variations in women's access to political office (Caul 1999), as well as challenges to these arguments based on data from developing countries (Yoon 2004) and the recent adoption and implementation of electoral gender quota policies (Dahlerup and Freidenvall 2005).

As noted in the introduction, predictions as to how women would use their right to vote played a central role in debates leading up to women's suffrage. Although some believed that women would vote in ways similar to men, others argued that women were likely to espouse quite different political priorities. Subjecting these assumptions to an empirical test, *Ronald Inglehart and Pippa Norris* analyze patterns of male and female voting behavior in more than sixty countries over time. They discover that a "traditional gender gap," whereby women vote more to the right than men, continues to prevail in many non-Western contexts. However, this gap has narrowed and reversed in many Western countries, producing a "modern gender gap," whereby women are not more likely to vote to the left than men. They find that this trend is strongest among younger age groups, suggesting that the process of generational turnover is likely to strengthen the modern gender gap over time. Reasons for these patterns, they suggest, stem from differences in men's and women's values, especially their divergent attitudes toward postmaterialism and the women's movement.

Turning to the question of women as elected officials, a common starting point is what has come to be known as the "supply and demand" model of political recruitment. Using evidence from the United Kingdom, *Pippa Norris and Joni Lovenduski* outline their seminal statement of this model. They propose that the number of women elected is the combined result of (1) the qualifications of women to run for political office and (2) the desire or willingness of elites to select female aspirants. The two key factors shaping the supply of potential candidates are (1) resources, like time, money, and experience, and (2) motivation, such as drive, ambition, and interest in politics. Once applicants come forward, their selection hinges on perceptions of their abilities, qualifications, and experience. Trends in these assessments are strongly shaped by the preferences and opinions of political elites, who may justify their decisions as based on merit, but in fact often employ various types of "information short-cuts" like sex as a proxy measure of abilities and character.

Richard L. Fox and Jennifer L. Lawless expand on the supply-side explanation by analyzing the initial decision to run for political office in the United States. Drawing on the results of a national survey, they find that women who share the same personal characteristics and professional credentials as men express significantly lower levels of ambition to hold elective office. They note that women are far less likely than men to be encouraged to run for office and are significantly less likely to view themselves as qualified to run. As a consequence, they argue that despite major changes in women's social and economic status in recent years, traditional sex-role socialization continues to play a role in limiting women's access to political office. *David Niven,* in turn, elaborates the demand-side explanation by examining elite attitudes toward the selection of male and female candidates. Through a survey, he seeks to ascertain whether the selection of fewer women than men is due to the biases of predominantly male elites against potential female candidates. He finds that the tendency not to select women is due to the preferences of male elites to find candidates similar to them through their stated preference for attributes that are stereotypically seen as "male."

A focus on general explanations for women's under-representation, however, overlooks the fact that there are significant variations across countries in terms of women's representation in national parliaments. *Miki Caul* reflects the dominant findings of this literature through a statistical analysis of women's representation in twelve advanced industrial countries at three points in time: 1975, 1985, and 1989. She examines a range of factors, including the electoral system, the degree of party institutionalization, the level of candidate nomination, the ideologies and values of political parties, the proportion of women in party offices, and the presence of formal rules to increase the numbers of women nominated. Drawing on this research, *Mi Yung Yoon* tests whether the same or different factors explain variations in women's representation in sub-Saharan Africa. Contrary to findings from developed countries, she discovers that education, labor force participation, and socioeconomic development do not have any positive effect. In contrast, patriarchal culture, proportional representation electoral systems, and gender quotas are statistically significant.

Elaborating on this last variable, *Drude Dahlerup and Lenita Freidenvall* observe the rapid diffusion of gender quotas around the world in recent years and identify two paths to increased representation for women. In countries that follow the "incremental track," the proportion of women increases gradually over time, and gender quotas—if adopted—appear only after women make substantial gains. In countries on the "fast track," in contrast, the number of women in elected office may increase dramatically following quota adoption. Together, these readings indicate that general trends in women, gender, and elections coexist with important cross-national and cross-temporal variations, which point to the contested nature—and uneven progress—of women's incorporation into the political process.

Chapter 15

THE DEVELOPMENTAL THEORY
OF THE GENDER GAP:
WOMEN'S AND MEN'S VOTING BEHAVIOR
IN GLOBAL PERSPECTIVE

Ronald Inglehart

Pippa Norris

During the postwar era the established orthodoxy in political science was that women in western democracies proved more right wing than men. Gender differences in party preferences were never as marked as the classic electoral cleavages of class, region, and religion, . . . but . . . "women's conservatism" was commonly noted as a persistent and well-established phenomenon. During the 1980s the conventional wisdom came under increasing challenge. On the one hand, commentators in many countries outside the United States detected a process of gender *dealignment*, finding minimal sex differences in voting choice and party preferences. On the other hand, in the United States a pattern of gender *realignment* became evident. The emergence of the modern gender gap in America is due to the way that women moved toward the Democrats since 1980 while men moved toward the Republicans on a stable, long-term, and consistent basis, thereby reversing the pattern of voting and partisanship common in the 1950s.

The process of gender realignment in the United States raises the question whether similar developments are now evident elsewhere. There are two perspectives on this issue. If the gender gap in American politics is caused by common structural and/or cultural trends affecting modern societies, such as increased female participation in the paid workforce, the breakup of traditional family units, or the transformation of sex roles,

then we would expect to find similar gender gaps in other nations. Yet, alternatively, if caused by specific factors which are distinctive to American politics, such as the traditional lack of a strong class cleavage in the electorate, the centrist pattern of two-party competition, or the salience of issues like abortion and affirmative action, then we would expect that the modern gender gap in the United States would prove to be *sui generis*, or at least highly contingent upon particular conditions found in particular countries, such as the predominant issue agenda, patterns of party competition, or cultural values. . . .

To provide a fresh look at this issue we focus on comparing gender differences in the voting preferences of the electorate, the most common meaning of the term "gender gap," in a wide range of countries. . . .Our argument is based on a developmental theory of the gender gap suggesting that long-term structural and cultural trends, which have transformed women's and men's lives, have gradually produced realignment in gender politics in postindustrial societies. For data we draw on the World Values Surveys (WVS), carried out in three waves in the early 1980s, the early 1990s, and the mid-1990s. In total these surveys allow us to compare sixty societies around the globe, although not all countries were included in each wave. . . . Gender differences in voting intentions are compared using a 10-point scale, derived from expert assessments of the position of parties across the left–right spectrum. . . .

Theoretical Framework

The Orthodox Account of Female Conservatism

. . . The early classics in the 1950s and 1960s established the orthodoxy in political science; gender differences in voting tended to be fairly modest but nevertheless women were found to be more apt than men to support center–right parties in Western Europe and in the United States, a pattern which we can term the *traditional gender gap* (Duverger, 1955: 65–66; Lipset, 1960: 143; Pulzer, 1967: 52; Butler and Stokes, 1974: 160; Campbell et al., 1960: 493). Inglehart (1977: 229) confirmed that in the early 1970s women remained more likely to support Christian Democrat and Conservative parties in Western Europe, particularly in Italy and Germany, although a new pattern appeared to be emerging in the United States. Most explanations of the traditional gender gap emphasized structural sex differences in religiosity, longevity, and labor force participation. . . . In this era women were also commonly assumed to be more conservative in their political attitudes and values, producing an ideological gap underpinning their party preferences. . . .

Theories of Gender Dealignment

This orthodoxy came under increasing challenge during the 1980s since scholars in many Western countries emphasized a pattern of gender dealignment in the electorate, or a weakening of women's traditional conservatism. . . . The old thesis of female conservatism was apparently no longer evident; instead, the situation in the 1980s seemed contingent upon political circumstances: in some established democracies women seemed to lean toward the right, in others to the left, particularly in Nordic societies (Oskarson, 1995), and in yet others no significant differences could be detected (Mayer and Smith, 1995; Norris, 1988; Oskarson, 1995; Studlar, McAllister, and Hayes, 1998). . . .

An overall pattern of gender dealignment seemed to fit theories suggesting that the impact of traditional social–party linkages had weakened in many established democracies, notably in terms of class and religion (Dalton et al., 1984; Crewe and Denver, 1985; Franklin et al., 1992; Norris and Evans, 1999). . . . This account stressed that voters have become more instrumental. Under these conditions no party could expect to enjoy a persistent and habitual advantage among women or men voters; instead contingent factors like government performance, party policies, and leadership images could be expected to come to the fore in voting decisions.

Theories of Gender Realignment

During the last decade, however, there has been much speculation, although little concrete evidence, that women were continuing to realign toward the left throughout advanced industrial societies, a situation that we will term the *modern gender gap*, replicating the pattern evident since the early 1980s in the United States. The process of "partisan realignment" is understood to produce an enduring and stable change in the mass coalitional basis of party politics (Norris and Evans, 1999). . . . The modern gender gap in American elections has rarely been substantial compared with differences based on race or religion, but nevertheless this has proved a consistent, stable, and politically significant factor in many contests, representing a long-term shift in the mass basis of party politics. . . .

The Developmental Theory of Gender Realignment

. . . We argue that a developmental theory can be used to explain this phenomenon, in which the transformation of sex roles in postindustrial societies has influenced the process of value change. As women's and men's lifestyles and cultural attitudes have been altered by the process of societal modernization we expect this to have a major impact on their political preferences. The theory is based on three major premises that are open to empirical investigation; namely, we expect to find systematic differences in the gender gap:

1. between societies based on their level of political and economic development;
2. within societies based on generational cohorts; and

3. within societies based on structural and cultural factors.

The developmental theory is based on the assumption that traditional societies are characterized by sharply differentiated gender roles that discourage women from jobs outside the home. . . . In postindustrial societies gender roles have increasingly converged due to a structural revolution in the paid labor force, in educational opportunities for women, and in the characteristics of modern families. These major changes in sex roles can be expected to influence women's and men's political behavior. . . . Women's support for parties of the left may be encouraged by pervasive patterns of horizontal and vertical occupational segregation. Working women are often overrepresented in low-paid jobs and as public sector professionals and service providers in education, health care, and welfare services. Women also experience continued pay disparities and lower socioeconomic status, with considerably higher levels of female poverty (United Nations, 1995). . . . Increased participation by professional women in higher education may have encouraged more liberal attitudes. Structural accounts have also commonly emphasized the process of secularization. Women have tended to be more religious in the past and this, particularly Catholicism, helped to explain greater female support for Christian Democratic parties in the postwar era (Lipset, 1960). . . .

Structural factors can be regarded as interacting with, and causing, shifts in cultural attitudes and values that may subsequently exert an independent and direct effect upon voting choice. The most influential cultural theories concern gender differences in postmaterialist values, the effects of feminist mobilization, and attitudes toward the role of government. . . . It is argued that this pervasive cultural shift has increased the salience of issues such as reproductive choice, sexual harassment in the workplace, and equal opportunities. . . . If the modernization process has influenced the gender gap, we would expect to find that support for postmaterialist values would be closely associated with female support for parties of the left.

Alternatively, Conover (1988) has argued that the electoral gap in America has been strongly influenced by mobilization by the women's movement around issues of gender equality. In this view it is not the general shift to postmaterialist values per se, but rather the growth of feminist identity and consciousness that has been the catalyst producing the modern gender gap in party support. . . . If so, we would expect to find the modern gender gap would be strongest among feminist women. This hypothesis can be tested by examining the size of the gender gap controlling for the effects of confidence in the women's movement and also attitudes toward abortion, understood as key indicators of sympathy for feminist ideals. . . .

Lastly, some suggest that the gender gap in America is due to greater support among women for a range of left-wing policy issues, rather than those that are explicitly gendered, . . . such as government spending on the welfare state and public services, pro-environmental protection, and pacifism in the use of military force. . . . We can examine this hypothesis by monitoring the gender gap after controlling for attitudes toward government, measured by examining a series of left-right attitude scales in the WVS toward the role of government in the economy and the responsibilities of the state in the provision of social welfare.

To summarize, the developmental theory suggests that structural and cultural trends common to postindustrial societies have realigned women toward parties of the left. This can be tested by examining the size and direction of the gender gap given a series of hypotheses. First, at national levels we would expect to find the reversal of the gender gap according to the society's level of economic development. . . .

Within postindustrial societies we would also predict that the gender gap would reverse by generational cohort, given the way that changes in lifestyles and cultural trends have transformed the lives of older and younger groups of women. . . . We would hypothesize that the modern gender gap should be evident among the younger generation, while the traditional gap should remain relatively strong among the older cohorts. These generational effects would not be expected in postcommunist or developing societies, since structural and cultural changes in these societies have taken very different pathways there. The forces of modernization have not yet transformed gender roles in most developing societies; and in the postcommunist world, the historical changes of recent decades have been very different from those operating in advanced industrial societies.

Lastly, . . . we would also expect to find that within societies the gender gap at the individual level would vary systematically according to structural and cultural factors which have changed women's and men's lives, namely women's participation in the paid labor force, their socio-economic status, education, and religiosity, as well as their attitudes toward postmaterialism, the women's movement, and government.

Trends in the Voting Gap

. . . We can start by comparing the gender gap in voting choice in eleven established democracies where we have information from the early 1980s to the early or mid-1990s. . . . The evidence for trends since the early 1980s is available for the eleven established democracies included in the first wave of the World Values Survey. If we compare the gender gap using the expert scale we find a mixed pattern in these societies in the early 1980s: in four countries (the Netherlands, the United States, Denmark, and Italy) women leaned toward the left while in six countries they leaned rightward. But the pattern of change over time is generally consistent: in countries where women were more conservative in 1981 this pattern weakens although it does not disappear everywhere, except for Spain. The modern gender gap, with women more left wing than men, is evident in each wave in the United States, consolidates over time in the Netherlands, and emerges by the 1990s in Canada and West Germany.

. . . We can compare the size and direction of the voting gap in the 1990s in 36 countries. What is striking is that in postindustrial societies in the 1990s the modern gender gap, with women significantly more left wing than men, is evident in almost half the nations under comparison. Women are significantly more right wing in only two (Finland and Spain), and in the remainder there is no significant gender difference. In contrast, in the eight developing societies women proved significantly more right wing in four and more left wing in only one (Argentina). Across all advanced industrialized democracies the gender gap in voting was +.10 (with women leaning left), whereas it was −.08 in postcommunist societ-

ies, and −.14 in developing societies (with women leaning right). This offers important evidence providing initial confirmation of our first hypothesis, that the gender gap is consistently associated at the national level with the process of economic and political modernization. The traditional right-wing gap remains prevalent in developing societies, but a pattern of convergence or gender realignment is evident in more developed societies. This lends support to the hypothesis that the shift toward the left among women is strongly influenced by the modernization process.

To test whether the pattern we have established is an artifact of the particular measure we used, or whether the patterns in voting are reflected more broadly in terms of the ideological position of women and men, we can compare nineteen countries where we have a consistent measure of left–right identity. . . . The "ideological gap" is calculated as the difference in the mean self-placement of women and men on these scales. . . . The results confirm that the position of men has remained relatively stable since the early 1970s, with some trendless fluctuations around the mean. . . . In contrast, women proved ideologically further to the right of men in the early 1970s, with a closure of the gap in the mid-1980s, and the emergence of women more to the left of men in the mid-1990s. . . .

The analysis of gender differences in left–right ideology in the wider range of societies included in the World Values Surveys in the early 1980s, the early 1990s, and the mid-1990s confirms this pattern: the results support the conventional wisdom about women's greater conservatism in the past. In the early 1980s women did see themselves as slightly more right wing than men in two-thirds of the countries where we have comparable data, and this pattern was particularly strong in Italy, Spain, and France. By the early 1990s the evidence shows that women had moved to center–left in about half the countries under comparison, with the modern gender gap becoming evident in the United States, Norway, and the Netherlands. By the last wave of the survey in 1995–97 this pattern is even clearer as women were on balance more left wing than men in all nations except Spain (where women have still become less conservative over time) and South Korea (which shows a mixed pattern over time and no significant difference in the mid-1990s).

. . . We also compared the ideological gap in 57 nations with data drawn from the most recent World Values Surveys available in the early or mid-1990s. The results confirm that by the 1990s women were significantly more right wing than men in only a few societies (6 out of 57 nations). In most nations women proved largely similar to men, but they were significantly more left wing in fourteen countries. . . . Most of the countries displaying the modern gender gap in ideology are postindustrial societies. . . .

Testing the Developmental Theory of Gender Realignment

To examine the reasons for gender realignment we need to analyze the effects of the generational, structural, and cultural factors discussed earlier. To do this we use ordinary least squared regression models with the 10-point left-right voting scale as the dependent variable. . . . In Model 1 we explore the impact of gender on the left-right voting scale without any controls. . . . Model 2 subsequently adds structural controls, including religiosity, labor force participation, education, age, and the respondent's socioeconomic status. . . . Model 3 adds controls for cultural factors, measured by support for postmaterial values, the women's movement and abortion, and attitudes toward government. . . .

[Analyzing] Model 1 confirms that gender was a significant predictor of voting choice in the 1990s, with women leaning left, confirming the existence of the modern gender gap. Model 2 shows that gender remains significant even after entering the structural controls. That is to say, the modern gender gap cannot be explained, as some previous research suggests (DeVaus and McAllister, 1989), as simply the result of gender differences in religiosity, class, age, or participation in the labor force. In established democracies the pattern of the gender gap by age group did prove to be an important indicator of generational change: among the youngest group women are far more left wing than men whereas among the over-65s the gender gap reversed, with women more conservative. Given the process of generational turnover this promises to have profound consequences for the future of the gender cleavage, moving women further left. Lastly, Model

3 also enters the attitudinal variables, which reduced the effect of gender although this still remained significant. Support for postmaterialist values and for the women's movement were the most important effects although all these variables proved significant. What this suggests . . . is that the modern gender gap is more strongly the product of attitudinal rather than structural variables. That is, women in advanced industrialized societies are shifting left because of a broad process of value changes, particularly the shift toward more egalitarian attitudes associated with postmaterialism and feminism.

[Analyzing] the results for postcommunist societies, we found a different pattern, with the traditional gender gap being prevalent in the 1990s. Women proved more right wing than men even after controlling for differences in social structure and in political attitudes. Cultural factors proved particularly weak. . . . The pattern by age group was also far more polarized than in established democracies, since the women who leaned further to the left than men were found between both the youngest and oldest cohorts. The pattern of secular generational trends in these nations is therefore more complex than we can predict in developed societies. When we compared the same models in developing societies, the results confirmed the persistence of the traditional gender gap, even after controlling for structural and cultural factors.

As observed earlier, however, there are important variations within these broad categories of societies. We break down the results further to compare patterns for the eighteen nations where we have the complete set of control variables. The results in Model 1 confirm that by the 1990s among advanced industrialized societies women proved significantly more left wing than men in six out of ten nations, there was no significant difference in three countries, and in one (Finland) women were more right wing. The modern gender gap was maintained in the United States, France, and Germany after introducing structural controls, but it became insignificant in every country except the United States once we controlled for cultural attitudes. This reinforces the earlier conclusions that structural and cultural factors play a role in the development of the modern gender gap, but of these it is value change that seems the most direct influence. Moreover, in postcommunist societies the only significant gender gap at the national level was found in East Germany, which closely reflects the West German tendency for women to lean to the left. Lastly, in the four developing nations analyzed here, the traditional gender gap proved strong and significant, even after introducing controls, in two countries (Chile and Mexico). This again reinforces the finding that any global analysis of the gender gap needs to take account of the type of society, as well as individual level factors. The process of modernization has had profound effects on men's and women's lives, and the modern gender gap is strongly linked to the process of economic and political development.

Conclusions and Discussion

. . . The developmental theory emphasizes that common developments transforming the lifestyles and values of women and men in postindustrial societies have produced changes in party preferences. To support this theory, this study established three main patterns. First, we found that in established democracies as recently as the early 1980s, women tended to be more conservative than men, in their ideology and voting behavior, as earlier studies suggested. The traditional gender gap continued to be evident in many postindustrial societies as late as the 1980s. Moreover, this pattern persists today in many developing societies where women continue to prove slightly more right wing than men, even after including a range of social controls.

Yet, most important, we also found that in many postindustrial societies by the 1990s women have shifted leftward, producing a modern gender gap similar to that which currently exists in the United States. It should be stressed that the process is far from uniform, probably reflecting particular circumstances within each country, such as the pattern of party competition, the predominant issue agenda, and the strength of the organized women's movement. Nevertheless, by the mid-1990s we established that women are now no longer more conservative than men, and are often more left-leaning, in many established democracies. In postindustrial societies the modern gender gap persists even after introducing a range of social controls, but the size of the gap diminishes once we take into account cultural factors. This finding suggests that the modern gender gap is more strongly the product of cultural differences between women and men in their value orientations, especially attitudes toward postmaterialism and the women's movement, rather than differences in their lifestyles.

Third, and perhaps most significantly for future developments, we demonstrated that in postindustrial societies the modern gender gap was strongest among the younger age groups while the traditional gender gap was evident among the elderly. If this is a generational rather than a life-cycle effect, as seems most likely, it suggests that the process of generational turnover will probably continue to move women leftward. In the long term, as younger voters gradually replace older generations, through secular turnover, the modern gender gap should therefore strengthen and get consolidated in established democracies. . . .

References

Butler, D., and D. E. Stokes (1974). *Political Change in Britain: The Evolution of Electoral Choice* (2nd ed.). London: Macmillan.

Campbell, A., P. Converse, W. E. Miller, and D. E. Stokes (1960). *The American Voter*. New York: Wiley.

Conover, P. J. (1988). "Feminists and the Gender Gap." *Journal of Politics*, 50: 985–1010.

Crewe, I., and D. T. Denver (1985). *Electoral Change in Western Democracies: Patterns and Sources of Electoral Volatility*. New York: St. Martin's Press.

Dalton, R. J., S. C. Flanagan, P. A. Beck, and J. E. Alt (1984). *Electoral Change in Advanced Industrial Democracies: Realignment or Dealignment?* Princeton, NJ: Princeton University Press.

DeVaus, D., and I. McAllister (1989). "The Changing Politics of Women: Gender and Political Alignments in 11 Nations." *European Journal of Political Research*, 17: 241–262.

Duverger, M. (1955). *The Political Role of Women*. Paris: UNESCO.

Franklin, M., T. T. Mackie, H. Valen, and C. Bean (1992). *Electoral Change: Responses to Evolving Social and Attitudinal Structures in Western Countries*. Cambridge: Cambridge University Press.

Inglehart, R. (1977). *The Silent Revolution: Changing Values and Political Styles among Western Publics*. Princeton, NJ: Princeton University Press.

Lipset, S. M. (1960). *Political Man: The Social Bases of Politics*. Garden City, NY: Doubleday.

Mayer, L., and R. E. Smith. (1995). "Feminism and Religiosity: Female Electoral Behavior in Western

Europe." In *Women and Politics in Western Europe* (S. Bashevkin, ed.). London: Frank Cass.

Norris, P. (1988). "The Gender Gap: A Cross National Trend?" In *The Politics of the Gender Gap* (C. Mueller, ed.). Beverley Hills, CA: Sage.

Norris, P., and G. Evans (1999). "Introduction: Understanding Electoral Change." In *Critical Elections: British Parties and Voters in Long-term Perspective* (G. Evans and P. Norris, eds.). London: Sage.

Oskarson, M. (1995). "Gender Gaps in Nordic Voting Behavior." *Women in Nordic Politics* (L. Karvonen and P. Selle, eds.). Aldershot: Dartmouth.

Pulzer, P. G. J. (1967). *Political Representation and Elections in Britain*. London: Allen & Unwin.

Studlar, D., I. McAllister, and B. Hayes (1998). "Explaining the Gender Gap in Voting: A Cross-National Analysis." *Social Science Quarterly*, 79.

United Nations (1995). *The World's Women 1995: Trends and Statistics*. New York: United Nations.

Chapter 16

Puzzles in Political Recruitment

Pippa Norris

Joni Lovenduski

. . . To understand recruitment, this study seeks to reintegrate the literature from two primary sub-fields in political science. Studies of political elites have been concerned with the social composition of parliament. Studies of party organizations have focused on how the process operates and what the selection process tells us about the distribution of power within parties. This [chapter] seeks to build on this literature, developing a more comprehensive theoretical model and analyzing new evidence—the British Candidate Study (BCS). The aim is to link our understanding of the process of candidate recruitment with the outcome for the social composition of parliamentary elites. This study provides a fresh exploration of three major questions:

(i) Who selects, and how?
(ii) Who gets selected, and why?
(iii) Does the social bias of the outcome matter?

Studies of Party Organizations: Who Selects and How?

. . . Candidate selection may seem at first sight like a routine and obscure function of political parties, conducted behind closed doors in small meetings long before the public drama and excitement of the election campaign. In marginal seats, who gets into parliament is determined by voters. But in safe seats with a predictable outcome the selectorate have *de facto* power to choose the MP. And in Britain, about three quarters of all seats are "safe," with majorities greater than 10 percent.[1] In choosing candidates the selectorate therefore determines the overall composition of parliament, and ultimately the pool of those eligible for government. In federal systems such as in Canada or the United States, there are multiple routes into government. But in Britain there is a single ladder into the highest offices of state; the first hurdle is adoption as a prospective parliamentary candidate in a local constituency.[2]

The main approach to studying recruitment in Britain has focused on identifying who controls selection decisions within parties, whether national leaders, local officers, or grassroots party members, and how this power has evolved over time. . . . The recruitment process has commonly been evaluated according to whether the process is "democratic" in the sense of involving local activists and grassroots members; "fair" in treating all applicants equally; "efficient" as a decision-making process; and "effective" in producing "good" candidates.

The question of internal party democracy, particularly the appropriate role for national and local organizations, has been one of the most controversial issues. . . . Struggles to control the process have always been one of the prime areas of intraparty conflict, as E. E. Schattschneider notes, because gatekeepers who select ultimately control the composition of the party leadership:

The nominating [i.e. candidate selecting] process . . . has become the crucial process of the party. The nature of the nominating procedure determines the nature of the party; he who can make nominations is the owner of the party.[3]

In [Austin] Ranney's words, factional struggles to control the nominating procedure are contests for "nothing less than control of the core of what the party stands for and does."[4] Placing candidates in safe seats, possibly for a lifetime political career, has more significant consequences than getting conference resolutions adopted, or supporters nominated to internal party bodies. . . .

The locus of control over candidate selection varies substantially cross-nationally. In most countries the recruitment process is governed primarily by internal party rules, rather than by law. A comparative approach indicates that decision making in the recruitment process varies along two dimensions. First, there is the question of the dispersion of power. Is the process centralized with the main decisions taken by the national party leadership, is it left to regional party officers, or is it dispersed with grassroots local party members exerting most influence? Secondly, there is the question of the formalization of decision making. Is the process informal, a matter of tacit norms with few binding rules and constitutional regulations, or is it formalized so that the procedures at each step are standardized, rule-governed, and explicit? These distinctions suggest six main types of selection process.

In *informal-centralized* systems (such as the French Union pour la Démocratic Française—UDF) there may be democratic constitutional mechanisms, but in practice the process is characterized by leadership patronage. Rules serve a largely symbolic function. Without any established tradition of internal party democracy, and with loose organizations, party members play little role in the process. In *informal-regional* systems (such as the Italian Christian Democrats) faction leaders bargain with each other to place their favored candidates in good positions.[5]

In *informal-localized* systems (such as in the Canadian Progressive Conservatives), local ridings decide on the general procedures used for selection, as well as the choice of individual candidate. Without established guidelines, practices vary widely; some constituencies may nominate at large-scale meetings open to all "members," while patronage by a few local leaders may be significant in others.

Reflecting weak organizations, this system may be open to manipulation by small groups.

Alternatively, in *formal-centralized* and *formal-regional* systems (such as in the Liberal party in the Netherlands, the old Italian Communist Party [PCI], or the old Japanese Liberal Democrats), party executives or factional leaders at national and regional level have the constitutional authority to decide which candidates are placed on the party ticket. Lastly the most common pattern in European parties is one of *formal-localized* recruitment. Here constitutional rules and national guidelines are established to standardize the process throughout the party. The fairness of the system, ensuring all applicants are treated alike, rests on the implementation of clear, transparent, and equitable rules. Within this framework the selection of individual candidates takes place largely by local agencies at constituency level.

Based on this classification, it becomes apparent that in the long term the main change in recruitment within British parties has been in process rather than power. There has been a gradual evolution from an "informal-localized" system based on patronage in the nineteenth century toward a more "formal-localized" system today based on more meritocratic standards. This change has gone further in some parties than others. . . .

It was commonly assumed that a formal-localized system was functional for British party organizations. Without some central management the process might become factionalized and divisive, since in moribund constituency associations small groups might "capture" the party label for their preferred candidate. Standard procedures for selection and appeal help ensure that the rules are seen as uniform and legitimate by all participants. All British parties, except the Greens, have national guidelines, and formal vetting of all proposed candidates by national officers. On the other hand it is usually assumed that too much control by the national party leadership might cause resentment at the grassroots level. The constituency association has to work closely with its candidate on a day-to-day basis for an effective grassroots campaign. Local members are most in touch with the needs of their area. Therefore, many believe that local associations should exercise most power over the choice of individual applicants, working within nationally standardized selection rules.

Changes in the Selection Process

. . . During the last decades many aspects of the Labour and Conservative selection process have changed significantly. Reforms have usually been initiated during periods in opposition, when parties have sought to regain electoral popularity by improving the quality of their candidates. The selection process has altered in accordance with the dominant ethos and traditional practices in each party. In the major parties the main impact of these changes has been twofold: to increase the formality of the process; and to shift power slightly away from the core constituency activists, simultaneously upward toward the central leadership and downward toward grassroots members. . . .

The Attitudes of Party Selectors

A reason for a fresh study lies in the need to move beyond the formal process to analyze the attitudes, values, and priorities of party selectors. . . . The institutional focus of organizational studies means we know more about the main steps in the process than the experience and attitudes of the key actors. What are selectors looking for in candidates, when they make their decisions? Do participants feel that selection procedures are fair, democratic, and efficient? Are party members and candidates satisfied with the process? What do members feel about the relative influence of national and local party agencies? To understand the experience and perceptions of the main actors we need to go beyond the formal steps in the process.

The Sociology of Political Elites: Who Gets Selected, and Why?

The study of party organizations focuses on how the process operates and who has power over recruitment. This perspective can be understood as one half of the equation. It is supplemented by the extensive literature on political elites, concentrating on the outcome of the process. The traditional sociological study of political elites sought to explain how those in power reinforced and consolidated their position.[6] . . . Studies have focused on *who* got into positions of power rather than *how* they got there. . . .

. . . Studies of legislative elites in many countries have established that legislators tend to be drawn from a privileged social background compared with the electorate.[7] The British parliament fits this pattern. Far from representing a microcosm of the nation, the "chattering classes" with professional occupations fill benches on both sides of the aisle.[8] Although the number of old Etonians and Harrovians has gradually decreased, many new members continue to follow the traditional path of attending public school and Oxford or Cambridge.[9] Over time the Labour and Conservative parties have become more middle class, with a decline in members from the traditional aristocracy and the manual working class, although there remains an important public–private sector split by party. In other regards the Commons has become slightly more diverse; after the 1992 election the Commons included sixty women (9.2 percent) and six Asian and black MPs (1 percent).[10] Concern about the gender and racial composition of parliament has risen during the last decade although the general social bias has been familiar for years. . . .

The Experience of Applicants

Most previous work has relied upon aggregate trends in the composition of the elite over time, for example their age or education, since this information is easily available from public records. Studies have too frequently counted what can be counted, without a broader theoretical framework. Individual-level survey evidence needs to be considered to understand how applicants experience the process, their perceptions of the selectorate, and their strategy in securing seats. What do they see to be the main obstacles in running for parliament? What are the most rewarding aspects? If elected, what are their primary goals? Unless we understand micro-level data—lifetime career patterns of individuals to see how some politicians move into elite positions while others fail—we will be limited to describing rather than explaining this phenomenon. We need to understand *who* are members of the legislative elite, but, more important, *why* and *how* they got there. Just as studies of party organization tended to neglect the outcome, so studies of the outcome have tended to neglect the process.

The Experience of Losers

Another reason for a new approach is that the winners—MPs—are only the tip of the iceberg. The elite literature describes the social background of MPs, and sometimes parliamentary candidates, but studies are usually silent about those in the wider pool who aspire to a political career but fail. . . . Studies have compared the social background of MPs with parliamentary candidates, the next strata down. But again this tells us little about the reasons for the social bias. We would expect significant differences in social background and political experience because MPs represent an older generation than candidates. . . .

Legislative Behavior: Does the Social Bias Matter?

Despite all the studies of trends in occupational class and education, previous research has not clearly established that the social background of politicians has a significant influence on their attitudes, values, and behavior. Does the social bias matter? There are reasons to be skeptical since we can identify MPs from an impeccably patrician background who are radical left wingers on the Labour benches, just as there are working-class Conservatives who are among the most enthusiastic "hangers and floggers." Some women members, such as Margaret Thatcher, acknowledged no sympathy with feminist concerns while others were ardent defenders of abortion rights, child care provision, and equal opportunities policy. Anecdotal evidence suggests a complex relationship between background and attitudes. . . .

Further, there are significant differences in the roles MPs adopt, and the priorities they give to different sorts of activities, such as individual casework, committee work, and attending debates. Studies have tried to explain these differences by party affiliation, type of constituency, and political generation.[11] But they have not examined the relationship between behavior and the social background of legislators. There are a range of plausible hypotheses to be tested, for example do "local" MPs who grew up in their constituency spend more time on constituency surgeries than "carpetbaggers"? Do women members give a higher priority to social policy than men? Does the social class of members relate to their political values? . . .

Research Design, Data, and Methods

. . . The main intellectual foundations for this study lie in the work on party organizations and political elites. . . . The research design reconceptualizes the candidate recruitment process. Based on a "supply and demand" model, the study distinguishes between the factors influencing the "supply" of candidates willing to come forward and the factors influencing the "demand" of party selectors in making their decisions.

The Supply and Demand Model

Demand The supply and demand model provides an analytical framework to understand factors influencing the selection process. The most common explanations of the outcome usually assume demand by selectors is critical. On the *demand-side* the model assumes selectors choose candidates depending upon their perceptions of the applicants' abilities, qualifications, and experience. Since candidates are rarely well known to most selectors, these perceptions may be colored by direct and imputed discrimination toward certain types of applicant. The term "discrimination" is used here in a neutral sense. Discrimination can be for or against certain groups, whether lawyers, farmers, trade unionists, southerners, women, or Asians.

Direct discrimination means the positive or negative judgment of people on the basis of characteristics seen as common to their group, rather than as individuals. Party selectors, faced with nonlocal candidates, often have minimal information on which to make their decisions. The curriculum vitae gives the bare bones. There may be hundreds of application forms. The interview process is relatively short and formal. Members may therefore rely upon background characteristics as a proxy measure of abilities and character; prejudice functions as an information short-cut. As a result, individuals are judged by their group characteristics.

Imputed discrimination is different. Here party members may personally favor a certain category of candidate ("I'd like to vote for a woman," "We need more blacks in parliament") or an individual applicant ("The Asian was the best-prepared speaker"). But members may be unwilling to choose such a candidate because they expect they would lose votes among the electorate ("But she'd never get in." "There aren't enough black voters in Cheltenham"). Demand-side explanations therefore suggest that the social bias in parliament reflects the direct and imputed discrimination of party selectors. These explanations are pervasive in popular thinking, and often reflected in the academic literature, although rarely substantiated. . . .

Supply The obvious cause of the social bias in parliament—discrimination by party members—is not necessarily the most significant one. Discrimination may be a popular explanation, but this might be based on inferences from the outcome, rather than any good evidence. In a plea of mitigation party members frequently claim their hands were tied: they would like to short-list more well-qualified woman, Asians from the local community, or experienced working-class candidates, they say, but few come forward.

Supply-side explanations suggest that the outcome reflects the supply of applicants wishing to pursue a political career. Constraints on resources (such as time, money, and experience) and motivational factors (such as drive, ambition, and interest) determine who aspires to Westminster. Most citizens, other than a few categories such as lunatics, traitors, and peers, are legally qualified to stand. Few do so given the risks and demands of life at Westminster. Supply-side explanations of the social bias in parliament suggest that the outcome reflects the resources and motivation of the pool of applicants seeking a political career.

Supply-side and demand-side factors interact. Potential applicants may be discouraged from coming forward by the perception of prejudice among party activists, complex application procedures, or anticipated failure. The concept of hidden unemployment ("Why apply? I won't get the job") is a perfect analogy for the "discouraged political aspirant." If seen as a "systems model," this produces a feedback loop from the outcome back to the pool of those who aspire to a political career. . . . Despite these qualifications there remains an important dis-tinction between the *supply* factors holding individuals back from applying for a position ("I'm not interested." "I don't have the right experience." "I can't afford to move." "I couldn't win") and the *demand* factors which mean that, if they apply, they are not accepted by selectors ("He's not locally known." "She's not got the right speaking skills." "He would not prove popular with voters"). The supply-side and demand-side distinction therefore provides a useful analytical framework to explore alternative explanations.

To operationalize this model, the process of getting into parliament can be conceptualized as a multistep ladder of recruitment. *Party strata* are groups at different levels on the ladder. *Party voters* are those who supported the party in the general election. *Party members* are the grassroots card-carrying activists at selection meeting.[12] In the next step up the ladder, *applicants* are those on the party list, the "pool of talent" who failed to be selected by a constituency in the 1992 election.[13] Next are parliamentary *candidates* (PPCs) adopted for a constituency in the 1992 election, who can be further classified by type of seat, as discussed later. At the top of the ladder are incumbent *Members of Parliament* (MPs) who were returned in the previous election. The term *party elite* refers to the combined group of applicants, candidates, and MPs. . . .

To explain the outcome of the process we need to know the total pool involved at every level: MPs, candidates, list applicants, party members, and voters. By comparing strata we can see whether the outcome of the selection process reflects the *supply* of those willing to stand for parliament or the *demands* of party activists when adopting candidates for local constituencies. This simple method, in brief, is the heart of our research design. . . .

Notes

1. This definition refers to multiparty marginals, that is, those where the difference between the parties in first and second place is less than 10 percent. From 1955 to 1992 about 73 percent of seats can be seen as safe by this definition. See Pippa Norris and Ivor Crewe, "The British Marginals Never Vanished: Proportionality and Exaggeration in the British Electoral System Revisited." *Electoral Studies* (June 1994).

2. It should be noted that the only exceptions for Cabinet office are entry via the House of Lords.

3. E. E. Schattschneider, *Party Government* (New York, Holt, Rinehart and Winston, 1942) p. 64.

4. Austin Ranney, "Candidate Selection" in David Butler, Howard R. Penniman and Austin Ranney, *Democracy at the Polls* (Washington DC, American Enterprise Institute, 1981) p. 103.

5. For studies of the process in Italy and France see chapters 4 and 7 in Michael Gallagher and Michael Marsh (eds.), *Candidate Selection in Comparative Perspective* (London, Sage, 1988).

6. For a review of elite theory see Geraint Parry, *Political Elites* (New York, Praeger, 1969).

7. Robert D. Putnam, *The Comparative Study of Political Elites* (Englewood Cliffs NJ, Prentice-Hall, 1976); Gerhard Loewenberg and Samuel C. Patterson, *Comparing Legislatures* (Boston, Little, Brown and Company, 1979); J. D. Aberbach, R. D. Putnam, and B. A. Rockman, *Bureaucrats and Politicians in Western Democracies* (Cambridge MA, Harvard University Press, 1981) pp. 40–83.

8. See Martin Burch and Michael Moran, "The Changing Political Elite," *Parliamentary Affairs* 38, 1 (1985), pp. 1–15.

9. In 1945, 83 percent of Conservative MPs and 19 percent of Labour MPs had attended public school. In 1992 the figures were 62 percent and 14 percent, respectively. There has also been a decline in the number from Oxford and Cambridge, although in 1992 one-third of all MPs had been educated there. See Burch and Moran, "The Changing Political Elite"; Byron Criddle, "MPs and Candidates," in David Butler and Dennis Kavanagh (eds.), *The British General Election of 1992* (London, Macmillan, 1992); George Borthwick, Daniel Ellingworth, Colin Bell, and Donald MacKenzie, "The Social Background of British MPs," *Sociology*, 25, 4 (November 1991), pp. 713–17.

10. It should be noted that the term "black" will be used to refer to ethnic identification based on the 1991 Census definitions including Black Caribbean, Black African, and Black other.

11. See Donald D. Searing, "New Roles for Postwar British Politics: Ideologues, Generalists, Specialists and the Progress of Professionalisation of Parliament," *Comparative Politics* (1987) 19, 4 pp. 431–53; Donald Searing, "The Role of the Good Constituency Member and the Practice of Representation in Great Britain," *Journal of Politics*, 47 (May 1985), pp. 348–81; J. Vincent Buck and Bruce E. Cain, "British MPs in Their Constituencies" *Legislative Studies Quarterly*, 15 (February 1990), pp. 127–43; Bruce E. Cain, John A. Ferejohn, and Morris P. Fiorina, *The Personal Vote: Constituency Service and Electoral Independence* (Cambridge MA, Harvard University Press, 1987); Philip Norton and David Wood, "Constituency Service by Members of Parliament: Does It Contribute to a Personal Vote?" *Parliamentary Affairs*, 43, 2 (April 199), pp. 196–208.

12. The BCS survey was compared with the larger Whiteley and Seyd survey of Labour party members (N = 5071). This confirmed that selectors are broadly socially representative of all members. Patrick Seyd and Paul Whiteley, *Labour's Grassroots: The Politics of Party Membership* (Clarendon Press, Oxford, 1992).

13. It should be noted that throughout this chapter the term "applicant" refers to those on the national lists of applicants. It does not refer to those who apply to particular constituencies. Further, the Labour and Conservative lists are not wholly comparable. The Conservative list is based on candidates approved by Conservative Central Office, therefore some "applicants" have already been weeded out. In contrast the Labour "A" (Trade Union nominees) and "B" (constituency nominees) has not been approved by the National Executive Council.

Chapter 17

ENTERING THE ARENA?
GENDER AND THE DECISION TO
RUN FOR OFFICE

Richard L. Fox

Jennifer L. Lawless

When the 108th Congress convened, 86% of its members were male (CAWP 2003). . . . The dearth of women in elective office is also evident at the state and local levels: 88% of state governors, 88% of big-city mayors, and 78% of state legislators are male (CAWP 2003). Particularly striking about these large gender disparities in elective office is that neither qualitative investigations nor empirical analyses reveal a political system rife with gender bias. . . .

In light of the seeming contradiction between a political system that elects few women and an electoral environment that is unbiased against women candidates, political scientists focus on two theoretical explanations for women's numeric underrepresentation. First, they point to the incumbency advantage, where reelection rates for legislative positions are consistently above 90%. . . . Second, researchers point to the "eligibility pool" to explain the low number of women candidates and elected officials (Conway, Steurnagle, and Ahern 1997; Darcy, Welch, and Clark 1994; Duerst-Lahti 1998; Thomas 1998). . . .

Common to both of these explanations is the expectation that, as more women enter the pool of qualified candidates, women will increasingly be presented with good opportunities for political success and electoral victory. Further, each explanation expects that potential women candidates will respond to political opportunities in the same ways that men traditionally have. The incumbency explanation relies on the premise that

both sexes, when presented with similar electoral opportunities for open seats, will employ similar cost-benefit analyses when deciding whether to enter the race (e.g., Kazee 1994; Schlesinger 1966; Stone and Maisel 2003). The eligibility pool explanation posits that as women's presence in the fields of law and business becomes more comparable to men's, so too will their economic status and their likelihood of seeking elected positions (Darcy, Welch, and Clark 1994). . . .

To assess prospects for gender parity in our electoral system based on these institutional explanations is to fail to consider a critical piece of the candidate emergence process: the manner in which gender interacts with the initial decision to run for office. . . . A wide body of literature on the impact of traditional gender socialization in the electoral process continues to find that sex plays a significant role in the manner in which actual candidates and officeholders retrospectively assess their initial decisions to run for office (e.g., Fowler and McClure 1989). Although this body of research does not speak directly to potential candidates, it identifies several specific ways in which the decision calculus involved in deciding whether to enter an electoral contest may differ significantly for potential women and men candidates. Studies comparing geographic regions, for instance, find that women are more likely to emerge as candidates when they live in areas with less traditional political cultures (e.g., Fox 2000; Hill 1981; Rule 1990). Other investigations find that women in politics are more concerned than men with balancing their career and familial responsibilities (Fox, Lawless, and Feeley 2001; Jamieson 1995; Witt, Paget, and Matthews 1994). Analyses also point to the fact that, since their entry into the public sphere has not traditionally been embraced, women candidates and officeholders are more concerned with their qualifications, substantive credentials, and policy expertise and motivations, all of which help them gain legitimacy in the political arena (Dodson 1998; Fowler and McClure 1989; Niven 1998; Sanbonmatsu 2002b; Swers 2002). . . .

This [chapter] presents the results of the Citizen Political Ambition Study, the first national survey of potential candidates in the "eligibility pool" for all levels of elective office. . . . Our unique research design allows us to assess whether men and women potential candidates who share the same personal characteristics and professional credentials hold similar levels of political ambition at the earliest stage of the candidate-emergence process. . . .

The Citizen Political Ambition Study

. . . This research design involves compiling a random, national sample of citizens who occupy the professions that are most likely to precede a career in politics. The sample is stratified by sex, so as to avoid informant bias and ensure an equal number of men and women potential candidates. . . .

We administered by mail a four-page survey to a national sample of 6,800 men and women, each of whom could be considered part of the "eligibility pool." . . . The survey asks respondents about their sociodemographic backgrounds, familial arrangements, political outlooks and experiences, and perceptions and willingness to run for office. The sample consists of an equal number of men and women in the three professions that tend to yield the highest proportion of political candidacies: law, business, and education (CAWP 2001; Dolan and Ford 1997; Gray, Hanson, and Jacob 1999; Moncrief, Squire, and Jewell 2001). A group of political activists supplements the national sample.

This conception of the eligibility pool serves as a stringent test case through which to explore gender differences in political ambition. Female lawyers and business leaders have already entered and succeeded in male-dominated fields, which suggests that the

women in the sample may have overcome the forces of traditional socialization to a greater extent than the overall population of potential women candidates. . . . Although this sampling design allows us to compare levels of political ambition across these professions, it does not allow us to determine whether the gender dynamics within each profession require more extraordinary commitments of time and effort by women than men. . . . We balance this gendered conception of the eligibility pool by equally representing educators and political activists, two professions from which women are more likely than men to emerge as candidates (CAWP 2001).

Our results are based on responses from 3,765 respondents (1,969 men and 1,796 women). After taking into account undeliverable surveys, this represents a 60% response rate, which is higher than that of typical elite sample mail surveys (see Carroll 1994; Fox, Lawless, and Feeley 2001; Stone and Maisel 2003). No remarkable sociodemographic, geographic, or professional differences distinguish the samples of men from women professional elites. . . .

Gender, Candidate Emergence, and Prospects for Women's Representation

General studies of political ambition conclude that, as rational actors, potential candidates are more likely to seek office when they face favorable political and structural circumstances. The number of open seats, term-limit requirements, levels of legislative professionalization, partisan composition of the constituency, and the party of the potential candidate relative to that of the incumbent are among the factors men and women consider when seeking elective positions or deciding whether to run for a higher office (Black 1972; Kazee 1994; Moncrief, Squire, and Jewell 2001; Rohde 1979; Schlesinger 1966; Stone and Maisel 2003). In conceptualizing ambition this way, the decision to run for office is primarily a strategic response to an opportunity structure; with the exception of general gauges of political interest, financial security, and political experience, potential candidates' personal circumstances are treated as relatively exogenous. This framework predicts that women and men from similar professional and sociodemographic backgrounds

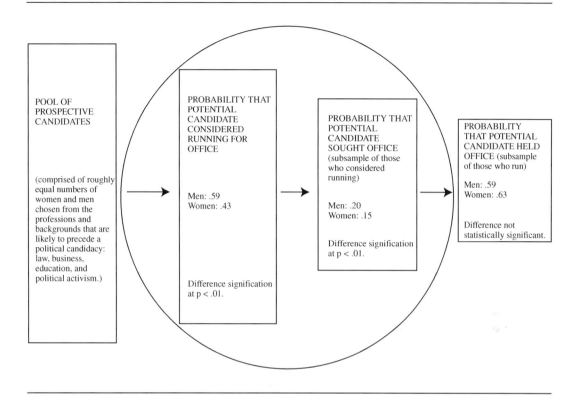

FIGURE **17.1: Candidate Emergence from the Pool of Prospective Candidates.**

are equally likely to move from the pool of eligible candidates into positions of elective office.

But this rational choice approach to ambition is almost certainly flawed when we consider potential candidates who do not currently hold office. In order to leave the pool of eligible candidates and run for office, potential candidates undergo a two-stage process that serves as a precursor to the strategic side of the decision to run. First, they must consider running for elective office; potential candidates will never emerge as actual candidates if the notion of launching a campaign and what that entails does not enter into their frame of consciousness. Only after the notion of a candidacy crosses a potential candidate's mind can he/she determine that the benefits to entering the electoral arena outweigh the costs. The central question before us, therefore, is whether sex interacts with either stage of this process by which qualified individuals select to be actual candidates.

Results from the Citizen Political Ambition Study reveal that gender does, in fact, play a substantial role in the initial decision to run for office. Figure 17.1 depicts the process by which potential candidates move into positions of political power. The leftmost box contains roughly equal samples of men and women who comprise the pool of potential officeholders: lawyers, business leaders and executives, educators, and political activists. The figure's final box illustrates the likelihood that a candidate wins the race. As we would expect from the body of literature on gender and elections, there is no statistically significant gender difference between men and women's likelihood of winning political contests: 63% of the women and 59% of the men in the eligibility pool who ran for office launched successful campaigns.[1] Of course, this finding means only that there appear to be no gender differences at the *end stage* of the electoral process.

The second and third boxes in the figure shed light on the gender dynamics of the candidate emergence process. The second box from the left is comprised of those members of the eligibility pool who "considered" running for any political office. More than half of the respondents (51%) stated that the idea of running for an elective position at least "crossed their mind." Turning to the gender breakdown of the respondents who considered a candidacy, though, a significant gender difference emerges: 59% of the men, compared to 43% of the women, considered running for office (difference significant at p < .01).[2] . . . Sex remains a significant predictor of considering a candidacy even after controlling for education, income, race, political party and attitudes, previous campaign experience, and whether the respondent ever received external encouragement to run for office, most of which are traditional correlates of political interest, participation, and ambition (see Bledsoe and Herring 1990; Burns, Schlozman, and Verba 2001; Fox, Lawless, and Feeley 2001; Stone and Maisel 2003; Verba, Schlozman, and Brady 1995). . . .

Such high levels of interest in considering a candidacy may appear suspect, even among a sample of professional elites. The measure, however, is aimed to capture even the slightest inclination of pursuing a candidacy. Nonetheless, in order to ensure that respondents' attitudes toward considering a candidacy were not merely an artifact of being asked the question, we asked potential candidates whether they took any of the steps required to mount a political campaign. More specifically, they were asked whether they ever investigated how to place their name on the ballot or ever discussed running with potential donors, party or community leaders, family members, or friends. Comparisons between men's and women's answers to all of these questions again highlight stark gender differences. Table 17.1 reveals that, across professions, men are always at least 50% more likely than women to have engaged in each of these fundamental campaign steps (gender differences significant at p < .01). Based on a variety of measures, what started out as a gender-balanced eligibility pool winnows to one that is dominated by men.

When we move to the third box in the figure and examine those members of the sample who actually ran for elective office, gender differences

again emerge, although they are of a smaller magnitude: 20% of the men, compared to 15% of the women, who considered running for office actually chose to seek an elected position (difference significant at p < .01). Once again, this gender difference withstands statistical controls for the aforementioned demographic, political, and structural variables. It is also noteworthy that women potential candidates' lower levels of political ambition are not a result of the fact that women are not as interested as men in politics and the seemingly male-dominated political arena (see Burns, Schlozman, and Verba 2001; Burt-Way and Kelly 1992; Carroll 1994; Darcy, Welch, and Clark 1994; Fox 1997). Women in the sample are more likely than men to express a high degree of interest in both local (49% of women, compared to 41% of men) and national (41% of women, compared to 31% of men) politics (differences significant at p < .01). Women, therefore, are at least as well positioned as men not only in terms of professional accomplishment and socioeconomic status, but also general interest in the political sphere.

Together, the second and third boxes of Figure 17.1 illustrate the precarious assumption on which current prescriptions for increasing the

Table 17.1. *Gender Differences in Considering a Run for Political Office (across Professions)*

Question: Have you ever...		
	Women	Men
Considered running for office?	43%	59%
Discussed running with friends and family?	22	33
Discussed running with community leaders?	9	15
Investigated how to place your name on the ballot?	6	13
Discussed running with party leaders?	6	12
Solicited or discussed financial contributions with potential supporters?	3	7
N	1,711	1,812

Note: For each item, the Chi square test comparing women and men is significant at p < .01.

number of women in positions of political power are predicated. Despite starting out with relatively equal proportions of similarly situated and equally credentialed women and men as potential candidates, and regardless of the fact that women are just as likely as men to win elections, men are nearly twice as likely as women to hold elected office: 7% of the men, compared to less than 4% of the women, from the initial pool of potential candidates, hold an elective position (difference significant at p < .01).

. . . Empirically, our results provide the first piece of evidence—nationwide—that women elites are significantly less likely than their male counterparts to emerge as candidates. Theoretically, our results indicate that the conventional institutional explanations that account for women's numeric underrepresentation are incomplete and somewhat misleading. The challenge to which we now turn is to account for the sources of the gender gap in the initial decision to run for office.

Traditional Gender Socialization and the Gender Gap in Political Ambition

Gender socialization theory offers the most compelling lens though which to understand the gender gap we uncovered in Figure 17.1. . . . Recent studies of gender in the electoral process, based largely on women who have already entered the electoral arena, identify four general areas in which vestiges of traditional gender role orientations may affect both the likelihood of considering a candidacy and the propensity to launch an actual campaign.

Political Culture

Evidence suggests that the political environment can have a gendered effect on citizens' attitudes about entering the political system. . . . Despite the fact that the men and women in the Citizen Political Ambition Study are similar in terms of geographic dispersion, we might expect that women in certain political environments will be less likely to think about running for office, whereas the political culture in which men exist will not have an impact on the decision to seek an elective position.

Family Responsibilities

. . . Contemporary studies of family gender dynamics reveal that women, even in two-career households, are still more likely than their spouses to spend time raising children and completing household tasks, such as cleaning and laundry (Burns, Schlozman, and Verba 2001; McGlen and O'Connor 1998). This division of labor often results in women candidates and elected officials feeling obligated to consider family responsibilities more carefully than do their male counterparts (Burrell 1998; Conway, Steuernagel, and Ahern 1997; Fowler and McClure 1989).

When we consider the household division of labor in the Citizen Political Ambition Study sample, we see that women who live with a spouse or partner are approximately seven times more likely than men to be responsible for more of the household tasks; the numbers are similar for childcare arrangements. These results might account for women's lesser likelihood of considering a run for office.

Self-Perceived Qualifications

. . . Regardless of their actual qualifications and credentials, women have likely been socialized to perceive themselves as less qualified to enter politics. In fact, when asked to place themselves on a continuum from "not at all qualified" to "very qualified" to run for office, the male potential candidates in our sample are nearly twice as likely as the female potential candidates (26%, compared to 14%) to deem themselves "very qualified" for an elected position (difference significant at p < .01).

We might also expect traditional socialization to play a role in the degree to which potential candidates rely on their self-perceived qualifications when considering a candidacy, since we know from the ambition theory literature that politicians tend to behave in way that maximizes their likelihood of attaining higher office (Schlesinger 1966). . . . We might expect women to be more likely than their male counterparts to emphasize their substantive credentials, perhaps in an effort to gain legitimacy for their candidacies (see Fowler and McClure 1989; Kahn 1996; Sanbonmatsu 2002b).

Ideological Motivations

Finally, traditional gender socialization may influence the decision to run for office in terms of ideological motivations. . . . Whereas men of all political proclivities might be equally likely to think about a candidacy, women may need an additional policy boost to spur them on to consider running for office, if for no reason other than the legitimacy conferred by a focus on women's issues and interests.

Traditional Gender Socialization and Considering a Candidacy

In order to explore the degree to which traditional gender socialization accounts for the gender gap in potential candidates' likelihood of considering running for office, measures of political culture, familial arrangements and responsibilities, self-perceived qualifications, and ideological motivations supplement the [earlier] logistic regression. . . . Somewhat surprisingly, sex remains a significant predictor of considering a candidacy even after controlling for the series of sociodemographic and political variables, as well as the "traditional socialization" variables. When we calculate the substantive effects of the logistic regression coefficients, . . . we see that, on average, women are 14 percentage points less likely than men to consider running for office. The "average" woman has a predicted probability of 0.56 of having considered a run for office; an identical man in the sample has a 0.70 likelihood of thinking about a candidacy (difference significant at p < .01).

Unexpectedly, most of the traditional gender socialization variables fail to meet conventional levels of statistical significance. Neither political culture nor family structures and arrangements influence the likelihood of considering a candidacy, although both men and women are less likely to think about running for office as they age. Women's circumstances of being the primary caretakers of the home and the children do not depress their likelihood of running. And ideological motivations do not have an impact on the propensity to consider running for office. The traditional barriers to women's entry into the political sphere, therefore, no longer appear to impede their likelihood of thinking about a political candidacy.

Of course, we cannot fully dismiss these variables' effects without examining the degree to which they interact with the sex of the respondent. . . . Only one interaction term—self-perceived qualifications—achieves statistical significance. The interaction between the sex of the respondent and the respondent's self-perceived qualifications is so strong, though, that it mitigates sex's independent effect. Table 17.2 which displays the substantive impact of perceived qualifications on the likelihood of considering a political candidacy, indicates that the gender gap narrows considerably and becomes statistically insignificant as women perceive themselves as increasingly qualified to run for political office. Men's likelihood of considering a candidacy increases from 0.60 to 0.87 as they move along the continuum of perceiving themselves as "not at all qualified" to "very qualified" for holding an elected position. The impact of self-perceived qualifications on women's predicted likelihood of considering a run is nearly double that for men. Women gain a 53 percentage point boost when they assess themselves as "very qualified." Although men have a higher base likelihood of considering a candidacy, women's perceptions

Table 17.2. Predicted Probabilities of Considering Running for Political Office, by Self-Perceived Qualifications

| | Respondent Considers Himself/Herself… | | | |
	Not at All Qualified	Somewhat Qualified	Qualified	Very Qualified
Male Respondent	.60	.71	.80	.87
Female Respondent	.30	.49	.69	.83
Gender Gap	30%	22%	11%	4%

Note: Predicted probabilities are based on setting the variables included in the regression to their respective means. Dummy variables are held constant at their modes.

of their qualifications work to lessen the political ambition gender gap. In fact, for women, self-perceived qualifications are the strongest predictor of considering a run for office.

One additional gendered finding emerges from the regression results. The consideration of a candidacy depends significantly on the degree to which an individual receives encouragement to run. When we calculate the predicted probabilities of considering running for office, we see that a woman who has never received encouragement to run for office, either from a political actor or a nonpolitical source, has only a 0.20 predicted probability of having considered it. Men's likelihood is significantly higher (0.32), but still falls far below the mean level of considering a run. When a respondent receives external support to run from both a formal political actor and a nonpolitical source, the likelihood of considering a candidacy more than doubles. Women's likelihood of considering running increases to 0.75; and men's predicted probability of considering a run grows to 0.85. Despite the fact that external support for a candidacy boosts both men and women's likelihood of considering a run for office, 43% of the men, compared to 32% of women, received encouragement to run from a party leader, elected official, or political activist (difference significant at p < .01). Thus, even if traditional gender socialization does not affect potential candidates' reliance on external support, these results corroborate the conclusions of scholars who suggest that vestiges of patterns of traditional gender socialization in candidate recruitment hinder the selection of women candidates (Sanbonmatsu 2002a; Niven 1998).

Traditional Gender Socialization and Running for Office

. . . The logistic regression coefficients shed light on the factors that lead men and women who have considered running for office to decide to enter actual electoral contests. Not only are most of the traditional gender socialization variables and interaction terms statistically insignificant, but sex is also not a statistically significant predictor of whether a potential candidate enters an actual race. Based on the logistic regression coefficients, the "average" male respondent has a 0.17 predicted probability

of entering a race; female potential candidates' likelihood is slightly greater than 0.12.

The regression results suggest that the gender gap in political ambition is significantly alleviated by the second step of the process, in large part because so many women weed themselves out by never having considered running. The variables that predict men's likelihood of entering an electoral contest also predict women's likelihood, and the magnitude of each variable's effect is not conditioned by sex. Even in terms of external support, gender differences seem to disappear. When we focus only on those potential candidates who considered a candidacy, we see that receiving encouragement for the idea still exerts an equal and significant impact on women and men, but at this stage, women and men are also equally likely to receive it (60% of men, compared to 57% of women). In short, as we move throughout the candidate-emergence process, the effects of gender seem to dissipate. But far fewer women than men reach this stage of the process.

These findings do not mean that sex is irrelevant at the second stage of candidate emergence. The gender gap in self-perceived qualifications is smaller at this stage, and women are no more likely than men to rely on these perceptions when determining whether to turn the consideration of a candidacy into an actual campaign. But women are still disadvantaged in terms of their self-assessed qualifications. Twenty-six percent of the women who considered running for office deem themselves "very qualified," compared to 36% of men (difference significant at p < .01). When a potential candidate considers himself/herself highly qualified, the likelihood of launching a candidacy increases by more than 63%. This translates into a 10 percentage point increase for men and a 9 percentage point increase for women. Men and women might rely similarly on this factor when determining whether to enter an electoral contest, but men and women potential candidates are not similarly situated in terms of how they perceive their own qualifications.

Conclusion and Implications

The results from the Citizen Political Ambition Study offer evidence that the leading theoretical explanations for women's continued exclusion from high elective office—incumbency and the eligibility pool—are inadequate. These theories assume that, because the electoral arena is gender neutral, women will, over time, become more likely to run for office, win elective positions, and bring gender parity to our electoral institutions. These explanations for women's underrepresentation do not, however, take into account the selection process by which potential candidates become actual candidates. The evidence uncovered in our study reveals that it is at the candidate emergence phase of the electoral process that critical gender differences exist. Women are far less likely than men to emerge from the pool of eligible candidates and seek elected positions. Thus, even though women who run for office are just as likely as men to emerge victorious, the substantial winnowing process in candidate emergence yields a smaller ratio of women than men. The pool of candidates who run for office, therefore, looks quite different than the eligibility pool of potential candidates with whom we began. . . .

Notes

1. The absence of a gender gap in the probability of winning an election is not due to the fact that women tend to run for lower status offices than do men. Eighty-eight percent if the men and 90% of the women who won their races sought local-level positions; 11% of the men and 10% of the women who won their races ran at the state level; and 1% of the men and none of the women who ran for a federal level office won their elections.
2. Although the proportion of respondents who considered running for office differs by profession, with lawyers and political activists most likely to have considered a candidacy, the gender differential is statistically significant at p < .01 within each subgroup.

References

Black, Gordon S. 1972. "A Theory of Political Ambition: Career Choices and the Role of Structural Incentives." *American Political Science Review* 66(1):144–59.

Bledsoe, Timothy, and Mary Herring. 1990. "Victims of Circumstances: Women in Pursuit of Political Office." *American Political Science Review* 84(1):213–23.

Burns, Nancy, Kay Lehman Schlozman, and Sidney Verba. 2001. *The Private Roots of Public Action: Gender, Equality, and Political Participation.* Cambridge: Harvard University.

Burrell, Barbara. 1998. *A Woman's Place Is in the House.* Ann Arbor: University of Michigan Press.

Burt-Way, Barbara J., and Rita Mae Kelly. 1992. "Gender and Sustaining Political Ambition: A Study of Arizona Elected Officials." *Western Political Quarterly* 44(1): 11–25.

Carroll, Susan J. 1994. *Women as Candidates in American Politics*, 2nd ed. Bloomington: Indiana University Press.

Center for American Women and Politics (CAWP). 2003. "Women in Elective Office 2003 Fact Sheet." New Brunswick: Center for American Women and Politics.

Center for American Women and Politics (CAWP). 2001. "Women State Legislators: Past, Present, and Future." New Brunswick: Eagleton Institute of Politics.

Conway, M. Margaret, Gertrude A. Steuernagel, and David W. Ahern. 1997. *Women and Political Participation.* Washington: Congressional Quarterly Press.

Darcy, R., S. Welch, and J. Clark. 1994. *Women, Elections, and Representation.* 2nd ed. Lincoln: University of Nebraska Press.

Dodson, Debra L. 1998. "Representing Women's Interests in the U.S. House of Representatives." In *Women and Elective Office*, ed. S. Thomas and C. Wilcox, New York: Oxford University, pp. 130–49.

Dolan, Kathleen, and Lynee E. Ford. 1997. "Change and Continuity among Women State Legislators: Evidence from Three Decades." *Political Research Quarterly* 50 (1):137–51.

Duerst-Lahti, Georgia. 1998. "The Bottleneck, Women as Candidates." In *Women and Elective Office*, ed. S. Thomas and C. Wilcox. New York: Oxford University Press, pp. 15–25.

Fowler, Linda L., and Robert McClure. 1989. *Political Ambition.* New Haven: Yale University Press.

Fox, Richard L. 2000. "Gender and Congressional Elections." In *Gender and American Politics*, ed. S. Tolleson-Rinehart and J. Josephson. Armonk: M. E. Sharpe, pp. 227–56.

Fox, Richard L. 1997. *Gender Dynamics in Congressional Elections.* Thousand Oaks: Sage.

Fox, Richard L., Jennifer L. Lawless, and Courtney Feeley. 2001. "Gender and the Decision to Run for Office." *Legislative Studies Quarterly* 26(3):411–35.

Gray, Virginia, Russell L. Hanson, and Herbert Jacob. 1999. *Politics in the American States*, 7th ed. Washington: CQ Press.

Hill, David. 1981. "Political Culture and Female Political Representation." *Journal of Politics* 43(1):159–68.

Jamieson, Kathleen Hall. 1995. *Beyond the Double Bind.* New York: Oxford University Press.

Kahn, Kim Fridkin. 1996. *The Political Consequences of Being a Woman.* New York: Columbia University Press.

Kazee, Tomas A. 1994. "The Emergence of Congressional Candidates." In *Who Runs for Congress? Ambition, Context, and Candidate Emergence*, ed. T. Kazee. Washington: Congressional Quarterly Press, pp. 1–22.

McGlen, Nancy E., and Karen O'Connor. 1998. *Women, Politics, and American Society*, 2nd ed. Upper Saddle River: Prentice Hall.

Moncrief, Gary F., Peverill Squire, and Malcolm E. Jewell. 2001. *Who Runs for the Legislature?* Upper Saddle River: Prentice Hall.

Niven, David. 1998. "Party Elites and Women Candidates: The Shape of Bias." *Women and Politics* 19(2):57–80.

Rohde, David W. 1979. "Risk-Bearing and Progressive Ambition: The Case of the U.S. House of Representatives." *American Journal of Political Science* 23(1):1–26.

Rule, Wilma. 1990. "Why More Women Are State Legislators: A Research Note." *Western Political Quarterly* 43(2):437–48.

Sanbonmatsu, Kira. 2002a. "Political Parties and the Recruitment of Women to State Legislatures." *Journal of Politics* 64(3):791–809.

Sanbonmatsu, Kira. 2002b. "Women's Election to the State Legislature." Presented at the annual meeting of the American Political Science Association, Boston.

Schlesinger, Joseph A. 1966. *Ambition and Politics: Political Careers in the United States.* Chicago: Rand McNally.

Stone, Walter J., and L. Sandy Maisel. 2003. "The Not-So-Simple Calculus of Winning: Potential U.S. House Candidates' Nominations and General Election Prospects." *Journal of Politics* 65(4):951–77.

Swers, Michele L. 2002. *The Difference Women Make.* Chicago: University of Chicago.

Thomas, Sue. 1998. "Introduction: Women and Elective Office: Past, Present, and Future." In *Women and Elective Office*, ed. S. Thomas and C. Wilcox. New York: Oxford University Press, pp. 1–14.

Verba, Sidney, Key Lehman Schlozman, and Henry E. Brady. 1995. *Voice and Equality: Civic Voluntarism in American Politics.* Cambridge: Harvard University.

Witt, Linda, Karen Paget, and Glenna Matthews. 1994. *Running as a Woman.* New York: Free Press.

Chapter 18

PARTY ELITES AND WOMEN CANDIDATES: THE SHAPE OF BIAS

David Niven

. . . It is in the study of party recruiters and their interaction with potential women candidates where many scholars argue we will find an explanation for the dearth of women candidates and office-holders in the U.S. (Carroll 1994; Clark, Hadley, and Darcy 1989; Darcy and Schramm 1977; Rule 1981).

Nevertheless, the most prominent studies on the subject have concluded that women are not subject to biased treatment by party leaders (Burrell 1994a; Darcy, Welch, and Clark 1994). Unfortunately, these works base their conclusions on indirect indications of elite behavior. Specifically, they incorporate party financial contributions to their nominees as a surrogate for party treatment of candidates. Of course, this measure tells us little concerning the hurdles candidates face on the way to the nomination. In other words, the pattern of contributions to nominated candidates is only of tangential interest if the elites are in any way limiting the number of women running.

With the financial contribution approach, we learn nothing of the treatment of the countless unknown potential candidates who have been successfully discouraged from running; we learn nothing of the behavior of party leaders behind closed doors. Thus, conclusions regarding the lack of bias emerge primarily when the experiences of the potential candidates who are most likely to have been subject to bias are excluded from the analysis. . . .

Instead of extrapolating elite attitudes and treatment of women from the financial contribution measure, a more revealing approach is available. The potential for expanding our understanding of why there are few women legislators seems most likely to be in direct examination of elite recruiter attitudes and their treatment of potential women candidates. This can be accomplished by asking potential women candidates about their experiences and by asking elite party people (sensitively constructed) questions about their preferences.

Methods and Hypotheses

To examine elite party recruiter attitudes, county party chairs are surveyed. . . . Party chairs have many different levels on which to exercise their influence in recruiting: direct contact with prospective candidates, trading of political favors with other interested people, organization of party loyalists, and strategic mentions of prospective candidates to the media. All can be marshaled toward the end of discouraging the unwanted and aiding the favored candidates (Abel and Oppenheimer 1994; Canon, Schousen, and Sellers 1994; Fowler and McClure 1989; Herrnson and Tennant 1994; Hertzke 1994; Kazee and Roberts 1994).

To complement the survey of party chairs, a survey of women holding local office was also conducted. Those elected on the local level represent a most fertile ground for finding people willing to contest for higher office in the future (Carroll 1994), thus locally elected women would be able to express the perceptions of potential female state legislative and Congressional candidates. This unconventional sample avoids the widespread problem of surveys relying on women nominated or elected to state legislatures or Congress, a sample that constricts variation on a key dimension, namely success of legislative candidacy. The women in this sample are only potential legislative candidates, a group that includes both those who have been encouraged and discouraged from seeking higher office, making the group uniquely qualified to express the extent and ramifications of bias.

The sample population for these surveys includes all county party chairs[1] and a sample of locally elected women[2] from the states of Ohio, New Jersey, Tennessee, and California. Mail surveys resulted in usable responses from 280 party chairs and 276 women. Sampling four states provides regional balance, as well as variation of state political cultures, attitudes toward women, and state legislative structures. . . . While obviously not as powerful as a sample population of all 50 states, one could argue that results found in these four varied states would be quite instructive regarding the situation in the nation as a whole.

If elites are biased against potential women candidates, party chair responses will be scrutinized to try to uncover what motivates biased behavior. It is hypothesized that bias against women candidates is most likely based on one of two perceptual processes, the outgroup effect or the distribution effect.

The Outgroup Effect

Why would party elites react negatively to female candidates? One potential answer begins with the fact that most party leaders are male; as many as 97% are male in some states. . . . If a party leader holds the view that most women are not as politically inclined as men, one would expect that prospective female candidates would be lumped into an outgroup in which the default assumption is that a woman is not as politically capable as a man. Outgrouping inhibits individuation, which by definition limits the ability of the qualified woman to distinguish herself from the party leader's notion of women in general. . . . When confronted with a woman who wants to run for office, the recruiter's perception of women could lead the recruiter to encourage the woman not to run.

Meanwhile, if party leaders see potential male candidates as part of the ingroup, they are likely to individually evaluate the competency of the person. Moreover, ingroup members are generally assumed to be similar to the perceiver in attitudes, values, and personality (Piliavin 1987). This assumption of similarity can be very significant when a subjective evaluation must be made, as similarity induces assumptions of competence (Klahr 1969). . . .

Distribution Effect

An alternate explanation for elite bias is the distribution effect, where the differential distribution into productive roles feeds the perception of gender-based differences (Eagly and Wood 1982). Because of sexual segregation in the work roles, men outnumber women in positions of achievement, and women more frequently have low status jobs. This results in abstractions of the sexes based on their distribution in productive roles (Eagly and Wood 1982; Yount 1986). . . .

In addition to assumptions based on the division of productive roles, another aspect of the distribution effect is the salience of the numerically rare. When one encounters a female in an occupation area dominated by males, the incongruity feeds doubts concerning the appropriateness of the woman's position (Eagly, Makhijani, and Klonsky 1992).

The distribution effect would occur in politics because women are more likely to pursue home-based or low-status work than are men and because women officeholders are comparatively rare. Party leaders, encountering a woman interested in political office, could subconsciously assume that men are more likely to succeed in politics because of the difference in distribution. This assumption colors their behavior, not because they view women as inherently incapable, but because their understanding of the political landscape (the distribution of gender among professionals and officeholders) leads them to believe men are more likely to succeed. . . .

Perhaps the most important distinction for the future between the outgroup and distribution explanations is that the distribution effect suggests that by altering the number of women in high-status positions, opposition to women will wane

(Eagly, Makhijani, and Klonsky 1992), making it progressively easier for women to pursue political office. . . . If women can overcome the obstacles in their path to contest and win political office, the distribution will change, changing the beliefs, and encouraging further change in the distribution. The outgroup effect, conversely, produces bias against those from other groups even as the other group strengthens itself politically (Giles and Evans 1985), as the talents of the outgroup may be downplayed in ego-protective conclusions (Snyder and Miene 1994). . . .

Bias against Women

Women holding local office serve here as a sample of potential women candidates for the state legislature and Congress. These women were asked, "In your experience, have party leaders discouraged potential women candidates from running for office because of their gender?" A stunning 64% responded affirmatively. Space was provided for the respondents to make comments on the question, and 46% of the women chose to relate some personal experience with discrimination. . . .

Among those who reported experiencing discrimination, many responses (42%) referred to some variant of "old-boy networks," where appointments, endorsements, and eventually nominations went to male friends of the men in charge, instead of going to the most qualified. Others (31%) recounted situations in which they were discouraged from running because of their gender or were ignored or rebuffed when they attempted to assume leadership on a specific issue (11%). The remaining 16% report multiple manifestations of bias.

Through the course of their political experiences these women report being told in various ways that when it came to running for office, they "don't belong here. You should be at home in your kitchen," that the job of holding office "really needs a man." To the extent their political activity was accepted it was accepted with severe limits, as one Ohio Republican reports being told that in her party "women only serve on the decorating and coffee committee." Nevertheless, these women continued to persevere, enduring insults along the way, including being "referred to as a dumb housewife," a "blonde bimbo," or "brainless bitches," being told they "spend money like a woman," or that holding office made women "frighteningly strong to their husbands." More startlingly, some women referred to even more pervasive bias that affected everything they did politically. In the words of one Ohio Democrat, the instances of discrimination she experienced in party politics were "too numerous to list, I could write a book!" . . .

Establishing that women are subject to bias within their party is a significant step in justifying a need to examine party recruiter behavior and the larger effort to identify bias. These simple data strongly suggest that potential women candidates are subject to bias (see also Werner 1993). Moreover, this lack of party support has quite dramatic effects on the officeholding plans of these women, as 85% report they would not run for higher office if their party was unsupportive.

Outgroup versus Distribution Effect

The responses of county party chairs to the survey instrument were utilized to assess their attitudes. Built into the survey were numerous opportunities for party chairs to evaluate relevant candidate traits. The evaluations involved reactions to occupations, reactions to personality traits, estimates of women's electoral chances in specific scenarios, and finally, reports on the gender ratio of the candidates the chair considers most capable of seeking state legislative office.

Occupation Test

In the first evaluation, the party chairs were asked to rate the favorability of candidates with different occupations. Specifically, the chairs, being told only the occupation of the candidates, were asked to rank each of the seven candidates based on their capacity to win a legislative race (1 to 7, 7 = most capable). The occupations listed were attorney, grade school teacher, television reporter, sales person, former professional athlete, police officer, and "someone with your primary occupation."

If the distribution effect influences the party chairs, then they should rate most favorably the occupations that tend to produce elected officials. . . . If the outgroup effect influences party chairs, then chairs should rate most favorably the occupations that are most closely related to their own background.

. . . Party chairs did not display a strong preference for the occupations that have the strongest presence, or distribution, in politics. While attorneys play the most significant role by far in legislative officeholding of the professions listed, attorney was not the top-rated category, and certainly did not stand far ahead of the field as its distribution in politics would suggest. The overall correlation between the occupations' ratings and their distribution was weak ($r = .17$) and statistically insignificant (at $p < .10$). Conversely, strong evidence for the outgroup effect exists as the clear top choice of party chairs was a candidate from the same profession as themselves. In other words, party chairs valued the occupation most closely associated with themselves, not the occupation most prevalent in politics.

This evidence could be misleading if responses to a candidate from the same profession as the chair vary based on the type or distribution of that profession. Further analysis reveals, however, that party chair reaction was quite favorable across all occupation categories.

It is both a strength and a weakness of this type of test that gender was not specifically mentioned to the respondents. The strength of this measure is that it is less likely to provoke defensive responses used to guard against the appearance of gender bias. The weakness, however, is that such efforts make it more difficult to show that respondents would react this way when gender was the clear focus of their attention. To extend these findings, and move closer to the target, party chairs were asked to react to a series of personality traits. This is another effort to examine how party chairs feel about male and female candidates without that purpose being explicitly apparent.

Personality Trait Test

The party chairs were given a list of 15 personality traits and were asked whether the trait was a positive or negative feature of a candidate. Then the party chairs were asked to rate the importance of the trait to electoral success on a scale from 1 (least important) to 7 (most important). The trait list was constructed to provide five traits associated with men, five associated with women, and five with no gender association.[3] To make the purpose of the test less obvious, the traits were randomly listed in the survey question. . . .

The results provide strong support for the outgroup effect and no support for the distribution effect. First, there is a slight negative association between distribution of female officeholders and ratings of female traits ($r = -.11$).[4] A correlation that is neither statistically significant, nor positive, is quite inconsistent with the distribution effect. Second, party chairs did not rate the traits that are most prevalent in politics most favorably. Party chairs rated the two least prevalent traits (average score 5.2) to be the two most positive of the five neutral traits (the more prevalent traits averaged 2.1). Again, the party chairs failed to treat that which is more commonly associated with officeholders as superior, challenging the distribution effect. Finally, male party chairs rate the male traits much higher than do the female party chairs. Male party chairs offer estimates of male trait value that are higher by a margin representing fully 10% of the range of the trait index (Male Trait Index: male chairs = 3.1/female chairs = 1.7, $p. < .01$).[5] Meanwhile, female chairs by an even wider margin rate the female traits higher than do male party chairs (Female Trait Index: male chairs = 1.9/female chairs = 3.4, $p. < 01$). Again, such a pattern should not occur if chairs were influenced by the distribution effect, but this is precisely the pattern one would expect if the outgroup effect were influencing perceptions.

On two measures, the occupation ranking and the personality trait response, party chairs have displayed strong support for the outgroup effect by favoring that which is more closely associated with themselves and devaluing descriptions of outgroup members. Their responses have lent no support to the distribution effect as prevalence has not produced more positive evaluations. Although the results to this point have been clear, gender has not been explicitly mentioned to the respondents. Therefore, one could argue that a stronger test of the applicability of the outgroup and distribution effects on gender bias would require the party chairs to respond more directly to gender (Linville and Jones 1980).

Electoral Chances of Women

The next evaluation, then, explicitly asks for estimates of the electoral chances of women. Specifically, the party chairs' opinions of a woman's chances for election to a set of political offices is solicited. The list progresses from local offices to national offices: including town/city council, state house, and Congress. The party chairs were asked to indicate on a scale of 0 to 100 the likelihood of a female candidate from their party defeating a male for the position in the general election. The scenario varied from a woman as incumbent to challenger and from a woman candidate emphasizing mainstream issues to a candidate emphasizing women's issues; thus, including the three levels of office, there were twelve different scenarios presented.[6] In order to lessen the chance for self-monitoring (avoiding giving an answer that reflects poorly on yourself), the survey emphasized that the question asks for a guess based on their experience and expertise and not whom they would prefer. In this way, the subjects should not feel that they are betraying any bias when they are rating the chances for victory of the hypothetical female.

These results add support to the outgroup effect and again do not conform to the distribution effect. First, the aggregate women candidates, electoral chance rating (average of all twelve estimates) is not strongly correlated with gender distribution (r = .09). Second, the results reveal that averaging their responses across the different conditions presented to them, women party chairs believed that women candidates had a significantly better chance of winning than did men party chairs. This finding again undermines the distribution effect, as a significant difference is not to be expected if the distribution effect were creating this behavior. Moreover, these differences between men and women party chairs exist in the same direction for all twelve situations presented (and are statistically significant in ten of the twelve).

Some might argue that the numbers hardly bespeak great prejudice against women, as most of the figures near 50%. However, according to male party chairs, the average chance for a woman candidate to succeed in the twelve scenarios is 47%. Clearly, 47% is less than 50%, and in a two-person race 47% is an expected loser, meaning the chair should go with another candidate. Additionally, 47% is an estimate based on half the candidacies being labeled "mainstream" on the issues. Left on their own to assume what kinds of issues women candidates would run on, party chairs might more likely imagine women running on "women's issues,"[7] for which their average estimate of the likelihood of female success ranges from a high of 47% to a low of 28%. Examining the estimates shown for women's issue candidates reveals that the cumulative average for such candidates offered only a 38% chance of success. In other words, 47%, which is a losing estimate, may be inflated by the "mainstream" label being given to half the women candidates.

While this examination of the results provides some additional support for the outgroup effect, another way to interpret the data is even more illuminating. One of the defining aspects of bias against a group is obviously the failure to attend to individuating information (Judd and Park 1988). Partly chairs were given different scenarios involving three different levels of office, two different issue areas emphasized, and two different types of candidate. This resulted in twelve different situations in which the party chair was asked to estimate the chances of a female candidate. To the extent party chairs are without bias, they should recognize and incorporate into their estimates the value of the information provided them. In other words, each of the twelve estimates should vary significantly based on the precise details involved. If the distribution effect is affecting party chair behavior, this variance should not be predicted by gender of the chair. If, however, the outgroup effect is affecting party chair behavior, then male party chairs should be less likely to acknowledge the individuating information of the outgroup candidate scenarios presented, and should, therefore, display less variance in their estimates than female party chairs display.

To examine this possibility, a score was created by calculating the variance for each individual party chair's estimates across the twelve scenarios.[8] The pattern that emerges shows that female party chairs do, in fact, have more variance in their responses to the scenarios presented them (male = 369/female = 499, p > .05). Women's estimates of women's chances vary significantly more with the details of the situation than do men's estimates. This provides further support for the outgroup effect as women utilized the individuating details describing ingroup members more than men chose to factor in those same details when describing the chances of outgroup members.

While this test also provides strong support for the contention that the outgroup effect is evident in party chair behavior, all of the tests presented have relied heavily on hypothetical situations. . . . Therefore, the last test involves gender both directly and in a real-world setting.

Gender of Future Candidates

Party chairs were asked the gender ratio of the top five people they have in mind for future state legislative races. Party chairs were also asked the gender of the person they consider to be the best of the five. The obvious danger of this type of question is that it may appear to the party chair to be socially unacceptable to answer this question truthfully if there are too few women in their top five. A basis for optimism, however, exists in that the chairs were told this was a study of the party leader/candidate relationship (not about women) and were reminded throughout the survey that there were no right answers. If the party chairs accepted the purported purpose of the study and did not feel threatened, then they might offer realistic answers to these sensitive questions. . . .

As is consistent with the previous findings, the number of women in the chairs' lists of prospective candidates is not strongly correlated with gender distribution (r = .12). Further, male chairs on average indicated that 1.5 of their top five candidates were women, while women responded that 2.2 of their top five candidates were women, a difference significant at p < .001. Perhaps more interesting is the question of who the top candidate is, since this will presumably be the person given the most opportunity and encouragement to run. Again, whether a woman is the top choice in the chairs' lists of prospective candidates is not strongly correlated with gender distribution (r = .15). Moreover, while only 24% of male party chairs indicated that their top candidate for a future state legislative race is a woman, 47% of female party chairs indicated that their top candidate is a woman, a difference also significant at p < .001.

In these questions, which seek to directly tap real party chair behavior, male party chairs display a distinct pattern for more strongly supporting ingroup candidates at the expense of outgroup candidates (women). The absence of strong correlations suggests that it is not the relative poor distribution of women in high-status positions that caused this response, but instead again this is evidence for an outgroup effect where those who lack surface similarity to the evaluator are less valued.

The significance of this last test, beyond adding more evidence in support of the outgroup effect, is that this test is based on real-life behavior and preferences. Male party chairs report that they are considering fewer women candidates for actual future races than are women chairs. Male chairs have more than twice as many men than women candidates in mind for future races and are about three times more likely to have a man as their top candidate prospect. Given that men far outnumber women as party chairs, and that the women candidates largely report an unwillingness to run for higher office without the support of their party, this pattern of preference for male candidates represents a most meaningful obstacle for potential women candidates (see also Niven 1996).

In sum, while the distribution effect was not firmly supported by any of the tests utilized, the outgroup effect was consistently supported by a variety of evaluations whose connection with gender ranged from none to explicit and whose relationship with actual behavior ranged from remote and hypothetical to very real.

Implications

. . . The most daunting implication of the prevalence of the outgroup effect is that male party chairs will continue to express reluctance to support women regardless of the amount of success women candidates achieve. Unlike the distribution effect which suggests negative evaluations of women would recede as women's success expanded, the outgroup effect offers no reason to expect that male elites will evolve into supporters of candidates who are unlike themselves. The outgroup effect persists because it is predicated on perceived distance. Success for outgroup members can be treated as an isolated anomaly or explained away through situational events (Schlenker and Miller 1977).

One way to reduce bias against women candidates, then, would be to increase the number of women in party leadership. While both major parties have professed interest in having more women run as candidates (Burrell 1994b), increasing the number of women party leaders has not been stressed. The number of women party chairs is slowly increasing (Baer 1993), and this bodes well for women candidates. However, women today still hold only a small minority of party chair positions and are likely to see their power remain limited for the same reasons women's candidacies are limited. . . .

Notes

1. A total of 516 county party chairs actively held office in the four states in fall 1995. Names and addresses of the county party chairs were provided by the state party offices of the two parties in each state. The response rate was 54%, with respondents having no statistically significant differences from the overall sample on demographic traits.

2. A sample of elected women was chosen to produce 516 cases, the same number available for party chairs. The sample consisted of 129 women randomly chosen from the lists available for each of the four states. Names and addresses of locally elected women in the four states were provided by the National League of Cities. The response rate was 53%, with respondents having no statistically significant differences from the overall sample on demographic traits.

3. There has been extensive work done on traits people associate with men and women (Alexander and Andersen 1993; Eagly and Mladinic 1989; Eagly and Steffen 1984; Hoffman and Hurst 1990; Huddy and Terkildsen 1993). These works were consulted in producing the traits used in the survey: (associated with women) loyal, yielding, modest, cautious, and compassionate; (associated with men) individualistic, aggressive, arrogant, competitive, outspoken; (neutral) adaptable, tactful, conventional, unpredictable, serious.

4. The correlations reported use the actual percentage of women state legislators in each state as a score of women's distribution. Other potential measures, such as the number of female members of Congress from the state, or the chairs' reported percentage of female officeholders in their county were used in separate analyses, and produced similar results.

5. Statistical significance for this and subsequent comparisons of means refer to 2-tailed T-tests.

6. Sniderman et al. (1991) find that describing an African American as a dependable worker tends to reduce or eliminate prejudiced reactions to that individual because the description violates the stereotypes of many respondents. In this situation, identifying the woman candidate as an incumbent or as emphasizing mainstream issues may violate the stereotype party leaders have of women candidates, thus it is necessary to provide the challenger and women's issues categories to prevent the description from artificially lowering displayed bias against women.

7. On the tendency to associate women candidates with certain issues, see Alexander and Anderson (1993) and Huddy and Terkildsen (1993).

8. The variance of the twelve estimates from each individual was first calculated, then the average variance for party chairs was calculated by determining the average of those scores. This method was chosen, instead of simply using the traditional aggregate variance, because the purpose was to try to isolate whether individuals recognized differences in the scenarios presented them. For example, if one party chair gave an estimate of 10% for each situation and another gave an estimate of 60% for each situation, these figures would produce variance as it is traditionally calculated. By individually calculating variance, and then averaging the scores, this situation would produce no variance, which more accurately reflects the lack of attention to individuating information in the example.

References

Abel, Douglas, and Bruce Oppenheimer. 1994. "Candidate Emergence in a Majority Hispanic District: The 29th District in Texas." In *Who Runs for Congress?* ed. Thomas Kazee. Washington, DC: Congressional Quarterly Press.

Alexander, Deborah, and Kristi Andersen. 1993. "Gender as a Factor in the Attribution of Leadership Traits." *Political Research Quarterly* 46:527–545.

Baer, Denise. 1993. "Political Parties: The Missing Variable in Women and Politics Research." *Political Research Quarterly* 46:547–576.

Burrell, Barbara. 1994a. *A Woman's Place Is in the House: Campaigning for Congress in the Feminist Era.* Ann Arbor, MI: University of Michigan Press.

Burrell, Barbara. 1994b. "Women's Political Leadership and the State of the Parties." In *The State of the Parties,* eds. Daniel Shea and John Green. Lanham, MD: Rowman and Littlefield.

Canon, David, Matthew Schousen, and Patrick Sellers. 1994. "A Formula for Uncertainty: Creating a Black Majority District in North Carolina." In *Who Runs for Congress?* ed. Thomas Kazee. Washington, DC: Congressional Quarterly Press.

Carroll, Susan. 1994. *Women as Candidates in American Politics.* Bloomington, IN: Indiana University Press.

Clark, Janet, Charles Hadley, and R. Darcy. 1989. "Political Ambition among Men and Women State Party Leaders." *American Politics Quarterly* 17:194–207.

Darcy, R., and Sarah Schramm. 1977. "When Women Run against Men." *Public Opinion Quarterly* 41:1–12.

Darcy, R., Susan Welch, and Janet Clark, 1994. *Women, Elections, and Representation.* New York: Longman.

Eagly, Alice, Mona Makhijani, and Bruce Klonsky. 1992. "Gender and the Evaluation of Leaders: A Meta-Analysis." *Psychological Bulletin* 111:3–32.

Eagly, Alice, and Antonio Mladinic. 1989. "Gender Stereotypes and Attitudes toward Women and Men." *Personality and Social Psychology Bulletin* 15:543–558.

Eagly, Alice, and Valerie Steffen. 1984. "Gender Stereotypes Stem from the Distribution of Women and Men into Social Roles." *Journal of Personality and Social Psychology* 46:735–753.

Eagly, Alice, and Wendy Wood. 1982. "Inferred Sex Differences in Status as a Determinant of Gender Stereotypes about Social Influence." *Journal of Personality and Social Psychology* 43:915–928.

Fowler, Linda, and Robert McClure. 1989. *Political Ambition.* New Haven, CT: Yale University Press.

Giles, Michael, and Arthur Evans. 1985. "External Threat, Perceived Threat, and Group Identity." *Social Science Quarterly* 66:50–65.

Herrnson, Paul, and Robert Tennant, 1994. "Running for Congress under the Shadow of the Capitol Dome: The Race for Virginia's 8th District." In *Who Runs for Congress?* ed. Thomas Kazee. Washington, DC: Congressional Quarterly Press.

Hertzke, Allen. 1994. "Vanishing Candidates in the 2nd District of Colorado." In *Who Runs for Congress?* ed. Thomas Kazee. Washington, DC: Congressional Quarterly Press.

Hoffman, Curt, and Nancy Hurst. 1990. "Gender Stereotypes: Perception or Rationalization." *Journal of Personality and Social Psychology* 58:197–208.

Huddy, Leonie, and Nayda Terkildsen. 1993. "Gender Stereotypes and the Perception of Male and Female Candidates." *American Journal of Political Science* 37: 119–147.

Judd, Charles, and Bernadette Park. 1988. "Out-Group Homogeneity: Judgements of Variability at the Individual and Group Levels." *Journal of Personality and Social Psychology* 54:778–788.

Kazee, Thomas, and Susan Roberts. 1994. "Challenging a 'Safe' Incumbent: Latent Competition in North Carolina's 9th District." In *Who Runs for Congress?* ed. Thomas Kazee. Washington, DC: Congressional Quarterly Press.

Klahr, David. 1969. "Decision Making in a Complex Environment: The Use of Similarity Judgements to Predict Preferences." *Management Science* 15:593–618.

Linville, Patricia, and Edward Jones. 1980. "Polarized Appraisals of Out-Group Members." *Journal of Personality and Social Psychology* 38:689–703.

Niven, David. 1996. "The Missing Majority: Recruitment of Women as State Legislative Candidates." Ph.D. dissertation. Ohio State University.

Piliavin, Jane. 1987. "Age, Race, and Sex Similarity to Candidates and Voting Preference." *Journal of Applied Social Psychology* 17:351–368.

Rule, Wilma. 1981. "Why Women Don't Run: The Critical Contextual Factors in Women's Legislative Recruitment." *Western Political Quarterly* 34:60–77.

Schlenker, Barry, and Rowland Miller. 1977. "Egocentrism in Groups: Self-Serving Biases or Logical Information Processing." *Journal of Personality and Social Psychology* 35:755–764.

Sniderman, Paul, Thomas Piazza, Philip Tetlock, and Ann Kendrick. 1991. "The New Racism." *American Journal of Political Science* 35:423–447.

Snyder, Mark, and Peter Mienc. 1994. "Stereotyping of the Elderly: A Functional Approach." *British Journal of Social Psychology* 33:63–82.

Werner, Brian. 1993. "Bias in the Electoral Process: Mass and Elite Attitudes and Female State Legislative Candidates; 1982–1990." Ph.D. dissertation. Washington University.

Yount, Kristen. 1986. "A Theory of Productive Activity: The Relationships among Self-Concept, Gender, Sex Role Stereotypes, and Work-Emergent Traits." *Psychology of Women Quarterly* 10:63–88.

Chapter 19

WOMEN'S REPRESENTATION
IN PARLIAMENT:
THE ROLE OF POLITICAL PARTIES
Miki Caul

Women are still under-represented in the parliaments of all advanced industrial democracies. . . . Virtually all prior comparative empirical research has focused on national-level patterns of women's parliamentary representation. A national-level analysis overlooks the fact that individual parties vary greatly in the proportion of women MPs within each nation. Parties differ in the number of women they nominate, where they rank women on party lists, and the proportion of women that they send to parliament. Parties are the real gatekeepers to elected office (Norris and Lovenduski, 1995; Norris, 1996). Because they play such an important role in the composition of parliament, we must understand how parties differ in encouraging or discouraging women's access to parliament.

This chapter analyzes party-level variation in women's representation in parliament. By treating the party as the unit of analysis, rather than the nation, we can isolate the role of the party in promoting women. . . . This study of parties in 12 advanced industrial democracies enables research to . . . determine which party characteristics are conducive to the parliamentary representation of women. . . .

Examining Party-Level Differences

This study systematically examines four general party characteristics that have been hypothesized to affect the proportion of women MPs: a party's organizational structure, its ideology, the proportion of women party activists, and party gender-related representation rules.

Party Organization

Three aspects of party organizational structure may influence women's representation: centralization, institutionalization, and the location of candidate nomination.

The first component, *centralization*, describes the distribution of control over decision making within the party hierarchy. . . . In a highly centralized party, leaders have the control to create openings for women—when they want to do so. . . . In response to pressures from other parties and the electorate, party leaders may seek votes by broadening the diversity of party MPs. Therefore, one might expect that women will be better represented where the party leaders *can* effectively make an effort to promote women candidates through the use of particular party policies.

Further, a centralized party organization may be more accountable for its inclusion of female candidates. Groups seeking increased representation have a central target for their demands. If those demands are not met, the groups can fault the party leaders. In a more decentralized system each locality must be individually pressured to support women.

The degree of *institutionalization* determines the nature of the process by which MPs are recruited. A high degree of institutionalization denotes a more rule-orientated process (Norris and Lovenduski, 1995). Highly institutionalized parties provide all potential MPs, especially those without ties to the power center, with a set of understandable rules. . . . If the rules do not overtly discriminate against women, women might have a better chance in a highly institutionalized environment.

In addition, with institutionalization, party leaders have less leeway to bend the rules in favor of certain candidates. Weakly institutionalized parties tend to bias candidate nomination in favor of those who have accumulated "personal political capital," resources based upon personal status or external group support (Guadagnini, 1993). . . .

Another important characteristic is the *level of nomination* for parliamentary candidates. One might hypothesize that localized nomination is more hospitable to women because they are more likely to work in community politics and may work their way up to the national level (Lovenduski and Norris, 1993). . . . In contrast, a centralized nomination pattern may provide a more structured internal party career ladder. . . .

Party Ideology

Another explanatory factor is party ideology. Left parties may be more likely to support women's candidacies than right parties because left parties espouse egalitarian ideologies (Duverger, 1955; Beckwith, 1986, 1992). Traditionally the women's movement has been linked to left parties (Jenson, 1995). Matland and Studlar (1996: 27) suggest that parties on the left may "feel a need to be sensitive to groups traditionally excluded from the circles of power"—and this may include women. . . .

Lovenduski and Norris (1993) contend that while left ideology may once have been a strong influence on women's parliamentary representation it is no longer as strong. Left parties may no longer be the only parties to support women because such support spreads across the ideological spectrum. . . . Therefore, the impact of party ideology on women's representation must be examined over time.

In addition, the traditional unidimensional left-right ideological continuum may be too simple to describe how ideology affects women's representation. . . . The rise of a "New Politics" cleavage adds a new dimension to our conceptualization of ideology. "This New Politics dimension involves conflict over a new set of issues: environmental quality, alternative lifestyles, *minority rights*,

participation, and *social equality*" (Dalton, 1986: 153; emphasis added). New Left parties may be even more closely linked to the women's movement than are the Old Left parties (Kitschelt, 1989; Jenson, 1995).

The year a party enters the political system may be another measure of "newness" that affects the representation of women. Single-nation evidence suggests that new parties may be more supportive of female candidacies. . . . New parties may be more likely to open their doors to a less powerful group such as women and to encourage them to run for office. New parties may be more likely to hold postmaterialist values such as equality and increased internal democracy (Dalton, 1991). In addition, new parties have few entrenched powerholders and are thus open to newcomers because no incumbents will be deposed in the process. . . .

Women Activists

During the 1970s, increasing numbers of women took their demands for increased participation to the political parties. . . . Once women began to enter the lower party ranks, they could directly increase pressure for representation at the highest level—parliament. In other words, women's participation inside the party as party activists at the local level, as organizers of intraparty women's groups, and as internal officeholders should buoy up women's power in the party. This power should increase women's opportunities to lobby for further support of women as candidates for parliament. Women's party activity also creates a new pool of politically experienced women. . . . Thus, those parties with higher proportions of women activists display correspondingly high proportions of women MPs.

Party Rules

Parties can increase the proportion of nominated female candidates by creating formal rules that prescribe a certain proportion of women among the party's candidates. Such direct action can take the form of a quota (mandated percentages of women) or a target (recommended percentages of women). Implementation of gender quotas or targets by parties not only reflects the acceptance that gender underrepresentation is a problem, it also demonstrates a willingness to act to fix the problem.

Gender goals and quotas within parties first emerged in the late 1970s. The number of parties implementing these goals and quotas rose throughout the 1980s (Caul, 1997). In advanced industrial societies, the number of parties establishing quotas and targets doubled between 1975 and 1985. . . . Parties that implement formal rules to promote women's representation should directly increase the number of females nominated.

Party organization and ideology may influence whether there are gender rules for candidates. Party organization affects a party's capacity to make enforceable rules concerning equal representation of candidates. For example, in the United States the weak and decentralized parties are unlikely to attempt to establish candidate quotas because they lack any mechanism to enforce them. Party ideology is likely to affect whether or not parties see fit to adopt quotas. A leftist party might reason that equal opportunity is not enough to help severely underrepresented groups, while more conservative parties may extend their "hands-off" approach to the economy to the gender of party candidates (Lovenduski and Norris, 1993: 320).

Electoral System

The focus of this research is on party-level differences. However, the electoral system remains an integral component in explaining women's representation. Several studies have established that a nation's electoral system strongly influences women's representation in national legislatures. Party-list PR systems produce more women in parliament than plurality systems (Duverger, 1955; Lakeman, 1994). The standard explanation is that parties in PR systems are more likely to add women to the list in order to broaden their appeal and balance the ticket. The perceived electoral risk with a female candidate decreases when a female is part of a group, rather than the sole candidate.

Data Analysis

The analysis is based on 68 parties in 12 advanced industrial democracies.[1] This study is limited to the United States and West European nations. . .

. A party was included in the study if it gained at least one seat in parliament at any one of the three time points under review. . . .

The participation of women is examined at three points in time: 1975, 1985, and 1989. These were selected because it was at the beginning of this time frame that women increased pressures for greater political representation. By 1975, attention had been called to the dearth of women MPs in advanced industrial democracies. By 1985, some parties had substantially increased their level of women's representation. Finally, by 1989, . . . it is possible to evaluate how new parties and new rules for gender parity affect party levels of women's representation.

Women MPs

. . . The data show that the percentage of women increases over time: from 12 percent in 1975 to 19 percent in 1985 and 23 percent in 1989. . . .

. . . There are substantial variations among parties in the percentage of women they send to parliament. For example, the Norwegian Labor Party had 19, 42, and 50 percent women MPs in 1975, 1985, and 1989, respectively. In stark contrast, Fianna Fáil of Ireland had 1, 6, and 6 percent women MPs in the same three years. Within Italy, the Communists sent 18, 19, and 32 percent female delegations to the national legislature, while the Liberal Party sent no women in any year. Similar variation exists within several nations.

Taking into account that basic party characteristics are fairly stable, a party's proportion of female MPs should be strongly correlated with the previous time point. Indeed, the data reveal that the parties that elect the highest proportion of women candidates in 1975 are among the highest in this respect at the next two time points. The correlation between the percentage of women MPs in 1975 and 1985 is .43; the correlation between 1985 and 1989 is .69 ($p < .05$ in all cases).

Predicting the Representation of Women

Party Organization

. . . The first hypothesis is that a more highly centralized party will better promote women MPs.[2]

The index of membership centralization is moderately related to women MPs in each year, yet the leadership index of centralization is only positively related to women MPs in 1975. More highly centralized parties appear only slightly more likely to have women MPs. A second set of party characteristics measures the degree of institutionalization. More highly institutionalized parties are in fact more likely to elect women to office at each time point. A more specific measure of party centralization is the pattern of candidate nomination. "Candidate nomination level" scores nomination at the local level as 1 and nomination at other levels as 2.[3] In 1985 and 1989, candidate nomination at the local level is associated with higher percentages of women MPs. This suggests that centralized control over nomination is *not* conducive to women's representation.

Party Ideology

Leftist parties may be more supportive of gender equality than rightist parties. As a first test of this idea, Figure 19.1 displays the average percentage of women MPs for different ideological families of parties in 1989. Overall, the chart supports the hypothesis. On the whole, the party types to

the left have higher percentages of women MPs than the parties to the right. Environmental and communist parties average the highest percentages of women. In stark contrast, the discontent and ultra-right parties send virtually no women to parliament. Surprisingly, the conservative and rural parties both have more women MPs on average than the left socialist parties.

But party type is an extremely blunt indicator of ideology. In order to measure party ideology rather than party labels, voter self-placement on the left-right ideological continuum is used. The moderately strong and statistically significant correlations between leftist self-location and percentage of women MPs supports the hypothesis.

Separate measures of Old Politics and New Politics ideology were also collected.[4] The correlations suggest that the more leftist the party, on old or new cleavages, the more women MPs the party tends to have. The most striking finding is that the summary indices for the New Politics dimension yield higher correlations than the Old Politics indices. Further, there is little support for the diffusion of women's representation across the ideological spectrum. Ideology does not play a stronger role in 1975 than in 1985 or 1989. The

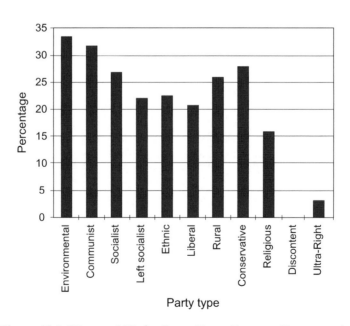

Figure 19.1: Women MPs by Party Type (Average Percentage).

correlations for the Old Politics indices actually grow stronger over time. This moderate strengthening of the Old Politics indicator suggests that Old Left parties may have responded in the late 1980s to New Left parties' efforts to promote women MPs in the early 1980s.

A related expectation is that the "newness" of the party is positively associated with women's representation. The correlation between the year a party was founded and the percentage of women MPs is weak in each case. Newer parties do not appear to be more hospitable to women.

Women Activists

With more women active at different levels within a party, the party may send more women to the national legislature. The percentage of women is examined at three internal levels within the party: representation on the party's national executive, among middle-level elites, and among local party activists.

The first striking finding is that the average percentage of women party activists at the local level is lower than the average percentage of women who are middle-level party elites. Further, both these averages are lower than the percentage of women on the national executive in 1975, 1985, or 1989! The average percentage of women local activists is 12 while among the middle-level elites it is 14 percent. The average proportion of women on party national executives is 16 in 1975, 24 in 1985, and, by 1989, the average grows to 27 percent. Parties appear to have more women at the top of the internal party ranks than at the lower-level elite positions. . . .

In each year there is a moderately strong and statistically significant relationship between the level of women in the party national executive and its level of MPs. The correlations grow stronger and more significant over time. This finding reveals a lag effect. In a party where there is a higher proportion of women on the national executive in 1975, by the next time point there is a higher percentage of women in parliament. In sum, women at upper levels within the party appears to encourage more women in parliament.

A high level of women working within the party ranks may also increase the party's promotion of female candidates. The middle-level elite indicators measure the percentage of women party elites who are delegates at 1977 national party conferences and the percentage of women working as local activists. The correlations suggest that high levels of women delegates and local activists also lead to high levels of women officeholders in later years.

Party Rules

Party rules range from strict quotas to softer recommendations for a certain proportion of women candidates. Accordingly, parties with explicit quotas score 2 points, while parties with targets score 1, and parties with no gender rules score zero. Each party was scored in this manner in 1975, 1985, and 1989.

Only three out of our 68 parties had any candidate gender goals or quotas in 1975. The number of parties with candidate gender rules grows by 1985, reaching its highest level in 1989 at 21 out of 68 parties. In 1989, those parties that have implemented candidate gender rules average 28 percent women in their delegation to parliament, while those parties without any form of gender rules average 22 percent women.

As one might expect, the influence of party candidate gender rules on the percentage of women MPs has a lagged effect. For candidate gender rules adopted in 1975 there is a low correlation in 1975 itself, and a higher and significant correlation in both 1985 and 1989. For those rules adopted by 1985 there is a weak positive correlation with MPs in 1985 itself. However, by 1989 the rules adopted in 1985 seem to have had their impact. The effects of the quotas instituted in the late 1980s may not show up until the mid-1990s.

Electoral Rules

As hypothesized earlier, parties in party-list PR electoral systems may have higher levels of women in their delegation to parliament. Parties in a party-list PR system scored 1 and parties in any other type of system scored zero. The resulting correlations reveal that parties embedded in party-list PR electoral rules do in fact send more women to parliament.

Multivariate Analysis

There are strong relationships for variables in each of the four categories. The next goal is to determine which characteristics work best together to maximize women's representation. To avoid possible multicollinearity problems, the strongest independent variables from each of the five categories were selected and entered into a multivariate regression analysis. From the party organization variables, both the index of institutionalization and the level of candidate nomination were selected as measures of party centralization.[5] From the party ideology variables, the New Politics index emerged as the strongest. From among the women activist indicators, the percentage of women on the national executive in 1985 was selected. In addition, the presence of rules in 1985 was selected.[6] The lagged variables were utilized as predictors because the bivariate relationships suggest that it takes time for these variables to have their desired impact. Finally, the type of electoral system in 1989 is included.

Causal Flow Chart

These party characteristics are linked. Their combined impact on women's representation may not be simultaneous, but rather linked in a chain of favorable influences. . . . The first and broadest influence is the electoral rules in which the parties are embedded. The electoral system should be linked to the ideologies of the parties and should also shape the internal organization of those parties. Specifically, a party-list PR system should increase a party's ability to adopt candidate rules because achieving gender balance on a list should be more feasible than mandating that one particular seat be filled by either gender.

Moving through the causal process, parties with New Left values have more women on their national executives and also should be willing to adopt candidate gender rules. In addition, a more highly institutionalized party may nominate more women to a rule-making body such as the national executive and is more apt to adopt and implement formal rules to help promote women. Also, the level of candidate nomination should have an impact on the ability of the party to implement those candidate rules.

At the next level, a reciprocal relationship may exist between the two most direct influences.[7] Parties may adopt internal gender targets and quotas for party decision-making bodies, such as the national executive. In turn, the presence of women on the national executive may encourage the adoption of candidate rules; women active at high levels within the party can add the direct pressure necessary to create and implement gender quotas and goals. Finally, women on the national executive and candidate rules may both have a direct and significant impact on the level of women in parliament.

Estimating the Model

. . . The first model predicts the level of women activists on the national executive of each party in 1989.[8] The resulting equation is as follows:

$$\text{Activists} = .28 - .02(\text{Inst.}) - .05(\text{Nom.}) - .52(\text{NewPol.}) + .09(\text{ES})$$

The only strong and significant indicator in this model is the New Politics index. Hence, in 1989 a party's New Left orientation alone best predicts its level of women activists.

The second model predicts the presence of candidate gender rules in 1989 and the resulting equation is:

$$\text{Rules} = -.28(\text{Inst.}) + .11(\text{Nom.}) - .27(\text{NewPol.}) + .18(\text{ES}) + .43(\text{Act.})$$

The index of institutionalization, the index of New Politics, and the level of women activists all predict the presence of candidate rules. Yet the indicator for women activists is the strongest. . . . We expected that high levels of New Left values and women on the national executive would advance the adoption of gender rules. It was previously hypothesized that parties with *high* levels of institutionalization would be more likely to adopt these rules. However, according to this multivariate model, once the other variables are controlled for, parties with *low* levels of institutionalization tend to have gender-related rules. In response, one might hypothesize that if candidate gender rules are largely a function of women on the national executive and their efforts to pressure the party, then rule-orientated parties are less flexible and more focused upon the party's program and thus reluctant to adopt measures to promote women.

The third model finally predicts the level of women MPs in 1989. The formula for the model is:

$$MPs = .01 \ (Inst.) - .14(Nom.) \\ - .13(NewPol.) - .35(ES) \\ + .39(Act.) + .39(Rules)$$

The type of electoral system and women activists both have a direct impact on the level of women MPs.

Comparing the models, while the impact of a party-list PR electoral system appears limited to the final outcome of women MPs, a high level of women activists on the national executive is important both to the implementation of candidate rules and to the level of women MPs directly. In contrast, the impact of the index of New Politics is mediated by the women activists variable. In sum, New Left values are important in elevating women within the party's internal hierarchy. Then, women use their new power to push for candidate gender rules and to promote women MPs.

According to the theoretical model, candidate gender rules should be a powerful influence on women's representation.[9] On the one hand, it is possible that gender goals and quotas do not have the strong effect that we had hypothesized. Upon close inspection of the data over time, of the parties with candidate gender rules in 1985, 5 out of the 15 decline or remain the same in their proportion of women MPs from 1985 to 1989. On the other hand, and based on the success of the lagged candidate gender rules variable in the bivariate analysis, one expects that gender quotas and targets take time to realize their full impact. It was not until the mid-1980s that many parties began adopting such candidate gender rules. As such, the effects of these new rules might not be visible until the 1990s.

Conclusions

. . . These findings reveal that certain party characteristics actually influence party-level variation in women's representation. High levels of institutionalization, a localized level of candidate nomination, and leftist and postmaterialist values all individually enable parties to increase the representation of women. Further, high levels of women working at internal party offices and the presence of formal rules designed to increase the number of women MPs are both conducive to women's representation.

It appears that women's party activism, especially at the high levels, triggers the other factors, such as quota rules, that facilitate women's representation in parliament. The finding that women's party activism is integral is especially encouraging in an era when women's activity in party politics has increased substantially. Not only can women party activists pressure the party for women's representation in parliamentary office, activists can also institutionalize the gains made by pressing to implement rules that call for guaranteed proportions of female candidates. . . .

Notes

1. The nations included in this study are: Austria, Belgium, Denmark, Finland, Germany, Ireland, Italy, Netherlands, Norway, Sweden, the UK, and the United States.
2. The index of institutionalization measures a party's programmatic orientation. All the party organization variables, plus party type, self-location, and women on the national executive, are collected from Lane and Ersson (1991). In order to uncover which measures tapped underlying subcharacteristics, the groupings of items under party organization, ideology, and women activists were factor analyzed using a principal components analysis involving the extraction of a varying number of factors, corresponding to each grouping of items. The only set of indicators that are intended to measure the same characteristic, but do not appear to tap the same dimension, are Lane and Ersson's summary index of integration (centralization) items. Therefore, I present the factor scores from each of these dimensions as the leadership and membership indices of centralization.
3. Candidate nomination level is taken from Lane and Ersson (1991) and these scores are verified and supplemented with the information on candidate selection in Gallagher et al. (1995), Gallagher and Marsh (1998), and Norris (1996).
4. The Old and New Politics indices were created from scores given to parties on select issues from Laver and Hunt (1992). The first two issues, which make up the Old Politics index, are "Increase Public Services vs Cut

Taxes" and "Public Ownership vs Anti." The third and fourth issues make up the New Politics issues: "Pro-Permissive Social Policy vs Anti" measures a party's position on abortion and homosexual law; and "Environment vs Growth" measures the party's support of protection of the environment, even at a cost to economic growth. I have selected the elite-level adjusted scores on these issues because we are interested in the attitudes of party elites.

5. There are two measures from the centralization category—the index of institutionalization and the level of candidate nomination—because both have equally strong correlations and it is therefore difficult to say which is *the* strongest indicator. I have also run the same multivariate analyses using only one or the other and the results are similar to the model with both.

6. When lagged variables are replaced by indicators from 1989 the models change very little. The same predictors remain strong in each model. However, the explained adjusted variance drops.

7. It is difficult to determine the sequence of the relationship between gender party rules and women party activists. From the case study literature it appears that women party activists began pressuring parties to open their hierarchies to women, and as more women gained clout within the party, changes occurred at even higher levels. Many parties set aside seats on the national executive for a representative of the women's wing. Perhaps these women used their position to press for opportunities for women candidates.

8. The models are estimated with a pairwise deletion of missing data because there are missing scores on some indicators. When the same multiple regressions are run with a listwise deletion of missing data the explained adjusted variance on each equation increases considerably.

9. Candidate gender rules is a highly intercorrelated indicator (as indicated by its strong correlations with several indicators and by its low tolerance levels in the multivariate regression). Therefore, its impact may be reduced by multicollinearity problems.

References

Beckwith, Karen (1986) *American Women and Political Participation*. New York: McGraw Hill.

Beckwith, Karen (1992) "Comparative Research and Electoral Systems: Lessons from France and Italy," *Women and Politics* 12 (3): 1–33.

Caul, Miki (1997) "Women's Representation in National Legislatures: Explaining Differences across Advanced Industrial Democracies," paper presented at the Western Political Science Association Meeting, 13–15 March, Tucson, Arizona.

Dalton, Russell J. (1991) "Responsiveness of Parties and Party Systems to the New Politics," in *Politische Klasse und politische Institutionen*. Opladen: Westdeuscher Verlag GmbH.

Dalton, Russell J. (1986) *Citizen Politics*. Chatham, NJ: Chatham House Publications.

Duverger, Maurice (1955) *The Political Role of Women*. Paris: United Nations Economic and Social Council.

Gallagher, Michael and Michael Marsh, eds (1988) *Candidate Selection in Comparative Perspective*. London: Sage.

Gallagher, Michael et al. (1995) *Representative Government in Modern Europe*. New York: McGraw Hill.

Guadagnini, Marila (1993) "A 'Partiocrazia' without Women: The Case of the Italian Party System," in Lovenduski and Norris (eds).

Jenson, Jane (1995) "Extending the Boundaries of Citizenship: Women's Movements of Western Europe," in Amrita Basu (ed.) *The Challenge of Local Feminisms*. Boulder, CO: Westview.

Kitschelt, Herbert (1989) *The Logics of Party Formation*. Ithaca, NY: Cornell University Press.

Lakeman, Enid (1994) "Comparing Political Opportunities in Great Britain and Ireland," in W. Rule and J. Zimmerman (eds) *Electoral Systems in Comparative Perspective*. Westport, CT: Greenwood Press.

Lane, Jan-Erik and Svante Ersson (1991) *Politics in Society in Western Europe*, 2nd edn. Newbury Park, CA: Sage.

Laver, Michael and W. Ben Hunt (1992) *Policy and Party Competition*. New York: Routledge.

Lovenduski, Joni and Pippa Norris, eds (1993) *Gender and Party Politics*. London: Sage.

Matland, Richard E. and Donley T. Studlar (1996) "The Contagion of Women Candidates in Single-Member District and Proportional Representation Electoral Systems: Canada and Norway," *Journal of Politics* 58 (3): 707–34.

Norris, Pippa (1996) "Legislative Recruitment," in Lawrence LeDuc et al. (eds) *Comparative Democratic Elections*. London: Sage.

Norris, Pippa and Joni Lovenduski (1995) *Political Recruitment: Gender, Race and Class in the British Parliament*. Cambridge: Cambridge University Press.

Chapter 20
EXPLAINING WOMEN'S LEGISLATIVE REPRESENTATION IN SUB-SAHARAN AFRICA
Mi Yung Yoon

Introduction

. . . Some sub-Saharan African countries show an impressive representation of women in parliament, while others lag behind. Women account for more than 20% of parliamentary seats in Mozambique, Namibia, Seychelles, South Africa, and Tanzania, but they account for less than 5% of seats in Djibouti, Lesotho, Niger, Nigeria, and Togo. What can explain these considerable cross-national variations? This study addresses this question by examining the relative significance of social, economic, cultural, and political factors that boost or hinder women's legislative representation. I study sub-Saharan African countries that held democratic legislative elections between January 1990 and June 30, 2001. For the countries that held more than one legislative election during this period, I include only the latest election for analysis. . . .

This study is different from previous studies of women's parliamentary representation in a couple of aspects. First, by focusing solely on sub-Saharan Africa, it fills a gap in the extant literature, which has focused on advanced industrialized democracies.[1] To put it bluntly, factors affecting female legislative representation in sub-Saharan Africa have been neglected and left unexplained in the literature.[2] Second, this study is the most extensive cross-national analysis of female legislative representation in sub-Saharan Africa. With the recent democratization in the continent, which began in 1990, the questions this study raises have emerged as new scholarly interests among Africanists. Yet,

with only one exception (Reynolds 1998), there has been no systematic empirical study of women's parliamentary representation in sub-Saharan Africa. Most of the few works on this subject are studies of one or a few cases,[3] and it is difficult to generalize on the basis of these findings. . . .

Social, Economic, and Cultural Variables

The extant literature of women's political representation sees female access to education, women's labor force participation, a country's economic condition, and that country's culture as the most important social, economic, and cultural factors that affect women's access to the legislature.[4]

Access to Education

. . . Female education in sub-Saharan Africa has not been given much priority (Ufomata 1998, 64), as is proven by the area's female enrollment rate, which is the lowest in the world (UNDP 2000, 164).[5] As a result, the gender gap in education has been more noticeable in sub-Saharan Africa than in other regions of the world. . . .

Participation in the Labor Force

. . . Women's labor force participation in the formal sector remains low in sub-Saharan Africa. The majority of the female workforce is either in labor-intensive subsistence farming or in the informal sector (for example, knitting, pottery, gardening, raising small livestock, dressmaking, vegetable and fruit selling, firewood selling, and others) (Kanji and Jazdowska l993, 13).

Economic Condition

. . . Extrapolating from the Kenyan experience, Nzomo (1993, 70) states that economic hardship has a negative impact on women's political representation because it decreases women's interest in running for elective offices. Other scholars argue that by discrediting male politicians who failed to manage the country's economy, harsh economic reality actually encourages women to become involved in politics (Foster 1993, 113; Mikell 1995, 409).

Culture

. . . Some Africanists argue that patriarchal culture, which relegates women to subordinate roles, has been a major barrier to female political representation in Africa because it not only discourages women from becoming candidates but also lowers their probability of winning elections (Geisler 1995; Gordon 1996, 113).

Political Variables

Analysts view electoral systems, party system fragmentation, and gender quotas as the most significant political variables.

Electoral Systems

Norris (1985), Rule (l981, 1987, 1994a, 1994b), Matland (1998), and Matland and Studlar (1996) found multimember proportional representation systems more favorable to women than single-member majority or plurality systems. . . .

Party System Fragmentation

Reynolds (1999, 553) states that the likelihood of women to be nominated is higher in a party system with a small number of large parliamentary parties because large parties are likely to have safe seats in which they can place female candidates. Most sub-Saharan African countries have inchoate

multiparty systems with many political parties that sprang up in the 1990s.

Gender Quotas

Gender quotas have been used to increase women's entry into parliament. . . . Two types of quotas are used in sub-Saharan Africa: the system of reserved seats established by national legislation (Sudan, Uganda, and Tanzania)[6] and quotas voluntarily established by political parties (Botswana, Côte d'Ivoire, Equatorial Guinea, Mali, Mozambique, Namibia, Senegal, and South Africa).[7] At present, no country in sub-Saharan Africa mandates all political parties to adopt a gender quota for national legislative elections.

Methods

Selection of Cases

Since 1990, more than 40 countries have held multiparty legislative elections in sub-Saharan Africa. Doubts have been raised, however, about the competitiveness of these elections because of electoral irregularities reported in many countries. . . . Elections in some countries have been declared meaningfully competitive and therefore democratic. This study includes only those countries because the political dynamics related to women's legislative representation might be quite different in countries where elections are meaningless. . . .

. . . On the basis of this criterion, 28 countries have been selected. Freedom House political rights scores are measured by such indicators as free and fair elections for political offices, fair electoral laws, equal campaigning opportunities, fair polling, honest tabulation of ballots, citizens' right to organize political parties and other political groupings, the existence of significant opposition, freedom from domination by powerful groups, and autonomy or participation of minority groups in the decision-making process. . . .

Dependent Variable

The dependent variable of this study is women's representation in national legislatures, measured by the percentage of women in each parliament.

For countries that have two chambers, the study considers the percentage of women in the lower house only because members of the upper house or Senate of those countries are appointed or elected indirectly.[8]

Explanatory Variables

I measure women's access to education by rendering the combined female primary, secondary, and tertiary level gross enrollment ratio as a percentage of the combined male primary, secondary, and tertiary level gross enrollment ratio.[9] I index the male enrollment ratio to equal 100. A larger percentage indicates a smaller gap in enrollment between men and women. I measure women's participation in the labor force using women's share of the adult labor force in percentages.[10] Here, "labor force" refers to wage earners in the formal sector and excludes homemakers and workers in the informal sector. For enrollment ratios and women's share of the adult labor force, I use the election year data. When election year data are unavailable, I use the data for the closest previous year. . . . I use the average annual percentage increase of the consumer price index in the 1990s before the election year as the barometer for an adverse economic condition because the rise of basic commodity prices has been the most critical complaint among the populace in Africa and, according to some analysts, has hurt women more than men.[11]

I measure patriarchal culture by the prevalence of female genital mutilation in percentage terms. The percentage for each country refers to the proportion of the female population affected by this practice. . . . It has been identified as one of the symbols of male-dominant culture. . . . The data for female genital mutilation are estimates from national surveys conducted mostly in the 1990s.[12]

For this study, I divide electoral systems into three categories: proportional representation systems, mixed systems, and majority-plurality systems. . . . Party system fragmentation is measured by the Laakso and Taagepera effective number of parliamentary parties (1979). . . .

I also divide gender quotas into three categories: substantial quotas, minor quotas, and no quotas. The substantial quota category includes

countries that reserve at least 15% of parliamentary seats for women, as well as countries where a political party that wins more than 50% of parliamentary seats employs at least a 30% quota for female candidates. . . . In sub-Saharan Africa, the highest percentage of a party quota for women is 33.3%, in the African National Congress in South Africa.

The minor quota category includes countries that reserve less than 15% of parliamentary seats for women and countries in which a political party that wins less than 50% of parliamentary seats has a gender quota. The no quota category includes countries with no party quota or reserved seats for women. . . .

Findings

To estimate the effects of the explanatory variables on women's parliamentary representation in sub-Saharan Africa, I used an ordinary least squares multiple regression model. . . . I hypothesized that the coefficients for access to education, participation in the labor force, proportional representation, mixed electoral system, and gender quotas would be positive, whereas the coefficients for patriarchal culture and party system fragmentation would be negative. Further, I expected the coefficient for economic condition to be either positive or negative. All of the coefficients have the expected signs except for those for mixed electoral system and party system fragmentation. Of the nine coefficients, four are much larger than their associated standard errors. The overall fit of the model measured by the F-statistics indicates that the dependent variable is not independent of the explanatory variables. It is statistically significant at $p = .000$ and rejects the null hypothesis that all of the coefficients except the constant are zero. The explanatory variables in the model explain 90.7% of the variance in the percentage of women in parliament.

The bulk of the literature suggests that some of the explanatory variables in the model might be correlated. . . . An inspection for multicollinearity with the variance inflation factor (VIF) does not call for any serious concern, however.[13]

Among the social, economic, and cultural variables, only patriarchal culture is statistically significant. . . . Women's access to education has little effect on female legislative representation in sub-Saharan Africa, perhaps because of the content of the education that women receive. According to Gordon (1991, 33), education for girls in Africa tends to emphasize stereotypical roles of women and does not train women to assume leadership roles. Measuring women's access to education with the percentage of female college graduates or with the gender gap in higher education only might have produced a different result for the education variable, if we assume that female politicians are likely to come from the well-educated population. Unfortunately, the data for female college graduates or for the gender gap in higher education are unavailable for most sub-Saharan African countries. Women's participation in the labor force also shows a negligible effect, probably because women are concentrated in low-skilled, low-paid jobs, which offer little of the training and resources necessary to pursue elective office.

Adverse economic condition has no significant effect, perhaps because of the pervasive poverty hurting most sub-Saharan African countries. . . . I also found no significant relationship between economic development and women's representation. This result suggests that economic development is not an important determinant. In fact, this generalization has been proven by studies of many developing countries—including several African countries—that have much higher rates of representation of women in parliament than do some of the most developed countries, such as France (12.1%), Italy (9.8%), Japan (7.3%), and the United States (13.8%).[14]

Among the political variables, substantial quota, minor quota, and proportional representation significantly influence the percentage of women in parliament in the expected direction. Women's parliamentary representation is 15.56% higher in countries with a substantial quota and 12.76% higher in countries with a minor quota than in countries with no quota. Women's representation is also 4.31% higher in proportional representation systems than in majority-plurality systems. There is no significant difference, however, between mixed systems and majority-plurality systems in determining female parliamentary representation. Contrary to expectation, the former elect fewer women to parliament than the latter.

Party system fragmentation has little impact on women's parliamentary representation. . . . What is important for greater legislative representation of women is the political will of major parties, particularly ruling parties, to nominate more women and place them in good constituencies or in winnable positions on their lists. In most African countries, a few political parties with superior competitive strength tend to win substantial shares of parliamentary seats. Other parties, new or crippled for a long time under pre-democratization, single-party, authoritarian rule, lack well-established support bases, party structures, and campaign strategies—all prerequisites for winning legislative seats. The hurried transition toward democracy has not allowed sufficient time for these young or oppressed political parties to develop such essentials. . . .

It is clear that political factors (proportional representation and gender quotas) play a crucial role in increasing the proportion of women in African parliaments. The effects of gender quotas appear substantial.[15] Even a minor quota increases women's parliamentary representation by 12.76%! To check the robustness of these findings, I ran two restricted models: one with the social, economic, and cultural variables and the other with the political variables. The results of these two restricted models confirm the main findings of this study but with a few changes. What are the implications of this study's findings for improving women's legislative representation in sub-Saharan Africa and for understanding women's legislative representation in general? . . .

This study found variables that affect legislative representation of women in advanced industrialized democracies, such as women's educational opportunities and labor force participation, to be irrelevant in sub-Saharan Africa, whereas proportional representation and culture were consistently relevant. These findings imply that the effects of women's education and labor force participation are different in developing societies; in the latter, education perpetuates the view that politics is not a women's domain, and an overwhelming majority of female wage earners are concentrated at the bottom rung of the formal economy. Proportional representation, on the other hand, is advantageous to women in advanced and developing democracies, although its positive impact might be greater in well-established democracies. Culture, which shapes people's views toward women's roles, appears to play a significant role, irrespective of levels of economic and political development. Egalitarian culture fosters women's involvement in electoral politics, but hierarchical culture impedes it. How favorably or unfavorably the society views women's involvement in politics depends on where its culture lies in the egalitarian-hierarchical cultural spectrum.

Notes

1. Among the studies that analyze the determinants of women's political representation in industrialized democracies are Matland 1998, Norris 1985, and Rule 1987, 1994a, 1994b.
2. This neglect is mainly due to the lack of data.
3. For case studies, see Geisler 1995, Goetz 1998a, 1998b, House-Midamba 1990, Shettima 1995, and Tripp 2000.
4. It is important to note that the discussions of these variables involve inevitably broad generalizations that do not apply to some countries.
5. Girls' combined primary, secondary, and tertiary level gross enrollment ratio in sub-Saharan Africa is 37%. This combined ratio refers to "the number of students at all these levels as a percentage of the population of official school age for these levels" (UNDP 2000, 278). For an extensive discussion on the factors that limit women's educational opportunities in sub-Saharan Africa, see Odaga and Heneveld 1995.
6. Sudan reserves 35 (9.72%) legislative seats for women; Tanzania, 48 (17.51%); and Uganda, 56 (18.42%) (Amongi 2002; Inter-Parliamentary Union 2001; Parliament of Tanzania 2003). I exclude Sudan and Uganda from this study because their legislative elections fail to satisfy the democratic election standard of my analysis. (See "Selection of Cases" in the Methods section of this article.)
7. The following table lists the political parties that employ gender quotas. The data were drawn from Inter-Parliamentary Union 1997, 2001; Jacobson 1996; Lowe-Morna 1999; MacGregor 2000; Socialist International Women 2002; and Yoon 2001.

   Senegal uses both proportional representation and majority systems; the Socialist Party gender quota is for proportional representation. The gender quotas of the African National Congress and the Front for the Liberation of Mozambique require that a woman occupy every third place on these parties' lists. The data for placement rules of other political parties are unavailable. Côte d'Ivoire and Equatorial Guinea are also excluded from study because they fail to meet the selection standard of my analysis.

Country	Party	Size of Quota (%)	Party's Share of Legislative Seats (%)
Botswana	Botswana Congress Party	30	2.1
	Botswana National Front	30	12.8
Côte d'Ivoire	People's Front of Côte d'Ivoire	30	43.0
Equatorial Guinea	People's Social Democratic Convergence	?	1.3
Mali	Alliance for Democracy in Mali	30	87.1
Mozambique	Front for the Liberation of Mozambique	30	53.2
Namibia	South West African People's Organization	30	76.4
Senegal	Socialist Party	25	8.3
South Africa	African National Congress	33.3	66.5

8. Most sub-Saharan African countries have unicameral systems. Only Burkina Faso, Ethiopia, Gabon, Lesotho, Liberia, Mauritania, Namibia, Nigeria, Senegal, South Africa, and Swaziland have bicameral systems. Of these countries, Ethiopia, Liberia, and Nigeria elect members of the upper house or Senate through direct elections. I have excluded some of these countries because their legislative elections fail to meet the democratic election standard of this study. Data for the dependent variable come from Inter-Parliamentary Union 2001.
9. I collected the data for these ratios from volumes of *Human Development Report*, published by the United Nations Development Programme. Here, "primary education" refers to elementary schools; "secondary education" to middle school, secondary schools, high schools, teacher training schools at this level, and vocational or technical schools; and "tertiary education" refers to universities, teachers colleges, and higher professional schools.
10. I culled the data for women's share of the adult labor force from volumes of the World Bank's *World Development Report* and *World Development Indicators*, and volumes of *African Development Report*, produced by the African Development Bank.
11. Data come from the World Bank's *World Development Indicators* 2000, the United Nations Development Programme's *Human Development Report* 2001, and volumes of *African Development Report*. Unemployment rates would be another good indicator of adverse economic conditions, but such data are unavailable for most African countries.
12. I culled data from AFROL 2003, Inter-Parliamentary Union 2003, United Nations Population Fund 2003,

and World Health Organization 2003. The countries where female genital mutilation is reportedly not practiced or rarely practiced are coded as "0" for this variable. Of the countries excluded from this study, Democratic Republic of the Congo, Eritrea, and Somalia show 5%, 95%. and 98% prevalence rates, respectively.

13. The VIF scores are 2.567 for education, 1.369 for labor force participation, 1.124 for economic condition, 2.266 for culture, 1.565 for proportional representation, 1.491 for mixed system, 1.735 for party system fragmentation, 1.527 for substantial quota, and 1.287 for minor quota. $VIF_i = 1/(1 − r_i^2)$, where r_i^2, is the coefficient of determination obtained by regressing the ith explanatory variable on the remaining explanatory variables in the model. Values for the VIF, therefore, range from 1 to infinity. The greater the extent of multicollinearity between an explanatory variable and the remaining explanatory variables, the greater the VIF. But VIFs cannot "determine which of the other regressors are causing the collinearity with the regressor that has a large VIF"; furthermore, there is no formal rule to determine what the cutoff value should be to designate a VIF as too large (Craney and Surles 2001, 393). For interpretation of VIFs, see Craney and Surles 2001, 392–94.

14. For percentage of women in parliament, see Inter-Parliamentary Union 2001.

15. We might ask if gender quotas would also have substantial effects in advanced industrialized democracies. Studies of female legislative representation in industrialized democracies do not include gender quotas as one of the variables.

References

Africa Development Bank. Various Years. *African Development Report.* New York: Oxford University Press.

AFROL. 2003. "Fighting Female Genital Mutilation in Africa." http://www.afro.com/Categories/Women/ backgr_fighting_fgm.htm (January 4, 2003).

Amongi, Betty Ongom. 2002. "Engendering Legislation and Government Policies in Uganda: Tactics and Strategies of Uganda Women Parliamentarians." Presented at the Third International Congress on Women, Work, and Health, Stockholm, Sweden.

Craney, Trevor, and James Surles. 2001. "Model-Dependent Variance Inflation Factor Cutoff Values." *Quality Engineering* 14: 391–403.

Foster, Annie. 1993. "Development and Women's Political Leadership: The Missing Link in Sub-Saharan Africa." *Flecher Forum of World Affairs* 17: 101–16.

Geisler, Gisela. 1995. "Trouble Sisterhood: Women and Politics in Southern Africa." *African Affairs* 94: 545–78.

Goetz, Anne Marie. 1998a. "Fiddling with Democracy." In *The Democratic Developmental State: Politics and Institutional Design,* ed. Mark Robinson and Gordon White. New York: Oxford University Press.

Goetz, Anne Marie. 1998b. "Women in Politics and Gender Equity in Policy: South Africa and Uganda." *Review of African Political Economy* 76: 241–62.

Gordon, April A. 1991. "Economic Reform and African Women." *Transafrica Forum* 8: 21–41.

Gordon, April A. 1996. *Transforming Capitalism and Patriarchy: Gender and Development in Africa.* Boulder, CO: Lynne Rienner.

House-Midamba. 1990. "The United Nations Decade: Political Empowerment or Increased Marginalization for Kenyan Women?" *Africa Today* 37: 37–48.

Inter-Parliamentary Union. 1997. *Men and Women in Politics: Democracy Still in the Making.* Reports and Documents, No. 28. Geneva, Switzerland.

Inter-Parliamentary Union. 2001. "Women in National Parliaments." http://www.ipu.org/ (July 2, 2001).

Inter-Parliamentary Union. 2003. "Female Genital Mutilation." http://ww.ipu.org/wmn-e/fgm-prov. htm (January 4, 2003).

Jacobson, Ruth. 1996. "Gender and Democratization: The Mozambican Election of 1994." *Internet Journal of African Studies,* No. 1 http:// www.brad.ac.uk/research/ijas/ rjijasel.htm (April 15, 2000).

Kanji, Nazneen, and Niki Jazdowska. 1993. "Structural Adjustment and Women in Zimbabwe." *Review of African Political Economy* 56: 11–26.

Laakso, Markku, and Rein Taagepera. 1979. "Effective Number of Parties: A Measure with Application to West Europe." *Comparative Political Studies* 12: 3–27.

Lowe-Morna, Colleen. 1999. "Women's Political Participation in SADC." http://www.idea.int/ideas_ work/22_s_africa/elections_7_womens_participation. htm (July 3, 2001).

MacGregor, Karen. 2000. "The Politics of Empowerment: Women in Parliament." *Indicator SA* 16: 26–33.

Matland, Richard E. 1998. "Women's Representation in National Legislatures: Developed and Developing Countries." *Legislative Studies Quarterly* 23: 109–25.

Matland, Richard E., and Donley T. Studlar. 1996. "The Contagion of Women Candidates in Single-Member District and Proportional Representation Electoral Systems: Canada and Norway." *Journal of Politics* 58: 707–33.

Mikell, Gwendolyn. 1995. "African Feminsim: Toward a New Politics of Representation." *Feminist Studies* 21: 405–24.

Namibian Women's Manifesto Network. 2002. "50–50: Women and Men in Government—Get the Balance Right." Windhoek, Namibia: Sister Namibia.

Norris, Pippa. 1985. "Women's Legislative Participation in Western Europe." *West European Politics* 8: 90–101.

Nzomo, Maria. 1993. "The Gender Dimension of Democratization in Kenya: Some International Linkages." *Alternatives* 18: 61–73.

Odaga, Adhiambo, and Ward Heneveld. 1995. *Girls and Schools in Sub-Saharan Africa: From Analysis to Action.* Washington, DC: World Bank.

Parliament of Tanzania. 2003. "Members of Parliament." http://www.bunge.go.tz/bunge/bunge.asp?Menu=1 (September 27, 2003).

Reynolds, Andrew. 1998. "Women in African Legislatures and Executives: The Slow Climb to Power." Johannesburg, South Africa: Electoral Institute of South Africa.

Reynolds, Andrew. 1999. "Women in the Legislatures and Executives of the World." *World Politics* 51: 547–72.

Rule, Wilma. 1981. "Why Women Don't Run: The Critical Contextual Factors in Women's Legislative Recruitment." *Western Political Quarterly* 34: 60–77.

Rule, Wilma. 1987. "Electoral Systems, Contextual Factors, and Women's Opportunity for Election to Parliament in Twenty-three Democracies." *Western Political Quarterly* 40: 477–98.

Rule, Wilma. 1994a. "Women's Underrepresentation and Electoral Systems." *PS: Political Science and Politics* 27: 689–92.

Rule, Wilma. 1994b. "Parliaments of, by, and for the People: Except for Women?" In *Electoral Systems in Comparative Perspective*, ed. Wilma Rule and Joseph F. Zimmerman. Westport, CT: Greenwood.

Shettima, Kole Ahmed. 1995. "Engendering Nigeria's Third Republic." *African Studies Review* 38: 61–98.

Socialist International Women. 2002. "The Quota System." http://www.socintwomen.org.uk/QUOTA/QUOTAEngl.html (January 4, 2003).

Tripp, Aili Mari. 2000. *Women and Politics in Uganda*. Madison: University of Wisconsin Press.

Ufomata, Titi. 1998. "Linguistic Images, Socialisation, and Gender in Education." *Africa Development* 23: 61–75.

United Nations Development Programme (UNDP). Various years. *Human Development Report*. New York: Oxford University Press.

United Nations Population Fund. 2003. "Working to End Gender Inequality." http://www.unfpa.org/gender/index.htm (January 4, 2003).

World Bank. Various years. *World Development Report*. Washington, DC: Oxford University Press.

World Bank. 2000, 2001. *World Development Indicators*. Washington, DC: World Bank.

World Health Organization. 2003. "Most Recent Prevalence Rates for FGM." http://www.who.int/frh-whd/FGM/FGM%20prev%20update.html (January 3, 2003).

Yoon, Mi Yung. 2001. "Democratization and Women's Legislative Representation in Sub-Saharan Africa." *Democratization* 8: 169–90.

Chapter 21

QUOTAS AS A "FAST TRACK" TO EQUAL REPRESENTATION FOR WOMEN: WHY SCANDINAVIA IS NO LONGER THE MODEL

Drude Dahlerup

Lenita Freidenvall

Although highly controversial, electoral gender quotas are being introduced in an increasing number of countries in all the major regions of the world. About forty countries have already introduced gender quotas for parliamentary elections by constitutional amendment or electoral law, most of them in recent years. In more than fifty countries, quotas requiring that a certain minimum of the parties' candidates for election to national parliament must be women are now stipulated in major political parties' own statutes. This development challenges previous theories of variations in women's political representation. . . .

Major historical leaps in women's parliamentary representation can occur without quota provisions, just as the mere introduction of quotas has not resulted in uniform increases in the numbers of women parliamentarians worldwide. However, this [chapter] focuses on electoral gender quotas as an affirmative action measure to increase women's representation. First, the [chapter] identifies two discourses: the incremental track versus the fast track to women's parliamentary representation. Second, it outlines the amazing new development in the introduction of quotas worldwide. Third, it analyzes the troublesome implementation process. Finally, the [chapter] discusses the implications of the incremental versus the fast track in terms of women's empowerment. The conclusion is that,

today, the Scandinavian countries may no longer be the model, at any rate not the only model, for ways to improve women's political representation. The introduction of a fast track, notably the introduction of legal electoral quotas in Latin American and other Third World countries, may represent an alternative and faster model, though this may also have its problems.[1]

The chapter is based on the first worldwide overview of the use of quotas (www.quotaproject. org).[2] Here, only electoral gender quotas are discussed, defined as legal rules (constitutional or legislative) or internal party regulations setting a minimum proportion of women, or both sexes, in the political parties' candidates for public election or among those elected.[3]

The Fast Track versus the Incremental Track

. . . Figure 21.1 shows what we call the fast versus the incremental track to high representation for women. By means of a strong quota regulation (40 percent) and forceful implementation procedures, women's representation in Costa Rica's parliament jumped overnight from 19 to 35 percent in 2002. In Denmark, where 38 percent of members of parliament are women (2001 election), the same move

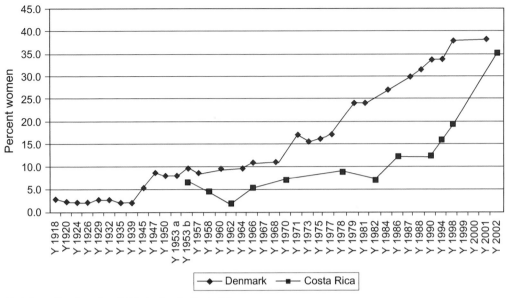

No information from the 1974 election in Costa Rica.
1953a and b: Two general elections took place in Denmark.

Figure 21.1: Women's Parliamentary Representation in Costa Rica and Denmark (Percentage).

took twenty years of incremental increase over eight elections. . . .

Figure 21.2 shows the two tracks as two different discourses—constructed as ideal types. Both discourses advocate equal representation for women, but their general perception of the historical and the future development varies, as does their identification of both the causes of underrepresentation and understanding of women's underrepresentation as a problem, and the proposed strategies. . . .

According to the incremental track discourse, the primary problem is that women do not have the same political resources as men. While there is prejudice against women, this will eventually disappear as society develops. There is thus an inherent concept of gradualism, leading to strategies such as women's capacity-building and parties' responsibilities to recruit more women.

From a liberal perspective, quotas as a specific group right conflict with the principle of equal opportunity for all. Explicitly favoring certain groups of citizens, i.e., women, means that not all citizens (men) are given an equal chance to attain a political career. The incremental track discourse thus points to the reluctance to give specific

categories the right to a guaranteed number of representatives based on their specificity, preferring equal opportunity to equal results. Concerns about the multiplicity of categories and groups that might claim quota provisions have also been raised (Maier and Klausen 2001), as well as arguments focusing on social cohesion, accountability, and fear of fractionalization (Phillips 1995).

In contrast, the fast track discourse rejects the idea of gradual improvement in women's representation. It is even assumed that an increase in resources might not automatically lead to equal representation. Exclusion and discrimination are regarded as the core of problem identification and understanding, the solution to which could very well be affirmative action. The fast track discourse represents the impatience of today's feminists, who are not willing to wait seventy to eighty years to achieve their goals. . . . Since the political parties are the real gatekeepers, they are the ones capable of increasing the proportion of nominated women candidates by defining formal rules that prescribe a certain proportion of women among the party's candidates. According to this understanding of women's underrepresentation, mandated quotas for the recruitment and election of female

The Incremental Track

1.   General perception:

  • Equal representation may take many decades, but will be achieved in due course as a country develops.

2.   Problem identification: Why so few women?

  • Women lack resources and public commitment.

  • Attitudes and ingrained prejudices limit women.

3.   Strategy:

  • Increase women's commitment and resources in civil society through education. labor force participation, social welfare provisions such as day-care centers.

  • Political parties should work more actively to recruit women. Capacity-building for women in the political parties through education, mentor programs, and provisions to help women combine family, work, and politics, such as babysitting facilities at political meetings, family activities at conferences, compensation for salary reduction, change of meeting hours.

  • Strong resistance to quotas, which is considered discriminatory (against men).

The Fast Track

1.   General perception:

  • Women's representation does not increase by some historical necessity. Backlash may even be possible.

  • Historical leaps in women's representation are necessary and possible.

2.   Problem identification: Why so few women?

  • Informal and formal discrimination against women (and other groups) is widespread in politics. Processes of exclusion and glass ceilings.

3.   Strategy:

  • Active measures, such as targets or quota provisions, which will force political parties to work more actively to recruit women.

  • Quotas are seen as a compensation for structural barriers, not as discrimination.

Figure 21.2: Two Tracks to Equal Political Representation.

candidates, possibly also including time-limit provisions, are needed.

Advocating the use of quotas thus represents a shift from one concept of equality to another. The incremental track is associated with the classic liberal notion of equality— "equal opportunity" or "competitive equality"—whereas quotas represent a shift toward "equality of results." . . . If barriers exist, compensatory measures must be introduced as a means to achieve equality of results. In this perspective, we will argue that quotas are not discrimination (against men), but a compensation for structural barriers that women face in the electoral process. . . .

Women as a Group

Electoral gender quotas also touch on the current theoretical debate about "women as a group" and draw attention to the problem of whether it is theoretically acceptable to continue saying "we" about a single category of women. . . . We will argue that, rather than using static concepts of "essentialism," the dilemmas and strategic choices of women in various contexts should be explored empirically. Research on quotas must therefore empirically analyze which groups of women are involved in the promotion of quotas as well as their alliances with men. . . .

The Use of Quotas—A Global Overview

In recent years, countries around the world have implemented constitutional quotas and/or quota regulations by law for elections to national parliament. Quota provisions are found in many different political systems, including countries with less democratic elections.

Depending on how difficult it is to amend a constitution, quotas by law are generally less robust than constitutional quota systems. At the implementation stage, the difference between the two different kinds of legal basis is insignificant, however. Democratic countries with constitutional quotas have usually laid down quota regulations in the electoral law as well. A simple division between *legal quotas* (constitutional and/or by law) and *party quotas* thus seems adequate.

Major political parties in more than fifty countries have now included quota regulations in their own bylaws, requiring a certain minimum proportion of women on the party's candidate list (www.quotaproject.org). . . . We reserve the concept of "party quotas" for countries where quota provisions are introduced solely by the individual political parties and not required by national legal rules. . . .

[There are] interesting regional variations. . . . *Latin America* represents one such cluster, where, in the space of very few years (1996–98), many countries, with Argentina as front-runner in 1991, introduced quota systems, mostly legal quotas. . . . Researchers have explained this amazing development, where totally male-dominated parliaments

passed quota laws, by factors such as the difficult transition to democracy in the region and the desire of political leaders to present their countries as "modern" by increasing women's representation (Marques-Pereira 2001; Htun and Jones 2002; Peschard 2003).

Quota regulations are also being adopted in several countries in *Asia*, and people there even talk about a new "quota fever." The radical move to introduce a 33 percent quota in village councils in India, Pakistan, and Bangladesh represents a very important step toward empowering women in countries with massive female illiteracy and a strict patriarchal regime. . . . There seems to be general agreement that profound changes are taking place, but also that, without massive support and capacity-building, these new women politicians, of whom many are illiterate, tend to become tokens (Chowdhury 2002; Raman 2002; Mohanty 2003; Rai 2003; Sharma 2003).

A distinction should be made between *Western Europe* and *Eastern Europe*. In the former, there are few legal quota systems, France and Belgium being the exceptions. However, party quotas are becoming more and more widespread. In contrast, in the former communist countries in Eastern and Central Europe and Russia (with the exception of countries in former Yugoslavia), quotas are very unpopular, and with few exceptions not used. . . . Resistance is fierce, also among women, because it reminds people of what is seen as the "forced emancipation" of Soviet rule. . . .

Several countries in *Africa* and the *Middle East* have introduced quotas. Uganda introduced a system of reserved seats for women as early as 1995. One of the most notable examples is South Africa, where the 30 percent quota system of the ANC party brought the Republic of South Africa to the top of the world ranking of countries with high women's representation (Ballington 2002; Goetz and Hassim 2003). In late 2003, Rwanda topped the world ranking, thus surpassing Sweden (www.ipu.org). In the 2003 election, twenty-four seats were reserved for women on women-only ballots, but another fifteen women were elected among the "free seats," thus giving women thirty-nine out of eighty parliamentary seats, or 48.8 percent. Women's representation in the *Arab* world is negligible, although quotas are currently being discussed there. Recently, by agreement among the political parties, Morocco elected thirty women on the "national list," and in the June 2003 election in Jordan, six seats were reserved for women for the first time. In Egypt, quotas were in use only between 1979 and 1986 (Abou-Zeid 1998).

Quotas for women are also being discussed in countries administered or occupied by the international community. In some cases, e.g., Bosnia and Herzegovina, the initiative came from international organizations in cooperation with local women's organizations (Jalusic and Antic 2001; Nordlund 2003). In the case of East Timor, however, the UN actually rejected a quota demand put forward by East Timor's women's organizations (Pires 2002). . . . This development makes it important to discuss further the concepts of empowerment "from above" versus "from below."

Do quotas work? . . . A majority of countries with more than 30 percent women in the national parliament have implemented quota provisions.[4] . . . However, some countries at the top of the list, such as Denmark and Finland, have not implemented any type of quotas for national parliament.

The use of quotas alone is not sufficient to ensure high levels of representation for women. Properly implemented, however, quotas can bring about substantial improvements in women's political representation. Thus, a high representation of women may be attained by the implementation of various types of quotas, but it can also be achieved without them.

Discrepancies between the provision of quotas and the actual representation of women . . . should not just be regarded as a question of time, i.e., women's representation will reach the required percentage in due course. After all, the very aim of quota systems is to produce a rapid and immediate change, i.e., in the next election.[5]

Information about the electoral systems of the top sixteen countries supports the well-known theory that electoral systems based on proportional representation are better at ensuring women's representation than the majority system (see also Rule 1987; Reynolds 1999). . . . Quota provisions are undoubtedly more compatible with PR electoral systems than with majority systems, even though quota provisions are being tried out in several majority systems, such as

the UK (party quotas in the form of short lists), France, India, and Bangladesh as well as Nepal (legal quotas).

Quotas for women are also being used in parliaments resulting from nondemocratic elections. It seems appropriate to use the term "quotas as reserved seats" for systems that guarantee women a certain number of seats in parliament independent of the electoral result, whereas "candidate quotas" (legal as well as party quotas) prescribe a certain percentage of women on the lists presented to voters at the election. In reality, the difference may in some cases be quite small, and many reserved-seat systems include some kind of election among the women candidates. In Uganda, an electoral college in each of the fifty-six districts elects a "woman representative" to parliament. Seats are also reserved for other groups, e.g., youth, the armed forces, and workers, and a few women are elected to so-called free seats. In all, women's representation in Uganda's parliament is as high as 24.7 percent (Christensen 1999; Tripp 2000; www.quotaproject.org). . . .

The Implementation of Quotas

. . . Passing quota regulations may be just a symbolic gesture if implementation is not regulated and there are no sanctions for noncompliance. . . . Several factors are important to the successful implementation of quota provisions. Here, we will discuss two very crucial dimensions: first, the specification of the quota provisions, including the question of a rank order for the candidates, and second, the sanctions for noncompliance and the eventual (non-)implementation of such sanctions. The following discussion is limited to candidate quotas.

The Minimum Requirement

Candidate gender quotas imply that women must make up a certain minimum number or percentage of the candidate lists (Dahlerup 1998). Today, most quota systems aim at ensuring that women constitute at least a "critical minority" of 20–30 percent. Quota provisions vary considerably, from Nepal's 5 percent to Costa Rica's 40 percent and France's 50 percent. A required minimum of 30 percent women is most common. . . .

Gender Neutral or Quotas for Women?

Most quota systems aim at increasing women's representation. . . . However, the rules are often formulated in a *gender-neutral* way. . . . A minimum requirement for women implies a maximum for the representation of men. In contrast, gender-neutral quotas involve a maximum for both sexes. An often-used rule is that neither gender should have more than 60 percent and less than 40 percent of the candidates. . . . A 50–50 quota is by mature gender neutral. . . .

Rules on the Ranking of Candidates

. . . A requirement of 30 percent women on the list may result in no women being elected at all. But even a radical 50–50 regulation, where women and men are alternated on the list, can, under special circumstances, result in the election of only men from the party in question. If, for example, a small party nominates a man as first on the list and a woman as second in a closed-list electoral system, and the party wins none or only one seat in all constituencies, then a 50–50 quota provision is of no help. In this case, as in majority systems, the central party has to intervene in order to break the tradition, which counteracts the tradition of local party autonomy in nominations.

. . . In countries such as Argentina, Paraguay, Bolivia, and Ecuador, rules were passed on the ranking of candidates on the electoral list, the so-called placement mandates or double quotas. In Argentina, the quota pioneer among Latin American countries, the decree of 1933 fixes the minimum number of seats guaranteed to women. . . .

In Costa Rica in 1999, after intervention from women's organizations, the Supreme Electoral Tribunal came up with the following radical interpretation of the quota law: women should not only have the required 40 percent of the candidates on the lists, but also 40 percent of the "electable" seats, interpreted as the number of seats that the party won in the constituency in the previous election . . . (Peschard 2003; Quesada 2003). . . .

Sanctions for Noncompliance

The distinction between legal quotas and party quotas becomes highly relevant in the case of sanctions for noncompliance. . . . In party quota systems, the sanctions are only political—critique from women's groups with the party or reactions from the voters. In contrast, legal quota systems often have some rules about sanctions in case of noncompliance. . . . It is important to note, however, that while regulated sanctions are important, there is no guarantee that they will be used, as in Peru and Brazil. In France, the rejection of lists which failed to meet the requirement worked, and women's representation on municipal councils in larger cities doubled. At the national level, only financial sanctions were available, which obviously did not deter the parties, and consequently women's representation increased only marginally, from 10.9 to 12.3 percent in the French National Assembly . . . (Sineau 2002). . . .

The conclusion is that . . . quota provisions that do not match the electoral system may just be symbolic. Furthermore, in the case of legal quotas, sanctions for noncompliance are crucial, provided that the sanctions themselves are implemented. . . .

Quotas and the Empowerment of Women

The Scandinavian notion that the introduction of quota systems is very difficult, if not impossible, if women do not already have a solid power base in parliament or in the political party in question is contradicted by the rapid diffusion of quota measures worldwide, particularly during the 1990s. Today, quotas have been introduced in countries where women's representation is low, and where women seemingly had little political influence. Gender quotas therefore appear in countries at all levels of development and in various social and economic political systems. . . .

One of the most important factors behind this new trend is the influence from a new international discourse supporting active measures to increase women's representation, as, for example, at the UN conference in Beijing in 1995. However, this does not explain why quotas are being introduced in some countries and not others, and why quota systems seem to expand in clusters. Consequently, the focus should be on the study of the *translation* of these new international and regional discourses through national actors, e.g., the women's movement . . . (Dahlerup and Freidenvall 2003; see also Krook 2004).

The crucial question to be discussed in the last part of this [chapter] is the extent to which, and under what circumstances, quotas will eventually empower women, which is after all the ultimate goal for most advocates of such measures.

In *quantitative* terms, quotas have proven effective at increasing the number of women in political assemblies, provided that the specific rules match the electoral system in question, and provided that sanctions for noncompliance exist and are properly enforced. . . .

Quotas are thus a means to open up systems of closed and male-dominated recruitment patterns. Quota systems do not accept the argument that there are not enough (competent) women, but demand that parties seriously begin to search for women and allow women at all levels in the party organization. . . .

However, quota systems do not remove all barriers to women in politics, such as women's double burden, the gender imbalance of campaign financing, and the many obstacles women meet when performing their job as elected politicians, and quotas may even contribute to the stigmatization of women politicians. But quota provisions properly implemented do obstruct and overcome some of the most crucial barriers to women's equal political representation. *Quota systems force parties to scrutinize and change their male-dominated gender profile and seriously start recruiting women who share their political conviction.* . . .

An evaluation of quota regulations in *qualitative* terms should be the subject of future research the world over. Among important themes are the possibilities for elected women to perform their job, changes in political culture, changes of public policy (substantial representation of women versus numerical representation), the interaction between the women's movement and elected women, and the alliance structure within political assemblies.

We suggest that the two tracks may have different implications for women's empowerment, seen within a limited time perspective: The *incremental track* to high representation usually ensures that elected women have some power base outside parliament, whether in terms of educational or job resources, or by their positions in politi-

cal parties, trade unions, or other organizations. While the *fast track* does have its advantages because of the speed of the changes, it can also create problems. The fast track, where women are given political positions "from above," so to speak, could turn them into tokens and leave them relatively powerless, unless the initiative is followed up by massive capacity-building, critique, and support of the many newcomers by women's organizations. . . .

Notes

1. In a forthcoming book (Dahlerup 2006), the quota systems in all major regions in the world are compared.
2. This website, representing the first global overview of electoral gender quotas (www.quotaproject.org), is the result of a joint venture between International IDEA and our research project, entitled 'Quotas—A Key to Equality? An International Comparison of the Use of Electoral Quotas to Obtain Equal Political Citizenship for Women' (www.statsvet.su.se/quotas). We would like to thank everybody who participated in the hard work of collecting data for this website: Julie Ballington and Virginia Beramendi-Heine at IDEA, Christina Alnevall and Anja Taarup Nordlund at our department, and Mona Lena Krook at Columbia University. This global overview would not have been possible without the help of a large number of researchers and women's organizations from all over the world.
3. Quotas for internal party structures are not discussed here, nor are quota provisions for public committees and boards.
4. In the 2003 election, 50 percent women and men were elected to the Welsh parliament. However, Wales is a part of the United Kingdom and not an independent state.
5. In some countries, like Belgium and Brazil, a gradual increase in the minimum requirement was built into the law.

References

Abou-Zeid, G. 1998. "In Search of Political Power—Women in Parliament in Egypt, Jordan and Lebanon," in Karam, A. (ed.) *Women in Politics: Beyond Numbers,* pp. 43–54. Stockholm: International IDEA.

Ballington, J. 2002. "Political Parties, Gender Equality and Elections in South Africa," in Fick, G., Meintjes, S. and Simons, M. (eds) *One Woman One Vote: The Gender Politics of South African Elections,* pp. 75–105. Johannesburg: EISA.

Chowdhury, N. 2002. "The Implementation of Quotas: Bangladesh Experience—Dependence and Marginality in Politics," paper presented at the Regional Workshop on "The Implementation of Quotas: Asian Experiences," IDEA, Jakarta, Indonesia, 25 September.

Christensen, T. G. 1999. *A Woman's Place Is in the House—State House!* Aarhus: Department of Political Science, University of Aarhus.

Dahlerup, D. 1998. "Using Quotas to Increase Women's Political Representation," in Karam, A. (ed.) *Women in Parliaments: Beyond Numbers,* pp. 91–106. Stockholm: International IDEA.

Dahlerup, D. 2006. *Women, Quotas, and Politics.* London: Routledge.

Dahlerup, D. and Freidenvall, L. 2003. "Quotas as a 'Fast Track' to Equal Political Representation for Women," paper presented at the IPSA World Congress in Durban, South Africa, 29 June–4 July.

Goetz, A. M. and Hassim, S. 2003. *No Shortcuts to Power: African Women in Politics and Policy Making.* London & New York: Zed Books.

Htun, M. N. and Jones, M. 2002. "Engendering the Right to Participate in Decision-Making: Electoral Quotas and Women's Leadership in Latin America," in Craske, N. and Molyneux, M. (eds) *Gender and the Politics of Rights and Democracy in Latin America,* pp. 32–56. England: Palgrave.

Jalusic, V. and Antic, M. G. 2001. *Women-Politics-Equal Opportunities: Prospects for Gender Equality Politics in Central and Eastern Europe.* Ljublijana: Politike.

Krook, M. L. 2004. "Promoting Gender-Balanced Decisions-Making: The Role of International Fora and Transnational Networks," in Christensen, H. R., Halsaa, B. and Saarinen, A. (eds) *Crossing Borders: Re-Mapping Women's Movement at the Turn of the 21st Century,* pp. 205–20. Odense: University Press of Southern Denmark.

Maier, C. S. and Klausen, J. (eds). 2001. *Has Liberalism Failed Women? Assuring Equal Representation in Europe and the United States.* New York: Palgrave.

Marques-Pereira, B. 2001. *La répresentation politique des femmes en Amérique latine.* Bruxelles: L'Harmattan.

Mohanty, B. 2003. "Women's Presence in Panchayats (Village Councils) in India: A New Challenge to Patriarchy," paper presented at the conference "Women and Politics in Asia," Halmstad, Sweden, 6–7 June.

Nordlund, A. T. 2003. "International Implementation of Electoral Gender Quotas in the Balkans—A Fact-Finding Report." Working Papers Series 2003:1 from the project "Quotas—A Key to Equality?" Stockholm: Stockholm University, Department of Political Science.

Peschard, J. 2003. "The Quota System in Latin America: General Overview," paper presented at the Regional Workshop on "The Implementation of Quotas: Latin American Experience." IDEA, Lima, Peru, 23–24 February.

Phillips, A. 1995. *The Politics of Presence.* Oxford: Oxford University Press.

Pires, M. 2002. "East Timor and the Debate on Quotas," paper presented at the Regional Workshop on "The Implementation of Quotas: Asian Experiences," IDEA, Jakarta, Indonesia, 25 September.

Quesada, A. I. G. 2003. "Concretando el mandato: Reforma juridica en Costa Rica," paper presented at the Regional Workshop on "The Implementation of Quotas: Latin American Experience," IDEA, Lima, Peru, 23–24 February.

Rai, S. M. 2003. "Quotas for Women in Local Government and Deliberative Politics: The Case of the Indian Panchayats," paper presented at the ECPR conference in Marburg, 18–21 September.

Raman, V. 2002. "The Implementation of Quotas for Women: The Indian Experience," paper presented at the Regional Workshop on "The Implementation of Quotas: Asian Experiences," IDEA, Jakarta, Indonesia, 25 September.

Reynolds, A. 1999. "Women in the Legislatures and Executives of the World: Knocking at the Highest Glass Ceiling," *World Politics* 51 (4): 547-72.

Rule, W. 1987. "Electoral Systems, Contextual Factors and Women's Opportunity for Election to Parliament in Twenty-Three Democracies," *Western Political Quarterly* 50 (3): 477–98.

Sharma, A. 2003. "Women's Political Participation and Leadership in the Governance of Municipal Institutions in an Indian State," paper presented at the conference "Women and Politics in Asia," Halmstad, Sweden, 6–7 June.

Sineau, M. 2002. "La parité en peau de chagrin (ou la résistible entrée des femmes à l'Assemblée nationale)," *Revue Politique et Parlementaire* 104 (1020–1): 211–18.

Tripp, A. M. 2000. *Women and Politics in Uganda.* Oxford: James Currey.

Part IV

WOMEN, GENDER, AND POLITICAL REPRESENTATION

This section contains readings on women, gender, and political representation, surveying normative arguments as to why women's presence might matter for public policy and empirical evidence regarding the role of women in producing gender-sensitive public policy. The first three readings are classic statements that have influenced almost all subsequent feminist thought on justifications for increasing women's presence in political office. As a group, they present both general and more contingent arguments for why the descriptive features of female officeholders might be important—or not—for ensuring the substantive representation of women's concerns (Phillips 1995; Young 2000; Mansbridge 1999). This work is critically challenged by the next article, which elaborates criteria for identifying "preferable group representatives" (Dovi 2002). The next two pieces draw on empirical evidence to assess these claims. The first is a seminal article that introduces various ways for analyzing links between the descriptive and substantive representation of women (Dahlerup 1988), while the second seeks to nuance this approach by exploring other actors and locations that may be involved in the substantive representation of women's concerns (Weldon 2002).

In an influential formulation, *Anne Phillips* identifies four possible reasons for increasing women's representation: (1) to provide role models, because the increased presence of women in politics may inspire other women to run; (2) to promote justice, as women constitute half the population so should therefore occupy half of all elected positions; (3) to articulate interests, on the grounds that men cannot advocate on behalf of women's needs; and (4) to take advantage of new resources that will improve democracy, because the participation of women will introduce different values and concerns to political debate, thereby enhancing the quality of political life. *Iris Marion Young* brings these arguments down to the microlevel, arguing that the process of political representation moves between moments of authorization and accountability, connecting the representative and the represented to one another in determinate ways. For this reason, she asserts that members of underrepresented social groups should be present in political institutions to facilitate group representation, because being similarly positioned in society creates a shared social perspective among group members.

Jane Mansbridge, however, cautions against these arguments about "women" as a group. In her view, there are only four contexts where disadvantaged groups like women benefit from increased descriptive representation: (1) where there is group mistrust, (2) where interests remain uncrystallized, (3) where there is a history of political subordination, and (4) where there is low de facto legitimacy. She argues that outside these specific contexts, there is a risk of promoting essentialism, or the notion that members of certain groups have an essential identity that all members of that group share and which no others can partake. Along related lines, *Suzanne Dovi* criticizes existing normative arguments for women's representation by posing the question of whether the presence of "any" woman will do. Concerned that a focus on sex may obscure the fact that women are divided by other identities, she argues that substantive representation requires the presence of "preferable group representatives." These are representatives who possess strong mutual relationships with dispossessed subgroups of historically disadvantaged groups; in the case of women, with women from disadvantaged race and class backgrounds. Only then, she claims, can the increased descriptive representation of women be matched by their increased substantive representation.

These theoretical arguments have developed alongside a growing empirical literature on women, gender, and political representation. In a well-known contribution, *Drude Dahlerup* identifies six areas where increased numbers—or a "critical mass"—of female representatives might have an impact on political life: (1) reactions to women politicians, with a decline in sexist treatment and sexual harassment; (2) the performance and efficiency of female politicians, with fewer women leaving politics; (3) the social climate of political life, with the arrival of a more consensual style and family-friendly working arrangements; (4) political discourse, with a redefinition of "political" concerns; (5) the policy-making agenda, with a feminization of the political agenda; and (6) the influence and power of women in general, with the broader social and economic empowerment of women. Using evidence from Scandinavia, she finds that women in politics are often important in all of these respects. However, she remains skeptical of the power of numbers, rejecting the concept of "critical mass" in favor of focusing on "critical acts."

Taking these arguments one step further, *S. Laurel Weldon* contends that assumed links between descriptive and substantive representation rest on a problematic understanding of the importance of female representatives for women's substantive representation and the relationship between individual experience and group perspective. Comparing the impact of various modes and sites of women's representation on policies to address violence against women in thirty-six democratic countries in 1994, she finds that women's movements and women's policy agencies may provide more effective avenues of expression for women's perspective than the presence of women in national legislatures. Collectively, therefore, the readings provide an introduction into a series of contentious debates within and across theoretical and empirical research on women's political representation.

Chapter 22
QUOTAS FOR WOMEN
Anne Phillips

I

. . . Arguments for raising the proportion of women elected have fallen broadly into four groups. There are those who dwell on the role model success-ful women politicians offer; those that appeal to principles of justice between the sexes; those that identify particular interests of women that would be otherwise overlooked; and those that stress women's different relationship to politics and the way their presence will enhance the quality of political life. The least interesting of these, from my point of view, is the role model. When more women candidates are elected, their example is said to raise women's self-esteem, encourage others to follow in their footsteps, and dislodge deep-rooted assumptions about what is appropri-ate to women and men. I leave this to one side, for I see it as an argument that has no particular purchase on politics *per se*. Positive role models are certainly beneficial, but I want to address those arguments that engage more directly with democracy.

The most immediately compelling of the remaining arguments is that which presents gender parity as a straightforward matter of jus-tice: that it is patently and grotesquely unfair for men to monopolize representation. If there were no obstacles operating to keep certain groups of people out of political life, we would expect positions of political influence to be ran-domly distributed between the sexes. There might be some minor and innocent deviations, but any more distorted distribution is evidence

of intentional or structural discrimination. In such contexts (that is, most contexts) women are being denied rights and opportunities that are currently available to men. There is a prima facie case for action.

There are two things to be said about this. One is that it relies on a strong position on the current sexual division of labor as inequitable and "unnatural." . . . My reasons lie in a feminist analysis of the sexual division of labor as "unnatu-ral" and unjust. The general argument from equal rights or opportunities translates into a specific case for gender parity in politics only when it is combined with some such analysis; failing this, it engages merely with the more overt forms of discrimination that exclude particular aspirants from political office. Justice requires us to elimi-nate discrimination (this is already implied in the notion of justice), but the argument for women's equal representation in politics depends on that further ingredient which establishes structural discrimination. . . .

The second point is more intrinsically problem-atic, and relates to the status of representation as a political act. If we treat the under-representation of women in politics as akin to their under-representation in management or the professions, we seem to treat being a politician as on a con-tinuum with all those other careers that should be opened up equally to women. In each case, there is disturbing evidence of sexual inequality; in each case, there should be positive action for change. The argument appeals to our sense of justice, but it does so at the expense of an equally strong feeling that being a politician is not just another kind of job. . . . While men have no "right" to monopolize political office, there is something rather unsatisfying in basing women's claim to political equality on an equal right to an interesting job.

. . . A rough equality in political participation has entered firmly enough into the understanding (if not yet the practice) of political equality for us to see an imbalance between the sexes as a legitimate cause for concern. Extending this, however, to the sphere of representation simply asserts what has to be established: that representation is just another aspect of participation, to be judged by identical criteria. The under-representation of women in elected assemblies is not simply analogous to their under-representation in the membership of political parties or the attendance at political meetings; for, while we can quite legitimately talk of an equal "right" to political participation, we cannot so readily talk of an equal "right" to be elected to political office. . . .

What we can more usefully do is turn the argument around, and ask by what "natural" superiority of talent or experience men could claim a right to dominate assemblies. The burden of proof then shifts to the men, who would have to establish either some genetic distinction which makes them better at understanding problems and taking decisions, or some more socially derived advantage which enhances their political skills. Neither of these looks particularly persuasive; the first has never been successfully established, and the second is no justification if it depends on structures of discrimination. There is no argument from justice that can defend the current state of affairs; and in this more negative sense, there *is* an argument from justice for parity between women and men. The case then approximates that more general argument about symbolic representation, stressing the social significance that attaches to the composition of political elites, and the way that exclusion from these reinforces wider assumptions about the inferiority of particular groups. But there is a troubling sense in which this still overlooks what is peculiar to representation as a political act. When democracy has been widely understood as a matter of representing particular policies or programs or ideas, this leaves a question mark over why the sex of the representatives should matter.

II

An alternative way of arguing for gender parity is in terms of the interests that would be otherwise discounted. . . . Women occupy a distinct position within society: they are typically concentrated, for example, in lower paid jobs; and they carry the primary responsibility for the unpaid work of caring for others. There are particular needs, interests, and concerns that arise from women's experience, and these will be inadequately addressed in a politics that is dominated by men. Equal rights to a vote have not proved strong enough to deal with this problem; there must also be equality among those elected to office.

One point made by Will Kymlicka is that this argument may not be enough to justify parity of presence.[1] . . . When the group in question is a numerically small minority, the threshold might prove larger than their proportion in the population as a whole; when the group composes half the population, the threshold might be considerably lower. . . . It is the argument from justice that most readily translates into strict notions of equality; the argument from women's interests need not deliver such strong results.

The above is a qualification rather than a counterargument, and in principle it still confirms the legitimacy of political presence. A potentially more damaging argument comes from those who query whether women do have a distinct and separate interest, and whether "women" is a sufficiently unified category to generate an interest of its own. If women's interests differed systematically from men's (or if women always thought differently on political issues), then the disproportionate number of men in politics would seem self-evidently wrong. . . . Does not the notion of a distinct "women's interest" just dissolve upon closer attention?

The idea that women have at least some interests distinct from and even in conflict with men's is, I think, relatively straightforward. Women have distinct interests in relation to child-bearing (for any foreseeable future, an exclusively female affair); and as society is currently constituted they also have particular interests arising from their exposure to sexual harassment and violence, their unequal position in the division of paid and unpaid labor, and their exclusion from most arenas of economic or political power.[2] But all this may still be said to fall short of establishing a set of interests shared by all women. If interests are understood in terms of what women express as their priorities and goals, there is considerable disagreement among women; and, while attitude surveys frequently expose a "gender gap" between women and men, the more striking development over recent decades has been the convergence in the voting behavior of women and men. There may be more mileage in notions of a distinct woman's interest if this is understood in terms of some underlying but as yet unnoticed "reality," but this edges uncomfortably close to notions of "false consciousness," which most feminists would prefer to avoid. Indeed, the presumption of a clearly demarcated woman's interest which holds true for all women in all classes and all countries has been one of the casualties of recent feminist critique, and the exposure of multiple differences between women has undermined more global understandings of women's interests and concerns.[3] If there is no clearly agreed woman's interest, can this really figure as a basis for more women in politics?

There are two things to be said about this. The first is that the variety of women's interests does not refute the claim that interests are gendered. . . . The argument from interest does not depend on establishing a unified interest of all women: it depends, rather, on establishing a difference between the interests of women and men.

Some of the interests of women will, of course, overlap with the interests of certain groups of men. . . . Women have no monopoly on generosity of spirit, and even in these more conflictual situations they can expect to find a few powerful allies among the men. What they cannot really expect is the degree of vigorous advocacy that people bring to their own concerns.

The second point is more complex, and arises with particular pertinence when a history of political exclusion has made it hard even to articulate group concerns. . . . The more fixed the interests, the more definite and easily defined, the less significance seemed to attach to who does the work of representation. So if women's interests had a more objective quality (and were transparently obvious to any intelligent observer) there might be no particular case—beyond what I have already argued about vigorous advocacy—for insisting on representatives who also happen to be women. We might feel that men would be less diligent in pressing women's interests and concerns, that their declared "sympathy" would always be suspect. But if we all knew what these interests were, it would be correspondingly easy to tell whether or not they were being adequately pursued.

Interest would then more obviously parallel political ideas or beliefs. It would become something we could detach from particular experience. . . . The alternative emphasis on changing the composition of decision-making assemblies is particularly compelling where interests are not so precisely delineated, where the political agenda has been constructed without reference to certain areas of concern, and where much fresh thinking is necessary to work out what best to do. In such contexts there is little to turn to other than the people who carry the interests, and who does the representation then comes to be of equal significance with what political parties they represent.

. . . If the field of politics has already been clearly demarcated, containing within it a comprehensive range of ideas and interests and concerns, it might not so much matter who does the work of representation. But if the range of ideas has been curtailed by orthodoxies that rendered alternatives invisible, there will be no satisfactory solution short of changing the people who represent and develop the ideas.

The more decisive problem with the argument from interests lies in the conditions for accountability to the interested group. Does the election of more women ensure their representation? At an intuitive level, an increase in the number of women elected seems likely to change both the practices and priorities of politics. . . . In the absence of mechanisms to establish accountability, the equation of more women with more adequate representation of women's interests looks suspiciously undemocratic. If the interests of women are varied, or not yet fully formed, how do the women elected know what the women who elected them want? By what right do they claim their responsibility to represent women's concerns? . . . However plausible it is to say that male-dominated assemblies will not adequately address the needs and interests of women, it cannot be claimed with equal confidence that a more balanced legislature will fill this gap.

III

The third way of formulating the case for gender parity approaches it from almost the opposite direction. It sees the inclusion of women as challenging the dominance of interest group politics, and expects women politicians to introduce a different set of values and concerns. . . . In some formulations of this, feminists have made a strong distinction between interest and need, arguing that the emphasis on interests treats politics as a matter of brokerage between different groups, and that the equation of politics with the rational calculation of interests is at odds with women's own understanding of their needs and goals.[4] . . . Need, by contrast, is thought to appeal to a more basic and common humanity; instead of asserting a stake in political battle, it formulates claims in more obviously moral terms.

This distinction engages directly with that common objection to a politics of presence which views it as increasing the role of interest in politics. When the demand for more women in politics is formulated in terms of interest, this seems to accept a version of politics as a matter of competition between interest groups; it talks the language of defense or protection, and treats politics as a zero-sum game. . . . The substitution of needs talk for interests talk may then offer a more radical challenge to the practices of contemporary democracy, querying the very nature of the game as well as the composition of the players.

My own position on this is somewhat agnostic. Interest can sound rather grasping and competitive, but it does at least serve to remind us that there may be conflicts between different groups. Need has more obvious moral resonance, but it originates from a paternalist discourse which lends itself more readily to decisions by experts on behalf of the needy group.[5] My own rather commonsensical solution is to use both terms together. . . . Neither needs nor interests can be conceived as transparently obvious, and any fair interpretation of either then implies the presence of the relevant group.

The broader claim made by those who disdain the politics of interest is that increasing the proportion of women elected introduces new kinds of behavior and values. It is often suggested, for example, that women will be less competitive,

more cooperative, more prepared to listen to others; that women bring with them a different, and more generous, scale of values; that women raise the moral tenor of politics. These arguments are always associated with women's role as caring for others, and often more specifically with their role as mothers. . . . The real problem with basing the case for more women in politics on their supposed superiority over men is that this loads too much on women's role as mothers.

The precise implications of this remain, however, ambiguous. The widely presumed association between women and a politics of care leaves it open whether women will concentrate on policies to enhance child care provision, thereby to increase women's participation in the labor market, or on policies that will raise the value and prestige of the care work that women do in the home. What resolves this in the Norwegian context is not so much gender as party. Women associated with parties on the left of the political spectrum are more likely to interpret a politics of care in terms of the first set of priorities, while women associated with parties on the right will tend to the second interpretation. In this as in other policy areas, party loyalties are usually decisive, and, though H. Skjeie notes a number of cases of women forming cross-party alliances on particular issues, she finds little evidence of women refusing the ultimate priorities of their parties. "The belief in women's difference could still turn into a mere litany on the importance of difference. Repeated often enough, the statement that 'gender matters' may in turn convince the participants that change can in fact be achieved by no other contribution than the mere presence of women."[6]

IV

This leads directly into the key area of contention, already signaled in my discussion of interest. Either gender does make a difference, in which case it is in tension with accountability through political parties, or it does not make a difference, in which case it can look a rather opportunistic way of enhancing the career prospects of women politicians. Aside from the symbolic importance of political inclusion, and women's equal right to have their chance at a political career (a fair enough argument, but not intrinsically about democracy), we can only believe that the sex of the representatives matters if we think it will change what the representatives do. Yet in saying this, we seem to be undermining accountability through party programs. We are saying we expect our representatives to do more—or other—than they promised in the election campaign. . . .

Though it is rarely stated in the literature, the argument from women's interests or needs or difference implies that representatives will have considerable autonomy; that they do have currently; and, by implication, that this ought to continue. Women's exclusion from politics is said to matter precisely because politicians do not abide by pre-agreed policies and goals—and feminists have much experience of this, gained through painful years of watching hard-won commitments to sexual equality drop off the final agenda. When there is a significant under-representation of women at the point of final decision, this can and does have serious consequences, and it is partly in reflection on this that many have shifted attention from the details of policy commitments to the composition of the decision-making group. Past experience tells us that all male or mostly male assemblies have limited capacity for articulating either the interests or needs of women, and that trying to tie them down to pre-agreed programs has had only limited effect. There is a strong dose of political realism here. Representatives *do* have autonomy, which is why it matters who those representatives are.

This is a fair enough comment on politics as currently practiced, and shifting the gender balance of legislatures then seems a sensible enough strategy for the enfeebled democracies of the present day. But one might still ask whether representatives *should* have such autonomy, and whether it would change the importance attached to gender composition if the politicians were more carefully bound by their party's commitments and goals. . . . The more radical the emphasis on accountability, the less significance attaches to who does the work of representation.

Bob Goodin offers one way out of this impasse, which stresses the importance of symbolic representation and the way this relates to people's self-images in politics.[7] . . . If the pattern

of representation gives no recognition to the communal attachments through which people live their lives, then this is felt to be intolerable, even when changing that pattern of representation has no discernible impact on the kinds of policies adopted. . . .

. . . People do recoil from the representation of themselves by such an "unrepresentative" sample, and do feel that changing this matters even if it subsequently proves to make no further difference. One of the principles associated with legal judgments is that justice must not only be done but be seen to be done. By the same token, we might well say that representatives must not only be representative but also be seen to be so. It would be foolish to underplay this element, but it would also be misleading to consider it the only thing at issue in demands for political presence. Women *do* think that it will—or should—make a difference when more women are elected as representatives. . . .

This points to a significant area of divergence between current feminist preoccupations and what has long been the main thrust in radical democracy. Radical democrats distrust the wayward autonomy of politicians and the way they concentrate power around them, and they typically work to combat these tendencies by measures that will bind politicians more tightly to their promises, and disperse over-centralized power. Feminists have usually joined forces in support of the second objective: feminism is widely associated with bringing politics closer to home; and women are often intensely involved in local and community affairs. But when feminists insist that the sex of the representatives matters, they are expressing a deeper ambivalence toward the first objective. The politics of binding mandates turns the representatives into glorified messengers: it puts all the emphasis on the content of the messages, and makes it irrelevant who the messengers are. In contesting the sex of the representatives, feminists are querying this version of democratic accountability.

. . . Much more can (and in my view should) be done to keep representatives accountable to the programs on which they were elected to office, and to bind them more closely to what they professed as their political beliefs. But there is no combination of reforms that can deliver express and prior commitments on every issue that will come to matter, and it is in those spaces where we have to rely on representatives exercising their own judgment that it can most matter who the representatives are. Behind the deceptive simplicity of the arguments for gender parity is this alternative—and more contested—understanding of representation.

The first part of the argument for gender parity in politics derives from principles of justice, and its power is essentially negative: by what possible superiority of talent or experience could men claim a "right" to monopolize assemblies? There is no convincing answer to this ultimately rhetorical question, and on this more limited ground of equal access to elected office it is easy enough to establish the case. There are all kinds of second-order questions, relating to how legitimate objectives can be best achieved; and all kinds of pragmatic judgments to be made on specific proposals, none of which flows directly from conclusions on overall objectives. But the real problem with the argument from justice is that it remains a subset of more general arguments for equal opportunities and affirmative action, and as such it gives too little weight to the difference between being a representative and being a lawyer or professor. It may be said that changing the composition of elected assemblies plays a particularly important symbolic role, that it involves a more powerful and visible assertion of women's equality with men than changing the composition of management or the professions. But this still confines it to the realm of symbolic representation, without any clear implications as to what further difference this representation should make.

The argument from either interests or needs, by contrast, anticipates a difference in the kinds of policy decision that will be made, and this more directly challenges existing conditions of representation and accountability. Representation as currently practiced rests on what most of the practitioners will admit is pretense: a pretense that the choices offered to the electorate exhaust the full range of possible alternatives; a pretense that party manifestos and programs wrap up coherent packages of interests and beliefs; a pretense that government is just a matter of implementing the choices the electorate has made. The pretense cedes tremendous power to those individuals who are eventually elected. . . .

. . . Changing the gender composition cannot guarantee that women's needs or interests will then be addressed. The only secure guarantees would be those grounded in an essential identity of women, or those arrived at through mechanisms of accountability to women organized as a separate group. The first has neither empirical nor theoretical plausibility; the second is impossible under current electoral arrangements, and perhaps unlikely in any event. So the case for gender parity among our political representatives inevitably operates in a framework of probabilities rather than certainties. It is possible—if highly unlikely—that assemblies composed equally of women and men will behave just like assemblies in which women have a token presence; it is possible—and perhaps very likely—that they will address the interests of certain groups of women while ignoring the claims of others. The proposed change cannot bring with it a certificate of interests addressed or even a guarantee of good intent. In this, as in all areas of politics, there are no definitive guarantees.

. . . Fair representation is not something that can be achieved in one moment, nor is it something that can be guaranteed in advance. Representation depends on the continuing relationship between representatives and the represented, and anyone concerned about the exclusion of women's voices or needs or interests would be ill-advised to shut up shop as soon as half those elected are women. . . . The shared experience of women as women can only ever figure as a *promise* of shared concerns, and there is no obvious way of establishing strict accountability to women as a group. Changing the gender composition of elected assemblies is largely an enabling condition (a crucially important one, considering what is *dis*abled at present), but it cannot present itself as a guarantee. It is, in some sense, a shot in the dark: far more likely to reach its target than when those shooting are predominantly male, but still open to all kinds of accident.

Notes

1. W. Kymlicka, *Multicultural Citizenship: A Liberal Theory of Minority Rights* (Oxford, 1995), ch. 7.

2. Since segregation is the fundamental ordering principle of gendered societies, women can be said to share at least one interest in common: the interest in improved access. See H. Skjeie, *The Feminization of Power: Norway's Political Experiment (1986–)* (Oslo, 1988).

3. See e.g. C. T. Mohanty, "Feminist Encounters: Locating the Politics of Experience," in M. Barrett and A. Phillips (eds.), *Destabilizing Theory: Contemporary Feminist Debates* (Cambridge, 1993).

4. J. Jacquette, "Power as Ideology: A Feminist Analysis," in J. S. Stiehm (ed.), *Women's Views of the Political World of Men* (New York, 1984).

5. This is one of the arguments made by Anna Jonasdottir, who sees needs talk as potentially paternalist, and not sufficiently insistent on the political involvement of those in need; see her "On the Concept of Interest, Women's Interests, and the Limitation of Interest Theory," in K. B. Jones and A. Jonasdottir, *The Political Interests of Women* (London, 1988).

6. H. Skjeie, "Rhetoric of Difference: On Women's Inclusion into Political Elites," *Politics and Society*, 19/2 (1991).

7. R. E. Goodin, "Convention Quotas and Communal Representation," *British Journal of Political Science*, 7/2 (1977).

Chapter 23

REPRESENTATION AND SOCIAL PERSPECTIVE

Iris Marion Young

. . . In the context of complex mass politics, a frequently heard complaint of exclusion invokes norms of representation. People often claim that the social groups they find themselves in or with which they claim affinity are not properly represented in influential discussions and decision-making bodies, including legislatures, commissions, boards, task forces, media coverage of issues, and so on. Such claims recognize that in a large polity with many complex issues formal and informal representatives mediate the influence people have. . . .

Policies, proposals, and arguments for the special representation of groups, however, face many objections. One of these . . . presumes a commitment to attend to rather than submerge social difference. The idea of group representation, this objection claims, assumes that a group of women, or African Americans, or Maori, or Muslims, or deaf people has some set of common attributes or interests which can be represented. But this is usually false. Differences of race and class cut across gender, differences of gender and ethnicity cut across religion, and so on. . . . The unifying process required by group representation tries to freeze fluid relations into a unified identity, which can re-create oppressive exclusions.[1]

. . . Implicitly much discourse about representation assumes that the person who represents stands in some relation of substitution or identity with the many represented, that he or she is present for them in their absence. Against such an image of representation as substitution or identification I conceptualize representation as a *differentiated* relationship among political actors engaged in a process extending over space and time. . . .

Representation as Relationship

. . . On this [conventional] image of democracy, representatives could only properly express the "will of the people" if they are *present for* their constituents, and act as they would act. On this image, the representative *substitutes* for the constituents, stands for them in a relation of identity. Critics of representation rightly note that it is not possible for one person to be present in place of many, to speak and act as they would if they were present. It is impossible to find the essential attributes of constituents, the single common good that transcends the diversity of their interests, experiences, and opinions. The objection that some people make to the notion of specific representation for marginalized gender or ethnic groups in fact can be extended to all representation. Political representatives usually have a large constituency that is diverse in its interests, backgrounds, experiences, and beliefs. . . .

If we accept the argument that representation is necessary, but we also accept an image of democratic decision-making as requiring a co-presence of citizens, and that representation is legitimate only if in some way the representative is identical with the constituency, then we have a paradox: representation is necessary but impossible. . . . A way out . . . involves conceptualizing representation outside a logic of identity. . . . [This] entails discarding images of the co-presence of citizens or that representatives must be present for citizens, and instead conceiving democratic discussion and decision-making as mediated through and dispersed over space and time. Rather than a relation of identity or substitution, political representation should be thought of as a process involving a mediated relation of constituents to one another and to a representative. . . .

Conceptualizing representation in terms of *différance* means acknowledging and affirming that there is a difference, a separation, between the representative and the constituents. Of course, no person can stand for and speak as a plurality of other persons. The representative function of *speaking for* should not be confused with an identifying requirement that the representative *speak as* the constituents would, to try to be present for them in their absence. It is no criticism of the representative that he or she is separate and distinct from the constituents. At the same time, however, conceiving representation under the idea of *différence* means describing a relationship between constituents and the representative, and among constituents, where the temporality of past and anticipated future leave their traces in the actions of each.

Conceiving representation as a differentiated relationship among plural actors dissolves the paradox of how one person can stand for the experience and opinions of many. There is no single will of the people that can be represented. Because the constituency is internally differentiated, the representative does not stand for or refer to an essential opinion or interest shared by all the constituents which she should describe and advocate.

Rather than construe the normative meaning of representation as properly standing for the constituents, we should evaluate the process of representation according to the character of the relationship between the representative and the constituents. The representative will inevitably be separate from the constituents, but should also be *connected* to them in determinate ways. Constituents should also be connected to one another. Representation systems sometimes fail to be sufficiently democratic not because the representatives fail to stand for the will of the constituents, but because they have lost connection with them. . . .

Anticipating Authorization and Accountability

In her classic work on representation Hanna Pitkin analyzes several meanings that attach to the term. Some writers understand what constitutes a representative as the fact that he or she is *authorized* to act by a set of official institutions that also bind together the represented group. Others focus on demands that a legitimate representative must be *accountable* to those whom he or she represents; otherwise the agent who claims to represent is simply acting on his or her own.

Pitkin discusses the debate about whether a representative is properly a *delegate* who carries the mandate of a constituency which he or she advocates, or rather ought to act as *trustee* who exercises independent judgment about the right thing to do under these political circumstances. Pitkin argues that the debate is misconstrued. Both sides are correct in their way; the specific function of legitimate representation consists in exercising independent judgment but in knowledge and anticipation of what constituents want.

. . . I follow Pitkin in theorizing representation as involving both authorization and accountability, and agree with her that the dichotomy of delegate–trustee is a false polarization.[2] . . . Representation consists in a mediated relationship, both among members of a constituency, between the constituency and the representative, and between representatives in a decision-making body. As a deferring relationship between constituents and their agents, representation moves between moments of authorization and accountability. Representation is a cycle of anticipation and recollection between constituents and representative, in which discourse and action at each moment ought to bear *traces* of the others.

. . . Representation is a differentiated relationship between constituents and representative where disconnection is always a possibility, and connection maintained over time through anticipation and recollection in moments of authorization and accountability. A representative process is worse, then, to the extent that the separation tends toward severance, and better to the extent that it establishes and renews connection between constituents and representative, and among members of the constituency.

. . . In most situations the specific constituency exists at best potentially. . . . The constituency is usually too large, or the varying activities of its members are too dispersed, or its definition and borders too vague, to expect a time when the constituency at one moment arrives at a collective will. Instead, in a well-functioning process a public sphere of discussion sets an issue agenda and the main terms of dispute or struggle. For parliamentary processes to be effective as representative, and not merely as a stage on which elites perform according to their own script, the democratic process of the authorization of representatives should be both participatory and inclusively deliberative.

. . . The representative ought to recollect the discussion process that led to his authorization and anticipate a moment of being accountable to those he claims to represent. The representative is authorized to act, but his judgment is always in question. Whether he acted on authority is a question deferred to a later time, when he will be held accountable. The representative acts on his or her own, but in anticipation of having to give an account to those he or she represents. While there is no authorized mandate for many decisions, representation is stronger when it bears the traces of the discussion that led to authorization or in other ways persuasively justifies itself in a public accounting.

In the process of calling representatives to account for what they have decided, citizens continue to form themselves into a constituency, and they engage anew in debate and struggle over the wisdom and implications of policy decisions. Such renewed opinion formation may bear the traces of the process of authorization, but it also has new elements, because previously the constituents did not know just how issues would be formulated in the representative body, and what expression, appeals, and arguments would be offered there. The responsibility of the representative is not simply to tell citizens how she has enacted a mandate they authorized or served their interests, but as much to persuade them of the rightness of her judgment.

In most actually existing democracies, the moment of accountability is weaker than the moment of authorization. . . . Strong communicative democracy, however, requires some processes and procedures where constituents call representatives to account over and above reauthorizing them. As with authorization, accountability should occur both through official institutions and in the public life of independent civic association. All existing representative democracies could be improved by additional procedures and fora through which citizens discuss with one another and with representatives their evaluation of policies representatives have supported. . . .

Modes of Representation

The representative should not be thought of as a substitute for those he or she represents, I have suggested, nor should we assume that the representative can or should express and enact some united will of the constituency. The representative can stand for neither the identity of any other person nor the collective identity of a constituency. There is an inevitable difference and separation between the representative and constituents, which always puts in question the manner and degree to which constituents participate in the process that produces policy outcomes. Yet representation is both necessary and desirable in modern politics. Rather than devaluing representation as such, participatory and radical democrats should evaluate the degree to which processes of authorization and accountability exist, are independent, and activate the constituency-inclusive participatory public opinion.

Another measure of the degrees of democracy, I suggest, is whether people are connected through relationships of authorization and accountability to a plurality of representatives who relate to different aspects of their lives. . . . Democracy can be strengthened by pluralizing the modes and sites of representation. Systems of political representation cannot make individuals present in their individuality, but rather should represent *aspects* of a person's life experience, identity, beliefs, or activity where she or he has affinity with others. Potentially there are many such aspects or affinity groups. I propose to distinguish here three general modes through which a person can be represented: according to interest, opinion, and perspective. . . .

What do I mean when I say that I feel represented in the political process? There are many possible answers to this question, but three stand out for me as important. First, I feel represented when someone is looking after the interests I take as mine and share with some others. Secondly, it is important to me that the principles, values, and priorities that I think should guide political decisions are voiced in discussion. Finally, I feel represented when at least some of those discussing and voting on policies understand and express the kind of social experience I have because of my social group position and the history of social group relations. . . .

Interest

I define interest as what affects or is important to the life prospects of individuals, or the goals of organizations. . . . I define interest here as self-referring, and as different from ideas, principles, and values. The latter may help define the ends a person sets for herself, where the interest defines the means for achieving those ends. . . . Interests frequently conflict, not only between agents, but also in the action of a single agent. . . .

Opinions

I define opinions as the principles, values, and priorities held by a person as these bear on and condition his or her judgment about what policies should be pursued and ends sought. This is the primary sphere of what Anne Phillips refers to as the "politics of ideas."[3] . . . By opinion, I mean any judgment or belief about how things are or ought to be, and the political judgments that follow from these judgements or beliefs. . . . A communicative democracy requires the free expression and challenging of opinions, and a wide representation of opinions in discussions leading to policy decisions.

Political parties are the most common vehicle for the representation of opinions. Parties often put forward programs that less express the interests of a particular constituency, and more organize the political issues of the day according to principles, values, and priorities the party claims generally to stand for. Smaller or more specialized associations, however, can and often do form to represent opinions in public life and influence public policy. . . .

Perspective

. . . Social group differentiation should be understood with a more relational logic, I argued, and individuals should be understood as positioned in social group structures rather than having their identity determined by them. . . . Group differentiation offers resources to a communicative democratic public that aims to do justice, because differently positioned people have different experience, history, and social knowledge derived from that positioning. I call this social *perspective*.

Because of their social locations, people are attuned to particular kinds of social meanings and relationships to which others are less attuned. Sometimes others are not positioned to be aware of them at all. From their social locations people have differentiated knowledge of social events and their consequences. . . . Structural social positions thus produce particular location-relative experience and a specific knowledge of social processes and consequences. Each differentiated group position has a particular experience or point of view on social processes precisely because each is part of and has helped produce the patterned processes. . . .

Following the logic of the metaphor of group differentiation as arising from differing positions in social fields, the idea of social perspective suggests that agents who are "close" in the social field have a similar point of view on the field and the occurrences within it, while those who are socially distant are more likely to see things differently. While different, these social perspectives may not be incompatible. . . .

[A] social perspective does not contain a determinate specific content. In this respect perspective is different from interest or opinion. Social perspective consists in a set of questions, kinds of experience, and assumptions with which reasoning begins, rather than the conclusions drawn. Critiques of essentialism rightly show that those said to belong to the same social group often have different and even conflicting interests and opinions. People who have a similar perspective on social processes and issues . . . nevertheless often have different interests or opinions, because they reason differently from what they experience, or have different goals and projects.

Perspective is a way of looking at social processes without determining what one sees. Thus two people may share a social perspective and still experience their positionality differently because they are attending to different elements of the society. Sharing a perspective, however, gives each an affinity with the other's way of describing what he experiences, an affinity that those differently situated do not experience. This lesser affinity does not imply that those differently positioned cannot understand a description of an element of social reality from another social perspective, only that it takes more work to understand the expression of different social perspectives than those one shares. . . .

One might object that the idea of an African American perspective, or a female gendered perspective, is just as open to criticism as the idea of a single group interest or opinion. . . . To be sure, each person has his or her own irreducible history which gives him or her unique social knowledge and perspective. We must avoid, however, the sort of individualism that would conclude from this fact that any talk of structured social positions and group-defined social location is wrong, incoherent, or useless. . . . The idea of perspective is meant to capture that sensibility of group-positioned experience without specifying unified content to what the perceptive sees. . . . So we can well find different persons with a similar social perspective giving different interpretations of an issue. Perspective is an approach to looking at social events, which conditions but does not determine what one sees.

Suppose we accept this claim that individuals positioned in similar ways in the social field have a similar group perspective on that society. What does this imply for individuals, who are positioned in terms of many group-differentiated relations? Since individuals are multiply positioned in complexly structured societies, individuals interpret the society from a multiplicity of social group perspectives. Some of these may intersect to constitute a distinctive hybrid perspective, a Black woman's perspective, perhaps, or a working-class youth perspective. . . . The multiple perspectives from which persons may see society may reinforce and enhance one another, or it may be impossible to take one without obscuring another. . . . However they are experienced, the availability of multiple perspectives provides everyone with the resources to take a distance on any one of them, and to com-

municate in certain ways with people with whom one does not share perspectives in others.

. . . It is useful to regard social perspective as helping to set a framework of interpretation. Doing so may indeed help individuals reason through what they find to be in their interests. Nevertheless, theorizing in this regard ought to recognize that sometimes individuals similarly positioned in social structures find that there are many interests they do not share. Representing an interest or an opinion usually entails promoting certain specific outcomes in the decision-making process. Representing a perspective, on the other hand, usually means promoting certain starting points for discussion. From a particular social perspective a representative asks certain kinds of questions, reports certain kinds of experience, recalls a particular line of narrative history, or expresses a certain way of regarding the positions of others. These importantly contribute to the inclusion of different people in the decision-making process and nurture attention to possible effects of proposed policies on different groups. Expressing perspective, however, does not usually mean drawing a conclusion about outcomes.

Let me give another example to illustrate the expression of perspective. Several years ago U.S. Senator Robert Packwood was accused of sexual harassment of several of his aides. After the story broke, many in the Senate seemed disinclined to bring the matter to hearing for potential ethics sanction. . . . In response nearly all the women legislators in both the House of Representatives and the Senate held a joint press conference to demand that the Senate hold hearings seriously to consider the charges against Packwood. These women did not agree on political values and they had many divergent interests; they did not agree in their opinions of whether Packwood was guilty of harassment. Their purpose was to influence the Senate's agenda, and in doing so they expressed a similar perspective on the meaning and gravity of accusations of sexual harassment, a perspective that many of the men seemed not to understand, at least at first.

Interests, opinions, and perspectives, then, are three important aspects of persons that can be represented. . . . None of these aspects reduce to the identity of either a person or a group, but each is an aspect of the person. None of these aspects of persons, moreover, is reducible to the others. They are logically independent in the sense that from a general social perspective one can immediately infer a set of neither interests nor opinions.

Unlike interests or opinions, moreover, social perspectives cannot easily be thought of as conflicting. Put together they usually do not cancel each other out, but rather offer additional questions and fuller social knowledge. . . .

Special Representation of Marginalized Groups

. . . One important way to promote greater inclusion of members of under-represented social groups is through political and associational institutions designed specifically to increase the representation of women, working-class people, racial or ethnic minorities, disadvantaged castes, and so on. . . .

Many doubt the justice or wisdom of efforts at the specific representation of social groups. Some claim that individuals should relate directly to political institutions without the mediation of groups, and that districts aggregating individual votes to obtain one representative is the only way to implement such political individualism.[4] . . . Others object to group representation because they suspect it of invidious and false essentializing. Several theorists raise objections to what is called "descriptive" or "mirror" representation.

. . . Any form or system of representation poses the problem of the one and the many, and, in my view, this problem is best addressed by active relationships of authorization and accountability between constituents and representatives. . . . The notion of representing a perspective in particular aims to respond to objections to group representation which claim that social groups cannot be defined by common interests or opinions. To the extent that what distinguishes social groups is structural relations, particularly structural relations of privilege and disadvantage, and to the extent that persons are positioned similarly in those structures, then they have similar perspective both on their own situation and on other positions in the society. . . .

Can only persons with certain ascriptive attributes represent the perspective of a structural social group? If representation consists in a relationship between a constituency and representative in which the constituency contests within itself about the issues to be represented and calls the representative to account, then a social group constituency certainly can and should ask how well a person with the presumed descriptive attributes in fact represents a social perspective. It may be possible, furthermore, though I would argue not very common, for persons without the descriptive attributes to represent a perspective. To do so, however, the person should stand in social relations that provide him or her with similar experiences and social knowledge to those with the descriptive attributes. An Asian American man who grew up in a predominantly African American neighborhood, who has many African American friends, and who now works for a community service in a neighborhood with many African Americans, for example, might be able to represent an African American perspective in many discussions, but most Asian American men could not because they are rather differently positioned.

[A] second question [is] whether we have really transcended the problem of the one representing the many by moving from representing group interest to representing group perspective. . . . For this reason a scheme of group representation would do best to *pluralize* group representation. Representation of the perspective of women in a commission or legislative body would be better done by means of a small committee of women rather than just one woman, for example. . . .

Quotas for women in party lists, or rules about a certain proportion of racial or ethnic minority group members in party conventions, are often acceptable and desirable ways of promoting the inclusion of diverse perspectives and interests. This method does not ghettoize group members, but includes them in wider party deliberations. Depending on the number of parties and the voting procedures, voters from all groups continue to have several candidate options. . . .

Legislatures are not the only governmental bodies, however, in which arguments for group representation can and should be applied. Courts, public hearings, appointed committees and commissions, and consultative processes are among the other deliberative and decision-making bodies that should be candidates for inclusive representation, even when citizens do not directly vote on their composition. . . . A more democratic representative government would have various layers and sites of elected, appointed, and volunteer bodies that discuss policy options, make policy decisions, or review policy effectiveness. . . .

Notes

1. For examples of works that make this sort of objection, see Anne Phillips, "Democracy and Difference," in *Democracy and Difference* (University Park: Pennsylvania State University Press, 1993); Chantal Mouffe, "Feminism, Citizenship and Politics," in *The Return of the Political* (London: Verso, 1993); Cathy J. Cohen, "Straight Gay Politics: The Limits of an Ethnic Model of Inclusion," in Ian Shapiro and Will Kymlicka (eds.), *Ethnicity and Group Rights*, Nomos 29 (New York: New York University Press, 1997).

2. Hanna Pitkin, *The Concept of Representation* (Berkeley: University of California Press, 1971).

3. Anne Phillips, *The Politics of Presence* (Oxford: Oxford University Press, 1995).

4. See Nancy Schwartz, *The Blue Guitar: Political Representation and Community* (Chicago: University of Chicago Press, 1988).

Chapter 24

SHOULD BLACKS REPRESENT BLACKS AND WOMEN REPRESENT WOMEN? A CONTINGENT "YES"

Jane Mansbridge

In at least four contexts, for four different functions, disadvantaged groups may want to be represented by "descriptive representatives," that is, individuals who in their own backgrounds mirror some of the more frequent experiences and outward manifestations of belonging to the group. For two of these functions—(1) adequate communication in contexts of mistrust, and (2) innovative thinking in contexts of uncrystallized, not fully articulated, interests—descriptive representation enhances the substantive representation of interests by improving the quality of deliberation. For the other two functions—(1) creating a social meaning of "ability to rule" for members of a group in historical contexts where that ability has been seriously questioned, and (2) increasing the polity's de facto legitimacy in contexts of past discrimination—descriptive representation promotes goods unrelated to substantive representation.

In the contexts of group mistrust, uncrystallized interests, a history suggesting inability to rule, and low de facto legitimacy, constitutional designers and individual voters have reason to institute policies that promote descriptive representation, even when such implementation involves some losses in the implementation of other valued ideals. As political parties, legislative committees, and voters weigh the pros and cons of descriptive representation, this analysis argues for attention to the specific historical contexts that make descriptive representation most useful.

The analysis will stress that the deliberative function of democracy requires descriptive representation far more than does the aggregative function. It is primarily when we ask how to improve deliberation—both vertically, between constituent and representative, and horizontally, among the representatives—that we discover the virtue of shared experience, which lies at the core of descriptive representation.

What Is "Descriptive" Representation?

. . . Few commentators have noticed that the word "descriptive," modifying representation, can denote not only visible characteristics, such as color of skin or gender, but also shared experiences, so that a representative with a background in farming is to that degree a descriptive representative of his or her farmer constituents. . . . "Being one of us" is assumed to promote loyalty to "our" interests.

Arguments against Descriptive Representation

Descriptive representation is not popular among normative theorists. Indeed most normative democratic theorists have rejected descriptive representation relatively summarily, often with some version of Pennock's trenchant comment, "No one would argue that morons should be represented by morons" (Pennock 1979, 314, based on Griffiths and Wollheim 1960, 190; see also Grofman 1982, 98; Pitkin [1967] 1972, chap. 4). Even among explicit advocates of group representation the ideal of descriptive representation finds little support. Will Kymlicka writes, "[T]he general idea of mirror [descriptive] representation is untenable" (1995, 139), and Iris Marion Young concurs: "Having such a relation of identity or similarity with constituents says nothing about what the representative does" (1997, 354). Empirical political scientists studying women and Black legislators have had similar negative assessments. . . .

These normative theorists and empirical researchers make an important, incontrovertible point. The primary function of representative democracy is to represent the substantive interests of the represented through both deliberation and aggregation. Descriptive representation should be judged primarily on this criterion. When nondescriptive representatives have, for various reasons, greater ability to represent the substantive interests of their constituents, this is a major argument against descriptive representation.

The Costs of a Lottery: Lesser Talent

The most frequent criticism of descriptive representation charges that descriptive representatives will be less able than others to perform the task of the substantive representation of interests: "No one would argue that morons should be represented by morons."

This criticism rests primarily on confusing two forms of descriptive representation, the "microcosmic" and the "selective" forms.[1] In "microcosmic" representation, the entire assembly is designed to form a microcosm, or representative sample, of the electorate. . . .

If microcosmic representation, achievable only by lottery or another form of representative selection, were to replace elected representative assemblies, one cost would indeed lie in the strong likelihood that choosing the members of a ruling assembly at random from the population would produce legislators with less ability, expertise, and possibly commitment to the public good than would choosing those legislators through election. . . .

Because lawmaking in large states and at the national level usually requires considerable talent and acquired skill, the costs of replacing current

elected assemblies with assemblies chosen simply by random selection from the population overwhelm the current benefits. Very few democratic theorists advocate substituting microcosmic representation for electoral representation. . . .

In the far more frequent "selective" form of descriptive representation, institutional design gives selected groups greater descriptive representation than they would achieve in existing electoral systems in order to bring the proportions of those groups in the legislature closer to their percentages in the population. Selective forms of descriptive representation are necessary, if at all, only when some form of adverse selection operates within an existing system to reduce the proportions of certain groups below what they would achieve by chance. Otherwise, one would expect all the characteristics of the population to be duplicated, more or less, in the legislature in proportion to their occurrence in the population. Selective representation should thus be conceived as compensating for the effects of some other process that interferes with an expected proportionality.

One version of the selective form of representation draws geographical district lines to encourage the election of representatives from proportionally underrepresented groups. In other versions of selective representation, parliaments and parties set aside a number of seats for members of specific descriptive groups, such as French speakers, Catholics, scheduled castes, or women. . . .

Representatives with selective descriptive characteristics need not be significantly less skilled or dedicated to the public good than representatives chosen for reasons that do not include descriptive characteristics. It is true that adding any criterion (e.g., that a representative have lived in a constituency five or more years, or be of a given gender or ethnicity) to a mix of criteria for selection will always dilute to some degree the impact of the other criteria for selection. The key question is, however, whether the reasons for the currently lower proportion of a given characteristic are functionally related to ability to perform the task of representation. . . . If the reasons for lower proportions of the characteristic are not functionally related to the task, and if the descriptive characteristic on which one is selecting is widely shared, one would expect any decrement in talent from adding a descriptive criterion to the mix of criteria for selection to be almost infinitesimally small.[2] . . . Although in microcosmic representation the costs in talent might be considerable, in selective representation those costs seem to be negligible.

The Costs of Selection: Which Groups, Why, and How Many from Each?

. . . The *deliberative* function of representative democracy aims at understanding which policies are good for the polity as whole, which policies are good for a representative's constituents, and when the interests of various groups within the polity and constituency conflict. It also aims at transforming interests and creating commonality when that commonality can be genuinely good for all. In its deliberative function, a representative body should ideally include at least one representative who can speak for every group that might provide new information, perspectives, or ongoing insights relevant to the understanding that leads to a decision. It should not, however, simply reproduce all views in the polity. The process of choosing representatives should select to some degree against those views that are useless or harmful to the polity as a whole (Mansbridge 1998).

The *aggregative* function of democracy aims at producing some form of relatively legitimate decision in the context of fundamentally conflicting interests. In its aggregative function, the representative assembly should, in moments of conflict, ideally represent the interests of every group whose interests conflict with those of others, in proportion to the numbers of the group in the population. . . .

In aggregation, interests are relatively easily represented by nondescriptive representatives. . . . On matters of pure aggregation, reelection incentives and other forms of accountability can make descriptive representation unnecessary. For aggregation alone, normative democratic theory demands only that power be exercised on behalf of particular interest bearers in proportion to their numbers in the population, not that this power be exercised by any particular mechanism.

In deliberation, perspectives are less easily represented by nondescriptive representatives.

Through reading, conversation, and living with left-handers, right-handers can learn many of the perspectives of this group that would be relevant to a deliberation. As we will see, however, in the contexts of communicative mistrust and uncrystallized interests this vicarious portrayal of the experience of others by those who have not themselves had those experiences is often not enough to promote effective deliberation—either vertically between constituents and their representatives or horizontally among the representatives. Although a representative need not have shared personally the experiences of the represented to facilitate communication and bring subtlety to a deliberation, the open-ended quality of deliberation gives communicative and informational advantages to representatives who are existentially close to the issues.[3]

Do deliberations require the participation of representatives of relevant perspectives in proportion to the incidence of those perspectives in the population? In theory, deliberation seems to require only a single representative, or a "threshold" presence, in the deliberation to contribute to the larger understanding (Kymlicka 1993, 77–78, 1995, 146–47; Mansbridge 1981; Phillips 1995, 47, 67ff.; Pitkin [1967] 1972, 84). Getting the relevant facts, insights, and perspectives into the deliberation should be what counts, not how many people advance these facts, insights, and perspectives. In practice, however, disadvantaged groups often need the full representation that proportionality allows in order to achieve several goals: deliberative synergy, critical mass, dispersion of influence, and a range of views within the group.

First, deliberation is often synergistic. More representatives usually produce more, and sometimes better, information and insight, particularly when they may need to explore among themselves new ideas that counter the prevailing wisdom. . . .

Second, representatives of disadvantaged groups may need a critical mass for their own members to become willing to enunciate minority positions. They may also need a critical mass to convince others—particularly members of dominant groups—that the perspectives or insights they are advancing are widely shared, genuinely felt, and deeply held within their own group.

Third, governing bodies usually include a variety of committees and subcommittees in whose deliberative spaces the most important features of policy are often hammered out. Having sufficient numbers of representatives to disperse into the relevant policy areas allows members of the disadvantaged group to influence decisions wherever those decisions would become better decisions by including these members' perspectives.

Finally and most important, because the content and range of any deliberation is often unpredictable, a variety of representatives is usually needed to represent the heterogeneous, varied inflections and internal oppositions that together constitute the complex and internally contested perspectives, opinions, and interests characteristic of any group. This range of views is not easily represented by only a few individuals. . . .

The demand for proportionality is accentuated by the fact that in practice almost all democratic assemblies are aggregative as well as deliberative, and achieving the full normative legitimacy of the aggregative function requires that the members of the representative body cast votes for each affected conflicting interest in proportion to the numbers of such interest bearers in the population (see Mansbridge 1981, 1996, 1998 for a fuller exposition of these ideas).

"Essentialism" as a Cost of Selection

The greatest cost in selective descriptive representation is that of strengthening tendencies toward "essentialism," that is, the assumption that members of certain groups have an essential identity that all members of that group share and of which no others can partake. . . . Insisting that others cannot adequately represent the members of a descriptive group also implies that members of that group cannot adequately represent others (Kymlicka 1993, 1995; Phillips 1992, 1995; Swain 1993; Young 1997).

This problem of essentialism haunts every group that hopes to organize politically around a facet of identity, including descriptive characteristics such as place of birth, gender, and race. Essentialism involves assuming a single or essential trait, or nature, that binds every member of a descriptive group together, giving them common

interests that, in the most extreme versions of the idea, transcend the interests that divide them. Such an assumption leads not only to refusing to recognize major lines of cleavage in a group, but also to assimilating minority or subordinate interests in those of the dominant group without even recognizing their existence (Fuss 1989; Spelman 1998; see Young 1994, 1997 for ways of conceiving of group existence with a minimum of essentialist thinking). The problem is exacerbated when the facets of identity assumed to bind the group together have biological markers, such as sexual organs or skin color, because such markers encourage seeing whatever commonalities are assumed central to the group as biological, not historical. . . .

The advocacy of descriptive representation can emphasize the worst features of essentialism. When an extreme descriptivist writes, "it is impossible for men to represent women" (Boyle 1983, 797),[4] that statement implies the corollary, that it is impossible for women to represent men. It also implies that any woman representative represents all women (and all women equally), regardless of the women's political beliefs, race, ethnicity, or other differences.

The essentializing features of descriptive representation can be mitigated by stressing the nonessentialist and contingent reasons for selecting certain groups for descriptive representation. The entire argument in this [chapter] is an argument from contingency. . . . It highlights the historical contexts in which descriptive representation is likely to advance the substantive representation of interests. That descriptive representation most closely approaches normative ideals when it reflects the inner diversity of any descriptively denominated group.

One might also approach contingency from another angle, by asking first what features of the existing electoral process have resulted in lower proportions of certain descriptive groups in the legislature than in the population—a result that one would not expect by chance and that suggests the possibility that "certain voices are being silenced or suppressed" (Phillips 1992, 88; also 1995, 53, 63). The next screening question should be whether the members of that group consider themselves able adequately to represent themselves. If the answer is yes, the third question, bearing on normative responsibility, might be whether there is any evidence that dominant groups in the society have ever intentionally made it difficult or illegal for members of that group to represent themselves. A history of strong prejudice would provide such evidence. If the answer to this third question is also yes, the group appears to be a good candidate for affirmative selective representation. If a group has been in the past excluded by law from the vote, to take an extreme example, it seems likely that the social, political, and economic processes that allowed one group in the past legally to forbid the political participation of another may well have their sequelae in the present, working through informal social, political, and economic structures rather than through the law.[5]

A formation like this points backward to contingent historical processes rather than inward to an essential nature. It also implies that when the systemic barriers to participation have been eliminated through reform and social evolution, the need for affirmative steps to ensure descriptive representation will disappear. The institution of descriptive representation itself becomes contingent.

Other Costs of Descriptive Representation

Another potential cost of selective descriptive representation, related to that of essentialism, involves the way developing institutions that encourage citizens to see themselves as members of a subgroup may erode the ties of unity across a nation, a political party, or a political movement (see, e.g., Phillips 1995, 22ff.). This serious cost has greater or lesser weight depending on the precise institutional arrangements. . . .

Yet another cost of selective descriptive representation applies specifically to a particular method for achieving this result—drawing electoral boundaries to create relatively homogeneous districts. This cost is the potential loss of influence in other districts. . . .

A final cost of selective descriptive representation lies in the possibility of reduced accountability. The descriptive characteristics of a representative can lull voters into thinking their substantive interests are being represented even when this is not the case. . . . One would expect this danger

of blind loyalty to be eased as more descriptive representatives competed for and entered the representative assembly, allowing constituents to compare more easily the virtues of one descriptive representative against another. . . .

Against these costs, one must weigh the benefits for substantive representation of enhanced deliberation through descriptive representation. These benefits, I argue, are greatest in contexts of communicative distrust and uncrystallized interests.

Contexts of Distrust: The Benefits of Enhanced Communication

The quality of the mutual communication between representative and constituent varies from group to group and era to era. Historical circumstances can interfere with adequate communication between members of one group and members of another, particularly if one group is historically dominant and the other historically subordinate. A history of dominance and subordination typically breeds inattention, even arrogance, on the part of the dominant group and distrust on the part of the subordinate group.

In conditions of impaired communication, including impairment caused by inattention and distrust, the shared experience imperfectly captured by descriptive representation facilitates vertical communication between representatives and constituents. Representatives and voters who share some version of a set of common experiences and the outward signs of having lived through those experiences can often read one another's signals relatively easily and engage in relatively accurate forms of shorthand communication. Representatives and voters who share membership in a subordinate group can also forge bonds of trust based specifically on the shared experience of subordination. . . .

In the United States, voters have many of their most vital interests represented through the "surrogate" representation of legislators elected from other districts. Advocates of particular political views who lose in one district, for example, can hope to be represented by advocates of those views elected in another district.[6] Surrogate representatives do not have to be descriptive representatives. But it is in this surrogate process that descriptive representation often plays its most useful role, allowing representatives who are themselves members of a subordinate group to circumvent the strong barriers to communication between dominant and subordinate groups. Black representatives, for example, are likely to be contacted by Blacks "throughout the region" and not just in their own districts. . . .

Contexts of Uncrystallized Interests: The Benefits of Experiential Deliberation

In certain historical moments, citizen interests on a given set of issues are relatively uncrystallized. The issues have not been on the political agenda long, candidates have not taken public positions on them, and political parties are not organized around them. . . .

When interests are uncrystallized, the best way to have one's most important substantive interests represented is often to choose a representative whose descriptive characteristics match one's own on the issues one expects to emerge. One might want to elect a representative from one's own geographical territory, class, or ethnicity. Then, as issues arise unpredictably, a voter can expect the representative to react more or less the way the voter would have done, on the basis of descriptive similarity. The original geographic representation of voters in the United States was undoubtedly intended in part to capture this form of descriptive representation.

In political systems where many issues, such as those involving economic class, are relatively crystallized, other issues, such as those involving gender, are surfacing and evolving rapidly on the political agenda. When this is the case, individuals for whom these relatively uncrystallized interests are extremely important may get their best substantive representation from a descriptive representative.[7] Here, the important communication is not vertical, between representative and constituent, but horizontal, among deliberating legislators. In this horizontal communication, a descriptive representative can draw on elements of experiences shared with constituents to explore the uncharted ramifications of newly presented issues and also to speak on those issues with a voice carrying the authority of experience.

In the United States, where party discipline is weak and representatives consequently have considerable autonomy, legislators often vote by "introspective representation," acting on the basis of what they themselves have concluded is the right policy for their constituents and the nation. When this is the case, voters exercise power not by changing the behavior of the representatives, as suggested in traditional mechanisms of accountability, but by electoral selection.[8] In this process, the voters often use descriptive characteristics, as well as party identification and indicators of character, as cues by which to predict whether a particular candidate, if elected, will represent their interests, both crystallized and uncrystallized. . . .

The accuracy of these cues, and degree to which they predict "identification" (Fenno 1978, 58–59) or "common interests" (Bianco 1994), depends on the degree to which the descriptive characteristics are in fact aligned with the interests of the majority of voters in their districts, so that representatives engaged in introspective representation will reflect the policies their constituents would choose if they had greater knowledge and time for reflection.

In introspective representation both postelection communication and traditional accountability between the representative and the constituent can be nonexistent, and the relation still fulfill democratic norms. Because this is not a traditional principal–agent relation but rather a relation only of selection, democratic norms require that in the selection process communication be open, accurate, and likely to help participants achieve a better understanding of their interests. We can also judge the relationship normatively by making a third-person estimate of the interests of the constituents and the degree to which the representative actually promotes those interests effectively in the assembly (Mansbridge 1998).

When legislators are engaged primarily in introspective representation, descriptive representation will enhance that representation most when interests are relatively uncrystallized—that is, when party identification and campaign statements provide poor clues to a representative's future actions. On the many issues relating to gender, for example, where views are changing and policies developing in a relatively ad hoc way to meet a rapidly evolving situation, descriptive representatives are, other things equal, more likely than nondescriptive representatives to act as their descriptive constituents would like them to act.

Issues of race, which are somewhat more crystallized in the United States than issues of gender, also produce moments when a descriptive representative acts in a context of relatively uncrystallized interests. In 1993, when Carol Moseley-Braun was the only Black member of the U.S. Senate, only she was galvanized into action when Senator Jesse Helms attached to one piece of legislation an unrelated amendment renewing the design patent of the United Daughters of the Confederacy—a design that featured the confederate flag. Moseley-Braun argued vehemently against the Senate's legitimating the flag by granting this patent, and succeeded in persuading enough senators to reverse themselves to kill the measure.[9]

As an African American, Moseley-Braun was undoubtedly more likely than even the most progressive White representative to notice and feel it important to condemn the use of the Confederate flag on the design patent of the United Daughters of the Confederacy. The flag issue had not previously appeared on the active political agenda of either the nation or the state of Illinois, Moseley-Braun's constituency. Moseley-Braun undoubtedly had never mentioned the issue in her election campaign. Nor could Moseley-Braun have feared reelection sanctions on this point, since without her intervention the amendment would have passed unnoticed. She did, it turns out, use the issue to consolidate her position with her Democratic constituency in the next election, but one can imagine a less dramatic issue in which this would not be the case. The most important reason for her action seems to have been the particular sensibility, created by experience, that led her to notice the Confederate flag and be offended by it. Her descriptive characteristics—going beyond skin color to her use of language and ties to her church—had earlier signaled that sensibility to her Black constituents. The visible characteristics were the outward signs of the shared experience that allowed her, as a representative, to react as most of her descriptive constituents would have liked.[10]

With respect to gender, many issues relating to sexual harassment and violence against women are politically salient but have not become sufficiently crystallized that the two main parties in the United States have developed distinctive and opposing positions in regard to them, or that candidates usually mention their positions on these issues in their campaigns. It is not surprising, then, that women legislators have usually been the ones to bring these issues to the legislative table. . . . Having more women in office unquestionably makes government policies more responsive to the interests of most women.[11] Proportional descriptive representation would undoubtedly reflect an even wider range of views among women, producing a more nuanced sensitivity to differences within that group. Reflecting internal group differences is a particularly important feature in deliberation when issues are uncrystallized and may be taking their first, and possibly defining, shape.

Disadvantaged groups also may need descriptive representation in order to get uncrystallized substantive interests represented with sufficient vigor (see Phillips 1995, 69 and passim, on the "degree of vigorous advocacy that people bring to their own concerns"). . . .

In the case of Anita Hill versus Clarence Thomas, for example, an issue involving sexual harassment (which could not have been on the agenda of the members of the U.S. House of Representatives when they ran for election) emerged in the Senate hearings on the nomination of Thomas for the Supreme Court. It was the women in the House of Representatives, where the number of women had reached a critical mass, who took decisive action. The famous photograph of five women legislators from the House of Representatives charging up the Senate steps to demand a delay in the Thomas nomination captured for many women voters the need to have representatives of their own gender in the legislative body.

Particularly on issues that are uncrystallized or that many legislators have not fully thought through, the personal quality of being oneself a member of an affected group gives a legislator a certain moral force in making an argument or asking for a favorable vote on an issue important to the group.[12]

Beyond Substantive Representation

Two other benefits of descriptive representation do not enhance substantive representation, but nevertheless deserve consideration in any discussion of the costs and benefits of descriptive representation. These benefits arise from the representative assembly's role in constructing social meaning and de facto legitimacy.

The Construction of Social Meaning

In certain historical conditions, what it means to be a member of a particular social group includes some form of "second-class citizenship." Operationally, this is almost always the case when at some point in the polity's history the group has been legally excluded from the vote. In these conditions, the ascriptive character of one's membership in that group carries the historically embedded meaning, "Persons with these characteristics do not rule," with the possible implication, "Persons with these characteristics are not able to (fit to) rule."[13]

Whenever this is the case, the presence or absence in the ruling assembly (and other ruling bodies, such as the executive and judiciary) of a proportional number of individuals carrying the group's ascriptive characteristics shapes the social meaning of those characteristics in a way that affects most bearers of those characteristics in the polity. . . .

Similarly, when descriptive characteristics signal major status differences connected with citizenship, then a low percentage of a given descriptive group in the representational body creates social meanings attached to those characteristics that affect all holders of the characteristics. Low percentages of Black and women representatives, for example, create the meaning that Blacks and women cannot rule, or are not suitable for rule. . . .

This is a historically specific and contextual dynamic. Normatively, making a claim for descriptive representation on these grounds requires historical grounding for the factual contention that the social meaning of membership in a given descriptive group incorporates a legacy of second-class citizenship. Such a claim could point, for confirmation, to a history of being legally deprived of the vote.

A major cost to this claim, in addition to the problem of essentialism discussed earlier, involves the way the very process of making a claim of historical disability to some degree undermines claims on other political tracks that members of the group have currently achieved the status of first-class citizens. As in any claim for justice based on disadvantage, signaling that disadvantage in public erodes the public presentation of the group as fully equal. This cost must be balanced against the benefit of creating new social meanings that include members of the group as truly "able to rule."

Claims like this one, based partly on the concept of reparations, do not in theory entail the cost of painting a group as disadvantaged, because claims for reparation can be and are made by political, economic, and social equals (or superiors). But claims for reparation do require both establishing a history of intentional injustice and arguing convincingly that a particular form of reparation (in this case establishing some form of selective descriptive representation) is the best way of redressing that injustice.[14]

The argument here for the creation of social meaning is an argument not for a right but for a social good. The argument is simply that if the costs are not too great, any measure is good that increases the degree to which the society as a whole sees all (or almost all) descriptive groups as equally capable of ruling.

De Facto Legitimacy

A second benefit to descriptive representation comes in the increased empirical (or sociological, or de facto) legitimacy of the polity. Seeing proportional numbers of members of their group exercising the responsibility of ruling with full status in the legislature can enhance de facto legitimacy by making citizens, and particularly members of historically underrepresented groups, feel as if they themselves were present in the deliberations (Gosnell 1948, 131, cited in Pitkin [1967] 1972, 78; also Guinier 1994, 35, 39; Kymlicka 1993, 83; Minow 1991, 286 n. 69, 291; Phillips 1995). Seeing women from the U.S. House of Representatives storming the steps of the Senate, for example, made some women feel actively represented in ways that a photograph of male legislators could never have done.

To a great degree this benefit is a consequence of previous ones. Easier communication with one's representative, awareness that one's interests are being represented with sensitivity, and knowledge that certain features of one's identity do not mark one as less able to govern all contribute to making one feel more included in the polity. This feeling of inclusion in turn makes the polity democratically more legitimate in one's eyes. Having had a voice in the making of a particular policy, even if that voice is through one's representative and even when one's views did not prevail, also makes that policy more legitimate in one's eyes.[15]

These feelings are deeply intertwined with what has often been seen as the "psychological" benefits of descriptive surrogate representation for those voters who, because of selective bias against their characteristics, are less than proportionately represented in the legislature. The need for role models, for identification, and for what Charles Taylor (1992) has called "equal dignity" and "the politics of recognition" can be assimilated under this rubric. In many historical moments, these factors may be of great importance to a particular constituency.

I stress the creation of social meaning and de facto legitimacy rather than, say, the need for role models on the part of individuals in the descriptively underrepresented group precisely because points like these have often been presented as questions of individual psychology.[16] Instead, I want to point out that the social meaning exists outside the heads of the members of the descriptive group, and that de facto legitimacy has substantive consequences. . . .

For similar reasons I do not contrast "symbolic" and "substantive" representation. In political contexts the word "symbol" often bears the unspoken modifier "mere." Moreover, symbols are often perceived as being "only" in people's heads rather than "real." Psychological needs are intangible, and it is easy incorrectly to contrast the "intangible" with the "real" (as Swain 1993, 211, points out). In most writing on this subject, the structural consequences of descriptive representation have been de-emphasized in favor of psychological ones in ways that I believe do not reflect their actual relative influence in contemporary political life.

Institutionalizing Fluid Forms of Descriptive Representation

Because there are always costs to privileging any one characteristic that enhances accurate substantive representation over others, voters and institutional designers alike must balance those benefits against the costs. And because I have argued that the benefits of descriptive representation vary greatly by context, it would be wise, in building descriptive representation into any given democratic institutional design, to make its role fluid, dynamic, and easily subject to change.

This analysis suggests that voters and the designers of representative institutions should accept some of the costs of descriptive representation in historical circumstances when (1) communication is impaired, often by distrust, (2) interests are relatively uncrystallized, (3) a group has once been considered unfit to rule, (4) de facto legitimacy is low within the group. The contextual character of this analysis suggests strongly that any institutionalization of descriptive representation is best kept fluid. Microcosmic forms of descriptive representation are best kept advisory and experimental for a good while, as they currently are. Selective forms are also best kept experimental. Permanent quotas are relatively undesirable because they are both static and highly essentializing. They assume, for example, that any woman can stand for all women, any Black for all Blacks. They do not respond well to constituents' many-sided and cross-cutting interests.

Drawing political boundaries to produce majority-minority districts is also both relatively static and essentializing. Cumulative voting in at-large districts (Guinier 1994) is far more fluid, as it allows individuals to choose whether they want to cast all their votes for a descriptive representative or divide their votes among different representatives, each of whom can represent one or another facet of the voters' interests. Such systems, however, have their own costs in party collusion to produce noncompeting candidates and the consequent voter demobilization.[17] Systems of proportional representation with party lists have well-known costs, but are still a relatively flexible way to introduce selective descriptive representation, as those lists can change easily in each election.[18] Similarly, experimental decisions by political parties to make a certain percentage of candidates descriptively representative of an underrepresented group are preferable to quotas embedded in law or constitutions. Such ad hoc arrangements can be flexible over time.

Less obtrusive, although also undoubtedly less immediately successful, are other "enabling devices," such as schools for potential candidates (Phillips 1995, 57), and reforms aimed at reducing the barriers to representation, such as those studied by the Canadian Royal Commission on Electoral Reform: "caps on nomination campaign expenses; public funding of nomination campaign expenses . . . ; the establishing of formal search committees within each party to help identify and nominate potential candidates from disadvantaged groups; and so on" (Kymlicka 1993, 62). Vouchers for day care or high-quality day care at the workplace of elected officials would reduce the barriers to political entry for parents of young children. Scholarships to law schools for members of historically disadvantaged and proportionally underrepresented groups would reduce another major barrier to entry.[19] This approach more generally aims at identifying and then reducing the specific structural barriers to formal political activity that serve to reduce the percentages in office of particular disadvantaged groups. . . .

This chapter represents a plea for moving beyond a dichotomous approach to descriptive representation. It argues that descriptive representation is not always necessary, but rather that the best approach to descriptive representation is contextual, asking when the benefits of such representation might be most likely to exceed the costs. Representation is in part a deliberative process. Recognizing this deliberative function should alert us to contexts of communication impaired by distrust and contexts of relatively uncrystallized interests. In both of these contexts, descriptive representation usually furthers the substantive representation of interests by improving the quality of deliberation. Systems of representation also have externalities, beyond the process of representation itself, in the creation of political meaning and legitimacy. Recognizing these externalities should alert us to contexts of past denigration of a group's ability to rule and contexts of low current legitimacy. In both of these contexts, descriptive rep-

resentation usually produces benefits that extend throughout the political system.

Notes

1. The term "microcosmic" comes from Birch 1993, 72; the term "selective" is my own.
2. If adding descriptive criteria in fact made a selection process dip significantly lower into the pool of potential representatives, polities could compensate for any expected descriptive decrement by reducing the negative impact of the other factors on selection (e.g., by instituting public funding for campaigns or increasing the salary of the legislators). The number of talented and dedicated individuals currently driven away from state and federal electoral politics by low salaries and the politically compromising activities of fund-raising is undoubtedly far higher than the number that would be overlooked if, say, ethnicity and gender played greater roles in the selection process.
3. Pitkin's ([1967] 1972) condemnation of descriptive representation recognized its uses in deliberation, but set up what I believe to be a false dichotomy between "talking" and "actively governing" (63, 84), as well as sometimes seeming to restrict the deliberative function to simply "giving information" (63, 81, 83, 84, 88, 90).
4. See also Phillips 1995, 52, quoting a group of Frenchwomen in 1789 ("a man, no matter how honest he may be, cannot represent a woman"), and Williams 1998, 133, quoting the Reverend Antoinette L. Brown in 1852 ("Man cannot represent woman").
5. The intent of this argument is not to restrict groups designated for selective representation to those who have been legally deprived of the vote or other rights of citizenship, but to draw normative attention to this characteristic on the grounds of past societal responsibility. Such responsibility is also involved when a form of discrimination, such as that against gays and lesbians, has run so deep that it has not been necessary legally to forbid their political participation. Historical discrimination is also usually responsible for communication impaired by distrust, a social meaning of lesser citizenship, and impaired de facto legitimacy, three of the four contexts that in the central argument in the text mandate particular concern for descriptive representation. See Phillips 1992, 1995; Kymlicka 1993, 1995; and Williams 1998 on historical and systemic disadvantage; Guinier (1994, 140) points out, however, that her argument does not rely primarily on the historic context of group disenfranchisement. Political marginalization, our concern here, need not require economic inferiority (Aminzade n.d.).
6. Surrogate representation is in many ways similar to what Burke called "virtual representation" ([1972] 1871, 293). It differs in applying to the aggregative as well as the deliberative function of democracy to will as well as wisdom, to changing preferences as well as relatively fixed and objective interests, and to negotiations among

self-interested groups as well as the good of the nation as a whole (Pitkin [1967] 1972, 169–75; see Williams 1998, 33ff., for a nuanced discussion of Burke's concept of a "description" of people). Burke therefore did not address questions of proportionality, as does my concept of surrogate representation, Weissberg's (1978) similar "collective representation," and Jackson and King's (1989) "institutional" representation. For a fuller analysis of surrogate representation, see Mansbridge 1998.

7. Two of Anne Phillips's four "key arguments" for descriptive representation turn on this issue. One is "the need to tackle those exclusions that are inherent in the party-packaging of political ideas" and the other "the importance of a politics of transformation in a opening up the full range of policy options" (1995, 25; see also 43–45, 50, 70, 151ff.). Her analysis, particularly of transformative politics, goes much further than I have the opportunity to do here. Holding other features of substantive representation equal, one might expect descriptive representatives in a field of uncrystallized interests to be most efficacious when dominant groups have kept key issues off the political agenda (see Bachrach and Baratz 1963).

8. Mansbridge 1998. Others have called this process representation by "recruitment" (Kingdon 1981, 45), "initial selection" (Bernstein 1989), or "electoral replacement" (Stimson, MacKuen, and Erikson 1995).

9. Adam Clymer, "Daughter of Slavery Hushes Senate," *New York Times*, 23 July, 1993. See also Gutmann and Thompson 1996, 135–36.

10. Her experience as an African American also helped Moseley-Braun find words to describe the issue that would convince the other senators to change their minds. See Williams 1998 on "voice."

11. Thomas (1994) summarizes the literature on gender differences among legislators and adds important data of her own. She and Mezey (1994) each point out that although on several feminist issues party affiliation predicts feminist position better than female gender, gender has its own independent effect. See also Berkman and O'Connor 1993; Skjeie 1991; Jonasdottir 1988; Strauss 1998. Representative diversity (and the critical mass of important subgroups within that diversity) in any descriptive group greatly increases the chances of diverse perspectives being represented in deliberation. For example, although there was one Black woman on the 16-member Illinois Commission on the Status of Women when it debated the Sexual Assault Act (which also changed the burden of proof in rape, requiring the alleged rapist rather than the victim to show that the victim had consented), it is not clear how deeply, if at all, the commission discussed the distinctive concerns of Black women on this issue. The differential conviction rates of African American and White men, the historical legacy of lynching, and the ongoing racism of most contemporary police forces complicate for Black women approval of any law such as this that shifts the burden of proof on consent in rape from the victim to the alleged rapist (see

Crenshaw 1991; Gilmore 1996, chap. 3; Richie 1996; Walker 1981).

12. I take this point from Representative Barney Frank (personal communication, June 1998), who as an openly gay legislator in the U.S. Congress serves as a surrogate descriptive representative for many on gay and lesbian issues.

13. The concept has a word in German: *Regierungsfähig*, "fit to rule."

14. Distinguishing between minority "nationalities" and minority "ethnic groups" within a nation-state, Kymlicka (1995) makes a convincing case on the basis of reparations for nationalities having forms of representation separate from those of the majority population. Although Kymlicka does not espouse descriptive representation for minority ethnic groups or women, a similar historically based case could be made for temporary forms of selective descriptive representation. See Williams 1998 on "memory," suggesting for selective descriptive representation only the two criteria of contemporary inequality and a history of discrimination. Using only these criteria would generate as candidates for selective representation Asians, Latinos, 18- to 21-year-olds, and the propertyless, among other groups.

15. Heilig and Mundt (1984) found that although moving from at-large to single-member district systems in the 1970s increased the number of Mexican American and Black members on city councils, the fiscal constraints of the cities were so great that even achieving a majority of the group on the council brought few results that greatly affected the citizens (see also Karnig and Welch 1980). At the same time, however, they found that council members from low-income districts were far more likely than at-large representatives to adopt an "ombudsman" role, helping constituents with personal problems and government services. Whatever the cause, the result seemed to be greater satisfaction among constituents after moving to a single-member district system (Heilig and Mundt 1984, 85, 152).

16. On role models see, e.g., the interview with Representative Craig Washington in Swain 1993, 193. Preston (1978, 198) and particularly Cole (1976, 221–23) stress what I call social meaning.

17. The state of Illinois practiced cumulative voting until the process was eliminated in 1982 in a cost-cutting effort that reduced the size of the assembly. The cumulative voting system produced greater proportional representation of Democrats and Republicans in the state legislature but not a great degree of voter choice, because for strategic reasons the two major parties often ran altogether only three candidates for the three seats available in each district (Sawyer and MacRae 1962; Adams 1996).

18. See Zimmerman 1992, 1994 for the positive and negative features of cumulative voting and different forms of proportional representation.

19. Directing attention to the eligible pool, Darcy, Welch, and Clark (1987, 101) indicate that the percentage of

women in state legislatures rose from 1970 to 1984 in tandem with the percentage of women in the law.

References

Adams, Greg D. 1996. "Legislative Effects of Single-Member vs. Multi-Member Districts." *American Journal of Political Science* 40(1): 129–44.

Aminzade, Ronald. N.d. "Racial Formation, Citizenship, and Africanization." *Social Science History*, Forthcoming.

Bachrach, Peter, and Morton Baratz. 1963. "Decisions and Non-Decisions: An Analytical Framework." *American Political Science Review* 57(3): 632–42.

Berkman, Michael B., and Robert E. O'Connor. 1993. "Do Women Legislators Matter?" *American Politics Quarterly* 21(1): 102–24.

Bernstein, Robert A. 1989. *Elections, Representation, and Congressional Voting Behavior*. Englewood Cliffs, NJ: Prentice Hall.

Bianco, William T. 1994. *Trust: Representatives and Constituents*. Ann Arbor: University of Michigan Press.

Birch, A. H. 1993. *The Concepts and Theories of Modern Democracy*. London: Routledge.

Boyle, Christine. 1983. "Home Rule for Women: Power Sharing between Men and Women." *Dalhousie Law Journal* 7(3): 790–809.

Burke, Edmund. [1972] 1871. "Letter to Sir Hercules Langriche." In *The Works of the Right Honorable Edmund Burke*, vol. 4. Boston. Little, Brown.

Cole, Leonard A. 1976. *Blacks in Power: A Comparative Study of Black and White Officials*. Princeton: Princeton University Press.

Crenshaw, Kimberlé. 1991. "'Mapping the Margins': Intersectionality, Identity Politics, and Violence against Women." *Stanford Law Review* 43(6): 1241–99.

Darcy, Robert, Susan Welch, and Janet Clark. 1987. *Women, Elections, and Representation*. New York: Longman.

Fenno, Richard F., Jr. 1978. *House Members in Their Districts*. Boston: Little, Brown.

Fuss, Diana, 1989. *Essentially Speaking: Feminism, Nature, and Difference*. New York: Routledge.

Gilmore, Glenda Elizabeth. 1996. *Gender and Jim Crow*. Chapel Hill: University of North Carolina Press.

Gosnell, Harold Foote. 1948. *Democracy: The Threshold of Freedom*. New York: Ronald Press.

Griffiths, A. Phillips, and Richard Wollheim. 1960. "How Can One Person Represent Another?" *Aristotelian Society*. Suppl. 34: 182–208.

Grofman, Bernard. 1982. "Should Representatives Be Typical of Their Constituents?" In *Representation and Redistricting Issues*, ed. Bernard Grofman et al. Lexington, MA: D. C. Heath.

Guinier, Lani. 1994. *The Tyranny of the Majority: Fundamental Fairness in Representative Democracy*. New York: Free Press.

Gutmann, Amy, and Dennis Thompson. 1996. *Democracy and Disagreement*. Cambridge: Harvard University Press.

Heilig, Peggy, and Robert J. Mundt. 1984. *Your Voice at City Hall: The Politics, Procedures, and Policies of District Representation*. Albany: State University of New York Press.

Jackson, John E., and David C. King. 1989. "Public Goods, Private Interests, and Representation." *American Political Science Review* 83(4): 1143–64.

Jonasdottir, Anna G. 1988. "On the Concept of Interest: Women's Interests and the Limitations of Interest Theory." In *The Political Interests of Gender*, ed. K. B. Jones and A. G. Jonasdottir. Beverly Hills: Sage.

Karnig, Albert K., and Susan Welch. 1980. *Black Representation and Urban Policy*. Chicago: University of Chicago Press.

Kingdon, John W. 1981. *Congressmen's Voting Decisions*. New York: Harper and Row.

Kymlicka, Will. 1993. "Group Representation in Canadian Politics." In *Equity and Community: The Charter, Interest Advocacy, and Representation*, ed. F. L. Siedle. Montreal: Institute for Research on Public Policy.

Kymlicka, Will. 1995. *Multicultural Citizenship*. Oxford: Oxford University Press.

Mansbridge, Jane. 1981. "Living with Conflict: Representation in the Theory of Adversary Democracy." *Ethics* 91(1): 466–76.

Mansbridge, Jane. 1996. "Using Power/Fighting Power. The Polity." In *Democracy and Difference: Contesting the Boundaries of the Political*, ed. Seyla Benhabib. Princeton: Princeton University Press.

Mansbridge, Jane. 1998. "The Many Faces of Representation." Working Paper, John F. Kennedy School of Government, Harvard University.

Mezey, Susan Gluck. 1994. "Increasing the Number of Women in Office: Does It Matter?" In *The Year of the Woman: Myths and Realities*, ed. Elizabeth Adell Cook, Sue Thomas, and Clyde Wilcox. Boulder, CO: Westview Press.

Minow, Martha L. 1991. "From Class Actions to Miss Saigon." *Cleveland State Law Review* 39(3): 269–300.

Pennock, J. Roland. 1979. *Democratic Political Theory*. Princeton: Princeton University Press.

Phillips, Anne. 1992. "Democracy and Difference." *Political Quarterly* 63(1): 79–90.

Phillips, Anne. 1995. *The Politics of Presence*. Oxford: Oxford University Press.

Pitkin, Hanna Fenichel. [1967] 1972. *The Concept of Representation*. Berkeley: University of California Press.

Preston, Michael. 1978. "Black Elected Officials and Public Policy: Symbolic and Substantive Representation." *Policy Studies Journal* 7(2): 196–201.

Richie, Beth. 1996. *Compelled to Crime: The Gender Entrapment of Battered Black Women*. New York: Routledge.

Sawyer, Jack, and Duncan MacRae. 1962. "Game Theory and Cumulative Voting in Illinois: 1902–1954." *American Political Science Review* 56: 936–46.

Skjeie, hege. 1991. "The Rhetoric of Difference: On Women's Inclusion into Political Elites." *Politics and Society* 19(2): 233–63.

Spelman, Elizabeth. 1998. *Inessential Woman: Problems of Exclusion in Feminist Thought*. Boston: Beacon Press.

Stimson, James A., Michael B. MacKuen, and Robert S. Erikson. 1995. "Dynamic Representation." *American Political Science Review* 89(3): 543–65.

Strauss, Julie Etta. 1998. "Women in Congress: The Difference They Make." Ph.D. dissertation, Northwestern University.

Swain, Carol M. 1993. *Black Faces, Black Interests: The Representation of African Americans in Congress.* Cambridge: Harvard University Press.

Taylor, Charles. 1992. *Multiculturalism and the Politics of Recognition.* Princeton: Princeton University Press.

Thomas, Sue. 1994. *How Women Legislate.* New York: Oxford University Press.

Walker, Alice. 1981. "Advancing Luna—and Ida B. Wells." In *You Can't Keep a Good Woman Down.* New York: Harcourt Brace Jovanovich.

Weissberg, Robert. 1978. "Collective vs. Dyadic Representation in Congress." *American Political Science Review* 72(2): 535–47.

Williams, Melissa S. 1998. *Voice, Trust, and Memory: Marginalized Groups and the Failings of Liberal Representation.* Princeton: Princeton University Press.

Young, Iris Marion. 1994. "Gender as Seriality: Thinking about Women as a Social Collective." *Signs* 19(3): 713–38.

Young, Iris Marion. 1997, "Deferring Group Representation." In *Ethnicity and Group Rights: NOMOS XXXIX*, ed. Ian Shapiro and Will Kymlicka. New York: New York University Press.

Zimmerman, Joseph F. 1992. "Fair Representation for Women and Minorities." In *United States Electoral Systems: Their Impact on Women and Minorities*, ed. Wilma Rule and Joseph F. Zimmerman. Westport, CT: Greenwood Press.

Zimmerman, Joseph F. 1994. "Alternative Voting Systems for Representative Democracy." *P.S.: Political Science and Politics* 24(4): 674–77.

Chapter 25

PREFERABLE DESCRIPTIVE REPRESENTATIVES: WILL JUST ANY WOMAN, BLACK, OR LATINO DO?

Suzanne Dovi

Democratic political institutions are often evaluated by the gender, ethnicity, and race of elected representatives (e.g., Guinier 1994; Paolino 1995). Implicit in these evaluations is the assumption that democratic political institutions that lack any representatives from historically disadvantaged groups are unjust. Moreover, these evaluations often assume that an increase in the number of representatives from historically disadvantaged groups can contribute to the substantive representation of those groups (e.g., Thomas 1991). . . . This method of evaluating democratic institutions often assumes that the more women, Blacks, and Latinos, the better for democratic institutions.[1]

These assumptions justify the political practice of setting aside certain political and institutional positions for members of historically disadvantaged groups. These positions are specifically designed to increase the number of representatives from historically disadvantaged groups—that is, the number of what I call "descriptive representatives." Contemporary political theorists have directly and indirectly supported these assumptions by offering several explanations for why political representatives for a historically disadvantaged group should come from that group (e.g., Mansbridge 1999; Phillips 1995; Sapiro 1981). . . . Although the reasons they advance differ significantly, these theorists sound a common theme: To be fully democratic, a society that has denied full political membership to certain groups must be strongly committed to including those groups

in its political life. Such a commitment, at least in many circumstances, requires society to take active steps to increase the number of descriptive representatives. On these grounds, these theorists endorse various institutional reforms such as party list quotas, caucuses, racial districting, and schemes for proportional representation. But these theorists have said remarkably little about the criteria that should guide democratic citizens in their choice of descriptive representatives.[2] The emphasis of this literature so far has been on establishing the *need for the presence* of some descriptive representatives, not on investigating *criteria for identifying preferable* descriptive representatives.

Which members of historically disadvantaged groups are preferable representatives for those groups? My primary aim is to argue for the need for criteria that will help answer this question. I take the value of having descriptive representatives in public positions as a given.[3] . . . I propose one criterion for identifying preferable descriptive representatives: Preferable descriptive representatives have strong *mutual* relationships with *dispossessed* subgroups. . . .

Justifying the Silence about Criteria

Silence about the criteria for evaluating descriptive representatives is not accidental. Theorists of group representation have offered two kinds of arguments to justify their silence. . . .

According to *the autonomy argument*, members of historically disadvantaged groups should decide for themselves who is a preferable descriptive representative.... According to this line of thinking, respecting the autonomy of historically disadvantaged groups requires theorists to refrain from advancing criteria for evaluating descriptive representatives....

The first version of the autonomy argument asserts that any proposed criterion for evaluating descriptive representatives presupposes that a historically disadvantaged group has an essential nature.... To explain why some members are less suitable descriptive representatives is to question the authenticity of those members' identity. Such explanations possess an implicit charge that "she isn't really a woman" or "he isn't really black."....

The second version of the autonomy argument emphasizes the autonomy of descriptive representatives.... To suppose that there is a fixed set of criteria by which descriptive representatives should be judged is to fail to appreciate how the *autonomy* afforded to representatives justifies the politics of presence. According to this second formulation, it would be misguided to provide a laundry list of "good policies" that a female representative should support and to insist that preferable female representatives can vote only in ways consistent with that list. After all, male representatives could also vote according to a laundry list. The more one knows how a descriptive representative should act, the less it is necessary to have a descriptive representative....

The second kind of argument for remaining silent about the criteria for judging descriptive representatives is *the contingency argument*. According to this argument, it is impossible to articulate the criteria that should be used to evaluate descriptive representatives because context matters.... For Mansbridge (1999), descriptive representatives are needed when marginalized groups distrust relatively more privileged citizens and when marginalized groups possess political preferences that have not been fully formed. She emphasizes that descriptive representatives are necessary only under certain conditions—that is, when descriptive representatives perform certain functions in certain contexts. Mansbridge's discussion provides some important insights into evaluating when descriptive representation is necessary. Implicitly, her work offers some general criteria for evaluating descriptive representatives—that is, by their ability to satisfy these different functions. However, her emphasis on identifying the contingent conditions under which descriptive representation is preferable to nondescriptive representation makes the actual choice of descriptive representatives secondary, if not irrelevant.

... Theorists of descriptive representation avoid a tough question: Who is a preferable descriptive representative? Answering this question is not easy, because it requires privileging the interests, values, and perspectives of certain members of historically disadvantaged groups over those of other members. Answers to this question can therefore have the effect of downplaying, if not excluding, certain interests, values, and perspectives. For this reason, answers to the question of who is a preferable descriptive representative are more likely to be disputed than answers to the question, "why have descriptive representatives?"

The Need for Criteria

... To articulate criteria for evaluating descriptive representatives runs the risk that those criteria can be used in unanticipated and possibly harmful ways. Some fear that articulating such criteria might also unduly influence members of historically disadvantaged groups.

Such concerns are understandable but ultimately unpersuasive. After all, to articulate such criteria is not necessarily to assume that all members of a historically disadvantaged group have some essential identity. In fact, the very real and politically relevant differences among members of historically marginalized groups point to the desperate need for a theoretical discussion of criteria. There is a difference between articulating particular policies that a descriptive representative must endorse to count as a legitimate descriptive representative and articulating general guidelines for identifying preferable descriptive representatives.... To maintain that a descriptive representative should pay special attention to overlooked interests does not require that she possess a particular view about those interests.[4] ... However, to say that descriptive representatives can legitimately interpret their group's interests in multiple ways is not to say that anything goes. Descriptive representatives who denounce their group affiliations or who deny that they have any particular obligation to their group would fail to achieve the ends for which descriptive representation was introduced (cf. Phillips's four arguments). Descriptive representatives who claim to represent only the common good might be desirable representatives for other reasons; however, they do not satisfy Phillips's "overlooked interests" argument.

. . . To pose criteria for judging descriptive representatives is not the same as imposing those criteria on members of historically disadvantaged groups. Obviously, to impose criteria on such groups, or on democratic citizens more generally, is wrongheaded. It is crucial according to my view that members of historically disadvantaged groups retain the ability to choose to adopt any proposed criterion.[5]

. . . Theorists can offer criteria for choosing among descriptive representatives and still maintain that members of historically disadvantaged groups must determine for themselves whether a specific criterion is appropriate at any particular moment. This leads to the second argument for remaining silent: the role of contingencies in evaluations of descriptive representatives.

Context undeniably does matter. . . . For instance, who is a preferable descriptive representative might depend on whose interests, opinions, and perspectives are currently being stigmatized and marginalized by existing political norms and institutional processes. . . . Which descriptive representatives are preferable might also depend on the reasons that descriptive representation is necessary, e.g., to increase the trust groups have in democratic institutions or to include overlooked interests on the policy agenda.

Espousing criteria is not the same as requiring that certain criteria be applied in all circumstances. Like most theorists of descriptive representation, I share the suspicion of a cookie-cutter approach to evaluating descriptive representatives. . . .

My final argument for articulating criteria for evaluating descriptive representatives is based on my understanding of a particular role that political theory can and should play. Increasingly, the need for political theory to inform contemporary political controversies has been recognized (Isaac 1998, chap. 7). . . . The suspicion is that simply having descriptive representatives is not sufficient to meet the requirements of a democratic commitment to the concerns of historically disadvantaged groups.

Descriptive representation can fail to revitalize democratic institutions. It can also undermine democratic institutions if the ruling elites of historically disadvantaged groups use their institutional positions to control those groups instead of mobilizing those groups or bringing their overlooked interests onto the policy agenda (e.g., Cohen 1999). For these reasons, it is important to clarify the criteria for judging descriptive representatives. Evaluations of democratic institutions need to go beyond merely quantitative considerations—that is, the number of descriptive representatives. Evaluations of democratic institutions need to consider the extent to which preferable descriptive representatives are present. The criteria for identifying preferable descriptive representatives need to identify principled reasons for preferring some descriptive representative to others that are in line with the arguments for group representation. By failing to discuss criteria for assessing descriptive representatives, this theoretical literature ignores certain persistent debates about descriptive representation in contemporary politics. It also disregards the possible dangers and disappointments of a politics of presence to democratic politics.

The Criterion for Evaluating Descriptive Representatives

My criterion for evaluating descriptive representatives is a general one: Democratic citizens should consider the degree to which a descriptive representative has mutual relationships with dispossessed subgroups as relevant to identifying preferable descriptive representatives. Preferable descriptive representatives will have strong *mutual* relationships with *dispossessed subgroups*. This criterion is composed of two aspects. First, preferable descriptive representatives should possess a particular kind of relationship (mutual), and second, they should have this kind of relationship *with* certain subgroups of historically disadvantaged groups (dispossessed).

Mutual Relationships

. . . What is distinctive about my criterion is its specification that representatives and members of historically disadvantaged groups must *mutually* recognize each other. Mutuality requires an inter-active relationship between representatives and citizens. Mutual relationships require a historically disadvantaged group to recognize its descriptive representatives in a particular way *as well as* a descriptive representative to recognize that group in a particular way. Such reciprocal recognition is necessary for descriptive representatives and their groups to coordinate consciously chosen political activities. Descriptive representatives without mutual relationships could be "representative" in the sense that their behavior responds to the policy preferences of their group, but such responsiveness is not sufficient to make the form of representation democratic.

Descriptive representatives with mutual relations would improve democratic representation by enabling historically disadvantaged groups to influence the political decision-making process. In doing so, historically disadvantaged groups act in concert with their descriptive representatives. . . .

In proposing this criterion, I am advocating a new approach to assessing the performance of descriptive representatives. . . . Assessing descriptive representatives solely by the way they cast their votes can lead to the conclusion that it does not matter who represents historically disadvantaged groups (Schwarz and Shaw 1976; Swain 1993). This approach ignores other reasons for having descriptive representatives, e.g., introducing overlooked interests or building trust in the political institutions. . . .

Assessments of descriptive representatives need to consider whether these representatives reach out to (or distance themselves from) historically disadvantaged groups. Preferable descriptive representatives facilitate social networks. Formal as well as informal ties provide the channels through which democratic relationships could work and thereby the means to revitalize democratic institutions. I introduce mutual relationships into discussions of descriptive representation because these discussions need to reflect the fact that what determines policy is not only what political actors do but also whom they know.

It is important to emphasize a consideration implicit in my claim that preferable descriptive representatives possess mutual relationships: The commitment to democratic representation requires that democratic citizens should not be apathetic. Preferable descriptive representatives will inspire their group to act in concert with them. Although it is possible that a descriptive representative could adequately "represent" the concerns of the apathetic insofar as the representative takes positions that reflect the interests or preferences of apathetic citizens, the descriptive representative's actions would not be democratic to the extent that apathetic citizens do not care about the activities of that representative. My criterion prefers descriptive representatives who can and do mobilize a historically disadvantaged group, encouraging the active engagement of that group. Requiring preferable descriptive representatives to have mutual relations is very demanding and therefore likely to support robust democracies.

To possess mutual relations, descriptive representatives must recognize and be recognized by members of a historically disadvantaged group in two ways. First, they must recognize each other as belonging to a historically disadvantaged group, and second, they must recognize each other as having a common understanding of the proper aims of a descriptive representative of the group. To recognize each other mutually in these two ways is to possess a mutual relationship.

Preferable descriptive representatives are those who recognize and are recognized by members of their historically disadvantaged group as being "one of us." In particular, they have a reciprocated sense of having a fate linked with that of other members of their group. . . . The notion of linked fate reflects the fact that a person's range of choices—that is, his or her perceived opportunities and goals—is both subjective and social. . . .

To have a sense of linked fate with a historically disadvantaged group partially entails having a substantive conception of that group that is relevantly similar to those held by other members of that group. Group membership can be based on shared visible characteristics, e.g., color of skin, or on shared experiences (Mansbridge 1999). The substantive content of group membership can vary. Some individuals can belong to more than one group and therefore experience conflicting allegiances to different groups. Members can also possess conflicting views on their group's politics. . . .

But preferable descriptive representatives for a given group share an understanding of the group's boundaries with that group. Descriptive representatives who possess a narrower (and more exclusive) understanding of those boundaries are unable, or at least less likely, to satisfy the arguments that justify group representation. For this reason, an African-American descriptive representative who denies that gay and lesbian blacks are members of the group (or who excludes conservatives, IV drug users, Muslims, or other religious African Americans) would be less preferable than one who includes those members in his or her understanding of the group.[6] After all, justifications for group representation tend to emphasize the extent to which descriptive representatives include overlooked interests, build trust, and foster deliberation. Descriptive representatives who overlook certain members of the group or who deem certain members "inauthentic" are less likely to fulfill these functions. Representatives who possess broader understandings of the group are more likely to overlap with the varied understandings of the represented and therefore satisfy the reasons for having an institutionalized voice. . . . Preferable descriptive representatives possess shared understandings of group membership that recognize salient differences of subgroups. . . .

To understand the importance of mutual recognition of belonging to the group for evaluating a descriptive representative, consider the following case. It is possible to imagine an African-American representative who grew up in a primarily white neighborhood, attended predominantly white private schools, has a white spouse, and has shown no demonstrable interest in the problems of other African Americans. In fact, such a representative could thrive politically by publicly distancing herself from the African-American community. The point of this example is not to question whether this woman is an "authentic" African American. I believe that she is.[7] Rather, it is to question whether such a representative could satisfy sufficiently the reasons that theorists for a politics of presence gave for increasing the number of descriptive representatives. After all, such a descriptive representative lacks the relationships necessary to satisfy these reasons. She might individually face certain obstacles and experience forms of discrimination because of her identity; however, she lacks the relationships with African Americans that could enable her to achieve

mutual recognition with them. The extent to which she disavows her relationships to African Americans indicates the extent to which she is less likely to possess mutual relationships with them. African Americans would be more likely to distrust her. She would also be less likely to advance overlooked interests of the African-American community and to mobilize that community. Who perceives that representative as "belonging" to the group and whom a representative claims to act on the behalf of are important considerations for evaluating the qualifications of descriptive representatives.

Individuals in mutual relationships not only recognize each other as belonging to the same group, but also recognize that they share an understanding of the proper aims of their representatives. To have shared aims is to possess a similar vision for the future direction of politics— one whose goal is the improvement of the social, economic, and political status of particular historically disadvantaged groups. My understanding of aims has two components: policy preferences and values.[8] A descriptive representative could disagree with members of a historically disadvantaged group about either component, yet still share aims.[9] Some members might experience a descriptive representative advocating certain public policies as a litmus test for shared aims with that representative, e.g., their position on abortion or affirmative action, while others see shared aims as resulting from a particular combination of policy preferences and values. Individuals can and will have different conceptions of what is necessary for having shared aims. Nevertheless, a descriptive representative who did not share either component with a historically disadvantaged group does not share aims with that group.

In this way, my criterion recognizes that people who share similar political values can justifiably disagree about the desirability of certain public policies. It also recognizes that individuals with different political values can agree about certain public policies. Consequently, I do not always want people who agree with my political values or with my policy preferences. I do want someone who shares my aims. The notion of shared aims recognizes the importance of the interaction between policy preferences and values for selecting preferable descriptive representatives. For this reason, shared aims must be measured in degrees: Descriptive representatives share aims with a historically disadvantaged group to greater or less degrees.

. . . Descriptive representatives are preferable to the degree that their actions are perceived by members of a historically disadvantaged group as improving their linked fate. My notion of aims is meant to capture the fact that members of historically disadvantaged groups, despite having different policy preferences and values, can still share a political vision aimed at relieving the plight of their communities. Thus, the actions of descriptive representatives are not irrelevant to who should be considered a preferable descriptive representative. Preferable descriptive representatives recognize themselves, and are recognized by members of a historically disadvantaged group, as sharing the aims of that group.

The importance of shared aims is most readily apparent when one lacks a representative who share one's aims. One is less likely to accept differences of opinions with those who have different aims than with those who share one's aims. . . . Both a sense of belonging to a group and shared aims are important for mutual relations, for individuals whose fates are linked can have different aims. . . .

Dispossessed Subgroups

. . . I use the term dispossessed . . . to refer to groups that are unjustly excluded from and/or stigmatized by the political process and consequently lack the political and economic resources necessary for effective representation. Often dispossessed subgroups suffer oppression not only as members of their overarching group but also as members of the subgroup. They are therefore members of historically disadvantaged groups, yet they face *further* political obstacles—what Cathy Cohen (1999, 70) describes as secondary marginalization—that is, the ways in which members of marginalized groups construct and police group identity to regular behavior, attitudes, and the public image of those groups. Perhaps it is in virtue of the combination of the forms of oppression that they lack the financial, time, and social resources necessary for political participation. Class, sexuality, drug use, geographic location, relationships to welfare, criminal records, and religion are all possible markers of dispossessed subgroups.

This second aspect of my criterion offers a way to return to the commitment found in the literature on group representation to those groups that *have been and continue to be* marginalized within the existing political system. A commitment to group representation entails a commitment to those whose interests have been overlooked, who have been and continue to be unjustly excluded from political participation, and whose presence could revitalize democratic institutions. Group representation therefore requires being vigilant about groups that lack a political voice. Preferable descriptive representatives would be those who seek out and establish mutual relationships with dispossessed subgroups.

To demonstrate the importance of mutual relationships with dispossessed subgroups, I focus on the ways in which class inequalities can constrain effective representation.[10] Such inequalities can undermine democratic citizens' political resources. My discussion of dispossessed subgroups is by no means limited to the experiences of poor subgroups of historically disadvantaged groups. Other subgroups that lack the political and economic resources for effective representation would also count as dispossessed. I use poor subgroups to illustrate my understanding of dispossessed subgroups for two reasons. First, this example highlights the necessity of mutual relationships for improving the substantive representation of historically disadvantaged groups. Second, this example demonstrates the interactions among different forms of oppression.

. . . Theorists of self-representation do not adequately acknowledge problems with poor subgroups of historically disadvantaged groups being represented by economically more privileged members of their group. Some explicitly deny that class should be incorporated into political solutions for presence. For example, Phillips argues that the politics solutions for presence should be treated as distinct from issues concerning class. Phillips offers several reasons for this distinction, e.g., the difficulty in defining class. However, Phillips (1995, 170–78) admits that these reasons for treating class separately are "insincere," stating that "when it comes down to it, the real reason for my silence on class is simply that it does not lend itself to the same kind of solutions."[11] This admission implies that considerations of class cannot be adequately incorporated into the types of institutional reforms necessary for increasing the number of descriptive representatives. Interestingly, this admission contradicts her arguments for a politics of presence. . . .

Others minimize the significance of socioeconomic factors by choosing examples that focus almost exclusively on only one form of oppression. Often these examples explore the ways that groups are formally excluded from political participation. For instance, Williams focuses on the structural obstacles faced by U.S. women and African Americans in their efforts to gain full political standing. She cites economic inequalities as indicators that institutional reforms are necessary, yet her proposed institutional reforms are aimed exclusively at formal political exclusions.

Williams's emphasis on formal political exclusions reflects the tendency among proponents of group representation to notice the oppressive nature of socioeconomic status without incorporating this observation into their arguments for group representation or into their proposed institutional reforms. . . .

William's analysis of self-representation would have benefited from an example in which the dynamic of multiple forms of oppression was considered. . . . Theorists of group representation tend to give examples in which the dynamics of race, class, and gender are prominent only a cursory treatment, if any treatment at all. They also tend to downplay how political norms and practices within the democratic institutions, e.g., recruitment practices, can marginalize certain subgroups. Consequently, their understandings of group representation ignore that inclusion in politics can promote instrumental political bargaining at the expense of transformative politics (Dryzek 1996; Reed 1999).

More specifically, theorists of group representation do not adequately address the particular barriers to effective representation experienced by poor subgroups of historically disadvantaged groups. . . .

Theorists who emphasize electoral reforms that increase the number of descriptive representatives also tend to ignore the kinds of resources necessary for poor subgroups to advance their political agendas. Traditional means for getting policy preferences onto the political agenda—studies, public relations campaigns, lobbying efforts—advantage citizens who are financially better off and resource-rich. Being able to stay informed

about political issues, let alone to participate in politics, requires time and economic resources. Elected officials increasingly spend their time fund-raising. Citizens with economic resources can buy access, but those without economic resources tend to have relatively less access. Consequently, those with economic resources do not necessarily need as much of an institutionalized voice as those who lack those resources. . . .

One should not assume that class "perspectives" are necessarily better represented if ethnicity, race, and gender are better represented in legislatures. After all, research has documented the economic disparities within various racial groups (e.g., Dawson 1994, chap. 2; Hochschild 1995; Wilson 1980). Such disparities are increasing. Although they continue as a group to be economically and socially worse off than whites, African Americans are increasingly economically divided in ways that affect housing, jobs, death rates, and the likelihood of being a victim of crime. . . .

My criterion for evaluating descriptive representation should not be interpreted as arguing that the self-representation of women or of African Americans or other minorities is secondary to the representation of the poor. Such an argument would merely mimic the common claim that identity politics is divisive while class is more unifying (Gitlin 1995). Nor am I repeating claims that class is more politically salient than race. . . . I maintain that who is a preferable descriptive representative depends on how different forms of oppression intersect; for example, how race can work in conjunction with class is relevant to determining who is a preferable descriptive representative. Democratic citizens need to evaluate descriptive representatives in ways that attend to how political institutions marginalize certain groups. Young was right that institutional reforms aimed at increasing the number of descriptive representatives can entrench certain interests, e.g., by privileging heterosexual Latinos at the expense of gay and lesbian Latinos. Moreover, evaluations of descriptive representatives are particularly messy when segments of a historically disadvantaged group reject a descriptive representative. For Young, the diversity within historically disadvantaged groups can be so great that schemes of group representation will necessarily result in the suppression of difference.

However, recognition of the diversity within historically disadvantaged groups does not change the fact that some groups are chronically underrepresented. In other words, it does not change the fact that some groups need institutional reforms to enhance their substantive representation. For the institutional reforms to work successfully, democratic citizens need to select descriptive representatives in ways that are sensitive to how institutional norms and practices unjustly marginalize dispossessed subgroups. My criterion offers one way to take into account the dynamic among different forms of oppression: Who is a preferable descriptive representative depends partially on whose interests, opinions, and perspectives are being excluded. Recall that a descriptive representative's shared aims and sense of belonging to a group provide some substantive guidance for what that representative should be doing. In this way, my criterion depends on context. Those selecting descriptive representatives (for appointments, committees, or public office) need to attend to the mutual relationships that descriptive representatives possess with dispossessed subgroups. They should not assume that "just any woman will do" or that "just any black will do." Institutional reforms aimed at increasing the number of descriptive representatives are more likely to revitalize democratic institutions if citizens assess descriptive representatives using my criterion.

For this reason, I submit that when one has a choice between two descriptive representatives, one who has strong mutual relationships to dispossessed subgroups and another who does not, one should (*ceteris paribus*) prefer the former. I have so far avoided the question of what to do when choosing among descriptive representatives who possess mutual relationships to different dispossessed subgroups. Such moments do not have generalizable or easy answers. In such circumstances, citizens face tough choices that require exercising their own political judgment. To recognize that the dispossessed too can have diverse interests is to acknowledge that my criterion might not settle the question of who is a preferable descriptive representative. However, the refusal to examine the criteria being used for selecting descriptive representatives can reinforce the norms and practices that unjustly exclude dispossessed subgroups. Public deliberations about the proper criteria could therefore help refine those decisions and prevent such exclusions. . . .

Notes

1. For an opposing view, see Cameron, Epstein, and O'Halloran 1996.
2. I use "democratic citizens" to refer to all citizens— that is, to both citizens who are members of historically disadvantaged groups and citizens who possess more privileged social locations.
3. The need for institutional reforms aimed at increasing the number of descriptive representatives for a certain historically disadvantaged group may be temporary. These reforms may be dropped, if and when the society has advanced to the point where a historically disadvantaged group is no longer politically marginalized.
4. Like representatives generally, good descriptive representatives should sometimes act as trustees and at other times act as delegates. The standards for good representation cannot be linked strictly to the policy preferences of the represented. Pitkin (1967, 166) expressed this point in the following way: "Neither 'follow their wishes' nor 'ignore their wishes' will do; the decision must depend on why they disagree . . . but the standard by which he [the representative] will be judged as a representative is whether he has promoted the objective interest of those he represents. Within the framework of his basic obligation there is room for a wide variety of alternatives." My criterion for assessing preferable descriptive representatives does not assume one particular understanding of the objective interests of historically marginalized groups.
5. A description of the conditions necessary for promoting this ability is clearly beyond the scope of this paper.
6. As can be seen, descriptive representatives with mutual relations do not necessarily possess "progressive" or "liberal" policy agendas.
7. To articulate reasons for preferring some descriptive representatives to others is not the same as questioning the authenticity of a descriptive representative's membership. A full discussion of the relationship between preferability and legitimacy is clearly beyond the scope of this chapter. Here I purposely limit my discussion to the desirability of particular descriptive representatives not their legitimacy. I recognize that all members of a historically disadvantaged group are in some sense legitimate descriptive representatives of that group. In other words, Reverend Jesse Jackson, Marian Wright Edelman, Shelby Steele, and Allan Keyes are all legitimate descriptive representatives for African Americans; however, who is a preferable descriptive representative for African Americans depends on who possesses strong mutual relationships with dispossessed subgroups. Such subgroups can include conservative and/or poor subgroups.
8. For a discussion of the difference between measuring political values and policy preferences, see Stoker 2001 and Rasiniski 2001.

9. To explicate the idea of an aim, it is necessary to differentiate an aim from what Young (2000, 134) calls the "modes of representation"—that is, three aspects of one's identity that need to be represented. Those three aspects are interests (policy preferences), opinions (values, priorities, and principles), and perspectives (starting points of conversations). While Williams (1998, 171) argues that interests and perspectives are more inextricably tied, Young stresses how these different aspects of a person's identity can conflict. For Young, the process of democratic representation relies on all three modes.

Young's analysis of the dynamic processes of representation, though, can divert attention from the proper standards for evaluating particular representatives. Individual representatives are less likely to satisfy all of these different modes of representation than are the processes of representation. I know of no representative who shares all of my interests, opinions, and perspectives. These modes of representation are too narrow to provide much guidance for identifying preferable descriptive representatives. For this reason, I argue that members of historically disadvantaged groups should seek descriptive representatives who share their aims.

10. I explicitly reject an understanding of class that is based on categories and classification schemes; rather, I am concerned with how class relations are produced and maintained through political institutions. Phillips argues that the category of class is substantively different from conceptions of race and gender. For example, one loses one's class when one becomes an elected official. For an alternative understanding of class, see Acker (2000, 197), who defines class as "social relations constructed through active practices, not as categories or classifications of people according to socioeconomic characteristics or occupational status."

11. For her full discussion of class, see Phillips 1995, chap. 7.

References

Acker, Joan. 2000. "Revisiting Class: Thinking from Gender, Race, and Organizations." *Social Politics* (Summer): 192–213.

Cameron, Charles, David Epstein, and Sharyn O'Halloran. 1996. "Do Majority-Minority Districts Maximize Substantive Black Representation in Congress?" *American Political Science Review* 90 (December): 794–812.

Cohen, Cathy. 1999. *The Boundaries of Blackness: AIDS and the Breakdown of Black Politics*. Chicago: University of Chicago.

Dawson, Michael C. 1994. *Behind the Mule: Race and Class in African-American Politics*. Princeton, NJ: Princeton University.

Dryzek, John. 1996. "Political Inclusion and the Dynamics of Democratization." *American Political Science Review* 90 (September): 475–87.

Gitlin, Todd. 1995. *Twilight of Common Dreams*. New York: Metropolitan Books.

Guinier, Lani. 1994. *The Tyranny of the Majority: Fundamental Fairness in Representative Democracy*. New York: Free Press.

Hochschild, Jennifer. 1995. *Facing Up to the American Dream: Race, Class, and the Soul of the Nation*. Princeton, NJ: Princeton University.

Isaac, Jeff. 1998. *Democracy in Dark Times*. Ithaca, NY: Cornell University.

Mansbridge, Jane. 1999. "Should Blacks Represent Blacks and Women Represent Women? A Contingent 'Yes.'" *Journal of Politics* 61 (August): 628–57.

Paolino, Phillip. 1995. "Group-Salient Issues and Group Representation: Support for Women Candidates in the 1992 Senate Elections." *American Journal of Political Science* 39 (May): 294–313.

Phillips, Anne. 1995. *Politics of Presence*. New York: Clarendon.

Pitkin, Hanna Fenichel. 1967. *The Concept of Representation*. Berkeley: University of California.

Rasiniski, Kenneth. 2001. "Commentary: The Study of Values," In *Citizens and Politics: Perspectives from Political Psychology*, ed. James Kuklinski. New York: Cambridge University.

Reed, Aldoph. 1999. *Stirrings of the Jug*. Minneapolis: University of Minnesota.

Sapiro, Virginia. 1981. "When Are Interests Interesting?" *American Political Science Review* 75 (September): 701–21.

Schwarz, John E., and L. Earl Shaw. 1976. *The United States Congress in Comparative Perspective*. New York: Holt. Rinehart and Winston.

Stoker, Laura 2001. "Political Value Judgments." In *Citizens and Politics: Perspectives from Political Psychology*, ed. James Kuklinski. New York: Cambridge University.

Swain, Carol M. 1993. *Black Faces, Black Interests: The Representation of African Americans in Congress*. Cambridge, MA: Harvard University.

Thomas, Sue. 1991. "The Impact of Women on State Legislative Policies." *Journal of Politics* 53 (November): 958–76.

Williams, Melissa. 1998. *Voice, Trust, and Memory: Marginalized Groups and the Failings of Liberal Representation*. Princeton, NJ: Princeton University.

Wilson, William Julius. 1980. *The Declining Significance of Race: Blacks and Changing American Institutions*. 2nd ed. Chicago: University of Chicago.

Young, Iris Marion. 2000. *Inclusion and Democracy*. Oxford: Oxford University.

Chapter 26

FROM A SMALL TO A LARGE MINORITY: WOMEN IN SCANDINAVIAN POLITICS

Drude Dahlerup

Does the Size of the Minority Count?

"Don't expect us to make much difference as long as we are only a few women in politics. It takes a critical mass of women to make fundamental changes in politics." Today, arguments like this can be heard among women politicians. This analytic term has been included in ordinary language before the concept of a critical mass has been properly developed in scientific analysis. . . .

Women in minority positions are the focus here. Recent literature has discussed what happens to women that, few in number, enter male dominated areas like politics and traditional male professions and crafts. Tokenism, invisibility, marginality, harassment, the Queen Bee Syndrome, exclusion from the informal network are some of the important problems discussed in the literature of women as a minority.

The term "critical mass" implies that the size of the minority is crucial, and that to women in politics a fundamental change may happen long before they reach the 50 (or maybe 60) percent of the seats.

The concept of a critical mass is borrowed from nuclear physics, where it refers to the quantity needed to start a chain reaction, an irreversible take-off into a new situation or process (Rendel 1978).

In physics, the concept of a critical mass is applied to a process that takes place in isolated entities or rooms. In social sciences, however, every entity we look at is normally characterized by some degree of interaction with its surround-ings. Therefore the analogy has its limitations. Yet, this chapter makes the point that we should not neglect that politics is also a workplace, an organization with its own rules, norms, and culture.

The idea of critical mass is most often applied to situations when women constitute *less* than 30 percent, in this way explaining why the entrance of women into politics has not made more difference—yet!

In this chapter, however, I discuss the relevance of the concept, based on the experiences of women in Scandinavian politics. . . .

The question is this: What is supposed to change when moving from a small to a large minority? Is it possible to identify a self-increasing process, which will start when the minority reaches a certain size? Are we in Scandinavia witnessing a critical mass at work? . . .

Some Methodological Remarks

. . . Several studies, using multivariate correlations analysis, have with different results tried—among many other variables—to measure the effect of the relative number of women in various local councils on the expenditures on for instance day care and care for the elderly. For the discussion of what will change when the minority grows, however, more qualitative approaches are needed.

. . . The empirical data used in this chapter on women in politics in the five Nordic countries comes from several sources: Lengthy interviews with 28 Nordic women politicians at the national and local level in a structured, nonrepresentative sample (Dahlerup 1985); results from a questionnaire sent to all national political parties in the five Nordic countries (Dahlerup: The POP Survey 1984) and results from a questionnaire sent to all women's organizations and equality committees within the same political parties at national level, provided such organizations existed in the party (Dahlerup: The WOC Survey 1984); information about what strategies women in the five countries have used to improve women's political representation (Dahlerup 1988); data on women's political representation in Haavio-Mannila et al. (1985). The surveys of local councillors made by Hellevik & Skard (1985) and Wallin et al. (1981) have provided useful information. . . .

Women as a "Minority Group"

Back in 1951, Helen Mayer Hacker wrote her famous article "Women as a Minority Group" (Hacker 1951). . . . Hacker's basic idea is that although they constitute 50 percent or more of the population, women—like minority groups—suffer from discrimination and unequal treatment. Women also display many of the psychological characteristics ascribed to minorities, such as self-hatred, feelings of inferiority, denying a feeling of group identification, and yet developing a separate subculture within the dominant culture. . . . Women who make it in the male world, on the other hand, will try to dissociate themselves from other women. This is a theory of women's "minority status" in society in general.

When Women Are Actually in the Minority

Although interlinked, the theory of women as a minority group should not be confused with theories of the problems women encounter when numerically in the minority, e.g., as politicians, engineers, mechanics, executives, or journalists.

The theory about women in actual minority positions looks at women *within* an organization. This is also the focus of this chapter.

The connection between the minority group status of women and women in actual minority positions derives from the fact that many of the problems women experience as minorities within

organizations are related to the "minority" status of women in society at large.

. . . Rosabeth Moss Kanter concludes that the problems of these women derive from women's minority position in the organization, not from the fact that they are women. Other minorities, such as blacks, will encounter the same problems (Kanter 1977).

My counterargument will be that the "minority" status of women or blacks outside the organizations interacts with their status inside the organization, thus creating greater problems than white males encounter when in a minority position.

Some minorities do fine inside an organization if they, directly or indirectly, get support and resources from outside. The successful careers of male nurses illustrate that "majority group status" in society at large might balance or even counterbalance an actual minority position inside the organization. Needless to say, women do not get power just because they are in the majority. . . .

Problems Women Encounter as a Minority in Male-Dominated Organizations

The following problems are compiled from the literature on women entering male-dominated professions and workplaces. . . . The question here is whether women in politics meet the same problems, and maybe only when in a small minority.

Consequence of women being in the minority in an organization (most of them shared with others in a minority position)

- high visibility
- become token, e.g., symbols of the entire sex (group), symbols of what women can do, stand-ins for all women
- role conflicts, e.g., too feminine or too masculine
- lack of allies in the organization
- exclusion from informal network
- lack of knowledge of the informal power structure and the recruitment process, lack of personal power
- higher dropout rate
- lower rate of promotion
- lower efficiency

- feel uncomfortable in the dominant culture of the organization
- over-accommodation ×
- sexual harassment ×
- lack of legitimate authority ×
- stereotyping ×
- no considerations for family obligations by the organization ×
- exposed to doubled standard ×

Problems marked with an × are considered *combined* consequences of the minority position and women's status in a patriarchal society in general. . . .

. . . Women politicians seem to be caught between two conflicting expectations:

(1) Women politicians must prove that they are just like (just as able as) male politicians, who in general have longer seniority and whose gender occupied the political arena long before women were allowed to participate.
(2) Women politicians must prove that it makes a difference when more women are elected. This second demand comes from the women's organizations and the feminist movement, who critically ask why it does not make more difference that there are now more women in politics. . . .

The Relative Numbers Count

In her study of women in a big American corporation, Rosabeth Moss Kanter makes the point that the size of the minority is significant. It is the proportion of social categories, here women and men, that makes an important difference. Moss Kanter identifies four types of groups on the basis of different proportional representation of socially different people, be it women/men or blacks/whites.

The *uniform group or organization* has only one significant social group and its culture dominates the organization.

The *skewed group* (the minority being no more than max. 15 percent) is controlled by the numerically dominant group and its culture. The minority become tokens; that is, they are considered symbols of their entire group, especially if they fumble. "They are made aware of their differences from the numerical dominants,

but then must often pretend that the differences do not exist, or have no implications," Moss Kanter writes (p. 239). Tokens are alone, yet the dynamics of interaction around them "create a pressure for them to seek advantage by dissociating themselves from other of their category and hence, to remain alone" (p. 239). This implies that tokens are unable to from alliances with each other.

Relaxing situations, e.g., after-work drinks and sports events, are often most stressful for tokens, who then lack the protection of defined positions and structured interaction. In short, according to Moss Kanter, organizational, social, and personal ambivalence surrounds people in token situations.

In the *tilted group* ("with ratios of perhaps 65:35," Kanter writes; from her figure, however, from 15 to about 40), the minority is becoming strong enough to begin to influence the culture of the group, and alliances between minority group members become a possibility. The "tokens" have changed into a "minority."

In the *balanced group* (about 60:40 and down to 50:50), culture and interaction reflect this balance, Moss Kanter argues. And for the individuals in such a balanced group the outcome will depend more on other structural and personal factors than their type (gender, race).

The basis of this reasoning is, of course, that there is a difference in culture and behavior between the minority and the majority group. The argument here is that alongside the similarities between women and men, also marked differences exist—not necessarily from birth, but from their different social positions and their different social experiences.

Moss Kanter does not talk about a "critical mass," but simply of the gradual change when the minority grows larger in an organization. The discussion of a critical mass adds to this the question of a possible point of acceleration in the influence of the minority when reaching a certain size, e.g., 30 percent. . . .

What Will Change with More Women in Politics?

. . . What might change if the political representation of women increases? What kind of changes are we looking for? Here follows a list of aspects that seem to be important in this respect:

1. Changes in the reaction to women politicians.
2. Changes in the performance and efficiency of the women politicians.
3. Changes in the social climate of political life (the political culture).
4. Changes in the political discourse.
5. Changes of policy (the political decisions).
6. Increase in the power of women (the empowerment of women). . . .

Changes in the Reaction to Woman Politicians

. . . It is not possible to conclude that the removal of the open resistance against women politicians derives solely from their increased numbers today. We are witnessing a general change in attitudes among both men and women toward women in public roles. However, the presence of women politicians in great numbers does make it seem rather hopeless to try to remove women from the public sphere today. So numbers do count.

Stereotyping is another well-known problem. . . . Following the growing number of women in politics, stereotyping decreases, because so many different types of women now occupy the political arena.

The removal of the open resistance against women in politics does not imply that women today have the same opportunities as men in politics. The fact that women are in the minority indicates the existence of barriers for women in politics.

Do women politicians experience discrimination, e.g., unfair treatment on account of gender? In my interviews with politicians I got four types of answers:

a. "There is no discrimination of women any more, rather the contrary," some women politicians said.
b. "Women are definitely discriminated against but personally I have not experienced it," said another group.
c. "Women are not discriminated against," a third group told me, but later in the interview the same women related many unpleasant episodes that certainly seemed like discrimination.

d. "Yes," a fourth group answered and told rather bitter stories of resistance, sexism, and male chauvinism—of how they had to fight to become accepted. . . .

In conclusion: changes have taken place in the perception of women as politicians by the voters. And the open resistance to women politicians by voters and male colleagues in the political workplace has almost disappeared. Less open kinds of discrimination, differential treatment, and "techniques of dominance" (Aas 1980) still exist, however.

It is suggested here that the increased number of women as politicians has had an impact, although within the framework of a general change in attitudes toward women in public roles. There has also been a growing resistance by the women politicians themselves to discrimination of women. However, it is not possible to conclude that these changes follow from any fixed number of women, e.g., 30 percent.

In this process of change, the example of just a few successful women in top positions, e.g., as prime minister or president, may have contributed substantially to the change in the perception of women as politicians. In such cases it is not the numbers that count, but the performance of a few outstanding women as role models.

Changes in the Performance and Efficiency of Women Politicians

. . . According to Rosabeth Moss Kanter's study, the "failure rate" or turnover of women in a minority position in the corporation was considerably higher than that of their male colleagues. Kanter suggests that the dropout rate will decrease when the size of the minority increases.

The media in the Nordic countries often carry stories about women who quit politics because they are overworked or do not like the atmosphere in the political institutions. But what are the facts?

A quick look at the women in parliament reveals that during the interwar period, most of the few women MPs did occupy their seats for a very long period and did not seem to have had a higher dropout rate than the men. . . .

Why should the dropout rate fall because the proportion of women increases? One answer could be that the role conflicts of women politicians diminish and that women begin to influence the political culture and hence begin to feel more at home in politics.

However, more women in politics does not in itself diminish the family obligations of women and the conflict between the need of the family and the political work. . . .

According to these studies, women politicians feel less satisfied with their job than their male colleagues, but nevertheless they stay on with almost the same frequency. So even if they constitute 20 to 30 percent today, women politicians have not obtained what one could call equal opportunity of carrying out their work as politicians.

Change in Political Culture

. . . What will change according to the women's organizations:

- The tone will be softer in politics.
- The meetings will be arranged with more consideration to family obligations—fewer late meetings, fewer meetings between 4 and 7 in the afternoon, no more meetings in restaurants!
- Meetings will be less formal and less ceremonious.
- Shorter speeches, less formal language, more to the point. . . .

Most interesting is that several women's organizations write that the women politicians not only will but already have changed the political workplace. . . .

The individual woman in an organization dominated by men is often faced with a dilemma. Either she lives up to the norms of how women behave, and keeps her female style, with the consequence that often she is not really accepted as a colleague. Or she may to some extent adapt to the style of the men, and consequently the public will call her a "man-woman"! . . .

Even if women politicians as a minority have been forced to and have to some extent wanted to adapt to the prevailing political culture, I will argue that the presence of women in the assemblies in itself makes some change. We know now that the entrance of just one woman into an all-male group (and vice versa) changes the discussion and behavior of that group. We all behave differently in front of a woman or a man. . . . I will argue that an increasing number of women politicians in itself changes some of the social conventions of politics as a workplace, because most of these women, not all of them, bring into the political institutions traits of women's culture as it manifests itself today, e.g., taking care of newcomers, consideration for the private problems of others, less tough style of debating, and so forth.

The higher the proportion of women in politics, the more social conventions will change, although again it is not possible to identity a special turning point, a critical mass. But numbers do count, event if the politicians themselves and the public are not aware of it.

But political culture is more than the social conventions of politics. The high level of conflict in politics seems to bother many female politicians ("politics is a football game to male politicians!"), but this is one of the many aspects of the political culture that women politicians do not seem to have been able to change. While changes in social conventions may happen without so many considerations, it takes a deliberate effort to change the more fundamental aspects of the political culture. Since politics is not physics, we should look for *critical acts, not for a critical mass.* . . .

Changes in the Political Discourse

. . . The political discourse is the language of politics, and the language and meaning attached to the different political issues. This includes also the discussion of what is considered political, and what is suppressed from the political debate by tradition or direct exclusion (Dahlerup 1982). . . .

Today, women's position has entered the political discourse. . . . Even if women politicians do not agree politically on many issues, an effect of a growing number of women in politics could be that the way to talk about women's position and the priority given to such issues changes. Again, we cannot isolate the effect of the growing number of women politicians from the effect of what happens outside the formal political arena. What we can see is that the issues of women's position in society have been placed on the formal political agenda by women politicians. . . .

Change in Policy

. . . Does making a difference mean that all women should form a coalition across party lines? The women MPs truly dislike this idea, because in Europe they are all elected on different party platforms. Or should women within each party make their voices heard and form coalitions with other women within the party?

Secondly, what ideas should these women bring forward? Values representing women's traditional culture? Or modern feminist ideas? Or ideas representing the points of view of different groups of women, e.g., by bringing the views of the unskilled women workers into the working-class parties, the views of the farmers' wives into the farmers' parties, or by expressing the different voices of socialist and liberal women? . . .

. . . The crucial point is whether women politicians develop some common ideas they want to fight for. Also here we must turn the question of a critical mass into a question of critical acts by the women politicians. In the Nordic countries women politicians have conducted critical acts on selected issues. These are described in the following.

Change in Women's Power

. . . Does the increase in women's political representation accelerate as recent electoral results seem to suggest? Will more women in the assemblies lead to a relative increase in women's share of the political leadership? . . .

. . . Although it is very difficult to isolate the effect of the growth in women's political representation from the general social development, certain changes may without much hesitation be connected with the increase in women's political representation, that is, with the move from a small to a large minority:

- The stereotyping of women diminishes without being removed totally.
- New role models of women in public life are created.
- The social conventions are somewhat changed, even if the main feature of the political culture remains untouched.

- The open resistance against women politicians is removed—now it seems hopeless to bring women back to the house.
- Still fewer voter express negative attitudes to being represented by a woman.

. . . Only on one point, namely, changes in the social climate, does it seem relevant to talk about a kind of "automatic" change when the minority grows large.

Maybe we should replace the concept of a *critical mass* with the new concept of a *critical act*, better suited to the study of human behavior. A critical act is one which will change the position of the minority considerably and lead to further changes.

Most significant is *the willingness and ability of the minority to mobilize the resources of the organization or institution* to improve the situation for themselves and the whole minority group. For women in politics this constitutes critical acts of empowerment. Here are some recent examples of critical acts by women in Scandinavian politics.

a. When women politicians recruit other women. . . .
b. Quotas for women. . . .
c. New legislation and new institutions. . . .

References

Dahlerup, D. 1982. "Overcoming the Barriers: An Approach to the Study of How Women's Issues are Kept from the Political Agenda," in Stiehm. J. H. ed. *Women's View of the Political World of Men*. New York: Transnational.

Dahlerup, D. 1984. *The POP Survey*.

Dahlerup, D. 1984. *The WOC Survey*.

Dahlerup, D. 1985. *Blomster & Spark. Samtaler med kvindelige politikere i Norden*. Nordisk Ministerrad: Nord-serien.

Dahlerup, D. 1988. *Vi hur pentel lange nok. Handbog i kvinderepresentation*. Nordisk Ministerrad: Nord serien.

Haavio-Mannila, E. et al. 1985. *Unfinished Democracy. Women in Nordic Politics*. Oxford: Pergamon Press.

Hacker, H. M. 1951. "Women as a Minority Group." *Social Forces* 30, 60–69.

Hellevik, O. and Skard. T. 1985. *Norske Kommunestyrer— plass for kvinner?* Oslo: Universitetsforlaget.

Kanter, R. M. 1977. *Men and Women of the Corporation*. New York: Basic Books.

Rendel, M. 1978. *Women as Political Actors. Legal Status and Feminist issues*. Paper, ECPR Workshop on Women as Political Actors. Grenoble.

Wallin, G. et al. 1981. *Kommunalpolitikerna*. Stockholm: Kommunaldepartementet.

Chapter 27

BEYOND BODIES:
INSTITUTIONAL SOURCES OF
REPRESENTATION FOR WOMEN IN
DEMOCRATIC POLICYMAKING

S. Laurel Weldon

Introduction

The literature on representation for marginalized groups has tended to focus on the question of whether women should represent women and blacks should represent blacks. But the idea that individuals can represent groups through their persons or behavior is based on a problematic understanding of the relationship between individual experience and group perspective. I propose that group perspective is a *collective* product of social groups, developed through intragroup interaction. This suggests that institutional structures and social movements, not just individuals, can be more or less representative of marginalized groups. I apply this argument in an examination of the impact of women's representation on policies to address violence against women in 36 democratic countries in 1994. Using OLS regression analysis, I find that women's policy agencies (such as women's commissions or women's bureaus) and women's movements provide more effective avenues of expression for women: in combination, they give women a stronger voice in the policy-making process than does the presence of women in the legislature. Thus, studies of representation for marginalized groups would do well to consider institutional changes and increased political mobilization as potential sources of political representation. The point is not that bodies provide *no* representation, but that bodies

are extremely limited as an avenue of *substantive* representation and that *multiple* sources of representation should be considered and compared. The contributions of and interactions between modes of representation can then be more effectively evaluated. . . .

The Limits of Individuals as Spokespersons for Marginalized Groups

Political theorists have argued that historically marginalized groups have a distinctive perspective that is unlikely to be articulated effectively in contexts from which members of those groups are absent. This perspective derives from shared experiences and/or social position, and it is manifest in narratives that members develop collectively. It often differs from or conflicts with the perspectives of dominant groups. Representation for marginalized groups should reflect group diversity and should not assume a false homogeneity of interest or identity. Substantive representation requires processes through which marginalized groups authorize and hold accountable those who speak for them. Finally, substantive representation requires that the group's voice or perspective is articulated and heard in policy processes (Mansbridge 1999; Phillips 1995; Williams 1998; Young 1997). The weakness in these arguments is the link between the personal experience of individuals and their knowledge of the group perspective. . . .

The assumption that a group perspective resides complete in any individual from the group implies that including individual members of the group is sufficient to represent the group perspective. Epistemologically, any individual has the knowledge to articulate a group's distinctive voice. This conclusion conflicts with the recognition of within-group diversity that these theorists explicitly recognize (Mansbridge 1999, 637–39; Williams 1998, 293). If she is a white, straight, middle-class mother, she cannot speak for African American women, or poor women, or lesbian women *on the basis of her own experience* any more than men can speak for women merely on the basis of theirs. Moreover, marginalized group perspectives are not transparent to *individual* members of the group. Group perspective is a *collective* phenomenon. . . .

Individual Experience, Group Perspective and Representation

. . . Group perspective is related to group members' individual experiences, but not in a direct, transparent way. . . . The distinctive voice of marginalized groups flows from group organization and mobilization; it is a product of the interaction among members of a social group (Weldon 2002). Only a small part of this group perspective is reflected in the experience of any particular individual. The group perspective is created when individual members of the group interact with other members of the group to define their priorities.

Group perspective can be thought of as a puzzle of which each member of the group has a piece. The more pieces of the puzzle, the better picture we have. When additional pieces are very similar to existing pieces (the same color or texture) we learn little about other areas or features of the puzzle. The greater the diversity in pieces, the better idea we have about the different areas and parts of the puzzle. Moreover, when members of the group come together, they can compare their puzzle pieces, and each person gains a greater understanding of the larger puzzle to which she or he holds a piece after seeing the puzzle pieces of others. Thus, the process of putting together the puzzle pieces is interactive rather than simply aggregative. One's puzzle piece likely gives one more information after interaction with others than before, but there is a point of diminishing returns: the last pieces are not as valuable as the first few.

It may seem as if this analogy suggests that interaction among women will produce agreement on the meaning or implications of the picture. But merely identifying similar obstacles or issues does not suggest that women will experience or interpret these phenomena in the same way. . . . Sharing a perspective on women's social position does not suggest agreement on the meaning of that position or the political dynamics that produce it.

Even when women have conflicting interests, the issues that divide them are strikingly similar. For example, middle-class and working-class women have conflicting interests in relation to the issue of wages for child care. The former would benefit from lower wages for child care while the latter would benefit from higher wages for child care. But in both cases, it is *women* who have responsibility for child care, and it is *women* for whom the issue has the most serious consequences. The important thing is to note that *all* of these women confront the issue of the relationship between motherhood and work. What they share is not a list of policy proposals, but more like a list of "women's issues."

. . . A group perspective is not as specific as a policy position or recommendation: It is more like an agenda of topics for discussion or list of problem areas (Weldon 2002). Because social perspectives are developed through interaction among the members of a social group, no individual member *on her own* has a full understanding of the conditions that confront the group. . . . Individual members of the group cannot legitimately claim to speak for the group without having participated in such interaction because they lack the epistemological bases (as well as the normative bases) for doing so.

Of course, interaction among women often involves conflict, and subordinated subsets of women often have difficulty getting their issues recognized as issues of importance by more privileged women. But debate among women makes these divisions *themselves* the topic of discussion, particularly when marginalized subsets of women can organize as such. . . .

. . . This view of group perspective . . . suggests that there is no reason to assume that the greater bodily inclusion of members of marginalized groups, in itself, should *significantly* increase their substantive representation. Small improvements can be expected, but significantly improving substantive representation for groups requires that representatives be able to articulate the *group* perspective. The individual alone cannot effectively articulate this perspective.[1]

. . . Mechanisms for the articulation of group perspectives must attend to both the interactive nature of such perspectives and the requirements of accountability and authorization.[2]

Institutional Sources of Representation

. . . Women's policy agencies are one way of creating state institutions that at least partially reflect women's perspective. A women's policy machinery can focus on issues of concern to women in their entirety: one need not segment problems confronting women (such as violence) into their health aspects, criminal justice aspects, and so on in order to address them (Weldon 2002). Stetson (1995) argues that those agencies that had centralized, cross-sectoral approaches to promoting gender equality were the most effective (288). These agencies must be set up to coordinate women's policies in an authoritative manner, having the power to direct policy making across a number of departments. This suggests that a subdepartmental desk in a low-ranking ministry is unlikely to be an effective mechanism for representing women in policy deliberations. Similarly, an agency with few resources will be unable to carry out the monitoring and analysis required. This suggests that a women's policy machinery must have a degree of independence, some of its own resources, and positional authority in order to be consistently effective in representing women.

The representativeness of the perspective articulated by women's policy agencies can be improved if the represented have the opportunity to comment on and critique the agency's proposals. Women's bureau consultations with women's movement organizations and activists can improve agency proposals. . . .

Where access is based on informal channels, it usually depends on good relations between women's movement activists and the individual bureaucrats. If consultation with women's groups is a formal part of the policy agency, then access is likely to be more uniform across policy areas and over time. It may be more difficult for new administrations (who may be hostile to women's groups) to shut women's organizations out of the policymaking process when formal, regularized channels for consultation exist and are part of the normal operation of government.

However, improving institutional capacity is not the same as providing the political will to address a problem. . . . In addition, providing mechanisms by which women's movements can be consulted will not be of much use if there is no one with whom to consult. This suggests that political support from external social movements is necessary to provide women's bureaus both the political pressure and input that is necessary to capitalize on improved institutional capacity. *Thus, when women's policy machineries have positional authority and adequate resources, they can improve substantive representation for women by providing a mechanism by which women's distinctive perspective can be articulated, and by providing some mechanism of authorization or accountability for women (through consultations with women's organizations). But this impact depends upon the presence of a women's movement, and we should expect little in the way of direct effects.*

Women's Movements as Sources of Political Representation

Women's movements, as mechanisms for the articulation of women's perspective, provide another important but generally unexplored avenue of representation (Dobrowolsky 1998). This is not to suggest that women's movements are a perfect incarnation of "women's voice." Women's movement articulations can only ever be partial articulations of women's perspectives because some subgroups of women are always dominated or excluded. Still, because women's movement activities provide an arena where women interact as women to define their priorities, women's movements are likely to come closer to articulating women's perspective than a disparate, unorganized group of women in the legislature.

However, it is not just the existence, but also the *autonomy* of women's groups that is important for their success in influencing policy (Busch 1992; Elman 1996). An autonomous women's movement is a form of women's mobilization that is devoted to promoting women's status and well-being independently of political parties and other associations that do not make the status of women their main concern. . . .

. . . If the women's movement is entirely contained in the state, the ability to criticize government policy may be curtailed. Autonomous groups can challenge the existing order of priorities by drawing attention to issues that are not on the agenda. *Thus, autonomous women's movements can improve the representation of women in the policy process.*

Interactions between Sources of Representation

Distinguishing multiple sources of representation makes it possible to conceptualize interactions between these different sources, and to theorize their combined impact on democratic political processes. Women's policy agencies provide an important avenue of representation for women, but this is only likely to have an effect on the policy process in the context of an autonomous women's movement. Strong, autonomous women's movements improve the institutional capabilities of government in addressing women's issues. This magnifies women's voice inside government. When the women's movement is strong, the women's policy machinery has more influence with other government departments. Bureaucrats inside the women's policy machinery seeking to articulate women's concerns can point to public pressure from the women's movement. Thus, a strong, autonomous women's movement improves the representative function performed by a women's policy agency.

Conversely, women's policy agencies can strengthen women's movements. By providing financial support for organizing and independent research, women's policy machineries provide additional resources to women's organizations. In addition, by providing research support and opportunities for input on policy development, women's policy machineries can assist women's movement activists in publicly articulating women's perspective. *Thus, strong, autonomous women's*

movements and effective women's policy agencies reinforce one another in improving women's representation. This effect is interactive: Each factor magnifies the effect of the other.

Women's Representation and Policies on Violence against Women

. . . In this section of this chapter. I examine the impact of different sources of political representation for women on policies to address violence against women. . . .

Government Responsiveness to Violence against Women

Violence against women takes a number of forms. This study focuses on the categories of sexual assault of women by men and battering of intimate female partners by males. Action on violence is an important indicator that a women's perspective is influencing policymaking, since it suggests that government is responding to the articulation of an issue of importance to women. Despite the many differences among the countries considered, similar features of the problem and the existing policy structure make it possible to identify a common set of needed actions to address violence against women. A cross-national data set developed by Weldon (2002) includes data on seven different aspects of government response to violence against women:[3]

1. Has there been any legal reform dealing with domestic violence?
2. Has there been any legal reform dealing with sexual assault?
3. Is there any national government funding for shelters for victims of domestic violence?
4. Is there any national government funding for rape crisis centers?
5. Are there any government-sponsored training programs for service providers?
6. Are there any government-sponsored public education initiatives?
7. Is there a central agency for coordinating national policies on violence?

Asking how many of these types of policy action a government undertakes provides a good measure of government responsiveness: A government that addresses more areas is enacting a broader, more multifaceted response. Although these seven types of policy action are important for different reasons, all seven policy areas are important for addressing violence against women.[4] The seven policy areas are weighted equally: The indicator simply sums the scores (1 for each area in which policy action occurs, 0 for a lack of action) across the seven areas. This variable therefore measures the *scope* of government response, that is, the amount or breadth of government activity, rather than the particular substantive focus or quality of the individual initiatives (Powell 1982; Putnam 1993).[5] Further, note that this indicator does not measure which governments enact the policies that result in the greatest reduction of violence. Indeed, some of the policy measures considered here are aimed at raising awareness or serving victims, rather than at directly reducing the overall incidence of violence.

The data set includes these seven aspects of national government response to violence against women for all stable democracies. The focus is on national government response because in general, action by the central government, even if it is only providing funding to local areas, is a key symbolic indicator that the political community is seriously addressing a problem. . . .

These data on government response are based on a variety of primary and secondary sources. . . . This analysis is for the year 1994.

Women's Movements and Political Representation

. . . The vast majority of nations in this study had active women's movements by 1994 (Weldon 2002).[6] Women's movements can be coded as *autonomous* if they have an organizational base outside political parties, unions, and other political institutions. . . .

In addition to gauging the autonomy of women's movements, we need some sense of whether they are strong or weak. . . . Such strength is indicated by the size and number of protest activities, the degree of support expressed for feminists in opinion polls, the degree of support for women's organizations, the diversity and membership of women's organizations, the proliferation and diversity of women's cultural institutions (such as

women's festivals, newspapers, concerts, and so on), and so on. Given what we know about democratic policymaking, it seems likely that strong women's movements will influence policy outcomes more than weak ones, but strong movements do not *always* influence policy outcomes.[7]

. . . Movements are coded as strong if they are described by expert observers as strong, influential, powerful, as mobilizing widespread public support, and the like. Comparative and country-specific accounts of women's movements explicitly assess the strength of women's movements over time and/or relative to other countries, relying on multiple data sources. . . . Where the movement is *both* strong and autonomous, the country is coded 1; otherwise it is coded 0.[8]

Women's Bureaus as a Form of Political Representation for Women

. . . We would expect women's bureaus to improve the political representation of women when they have:

1. formalized channels of access for women's organizations, and
2. the independence and resources needed to formulate and implement aspects of a women's agenda.

If the women's policy agencies in the 36 stable democracies in this study are categorized according to these criteria, only 8 of the 36 agencies actually meet these criteria (the agencies in Australia, Canada, Costa Rica, The Netherlands, Belgium, Venezuela, Portugal, and Germany). Countries are coded a 1 on this variable if they meet both conditions, and 0 if they do not.[9]

The Interaction between Women's Movements and Political Institutions

As argued above, such a women's policy machinery does not, on its own, guarantee any government response to violence against women. Rather, it is the interaction of the apparatus with a strong, autonomous women's movement that results in better representation for women in democratic policy processes. Where such women's movements interact with effective policy machineries, we should see greater responsiveness to violence against women. This interactive effect can be captured by using a multiplicative term (**strong and autonomous women's movement * effective women's policy machinery**) in the regression analysis.

Representation by Women Legislators

. . . I have argued that, in itself, *a greater number or proportion of women (even the presence of a critical mass) in the legislature would not have a consistently large effect on government responsiveness to violence against women.*

The Proposed Model

In general, then, the interaction between strong and autonomous women's movements and institutional structure produces better representation in the policy process, which is here measured by responsiveness to violence against women. We might also expect strong and autonomous women's movements to have an impact independent of this interaction, since such agencies are not necessary for women's movement influence. We would not necessarily expect such an independent effect from women's policy agencies. In addition, the number of women in the legislature does not determine responsiveness to violence against women. Level of development and culture are thought to be fundamental factors influencing politics and policy.[10] I control for these factors using dummy variables to measure level of development, region, and dominant religion (the latter two as proxies for culture).

Analysis

I employ OLS regression to examine the association of different sources of political representation for women with responsiveness to violence against women. Multivariate regression analysis can be used to examine whether (and how strongly) each of these modes of representation is associated with more government action on violence against women. (Table 27.1). Scope of government response is coded from 0 to 7, depending on the number of areas of policy action that a national government undertakes. If

a mode of representation produced better policy outcomes for women, we would expect the mode to be associated with governments addressing an increased number of additional areas.

As expected, there is no linear relationship between proportion of women legislators and government responsiveness to violence against women (Model 1, Table 27.1). More generally, a critical mass effect is not visible in this policy area. Of those governments where women comprise more than 30% of the legislature, none have addressed more than four policy areas (Weldon 2002, 99). Moreover, among those governments that have been the most responsive to violence against women (i.e., have adopted five or more policies), percent of women in the legislature varies from 6.4% to 21.2% (Weldon 2002, 98).[11] It may be that individual feminist women are important in getting policies passed as policy entrepreneurs. Indeed, it may be that the presence of at least one woman is a necessary condition for policy development. But there is no linear relationship between the overall number of women in the legislature or in cabinet and government responsiveness to violence against women.

The presence of a strong, autonomous women's movement is more strongly positively associated with scope than the proportion of women, with standardized Betas of .50 and .00, respectively (Model 1, Table 27.1). Controlling for level of development (Model 1, Table 27.1), the presence of a strong and autonomous women's movement is associated with about one or two additional areas of policy action on violence against women (1.90+/− 0.55). This supports the argument that the existence of strong, independent women's movements improves women's representation in the policy process more effectively than increasing women's presence in the legislature.

In contrast, the presence of an effective women's policy machinery is not associated with government responsiveness to violence against women (Table 27.1, Model 1). This may seem to contradict the hypothesis that these institutions have an effect on government responsiveness to violence against women. But I argued above that the policy impact of these institutions depended on the presence of a strong and autonomous women's movement, and that we should

Table 27.1. *Regression Coefficients, Dependent Variable = Scope of Govt. Response to Violence against Women, 36 Stable Democratic Countries, 1994*

Model	Independent Variables	B	SE	Beta	T	Sig.*	R^2
1	Level of development	1.20	.64	.30	1.87	.07	.37
	Strong and autonomous women's movement	1.90	.55	.50	3.44	.00	
	Percent of women in legislature	.00	.02	.00	−.02	.98	
	Effective women's policy machinery	.45	.66	.10	.68	.49	
2	Level of development	1.09	.54	.27	2.03	.05	.43
	Strong and autonomous women's movement	1.39	.59	.36	2.33	.02	
	Effective women's policy machinery	−.86	.96	−.19	−.90	.37	
	Eff. women's policy machinery * strong, aut. wm	2.33	1.27	.42	1.82	.07	
3	Level of development	−.28	1.43	−.07	−.20	.85	.61
	Strong and autonomous women's movement	.80	.67	.21	1.21	.24	
	Eff. women's policy machinery * strong, aut. wm	2.30	1.34	.43	1.71	.10	
	Logged number of reps	.01	.42	.04	.17	.87	
	Region–Africa	−1.12	1.84	−.14	−.60	.55	
	Region–Asia	2.31	1.48	.34	1.56	.13	
	Region–Latin America	−.88	1.68	−.18	−.53	.61	
	Region–North America	2.44	1.23	.30	1.99	.06	
	Region–Oceania	1.22	1.25	.18	.98	.34	
	Dominant religion–Protestant	.00	.65	−.01	−.06	.94	
	Dominant religion–other	−2.3	1.3	−.47	−1.7	.08	

* I report statistical significance as a matter of interest, but I consider this set of countries to be a complete set of stable democracies (i.e., a population), and I am not employing sampling techniques.

not expect to see an independent effect. If this argument holds, then a term capturing the interaction between effective women's policy agencies and strong and autonomous women's movements should be strongly associated with government response to violence against women, and should explain more than either term alone.

An indicator representing the interaction of a strong, autonomous women's movement and the presence of a women's policy machinery (one that provides access and resources) is a very strong predictor of government responsiveness to violence against women (Table 27.1, Models 2 and 3), being associated with more areas of government action than either of the two parts alone (Model 2). The interaction of a strong, autonomous women's movement and an effective women's policy agency is associated with about two additional areas of

policy action (B = 2.33+/−1.27) (Model 2). This association seems to hold even controlling for level of development, region, and religion (Model 3).

In sum, then, strong, independent women's movements and effective women's bureaus interact to provide an effective mode of substantive representation for women. Indeed, in the area of policies on violence against women, cross-national data suggest that women's bureaus and women's movements together are more effective than large numbers of women in the legislature at securing policy action.

Conclusion

. . . Discussions of substantive democratic representation should consider multiple sources of political representation. Considering a number of modes of representation makes it possible to compare different modes of representation, and explore interactions between them. In this study, the interaction between modes of representation appears to be critical: The interaction between women's movements and institutional structures is more important for understanding policy responsiveness to violence against women than the proportion of women in the legislature.

This is not to suggest that individual members of marginalized groups provide no representation. Indeed, the presence of such representatives can have important symbolic and sometimes substantive effects on policy processes. But descriptive representation is severely limited as an avenue for providing substantive representation. Of course, as noted, social movements and women's policy agencies are also limited in terms of substantive representation: Some women feel excluded or dominated in women's movements and lines of accountability are unclear. Women's policy agencies are characterized by similar exclusions and weaknesses. Examining multiple sources of representation provides a more complete picture of possibilities for—and limits on—influence in democratic policy processes.

More generally, this analysis shows the value of examining the structural conditions in which policy is made (Ashford 1978; Bobrow and Dryzek 1987). Examining the social order, the patterns of political inclusion and exclusion established by institutions and norms, is important for understanding democratic policymaking (March and Olsen 1989). Understanding the impact of such patterns, I have shown, is key to understanding whether and how social groups are represented in democratic policy processes. Thus, the study of women and politics, and of democratic policymaking more generally, should focus as much on political structures such as institutions, social movements, and other macrolevel phenomena as it does on individual-level variables and characteristics.

Notes

1. At best, an individual member of the group, without interacting with others from the social group, can articulate a truncated version of the group perspective,

if she is so inclined. This is a weak version of the argument that in cases where group perspectives are uncrystallized, the reactions of members of marginalized groups in legislatures can help to define the interests of marginalized groups (see Mansbridge 1999; Phillips 1995).

2. Even though social choice theory has treated the relation between individual and group preferences in depth, I do not employ that approach here. Methodological individualist tools are relatively poorly suited to a theorization of social group perspective because such perspectives are not achieved by aggregating individual preferences, and perspective is much less determinative than a specific preference.

3. This dependent variable has eight categories (0 to 7), and so can be used in an OLS regression equation. Since the dependent variable is not an event count, a Poisson regression function is not appropriate (Winkelmann 1997).

4. Note that this means that governments sometimes obtain the same score by enacting different policies. This is generally considered a problem with this sort of indicator, but for our purposes this feature of the indicator is of little interest. Policy experts and activists argue that there is no single policy solution and that an appropriate policy response is one that attacks the problem on all fronts (Busch 1992; United Nations 1998; Chalk and King 1998; Elman 1996). For this reason, the dependent variable is measured in terms of the number of different sorts of things that governments are doing (scope) rather than by which of the seven policy areas they address. On this measure, a government that undertook only a criminal justice response or only public education initiatives would receive a lower score than one that undertook both criminal justice and public education initiatives.

5. Unfortunately, the usual criteria for assessing composite dependent variables are inappropriate for this measure of scope, and for my research question more generally. For example, a common mode of assessing a composite indicator is to examine correlations among the items. The items in this indicator (policy areas) are conceptually related to the problem of violence against women, and are widely considered important elements of comprehensive response to the problem. But they need not be correlated with each other in order to indicate the breadth of government response. For example, funding for battered women's shelters is often distinct from funding for rape crisis centers: governments often fund one, but not the other, even though both are important elements of any government response to violence against women. If the adoption of these two different types of policies is only weakly correlated, should I conclude that one of them is unnecessary or unrelated to the underlying concept, the scope of government response to violence against women? I think the answer is no, since we can see that they are both clearly related to government response to violence against women. Eliminating one of these items would weaken, not strengthen, the measure,

because the very concept of the scope of government action suggests that policy will range across distinct areas. One would not necessarily expect government provision of public education programs to be related to government funding for rape crisis centers.

6. Women's movements are not equivalent to women's organizations. The idea that organized interests provide a form of representation has a long history, and is one of the core ideas of pluralism (see Williams 1998 for a discussion). I am arguing that women's movements, which include but are not limited to women's organizations, provide such a representative function. Movements include a broad range of activities such as protests, cultural productions, and "personal politics" (Costain 1998; Ferree and Martin 1995; Katzenstein 1995).

7. Women's movement strength is thus logically separable from policy influence, preventing what would otherwise be a tautological claim: that women's movements influence policymaking when they are influential in policymaking.

8. Note that a women's movement is never coded as strong simply because it appears to have influenced policies on violence against women. The codings are taken from Weldon (2002), Table 3.1.

9. The machinery is coded 1 only if both conditions are met, because neither condition alone is theoretically sufficient for political influence. Examination of the interactions between these two dimensions supports this coding.

10. Unfortunately, the cross-national data on levels of violence are not of sufficient quality to warrant inclusion in a regression analysis. The data that do exist, and are somewhat comparable, suggest that level of violence bears little relationship to government response (Weldon 2002).

11. Nor are absolute numbers of women linearly related to government responsiveness, even focusing on women in more influential positions, such as the proportion of women in cabinet (not shown).

References

Ashford, D. 1978. *Comparative Public Policies*. Beverly Hills: Sage.

Bobrow, Davis B., and John S. Dryzek 1987. *Policy Analysis by Design*. Pittsburgh: University of Pittsburgh Press.

Busch, Diane Mitsch. 1992. "Women's Movements and State Policy Reform Aimed at Domestic Violence against Women: A Comparison of the Consequences of Movement Mobilization in the United States and India." *Gender and Society* 6(4): 587–608.

Chalk, Rosemary, and Patricia King, eds. 1998. *Violence in Families*. National Research Council and Institute of Medicine. Washington, DC: National Academy Press.

Costain, Anne N. 1998. "Women Lobby Congress." In *Social Movements and American Political Institutions*, eds. Anne N. Costain and Andrew S. McFarland. Lanham, MD: Rowman and Littlefield.

Dobrowolsky, Alexandra. 1998. "Of 'Special Interest': Interest, Identity and Feminist Constitutional Activism in Canada." *Canadian Journal of Political Science/Revue canadienne de science politique* 31(4): 704–42.

Elman, R. Amy. 1996. *Sexual Subordination and State Intervention: Comparing Sweden and the United States*. Providence: Berghahn Books.

Ferree, Myra Marx, and Patricia Yancey Martin, eds. 1995. *Feminist Organizations: Harvest of the New Women's Movement*. Philadelphia: Temple University Press.

Katzenstein, Mary. 1995. "Discursive Politics and Feminist Activism in the Catholic Church." In *Feminist Organizations: Harvest of the New Women's Movement*, eds, M. M. Ferree and P. Y. Martin. Philadelphia: Temple University Press.

Mansbridge, Jane. 1999. "Should Blacks Represent Blacks and Women Represent Women? A Contingent 'Yes.'" *Journal of Politics* 61(3): 628–57.

March, James, and Johan Olsen. 1989. *Rediscovering Institutions: The Organizational Basis of Politics*. New York: Free Press.

Phillips, Anne. 1995. *The Politics of Presence*. Oxford: Clarendon Press.

Powell, G. Bingham. 1982. *Contemporary Democracies: Participation, Stability and Violence*. Cambridge: Harvard University Press.

Putnam, Robert D. 1993. *Making Democracy Work: Civic Traditions in Modern Italy*. Princeton, NJ: Princeton University Press.

Stetson, Dorothy McBride. 1995. "The Oldest Women's Policy Agency: The Women's Bureau in the United States." In *Comparative State Feminism*, eds. Dorothy McBride Stetson and Amy G. Mazur. Thousand Oaks: Sage.

United Nations. 1998. Commission on the Elimination of All Forms of Discrimination against Women (CEDAW). *Report of the Special Rapporteur on Violence against Women, Its Causes and Consequences*. New York: United Nations. http://www. un.org/womenwatch/daw/csw.

Weldon, S. Laurel. 2002. *Protest, Policy and the Problem of Violence against Women : A Cross-National Comparison*, Pittsburgh: University of Pittsburgh Press.

Williams, Melissa. 1988. *Voice, Trust and Memory: Marginalilzed Groups and the Failings of Liberal Representation*. Princeton, NJ: Princeton University Press.

Winkelmann, Rainer. 1997. *Econometric Analysis of Count Data*. 2nd ed. New York: Springer.

Young, Iris. 1997. "Deferring Group Representation." In *Nomos: Group Rights*, eds. Will Kymlicka and Ian Shapiro. New York: New York University Press.

Part V

WOMEN, GENDER, AND SOCIAL POLICIES

This section collects together readings on women, gender, and public policies, presenting an array of theoretical and empirical approaches for studying gendered origins and outcomes of public policy. Building on the previous section, the first two readings document and analyze the power dynamics in legislatures that influence how women as a group are able to shape broader policy-making processes (Tamerius 1995), as well as the ways in which the authority of women to speak for "women" is undermined by gender and racial biases that tend to silence minority women (Hawkesworth 2003). Focusing on specific policy areas, the next four selections offer various strategies for gendered policy analysis. They outline a "what's the problem approach" for studying the gendered nature of public policy (Bacchi 1996), develop a set of arguments for disaggregating what is meant by "gender policy" (Htun 2003), discuss historical approaches for thinking about "equality" and "difference" in state policies for women (Sarvasy 1992), and focus on the theoretical underpinnings of recent developments to promote equality between women and men through "gender mainstreaming" (Squires 2005).

Working from some of the key findings of the literature on links between the descriptive (numbers) and substantive (outcomes) representation of women, *Karin Tamerius* addresses the apparent lack of sex differences in legislative voting behavior, which have been utilized to argue that women do not appear to "make a difference" when elected to political office. She notes that this finding fails to take account of the gendered nature of this conventional measure of "policy impact," which presumes that enactment—not agenda-setting and policy formulation—are the most important stages of the policy-making process. Applying her revised approach to the U.S. House of Representatives, Tamerius's analysis reveals that differences between male and female legislators on women's issues are the biggest at the earliest stages of the policy-making process, which require the greatest amount of support, commitment, awareness, and expertise in relation to specific policy issues. *Mary Hawkesworth* offers a parallel critique, observing that it is difficult to capture many of the nuances of policy-making behavior using traditional methods of legislative analysis. Examining policy making in the U.S. Congress, she elaborates the concept of "racing-gendering" to refer to political processes that silence, stereotype, enforce invisibility, exclude, and challenge the epistemic authority of Congresswomen of color. Through these raced and gendered dynamics, she argues, minority women are frequently precluded from speaking for "women" in legislative contexts, despite their increased presence in elected assemblies.

Moving to the content of public policy itself, *Carol Lee Bacchi* notes that many policies, including those not traditionally thought of as "women's issues," are infused with beliefs about gender relations, in terms of what is viewed as a "problem" and how these "problems" are framed and translated into policy prescriptions. On this basis, she contends that public policies should not be understood as neutral technical matters, but rather in terms of competing interpretations or representations of political issues. She develops her "what's the problem" approach as a means to reveal how policy debates and proposals contain explicit or implicit diagnoses of the "problem," which in turn influence the choice of solution to pursue. *Mala Htun* elaborates a distinct critique of policy making. Comparing the cases of Argentina, Brazil, and Chile, she seeks to understand how and why states make decisions about gender-related issues. Focusing on rights to abortion, divorce, and gender equality in the family, she assesses the various roles played by transitions from dictatorship to democracy, relations between the church and state, activities of liberal and feminist reformers, and pressures from growing international norms. Based on her study, she presents a new "disaggregated" approach to studying gender policy and the state that does not treat "women's rights" as a single issue area, but rather as a collection of various issues that may not all be addressed in the same way.

Addressing policies that explicitly aim to improve women's status, *Wendy Sarvasy* studies the writings of early-twentieth-century feminists in the United States to reconstruct the evolution of their ideas about sex and gender equality. She argues that the work of these women suggests a feminist theoretical process for how to achieve gender equality: they showed how unequal power relations turned biological differences into socially constructed, substantive gender inequalities; they formulated public policies based on a new conception of gender equality to alleviate these substantive inequalities; and they sought to use the emancipated aspects of women's different experiences and outlooks to create a more egalitarian political and social environment. Focusing on policy developments in more recent decades, *Judith Squires* theorizes the history of gender equality strategies in terms of a typology of inclusion, reversal, and displacement. Inclusion involves a focus on equality as sameness, reversal entails an emphasis on sexual difference, and displacement seeks to go beyond existing binaries to meet the varied needs of women and men. Analyzing the strategy of "gender mainstreaming," she focuses on the potential of displacement as a transformative approach that is best able to respond to increasingly important demands of diversity, namely, efforts to include race and class in discussions of gender equality policy. Together, the readings point to the vivid political struggles that inform policy-making processes, shaping the degree to which public policies reinforce or reform existing dynamics of inequality.

Chapter 28

SEX, GENDER, AND LEADERSHIP IN THE REPRESENTATION OF WOMEN

Karin L. Tamerius

. . . Recent advances by women in the political arena have attracted new attention to a number of old but important questions about the relationship between sex, gender, and representative governance: Are the women in public office more supportive of women's issues than their male counterparts? Are they more attentive to the needs and concerns of the women in their constituencies? Do they work harder to enact policies for women into law? In short, does the sexual integration of our political institutions lead to greater representation of women's interests?

. . . Ever since women first began to achieve public office in significant numbers, researchers have been attempting to assess their impact on the "feminist" content of policy. The general conclusion to emerge from these studies—located primarily in state legislatures and Congress—is that women matter, but they do not matter much. The main indicator used to gauge sex differences in the representation of women in government institutions is the roll call voting of elected officials on "women's issues." All else being equal, sex has not been shown to be an important determinant. Although women at all levels of public office tend to vote in a slightly more feminist direction than their male colleagues, these differences rarely have been substantively significant.[1] Moreover, in the rare instances when meaningful differences have been found, . . . it still appears that electing women to public office is at best an inefficient way of enhancing the representation of women's interests. Since inevitably the most powerful predictor of feminist voting is party membership, it follows

that organizations seeking to promote women's welfare through government action would be best advised to direct their electoral resources toward Democratic candidates of either sex.

. . . I argue in this chapter that the largely negative findings of earlier studies are in fact perfectly compatible with a feminist worldview, even one that says that having more women in government will significantly enhance the representation of women's interests. It is my contention that previous work on this topic failed to uncover substantial sex differences not because the feminist project has failed or been misguided, but because difference was operationalized with scant regard to the stated and unstated theories of gender and politics that underlie feminist predictions. Rather than considering what we mean when we say that women will alter the substance of government and choosing tools well suited to investigating those propositions, researchers have simply appropriated traditional indicators of difference and applied them to the study of gender. Yet, as the work of a number of feminist epistemologists attests, such an approach is bound to provide a distorted image of the nature and consequences of women's political participation.[2]

The major shortcoming of previous studies from a feminist perspective is the failure to take into account the gendered nature of conventional measures. Regrettably, the stock research implements of modern political science did not arise untainted from the sexually divided environment of their origination. Developed largely by men to answer questions of interest to men about the political behavior of men, many existing tools contain an inherent male bias. In the study of legislative behavior, for example, the traditional emphasis on roll call voting, which assumes that enactment is the most important stage in the legislative process, privileges majority and, therefore, male interests. Since policies of concern to the majority of members are bound to make it to the floor eventually, early maneuvers are unlikely to have a major impact on whether a policy is ultimately adopted. From the perspective of women and other legislative minorities, however, critical stages of the legislative process are more properly identified as agenda setting and policy formulation, since the vast majority of policies of interest to underrepresented groups, including feminist bills, never receive consideration on the floor.

While the existence of such male biases does not mean that conventional indicators such as roll call votes should never be used to study sex differences, these biases do mean that we need to seriously investigate their implications and appropriateness for assessing gendered constructs before employing them in our empirical research. At the same time, we should not hesitate to develop novel alternatives capable of providing more accurate depictions of "female-oriented" behavior when conventional measures prove unequal to the task.[3] . . .

. . . The study reported here is an attempt to do just that. Drawing on theoretical and empirical work in gender and politics, legislative politics, and a series of interviews with more than a dozen members of Congress,[4] I develop and evaluate a model of sex differences in legislative behavior that posits several ways in which being female may impel a representative toward legislative leadership on feminist issues.

Why Expect Sex Differences in Representation?

In striving to develop realistic and defensible predictions about the impact of female legislators on governance, I began by looking for ways in which being a woman or man structures a representative's relationship with women's issues. My investigation yielded a number of factors that, in theory, have the potential to produce gendered

representation. Falling into two distinct yet causally related categories—sex differences in *experience* and sex differences in *attitudes* and *resources*—these determinants may conspire with the demands of representative institutions to produce sex differences in *feminist legislative leadership*—active involvement in the establishment and promotion of a feminist legislative agenda.

Sex Differences in Experience

A central notion of feminist standpoint theory is that women and men have different experiences in life that have consequences for how their interests are represented in politics. . . . In this study four gendered aspects of representatives' experiences—*content*, *perspective*, *mutuality*, and *association*—are expected to be particularly crucial in fashioning legislative involvement with women's concerns.

Content

The first feature that distinguishes the experiences of female and male legislators is their gendered content. Although the women and men who serve in public office tend to come from similarly privileged backgrounds, they are still likely to experience life in substantively different ways. Sex disparities in the types of experiences legislators have arise in part from fundamental biological distinctions (such as the capacity to become pregnant) but also from pervasive sexual divisions within society. Among the social factors that are likely to result in divergent experiences for women and men are sex differences in socialization, prejudicial treatment, occupation, socioeconomic status, domestic roles, and criminal victimization.

Perspective

A second distinction to be made about the experiences of female and male legislators is their gendered perspective. Simply put, women's experiences happen to women while men's experiences happen to men. This divergence in outlook limits the amount of insight either sex can have into what it is like to be the other since the interpretation, salience, and feeling of any experience is likely to be mediated at least in part by whether it is happening to us or someone else. While the "objective" experience—what happens—may be the same, we can only perceive it subjectively, through a gendered lens. Consequently, just about the only way men can experience womanhood or, conversely, women can experience manhood, is with the assistance of their imaginations.

Mutuality

A third factor that distinguishes the experiences of female and male legislators is gendered mutuality. In simple terms, women's experiences tend to be shared by other women while men's experiences tend to be shared by other men. Since the degree to which members of a social group identify with each other depends in large part on the commonality of their experiences, this divergence is likely to strengthen ties within the sexes while weakening bonds between them.

Association

A final aspect that differentiates the experiences of female and male legislators is their gendered association. Despite strong familial and emotional ties, women and men often work and socialize in sexually exclusive groups. Within the context of American politics, for example, male politicians historically have operated through political old-boys networks inimical to the participation of women. Partly in response to the male dominance of these informal associations, many female politicians have opted to work closely with political organizations for women. Not only do such groups often provide a starting point for women's political careers—affording much needed experience, encouragement, and funding—but they frequently continue to work closely with female legislators long after they are elected to public office.

Sex Differences in Attitudes and Resources

Although feminist standpoint theory has successfully focused attention on the political relevance of legislators' experience, it has made little attempt to specify the mechanisms by which experience as a woman or man might be translated into gen-

dered representation. In the model described here, it is hypothesized that experiences affect political engagement with issues of particular concern to women in two ways: first, by altering legislators' attitudes—*support* and *commitment*—toward women's issues, and, second, by providing legislators with resources—*awareness* and *expertise*—that facilitate feminist activism.

Support

One consequence of sex disparities in experience is that female legislators may be especially supportive of policies for women. Women's experiences may shape their policy attitudes by providing compelling evidence of the need for government action on feminist concerns. A female legislator who has suffered discrimination in hiring, for example, has personal confirmation that the problem of sex discrimination exists, while a male legislator who has had no such experience may remain skeptical. At the same time, because a female legislator who has experienced discrimination is afforded unique insight into its emotional and financial ramification, she may be inclined to judge the problem more severe than do her male counterparts.

Women do not need to confront problems directly, however, to have their policy attitudes shaped by their experiences. Female legislators may become convinced of the need for feminist policies simply through their frequent association with other women. For example, a legislator may be persuaded to support an antidiscrimination policy because she has had the opportunity to speak with victims of sex discrimination about their experiences. Similarly, being involved with organizations that possess substantial information about the severity and extent of prejudice may encourage a female legislator to alter her assessments of the need for policies designed to fight sex bias in the workplace. . . .

Commitment

A second consequence of sex disparities in experience may be that female legislators are especially committed to policies for women. Gendered experiences may cause female legislators to make feminist issues a priority for two reasons. First, . . . their unique perspective on women's issues may enhance their assessments of problem severity, making them more inclined to place women's issues high on the list of national concerns. Second, female legislators may feel a special responsibility for helping women with their problems as a result of their common experiences and group membership. . . .

Awareness

A third consequence of sex disparities in experience is that female legislators may be especially aware of issues of concern to women. Theoretically, gendered experiences give female officials an advantage in identifying the problems facing women in two respects. First, female legislators may be more aware of women's problems because they have encountered those problems in their own lives. A congresswoman who has been the victim of spousal abuse, for example, is apt to be more cognizant of crimes against women than are her male colleagues who have never suffered domestic violence. Second, female legislators may learn about women's problems through their association with other women. For example, one of the primary goals of feminist organizations is to bring problems of particular concern to women to the attention of female legislators. . . .

Expertise

A final consequence of sex disparities in experience is that female legislators may be especially expert on women's issues. In addition to imparting information about the types of problems women confront, experiences may also afford information about how those problems can best be resolved. To begin with, female legislators may acquire policy information by facing gender-based problems in their own lives. For example, a female legislator and mother who has had difficulty securing reliable and affordable day care for her children may be more apt to recognize that a jobs program for unemployed women will not succeed unless it makes adequate provisions for child care. At the same time, female legislators may acquire policy expertise from their associative experiences with other women. Feminist organizations are particularly important in this regard, since they often acts as clearinghouses for information relating to women and women's concerns. . . .

Sex Differences in Feminist Legislative Leadership

As noted earlier, one consideration that has been lost in the debate over the impact of female officeholders on the representation of women is that gender is likely to interact with legislative institutions in ways that are not captured by conventional conceptions of political difference. For this reason, before attempting to measure the effect of women's gendered attitudes and resources, it is important to examine the roles support, commitment, awareness, and expertise play in the legislative process. In the model delineated here, it is hypothesized that because of the widely varying demands of legislative activities, gendered attitudes and resources will result in sex differences in legislative leadership on feminist issues.

A widely known, but little heeded, fact of legislative politics is that different activities demand different things from the representatives who engage in them. Among the factors that distinguish among legislative activities is the amount of attitudinal support they require. In simple terms, there are some activities representatives are willing to undertake when their support for a policy is low, others they are willing to undertake when their support for a policy is moderate, and still others they are willing to undertake only when their support for a policy is high. For example, roll call voting is one activity that does not require high levels of policy support since a legislator need only prefer a policy to its alternative to cast a vote in support of it. In contrast, activities like cosponsorship, speechmaking, and sponsorship imply high levels of policy endorsement.

A second factor that distinguishes among legislative activities is the level of commitment they require from representatives who engage in them. Legislative sponsorship, for example, is a high-commitment activity because it requires large outlays of a legislator's time and energy. Not only does the sponsor of a bill tend to play a primary role in drafting the legislation, but she or he is usually also responsible for soliciting support from other legislators in order to build a coalition that will carry the bill to passage. Alternatively, activities such as voting, cosponsorship, and, to a lesser degree, speechmaking are low-commitment activities because they require legislators to expend comparatively few resources.

A third factor that distinguishes among legislative activities is the amount of issue awareness they require. Put simply, legislators must be highly conscious of an issue of concern to the public in order to engage in certain activities, but may engage in others while relatively unaware. For example, in order to sponsor legislation, a legislator must first know that a problem requiring government attention exists. In contrast, voting requires little awareness of issues because by the time legislation has gone to the floor for a vote, a problem has already been identified and the task before legislators is simply to accept or reject a proposal for solving it. At the same time, activities such as speechmaking and cosponsorship fall somewhere between these two extremes because neither demands that a legislator initiate action on a problem and yet both activities are often undertaken before an issue has been subject to much public debate.

A final factor that distinguishes among legislative activities is the amount of policy expertise they require. . . . Voting is one legislative activity that requires little substantive knowledge since representatives are able to rely on cues from a variety of sources when making their voting decisions.[5] In contrast, legislators must be relatively well informed to sponsor a bill and guide it through the legislative process. Other activities such as cosponsorship and speechmaking require legislators to be reasonably informed, but do not demand that they be experts.

Given these systematic differences in the attitudinal and resource burdens imposed by legislative activities, and given the expectations about sex differences in attitudes and resources discussed earlier, the potential consequences of gender in representative institutions are now readily apparent. Specifically, activities that require the greatest amount of support for, commitment to, awareness of, and expertise on women's issues should elicit the largest sex differences, while activities that require the least amount of support, commitment, awareness, and expertise should elicit the smallest differences. By taking a look at some of the most common legislative activities and the attitudinal and resource demands each imposes, several clear predictions for sex differences in feminist legislative behavior emerge. As shown in table 28.1, when activities are ranked according to predicted sex differences, the resulting order of magnitude is as follows: roll call voting (smallest), cosponsorship, speechmaking, and sponsorship (largest).

In light of these predictions, conceptualizing difference in feminist terms appears to mean more than simply thinking of female legislators as more feminist in orientation than men. It also means thinking of women as leaders on feminist issues—the people who assume responsibility for shaping the legislative agenda and doing the work necessary to get feminist policies enacted into law. From this perspective, the reason previous studies of sex differences in governance failed to uncover compelling evidence of female legislators' impact on politics is because they relied on roll call voting—the indicator theoretically associated with the least dramatic aspect of gendered representation.

Measuring Difference

Assessing the influence of sex on feminist legislative behavior is a difficult task. Like most political terms, the feminist label refers to a highly

Table 28.1. Predicted Sex Differences by Activity Type: Feminist Legislative Leadership

Activity Requirements	Roll Call Voting	Cosponsorship	Speeches	Sponsorship
Support	Moderate	High	High	High
Commitment	Low	Low	Moderate	High
Awareness	Low	Low	Moderate	High
Expertise	Low	Low	Moderate	High
Predicted Sex Differences	Small	Small/Medium	Medium	Large

subjective and mutable concept that shifts in meaning depending on how and by whom it is used. While few would deny that in general feminism seeks to advance the well-being of women, there are conflicting notions about what constitutes women's welfare and about how that welfare can be best advanced. . . .

. . . My own admittedly imperfect answer was to employ a definition of feminist that is consistent with liberal feminism, the most common form of feminism in American politics and the version most strongly associated with such groups as the National Women's Political Caucus (NWPC) and the National Organization for Women (NOW). Under this definition, legislators' behaviors were defined as feminist if their primary purpose was to promote the well-being of women through one or more of the following: eliminating discrimination on the basis of sex, redressing grievances of women who have suffered discrimination on the basis of sex, addressing needs arising from women's unique physiologies or socioeconomic conditions, or achieving public recognition of women's contributions to society. . . .

The locus of this study was the U.S. House of Representatives during the 101st Congress (1989–90). The sample included all twenty-four women and a matched group of twenty-four men who served in the House during this entire period. The matching procedure selected those men who shared the same party, seniority, and ideology as the women.[6] When possible, men were also paired with women on the basis of region and age. The purpose of using a matched sample was to measure the independent effect of sex on feminist legislative leadership. In accordance with the typology developed earlier, four types of legislative activities were examined: feminist roll call voting, feminist speechmaking, feminist cosponsorship, and feminist sponsorship.

Findings

The first dependent variable I examined was feminist roll call voting. . . . As in previous research, there was a measurable sex disparity in the voting behavior of the representatives. Seventy-seven percent of the votes congresswomen cast on the seventeen issues were feminist, compared with 70 percent of the votes cast by the congressmen. In accordance with predictions, however, this difference was far from large, equivalent to about one more feminist vote per congresswoman, indicating that sex is not a major determinant of roll call voting on women's issues. In addition, party was a better predictor of feminist voting than sex, with 78 percent of the Democrats' votes being feminist compared to just 65 percent of the Republicans' votes.

The second variable I examined was feminist bill cosponsorship. . . . All told, the congresswomen cosponsored legislation 11,962 times. Of these instances, 1,088 (9 percent) involved feminist bills. In contrast, the congressmen signed their names to legislation 9,541 times, and of these cases, 569 (6 percent) involved feminist bills. Since in practical terms this difference amounts to about 23 more pieces of feminist legislation per congresswoman, legislative cosponsorship is clearly an area in which the behavior of women and men in Congress is substantially different. Moreover, sex was a more important determinant of cosponsorship than partisanship, which had no discernible impact on the dependent variable; both Democrats and Republicans dedicated about 10 percent of their cosponsorship activity to feminist bills.

The third dependent variable I examined was feminist speeches on the floor of the House. Sex differences in this area were also highly pronounced. . . . Of the 2,841 speeches given by the congresswomen, 241 were feminist. During the same period, congressmen gave 1,941 speeches of which 81 were feminist. This means that on average the women gave about 6 more feminist speeches per person than did their male counterparts. As with feminist cosponsorship, the effect of sex on feminist speechmaking was greater than the effect of party, which accounted for less than a 1 percent difference between members. On average, about 8 percent of the speeches given by both Democrats and Republicans were feminist.

Sponsorship of feminist legislation was the final dependent variable, and was measured in the same manner as the cosponsorship variable. Overall, the congresswomen sponsored legislation 582 times, and in 69 of these instances the legislation they sponsored was feminist. In contrast, the congressmen sponsored legislation 328 times, and in only 6 of these instances did the legislation

Table 28.2. *Sex Distribution by Feminist Activity Type*

Feminist Activities	Women	Men	Totals
Roll Call Votes	52%	48%	100%
Cosponsors	66%	34%	100%
Speeches	75%	25%	100%
Sponsors	92%	8%	100%

fall into the feminist category. In practical terms, this means that female members sponsored about 2 more pieces of feminist legislation per person than did the congressmen. As with feminist speechmaking and bill cosponsorship, feminist bill sponsorship variation by party was almost imperceptible; both Democrats and Republicans spent about 11 percent of their sponsorship activity on feminist bills.

In order to determine whether these sex differences varied in magnitude depending on the types of activities in which the representatives were engaged, I compared the sex distributions of different feminist activities. As shown in table 28.2, the gap between women's and men's feminist legislative involvement increased consistently in the predicted direction: the greater the attitudinal and resource demands imposed by an activity, the larger the sex disparity. While in this study women cast just over half of the feminist votes, they constituted 66 percent of the cosponsors of feminist legislation, 75 percent of the profeminist speakers, and 92 percent of the sponsors of feminist legislation. This finding conforms closely to the model of feminist legislative leadership developed earlier. Although not definitive, the results are consistent with an interpretation that posits heightened support, commitment, awareness, and expertise among female members of Congress as primary determinants of sex disparities in feminist legislative leadership. While congressmen are not averse to feminist policies, congresswomen provide the bulk of the leadership on feminist issues. . . .

Notes

1. Frieda L. Gehlen, "Women Members of Congress: A Distinctive Role," in *A Portrait of Marginality*, ed. Marianne Githens and Jewell Prestage (New York: McKay, 1977); Sheila Gilbert Leader, "The Policy Impact of Elected Women Officials," in *The Impact of the Electoral Process*, ed. Louis Maisel and Joseph Cooper (Beverly Hills, Calif.: Sage Publications, 1977); David Hill, "Women State Legislators and Party Voting on the E.R.A.," *Social Science Quarterly* 64 (1982): 318–26; Janet A. Flammang, "Female Officials in the Feminist Capital: The Case of Santa Clara County," *Western Political Quarterly* 38 (1985): 94–118; Sue Thomas, "Voting Patterns in the California Assembly: The Role of Gender," *Women and Politics* 9 (1989): 43–53; Samantha L. Durst and Ryan W. Rusek, "Different Genders, Different Votes? An Examination of Voting Behavior in the U.S. House of Representatives," paper presented at the annual meeting of the American Political Science Association, Washington, D.C., September 2–5, 1993.
2. Kathleen B. Jones and Anna G. Jonasdottir, eds., *The Political Interests of Gender: Developing Theory and Research with a Feminist Face* (London: Sage Publications, 1988).
3. Ibid.
4. Sixteen interviews (nine with women and seven with men) were conducted in person during May, June, and July 1991. The sessions ranged in length from fifteen minutes to one hour, and, because of members' time limitations, not all questions were asked in every interview. To encourage members to speak freely about their attitudes and activities, respondents were promised anonymity and the sessions were recorded with written notes (taken during and immediately following the interviews) rather than with a tape recorder.
5. John W. Kingdon. *Congressmen's Voting Decisions*, 3d ed. (Ann Arbor: University of Michigan Press, 1989).
6. Ideology was measured with rankings from the Americans for Democratic Action (ADA) and the American Conservative Union (ACU) for 1987, 1988, and 1989.

Chapter 29

CONGRESSIONAL ENACTMENTS
OF RACE–GENDER:
TOWARD A THEORY OF
RACED–GENDERED INSTITUTIONS

Mary Hawkesworth

In their path-breaking work, *A Portrait of Marginality*, Marianne Githens and Jewel Prestage (1977, 339) noted that from its inception American politics has been "man's business" (i.e., it has been "gendered") and "white folks' business" (i.e., it has been "raced"). "As a consequence, black women have been doubly excluded from the political arena." The form of exclusion that Githens and Prestage sought to illuminate was the pervasive and persistent underrepresentation of women of color in elective offices. In 1977, when *Portrait of Marginality* was published, women of color held 3% of the elected offices in the United States and five seats in the U.S. Congress (King 1977, 347).[1] A quarter century later, women of color hold 3.7% of the seats in the U.S. Congress, 3.6% of the seats in state legislatures, and 3.09% of the mayoral and council offices at the municipal level (Center for American Women and Politics 2002; National League of Cities 2002). In addition to underrepresentation, studies of elected women of color consistently document forms of marginalization including stereotyping complemented by a policy of invisibility, exclusion of women of color from leadership positions within legislatures, and lack of institutional responsiveness to the policies women of color champion (Bryce and Warwick 1977; Bratton and Haynie 1999; Swain 2000). . . .

When women legislators of color report persistent marginalization within legislative institutions despite years of seniority and impressive legislative accomplishments, they offer political scientists a clue that there is more going on in legislative institutions than has yet been captured in the literature [on race, gender, and politics]. This chapter explores the experiences of marginalization reported by Congresswomen of color in the 103rd and 104th Congresses in an effort to make visible power relations that have profound effects, constructing raced and gendered hierarchies that structure interactions among members as well as institutional practices, while also shaping public policies.

Toward that end, I first develop a conception of racing–gendering as an active process that differs significantly from the conceptions of race and sex as individual attributes or demographic characteristics. I then suggest that investigating the processes of racing–gendering requires methodological innovation to make visible that which traditional methodologies have rendered invisible. I provide examples of racing–gendering in Congress and indicate how these marginalizing experiences of Congresswomen of color challenge a number of received views in Congress studies. I explore the persistence of racing–gendering across two Congresses, the Democratic-controlled 103rd and the Republican-controlled 104th, to demonstrate that Congresswomen of color perceive racing–gendering to be ongoing processes regardless of the party in power. In the final sections, I identify new explanatory possibilities created by the theory of racing–gendering in Congress and consider some of the implications of this account for understandings of the internal operations of political institutions, the substantive representation of the interests of historically marginalized groups, and the quality of democracy in the United States.

From Race and Sex to Racing–Gendering

Political scientists have tended to treat race and sex as biological or physical characteristics rather than as political constructs. According to this "primordial view" (Taylor 1996), race and sex precede politics. As part of the "natural" or "given" aspects of human existence, race and sex are apolitical, unless intentionally mobilized for political purposes. The effects of race or sex upon politics, then, are matters for empirical investigation but there is no reason to believe that politics plays any role in shaping the physical characteristics of individuals or the demographic characteristics of populations.

Within the past few decades, critical race theorists and feminist theorists have challenged the primordial view of race and sex, calling attention to processes of racialization and gendering through which relations of power and forms of inequality are constructed, shaping the identities of individuals. Through detailed studies of laws, norms, and organizational practices that enforced racial segregation and separate spheres for men and women, scholars have excavated the political processes through which hierarchies of difference have been produced and maintained. They have demonstrated that the imputed "natural" interests and abilities of women and men of various races are the result of state-prescribed limitations in education, occupation, immigration, citizenship, and office-holding (e.g., Connell 1987; Flammang 1997; Haney Lopez 1996; Siltanen 1994). Politics has produced race and gender not only by creating and maintaining raced and gendered divisions within the population but by defining race and gender characteristics and according differential rights on the basis of those definitions (Yanow 2002). . . .

Feminist scholars of color have coined the term *intersectionality* to capture the intricate interplay of social forces that produce particular women and men as members of particular races, classes, ethnicities and nationalities (Crenshaw 1989, 1997). Intersectionality suggests that the processes of racialization and gendering are specific yet interrelated. Racialization may produce marked commonalities or privilege between men and women of the dominant race/ethnic groups and of disadvantage among men and women of the subordinate racial/ethnic groups. Gendering may produce particular commonalities (deportment, adornment, stylizations of the body, voice intonations and inflections, skilling or deskilling, interests, aspirations) among women across race and ethnic groups and among men across race and ethnic groups.

The term *racing–gendering* attempts to foreground the intricate interactions of racialization and gendering in the political production of distinctive groups of men and women. Racing–gendering involves the production of difference, political asymmetries, and social hierarchies that simultaneously create the dominant and the subordinate. To investigate racing–gendering, then, it is crucial to attend to specifics and to interrelationships. The processes that produce a white male, for example, will differ from, while being fully implicated in, the processes that produce a black man, a Latino, a Native American man, a white woman, a black woman, a Latina, an Asian American woman, or a Native American woman.

Racing and gendering are active processes with palpable effects. Racing–gendering occurs through the actions of individuals, as well as through laws, policies, and organizational norms and practices. The identities of women of color are constituted through an amalgam of practices that construct them as "other" (to white men, men of color, and white women), challenging their individuality and their status as fully human. The manifold practices through which racing–gendering are generated and sustained are complex and many-layered. They surface epistemically in the particular knowledges ascribed to women of color and in the forms of knowledge alleged to lie beyond their grasp. They surface contradictorily as in the opposing phenomena of invisibility (when whites consistently fail to see or ignore women of color; confuse them because "they all look alike"; deny them recognition) and hypervisibility (any woman of color stands for all women of color; one or two women of color in a room is somehow too many). Silencing, excluding, marginalizing, segregating, discrediting, dismissing, discounting, insulting, stereotyping, and patronizing are used singly and in combination to fix women of color "in their place."

Tokenism has been a talisman of racing–gendering. As tokens, some women of color are admitted to membership in elite institutions but their inclusion carries an expectation that they accept the agenda of the dominant members (Hurtado 1996; Lorde 1984). Their talents are recognized only on the condition that they are used to support the status quo. Any attempt to expand the agenda or change the operating procedures by a token produces quite different racing–gendering tactics by those dominant within the institution. Hurtado (1996, 135, 166) has suggested that women of color who act in accordance with their own agendas confront "topic extinctions" and the "*pendejo* game." Topic extinctions refer to the total silence that greets substantive suggestions and policy agendas advanced by women of color. Whether fueled by willed indifference, evidence blindness, or a refusal to hear, such silence ensures that women of color fail to achieve their objectives. In the *pendejo* game, white men and white women in positions of power "play dumb," pretending that they do not understand the policy suggestions or substantive arguments of women of color and requesting further explication and deeper elaboration. While women of color devote time and energy trying to educate members of the dominant group about the issues, those in power pretend to listen but do not hear; hence, everything remains the same. The demand for additional information is simply a delaying tactic that ensures that the agenda advanced by women of color is deferred.

Racing–gendering can also involve certain "Catch 22s": Women of color are simultaneously pressured to assimilate to the dominant norms of the institution and denied the possibility of assimilation. They are not allowed to assume the position of the unmarked (white/male) member because racing–gendering practices continue to set them off as different. Indeed, racing–gendering involves asymmetrical power relations that simultaneously constitute the marked and unmarked members. Whites and men constitute themselves as the unmarked norm in the very process of constructing people of color and women as marked, different. Whether deployed intentionally or unwittingly,[2] racing–gendering practices produce relations of power that alter the conditions of work and the conditions of life for women of color in subtle and not so subtle ways. They ensure that the playing field is not equal.

In addition to a variety of direct effects, racing–gendering practices also produce unintended consequences: anger and resistance. In Hurtado's (1996, 21) words, " To be a woman of color is to live with fury." In response to racing–gendering, women of color mobilize anger for purposes of social change. Locke (1997, 378) has argued that women of color have "struggled since our nation's founding against peripheral status and the consequences of exclusion." Within the institutions in which they work and within their communities, a "central tactic of resistance is to use anger effectively" (Hurtado 1996, 21). In the struggle against exclusion and marginalization, women of color in electoral politics have envisioned themselves as social change agents "trying to achieve the visibility and recognition that were symbolically reserved for white men" (Darling 1998, 157). In exploring the dynamics of racing–gendering in the U.S. Congress, it is important to consider that the identities of Congresswomen of color may be constituted not only through the racing–gendering practices that silence, marginalize, and constrain but also through resistance and the political mobilization of anger that racing–gendering engenders. Indeed, I argue that the anger and resistance engendered by Congresswomen of color's experiences of racing–gendering in the halls of Congress help explain certain of their policy preferences and the intensity with which they pursue legislation that they know to be doomed.

Methodology

. . . To illuminate factors that contribute to Congresswomen of color's experience of marginalization, I interpret interview data from Congresswomen in the 103rd and 104th Congresses in light of recent scholarship in critical race theory, feminist theory, and African American history. I draw upon the concept of intersectionality and the theory of gendered institutions to investigate racing–gendering in the U.S. Congress, identifying interpersonal interactions and institutional practices that situate and constrain Congresswomen of color differently from white Congressmen and women, and differently from Congressmen of color.

While this study is informed by hermeneutics, it also employs a multimethod approach, combining textual analysis of interview data with a case-study of welfare reform in the 103rd and 104th Congresses. The interview data are drawn from a long-term study of women in Congress conducted by the Center for American Women and Politics. My textual analysis is based upon transcripts from interviews with 81 Congresswomen, including 15 Congresswomen of color who served in the 103rd and 104th Congresses (11 African American women, 3 Latinas, and 1 Asian American woman), supplemented by certain policy debates recorded in the *Congressional Record*. . . . During the interviews Congresswomen were asked about their legislative priorities and accomplishments, their efforts to represent women, and their relationship to the Congressional Caucus for Women's Issues, as well as their role in passing legislation in the areas of crime, health, health care reform, reproductive rights, violence against women, welfare, and international trade.

There were many similarities in the responses of white Congresswomen and Congresswomen of color. All agreed that they felt an obligation to represent women, although they differed in their understanding of what constituted a women's issue, which women they sought to represent, and how they thought it best to represent those women. They also agreed that they were willing to work across party lines to achieve legislation they thought would help women, and they agreed that the Congressional Caucus for Women's Issues played an important role in coordinating bipartisan coalitions in support of particular pieces of legislation.

The interview transcripts also revealed a range of differences in the responses of white Congresswomen and Congresswomen of color. In discussing their legislative priorities and in identifying their specific roles in support of or in opposition to particular bills, Congresswomen of color provided narratives that differed markedly from those of their white counterparts. African American Congresswomen, in particular, related tales of insult, humiliation, frustration, and anger

that distinguished their responses from those of their white counterparts. These tales provide concrete examples of racing–gendering in Congress that form the core of the analysis in the next two sections. . . .

Racing–Gendering Enactments in Congress

. . . Invisibility can mean markedly different things in Congress, depending on the context and depending on whether it is deployed tactically by a member or imposed unwillingly upon a member. When one is a member of the minority party, working with and through members of the majority party may be the only tactic possible to accomplish a legislative end. . . . In principle, such tactical invisibility is race and gender neutral. . . .

Congresswomen of color can be rendered invisible even when they are not deploying tactical invisibility to accomplish their legislative goals. . . .

Topic extinctions and silencing can undermine the legislative efforts of Congresswomen of color, contributing to a form of invisibility accompanied by ineffectiveness. Congresswomen of color have also been rendered invisible, however, in instances of significant legislative achievement. The role of Congresswomen of color in pressing for minimum wage legislation in the 104th Congress is well documented in the *Congressional Record*. The demand for a "livable wage" was a recurrent motif in their floor statements during the debates over welfare reform. Arguing that poverty could be eliminated for the working poor only if the minimum wage were increased sufficiently to lift those who worked full-time above the federal poverty level, Congresswomen of color organized to put minimum wage legislation on the agenda. In the tradition of legislative entrepreneurs (Kingdon 1984) and coalition leaders (Arnold 1990), Democratic Congresswomen of color wrote to the Minority Leader to press him to put a minimum wage bill at the top of his priorities. They wrote multiple "Dear Colleague" letters to all members of Congress in an effort to persuade Democrats and Republicans of the importance of an increase in the minimum wage for working women, who constitute over 60% of minimum wage workers. They circulated evidence generated by economists that an increase in the minimum wage was correlated with an increase in business activity rather than a decrease as opponents of the measure suggested (Clayton 1997). When the Republican House leadership was reluctant to schedule a vote on the proposed legislation, Representative Ileana Ros Lehtinen [R-FL], who was a cosponsor of HR 3265, the Minimum Wage Increase Act of 1996, worked with Jack Quinn [R-NY] to pressure the leadership to hold a straight up or down vote. When the vote was held, the legislation passed. Despite the activism of Congresswomen of color on both sides of the aisle in support of the Minimum Wage Increase Act, when the press conference was called to announce the enactment of the legislation, all the spokespersons for the Administration and for the Congress were male.

Representative Patsy Mink [D-HI] (1997) reported that the all-male delegation taking credit for the legislation was not inadvertent. On the contrary, she had lobbied the Secretary of Labor without success to include some women in the press conference. Thus Republican men who had been most opposed to the legislation while it was under consideration in Congress claimed full credit in public for its passage. In casting themselves as the real representatives of women's interests in Congress, these white men effectively rendered invisible the intensive labor of Congresswomen of color to advance the interests of the nation's working poor. . . .

One tactic underrepresented groups in Congress developed to try to minimize the personal costs of raced–gendered interactions was the creation of legislative service organizations (LSOs), such as the Congressional Black Caucus and the Congressional Caucus for Women's Issues, which could not only serve as support networks for members, but also provide a mechanism for collective action outside of party structures. Funded by contributions from members' staff allowances, the legislative service organizations hired staff to conduct research, draft legislation, and help the members devise successful legislative strategies to advance shared interests.

In the opening days of the 104th Congress, House Speaker Newt Gingrich [R-GA] introduced a number of structural changes to streamline House operations. The abolition of 28 legislative service organizations including the Congressional Black Caucus (CBC) and the Congressional Caucus for Women's Issues (CCWI) is of particular interest in the context of racing–gendering practices; for Gingrich's decision to eliminate the LSOs was perceived by many as an effort to mute the organized voice of blacks and the organized voice of women within the halls of Congress. The withdrawal of office space, furnishings, and equipment and the edict prohibiting members from using their staff allowances to support such collective endeavors were perceived as an assault motivated by racism and sexism. . . . Confiscation, dispossession, physical removal, and lockouts are not tactics typically deployed between equals. Nor do such draconian measures make much sense in terms of rational power maximization. Since almost all of the members of the CBC were Democrats, the tactics they had attempted to employ as a voting bloc to gain leverage within the Democratic party would not have worked with the new Republican majority. For this reason, they posed little threat to the Republican leadership of the House. Within the context of racing–gendering, however, the demarcation of government property as off-limits for the CBC staff takes on ominous meaning: for it racializes congressional space, constructing the black members of the House as somehow not fully part of the government, not entitled to use their resources to advance black interests. To physically bar black staff working without pay from House office buildings is to send a message about the Majority Leader's preference for the House as a white enclave. Thus the forcible eviction of the CBC staff from the Capitol was taken by Congresswomen of color as a particularly egregious example of institutional racism.

For Congresswomen of color, eliminating rights of participation, hampering efforts to devise collective strategies, and dampening the organized voice of underrepresented groups constituted unmistakably raced and gendered politics. While the institutional rule changes that sustained this politics of exclusion were neutral on their face, they were experienced by Congresswomen of color as race–gender specific in their effects. As such, they engendered new strategies for collective action. . . . Within Congress, the CBC and the CCWI reorganized as Congressional Members Organizations (CMOs), a form of organization that was not prohibited by Gingrich's institutional restructuring, and continued to meet to devise strategies to provide substantive representation for what they perceived as their national constituencies, women and people of color. . . .

Explanatory Possibilities of a Theory of Racing–Gendering

To this point, most of the examples of racing–gendering have been drawn from the 104th Congress. Some might then claim that what appears to be racing–gendering is really a matter of partisan politics. I have noted that such a reductive move is incompatible with the views of Congresswomen of color themselves. To support further the claim that racing–gendering is distinctive from partisan maneuvers, I want to expand the analysis to compare instances of racing–gendering in the Democratically controlled 103rd Congress with those in the Republican-controlled 104th Congress in one policy area, welfare reform. Welfare policy is a particularly appropriate case for the examination of racing–gendering for a number of reasons.

Since its inception, U.S. welfare policy has reinforced structural inequalities rooted in race–gender (Fraser 1989; G. Mink 1995). Restricted primarily to women recipients deemed morally worthy by the state bureaucrats, welfare has been "dispensed in a disparate and racially unequal manner not just in the Jim Crow era, but since the Voting Rights Act" (Darling 1998, 161). Racial bias in determinations of eligibility ensured that "African American and Latinos remained underrepresented on the welfare rolls, despite high levels of need" (Mettler 2000, 12). Although racial disparities in the allocation of benefits have typified welfare policy, and the majority of welfare recipients are white, cultural stereotypes of the typical welfare recipient are highly racialized. Several studies have demonstrated that the racist attitudes fueling the misperception of welfare recipients as overwhelmingly black influence white opposition to welfare (Gilens 1995, 1996). There is also evidence that entrenched racism has shaped decades of policymakers' efforts to reform welfare (Lieberman 1995; Quadagno 1994).

Welfare reform is also an appropriate focus, for it helps to illuminate the explanatory possibilities of the theory of racing–gendering in Congress. I will argue that the theory of racing–gendering provides a better explanation of the motivations and intensity of involvement of Congresswomen of color in welfare reform legislation than other accounts of congressional behavior. According to studies of constituency influence in Congress, welfare recipients are not a constituency likely to receive strong representation in the halls of Congress. As Hall (1996, 201) has pointed out, "The proposition that lower-class interests will suffer from relatively weak representation in the American political system dates at least back to E. E. Schattschneider's *The Semi-Sovereign People* (1960)." While welfare recipients are concentrated in the geographic constituencies of legislators representing inner cities, they are neither an attentive public nor the "primary constituency" (i.e., strongest supporters) of urban representatives (Fenno 1978). They do not donate time or money to campaigns and often they do not vote. They do not tend to be well informed about legislation pending in Congress. And with the exception of the activism mobilized by the National Welfare Rights Organization in the early 1970s (Sparks 1997), they tend to be unorganized. Why then did Congresswomen of color devote such time and energy to the representation of an unorganized majority-white underclass? . . .

The theory of racing–gendering can offer some insights into such questions. Through the following case study, I attempt to show that the intense involvement of Congresswomen of color in welfare reform legislation over the course of the 103rd and 104th Congresses can best be understood as an instance of resistance engendered in response to racing–gendering in Congress. I argue that as white Democrats and Republicans shifted the terrain of welfare debates from poverty alleviation to pathologizing and racializing the poor, Congresswomen of color mobilized at considerable political cost to make a public stand on the issue. In addition to the political harms of going against their own party and their President in the 103rd Congress and against the Republican majority in the 104th, the cost Congresswomen of color paid for their resistance was subjection to intensified forms of racing–gendering in Congress. Their willingness to incur those costs can be understood as a political manifestation of willed resistance to racing–gendering. In the case of welfare reform, to live with anger is to legislate against the grain. The theory of racing—gendering in Congress thus illuminates a form of minority participation at great remove from the "expression of minority opinion central to the practice of democratic consent" (Hall 1996, 238). Far from legitimating the legislative process and the policy it produces, legislating against the grain provides a trenchant indictment of the system.

A Case Study of Welfare Reform

In the 103rd Congress when welfare reform was placed on the political agenda by President Clinton and by the Republican minority, Congresswomen of color were fully supportive of the prospect of reforming the welfare system. The reforms they sought, however, placed them at odds with dominant forces in the Democratic and Republican parties. The Congresswomen of color sought a welfare reform that would eliminate poverty. Thus, they sought legislation that would address the structural causes of poverty, such as low wages and unemployment. They also sought strategies to address the needs of welfare recipients, such as lack of training, lack of transportation, and lack of child care, which constituted major barriers to workforce participation. . . .

Central to the concerns of Congresswomen of color was the circulation of racialized stereotypes about welfare recipients, particularly the construction of welfare recipients as women of color—too lazy to work—who sought to cheat the system. To counteract the "stereotypes that were alive and well" (McKinney 1997), Congresswomen of color tried to inject social science research into the debate. On October 23, 1993, Representatives Patsy Mink [D-HI] and Maxine Waters [D-CA] joined their colleagues Ed Pastor [D-AZ] and Lynn Woolsey [D-CA] in cochairing a conference on Women and Welfare Reform: Women's Opportunities and Women's Welfare. Sponsored by the Institute for Women's Policy Research in Washington, DC, the conference brought together academics and policymakers in an effort to "break myths and create solutions," The elements of progressive welfare reform outlined at this conference became the basis for the alternative welfare reform legislation introduced by Patsy Mink

and supported by all the Congresswomen of color. The alternative welfare reform included a proposal for a living wage, . . . education and training opportunities to equip welfare recipients for jobs that would enable them to escape poverty, job creation to counteract unemployment, child care to meet the needs of working parents, and transportation allowances to make remote worksites accessible. The Congresswomen of color supported enhanced entitlements to eradicate poverty, but their policy recommendations remained far more progressive than the proposals endorsed by the Democratic task force, which were announced by President Clinton in June 1994. Introduced immediately prior to Congress's summer recess and the fall congressional elections, the Clinton proposal to "end welfare as we know it" died with the 103rd Congress.

The experiences of the Democratic women of color in the 103rd Congress as the Democratic majority crafted welfare legislation exemplify marginalization. Many reported that they could not gain access to key white male decision makers and, as such, could not influence the shape of the legislation. Despite repeated efforts to shift the terms of debate away from erroneous perceptions of welfare cheats and cycles of dependency, neither the social science knowledge they circulated nor the personal experiences they related were taken as authoritative or compelling. Even Representative Patsy Mink's substitute proposal, which garnered 90 Democrats' votes in the House, was dismissed rather than selectively incorporated into the President's plan.

Welfare Reform in the 104th Congress

In contrast to the concern with structural causes of poverty, which lay at the heart of the approach to welfare reform taken by Congresswomen of color, the Republican proposals for welfare reform framed poverty as a matter of personal responsibility, particularly in relation to marriage and responsible fatherhood and motherhood. Asserting that the nation confronted a "crisis of out-of-wedlock births," the Republicans proposed legislation designed to "ensure that the responsibility of having a child belongs to the mother and father, rather than to the mother and the U.S. taxpayer" (Meyers 1993).[3] Several of the key provisions of the Republican welfare reform targeted teen pregnancy in particular and out-of-wedlock births more generally on the assumption that "the increase in the number of children receiving public assistance is closely related to the increase in births to unmarried women" (The Personal Responsibility and Work Opportunity Reconciliation Act of 1996, Public Law 104-193, 42 USC 601, Sec. 101 [5]C). In the words of Dick Armey [R-TX] (1995), "We need to understand . . . that it is illegitimacy and childbirth, fatherless children, that is so much at the heart of the distress that seems to be unending and growing worse and larger each year. So we insist that we must have a new approach that brings down illegitimacy, and quite rightly so many of us say, yes, bring down illegitimacy, but not through increased abortions." . . .

Congresswomen of color perceived the attack on single mothers at the heart of welfare reform proposals as an attack on the black family, an attack that resurrected pathological theories of poverty, which had circulated in policy circles since the Moynihan Report in the 1960s. To counter Republican claims about the causes of poverty, Congresswomen of color turned to social science. To engage the mistaken notion that single-parent families are the cause of increasing poverty in the United States, Representative Patsy Mink (1997) circulated to all members of the House and Senate copies of a 1995 study (Brown 1995) conducted by the Center on Hunger, Poverty and Nutritional Policy at Tufts University. Drawing upon the research of 76 scholars who specialize in the areas of poverty and welfare, Mink contested the conflation of single-motherhood with poverty and presented an alternative account. . . . Despite Representative Mink's attempt to invoke the authority of the social science community and the U.S. Census Bureau to shift the terms of the welfare debate, the empirical evidence did nothing to dispel the correlation mistaken for causation at the heart of the Personal Responsibility and Work Opportunity Reconciliation Act (PRWORA).

Congresswomen of color were deeply concerned that the Republican focus on out-of-wedlock births, unwed mothers, and single-women heads-of-household was a thinly veiled attack upon poor women of color. During a number of increasingly vitriolic floor debates the legitimacy of their concern became apparent as even the pretense of using race-neutral language to characterize the poor disappeared and Republican legislators denounced illegitimacy in the black community. For example, in his floor speech Representative Cunningham [R-CA] (1995) linked illegitimacy in the black community not only with welfare, but with crime and drug addiction.[4] Representatives Patsy Mink [D-HI] (1995), Sheila Jackson Lee [D-TX] (1995a, b), Maxine Waters [D-CA] (1996), Eva Clayton [D-NC] (1995a–c), and Nydia Velazquez [D-NY] (1995) repeatedly emphasized in floor debate that the majority of welfare recipients were white, but their factual claims failed to dispel racialized welfare myths. In the words of Representative Barbara Collins [D-MI] (1998), "The Congress unfortunately had the image of a welfare recipient as an urban black woman, who irresponsibly had children, was lazy, refused to work, was uneducated. Whereas the truth of the matter was that the majority of welfare recipients were white, white women and white families,"[5]

As a white woman and the only member of Congress to have once been a welfare recipient, Representative Lynn Woolsey [D-CA] (1998) also took to the House floor to tell her colleagues that most welfare recipients were white. "My strategy was to be out there, to take the heat and show people . . . that welfare moms were like me, that I was the typical welfare mom. They had to see that. Then I'd hear on the other side of the aisle, 'Yeah, but you're different.'" The racialization of the poor had conflated welfare recipient and black women so powerfully in the minds of some members of the House that they refused to accept that the typical welfare recipient is a white woman who resorts to welfare for a short time after a divorce in order to support her kids while she gets back on her feet. Facts that did not conform to raced–gendered stereotypes about welfare recipients were simply dismissed.

Since argument rooted in personal experience was not carrying much weight in welfare reform debates, Congresswomen of color relied heavily on social science research in their efforts to dispel other erroneous and damaging myths about welfare. In floor debates, Republicans constructed welfare recipients as "welfare addicts who will do anything to stay on the public dole" (Vucanovich 1995) and as people who need "tough love" to free "a whole class of people that have been held in bondage for generation after generation and cannot get out of bondage" (Chenowith 1995). In contrast to this image of perpetual dependency, Patsy Mink (1995) repeatedly emphasized that the majority of welfare recipients resort to welfare when beset by crises such as illness, unemployment, domestic violence, and divorce and remain on welfare for less than a year; indeed 80% of recipients rely on welfare for less than 2 years. Representative Lucille Roybal-Allard [D-CA] (1996) emphasized domestic violence as the reason that many women resort to welfare for short periods of time. "A recent study by the Taylor Institute of Chicago . . . found that 50–80% of women on AFDC are current or past victims of domestic violence. . . . For victims of abuse, the welfare system is often the only hope they have for escape and survival." As in the case of causal claims about poverty and empirical claims about the demographic characteristics of welfare recipients, social scientific evidence about welfare use made no impact on the terms of Congressional debate. Reflecting upon these frustrating floor debates, Representative Eva Clayton [D-NC] (1997) said, "I was trying to speak out for reason. I'm not sure I succeeded in that. . . . I would like to think that my role was to present common sense. Again I don't think I succeeded in that."

In addition to empirical arguments based upon social science research, Congresswomen of color raised constitutional arguments about the permissibility of discriminating against legal immigrants, punishing children for actions of their parents, and violating the rights of poor women to privacy in reproductive decision making (Meek 1995; Velazquez 1995). They also tried to humanize welfare recipients, to depict welfare recipients as mothers struggling against adversity to meet the needs of their children and as children who themselves are grappling with material deprivation that marginalizes them from the mainstream. Challenging the stereotype of the welfare cheat who gets pregnant to qualify for or to increase welfare benefits, Representative Sheila Jackson Lee [D-TX] (1995a) asserted unequivocally on the basis of her own interactions with welfare recipients and on the basis of social science evidence that "women do not get pregnant to get welfare." Representative Patsy Mink also quoted evidence from the Census Bureau and the Department of Health and Human Services to prove that there is no causal relationship between the availability of welfare benefits and the size or structure of poor families. . . .

Congresswomen of color were among the most outspoken opponents of welfare reform in congressional debates. Like her Democratic counterparts in the House, Senator Carol Moseley-Braun (D-IL), the only woman of color in the Senate, was an outspoken critic of the welfare reform bills in the Senate. She too tried to persuade her fellow Senators that the legislation under consideration would not address the underlying problem of welfare: poverty. . . . Like her counterparts in the House, Senator Moseley-Braun tried to use her power on the Senate Finance Committee to alter the welfare reform bill. She drafted a substitute proposal, The Personal Self-Sufficiency Act, which she introduced as an amendment to the draft welfare bill prepared by Committee Chair Bob Packwood. Her amendment was defeated in the Finance Committee by a 12–8 vote. She also tried to amend the welfare reform bill from the Senate floor, but her amendment was again defeated, by a 58–42 vote.

In the House and in the Senate, women of color worked arduously to air an alternative vision of welfare recipients and to advance an alternative version of welfare reform. According to one congressional staffer, "They spoke disproportionate to their seniority" on welfare reform (Hawkesworth et al. 2001). Yet their words seemed to have no effect. The statistical evidence they adduced was discounted. Their cogent arguments were dismissed. Authoritative knowledge was deemed to lie beyond their grasp. Gayatri Spivak (1988) has suggested that the refusal of the dominant to hear the voices of and for the oppressed is a perennial tactic in technologies of race–gender. It is a form of racing–gendering that permeated welfare reform debates in the 103rd and the 104th Congresses, ensnaring Congresswomen of color in a prolonged and painful *pendejo* game.

. . . The distorted racialized stereotypes of welfare recipients continued to circulate in discussions of welfare reform on the floor and in committees of the House and Senate until the Congress passed The Personal Responsibility and Work Opportunity Reconciliation Act in August 1996. Representative Waters, like many of the Congresswomen of color, transformed her anger at the calumnies against the poor into efforts to mobilize public opposition to welfare reform.

Mobilization of anger is a tactic that several Congresswomen of color reported deploying in response to the welfare reform legislation. Representative Corrine Brown [D-FL] (1998), for example, said that she felt it was her responsibility "to educate my constituents as to what was going on so they could be enraged and call their Senators. . . . In August I conducted 50 town meetings [to which] anybody could come and listen." In response to the proposal to drastically cut the school lunch program, Representative Eva Clayton [D-NC] (1997) "organized Forums called 'Feed the Folk's down in our district, and we must have received about 1300 different petitions to save the school lunch program."

In addition to their efforts to mobilize the anger of voters in their districts, I would suggest that the intensive and varied participation of Congresswomen of color in welfare reform efforts behind the scenes, in committees, and on the floor be understood as a mode of resistance against racing–gendering. Through a wide array of tactical maneuvers, Congresswomen of color attempted to stem the stigmatization, racialization, and punitive regulation of poor women. They proposed multiple amendments to the welfare reform bills. Although none of the 20 amendments that Representative Carrie Meek [D-FL] introduced as a member of the budget committee passed, two amendments proposed by Congresswomen of color to the House Rules Committee did succeed and were eventually approved by the House.[6] Representative Eva Clayton succeeded in inserting language that required that individuals employed or participating in a work or workfare program be paid at least at the minimum wage. Ileana Ros-Lehtinen [R-FL] secured an exemption for mentally or physically disabled immigrants from provisions excluding legal immigrants from access to state and local public benefits. . . .

In their efforts to legislate against the grain, Congresswomen of color deployed the full repertoire of strategies available to legislators. In the 103rd Congress, they used their power within the Democratic Party to try to shape the content of President Clinton's welfare reform proposal. They cochaired scholarly conferences to try to shape public perceptions of the poor, as well as the content of welfare legislation. They used their power in committees to try to amend Republican-sponsored legislation in the 104th Congress. They drafted one of two Democratic alternative bills to H.R. 4 considered in the House, as well as one of the Democratic alternative bills considered in the Senate during the first session of the 104th Congress. They secured a special order to allow a floor debate of the welfare legislation in the House of Representatives. They used their intellectual and rhetorical power in floor debates to try to alter congressional understandings of poverty. They scheduled press conferences featuring welfare recipients to try to get alternative images of the poor before the Congress and the public. They wrote "Dear Colleague" letters and circulated them with comprehensive social scientific studies in an effort to break the hold of pernicious stereotypes of the poor. They held town meetings across their constituencies to mobilize voters against the pending legislation. Even in the final hours they joined with a bipartisan group of 26 women members from both houses in sending a letter to the Conference Committee to try to shape the compromise bill that would eventually become law. But ultimately they failed to convince their colleagues to move beyond what they perceived to be racist stereotypes and policies that punished the poor. In the end, they used the power of their votes in Congress to oppose both versions of the welfare reform legislation. All 15 Congresswomen of color—14 Democrats and one Republican—voted against The Personal Responsibility Act and The Personal Responsibility and Work Opportunity Reconciliation Act. Their opposition was intense and consistent across two Congresses, but there is no indication that in airing their minority view, they accorded legitimacy to the process or to the bill that resulted from it. On the contrary, their stories of marginalization and thwarted effort, of the silencing of reason and evidence, and of the pervasive racing–gendering of welfare recipients and Congresswomen of color provide a resounding indictment of this form of majority rule. . . .

Notes

1. King notes that the preponderance of these elected officials held positions on local school boards. Congresswomen of color included Patsy Mink [D-HI], Shirley Chisholm [D-NY], Barbara Jordan [D-TX], Yvonne Braithwaite Burke [D-CA], and Cardiss Collins [D-IL].

2. In her study of state legislators, Thomas (1994, 37) found that male legislators routinely deny that they engage in stereotyping and sexist behavior or that women legislators are in any way limited in their legislative roles by stereotypes or sexism. Yet when asked to compare women's and men's performance in the legislature, the male legislators tended to identify certain "deficiencies" that impaired women's legislative effectiveness. The imputed deficiencies conformed to sexist stereotypes. For the purposes of my argument, it does not matter whether the racing–gendering is done intentionally or unintentionally. My goal is simply to demonstrate that these practices exist and have effects within legislatures.

3. Representative Jan Meyers [R-KS] was one of the first Republicans to frame welfare reform in terms of personal responsibility. This quote was taken from a floor speech accompanying her introduction of welfare reform legislation in early 1993. Although this bill died in Committee during the 103rd Congress, many of its provisions were incorporated in the 1994 Republican welfare reform.

4. The Personal Responsibility and Work Opportunity Reconciliation Act also strings together a series of claims about children of single-parent families and failure in and expulsion from schools and rates of violent crime (42 USC 601, Sec. 101 [9]I-M).

5. The bipartisan reference to the Congress in this statement is intentional, since many white Democrats as well as Republicans were articulating racialized claims about welfare recipients.

6. Eleven other amendments submitted by Congresswomen of color to the Rules Committee were not accepted (*Congressional Record*, 104th Cong., 1st sess., March 21, 1995).

References

Armey, Dick. 1995. *Congressional Record*, 104th Cong., 1st sess., p. H3444, March 22.

Arnold, R. Douglas. 1990. *The Logic of Congressional Action*. New Haven, CT: Yale University Press.

Bratton, Kathleen, and Kerry Haynie. 1999. "Agenda Setting and Legislative Success in State Legislatures: The Effects of Race and Gender." *Journal of Politics* 61 (August): 658–79.

Brown, Corrinne. 1998. Center for American Women and Politics Interview, March 12.

Brown, J. Larry. 1995. "Key Welfare Reform Issues: The Empirical Evidence." Center on Hunger, Poverty, and Nutritional Policy. Tufts University.

Bryce, Herrington, and Alan Warrick. 1977. "Black Women in Electoral Politics." In *A Portrait of Marginality*, ed. Marianne Githens and Jewell Prestage, New York: David Mckay, 395–400.

Center for American Women and Politics. 2002. "Fact Sheet: Women of Color in Elective Office, 2002." New Brunswick, NJ.

Chenowith, Helen. 1995. *Congressional Record*, 104th Cong., 1st sess., p. H3720, March 23.

Clayton, Eva. 1995a. *Congressional Record*, 104th Cong., 1st sess., p. H1684, February 13.

Clayton, Eva. 1995b. *Congressional Record*, 104th Cong., 1st sess., p. H3445, March 22.

Clayton, Eva. 1995c. *Congressional Record*, 104th Cong., 1st sess., p. H3511, March 22.

Clayton, Eva. 1997. Center for American Women and Politics Interview, November 4.

Collins, Barbara Rose. 1998. Center for American Women and Politics Interview, February 18.

Connell, Robert. 1987. *Gender and Power*. Stanford, CA: Stanford University Press.

Crenshaw, Kimberle. 1989. "Demarginalizing the Intersection of Race and Sex: A Black Feminist Critique of Antidiscrimination Doctrine, Feminist Theory and Antiracist Politics." *University of Chicago Legal Forum* 1989: 139–67.

Crenshaw, Kimberle. 1997. "Beyond Racism and Misogyny." In *Women Transforming Politics*, ed. Cathy Cohen, Kathy Jones, and Joan Tronto. New York: New York University Press.

Cunningham, Randy. 1995. *Congressional Record*, 104th Cong., 1st sess., p. H3446, March 21.

Darling, Marsha. 1998. "African American Women in State Elective Office in the South." In *Women and Elective Office*, ed. Sue Thomas and Clyde Wilcox. New York: Oxford University Press.

Fenno, Richard F., Jr. 1978. *Home Style*. Boston: Little, Brown.

Flammang, Janet. 1997. *Women's Political Voice*. Philadelphia: Temple University Press.

Fraser, Nancy. 1989. "Women, Welfare, and the Politics of Need Interpretation." In *Unruly Practices*, ed. Nancy Fraser. Minneapolis: University of Minnesota Press.

Gilens, Martin. 1995. "Racial Attitudes and the Opposition to Welfare." *Journal of Politics* 57 (November): 994–1014.

Gilens, Martin. 1996. "Race Coding and White Opposition to Welfare." *American Political Science Review* 90 (September): 593–604.

Githens, Marianne, and Jewell Prestage. 1997. "A Minority within a Minority." In *Portraits of Marginality: The Political Behavior of the American Woman*, ed. Marianne Githens and Jewell Prestage. New York: David McKay, 339–45.

Hall, Richard. 1996. *Participation in Congress*. New Haven, CT: Yale University Press.

Haney Lopez, Ian. 1996. *White by Law*. New York: New York University Press.

Hawkesworth, Mary, Debra Dodson, Katherine Kleeman, Kathleen Casey, and Krista Jenkins. 2001. *Legislating* by *Women and for Women: A Comparison of the 103rd and 104th Congresses*. New Brunswick, NJ: Center for American Women and Politics.

Hurtado, Aida. 1996. *The Color of Privilege: Three Blasphemies on Race and Feminism*. Ann Arbor: University of Michigan Press.

Jackson Lee, Sheila. 1995a. *Congressional Record*, 104th Cong., 1st sess., p. H3554, March 22.

Jackson Lee, Sheila. 1995b. *Congressional Record*, 104th Cong., 1st sess., p. H3872, March 28.

King, Mae. 1997. "The Politics of Sexual Stereotypes. In *A Portrait of Marginality*, ed. Marianne Githens and Jewell Prestage. New York, David McKay, 346–65.

Kingdon, John. 1984. *Agendas, Alternatives, and Public Policies*. Boston: Little, Brown.

Lieberman, Robert C. 1995. "Race and the Organization of Welfare Policy." In Paul E. Peterson, ed., *Classifying by Race*. Princeton, NJ: Princeton University Press, 157–87.

Locke, Marnie. 1997. "From 3/5ths to Zero: Implications of the Constitution for African American Women, 1787–1870." In *Women Transforming Politics*, ed. Cathy Cohen, Kathy Jones, and Joan Tronto. New York: New York University Press.

Lorde, Audre. 1984. *Sister Outsider*. New York: Crossing Press.

McKinney, Cynthia. 1997. Center for American Women and Politics Interview. October 29.

Meek, Carrie. 1995. *Congressional Record*, 104th Cong., 1st sess., p. H15524, December 21.

Mettler, Suzanne. 2000. "States Rights, Women's Obligations: Contemporary Welfare Reform in Historical Perspective." *Women and Politics* 21 (1): 1–34.

Meyers, Jan. 1993. *Congressional Record*, 103rd Cong., 1st sess., p. H1084, March 10.

Mink, Gwendolyn. 1995. *The Wages of Motherhood: Inequality in the Welfare State*. Ithaca, NY: Cornell University Press.

Mink, Patsy. 1995. *Congressional Record*. 104th Cong., 1st sess., pp. H1685–1686, February 13.

Mink, Patsy. 1997. Center for American Women and Politics Interview, November 4.

National League of Cities. 2002. "Women of Color in Local Elective Offices" [includes all cities with populations greater than 10,000].

Quadagno, Jill. 1994. *The Color of Welfare: How Racism Undermined the War on Poverty*. New York: Oxford University Press.

Roybal-Allard, Louise. 1996. *Congressional Record*, 104th Cong., 2d sess., H7508, July 12.

Siltanen, Janet. 1994. *Locating Gender: Occupational Segregation, Wages and Domestic Responsibilities*. London: UCL Press.

Sparks, Holloway. 1997. "Dissident Citizenship: Democratic Theory, Political Courage, and Activist Women." *Hypatia: A Journal of Feminist Philosophy* 12 (December): 74–109.

Spivak, Gayatri. 1988. "Can the Subaltern Speak?" In *Marxism and the Interpretation of Culture*, ed. Cary Nelson and Lawrence Grossberg. Champaign–Urbana: University of Illinois Press.

Swain, Carol. 2000. "Minorities in the House: What Can We Expect in the Next Century?" In *The U.S. House of Representatives: Reform or Rebuild*, ed. Joseph Zimmerman and Wilma Rule. Westport, CT: Praeger, 36–50.

Taylor, Rupert. 1996. "Political Science Encounters 'Race' and 'Ethnicity.'" *Racial and Ethnic Studies* 19 (October): 884–95.

Thomas, Sue. 1994. *How Women Legislate*. New York: Oxford University Press.

Velazquez, Nydia. 1995. *Congressional Record*, 104th Cong., 1st sess., p. H15520, December 21.

Vucanovich, Barbara. 1995. *Congressional Record*, 104th Cong., 1st sess., p. H2587, March 3.

Waters, Maxine. 1996. *Congressional Record*, 104th Cong., 2d sess., p. H7749, July 17.

Woolsey, Lynn. 1998. Center for American Women and Politics Interview. February 12.

Yanow, Dvora. 2002. *Constructing "Race" and "Ethnicity" in America: Category-Making in Public Policy and Administration*. Armonk, NY: M. E. Sharpe.

Chapter 30
TAKING PROBLEMS APART
Carol Lee Bacchi

Have you ever read a newspaper article about a controversial topic and thought that you would have approached the issue from a completely different angle? Have you ever compared the two perspectives, yours and that of the columnist or reported speaker, and noted that the contrast in views had all sorts of consequences, including how to deal with the issue? If so, you have already been applying the approach which I will outline in this [chapter], an approach I call "What's the Problem?"—a shorthand for "what's the problem represented to be?" At its most basic, the insight is commonsensical—how we perceive or think about something will affect what we think ought to be done about it. . . . The flip side of this, and the guiding premise of a What's the Problem? approach, is that every policy proposal contains within it an explicit or implicit diagnosis of the "problem," which I call its problem representation. A necessary part of policy analysis hence includes identification and assessment of problem representations, the ways in which "problems" get represented in policy proposals.

While this might appear commonsensical, it is not the way we are taught or encouraged to think about political issues. These are often talked about or written about as if there were only one possible interpretation of the issue at stake. I do not mean that we are not offered competing opinions on particular issues; this of course is the stuff of party political banter. But we are not encouraged to reflect upon the ways in which issues take shape within these discussions. This is illustrated most clearly in policy studies, where students are often asked to study the policy process *as if* policies were attempts, more or less successful, to "deal with" a range of issues or "problems." Even when students are warned that indeed those affecting and initiating policy have assumptions and values, the investigation seldom reaches into the effects these will have on the way the people concerned describe or *give shape to* a particular political issue.

In contrast, the approach developed [here] takes as its starting point that it makes no sense to consider the "objects" or targets of policy as existing independently of the way they are spoken about or represented, either in political debate or in policy proposals. Any description of an issue or a "problem" is an interpretation, and interpretations involve judgment and choices. Crucially, we also need to realize that interpretations are interventions since they have programmatic outcomes; that is, the interpretation offered will line up with particular policy recommendations (see Fraser, 1989: 166–75). More directly, policy proposals of necessity contain interpretations and hence representations of "problems." Therefore, we need to shift our analysis from policies as attempted "solutions" to "problems," to policies as constituting competing interpretations or representations of political issues.

I use the phrase "What's the Problem?" as a way of achieving this refocusing. The phrase is intended to provoke an analysis which begins with asking of any particular policy proposal or policy the questions what is the "problem" represented to be; what presuppositions are implied or taken for granted in the problem representation which is offered; and what effects are connected to this representation of the "problem?." Important follow-up questions would probe what is left unproblematic in particular representations, and how "responses" would differ if the "problem" were represented differently. The focus on interpretations or representations means a focus on discourse, defined here as the language, concepts, and categories employed to frame an issue. . . . This means that the objects of study are no longer "problems" but problematizations—"all those discursive practices that introduce something into the play of true and false and constitute it as an object for moral reflection, scientific knowledge or political analysis" (Foucault, 1984: 257, 265, cited in Reekie, 1994: 464). The focus on effects means that in this analysis discourse refers not just to ideas or to ways of talking, but to practices with material consequences. . . .

This [chapter] applies a What's the Problem? approach to a number of issues directly affecting the lives of many women, issues frequently taken as the focus in courses on women and policy. In doing this, I am not endorsing the common reference to "women's issues," a notion I intend to challenge. *Every* issue affects the lives of women and a What's the Problem? approach could be applied to any policy area. In addition, a What's the Problem? approach offers a way to think beyond single issues, and questions the kind of separation implied by a listing of discrete policy areas. In contrast to many studies of policy, a What's the Problem? approach encourages us to think about the interconnections between policy areas, and to reflect upon which issues remain unaddressed or undiscussed because of the ways certain "problems" are represented. . . .

A What's the Problem? approach encourages deeper reflection on the contours of a particular policy discussion, the shape assigned a particular "problem." In many cases, it is not a matter of deliberately refusing to act but of talking about a "problem" as if "acting" is simply inappropriate or not an issue. Frances Olsen (1985) has noted the ways in which labeling items on a political "public" agenda or "private" serves to achieve this effect. So, the "private" domestic sphere of "private" enterprise is by this labeling located outside of "public" accountability (see also Plumwood, 1995).

Olsen also emphasizes that decisions by governments affect the circumstances which provide the background to decisions we make about how we live our lives; hence, governments are "intervening" all the time, even when they are not "acting" in the traditional sense—not providing publicly funded child care or free-standing abortion clinics, for example. Importantly, for the point being made here, these issues might never come up for discussion, and hence it would be impossible to identify and talk about *deliberate* inaction. In this way, a What's the Problem? approach is markedly different from analyses that ask why and how some issues *make it* to the political agenda, while others do not (see, for example, Bachrach and Baratz, 1963; Cobb and Elder, 1983; Kingdom, 1995). Its starting point is a close analysis of items that *do* make the political agenda to see how the construction or representation of those issues limits what is talked about as possible or desirable, or as impossible or undesirable. . . .

It seems appropriate at this point to offer an example to illustrate the different kind of thinking a What's the Problem? approach entails. If we were thinking about political discussions of pornography, we would ask not what is the problem with pornography, but rather, what kind of a problem is pornography represented to be within different policy recommendations? This question opens up a space for reflecting upon the competing understandings of pornography offered by moral conservatives, defenders of free speech, feminists who find themselves in sympathy at some level with one of these interpretations, and feminists who wish to contrast their analyses with each of the other approaches. Representations of a "problem" can encompass two interrelated levels of analysis and judgment. There can be different impressions offered of what is a concern. There can also be different impressions offered of the causes of a "problem." So, with pornography, the concern may be expressed as moral degradation, *or* as an abuse of women, while the "cause" could be described as a lack of moral restraint, *or* as men's desire to control women. This example indicates that a great deal is at stake in competing representations of "problems." As Deborah Stone (1988: 162) forcefully states, "[S]truggles over causal definitions of problems, then, are contests over basic structures of social organization."

A little elaboration is required at this point. It might have occurred to some readers that, for defenders of free speech, pornography is *not* a "problem." As Merton (1966: 786) noted some years ago, "the same social condition will be defined by some as a social problem and by others as an agreeable and fitting state of affairs." However, those who call pornography a "problem" provoke a response from those who dispute its problem status. A What's the Problem? approach insists that it is crucial to reflect upon the representations offered both by those who describe something as a problem and by those who deny an issue problem status. Its purpose is to create a space to consider *competing constructions of issues addressed in the policy process, and the ways in which these constructions leave other issues untouched.* The approach can be applied to debates surrounding policy issues in public venues such as parliaments or the media, to policy documents such as committee reports, and to policy proposals in the shape of legislative or judicial decrees. For committee-produced documents, it is important to note that several problem representations may lodge within a single document, causing tensions and contradictions (see Maddox, 1997: 3). Still, the key insight of a What's the Problem? approach remains—the need to uncover problem representations and to see where they, and by implication, where they do not, lead.

I suggest thinking about problem representations as nested one within the other, necessitating repetition of the question "What's the problem represented to be?" at each level of analysis (see Fraser, 1989: 163). Thinking of pay equity, for example, the *concern* is often represented to be either the undervaluing of women's work or the low wages some women receive. However, the undervaluing of women's work is also often offered as a *cause* of the low wages some women receive. Causes of the undervaluing are commonly represented to be either discrimination or gender segregation of the labor force. Gender segregation itself can be represented to be a problem of discrimination or a matter of women's "choices." Discrimination is also represented to be different kinds of problems in different literatures. This example highlights the need to reflect upon the implications of different problem representations in successive layers of analysis. . . .

. . . [A] What's the Problem? approach insists upon a close scrutiny of the ways in which "social problems" are represented and what follows from these representations. It challenges the common presumption that achieving social problem status for one's cause is in itself a sign of success, a commitment to important change. Rather, it depends upon the way in which the problem is represented. For example, describing racism as the product of individual prejudice provides little leverage to challenge structural discrimination. Similarly, seeing sexual harassment as the unruly behavior of a few predatory men deters an analysis of the role played in sexual harassment by the greater social prestige attached to the status "male." While not wanting to discount the challenges and resistances posed by groups of people who mobilize to press for change, we need, in my view, to consider more closely the shape of the challenges they pose, the ways in which they perceive and represent "problems," and the reasons for this. Here we need to reflect upon why certain reform responses get taken up, why others get dismissed, and what happens to reform proposals in the process of being "taken up." . . .

Context is highly important in a What's the Problem? analysis. This is because "problems" are often constituted differently due to location-specific, institution-specific, and history-specific factors. Attention to these specifics will provide insights into why some versions of a "problem" appear in one place and other versions appear elsewhere, and/or why an issue problematized in one setting remains unproblematized in another. . . .

. . . To put it briefly, I argue that it is impossible to talk about any social condition without putting an interpretation to it. Hence, all we as analysts have access to are the interpretations. So, while I believe that there are a multitude of disturbing social conditions, once they are given the shape of an interpretation, once they are characterized as a "problem" or as a "social problem," they are no longer "real." They are interpretations or constructs of the "real." We can have no direct access to the "real." In the words of Bannister and Fransella (1977: 18), "we cannot contact an interpretation-free reality directly." This is what is meant by the sometimes misunderstood phrase that people do not "discover" problems; they "create" them. It is the particular shape, the problem representation, assigned a "problem" which is created.

I feel the need to spell this out clearly because it is easy for some who see "real" challenged in this way to conclude that this means that "social problems" are unreal, are inventions. In fact, there are many in the community who would leap at such an interpretation—all those, for example, who would challenge the "problem" status of issues like racism, sexism, or pollution. I hope it is clear that this is not my intention in saying that it is impossible to identify "real" "social problems." A What's the Problem? approach accepts that there are numerous troubling conditions, but states that we cannot talk about them outside of their representations, and their representations hence become what is important—because of the shape they give to the problem, and because of what they imply about what should be done or should not be done.

. . . [A] What's the Problem? approach is useful for any policy field. It provides a way of studying policy which opens up a range of questions that are seldom addressed in other approaches: how every proposal necessarily offers a representation of the problem to be addressed, how these representations contain presuppositions and assumptions which often go unanalyzed, how these representations shape an issue in ways which limit possibilities for change. It also offers a framework for examining gaps and silences in policy debate by asking what remains unproblematized in certain representations. Here I offer an elaborated set of questions which could be used to initiate a What's the Problem? approach of any selected issue, remembering the dangers of single-issue analysis and the need to reflect upon interconnections between policy areas:

- What is the problem of (domestic violence, abortion, etc.) represented to be either in a specific policy debate or in a specific policy proposal?
- What presuppositions or assumptions underlie this representation?
- What effects are produced by this representation? How are subjects constituted within it? What is likely to change? What is likely to stay

the same? Who is likely to benefit from this representation?
- What is left unproblematic in this representation?
- How would "responses" differ if the "problem" were thought about or represented differently?

While these questions directly target policy *proposals*, they can also be used to clarify the assumptions and implications of understandings of an issue offered by those who *deny* an issue "problem" status. . . .

References

Bachrach, Peter and Baratz, Morton S. (1963) "Decisions and Nondecisions: An Analytical Framework," *American Political Science Review*, 57 (3): 632–42.

Bannister, Don and Fransella, Fay (1977 [1971]) *Inquiring Man: The Theory of Personal Constructs*. Harmondsworth: Penguin.

Cobb, Roger and Elder, Charles (1983) *Participation in American Politics*, second edition. Baltimore, MD: Johns Hopkins University Press.

Foucault, Michel (1984) "The Concern for Truth" in L. D. Kritzman (ed.) *Politics, Philosophy, Culture: Interviews and Other Writings 1977–1984*. New York: Routledge, pp. 255–67.

Fraser, Nancy (1989) *Unruly Practices: Power, Discourse and Gender in Contemporary Social Theory*. Minneapolis, MN: University of Minnesota Press.

Kingdom, Elizabeth (1995) "Body Politics and Rights" in Jo Bridgeman and Susan Millns (eds.) *Law and Body Politics: Regulating the Female Body*. Aldershot: Darmouth, pp. 1–21.

Maddox, Marion (1997) "A Critique of the National Action Plan for the Education of Girls," unpublished paper. University of Adelaide, Politics Department.

Merton, Robert K. (1966 [1961]) "Epilogue: Social Problems and Sociological Theory" in Robert K. Merton and Robert Nisbet (eds) *Contemporary Social Problems*. New York: Harcourt Brace Jovanovitch, pp. 778–823.

Olsen, Frances (1985) "The Myth of State Intervention in the Family," *University of Michigan Journal of Law Reform*, 18 (4): 835–64.

Plumwood, Val (1995) "Feminism, Privacy and Radical Democracy," *Anarchist Studies*, 3: 97–120.

Reekie, Gail (1994) "Reading the Problem Family: Post-Structuralism and the Analysis of Social Problems," *Drug and Alcohol Review*, 13: 457–65.

Stone, Deborah A. (1988). *Policy Paradox and Political Reason*. New York: HarperCollins.

Chapter 31

SEX AND THE STATE IN LATIN AMERICA

Mala Htun

One of the more contentious developments of modern politics is the claim of the state to regulate family life and gender relations. How and on what grounds should states organize the rights of parents over children, allocate property within marriage, offer the possibility of and grounds for divorce, and allow women the choice to terminate a pregnancy? In most countries around the world, laws on these issues historically conformed to religious and patriarchal models. State policy granted men almost complete power in the family and limited citizen discretion over decisions about marriage and reproduction. Between the 1960s and the 1990s, the rise of the feminist movement brought new ideas about women's roles, while changes in social practices and the consolidation of democratic politics put pressure on old laws. Lawyers, feminist activists, and liberal and socialist politicians organized to demand reform of laws on family equality and divorce; many also favored decriminalizing abortion. Some states introduced major liberalizing changes. . . . Other countries continued to uphold restrictive laws, often stressing the importance of traditional gender norms to cultural integrity and national identity.

This [chapter] studies the experiences of Argentina, Brazil, and Chile during the last third of the twentieth century to understand how and why states make decisions about policy on gender issues. Through comparative analysis, it assesses how the transition from dictatorship to democracy, relations between church and state, the mobilization of liberal and feminist reformers, and international norms shaped state policy on abortion, divorce,

and gender equality in the family. . . . [It] proposes a new, disaggregated approach to studying gender policy and the state. All three countries in this study modified laws to grant women greater rights in marriage. By contrast, only two out of three legalized divorce and none liberalized abortion. This suggests that differences among gender issues are politically consequential. Rather than treating "women's rights" or "feminist policies" as a single issue area, we should disaggregate gender issues.

. . . Issues differ in how they are processed politically, the groups that weigh in on policy debates, and the ideas at stake in change. Some policy issues provoke rhetorically charged public debate informed by clashing worldviews, principled beliefs, and religious and ethical traditions. Other policy issues occupy small groups that spend days arguing over details of syntax and sequence. The prospect of change on some issues threatens the status of Catholic values, prompting bishops to defend the Church's position in the public sphere. The Church is disinterested in other issues and neglects to flex its muscles in policy debates. These differences among issues stem in large part from how policies are framed (Yishai 1993: 208). "Absolutist" policies tend to be seen in symbolic terms, provoke gut responses and value clashes, and "more likely deal with policy ends than means" (Carmines and Stimson 1980: 80). Religious institutions are likely to weigh in on changes to an absolutist agenda. "Technical" policies, by contrast, demand expert knowledge and provoke little public controversy. Change on technical issues is less likely to put religion on the defensive. In short, "gender rights" is not one issue but many. Opportunities for reform on one issue may not lead to reform on others. To explain policy change, we must disaggregate gender issues.

The [chapter] emphasizes the role of "issue networks"—elite coalitions of lawyers, feminist activists, doctors, legislators, and state officials—in bringing about policy change. These issue networks, inspired by ideas of modernity, equality, and liberty; changes in other countries; and international treaties, constituted the impetus behind reform. The growth of the second-wave feminist movement, in particular, helped put gender equality and reproductive rights on the policy agenda in many countries. Feminist movements in all three countries raised public awareness about questions of gender, lobbied state officials, and worked with or within the state to help formulate state policy. Yet many members of issue networks were not feminist activists but middle-class male lawyers. These lawyers, who played decisive roles in early abortion reform, the legalization of divorce, and changes promoting equality in the family, have been the unsung heroes of much of gender law liberalization in Latin America. Their activism on gender rights serves as important evidence that gender, far from being a "woman question," involves and affects all of society.

The possibilities for policy change depended on whether and how these elite issue networks were able to hook into state institutions. Institutional features of military and democratic regimes and the relationship between church and state shaped this "fit" between issue networks and the state (the notion of "fit" comes from Skocpol 1992: 54–7). Military governments created technical commissions charged with modernizing the civil law, opening a privileged window of influence for lawyers to bring cosmopolitan legal theories to bear on domestic policy. The closed nature of these governments insulated technical decisions from societal input, thus expediting change. As a result, military rulers in Argentina, Brazil, and Chile presided over important reforms advancing gender equality in the family. Under democratic rule, the success of issue networks was more varied, for it depended on the weight of the authoritarian legacy, the political party system, and the strength of executive and partisan commitment to

women's rights. Not all democratic governments were able to complete an agenda of gender equality, reneging on promises made during the transition and contributing to the trend toward illiberal democracy in the region (Diamond 1999; O'Donnell 1994; Zakaria 1997).

The other major factor shaping issue network success was the relationship between church and state. For partisans of legal divorce to succeed, the bishops had to be overpowered and defeated. The eruption of church-state conflict over human rights, economic policy, and authoritarian rule performed this function, opening a window of opportunity for liberal issue networks to promulgate divorce.

Abortion is a special case, because it provoked considerably more moral conflict than other issues. Even when citizens in Latin America came to accept divorce, they remained deeply ambivalent about abortion. Though the practice is widespread, abortion laws are rarely enforced. Since middle-class women generally have access to safe abortions in private clinics, many see little reason to press for the liberalization of abortion laws. It is primarily poor women who suffer the consequences of clandestine abortions. At the same time, the political clout of abortion opponents grew, particularly after John Paul II became pope of the Roman Catholic Church and antiabortion movements organized at the global level. Whereas abortion was once considered a technical issue of interest to criminologists and health practitioners, by the 1970s the abortion debate became polarized around a clash of absolutist values, frustrating political compromise over abortion legislation.

. . . In spite of their superficial similarities, the timing and content of gender policy in Argentina, Brazil, and Chile differed significantly. This variation is striking across countries and across issues. Brazil started to change its laws first, and these changes continued throughout the period of military rule. Argentina introduced major civil law reforms during military rule, though most of its changes came after the 1983 democratic transition. Chile, by contrast, which waited until 1989 to grant married women full civil status (also under military rule), has still not legalized divorce, and abortion remains illegal under all circumstances. In fact, no Latin American country has liberalized its laws on abortion since the 1940s.[1]

How can we make sense of this variation? . . .

Latin American Legal Systems

Due to the . . . nature of civil and criminal laws in Latin America, gender-related legal reform involves more than a mere policy shift. It can represent a transformation in the social and moral norms governing an important sphere of human behavior. When gender rights change, so do definitions and understandings of gender roles and relationships. Liberals who favor the legalization of divorce seek to replace the traditional image of marriage as an indissoluble and sacred relationship with a modern notion of a civil contract rooted in the will of individuals. Conservatives who resist divorce insist that marriage is not a contract but a bedrock institution of the social order. Prochoice groups favoring the decriminalization of abortion aim to make motherhood elective, not compulsory. Antiabortion groups maintain that an ethic of life in the post-Holocaust era requires the unconditional defense of the weak and innocent, including the unborn. As so much is at stake, government officials, elected representatives, and other policy experts take change in gender rights very seriously. They do not want to impose one vision of gender on the rest of society but to convince other citizens that it is the appropriate vision for the times. Gender-related legal reform is not usually imposed through executive decree or party discipline, but evolves through prolonged deliberation. Legislative decision making on divorce and abortion, for example, usually follows the principle of *voto de consciencia*, according to which parties free each legislator to vote her or his conscience on the issue. . . .

Issue Differences

. . . Different gender policy issues may engender distinct types of politics. Specifically, policies differ in terms of the involvement of the Roman Catholic Church and whether they are treated as "technical" or "absolutist." Roman Catholic bishops opposed policy change on divorce and abortion,[2] but did not contest, and sometimes even supported, advancing gender equality in the family. . . . Church doctrine began to change in the 1960s. From its earlier support of a patriarchal household, the Church came to endorse men and women's equal rights in family matters. The presence or absence of Church opposition was highly consequential for the politics surrounding policy change. Gender equality, moreover, was often treated as a technical issue of civil law. One had to have legal training (and considerable patience) to understand the nuances of marital property arrangements. Divorce and abortion, by contrast, were policies that invoked gut responses from novice and expert alike. Divorce and abortion called on people to assume absolutist moral positions; with rare exceptions, these two issues were never treated as technical matters.

. . . Decision making on technical policies could often be delegated to small commissions of experts. These commissions applied specialized knowledge to issues such as marital property and parental rights and the conditions under which abortion should be legally permitted. Working out the details of these reforms often took years, for it involved organizing studies, consulting data, and revising numerous drafts. Significantly, even when they closed Congress, military governments did not shut down expert commissions; in fact, military rulers frequently created such commissions to formulate state policy. Absolutist policies, by contrast, were decided in Congress. Decision making on these policies was preceded by principled deliberation among elected representatives, policy experts, activists, members of the media, and so on. While some ended up convinced by the views of their opponents, many continued to disagree. Resolving conflicts over an absolutist agenda thus require a congressional vote. After the 1970s, no president—not even a military president—was willing to impose radical changes to divorce and abortion law by executive decree on the recommendations of a small group of experts.[3] . . .

Issue differences need to be taken into account by theories of change. To be sure, the gender policy issues considered in this [chapter] share some common features. Laws on gender are normative as opposed to merely distributive, redistributive, or regulatory. . . . The normative power of the law enhances the role of deliberation, emotion, and the weight of principled ideas in policy change. But it would be a mistake to assume that all normative policies follow the same logic. Just because ideas are at stake doesn't mean they are the same ideas. Emotional investment, too, can vary in degree. For example, though divorce and abortion both engendered ethical conflict, the degree of moral polarization surrounding abortion made the issue far more politically intractable than divorce. By disaggregating gender issues, we may . . . reduce the scope of the application of causal theories and thereby enhance their explanatory power. Though we may never have a *general* theory of gender and the state, we may be able to arrive at *specific* theories of the politics surrounding different gender issues.

Issue Networks

New paradigms of gender rights became politically salient in Latin America when they were debated within elite "issue networks" of lawyers, feminists, and reformist politicians. . . . Issue networks involve people at many levels, such as interest groups who directly lobby policy makers, knowledgeable individuals who publish and offer expert advice, professional associations, grassroots movements circulating information about social conditions, and state officials with particular policy interests or competencies (Berry 1989; Heclo 1978; . . . Baumgartner and Jones 1993). This concept usefully captures the range of actors and interests who have contributed to gender-related reform in Latin America in the last third of the twentieth century. Feminist activists interested in women's emancipation participated in gender-related issue networks, and so did jurists influenced by legal changes in other countries and rational principles of law, liberal and socialist politicians interested in social reform, doctors, and representatives of the media. Issue networks were the key advocates for gender rights reform. These networks, which mobilized around specific issues such as divorce, abortion, or family law reform, brought issues to the public agenda, circulated information and recommendations, and mobilized public opinion.

"Issue networks" may be influenced by, or even grow out of, social movements. Yet "social movements" is a much broader term, which can be understood to refer to sequences of collective action among social actors seeking a variety of goals . . . (Cohen and Arato 1992: 526; Tarrow 1998: 2). Issue networks, by contrast, mobilize around specific policy issues, and may involve actors from both state and society. What links members of issue networks is interest in a particular policy area, not collective identity, occupational category, place of residence, shared values, or ideological orientation (though members of issue networks may share these things). . . .

Issue networks were the mechanism through which international developments influenced domestic political changes. International conferences, interstate agreements, and demonstration effects generated ideas and proposals within domestic issue networks. . . . Beginning in the 1940s, lawyers attending the annual meetings of the Inter-American Bar Association (IABA) deliberated civil law reforms to grant married women more rights is family matters. . . . Lawyers who attended these conferences came home armed with proposals for domestic policy reform. In this way, many members of domestic issue networks were simultaneously participants in transnational advocacy networks (Keck and Sikkink 1998).

Later, international agreements such as the Inter-American Convention on Women's Civil and Political Rights (1949) and the United Nations' Convention on the Elimination of All Forms of Discrimination against Women (CEDAW) . . . helped consolidate global norms of gender equality that helped issue networks to pressure local governments for change. In theory, the CEDAW has the force of law in ratifying countries. This boosts the standing of gender equality advocates, who may make the argument not that their government change its policies, but that it comply with already existing law. Liberal issue networks also inspired reforms in other countries. After the vast majority of North American and European states reformed laws on divorce, family relations, and abortion in the 1970s and 1980s, many members of Latin American issue networks argued that their countries had to adopt similar reforms in order not to lag behind the rest of the "civilized world."

International influences were also channeled through conservative issue networks. United Nations conferences in Cairo in 1994, Beijing in 1995, and New York in 2000 provided a focal point for antiabortion groups and created an opportunity for Latin American antiabortion activists to build connections and acquire skills and resources. These groups mobilized to prevent the consensus documents produced by U.N. meetings from endorsing broad definitions of reproductive

rights, which they argued legitimized the legalization of abortion (Franco 1998; Shepard 1999a). Antiabortion transnational advocacy networks also fed domestic political mobilization. Abortion reforms in Western Europe and the United States left behind disgruntled opponents who took an interest in preventing similar reforms in other countries. . . . Meanwhile, studies about the pernicious consequences of divorce law liberalization in the United States motivated Latin American conservatives to contest divorce reform at home (Diaz Vergara 1997). High rates of teenage pregnancy in the United States, interpreted as the result of liberal state policies on reproductive issues, shored up the arguments of Latin Americans opposed to sex education, family planning, and abortion (e.g., Santa Cruz 1996: 20). . . .

State Institutions

. . . For many years, major works of Latin American studies had used regime type and transition as proxies for the institutional configurations that mattered for political outcomes. Yet as we have seen, liberalizing reforms on gender and the family occurred under both military and democratic regimes, before and after democratic transitions. This lack of correspondence between forms of political regime and liberalizing gender policies caused scholars to call for a more complex analysis of the relationship between institutions and gender-related reform (Alvarez 1990; Jaquette 1994; Molyneux 2000; Waylen 1998). . . . In this spirit, the present study analyzes how middle-level features of military and democratic governments and the relationship between church and state shaped the prospects for reform.

Military Governments

Military coups and military governments have been a recurrent feature of Latin American politics in the twentieth century. . . . The military coups of the 1960s and 1970s differed from their predecessors. . . . Whereas earlier coups lacked any defined programmatic goals beyond restoring order or saving the fatherland, later coups were backed by a specific political ideology elaborated by senior military leaders. Coups of the 1960s and 1970s were

organized and executed by the military acting as an institution and aiming to reorder state and society (Cardoso 1979). Military rulers developed a national security ideology that justified their seizure of power to avert threats posed by politically mobilized popular classes and leftist movements; they also felt that military governance would create the political stability necessary to encourage investment . . . (O'Donnell 1979; Stepan 1978, 1988).

Military discourse had a significant gendered component. . . . Latin American military governments expressed their right and reason to rule in gendered terms, and appealed to traditional virtues of feminine care and devotion (Chuchryk 1989, 1994; Filc 1997; Kirkwood 1990; Munizaga and Letelier 1988; Tabak 1983; Valenzuela 1987). Military ideologies thus reinforced traditional gender roles and identities, presenting a seeming obstacle to liberalizing change on gender rights. . . . To be sure, the patriarchal military project was not seamless. Latin American militarism produced contradictory effects on gender relations and women's positions. In spite of their conservative discourse, military economic policies pushed unprecedented numbers of women into the work force, breaking down public-private distinctions and creating social dynamics that challenged traditional gender roles (Alvarez 1990; Jaquette 1994; Waylen 1998).

Given these conservative ideologies, how could military governments preside over important reforms on married women's civil rights and, in the Brazilian case, legalize divorce? To understand why, we need to look at the policy-making institutions created by military governments as well as how church-state relations developed under military rule. . . . Military governments overhauled national laws, constitutions, state bureaucracies, economic policy, and state-owned enterprises in line with principles of technical efficiency and cosmopolitan standards of modernity. . . . Legal technocrats included lawyers, legal scholars, and judges who published in professional journals and participated in national and international legal conferences. When they decided to modernize the law, military rulers created small commissions of legal technocrats to draft proposals for change based on the newest ideas and approaches. For example, the Argentine government of General Juan Carlos Ongania organized dozens of legal commissions to overhaul the country's civil, commercial, and criminal legislation. The existence of these commissions provided a window of opportunity for elite issue networks to influence state policy, even under authoritarian conditions. . . .

Democratic Governments

Latin American countries commonly made the transition to democracy in the 1980s and 1990s. Yet the political institutions of democratic governance—electoral rules, federalism, presidentialism, legislative procedures, party systems, and so on—contain important variations that have proven consequential for democratic stability, political practice, and policy outcomes. . . .

These institutional differences help to account for distinct patterns of policy making across countries. In Brazil, a combination of a fragmented party system, weak party discipline, and "robust federalism" thwarted the executive's attempts to fight inflation and reform the state during three administrations in the mid- to late 1980s and early 1990s (Mainwaring 1999). Problems with the party system can be largely attributed to Brazil's electoral rules, which combine an extreme form of proportional representation (a low threshold and high district magnitude) with a preference-voting system that encourages personalistic behavior. Historically, moreover, Brazilian legislators have enjoyed the automatic right to stand for reelection, further reducing the leverage of party leaders. . . . Nonetheless, there is evidence that this traditional pattern may have changed as parties became more disciplined throughout the 1990s. . . .

In Argentina, by contrast, a two-party-dominant system and moderate to high degree of party discipline in the legislature contributed to the country's *relative* policy success, particularly its ability to weather a severe economic crisis at the end of the 1980s. Electoral rules, including a closed-list proportional representation system, relatively low district magnitude (an average of five deputies per district), and plurality elections for senators and governors, helped maintain the two-party system and party discipline, as did the ability of party leaders in Congress to affect, by determining committee memberships and allocating budgetary resources, legislators' ability to deliver goods to their constituencies (Jones 2002). . . .

To be sure, Argentine democracy has its problems, including lack of judicial independence, limited provincial autonomy, and the excessive use of presidential decree powers, though many of these issues were addressed in the 1994 constitutional reforms (Jones 1997: 277–78). The relative inclination of Argentina's parties and institutions toward policies of national importance is reflected in the Radical Party's championing of liberal changes to family law, and of a multipartisan advocacy of divorce, in the mid-1980s. Argentine liberal lawyers and feminist activists found common ground with liberal parties in Congress and actors in the executive branch committed to reform.

Chile's democratic political institutions have been far more affected by an authoritarian legacy than counterparts in Brazil or Argentina. Democrats agreed to respect the constitution promulgated by military rulers in 1980, which established, among other problematic features, the presence of eight "institutional" senators appointed by Pinochet (the so-called *designados*). The presence of the *designados* increased the power of the socially conservative voting bloc in the Senate, frustrating reform on even mildly controversial gender issues (Londregan 2000). Military rulers also changed the electoral norms to create incentives for a de facto two-party system by creating sixty two-member districts to elect the lower house and requiring that a party or coalition receive twice as many votes as the runner-up in order to capture both seats (Rabkin 1996; Siavelis 1997). These rules required Chile's historic multiparty system essentially to squeeze itself into a two-coalition framework. The two coalitions have proven durable and unified throughout the 1990s (Carey 2002). Nonetheless, to maintain unity and their hold on power against opposition from the right-wing coalition, members of the governing coalition, comprised of Christian Democratic, Socialist, and Democratic (PPD) parties, have sought to avoid potentially divisive issues such as divorce and abortion. . . .

Church-State Relations

The final variable affecting the "fit" between issue networks and the state is church-state relations.

Seen most broadly, the process of gender law liberalization described in this study involved the replacement of laws inspired by traditional Roman Catholic ethics on male authority, indissoluble marriage, and the crime of abortion with new laws inspired by feminism and liberalism. Though this makes the Church an integral part of the story, it is important to bear in mind that Roman Catholic bishops did not contest all gender-related policy changes. By the 1960s, Roman Catholic doctrine had replaced a traditional model of male authority with acceptance of sex equality within marriage. As a result, the bishops did not act to oppose reforms advancing family equality. Church doctrine on divorce and abortion did not change. The Church always opposed the legalization of divorce and the decriminalization of abortion. Yet historically the Church acted to oppose divorce more vehemently than abortion because of the threat to its values posed by pro-divorce movements. Issue networks of lawyers, socialists, and liberals had mobilized to demand divorce since the nineteenth century. A large movement proposing alternative ideas about abortion, however, emerged only in the late twentieth century. The general social consensus that abortion was morally wrong assured the Church that its position was safe, and it chose not to contest some early, liberalizing reforms to abortion laws. After the middle of the twentieth century, the diffusion of feminist liberal ideas about elective abortion compelled the Church firmly to defend the sanctity of embryonic life under all circumstances.

The evolution of Church doctrine and the perceived threat to core Church principles shaped the Church's decision on whether or not to contest reforms. Yet even when the Church contested reform, it could still be defeated. Cracks in the Church-state relationship opened a window of opportunity for liberal issue networks to defeat the Church. How did this come about? Though the Latin American Church had historically allied itself with the conservative oligarchy and the military, many bishops transferred their allegiances in the 1970s and 1980s. Latin American bishops influenced by liberation theology condemned the human rights abuses of military governments, introduced new participatory structures, and worked with social movements and labor unions to demand social justice (Gilfeather 1979; Levine and Mainwaring 1989; Mainwaring and Wilde 1989; Moreira Alves 1984; Smith 1982). In many countries, the Church hierarchy formally opposed the military government and supported social movement networks struggling to bring about an end to authoritarian rule (Mainwaring 1986; Smith 1982).

These shifting relationships between Church and state produced by military rule and democratic transition were consequential for Church influence over policy issues it cared about. During periods of Church-state cooperation, state leaders realized benefits from the Church's political support and were unwilling to make moves that would incur episcopal wrath. When the Church turned against the state, opportunities emerged for opposing coalitions to step in and produce shifts in gender rights legislation. When national governments clashed with the Church over policy issues such as human rights, economic development, and education, liberal issues networks could overpower the Church. At other times, the Church elected to contest reform and succeeded.

In summary, differences among issues, political institutions, and Church-state relations shaped the ability of issue networks to produce policy change. . . .

Notes

1. One exception must be mentioned here. In 2000, the legislature of Mexico City approved changes to the city's criminal code to expand the conditions of legal abortion. Based on a bill introduced by then mayor Rosario Robles, the reforms granted women permission to abort if the pregnancy threatened their health (not just their life), or in the event of fetal abnormalities.
2. Before *Roe v. Wade*, however, the Church declined to contest some reforms that exempted from criminal punishment abortions performed on women who had been raped.
3. A partial exception must be mentioned here. In 1989, the outgoing Chilean military government modified the country's Health Code to make therapeutic abortions (performed in case of grave risks to the mother's life or health) illegal. This reform was supported by military elites but not preceded by deliberation among regime officials or society at large. I call this a "partial" exception because the criminal code, which criminalized abortion under all circumstances, was not modified.

References

Alvarez, Sonia. E. 1990. *Engendering Democracy, in Brazil: Women's Movements in Transition Politics.* Princeton: Princeton University Press.

Berry, Jeffrey M. 1989. "Subgovernments, Issues Networks, and Political Conflict." In Richard Harris and Sidney Milkis, eds., *Remaking American Politics.* Boulder: Westview Press. Pp. 239–60.

Baumgartner, Frank R., and Bryan D. Jones. 1993. *Agendas and Instability in American Politics.* Chicago: University of Chicago Press.

Cardoso, Fernando Henrique. 1979. "On the Characterization of Authoritarian Regimes in Latin America." In David Collier, ed., *The New Authoritarianism in Latin America.* Princeton: Princeton University Press. Pp. 33–57.

Carey, John. 2002. "Parties, Coalitions, and the Chilean Congress in the 1990s." In Scott Morgenstern and Benito Nacif, eds., *Legislative Politics in Latin America.* New York: Cambridge University Press. Pp. 222–53.

Carmines, Edward G., and James A. Stimson. 1980. "The Two Faces of Issue Voting." *American Political Science Review* 74, no. 1 (March): 78–91.

Chuchryk, Patricia. 1989. "Subversive Mothers: The Women's Opposition to the Military Regime in Chile." In Sue Ellen Charlton, Jana Everett, and Kathleen Staudt, eds., *Women, the State, and Development.* Albany: SUNY Press. Pp. 130–51.

Chuchryk, Patricia. 1994. "From Dictatorship to Democracy: The Women's Movement in Chile." In Jane Jaquette, ed., *The Women's Movement in Latin America.* Boulder: Westview. Pp. 65–107.

Cohen, Jean, and Andrew Arato. 1992. *Civil Society and Political Theory.* Cambridge: MIT Press.

Diamond, Larry. 1999. *Developing Democracy: Toward Consolidation.* Baltimore: Johns Hopkins University Press.

Díaz Vergara, Carlos. 1997. "Consecuencias económicas y sociales de la aceptación de una ley de divorcio vincular." In *Controversia sobre familia y divorcio.* Santiago: Ediciones Universidad Católica de Chile. Pp. 33–65.

Filc, Judith. 1997. *Entre el parentesco y la política: Familia y dictadura, 1976–1983.* Buenos Aires: Editorial Biblos.

Franco, Jean. 1998. "Defrocking the Vatican: Feminism's Secular Project." In Sonia E. Alvarez, Evelina Dagnino, and Arturo Escobar, eds., *Cultures of Politics: Politics of Cultures.* Boulder: Westview. Pp. 278–89.

Gilfeather, Katherine. 1979. "Women Religious, the Poor, and the Institutional Church in Chile." *Journal of Interamerican Studies and World Affairs* 21, no. 1 (February): 129–55.

Heclo, Hugh. 1978. "Issue Networks and the Executive. Establishment." In Anthony King, ed., *The New American Political System.* Washington: American Enterprise Institute. Pp. 87–124.

Jaquette, Jane S. 1994. "Introduction: From Transition to Participation—Women's Movements and Democratic Politics." In Jane S. Jaquette, ed., *The Women's Movement in Latin America.* Boulder: Westview. Pp. 1–11.

Jones, Mark P. 1997. "Evaluating Argentina's Presidential Democracy: 1983–1995." In Scott Mainwaring and Matthew Soberg Shugart, eds., *Presidentialism and Democracy in Latin America.* New York: Cambridge University Press. Pp. 259–99.

Jones, Mark P. 2002. "Explaining the High Level of Party Discipline in the Argentine Congress." In Scott Morgenstern and Benito Nacif, eds., *Legislative Politics in Latin America.* New York: Cambridge University Press. Pp. 147–84.

Keck, Margaret, and Kathryn Sikkink. 1998. *Activists beyond Borders: Advocacy Networks in Transnational Politics.* Ithaca: Cornell University Press.

Kirkwood, Julieta. 1990. *Ser política en Chile: Los Nudos de la sabiduría feminista.* Santiago: Editorial Cuarto Propio.

Levine, Daniel, and Scott Mainwaring. 1989. "Religion and Popular Protest in Latin America: Contrasting Experiences." In Susan Eckstein, ed., *Power and Popular Protest: Latin American Social Movements.* Berkeley: University of California Press. Pp. 203–40.

Londregan, John. 2000. *Legislative Institutions and Ideology in Chile.* New York: Cambridge University Press.

Mainwaring, Scott. 1986. *The Catholic Church and Politics in Brazil, 1916–1985.* Stanford: Stanford University Press.

Mainwaring, Scott. 1999. *Rethinking Party Systems in the Third Wave of Democratization: The Case of Brazil.* Stanford: Stanford University Press.

Mainwaring, Scott, and Alexander Wilde. 1989. "The Progressive Church in Latin America. An Interpretation." In Mainwaring and Wilde, eds., *The Progressive Church in Latin America.* Notre Dame: University of Notre Dame Press. Pp. 1–37.

Molyneux, Maxine. 2000. "Twentieth-Century State Formations in Latin America." In Elizabeth Dore and Maxine Molyneux, eds., *Hidden Histories of Gender and the State in Latin America.* Durham: Duke University Press. Pp. 33–81.

Moreira Alves, Maria Helena. 1984. "Grassroots Organizations, Trade Unions, and the Church: A Challenge to the Controlled *Abertura* in Brazil." *Latin American Perspectives* 11, no. 1 (Winter): 73–102.

Munizaga, Giselle, and Lilian Letelier. 1988. "La Mujer y la acción hegemonizadora del regimen militar." In *Mundo de mujer: Continuidad y cambio.* Santiago: Centro de Estudios de la Mujer. Pp. 525–62.

O'Donnell, Guillermo. 1979. *Modernization and Bureaucratic Authoritarianism: Studies in South American Politics.* Berkeley: Institute of International Studies, University of California.

O'Donnell, Guillermo. 1994. "Delegative Democracy." *Journal of Democracy* 5 (January): 55–69.

Rabkin, Rhoda. 1996. "Redemocratization, Electoral Engineering, and Party Strategies in Chile, 1989–1995." *Comparative Political Studies* 29, no. 3 (June 1996): 335–56.

Santa Cruz, Lucia. 1996. "Sexo y Estado." *Libertad y Desarrollo,* no. 58 (October): 18–21.

Shepard, Bonnie. 2000. "The 'Double Discourse' on Sexual and Reproductive Rights in Latin America: The Chasm between Public Policy and Private Action." *Health and Human Rights* 4, no. 2: 121–43.

Siavelis, Peter. 1997. "Executive Legislative Relations in Post-Pinochet Chile: A Preliminary Assessment." In Scott Mainwaring and Matthew Soberg Shugart, eds., *Presidentialism and Democracy in Latin America*. Cambridge: Cambridge University Press. Pp. 321–62.

Skocpol, Theda. 1992. *Protecting Soldiers and Mothers: The Political Origins of Social Policy in the United States*. Cambridge: Harvard University Press.

Smith, Brian. 1982. *The Church and Politics in Chile: Challenges to Modern Catholicism*. Princeton: Princeton University Press.

Stepan, Alfred. 1978. *The State and Society: Peru in Comparative Perspective*. Princeton: Princeton University Press.

Stepan, Alfred. 1988. *Rethinking Military Politics: Brazil and the Southern Cone*. Princeton: Princeton University Press.

Tabak, Fanny. 1983. *Autoritarianismo e participação política da mulher*. Rio de Janeiro: Graal.

Tarrow, Sidney. 1998. *Power in Movement: Social Movements and Contentious Politics*, 2nd ed. Cambridge: Cambridge University Press.

Valenzuela, María Elena. 1987. *La mujer en el Chile militar*. Santiago: CESOC.

Waylen, Georgina. 1998. "Gender, Feminism, and the State: An Overview." In Vicky Randall and Georgina Waylen, eds. *Gender, Politics, and the State*. New York: Routledge. Pp. 1–17.

Yishai, Yael. 1993. "Public Ideas and Public Policy: Abortion Politics in Four Democracies." *Comparative Politics* 25, no. 2 (January): 207–28.

Zakaria, Fareed. 1997. "The Rise of Illiberal Democracy." *Foreign Affairs* 76, no. 6 (November/December): 22–43.

Chapter 32
BEYOND THE DIFFERENCE VERSUS EQUALITY POLICY DEBATE: POSTSUFFRAGE FEMINISM, CITIZENSHIP, AND THE QUEST FOR A FEMINIST WELFARE STATE

Wendy Sarvasy

Women activists in the United States did not retire from public life after the ratification of the suffrage amendment but continued to pursue the interdependent aims of women's complete citizenship and the creation of a feminist welfare state. They assumed that a feminist welfare state with its guiding principle of gender equality would provide the context for the new women citizens and that the process of women becoming citizens would advance feminist welfare state development. They also assumed that both projects required a conception of gender equality that combined in new ways identical treatment and difference. To articulate this notion, they proposed a series of public policies expanding women's formal equality in the areas of jury duty, naturalization law, and family law. They also marshaled support for the first federal health care program that addressed the different needs of women and infants. Yet because women did not receive half the power along with the vote, feminists' attempts to institutionalize a new conception of gender equality within a hostile political climate fractured the women's movement. Placed in a defensive posture, feminists advocated either the presuffrage tradition of sex-based labor laws that emphasized women's differences from men or the postsuffrage commitment to an equal rights constitutional amendment that emphasized women's equality with men. Despite this difference/equal-

ity split, however, a core of feminist reformers held onto the comprehensive vision. They groped for a theoretical and practical synthesis of equality and difference as the basis for women's citizenship and as the defining characteristic of public policies in a feminist welfare state.

My aim is to reconstruct their feminist process of synthesis. Though these women disagreed about how to achieve a combination of formal equality and gender difference, their writings suggested a feminist theoretical process of how to reconceive gender equality: they showed how unequal power relations turned biological differences into socially constructed, substantive gender inequalities; they formulated public policies based upon a new conception of gender equality to alleviate these substantive inequalities; and they sought to use the emancipated aspects of women's different experiences and outlooks to create a more egalitarian political and social environment. . . .

To recapture the innovative aspects of postsuffrage feminism, I will focus on feminist analyses of mothers' pensions—the state programs of income supplements for poor mothers and their children, which preceded the 1935 federal Aid to Dependent Children (ADC) program. I have chosen mothers' pensions because this policy has been central in shaping our understanding of women's relationship to the welfare state, because its feminist aspects have been overlooked by the histories of the welfare state, and because feminists who disagreed among themselves on protective legislation and the Equal Rights Amendment (ERA) supported mothers' pensions. The mothers' pension discourse turned out to be an arena in which feminists worked out their new understanding of gender equality. On the surface, support of the mothers' pension concept appeared to require acceptance of special treatment for mother-headed families based upon a theory of gender difference. Yet women reformers used the issue to justify the development of universal entitlements and to show the compatibility of equal rights and social programs for mothers.

Specifically, I will use feminist analyses of mothers' pension programs to argue that a new synthesis of difference and equality embodied in social policy was required to achieve the interdependent aims of women's full citizenship and the creation of a feminist welfare state. To demonstrate this argument, I will begin by describing the feminists who shared a commitment to the development of a feminist welfare state. Then I will construct four different resolutions of the tension between gender difference and formal gender equality that illustrate the feminist process of synthesis. With each resolution, I will discuss the implications for a new conception of women's citizenship and for the use of the policy debate over gender equality as an ideological mechanism for furthering feminist welfare state development. . . .

Structuring Gender-Differentiated Needs into Universal Programs

When, in 1924, Florence Kelley characterized mothers' pensions as "a discrimination established in almost all the states in favor of women," she provided a politically potent argument against the ERA: it would abolish a popular program that benefited poor female-headed families. To dramatize her point, she gave the example of a young mother who was left with the care of two-month-old twins when her young electrician husband died of pneumonia. The widow had no marketable skills and soon went through her husband's life insurance and the savings of her older sister. To Kelley, the idea that this mother should be forced into the dual role of wage earner

and caregiver was unthinkable because the babies would have to be weaned prematurely and because "the earnings of an unskilled wage-earning woman afford no margin for paying a substitute in the home."[1] The implication of Kelley's story was that the feminists who supported the ERA were inhuman monsters who would pull babies from their mothers' breasts in the name of the principle of equality. This polemical presentation of the anti-ERA position on mothers' pensions was effective because it put the National Woman's Party (NWP) on the defensive. Yet Kelley's argument did not do justice to a more comprehensive approach to mothers' pensions, which was being developed by a group of fellow anti-ERA feminists who drew lessons from the limited state programs for how to create gendered universal social programs capable of alleviating gender difference as substantive inequality. . . .

To achieve this resolution, broad social policy would have to build upon investigations of women's different needs and problems. This aim was suggested by Agnes L. Petersen, assistant director of the U.S. Women's Bureau, in an article addressed to the general topic, "Four Ways to Support a Family." Petersen defended an ideal mothers' pension program in part because it "should serve to collect valuable facts and provide a working laboratory for the study and diagnosis of the economic and social ills of our family life."[2] Studies by Edith Abbott, [Sophonisba] Breckinridge, and [Mary F.] Bogue did reveal certain gender-specific problems: the difficulty of combining low-wage work and caretaking, the effects of having children out of marriage, and specific health issues for women and children.

Uncovering "the valuable facts," however, depended upon asking feminist questions so that women's differentiated needs could structure the emerging welfare state programs in a feminist direction. To have the mothers' pension programs make such a contribution, research would have to be guided by two assumptions. First, the pensioners could not be seen as deviants. Petersen, in particular, connected the situation of poor mother-headed families to the increasing number of married women who were in the paid labor market. . . . With this focus, the feminist analysis of the importance of mothers' pensions offered a way to counter the hegemonic familistic framework that assumed that social programs should strengthen only the father-headed model of the family.

The second feminist assumption was that social policies for families would have to be connected to labor law legislation that would guarantee adequate wages for women. . . . Abbott and Breckinridge argued that pensions were inadequate because they were tied to low wage levels: "It is probably true that until the great majority of independent wage earners have incomes that are adequate, relief will never be really adequate." They also showed in their analysis of an ethnically and racially diverse group of women who lost their eligibility due to new restrictions in the law (including a new citizenship requirement) that even the most able mothers "would doubtless have maintained better homes with the help of the pension from the Court and have given their children a better start in life."[3] . . .

By using analyses of the mothers' pension programs to focus attention on women's dual role and the interconnection between pensions and women's low wages, these feminists established that their aim was not a two-track system characterized by universal benefits geared to men's needs and inadequate means-tested mothers' pensions geared to women.[4] Instead, they suggested concrete ways that broad social policy could address gender differences that translate into substantive inequality.[5] Moreover, the perspective of the feminists was not wedded to the concept of a means-tested mothers' pension but explicitly addressed what Petersen called "the rights of mothers to economic security for their children."[6] If adequate women's wages could be achieved through legislative sensitivity to the implications of gender-segregated and racially segregated labor markets—phenomena well understood by these analysts—then even Kelley might have accepted the option of mothers working outside the home and paying for child care.[7] Thus, for these policy analysts, the problem was not simply how to supersede mothers' pensions with universal programs but how to structure the latter so that they could address the gender-specific problems of mother-headed families. . . .

The feminist aim of using a gender-specific program to expand universal entitlements showed how the gender-equality dynamic created by attempts to overcome the tension between equality and difference could advance welfare state development. Justifying a special program for women and children was not the ultimate goal of the feminist analysis of mothers' pensions. The feminists instead attempted to redefine the concept of equality embodied in the notion of universal social programs. Rather than emphasize a notion of universal as identical treatment, they suggested that different gender-specific needs could be accommodated within a universal framework. As they pushed for national systems of health insurance, unemployment insurance, and old age pensions to eradicate the inequalities experienced by mother-headed families, they suggested a process of policy formulation that could achieve two purposes: the eradication of substantive gender inequalities and the advancement of formal social rights for both men and women citizens.

Creating Greater Substantive Gender Equality through Equal Rights

The left wing of the NWP developed the theoretical importance of mothers' pensions for an understanding of gender equality in response to the political effectiveness of the polemical attacks from Kelley and others. When NWP members went to Congress to build support for the ERA, they were forced to confront the assertion that the adoption of the amendment would put mothers' pensions in jeopardy. Members of the NWP certainly supported these popular state programs, but without the polemics over equality and difference they might not have spent so much time discussing them. As the 1920s progressed, they developed a strategic defense of mothers' pensions as ADC and placed ADC within the context of growing European support for a family or child allowance. Both approaches, taken up in *Equal Rights*, in testimony before Congress, and in a 1928 pamphlet, emphasized the compatibility between equal rights and governmental support of children. Specifically, the analysis suggested a second resolution of the difference/equality tension: formal equality could help overcome gender difference as substantive inequality.

The NWP-aligned social reformers began their analysis of ADC with the obvious point: the program was not a privilege for women because they did not receive a stipend as caregivers. The aid was intended to support only the needy children. As studies for the Children's Bureau showed, the grants were not adequate for the children, let alone for the mothers. Where was the privilege? Quoting from legal experts such as Judge Ben Lindsey of Denver, who supported the ERA and radical social reform, and from Children's Bureau documents, Lavinia Dock declared that the programs were for the good of the nation as a whole and not simply a "sex privilege." Maud Younger similarly argued that the programs should be seen within the context of free school lunches and day nurseries.[8] While this line of argument was persuasive, a complete response to the charge that the ERA would undermine the advance of social programs for women and children required an even more explicit treatment of the equal rights aspect of ADC. . . .

The gender-neutral analysis of ADC and child allowances suggested a new formal equality framework that could challenge two types of substantive gender inequality, thereby establishing a more egalitarian social and political context for the new women citizens. First, there would no longer be a justification for stigmatizing the female-headed family, since the assumption of either the means-tested, gender-neutral ADC program or the universal child allowance program was that many types of families, not just women-headed ones, were in need of income supplements to raise children. While the mother-headed family would still suffer from the inadequate wages of the gender-segregated and racially segregated labor markets, the income supplement as a social right offered a means for improving the status and power of women.

Second, there would no longer be a justification for distinguishing between married and unmarried mothers. The establishment of equal social and legal rights for mothers and their illegitimate children was a key motivation for European feminist versions of child allowances. The feminists in the United States shared the concerns of their European counterparts.[9] Some of the feminists tried to address the issue through an equal rights framework. Unfortunately, they did not control most of the state mothers' pension programs. Still, the gender-neutral formulation, with its emphasis on the needs of the children rather than the marital status or sex of the caregiver, offered a simple way to respond to a particular gendered need, illustrating how universal formulations

could be used to offset a controversial aspect of substantive gender equality. . . .

While the gender-neutral formulation of the ADC program suggested a formal equality framework for transforming notions of citizenship, it also offered insights into how feminist attempts to resolve the difference/equality tension through public policy could advance movement toward a welfare state. When feminists advocated that all needy children should be included within the means-tested ADC programs, they were implicitly challenging the assumptions that prevented men from receiving income supplements for their families. In the United States, poor, able-bodied men traditionally had been categorized as nondeserving and excluded from public and private forms of aid. The feminists, in defending the ERA and its formal equality framework, challenged the distinction between the deserving and nondeserving poor and showed how low-income men as well as women could benefit when programs of income supplements for children were defined in gender-neutral terms. In effect, the formal equality stance of the pro-ERA feminists offered a radical critique of class inequality as it offered a new way to understand the relationship between gender difference and formal equality. . . .

Using Gender Difference to Redefine Formal Gender Equality

The feminist discourse on mothers' pensions intersected with another feminist issue in the 1920s: independent citizenship for married women. This issue gained prominence because some women were denied the right to vote when their citizenship status was determined by their husbands' status.[10] The dramatic cases that unified the women's movement were of native-born American women who married foreign citizens and then lost their American citizenship because of a 1907 law that legislated the concept of family unity based upon the husband's nationality. To correct this situation, the Cable Act of 1922, supported by the women's movement, established the concept of citizenship independent of marital status. This new law established identical treatment for men and women but created new substantive inequalities for foreign-born women married to

American citizens (including foreign-born men who had become naturalized citizens).[11] Between 1855 and 1922, immigrant women did not have to worry about naturalization examinations, which tested ability to speak English, and knowledge of history, government, geography, and the laws; their citizenship followed their husbands'. Because of the Cable Act, the immigrant women had to go through the whole ordeal of the naturalization process on their own, and their hesitancy to take the examination could eventually deny them a mothers' pension. . . .

For Abbott and Breckinridge, the situation of the immigrant woman under the Cable Act raised important questions about the relationship between gender difference as substantive inequality and formal gender equality. As Abbott explained, "Here in the United States we must remember that although we establish theoretical equality with reference to citizenship, actual equality will come only as one by one all the disadvantages from which women and particularly immigrant women have suffered are removed."[12] Abbott and Breckinridge used mothers' pensions to illustrate the gap between formal or theoretical equality and substantive or actual equality. Through their analyses of mothers' pensions and independent citizenship, they presented a third resolution of the difference/equality tension: gender difference could be used as a basis for restructuring legal or formal gender equality. . . .

The relationship between independent citizenship and mothers' pensions suggested that the feminist resolution of the tension between difference and equality could advance the welfare state project only if it proceeded from the vantage point of the most vulnerable women. Otherwise, some women might be denied citizenship status and thus be prevented from participating in the welfare state and from supporting its expansion. By arguing that identical treatment must be modified to include options and to reflect women's daily lives, Breckinridge and Abbott made clear that the different substantive inequalities among women must be addressed in the process of reconceptualizing gender equality and shaping public policy to reflect that evolving concept. In this way, a feminist welfare state would be able to respond to women's experiences and needs as well as to men's and to attract greater popular support.

Conclusion

This chapter has illustrated a feminist method of synthesis characterized by three steps: the uncovering of the negative aspects of gender difference as substantive gender inequality, the proposing of public policy remedies that embodied a new relationship between equality and difference, and the drawing out of the emancipatory potential of gender difference within a new context of greater substantive and formal gender equality. This three-part process provides both a framework for reconceiving women's citizenship and an ideological motor for developing a feminist welfare state. . . .

Notes

1. Florence Kelley, "Why Other Women Groups Oppose It," *Good Housekeeping* 78, no. 3 (March 1929): 162.
2. Agnes L. Petersen, "Mothers' Pensions," *Survey* 57, no. 5 (December 1, 1926): 281.
3. Edith Abbott and Sophonisba P. Breckinridge, *The Administration of the Aid-to-Mothers Law in Illinois*, Children's Bureau Publication 82 (1921), reprinted in *The Family and Social Service in the 1920s: Two Documents* (New York: Arno, 1972), 48, 69, 111, 157.
4. For a different interpretation, see Barbara Nelson, "The Gender, Race, and Class Origins of Early Welfare Policy and the Welfare State: A Comparison of Workmen's Compensation and Mothers' Aid," in *Women, Change, and Politics*, ed. Patricia Curin and Louise Tilly (New York: Sage, 1990), 413–35. She shows how during the Progressive period two gender-based state policy channels emerged: workmen's compensation for white men and mothers' aid for white mothers. Her analysis does not include the place of sex-based labor laws or how reformers attempted to create policies to address the needs of working mothers.
5. Though they did not make the case, their analysis suggested that unemployment insurance, e.g., could structure its benefits to accommodate a diversity of women's paid work patterns as well as the needs of male breadwinners. For a contemporary analysis of the implications of structuring employment insurance to respond to men's working patterns only, see Diana Pearce, "Toil and Trouble: Women Workers and Unemployment Compensation," *Signs* 10, no. 3 (Spring 1985): 439–59.
6. Petersen, "Mothers' Pensions," 281.
7. See Sophonisba P. Breckinridge, *Women in the Twentieth Century: A Study of Their Political, Social, and Economic Activities* (New York: McGraw-Hill, 1933), 229.

8. For examples of such arguments, see Eleanor Taylor Marsh, "Equal Rights and Mothers' Pensions," *ER* 1 (January 19, 1924): 390; "Mothers' Pensions and the Amendment" (editorial), *ER* 11 (May 3, 1924): 92; and Lavinia L. Dock, "Concerning Equal Rights," *ER* 12 (June 20, 1925): 147; U.S. Senate Subcommittee of the Committee on the District of Columbia Hearings on Mothers' Aid in the District of Columbia, *Statement of Miss Maud Younger, of the National Woman's Party,* S. 120 and S. 1929, 69th Congress, 1st sess., January 11, 1926, 37.

9. Mary Beard characterized the broad mothers' pension discourse on unmarried mothers in the following terms: "While women do not stand as a unit for recognition of the unmarried mother where they do support home pensions, there is evidence of strong advocacy of [sic] among women of her inclusion in the benefits of this legislation. At all events women are opening their eyes to the problem" (Mary Ritter Beard, *Woman's Work in Municipalities* [New York: Appleton, 1915], 70).

10. For a comprehensive analysis of independent citizenship, see Virginia Sapiro, "Women, Citizenship, and Nationality: Immigration and Naturalization Policies in the United States," *Politics and Society* 13, no. 1 (1984): 1–26.

11. The Cable Act did not address the needs of Chinese women who were ineligible for citizenship due to racist citizenship laws. In *Chang Chan v. Nagle* (1925), the Supreme Court decided that a Chinese wife of a native-born American was not eligible for citizenship; she remained an alien. This ruling affected the citizenship rights of American-born widows of Chinese husbands, who were not allowed to reclaim their original citizenship when their husbands died, and wives of aliens who were ineligible for naturalization. Breckinridge notes these examples of "hardship," but her main focus is on white immigrant women. Sophonisba P. Breckinridge, *Marriage and the Civic Rights of Women* (Chicago: University of Chicago Press, 1931), 31–32.

12. Grace Abbott, "After Suffrage—Citizenship," *Survey* 44, no. 19 (September 1, 1920): 656–57.

Chapter 33

IS MAINSTREAMING TRANSFORMATIVE? THEORIZING MAINSTREAMING IN THE CONTEXT OF DIVERSITY AND DELIBERATION

Judith Squires

Introduction

Is gender mainstreaming a transformative strategy, a bureaucratic tool of integration, or an agenda-setting process? I will explore this question in relation to the current policy concern with "diversity" and recent theoretical debates concerning the pursuit of democratic inclusion.

The first part of the [chapter] outlines the threefold typology of inclusion, reversal, and displacement (Squires 1999) and locates mainstreaming within this typology. I argue that while it is possible to depict mainstreaming as a strategy of displacement (where equal treatment and positive action are viewed as strategies of inclusion and reversal, respectively), one can also find each of the strategies of inclusion, reversal, and displacement *within* mainstreaming practices. I then go on to map these three approaches to mainstreaming, outlining the strengths and weaknesses of each. While acknowledging the strengths as well as the weaknesses of the integrationist and agenda-setting approaches, I argue in particular for the need to develop the potential of the transformative approach. In order to develop its currently under-specified potential, I consider the benefits of integrating theories of democratic inclusion into this mainstreaming model. I suggest that, augmented by a commitment to democratic inclusion, this transformative model of mainstreaming is best placed to respond to the—increasingly important—demands of diversity. . . .

Gender mainstreaming is widely perceived, within the European Union and among interna-tional organizations, to be a new equality strategy. There has been considerable progress in developing mainstreaming as a set of tools and methods (Yeandle et al. 1998), yet the transformative potential and theoretical coherence of mainstreaming as an equality strategy has been obscured by the piecemeal implementation of mainstreaming tools formulated within specific policy contexts (Hoskyns 1992). . . . There have [also] been relatively few sustained attempts to consider mainstreaming in the context of a diversity agenda or in relation to democratic theory. . . .

I suggest that, at a time when EU directives require member states to promote equality in relation to sexual orientation, age, and religion, in addition to race, gender, and disability, it simply doesn't make sense to look at gender equality in isolation from other forms of equality. Equality can no longer be considered in isolation from diversity. Understanding what mainstreaming might entail in the context of diversity and not just gender represents a significant challenge. Given the plurality of equality agendas held by diverse groups and the difficulty of ascertaining these by bureaucratic mechanisms, the role of inclusive deliberation should be stressed. This transforms mainstreaming from a technocratic tool into an institutional manifestation of deliberative democracy.

Mainstreaming as a Gender Equality Strategy

Accounts of mainstreaming vary. Mainstreaming is variously understood to entail mainstreaming equal opportunities, equal treatment, women's perspectives, gender, gendered perspectives, or, more recently, diversity. . . .

. . . I would suggest that there are three analytically distinct ways of conceptualizing mainstreaming, informed by three distinct theoretical frameworks, which I have previously defined as inclusion, reversal, and displacement (Squires 1999). Those pursuing a strategy of inclusion usually aspire to objectivity (whether cognitive or moral), conceive of people as autonomous, and espouse an equality politics (and are often labeled as liberal feminist). Those pursuing a strategy of reversal usually adopt an interpretative methodology, talk of "Woman" or "women," and espouse a difference politics (and are often labeled as radical feminist). Those pursuing a strategy of displacement adopt a genealogical methodology, speak of subject positions and of gendering (as a verb) rather than gender (as a noun), and espouse a diversity politics (and are often labeled as postmodern). The strategy of inclusion seeks gender-neutrality; the strategy of reversal seeks recognition for a specifically female gendered identity; and the strategy of displacement seeks to deconstruct those discursive regimes that engender the subject.

The place of mainstreaming in relation to this threefold typology is rather complex. I would suggest that mainstreaming is widely conceived to represent a displacement of the equality/difference debate, and as such might best be viewed as a strategy of displacement. However, I would also suggest that mainstreaming itself is variously conceived, such that it entails within its conceptual boundaries this same threefold typology. As such, it is best viewed not as resolution or displacement of the equality/difference debate, but as yet another manifestation of it. . . .

Mainstreaming as a Strategy of Displacement

Debates about equality within feminist writings have been shaped by a perception . . . that equality and difference are antagonistic aims. Those committed to liberal principles of equality have argued for the need to transcend sexist presumptions about gender difference, to grant women equal rights with men, and to enable women to participate equally with men in the public sphere. . . .

By contrast, those who adopt a difference perspective feel that in the context of a patriarchal society, the pursuit of equality will inevitably result in requiring everyone to assimilate to the dominant gender norm of masculinity. The central normative issue here is whether gender equality requires de-gendering or the equal valuation of different contributions by women and men.

Yet it is now increasingly accepted that equality and difference are only incompatible if equality is understood as sameness (Bacchi 1999, 266; Lister 1997, 96; Squires 1999, 127–32). While equality is understood in this way, gender consistently emerges as a problem of difference: "Equality as sameness is a gendered formulation of equality, because it secures gender privilege through naming women as difference and men as the neutral standard of the same" (Brown 1995, 153). Neither the sameness nor the difference perspectives therefore entail a transformation of the norms of equivalence themselves. For this, we need to render visible the ways in which particular institutions and laws perpetuate inequality by privileging particular norms. This is what I label a diversity perspective. . . .

One can see the same three approaches manifest in gender equality strategies. Teresa Rees, for example, suggests that one can identify three phases in the European Commission's approach to gender equality over the last three decades: equal treatment in the 1970s, positive action in the 1980s, and gender mainstreaming in the 1990s (Rees 2002, 48). . . . Equal treatment is a "legal redress to treat men and women the same." Positive action recognizes that there are differences between men and women and that specific measures are required to address disadvantages experienced by women as a consequence of those differences.[1] Mainstreaming "ideally should involve identifying how existing systems and structures cause indirect discrimination and altering or redesigning them as appropriate"(Rees 2002, 46–48). The aim of the mainstreaming strategy is to counteract gender bias within existing systems and structures: it addresses "those very institutionalized practices that cause both individual and group disadvantage in the first place" (Rees 2002, 3). It is because it takes a systems approach that it is felt to have more transformative potential than previous equality policies. . . .

Three Varieties of Mainstreaming

However, while one can conceptualize mainstreaming as a strategy of displacement, I would also suggest that one finds the three strategies of inclusion, reversal, and displacement manifest within mainstreaming practices themselves.

For example, accounts of how mainstreaming has emerged as a notable policy innovation, and what it entails, vary significantly. Some commentators argue that a "small number of key actors in the European Commission" envisioned the strategy (Booth and Bennett 2002, 440). Others suggest that increased political opportunities and mobilizing structures for social movements have been central (Pollack and Hafner-Burton 2000, 434). Still others emphasize the role of transnational networks and international nongovernmental organizations (True and Mintrom 2001, 28–29). These three accounts of the derivation of mainstreaming generate three distinct correlative accounts of the nature of mainstreaming. . . . Those who perceive mainstreaming to be a product of bureaucratic policy process conceive of it as a way of mainstreaming formal equality of opportunities, while those who perceive mainstreaming to be a product of women's movement campaigning conceive of it as a way of mainstreaming women's voices, and those who perceive mainstreaming to be a product of transnational norm diffusion conceive of it as an open-ended and potentially transformative project. . . .

Notwithstanding the intermingling of these three models of mainstreaming in practice, . . . it is analytically useful to understand approaches to mainstreaming via a threefold typology, labeled as "integrationist, agenda-setting, and transformative" approaches (Jahan 1995, 126). The first approach is now fairly widely accepted to entail a focus on experts and the bureaucratic creation of evidence-based knowledge in policy-making, while the second model is perceived as entailing a focus on the participation, presence, and empowerment of disadvantaged groups (usually women in this context) via consultation with civil society organizations (see Beveridge and Nott 2002, 301; Lombardo 2003). The features of the third, transformative model of mainstreaming are much less easy to discern—in theory or in practice. . . . Given the existence of these three distinct conceptions

of mainstreaming, it becomes clear that while mainstreaming might on the one hand be taken to represent a displacement of the equality/difference dichotomy, it might also on the other hand be viewed as a catchall concept that incorporates the tension within its boundaries.

I would suggest that of the three analytically distinct conceptualizations of mainstreaming, only the transformative conceptualization represents a displacement of the equality/difference dichotomy. Yet elements of all three analytical conceptualizations might coexist within the actual implementation of the strategy. . . . Moreover, . . . the implementation of mainstreaming strategies suggests that different definitions of mainstreaming are used according to institutional context (see Yeandle et al. 1998). This has led some scholars to suggest that the three approaches to mainstreaming should be viewed as complementary rather than competing. In this way, mainstreaming ceases to be understood as a distinctive equality strategy that moves beyond the previous strategies of equality of opportunity and positive action, and comes to be viewed as a broad strategy that entails the incorporation of the other two strategies as and when appropriate. . . .

Evaluating the Three Mainstreaming Models

Many articulations of mainstreaming are primarily either integrationist or agenda-setting, and manifest specific problems relating to each (Table 33.1). Integrationist mainstreaming relies on experts within existing bureaucracies to pursue neutral policy-making. The main concern here is that of rhetorical entrapment. Agenda-setting mainstreaming relies on women's groups within civil society to articulate their group perspectives. The main concern here is that of reification.

Strengths and Weaknesses of the Integrationist Model

One of the key strengths of the integrationist model of mainstreaming is its effectiveness in allowing gender experts an important role in the policy formation process (Woodward 2003). This in turn ensures that policy-making is based on

Table 33.1. Mainstreaming Strategies

Mainstreaming	Inclusion	Reversal	Displacement
Model	Integrationist	Agenda-setting	Transformative
Actors	Experts	Identity groups	Political citizens
Aims	Neutral policy-making	Recognizing marginalized voices	Denaturalizing and thereby politicizing policy norms
Processes Indicators	Bureaucratic policy instruments	Consultative politics of presence	Deliberative cultural transformation
Strengths	Effective integration	Group perspectives recognized	Sensitive to diversity
Weaknesses	Rhetorical entrapment	Reification, "women only"	Complexity, lack of specificity

"gendered" knowledge, rather than on ideology or stereotypes (Beveridge and Nott 2002, 301). However, to be effective, gender mainstreaming must be understood and implemented by the regular actors in the policy-making process. . . .

. . . There is the danger that, once accepted as a norm that resonates with the dominant policy frame, mainstreaming will be adopted as a *technocratic tool* in policy-making, depoliticizing the issue of gender inequality itself. Tellingly, Gender Impact Assessments have largely been introduced where they are not too demanding in terms of costs, time, and expertise (Verloo 2001, 15). This demand to limit the scope of mainstreaming tools such that they fit easily within existing policy processes potentially delimits the potential of mainstreaming itself. It raises questions about the political accountability of experts, reduces the scope for wider consultation with "non-experts," and so reduces the likelihood that the policy agenda will reflect the particular experiences and concerns of women that do not resonate with the preexisting policy framework. Its strength lies in its ability to realize effective integration; its weakness lies in its tendency to fall into rhetorical entrapment.

Strengths and Weaknesses of the Agenda-Setting Model

The key strength of the agenda-setting model, by contrast, lies in its aspiration to recognize the perspectives and concerns of women outside the policy-making elite, countering the top-down approach to agenda-setting and problem solving. Rather than relying on bureaucratic policy instruments, this approach focuses on the importance of consultation with nongovernmental organizations and social movements. . . . The potential weakness of this "agenda-setting" model is that, in focusing on particular organizations as representative of women's views, this strategy might privilege certain gendered identities over others, entrenching political opportunities in structures that require one to speak "as a woman" first and foremost. The concern is that this may formalize and freeze identities that are actually subject to constant change and thereby undermine solidarity across groups. . . . So, while the strength of this model is its ability to recognize group perspectives from outside the existing policy-making elite, its weakness is its tendency to reify group identities, obscuring both intra-group divisions and intergroup commonalities.

The Strengths and Weaknesses of the Transformative Model

. . . The weaknesses inherent in these two models suggest that there are good reasons to consider the transformative model of mainstreaming as the way forward, ideally avoiding the problems of both rhetorical entrapment and reification, while still promoting equality via the systematic integration of diverse perspectives into the policy-making process. The clear weakness of this model is, of course, its lack of specificity. This lack of specificity takes two forms: practical and conceptual. Its lack of practical specificity arises from the fact that it remains primarily theoretical, with very few practical features or concrete articulations. Its lack of conceptual specificity arises from its theoretical commitment to denaturalizing and thereby politicizing policy aims, rather than establishing and implementing alternative policy aims in their place. . . .

Diversity Mainstreaming?

It has long been accepted that one significant challenge for contemporary equality theorists is to engage with the intersecting hierarchies of gender, race, economic class, sexuality, religion, disability, and age. As Patricia Hill Collins suggests, "viewing gender within a logic of intersectionality redefines it as a constellation of ideas and social practices that are historically situated within and that mutually construct multiple systems of oppression" (Hill Collins 1999, 263). This discursive shift brought "diversity" to the fore as central to the theoretical conceptualization of equality.

Meanwhile, contemporary equality policies in the first world tend to focus on issues of cultural and political inequality rather than inequalities in distributional goods. Those who are considered to be "unequal" are increasingly seen to be ethnic minorities, disabled, the elderly, gays and lesbians, religious minorities, and so on, rather than the poor. As a consequence, we have witnessed the emergence of a commitment to pursuing and theorizing equality in a way that acknowledges and celebrates differences. While attempts to address economic inequalities have traditionally focused on distributive issues, seeking to erase the (economic) differences between people as the means of securing their equality, attempts to address cultural and political inequalities usually entail calls that (cultural) differences be recognized and respected, rather than denied or eroded, as a precondition for securing their equality. Equality now appears, in both policy and theory debates, to require a respect for diversity.

. . . Regional and national governments are attempting to negotiate both diversity management and gender mainstreaming under a broad commitment to "equality and diversity." When evaluating the strengths and weaknesses of the three models of gender mainstreaming, one of our concerns might therefore reasonably be the extent to which these models are capable of mainstreaming with relation to all of the various equality strands, and not just gender.

Yet there are concerns about the emergence of the "diversity" agenda that need to be considered. While the shift from the pursuit of "equality" to a celebration of "equality and diversity" could be viewed as a positive policy response to the long-standing theoretical concerns with inter-sectionality, it is worth noting that "diversity management" has its roots in corporate human resource management and is here conceived of primarily as a means to produce economic productivity rather than social justice (Wrench 2003). Diversity initiatives are widely argued to improve the quality of organizations' workforces and act as a catalyst for a better return on companies' investment in human capital. They are also argued to help businesses to capitalize on new markets, attract the best and the brightest employees, increase creativity, and keep the organization flexible (see Cartwright 2001, Price 2003, Thompson 1998). In this context, some theorists adopt a highly skeptical view of "diversity," locating the emergence of diversity management within the logic of Taylorized capitalism (Hennessy 2000) and bemoaning the replacement of a moral issue by a business strategy (Wrench 2003, 10). Given this, any attempt to find a possible synergy between diversity management and gender mainstreaming must necessarily proceed with caution. . . .

Given the nature of the integrationist model, the pursuit of "equality and diversity" from this framework is likely to rely upon "diversity experts," and to adopt the language of "diversity management" employed within the corporate sector.[2] To conceive of diversity mainstreaming from this perspective is to focus attention on the market and to embrace the neo-liberal rhetoric of economic competitiveness. Its strength would be that it resonates with the dominant logic of government, but its weakness would be that it ceases to be about gender justice and instead focuses on individuals' inclusion in the sphere of employment.

On the other hand, the pursuit of "equality and diversity" via the agenda-setting model of mainstreaming is likely to entail widespread consultation with a whole range of (frequently competing and conflicting) identity groups. The inevitable negotiations that will result around perceived "hierarchies of oppression" may well lead to fragmentation and the further erosion of a sense of public-spiritedness. For example, many feminists have suggested that multiculturalism and feminism not only stand in tension to each other, but that multiculturalism is bad for women. . . . To conceive of diversity mainstreaming from a group rights perspective is to focus attention on cultural identity and to embrace a potentially essentialist affirmative politics of authenticity. Its strength would be that it might create new political opportunity structures that would empower the spokespersons of particular groups, but its weakness would be that it reduces the incentive for people to speak across groups and thereby makes the pursuit of genuine diversity more difficult.

What then would the transformative model of mainstreaming entail with relation to the pursuit of "equality and diversity"? I would suggest that it would require, minimally, that greater attention be paid to democratic inclusion within the mainstreaming process. . . .

Inclusion Deliberation and Diversity Mainstreaming

At the heart of the mainstreaming process is a concern to determine, scrutinize, and transform the norms of equivalence currently used to evaluate competing equality claims, such that they cease to reproduce structural inequalities. . . . Enabling excluded groups to unsettle institutionally accepted conceptions of equality will require a parity of participation, which makes democratic inclusion central to both the meaning and realization of equality.[3]

Political theorists have recognized that democratic debate and decision-making are themselves necessary preconditions for impartial equality policies. . . .

It therefore makes sense for theories of mainstreaming to engage with theories of deliberative democracy, which have attempted to explore "discursive mechanisms for the transmission of public opinion to the state" (Dryzek 2000, 162). Advocates of deliberative democracy—in a move akin to that made by advocates of mainstreaming—suggest that the idea of democracy revolves around the transformation, rather than simply the aggregation, of preferences. The basic impulse behind deliberative democracy is the notion that people will modify their perceptions of what society should do in the course of discussing this with others. The point of democratic participation is to manufacture, rather than to discover and aggregate, the common good. . . .

. . . What deliberative democrats offer theorists of gender mainstreaming is a concern with the quality and form of engagement between citizens and participatory forums, stressing in particular the importance of political equality and inclusivity, and of unconstrained dialogue (Smith 2005, 39) Deliberative democrats, like gender mainstreaming theorists, suggest that if the decision-making process is inclusive and dialogue unconstrained, then a greater understanding between different perspectives is more likely to be realized, and outcomes more widely accepted by participants are likely to be achieved.

The emphasis that deliberative democrats place on inclusion and dialogue offers rich resources to counter the technocratic tendency in the integrationist model of mainstreaming. Whereas the integrationist model emphasizes the importance of "gender expertise" and creates an elite body of professional gender experts, a deliberative rendering of transformative mainstreaming would emphasize the importance of dialogue with diverse social groups. This is particularly significant given that the move to consider equality and diversity rather than simply gender equality renders the process of mainstreaming infinitely more complex. Deliberative innovations such as citizens' juries, consensus conferences, deliberative opinion polls, and deliberative mapping are growing in number and significance (see Smith 2005, 39–55). Evidence suggests that these mechanisms do indeed facilitate the capacity to produce recommendations on complex, public policy issues that are informed by a wide variety of experiences and viewpoints (Smith 2005, 55). For this reason, gender mainstreaming theorists have much to gain from exploring the possible synergies between deliberative innovations and their own equality strategies. . . .

However, while the deliberative democracy literature has focused on the importance of active civil society and the reinvigoration of the public sphere, there is surprisingly little attention as to how the deliberations from within civil society are to be transmitted to the more formal arena of political decision-making. . . .

I would suggest that these mechanisms should be considered with relation to mainstreaming policies, and that the potential of integrating these deliberative transmission mechanisms into a transformative model of mainstreaming be explored. This would generate a model of mainstreaming that is deliberative, rather than bureaucratic or consultative; that aims primarily to denaturalize and thereby politicize policy norms, rather than to pursue neutral policy-making or to recognize marginalized voices. The strengths of this potential model are that it would be sensitive to diverse citizen perspectives without reifying group identities, and that it would allow for deliberations within civil society to be transmitted to the formal arena of political decision-making without becoming rhetorically entrapped. . . .

Notes

1. The justification of positive action does not require the recognition of difference, and it may be defended in terms of correcting for past unequal treatment (see Rachels 1978). Nonetheless, a recognition of difference is most likely to lead to the support of positive action policies, and the implementation of such policies frequently results in the entrenchment of group identities that do reify differences.
2. The assumption, implicit in this argument, is that the criteria of equivalence, and the conception of "the good" upon which these rest, will be a product of democratic deliberation. In this way, transformative mainstreaming works to politicize and thereby denaturalize hegemonic equality criteria, but does not itself entail alternative criteria. This makes it a procedural model at heart.
3. Thanks to Ze'ev Emmerich for this point.

References

Bacchi, Carol Lee. 1999. *Women, Policy and Politics: The Construction of Policy Problems.* London: Sage.

Beveridge, Fiona, and Sue Nott. 2002. "Mainstreaming: A Case for Optimism and Cynicism." *Feminist Legal Studies* 10: 299–311.

Booth, Christine, and Cinnamon Bennett. 2002. "Gender Mainstreaming in the European Union: Towards a New Conception and Practice of Equal Opportunities?" *The European Journal of Women's Studies* 9 (4): 430–46.

Brown, Wendy. 1995. *States of Injury: Power and Freedom in Late Modernity.* Princeton, NJ: Princeton University Press.

Cartwright, Roger. 2001. *Managing Diversity.* Capstone Express Exec.

Dryzek, John. 2000. *Deliberative Democracy and Beyond.* Oxford: Oxford University Press.

Hennessy, Rosemary. 2000. *Profit and Pleasure: Sexual Identities in Late Capitalism.* New York: Routledge.

Hill Collins, Patricia. 1999. "Moving beyond Gender: Intersectionality and Scientific Knowledge." In *Revisioning Gender,* ed. Myra Marx Ferree, Judith Lorder, and Beth Hess. London: Sage.

Hoskyns, Catherine. 1992. "The European Community's Policy on Women in the Context of 1992." *Women's Studies International Forum* 15 (1): 21–28.

Jahan, Rounaq. 1995. *The Elusive Agenda: Mainstreaming Women in Development.* London: Zed Books.

Lister, Ruth. 1997. *Citizenship: Feminist Perspectives.* Basingstoke: Macmillan.

Lombardo, Emanuela. 2003. "Integrating or Setting the Agenda? Gender Mainstreaming in the Two European Conventions on the Future of the EU and the Charter of Fundamental Human Rights." Paper presented at the ECPR General Conference, Marburg. Available at http://www.essex.ac.uk/ecpr/events/generalconference/papers/.

Pollack, Mark, and Emilie Hafner-Burton. 2000. "Mainstreaming Gender in the European Union." *Journal of European Public Policy* 7 (3): 432–56.

Price, Alan. 2003. *Human Resource Management in a Business Context.* Thomson Learning.

Rachels, James. 1978. "What People Deserve." In *Justice and Economic Distribution,* ed. J. Arther and W.H. Shaw, 150–63. Prentice Hall.

Rees, Teresa. 1999. "Mainstreaming Equality." In *Engendering Social Policy,* ed. Sophie Watson and Lesley Doyal. Buckingham: Open University Press.

———. 2002. "The Politics of 'Mainstreaming' Gender Equality." In Esther Breitenbach, Alice Brown, Fiona Mckay, and Janette Webb, eds. *The Changing Politics of Gender Equality in Britain.* Basingstoke: Palgrave, 45–69.

Smith, Graham. 2005. *Beyond the Ballot: Democratic Innovations from around the World.* London: The Power Inquiry.

Squires, Judith. 1999. *Gender in Political Theory.* Cambridge: Polity Press.

Thompson, N. 1998. "The Organisational Context." In *Promoting Equality: Challenging Discrimination and Oppression in the Human Services.* London: Macmillan.

True, Jacqui, and Michael Mintrom. 2001. "Transnational Networks and Policy Diffusion: The Case of Gender Mainstreaming." *International Studies Quarterly* 45: 27–57.

Verloo, Mieke. 2001. "Another Velvet Revolution? Gender Mainstreaming and the Politics of Implementation." IWM Working Paper, no. 5. Available at http:// www.iwm.at/p-iwmwp.htm#Verloo.

Woodward, Alison. 2003. "European Gender Mainstreaming: Promises and Pitfalls of Transformative Policy Making." *Review of Policy Research* 20 (1): 65–88.

Wrench, John, 2003. "Managing Diversity, Fighting Racism or Combating Discrimination: A Critical Exploration." Council of Europe and European Commission Research Seminar, Budapest 10–15 June 2003. Available at http://www.gleiche-chancen.at/ htm/Wrench_budapest.pdf.

Yeandle, Sue, Chris Booth, and Cinnamon Bennett. 1998. "Criteria for Success of a Mainstreaming Approach to Gender Equality." CRESR, research report.

Part VI
WOMEN, GENDER, AND THE STATE

This section brings together readings on women, gender, and the state, focusing on general debates on women, gender, and the state; uses of the state to promote feminist political goals; and gendered implications of changes in state structures. The section begins with a classic statement of the radical feminist view of the state (MacKinnon 1989), which the second reading places within the context of later feminist theories of the state (Kantola 2006). It then moves on to another seminal contribution, which explores the ways in which gender relations and welfare states mutually influence one another (Orloff 1996). Subsequent research has used these insights to investigate how feminists may target the state for women-friendly policy change by adopting context-specific political strategies (Chappell 2000), promoting "state feminism" and women's policy agencies (Stetson and Mazur 1995), and lobbying particular government and party allies (Threlfall 1998), even as opportunities for access to state structures are reconfigured over time (Banaszak, Beckwith, and Rucht 2003).

Catharine A. MacKinnon originates what has come to be known as the radical feminist theory of the state. This view has often been used as an argument against feminist engagement with state actors and institutions on the grounds that the state is "inherently" male and patriarchal, although this is not the author's argument. In her analysis, the state coercively and authoritatively constitutes the social order in the interests of men as a gender, through its legitimating norms, forms, relation to society, and substantive policies. Situating this selection in relation to broader feminist theories and debates, *Johanna Kantola* provides an overview of approaches to studying gender and the state. She distinguishes and elaborates liberal, radical, Nordic, and poststructural feminist theories. She then explores how feminists themselves may discursively construct the state in order to alter its gendered and gendering nature, using the example of debates on child care and domestic violence in Finland and the United Kingdom.

To better understand these processes, *Ann Orloff* presents a framework for analyzing how gender relations and welfare states mutually influence one another. She argues that such a lens is a crucial improvement on existing theories of the welfare state. To build her case, she traces the historical development of state social provision to demonstrate its gendered effects and explores comparative variations in the linkages between specific characteristics of gender relations and particular features of welfare states. Interested in how these patterns might be changed, *Louise Chappell* undertakes a comparative analysis of feminist strategies and political opportunities in Australia and Canada. She argues that similar institutions in different countries provide varying opportunities for feminists, to which feminists respond by adopting certain strategies over others: feminists in Australia have targeted bureaucratic arenas, while feminists in Canada have focused on constitutional arenas. Chappell concludes that the relationship between feminists and political institutions is interactive and dynamic, rather than predictable and permanent.

Extending this theme of institutions and change, *Dorothy McBride Stetson and Amy Mazur* examine women's policy agencies in Europe and the United States and seek to establish the degree to which they can be considered a form of "state feminism." To this end, they outline criteria for assessing state feminism that combines attention to state capacity, or the extent to which women's policy agencies influence the formation of feminist public policies, and state-society relations, or the extent to which women's policy agencies develop opportunities for feminist and women's advocacy organizations to have access to the policy process. *Monica Threlfall* expresses some skepticism about the term "state feminism," observing that it appears under at least three distinct guises around the world, despite tendencies in the literature to talk about state feminism as a unified concept. According to her, "state feminism" has been used to refer to women-led political projects, male politician-led political projects, and women's policy machineries. For this reason, she argues that the term is no longer useful because it has been used in such widely divergent contexts that it has lost analytical precision. Further, she suggests, what is often seen as "state feminism" is in many ways a kind of "party feminism," championed by the party in power at a particular moment in time.

Adding another layer of complexity, *Lee Ann Banaszak, Karen Beckwith, and Dieter Rucht* observe interactive changes in states and the strategies of women's movements in recent years. These new dynamics stem from four distinct processes of state reconfiguration: uploading, the shifting of power and responsibility to higher state levels; downloading, the shifting of power and responsibility to lower state levels; lateral loading, the shifting of power and responsibility to nonelected state bodies; and offloading, the shifting of power and responsibility to nonstate actors. To illustrate how women's movements have responded to these changes in state forms, the authors draw on examples from Britain, France, and Germany. As a group, the readings thus offer a variety of vantage points for analyzing the ways in which ideas about "gender" shape state policy and, in turn, how state decisions may reinforce or alter gender relations.

Chapter 34

THE LIBERAL STATE

Catharine A. MacKinnon

Feminism has no theory of the state. . . .

Feminism has not confronted, on its own terms, the relation between the state and society within a theory of social determination specific to sex. As a result, it lacks a jurisprudence, that is, a theory of the substance of law, its relation to society, and the relationship between the two. Such a theory would comprehend how law works as a form of state power in a social context in which power is gendered. It would answer the questions: What is state power? Where, socially, does it come from? How do women encounter it? What is the law for women? How does law work to legitimate the state, male power, itself? Can law do anything for women? Can it do anything about women's status? Does how the law is used matter?

In the absence of answers, feminist practice has oscillated between a liberal theory of the state on the one hand and a left theory of the state on the other. Both theories treat law as the mind of society: disembodied reason in liberal theory, reflection of material interest in left theory. In liberal moments, the state is accepted on its own terms as a neutral arbiter among conflicting interests. The law is actually or potentially principled, meaning predisposed to no substantive outcome, or manipulable to any ends, thus available as a tool that is not fatally twisted. Women implicitly become an interest group within pluralism, with specific problems of mobilization and representation, exit and voice, sustaining incremental gains and losses. In left moments, the state becomes a tool of dominance and repression, the law legitimating ideology, use of the legal system a form of utopian

idealism or gradualist reform, each apparent gain deceptive or co-optive, and each loss inevitable.

Liberalism applied to women has supported state intervention on behalf of women as abstract persons with abstract rights, without scrutinizing the content and limitations of these notions in terms of gender. Marxism applied to women is always on the edge of counseling abdication of the state as an arena altogether—and with it those women whom the state does not ignore or who are in no position to ignore it. As a result, feminism has been left with these tacit alternatives: either the state is a primary tool of women's betterment and status transformation, without analysis (hence strategy) of it as male; or women are left to civil society, which for women has more closely resembled a state of nature. The state and, with it, the law have been either omnipotent or impotent: everything or nothing. The feminist posture toward the state has therefore been schizoid on issues central to women's status. Rape, abortion, pornography, and sex discrimination are examples. To grasp the inadequacies for women of liberalism on the one hand and Marxism on the other is to begin to comprehend the role of the liberal state[1] and liberal legalism[2] within a post-Marxist feminism of social transformation.

Gender is a social system that divides power. It is therefore a political system. That is, over time, women have been economically exploited, relegated to domestic slavery, forced into motherhood, sexually objectified, physically abused, used in denigrating entertainment, deprived of a voice and authentic culture, and disenfranchised and excluded from public life. Women, by contrast with comparable men, have systematically been subjected to physical insecurity; targeted for sexual denigration and violation; depersonalized and denigrated; deprived of respect, credibility, and resources; and silenced—and denied public presence, voice, and representation of their interests. Men as men have generally not had these things done to them; that is, men have had to be Black or gay (for instance) to have these things done to them as men. Men have done these things to women. Even conventional theories of power—the more individuated, atomistic, and decisional approaches of the pluralists, as well as the more radical theories, which stress structural, tacit, contextual, and relational aspects of power—recognize such conditions as defining positions of power and powerlessness.[3] If one defines politics with Harold Lasswell, who defines a political act as "one performed in power perspectives,"[4] and with Robert Dahl, who defines a political system as "any persistent pattern of human relationships that involves, to a significant extent, power, rule, or authority,"[5] and with Kate Millett, who defines political relationships as "power structured relationships,"[6] the relation between women and men is political.

Unlike the ways in which men systematically enslave, violate, dehumanize, and exterminate other men, expressing political inequalities among men, men's forms of dominance over women have been accomplished socially as well as economically, prior to the operation of law, without express state acts, often in intimate contexts, as everyday life. So what is the role of the state in sexual politics? Neither liberalism nor Marxism grants women, as such, a specific relation to the state. Feminism has described some of the state's treatment of the gender difference but has not analyzed the state's role in gender hierarchy. What, in gender terms, are the state's norms of accountability, sources of power, real constituency? Is the state to some degree autonomous of the interests of men or an integral expression of them? Does the state embody and serve male interests in its form, dynamics, relation to society, and specific policies? Is the state constructed upon the subordination of women? If so, how does male power become state power? Can such a state be made to serve the interests of those upon whose powerlessness its power is erected? Would a different

relation between state and society, such as may exist under socialism, make a difference? If not, is masculinity inherent in the state form as such, or is some other form of state, or some other way of governing, distinguishable or imaginable? In the absence of answers to these questions, feminism has been caught between giving more power to the state in each attempt to claim it for women and leaving unchecked power in the society to men. Undisturbed, meanwhile, like the assumption that women generally consent to sex, is the assumption that women consent to this government. The question for feminism is: what is this state, from women's point of view?

The state is male in the feminist sense:[7] the law sees and treats women the way men see and treat women. The liberal state coercively and authoritatively constitutes the social order in the interest of men as a gender—through its legitimating norms, forms, relation to society, and substantive policies. The state's formal norms recapitulate the male point of view on the level of design. In Anglo-American jurisprudence, morals (value judgments) are deemed separable and separated from politics (power contests), and both from adjudication (interpretation). Neutrality, including judicial decision making that is dispassionate, impersonal, disinterested, and precedential, is considered desirable and descriptive.[8] Courts, forums without predisposition among parties and with no interest of their own, reflect society back to itself resolved. Government of laws, not of men, limits partiality with written constraints and tempers force with reasonable rule-following. . . .

Formally, the state is male in that objectivity is its norm. Objectivity is liberal legalism's conception of itself. It legitimates itself by reflecting its view of society, a society it helps make by so seeing it, and calling that view, and that relation, rationality. Since rationality is measured by point-of-viewlessness, what counts as reason is that which corresponds to the way things are. Practical rationality, in this approach, means that which can be done without changing anything. In this framework, the task of legal interpretation becomes "to perfect the state as mirror of the society."[9] . . . Such law not only reflects a society in which men rule women; it rules in a male way insofar as "the phallus means everything that sets itself up as a mirror."[10] . . .

The state is male jurisprudentially, meaning that it adopts the standpoint of male power on the relation between law and society. This stance is especially vivid in constitutional adjudication, thought legitimate to the degree it is neutral on the policy content of legislation. The foundation for its neutrality is the pervasive assumption that conditions that pertain among men on the basis of gender apply to women as well—that is, the assumption that sex inequality does not really exist in society. The Constitution—the constituting document of this state society—with its interpretations assumes that society, absent government intervention, is free and equal; that its laws, in general, reflect that; and that government need and should right only what government has previously wronged. . . .

In this light, once gender is grasped as a means of social stratification, the status categories basic to medieval law, thought to have been superseded by liberal regimes in aspirational nonhierarchical constructs of abstract personhood, are revealed deeply unchanged. Gender as a status category was simply assumed out of legal existence, suppressed into a presumptively preconstitutional social order through a constitutional structure designed not to reach it. Speaking descriptively rather than functionally or motivationally, the strategy is first to constitute society unequally prior to law; then to design the constitution, including the law of equality, so that all its guarantees apply only to those values that are taken away by law; then to construct legitimating norms so that the state legitimates itself through noninterference with the status quo. Then, so long as male dominance is so effective in society that it is unnecessary to impose sex inequality through law, such that only the most superficial sex inequalities become *de jure*, not even a legal guarantee of sex equality will produce social equality.

The posture and presumption of the negative state, the view that government best promotes freedom when it stays out of existing social arrangements, reverberates throughout constitutional law. . . .

. . . If one group is socially granted the positive freedom to do whatever it wants to another group, to determine that the second group will be and do this rather than that, no amount of negative freedom legally guaranteed to the second group will make it the equal of the first. For women, this has meant that civil society, the domain in which women are distinctively subordinated and deprived of power, has been placed beyond reach of legal guarantees. Women are oppressed socially, prior to law, without express state acts, often in intimate contexts. The negative state cannot address their situation in any but an equal society—the one in which it is needed least. . . .

The underlying assumption of judicial neutrality is that a status quo exists which is preferable to judicial intervention—a common law status quo, a legislative status quo, an economic status quo, or a gender status quo. For women, it also tends to assume that access to the conventional political realm might be available in the absence of legal rights. At the same time it obscures the possibility that a substantive approach to women's situation could be adequate to women's distinctive social exploitation—ground a claim to civil equality, for example—and do no more to license judicial arbitrariness than current standards do. From women's point of view, adjudications are already substantive; the view from nowhere already has content. . . .

If the content of positive law is surveyed more broadly from women's point of view, a pattern emerges. The way the male point of view frames an experience is the way it is framed by state policy. Over and over again, the state protects male power through embodying and ensuring existing male control over women at every level—cushioning, qualifying, or *de jure* appearing to prohibit its excesses when necessary to its normalization. *De jure* relations stabilize de facto relations. Laws that touch on sexuality provide illustrations of this argument. As in society, to the extent possession is the point of sex, rape in law is sex with a woman who is not yours, unless the act is so as to make her yours. Social and legal realities are consistent and mutually determinate: since law has never effectively interfered with men's ability to rape women on these terms, it has been unnecessary to make this an express rule of law. Because part of the kick of pornography involves eroticizing the putatively prohibited, obscenity law putatively prohibits pornography enough to maintain its desirability without ever making it unavailable or truly illegitimate. Because the stigma of prostitution is the stigma of sexuality is the stigma of the female gender, prostitution may be legal or illegal, but so long as women are unequal to men and that inequality is sexualized, women will be bought and sold as prostitutes, and law will do nothing about it.

Women as a whole are kept poor, hence socially dependent on men, available for sexual or reproductive use. To the extent that abortion exists to control the reproductive consequences of intercourse, hence to facilitate male sexual access to women, access to abortion will be controlled by "a man of The Man."[11] So long as this is effectively done socially, it is unnecessary to do it by law. Law need merely stand passively by, reflecting the passing scene. The law of sex equality stays as far away as possible from issues of sexuality. Rape, pornography, prostitution, incest, battery, abortion, gay and lesbian rights: none have been sex equality issues under law.[12] In the issues the law of sex discrimination does treat, male is the implicit reference for human, maleness the measure of entitlement to equality. In its mainstream interpretation, this law is neutral: it gives little to women that it cannot also give to men, maintaining sex inequality while appearing to address it. Gender, thus elaborated and sustained by law, is maintained as a division of power. . . .

The law on women's situation produced in this way views women's situation from the standpoint of male dominance. It assumes that the conditions that pertain among men on the basis of sex—consent to sex, comparative privacy, voice in moral discourse, and political equality on the basis of gender—apply to women. It assumes on the epistemic level that sex inequality in society is not real. Rape law takes women's usual response to coercion—acquiescence, the despairing response to hopelessness to unequal odds—and calls that consent. Men coerce women; women "consent." The law of privacy treats the private sphere as a sphere of personal freedom. For men, it is. For women, the private is the distinctive sphere of intimate violation and abuse, neither free nor particularly personal. Men's realm of private freedom is women's realm of collective subordination. The law of obscenity treats pornography as "ideas." Whether or not ideas are sex for men, pornography certainly is sex for men. From the standpoint

of women, who live the sexual abuse in pornography as everyday life, pornography is reality. The law of obscenity treats regulation of pornography from the standpoint of what is necessary to protect it: as regulation of morals, as some men telling other men what they may not see and do and think and say about sex. From the standpoint of women, whose torture pornography makes entertainment, pornography is the essence of a powerless condition, its effective protection by the state the essence of sexual politics. Obscenity law's "moral ideas" are a political reality of women's subordination. Just as, in male law, public oppression masquerades as private freedom and coercion is guised as consent, in obscenity law real political domination is presented as a discourse in ideas about virtue and vice.

Rape law assumes that consent to sex is as real for women as it is for men. Privacy law assumes that women in private have the same privacy men do. Obscenity law assumes that women have the access to speech men have. Equality law assumes that women are already socially equal to men. Only to the extent women have already achieved social equality does the mainstream law of equality support their inequality claims. The laws of rape, abortion, obscenity, and sex discrimination show how the relation between objectification, understood as the primary process of the subordination of women, and the power of the state is the relation between the personal and the political at the level of government. These laws are not political because the state is presumptively the sphere of politics. They are integral to sexual politics because the state, through law, institutionalizes male power over women through institutionalizing the male point of view in law. Its first state act is to see women from the standpoint of male dominance; its next act is to treat them that way. This power, this state, is not a discrete location, but a web of sanctions throughout society which "control[s] the principal means of coercion" that structures women's everyday lives.[13] . . .

Notes

1. Recent work attempting to criticize and yet rehabilitate the liberal state, such as Bruce Ackerman, *Social Justice in the Liberal State* (New Haven: Yale University Press, 1980), does not solve these problems. Ackerman, for example, does not question

the social sources and sites of power, but only its distribution.

2. Karl Klare, "Law-Making as Praxis," *Telos* 40 (Summer 1979): 123–135; Judith Shklar, *Legalism* (Cambridge, Mass.: Harvard University Press, 1964).

3. Scholars of power in its political aspect traditionally analyze legitimated physical force. Thus, the organization called "government," the science of which is political science, after Weber became that which successfully upholds its claim to regulate exclusively the legitimate use of physical force in a physical territory; Robert A. Dahl, *Modern Political Analysis* (Englewood Cliffs, N.J.: Prentice-Hall, 1976), p. 3. (See Max Weber, *Theory of Social and Economic Organization* [New York: Free Press of Glencoe, 1957], p.154.) Dahl and C. E. Lindblom use "control" in a similar way: "In loose language, A controls the responses of B if A's acts cause B to respond in a definite way"; *Politics, Economics, and Welfare* (New York: Harper & Brothers, 1953), p. 94. Pluralist theorists of power have been critical of treating power as a lump in a zero-sum game: you either have it or you don't. Still, for them, it has to do with getting what one wants, with rewards and deprivations, with A getting B to do something A wants independent of what B wants, either from A telling B or from B anticipating what A wants. "A power relation, actual or potential, is an actual or potential causal relation between the preferences of an actor regarding an outcome and the outcome itself"; Jack H. Nagel, *A Descriptive Analysis of Power* (New Haven: Yale University Press, 1975), p. 29. Because he wants it, it happens. On other causal aspects, see Herbert A. Simon, "Notes on the Observation and Measurement of Political Power," *Journal of Politics* 15 (1953): 500–516. Carl J. Friedrich similarly formulates a "rule of anticipated reactions": "if A's desire for X causes B to attempt to bring about X"; *Constitutional Government and Democracy* (New York: Harper & Brothers, 1937), pp. 16–18. According to Dahl, "A has power over B to the extent that he can get B to do something that B would not otherwise do"; Robert A. Dahl, "A Critique of the Ruling Elite Model," in *Political Power*, ed. Roderick Bell, David Edwards, and Harrison Wagner (New York: Free Press, 1969), p. 80. See also Nelson Polsby, *Community Power and Political Theory* (New Haven: Yale University Press, 1962), and R. Dahl, "Power," *International Encyclopedia of the Social Sciences*, vol. 12 (New York: Macmillan, 1968), 405–415. These formulations, while envisioning a somewhat atomistic and individuated social world and a discrete set of decisional interactions, nevertheless do characterize many of the behaviors claimed by feminists as exhibiting power relations between women and men.

Other concepts of power urged by critics of the traditional approaches capture further dimensions of male power as a political system, emphasizing the more structural, contextual, tacit, and relational dimensions of power. See, e.g., Peter Bachrach and Morton Baratz, "Two Faces of Power," in Bell, Edwards, and Wagner, *Political Power*, p. 94. To these facets, Steven Lukes adds control over agenda, latent as well as observable conflict, and objective as well as subjective interests, emphasizing the "sheer weight of institutions" over explicit decisions; *Power: A Radical Analysis* (London: Macmillan, 1974), p. 18. These concepts also characterize gender relations as power, hence political, relations.

Given the heated disagreements among these men, it is remarkable the extent to which Robert Dahl is correct in characterizing them all when he observes that political science (which is the study of politics, which is, inter alia, about power) has defined the man/woman division outside its confines, because it is seen to relate to "ancient and persistent biological and physiological drives, needs and wants . . . to satisfy drives for sexual gratification, love, security and respect are insistent and primordial needs. The means of satisfying them quickly and concretely generally lie outside political life"; *Modern Political Analysis*, pp. 103–104. In other words, because the subordination of women is seen as universal and natural, it is not seen as a system of domination, hence a system of power, hence as political at all.

4. Harold D. Lasswell and Abraham Kaplan, *Power and Society* (New Haven: Yale University Press, 1950), pp. xiv, 240.

5. Dahl, *Modern Political Analysis*, p. 3. See also Dahl and Lindblom, *Politics, Economics, and Welfare*. Of course, this is not to say that power is all there is to politics.

6. Kate Millett, *Sexual Politics* (Garden City, N.Y.: Doubleday, 1970), p. 31.

7. See Susan Rae Peterson, "Coercion and Rape: The State as a Male Protection Racket," in *Feminism and Philosophy*, ed. Mary Vetterling-Braggin, Frederick A. Elliston, and Jane English (Totowa, N.J.: Littlefield, Adams, 1977), pp. 360–371; Janet Rifkin, "Toward a Theory of Law and Patriarchy," 3 *Harvard Women's Law Journal* 83–96 (Spring 1980). Additional work of interest on this subject includes Sherry B.Ortner, "The Virgin and the State," *Feminist Studies* 4 (October 1978): 19–36; Viana Muller, "The Formation of the State and the Oppression of Women: Some Theoretical Considerations and a Case Study in England and Wales," *Review of Radical Political Economics* 9 (Fall 1977): 7–21; Irene Silverblatt, "Andean Women in the Inca Empire," *Feminist Studies* 4 (October 1978): 37–61; Karen Sacks, "State Bias and Women's Status," *American Anthropologist* 78 (September 1976): 565–569.

8. Herbert Wechsler, "Toward Neutral Principles of Constitutional Law," 73 *Harvard Law Review* I (1959), though a defense of legalized racism, is taken as axiomatic.

9. Laurence Tribe, "Constitution as Point of View" (Mimeograph, Harvard Law School, 1982), p. 13.

10. Madeleine Gagnon, "Body I," in *New French Feminisms*, ed. Elaine Marks and Isabelle de Courtivron (Amherst: University of Massachusetts Press, 1980), p. 180. The mirror trope has served as metaphor for

the epistemological/political reality of objectification in feminist work. "Into the room of the dressing where the walls are covered with mirrors. Where mirrors are like eyes of men, and the women reflect the judgments of mirrors"; Susan Griffin, *Woman and Nature: The Roaring inside Her* (New York: Harper & Row, 1978), p. 155. "She did suffer, the witch / trying to peer round the looking / glass, she forgot / someone was in the way"; Michelène, "Réflexion," quoted in Sheila Rowbotham, *Woman's Consciousness, Man's World* (Harmondsworth: Penguin, 1973), p. 2; see also ibid., pp. 26–29, and Mary Daly, *Beyond God the Father: Toward a Philosophy of Women's Liberation* (Boston: Beacon Press, 1973), pp. 195, 197. Virginia Woolf wrote the figure around ("So I reflected . . ."), remarking "the necessity that women so often are to men" of serving as a looking glass in which a man can "see himself at breakfast and at dinner at least twice the size he really is." Notice the doubled sexual/gender meaning: "Whatever may be their use in civilized societies, mirrors are essential to all violent and heroic action. That is why Napoleon and Mussolini both insist so emphatically upon the inferiority of women, for if they were not inferior, they would cease to enlarge"; *A Room of One's Own* (New York: Harcourt, Brace & World, 1969), p. 36.

11. Johnnie Tillmon, "Welfare Is a Women's Issue," *Liberation News Service*, February 26, 1972; reprinted in Rosalyn Baxandall, Linda Gordon, and Susan Reverby, eds., *America's Working Women* (New York: Random House, 1976), pp. 355–358.

12. Sexual harassment, designed in pursuit of the jurisprudential approach argued here, is an exception. So is a recent decision by the Ninth Circuit, *Watkins v. Army*, 837 F.2d 1429 (9th Cir. 1988), which holds that to deprive gays of military employment on the basis of homosexual status is a violation of the Equal Protection Clause.

13. Charles Tilly, ed., "Western State-Making and Theories of Political Transformation," in *The Formation of National States in Western Europe* (Princeton: Princeton University Press, 1975), p. 638.

Chapter 35

GENDER AND THE STATE: THEORIES AND DEBATES

Johanna Kantola

. . .

Feminist Theories of the State

How have feminists theorized the state? What are the critiques of these theories? . . . Feminism was long dominated by a deep uneasiness about the state, which was seen as patriarchal and therefore beyond reform politics. This discomfort culminated in arguments that feminists did not have a theory of the state (MacKinnon 1989) and that it was not a feminist concern to theorize it (Allen 1990). Despite this, a variety of feminist perspectives on the state exists (Kantola 2006). . . .

The Neutral State

Liberal feminist theories of the state have been influential in offering feminists some powerful policy instruments. They see the state as a neutral arbiter between different interest groups. Whilst liberal feminists recognize that state institutions are dominated by men and that policies reflect masculine interests, they argue that the state is to be "re-captured" from the interest group of men. In other words, the state is a reflection of the interest groups that control its institutions. To many liberal feminists, more women in the state would entail more women's policy. They seek initiatives, legislation, and policies that promote equality and address women's concerns (Watson 1990, Waylen 1998). Liberal feminists stress the principle of formal equal treatment before the law (see Friedan

1962). Differences between women and men ought not to be pertinent in the public sphere; both are to be treated as equal citizens. . . .

While a number of the liberal feminist arguments have been powerful, there are problems that caution against the uncritical use of the liberal feminist notion of the state. The concept of the state is very narrow and understands it mainly in terms of institutions, which is rejected by critics. They argue that liberal feminists fail to understand the structural relations of women's lives—the family, the sexual division of labor, sexclass oppression—as part of the political life of society (Eisenstein 1986: 181). As it does not challenge the deep structures of male dominance, it could be argued that it creates space for a new form of patriarchy, one which is subtler and may be more stable and powerful than earlier forms (Pringle and Watson 1990: 231). Legislation provides formal equality but, at the same time, diverts attention away from powerful economic, social, and psychological bases for inequality. For Kathy Ferguson (1984), liberal feminism has become a voice subservient to dominant patriarchal discourses. An exclusive focus on integrating women into state institutions produces a situation that perpetuates dominant patriarchal discourses and norms rather than challenges them. . . .

The Patriarchal State

Radical feminists, in turn, offer important tools for feminist theories of the state by stressing its patriarchal nature. Their critical analyses help to reveal the role of the state in perpetuating gender inequalities. Radical feminist focus on women's concerns, such as reproduction and sexuality, opens feminist debates to crucial issues that are often regarded as lying outside state politics and analyses of states. . . .

While liberal feminists understand the state in terms of its political institutions, radical feminists extend their focus to the wider structures of the state and society. This is one of the key contributions of radical feminism and extremely useful for any analysis of the state. Radical feminist work shows the patriarchal nature of the formal and informal practices followed in decision-making. The concept of patriarchy informs feminist strategies and political goals: the whole structure of male domination must be dismantled if women's liberation is to be achieved (Acker 1989: 235). Civil society, rather than the state, is the sphere in which women should concentrate their energies in order to challenge patriarchy. . . .

Radical feminism employs the concepts of gender and sexuality. . . . States enforce the equation of women with sexuality. However, via consciousness-raising it becomes possible to rediscover what is truly female and to struggle to speak with women's own voice. Whereas liberal feminists understand differences between the sexes as nonpertinent, radical feminists celebrate and value them. At best, this creates new visions, for example, about alternative, antihierarchical ways of working (Ferguson 1984: 5).

Despite these useful insights into gender and the state, there are a number of problems with radical feminist theorizing. Particularly, radical feminists tend to essentialize the state as patriarchal. They seek to specify a single cause of women's oppression, namely the exploitative structure of patriarchy. In the model, the state becomes a key source of patriarchal power and power becomes men's power, authority, or dominance over women. For critics, neither the state nor masculinity has a single source or terrain of power (Barrett and Phillips 1992: 3, Brown 1995: 179).

Radical feminism is insensitive to differences between women and risks claiming that states oppress women everywhere in the same way (Acker 1989: 235). The universalizing tendencies are strongly rejected by black feminists, who point out that their solidarity is often with black men rather than with white women. Black feminist

criticism is directed at both radical and liberal feminists. They fail to understand the different meanings that concepts such as work and family have for black women (Amos and Parmar 1984, Mirza 1997). Western feminist state theory largely ignores the experience of Third World women under the postcolonial state. The assumptions made are West-centered but the theorizing takes on a universalizing language (Rai 1996: 5). . . .

The Capitalist State

Whereas for radical feminists the state is patriarchal, for Marxist feminists the state is essentially capitalist (McIntosh 1978: 259). The state is not just an institution but also a form of social relations. Women's subordination plays a role in sustaining capitalism through the reproduction of the labor force within the family. Women are oppressed in work and in exclusion from it, and Marxist feminists argue that the familial ideology is to blame. When criticizing welfare states, Marxist feminists argue that the state helps to reproduce and maintain the familial ideology primarily through welfare state policies. In contrast to radical feminism, Marxist feminists argue that women are important in the struggle against capitalism as workers, not as women (McIntosh 1978) and the category of women is employed in reproductive terms (Sargent 1981: xxi).

Socialist feminism attempts to combine the insights of both Marxist and radical feminism. From radical feminists, socialist feminists derive an understanding of the system of oppression called patriarchy, and from Marxist feminists the importance of the class oppression defining the situation of all workers. The two approaches are combined in analyses of this "dual system" of capitalism and patriarchy. . . . Michèle Barrett identifies a number of ways in which the state promotes women's oppression: women are excluded from certain sorts of work by protective legislation, the state exercises control over the ways sexuality is represented through pornography laws, and the state's housing policy is resistant to the needs of non-nuclear families (1980: 231–7).

. . . Many feminists are increasingly concerned about capitalist structures in their most neoliberal forms, their linkages to the state and their impact on gender relations, and argue for the need to theorize these. Nevertheless, these approaches have some significant shortcomings. Sophie Watson argues that despite the Marxist and socialist feminist emphasis on the state as a form of social relations, the state still appears to be an "entity which limits and determines our lives, which acts in the interests of capital, which defines who we are and what we need, which deflects class conflict and which obscures class divisions" (1990: 4). More specifically, Marxist feminist accounts employ reductionist and functionalist arguments to explain the persistence of sexual divisions and the patriarchal family form, which ends up subsuming gender relations within the all-powerful system of something called the 'needs of capital' (Watson 1990: 6).

In other words, Marxist feminists are criticized for privileging Marxist categories of analysis at the expense of feminist ones. . . . Privileging Marxist categories means that Marxist feminists continue to suffer from the problems faced by Marxists: structuralism, determinism, and an overemphasis on economics. Socialist feminists provide more nuanced analyses of the two systems. However, at times the capitalist and patriarchal structures of the society remain so dominant in their analyses that there is hardly any room for positive social change.

The Women-Friendly Welfare State

Liberal, radical, Marxist, and socialist feminist theories are challenged from a number of different perspectives within feminist theory. Nordic feminists, femocrats in Australia, and gender and development scholars highlight the differences between states. These scholars are united in arguing that there is a need to move beyond narrow understandings of the state as outlined above. For example, development scholars reveal the fundamentally different meaning of the state in non-Western countries. Like Western debates, this literature is concerned to examine the processes and functions of state institutions in exercises of power in various areas of the public and private lives of women and women's resistance to these intrusions (Rai and Lievesley 1996: 1). However, there are important differences. Postcolonialism, nationalism, economic modernization, and state

capacity emerge as key issues in the Third World literature, whereas Western feminists often take these issues for granted, focusing instead on how best to engage with the state (Chappell 2000: 246). . . .

Nordic feminist analyses of the state are markedly different from radical and Marxist feminist perspectives. . . .

Helga Maria Hernes (1987) defines Nordic states as potentially women-friendly societies, which signifies that women's political and social empowerment happens through the state and with the support of state social policy. The social democratic citizenship tradition results in a more optimistic acceptance of the state as an instrument for social change than radical, Marxist, or socialist feminism. For Hernes, Nordic women act in accordance with their own culture in turning to the state, even in those instances where they wish to build alternative institutions (1988: 210).

Studies of the Nordic women-friendly welfare states are concerned with the roles of women as political actors. It is argued that women become empowered as political subjects through the institutionalization of gender equality. An exclusive focus on patriarchy, in contrast, risks reducing women to victims of patriarchal structures, which means that their contribution to maintain or change gender relations becomes invisible (Siim 1988).

Nordic feminism is more pessimistic in its analysis of gender and the state than liberal feminism. The private dependency of women on individual men is transformed into public dependency on the state in the women-friendly welfare states (Dahlerup 1987). The expansion of the public sector, even if it benefits women, is planned and executed by a male-dominated establishment. The parameters for distribution and redistribution policies are increasingly determined within the framework of the corporate system, where women have an even more marginal role to play than in the parliamentary system. Thus, women are the objects of policies. The tendency is exacerbated by the observation that women's lives are more dependent and determined by state policies than men's (Hernes 1988a: 77). . . .

Whilst radical feminists assume that all women are oppressed by the state in the same way, Nordic feminists have the opposite problem: they seem to claim that all women are liberated through the state in the same way. Indeed, because the term "women-friendly welfare state" is premised on the idea of the common and collective interests of women, the category of women is very homogeneous. Hernes herself notes that egalitarian values have their limitations when it comes to introducing pluralism of any form (1987: 17). The concerns of, for example, lesbians and ethnic minorities have yet to enter the agenda of women-friendly welfare states. Gender equality signifies, first and foremost, equality for white, heterosexual, working mothers in the Nordic context. Diversity and fluidity within the category of women and women's identity are missing from Nordic feminist analyses of women-friendly welfare states.

Furthermore, like liberal feminists, Nordic feminists tend to opt for the sameness route to equality, which signifies the idea of gender equality as a condition where men's and women's lives are uniform (Lindvert 2002: 100). The normative foundation of the women-friendly welfare state rests on a dual-breadwinner model where both women and men are waged workers. In other words, the feminist discourse about women-friendliness is based on the premise that women's labor market participation is a key to gender equality (Borchorst and Siim 2002: 92). Measures associated with civil rights, rather than social rights, and their importance are neglected in the women-friendly welfare state literature. Liberal countries—the United States, Canada, Australia, and Britain—offer a somewhat different set of gender-equality measures from the social democratic states (O'Connor, Orloff, and Shaver 1999). These include reproductive or body rights, antidiscriminatory regulations, and workplace policies. The measures are associated with civil rights rather than with social rights.

Nancy Fraser argues that neither a politics of redistribution—remedying social inequalities—nor a politics of recognition—revaluing disrespected identities—is sufficient on its own (1995, 1997). Nordic feminists problematically show partiality toward the politics of redistribution and gender equality is separated from cultural politics (Siim 2000: 126). Such fundamental civil right issues as the right to bodily integrity (violence against women) have been notoriously slow to arrive on the Nordic agenda.

The Differentiated State

The final feminist approach to the state . . . is the poststructural feminist one. It seems to provide some answers to the problems identified with Nordic feminist theories of the state. Poststructural feminist approaches highlight differences within states. Rosemary Pringle and Sophie Watson challenge the unity of the state and argue that the state consists of a set of arenas that lack coherence (1990, 1992). In poststructural analyses, the state is a differentiated set of institutions, agencies, and discourses and has to be studied as such. The approaches shift the emphasis to state practices and discourses rather than to state institutions. The state is depicted as a discursive process, and politics and the state are conceptualized in broad terms. The state is not inherently patriarchal but was historically constructed as patriarchal in a political process whose outcome is open. The patriarchal state can be seen, then, not as the manifestation of patriarchal essence, but as the center of a reverberating set of power relations and political processes in which patriarchy is both constructed and contested (Connell 1987, 1994). Particular discourses and histories construct state boundaries, identities, and agency.

In comparison to the approaches discussed above, the poststructural contribution is to highlight the differentiated nature of the state and to question the unity of state responses (Franzway, Court, and Connell 1989). An important question for poststructural feminists is what the most effective strategies are for empowering women in their engagements with the state (Randall 1998: 200). In other words, the feminist aim becomes to make sense not only of the state's impact on gender, but also of the ways in which the state can be made use of and changed through feminist struggles. The analyses allow the complex, multidimensional, and differentiated relations between the state and gender to be taken into account. They recognize that the state can be a positive as well as a negative resource for feminists. . . .

While emphasizing the gendered nature of concepts such as the welfare state or citizenship, poststructural feminists also take into account national variations. Helpfully, the approaches turn away from the theorization of relations between gender and the state in general terms and focus instead on the construction of gender within specific state discourses and practices (Mottier 2004: 81). Within a framework of diverse discourses and power relations, gender diversity and differences in women's experiences come to the fore (Kantola and Dahl 2005).

Poststructural feminist theorizing of the state thus signifies important developments for feminist debates. Nevertheless, it would be problematic to opt for it uncritically. Poststructural feminist understandings of the state are criticized for an overemphasis on discursive processes, which shift attention away from institutions and policies. Foucauldians, in particular, concentrate on relations and techniques of governance, treating institutions as an effect of processes and practices rather than as their origin (Cooper 1998: 10). . . . It is often argued that due to the poststructural feminist lack of focus on institutions and institutional mechanisms, the approaches underestimate the difficulty of achieving change compared with the relative ease of reproducing status quo power relations (Cooper 1994: 7). A further implication of the oversight of state institutions is the neglect of the linkages between state bodies, for example, the influence the central government exerts over the local government (Cooper 1994: 7; O'Connor, Orloff, and Shaver 1999:11). Poststructural feminism can also be argued to lack specificity. The state is treated as a terrain of struggle, without much thought being given to how the state differs from other such terrains (Cooper 1994: 7). . . .

References

Acker, Joan (1989) "The Problem with Patriarchy," *Sociology* 23 (2) pp. 235–40.

Allen, Judith. (1990) "Does Feminism Need a Theory of 'The State'?" in Sophie Watson (ed.) *Playing the State* (London: Verso) pp. 21–37.

Amos, Valerie and Pratibha Parmar (1984) "Challenging Imperial Feminism," *Feminist Review* 17 pp. 3–19.

Barrett, Michèle (1980) *Women's Oppression Today: Problems in Marxist Feminist Analysis* (London: Verso).

Barrett, Michèle and Anne Phillips (eds.) (1992) *Destabilizing Theory* (Cambridge: Polity Press).

Borchorst, Anette and Birte Siim (2002) "The Women-Friendly Welfare States Revisited," *NORA: Nordic Journal of Women's Studies* 10 (2) pp. 90–98.

Brown, Wendy (1995) *States of Injury: Power and Freedom in Late Modernity* (Princeton, NJ: Princeton University Press).

Chappell, Louise (2000) "Interacting with the State," *International Feminist Journal of Politics* 2 (2) pp. 244–75.

Chappell, Louise (2003) *Gendering Government: Feminist Engagement with the State in Australia and Canada* (Vancouver: University of British Columbia Press).

Connell, Robert W. (1987) *Gender and Power* (Cambridge: Polity Press).

Connell, Robert W. (1994) "The State, Gender, and Sexual Politics: Theory and Appraisal," in H. Radtke and H. Stam (eds.) *Power/Gender* (London: Sage), pp. 136–73.

Cooper, Davina (1994) *Sexing the City* (London: Rivers Oram Press).

Cooper, Davina (1998) *Governing out of Order: Space, Law and the Politics of Belonging* (London and New York: Rivers Oram Press).

Dahlerup, Drude (1987) "Confusing Concepts—Confusing Reality: A Theoretical Discussion of the Patriarchal State" in Anne Showstack Sassoon (ed.) *Women and the State* (London: Routledge) pp. 93–127.

Eisenstein, Zillah (1986) *The Radical Future of Liberal Feminism* (Boston: Northeastern University Press).

Ferguson, Kathy (1984) *The Feminist Case against Bureaucracy* (Philadelphia: Temple University Press).

Franzway, Suzanne, Diane Court, and R. W. Connell (1989) *Staking a Claim: Feminism, Bureaucracy and the State* (Cambridge: Polity Press).

Fraser, Nancy (1995) "False Antitheses: A Response to Seyla Benhabib and Judith Butler," in Seyla Benhabib et al. (eds.) *Feminist Contentions: A Philosophical Exchange* (London: Routledge) pp. 59–74.

Fraser, Nancy (1997) *Justice Interrupts: Critical Reflections in the "Post-Socialist" Condition* (Routledge: London).

Friedan, Betty (1962) *The Feminine Mystique* (New York: Dell).

Hernes, Helga Maria (1987) *Welfare State and Woman Power* (Oslo: Norwegian University Press).

Hernes, Helga Maria (1988) "Scandinavian Citizenship," *Acta Sociologica* 31 (3) pp. 199–215.

Hernes, Helga Maria (1988a) "Women and the Welfare State: The Transition from Private to Public Dependence," in Anne Showstack Sassoon (ed.) *Women and the State* (London: Routledge) pp. 72–92.

Kantola, Johanna (2006) "Feminism," in Colin Hay, Michael Lister, and David Marsh (eds.) *The State: Theories and Issues* (Basingstoke: Palgrave Macmillan) pp. 118–34.

Kantola, Johanna, and Hanne Marlene Dahl (2005) "Feminist Understandings of the State: From Differences between to Differences Within," *International Feminist Journal of Politics* 7 (1) pp. 49–70.

Lindvert, Jessica (2002) "A World Apart: Swedish and Australian Gender Equality Policy," *NORA* 2 (10) pp. 99–107.

MacKinnon, Catharine (1989) *Towards a Feminist Theory of the State* (London: Harvard University Press).

McIntosh, Mary (1978) "The State and the Oppression of Women," in A. Kuhn and A. Wolpe (eds.) *Feminism and Materialism: Women and Modes of Production* (London: Routledge and Kegan Paul) pp. 254–89.

Mirza, Heidi Safia (ed.) (1997) *Black British Feminism: A Reader* (London: Routledge).

Mottier, Veronique (2004) "Feminist Political Theory," *European Political Science* 4 (3) pp. 79–84.

O'Connor, Julia, Ann Shola Orloff, and Sheila Shaver (1999) *States, Markets, Families: Gender, Liberalism and Social Policy in Australia, Canada, Great Britain and the United States* (Cambridge: Cambridge University Press).

Pringle, Rosemary and Sophie Watson (1990) "Fathers, Brothers, Mates: The Fraternal State in Australia," in Sophie Watson (ed.) *Playing the State* (London: Verso) pp. 229–43.

Pringle, Rosemary and Sophie Watson (1992) "'Women's Interests' and the PostStructuralist State," in Michèle Barrett and Anne Phillips (eds.) *Destabilizing Theory* (Cambridge: Polity Press) pp. 53–73.

Rai, Shirin (1996) "Women and the State in the Third World: Some Issues for Debate," in Shirin Rai and Geraldine Lievesley (eds.) *Women and the State: International Perspectives* (London: Taylor and Francis) pp. 5–22.

Rai, Shirin and Geraldine Lievesley (eds.) (1996) *Women and the State: International Perspectives* (London: Taylor and Francis).

Randall, Vicky (1998) "Gender and Power: Women Engage the State," in Vicky Randall and Georgina Waylen (eds.) *Gender, Politics and the State* (London: Routledge) pp.185–205.

Sargent, Lydia (1981) "New Left Women and Men: The Honeymoon is Over," in Lydia Sargent (ed.) *Women and Revolution: The Unhappy Marriage of Marxism and Feminism* (London: Pluto Press) pp. xi–xxxii.

Siim, Birte (1988) "Towards a Feminist Rethinking of the Welfare State," in Kathleen Jones and Anna Jónasdóttir (eds.) *The Political Interests of Gender* (Oxford: Sage) pp. 160–86.

Siim, Birte (2000) *Gender and Citizenship: Politics and Agency in France, Britain and Denmark* (Cambridge: Cambridge University Press).

Watson, Sophie (1990) "The State of Play: An Introduction," in Sophie Watson (ed.) *Playing the State* (London: Verso) pp. 3–20.

Watson, Sophie (1992) "Femocratic Feminism," in Mike Savage and Anne Witz (eds.) *Gender and Bureaucracy* (Oxford: Blackwell) pp. 186–204.

Waylen, Georgina (1998) "Gender, Feminism and the State: An Overview," in Vicky Randall and Georgina Waylen (eds.) *Gender, Politics and the State* (London: Routledge) pp. 1–17.

Chapter 36

GENDER IN THE WELFARE STATE

Ann Orloff

Introduction

Gender relations, embodied in the sexual division of labor, compulsory heterosexuality, discourses and ideologies of citizenship, motherhood, masculinity and femininity, and the like, profoundly shape the character of welfare states. Likewise, the institutions of social provision—the set of social assistance and social insurance programs, universal citizenship entitlements, and public services to which we refer as "the welfare state"—affect gender relations in a variety of ways. . . . However, comparative study has so far given little systematic attention to gender. Most feminist work, though concerned with elaborating a gendered analysis of welfare states, has not been systematically comparative. . . . This means that we lack a sense of the range of variation in how gender relations and welfare states mutually influence each other. . . .

Gender and the Welfare State

Over the past two decades, we have amassed a large body of research showing that state policies of all kinds are shaped by gender relations and in turn affect gender relations. Until recently, one of two broad understandings of the relationship between the state and gender has predominated in analyses of social policy. The first sees states contributing in one way or another to the social reproduction of gender hierarchies. In contrast, the second sees states varying in terms of their ameliorative impact on social inequality, including gender inequality.

The Social Reproduction of Gender Hierarchy

One school of thought emphasizes the ways in which state social policies regulate gender relations and contribute to the social reproduction of gender inequality through a variety of mechanisms (see Jenson 1986 for a review). Analysts saw the emergence of modern welfare states as a transition from "private" to "public" patriarchy (e.g., Holter 1984). Key mechanisms for the maintenance of gender hierarchy include: (i) gendered divisions of labor, with men responsible for families' economic support and women responsible for caregiving and domestic labor as well as for producing babies; (ii) the family wage system, in which men's relatively superior wages (and tax advantages) are justified partly in terms of their responsibility for the support of dependent wives and children; women are excluded from the paid labor force (or from favored positions within it) and therefore are economically dependent on men; (iii) traditional marriage (which implies the gender division of labor) and a concomitant double standard of sexual morality. . . . Many have called attention to the ways in which these various mechanisms—even when not associated with women's absolute material deprivation—are coupled with women's exclusion from political power (e.g. Lewis & Åström 1992, Nelson 1984, Hernes 1987, Borchorst & Siim 1987).

. . . More recently, there has been a greater focus on the ways in which state practices themselves constitute gender. Thus, some have focused particularly on the construction of gendered citizenship, with its encodings of male "independence" based on wage-earning (rather than the older basis in military service) and female "dependence," and associated gender-differentiated social provision (Gordon & Fraser 1994, Knijn 1994, Saraceno 1994, Cass 1994, Pateman 1988, Lister 1990). Another formulation highlights the state's production of gender differentiation (and inequality) through the process of claiming benefits from the state: men tend to make claims on the welfare state as workers while women make claims as members of families (as wives or mothers) and through the very existence of "masculine" and "feminine" programs—the former protecting against labor market failures and targeting a male clientele, the latter providing help for family-related problems and targeting a female clientele (e.g. Fraser 1989). . . . In the United States especially, scholars speak of a "two-tier" or "two-track" welfare state in which programs targeted on men and labor market problems tend to be contributory social insurance while those primarily for women and family-related are means-tested social assistance. . . .

Ameliorating Gender Inequalities?

The second understanding of gender relations and the welfare state is based on the common idea that welfare states work to ameliorate social inequalities; feminist versions of this view focus on gender as well as class inequalities, especially in vulnerability to poverty. These analysts generally note that although poverty rates for the population as a whole fell in the post–World War II era, women made up an increasing proportion of poor adults, and households headed by women became an ever-larger proportion of all poor households; these trends are due partly to the improving situation of other demographic groups (e.g., the elderly) but also to some women's deteriorating position in the labor market and the rising rates of solo motherhood (McLanahan, Sorenson, and Watson 1989). Income transfer programs sometimes offer buffers against women's poverty (Piven 1985). . . . The implication of these studies is that disadvantaged groups—including women—have an interest in higher spending. . . .

A focus on poverty rates alone can be misleading; when marriage rates are high, one sees relatively low poverty rates for women and low gender poverty gaps, but the extent of women's vulnerability to poverty is occluded. Moreover, quantitative poverty studies typically overlook the ways in which regulation may accompany benefits, as in the case of many benefits for solo parents that are conditioned on cooperation in paternity establishment (Monson 1996). In addition, the ways in which the systemic characteristics of social provision affect gender interests are ignored. For example, in the United States, increased levels of income transfers would not address the political marginalization of the status of "client" in a context where citizenship is linked strongly to the status of "worker" (Nelson 1984); nor would this strategy counter stereotypes of dependency deeply embedded in relations of class, race/ethnicity, and gender (Roberts 1995, Quadagno 1994, Collins 1990). Others have argued that the residual character of American social provision undermines popular support for social spending generally, and in such a context, calls for increased benefits in targeted programs such as Aid to Families with Dependent children (AFDC) may actually exacerbate the political difficulties of welfare (Weir et al. 1988). In other words, access to cash benefits is not always an unmixed blessing. . . .

Maternalism and the Origins of Welfare States

Recent studies of the origins of modern social provision have challenged some key assumptions of both mainstream and earlier feminist scholarship. First, these studies have revealed the significant amount of state activity aimed at the welfare of mothers and children and the activities of women reformers, ignored in the mainstream literature's focus on labor market regulation and class actors. Second, they have challenged some of the assumptions of the social reproduction analysts by highlighting women's participation (even as subordinate actors) in the shaping of policies directed at women and families.

Many women (and some male) reformers were motivated by the ideas and discourses of maternalism. Koven and Michel (1993, p. 4) define maternalism as "ideologies and discourses which exalted women's capacity to mother and applied to society as a whole the values they attached to that role: care, nurturance and morality." The widespread acceptance of ideals of gender differentiation did not deter women from entering the political sphere—indeed, they entered it largely on the basis of "difference," claiming their work as mothers gave them unique capacities for developing state policies that would safeguard mothers and children, leading to "equality in difference." Koven and Michel emphasize the ambiguous meanings and uses of maternalism, noting that it can encompass pronatalists most concerned with population increase, women who accepted the ideal of a family wage for men as the source of support for mothers, and feminists who called for an independent state-supplied income for mothers (Pedersen 1993, Lake 1992). . . .

The few explicitly comparative studies of this period offer some clues to which factors were most significant in shaping the character of social policies aimed at the support of motherhood, parenthood, and children—variations that in many cases continue to distinguish the systems of social provision in the contemporary west. Of particular significance are: (i) the balance of power among labor, employers, and the state; (ii) discourses and ideologies of motherhood, especially whether or not mothering was seen as compatible with paid work; and (iii) concerns about population quality and quantity, particularly in the context of international military competition.

Jenson's (1986) comparison of British and French policies for the support of reproduction was influential in questioning the generalizations about women and the state that predominated in the early 1980s. Both French and British elites operated within an international context that raised concerns about population, particularly about declining birthrates and rates of infant mortality perceived to be too high. Yet Jenson showed that differences in the capacities of organized workers and employers, different levels of demand for female labor, and different discourses about motherhood and paid work produced strikingly different policies. British policy worked to make the support of babies primarily dependent on fathers' wages, while France developed policies that allowed for mothers' paid work, offering both material support and health-related services to working mothers and their children. . . .

Analyses of maternalism have provided some opening for consideration of the ways in which race, ethnicity, and nationalism have also shaped gendered policies. In the United States, a number of studies have shown that maternalist policies such as mothers' pensions and the Sheppard-Towner maternal health programs were not equally aimed at or accessible to African Americans and other women of color (Bellingham & Mathis 1994, Goodwin 1992, Gordon 1994, Mink 1994, Boris 1995). Thus, the motherhood (and infant life) to be supported was bounded in racial and ethnic terms; analysts disagree about the extent to which this reflects the interests of maternalist reformers or is simply a reflection of the power of racist forces in American society. Similar considerations obtained in Australian policy, which simultaneously supported white motherhood (largely through state-regulated male wages, but also with maternalist measures), banned non-European immigration under the rubric of the "White Australia" policy, and systematically deprived aboriginal mothers of custody of their children (Lake 1992, Shaver 1990, Burney 1994). A debate in Germany about the character of social provision under National Socialism features disagreement about the interests of dominant-group women. Bock (1991) emphasizes that only some groups' reproduction was supported—pronatalism for "Aryans" was accompanied by antinatalism for Jews, Gypsies, and "defectives." . . .

Comparing Gender in Contemporary Welfare States

. . . A particularly promising development in comparative scholarship has come with the elaboration of the concept of "social policy regimes," which offers a way to analyze the qualitative variation across national systems. As Shaver (1990) describes them, social policy regimes are institutionalized patterns in welfare state provision establishing systematic relations between the state and social structures of conflict, domination, and accommodation. Such patterns refer to the terms and conditions under which claims may be made on the resources of the state, and reciprocally, the terms and conditions of economic, social, and political obligation to the state. These regimes are to be found in both individual institutions of the welfare state and in common patterns cutting across domains of social provision, such as health or income maintenance.

Mainstream analysts of regime types have been concerned with the effects of welfare states on class relations and particularly with whether the state can "push back the frontiers of capitalism" (Esping-Andersen 1990). Feminist analysts using the regime type concept are interested in the gendered effects of state social policy; some are also attempting to define and measure gender interests. . . .

Much recent feminist work on regime types builds on Esping-Andersen's *Three Worlds of Welfare Capitalism* (1990). . . . Esping-Andersen proposes three dimensions that characterize welfare states, including the relationship between the state and the market in providing income and services and the effects of the welfare state on social stratification. Central to the understanding of how welfare states affect class relations are the concepts of social rights and the "decommodification of labor," defined as the degree to which the individual's typical life situation is freed from dependence on the labor market. These rights affect the class balance of power by insulating workers to some extent from market pressures and by contributing to working-class political capacities.

Esping-Andersen has constructed a typology of regimes representing "three worlds of welfare capitalism"—liberal, conservative-corporatist, and social-democratic—based on where they fall out on the three dimensions. Liberal regimes promote market provision wherever possible, encourage social dualisms between the majority of citizens who rely mainly on the market and those who rely principally on public provision, and do little to offer citizens alternatives to participating in the market for services and income. The welfare state is well-developed in both social-democratic and conservative-corporatist regimes, bringing almost all citizens under the umbrella of state provision, but in other ways the two types differ. The former are universalistic and egalitarian, while the latter preserve status and class differentials. Only social-democratic regimes promote significant decommodification of labor, for conservative-corporatist regimes condition their relatively generous benefits on strong ties to the labor market. Significant for gender relations is the fact that conservative regimes promote subsidiarity (thereby strengthening women's dependence on the family), while social-democratic regimes have promoted an individual model of entitlement and provide services

allowing those responsible for care work—mostly married mothers—to enter the paid labor force. Liberal regimes, he argues, are indifferent to gender relations, leaving service provision to the market. . . . Esping-Andersen classified the United States, Canada, Australia, and . . . Great Britain as liberal regimes; the Nordic countries are identified as social-democratic regimes; and Austria, France, Germany, Italy, and the Netherlands are conservative-corporatist regimes.

Many feminist analysts have critiqued Esping-Andersen for the gender-blindness of his scheme: His citizens are implicitly male workers; his dimensions tap into states' impact on class relations and the relationship between states and markets without considering gender differences within classes or the relations between states and families; he leaves invisible women's work on behalf of societal welfare (i.e. unpaid caring/domestic labor); and his framework fails to consider states' effects on gender relations, inequalities, and power (see, e.g., Langan & Ostner 1991, O'Connor 1993, Orloff 1993, Sainsbury 1994a, b, c, Bussemaker & van Kersbergen 1994, Borchorst 1994). . . . Swedish women's employment depends on the state both for jobs and for the services that make employment for those with caregiving responsibilities a possibility. German women are largely marginalized by an employment regime that revolves around the needs of predominantly male industrial workers, a relatively underdeveloped service sector, and state policies that prize subsidiarity over the public provision of services. In the United States, women's rising employment and the advances women have made into the upper ranks of the labor force are largely market-driven, although state anti-discrimination activity has been important in opening opportunities in the realm of private employment. While some U.S. women have benefited from private employment opportunities and can afford private provision of services, others have suffered from the low wages and benefits of the lower rungs of the service sector.

Analysts have tried to make sense of gendered relations and patterns using the regime-type framework, evaluating whether or not liberal, conservative, and social-democratic regime types have distinctive effects on gender relations. Extending the analysis of regime types to consider the ways in which care work (broadly defined) is organized and supported has been a key area of concern for those interested in states and gender relations. . . . Gustafsson (1994) finds that childcare policies in the United States, the Netherlands, and Sweden reflect the regime-type differences specified by Esping-Andersen, that is, that public services are best developed in Sweden, market provision of services is prominent in the United States, and the Netherlands offers little public provision, in effect opting to support mother's caregiving work rather than offering daycare. . . .

Sainsbury (1993) considers the effects on women of one aspect of social rights, the bases for making welfare claims, and the programmatic characteristics (i.e., social assistance, social insurance, or universal entitlements) of four different welfare states—the United States, the United Kingdom, the Netherlands, and Sweden. . . . She shows that, indeed, whether claims are based on labor market status, need, or citizenship is significant for gendered outcomes; women do best in Sweden, a system with strong universal characteristics, and fare worst in the United States and Britain, the countries with claims based principally on labor market participation. . . .

Gendered Dimensions for Assessing Welfare States

All of the approaches I have reviewed have helped to show the importance of gender relations in the welfare state and the significance of welfare states for the situations of men and women and their relationships. Yet these studies share some analytic weaknesses: an inadequate theorization of the political interests of gender and a failure to specify the dimensions of social provision and other state interventions relevant for gender relations (Orloff 1993, Borchorst 1994). . . .

Gender Interests

Defining gender interests is necessary to the task of assessing the gendered effects of welfare states, but not simple. A prominent theme in recent feminist scholarship concerns conflicts of interests. For example, in addition to pointing

out that men and women may have conflicting interests based on who has family wage–paying jobs or who has access to domestic or sexual services, feminist analysts have noted ways in which women's interests cohere and/or compete with children's interests. Others argue that it is falsely homogenizing to speak of women's interests per se, since the "interests that women (or men) have" (the descriptive sense of the concept) vary by class, race, ethnicity, nationality, sexual orientation, and so on (e.g., Molyneux 1985, Collins 1990). . . .

Political power and participation are also of concern in understanding interests. Jónasdóttir (1988) contends that everyone has an interest in participating in the construction of choices in the policy areas that affect them. Thus, being the subject as well as the object of policy is a critical aspect of women's and men's interests (see also Lewis 1992, Orloff 1993, Lister 1990, O'Connor 1993, Nelson 1984). Participation takes on a specifically gendered character in that women have been so long formally and informally excluded from the policymaking that shapes the structures of their incentives to work for pay and bear children, and to care for children, their husbands, or the disabled.

Gendered Dimensions for Assessing Welfare States

Feminist analysts note that Esping-Andersen's framework was developed to address issues of class rather than gender power. Therefore, they argue, one cannot fully tap into states' effects on gender relations simply by looking at how women and men fare in different regime types using his (or others') gender-blind dimensions. Rather, specifically gendered dimensions based on an understanding of gendered interests are needed to assess the impact of state policies on gender relations.

Lewis (1992) argues for considering policy regimes in terms of their different levels of commitment to a male breadwinner–female housewife household form, which in ideal-typical form would "find married women excluded from the labour market, firmly subordinates to their husbands for the purposes of social security entitlements and tax, and expected to undertake the work of caring (for children and other dependents) at home without public support" (p. 162). Women's interests, she thereby implies, are least well served by policies supporting this traditional set of arrangements, but they fare somewhat better when policy supports dual-earner households. She contrasts France, Sweden, Britain, and Ireland, finding Britain and Ireland strongly committed to the breadwinner form, France less strongly so, and Sweden only weakly so, tending to a dual-breadwinner form. . . .

Sainsbury (1994c) proposes examining states in terms of their similarity to one of two gendered ideal-types: the breadwinner model (similar to Lewis's conception) and what she calls an individual model, where both men and women are earners and carers, benefits are targeted on individuals, and much caring work is paid and provided publicly. . . . She draws out specific dimensions of variation that differentiate the two models: the character of familial ideology, entitlement (including its basis, recipient, benefit unit, contribution unit, and mode of taxation), employment and wage policies, and organization of care work. . . .

Orloff (1993) proposes to consider how benefits contribute to women's capacity to form and maintain an autonomous household, a dimension that indicates "the ability of those who do most of the domestic and caring work—almost all women—to form and maintain autonomous households, that is, to survive and support their children without having to marry to gain access to breadwinners' income." This should enhance women's power vis-à-vis men within marriages and families (see also Hobson 1993). Men typically gain this capacity through their market work, backed up by income maintenance programs. State policies have differed in how (if at all) this capacity is achieved for women; some regimes have promoted women's employment through varying combinations of childcare services, wage subsidies, or improved-access policies, or by reducing levels of and eligibility for public support; this overlaps, then, with the dimension of access to paid work. Other regimes have offered support for solo mothers to stay at home to care for their children; this maintains core features of the gender division of labor—women remain responsible for caretaking—but undermines economic dependence on husbands. Orloff (1996) argues that the capacity to form and maintain a household embodies "the right to a family," implying more than individual independence, and reflects the character of laws regulating sexuality, marriage, and household formation (e.g. laws on divorce, custody, homosexuality). . . .

Conclusion

On the basis of this review, I recommend that future research include a comparative dimension; case studies should be situated in the context of the range of cross-national variation in relations between welfare states and gender relations. Moreover, I would encourage the use of gendered dimensions of variation to give greater specificity to findings and to allow the further development of a body of comparable findings concerning the mutual effects of gender relations and welfare states. These findings may also speak to the question of the extent to which different gendered interests are reflected in state social provision, including the "woman-friendliness" of the state (Hernes 1988). . . .

References

Bellingham B, Mathis MP. 1994. Race, citizenship, and the bio-politics of the maternalist welfare state: "Traditional" midwifery in the American South under the Sheppard-Towner Act, 1921–29. *Soc. Polit.* 1:157–89.

Bock G. 1991. Antinatalism, maternity and paternity in National Socialist racism. See G. Bock & P. Thane. 1991. *Maternity and Gender Policies: Women and the Rise of the European Welfare States. 1880s–1950s.* New York: Routledge, pp. 233–55.

Borchorst A. 1994. Welfare state regimes, women's interests, and the EC. See Sainsbury 1994a, pp. 26–44.

Borchorst A, Siim B. 1987. Women and the advanced welfare state—a new kind of patriarchal power? See AS Sassoon ed. 1987. *Women and the State. The Shifting Boundaries of Public and Private.* London, UK: Hutchinson, pp. 128–57.

Boris E. 1995. The racialized gendered state: Constructions of citizenship in the United States. *Soc. Polit.* 2:160–80.

Burney L. 1994. An Aboriginal way of being Australian. *Aust. Fem. Stud.* 19:17–24.

Bussemaker J, van Kersbergen K. 1994. Gender and welfare states: Some theoretical reflections. See Sainsbury 1994a, pp. 8–25.

Cass B. 1994. Citizenship, work and welfare: The dilemma for Australian women. *Soc. Polit.* 1:106–24.

Collins PH. 1990. *Black Feminist Thought. Knowledge, Consciousness, and the Politics of Empowerment.* New York: Routledge.

Esping-Andersen G. 1990. *The Three Worlds of Welfare Capitalism.* Princeton, NJ: Princeton Univ. Press.

Fraser N. 1989. Women, welfare and the politics of need. In *Unruly Practices*, pp. 114–60. Minneapolis, MN: Univ. Minn. Press.

Goodwin J. 1992. An American experiment in paid motherhood: The implementation of mother's pensions in early twentieth century Chicago. *Gender Hist.* 4:323–42.

Gordon L. 1994. *Pitied but Not Entitled: Single Mothers and the History of Welfare*. New York: Free Press.

Gordon L, Fraser N. 1994. "Dependency" demystified: Inscriptions of power in a keyword of the welfare state. *Soc. Polit.* 1:14–31.

Gustafsson S. 1994. Childcare and types of welfare states. See Sainsbury 1994a, pp. 45–61

Hernes H. 1987. *Welfare State and Woman Power*. Oslo, Norway: Norway Univ. Press.

Hernes H. 1988. The welfare state citizenship of Scandinavian women. See K. Jones & A. Jónasdóttir 1988. *The Political Interests of Gender*. Newbury Park, CA: Sage, pp. 187–213.

Hobson B. 1993. Feminist strategies and gendered discourse in welfare states. See Koven and Michel 1993, pp. 396–430.

Holter H, ed. 1984. *Patriarchy in a Welfare Society*. Oslo: Universitetsforlaget.

Jenson J. 1986. Gender and reproduction: Or, babies and the state. *Stud. Polit. Econ.* 20:9–45.

Jónasdóttir AG. 1988. On the concept of interest, women's interests, and the limitations of interest theory. See Jones & Jonasdottir 1988, pp. 33–65

Knijn T. 1994. Fish without bikes: Revision of the Dutch welfare state and its consequences for the (in)-dependence of single mothers. *Soc. Polit.* 1:83–105.

Koven S, Michael S, eds. 1993. *Mothers of the New world: Maternalist Politics and the Origins of the Welfare State*. New York: Routledge.

Lake M. 1992. Mission impossible: How men gave birth to the Australian nation—nationalism, gender and other seminal acts. *Gender Hist.* 4:305–22.

Langan M, Ostner I. 1991. Gender and welfare: Toward a comparative framework. In *Toward a European Welfare State*? ed. G Room, pp. 127–50. Bristol, UK: Sch. Adv. Urban Stud.

Lewis J. 1992. Gender and the development of welfare regimes. *J. Eur. Soc. Policy* 3:159–73.

Lewis J, Åström G. 1992. Equality, difference, and state welfare: Labor market and family policies in Sweden. *Fem. Stud.* 18:59–86.

Lister R. 1990. Women, economic dependency and citizenship. *J. Soc. Policy* 19:445–67.

McLanahan S, Sorenson A, Watson D. 1989. Sex differences in poverty, 1950–1980. *Signs* 15:101–22.

Mink G. 1994. *Wages of Motherhood: Inequality in the Welfare State, 1917–1942*. Ithaca, NY: Cornell Univ. Press.

Molyneux M. 1985. Mobilization without emancipation? Women's interests, the state and revolution in Nicaragua. *Fem. Stud.* 11:227–54.

Monson R. 1996. *State-ing sex and gender in paternity establishment and child support policy*. PhD thesis. Univ. Wis.-Madison.

Nelson B. 1984. Women's poverty and women's citizenship: Some political consequences of economic marginality. *Signs* 10:209–32.

O'Connor J. 1993. Gender, class and citizenship in the comparative analysis of welfare state regimes: theoretical and methodological issues. *Br. J. Sociol.* 44:501–18.

Orloff AS. 1993. Gender and the social rights of citizenship: The comparative analysis of gender relations and welfare states. *Am. Sociol. Rev.* 58:303–28.

Orloff AS. 1996. Gender in the liberal welfare states: Australia, Canada, the United Kingdom and the United States. In *State/Culture*, ed. G Steinmetz. Ithaca: Cornell Univ. Press.

Pateman C. 1988. The patriarchal welfare state. In *Democracy and the State*, ed. A Gutmann, pp. 231–78. Princeton, NJ: Princeton Univ. Press.

Pedersen S. 1993. *Family, Dependence, and the Origins of the Welfare State: Britain and France, 1914–1945*. New York: Cambridge Univ. Press.

Piven FF. 1985. Women and the state: Ideology, power, and the welfare state. In *Gender and the Life Course*, ed. A. Rossi, pp. 265–87. New York: Aldine.

Quadagno J. 1994. *The Color of Welfare. How Racism Undermined the War on Poverty*. New York: Oxford Univ. Press.

Roberts D. 1995. Race, gender, and the value of mothers' work. *Soc. Polit.* 2:195–207.

Sainsbury D. 1993. Dual welfare and sex segregation of access to social benefits: Income maintenance policies in the UK, the US, the Netherlands and Sweden. *J. Soc. Policy* 22:69–98.

Sainsbury D, ed. 1994a. *Gendering Welfare States*. Thousands Oaks, CA: Sage.

Sainsbury D. 1994b. Introduction. See Sainsbury 1994a, pp. 1–8.

Sainsbury D. 1994c. Women's and men's social rights: Gendering dimensions of welfare states. See Sainsbury 1994a, pp. 150–69.

Saraceno C. 1994. The ambivalent familism of the Italian welfare state. *Soc. Polit.* 1:60–82.

Shaver S. 1990. *Gender, Social Policy Regimes and the Welfare State*. Presented at Annu. Meet. AM. Sociol. Assoc., Washington, DC.

Weir M, Orloff AS, Skocpol T, eds. 1998. *The Politics of Social Policy in the United States*. Princeton, NJ: Princeton Univ. Press.

Chapter 37

INTERACTING WITH THE STATE: FEMINIST STRATEGIES AND POLITICAL OPPORTUNITIES

Louise Chappell

In recent years, feminists have engaged in new and interesting debates about the relationship between gender and the state. . . . They have been concerned to shift our understanding of feminist engagement of the state away from earlier dichotomous accounts which treated the state as *either* inherently patriarchal and oppressive of women, *or* as gender neutral and able to enhance women's emancipation, to a mid-position which emphasizes the *interaction* between the state and gender, without privileging one or the other. This approach enables us to look afresh at feminist engagement with the state. Through a comparative study of the feminist activists in Australia and Canada this chapter demonstrates that feminist strategies are not only shaped by, but they themselves can shape, the nature of the political opportunity structure at feminists' disposal. . . .

Methodological Considerations

This chapter offers a detailed analysis of feminist engagement with political institutions in two western liberal states, Australia and Canada, during the past two decades. In doing so, it utilizes a "most similar systems" comparative method. . . .

These similarities raise an important question. . . . Why is it, given these similarities, that feminists in the two countries have pursued such different strategies with those in Canada emphasizing lobbying and, in recent years, looking to the constitutional and legal realm while their Australian sisters have targeted the executive arena? One

possible explanation, proffered by Australian political scientist Marian Sawer, is that feminists in the two countries have different ideological positions, especially in relation to feminist engagement with the state. In her view, Canadian feminists have been more distrustful of the state, and have therefore been less inclined to enter state institutions (1994: 65). . . . Conversely, there is evidence to suggest that, in line with the mainstream political culture, many Australian feminists have adopted a much more positive approach to engaging with the state (see Sawer 1991; Eisenstein 1996).

While there is undoubtedly some variation in the degree to which Australian and Canadian feminists have been distrustful of the state, it would be wrong to overemphasize ideological differences as an explanatory variable. Not only have both Australian and Canadian feminists been influenced by American feminist liberationist ideas of the need for consciousness raising, a distrust of the state, and an antipathy to hierarchical forms of organization (for Canada see Vickers 1992; for Australia Burgmann 1993), but also, in both countries feminists have engaged directly with the state. . . . If we take the broad political context of both countries into account, it can be argued that Canadian feminists are not necessarily more suspicious of the state than their Australian sisters, rather that they have targeted different institutions. In other words, that their "pro-statism" has manifested itself in different ways.

If we can discount ideology as the key explanatory variable for the differences in feminist political strategies in Australia and Canada, how can they be explained? It is the contention here that these variations have arisen as a result of differences in both the operation of political institutions in each country and the political opportunities these institutions afford. . . .

. . . In Canada, Anglo-feminists were quick to identify the opportunities for advancing their aims through the entrenchment of a bill of rights in the Constitution. Having successfully lobbied for the inclusion of sex equality rights in the Charter of Rights and Freedoms, they then engaged in Charter litigation through which they were able to create new opportunities by way of feminist jurisprudence. In contrast, Australian feminists have long identified a range of impediments within the constitutional and legal realms. With no bill of rights and procedural and financial constraints limiting their ability to intervene in court cases, they have been unable to use the constitutional and judicial arena to pursue their aims. Instead, they have looked to the bureaucratic arena, where a culture of tolerance for internal advocates and supportive Australian Labor Party (ALP) governments have made it possible for them to achieve significant gains. In both cases we see that feminists have identified and exploited *existing* political opportunities, and, especially in the Canadian case, have been able to *create* new opportunities through their litigation strategy. In view of such findings, we cannot assume that feminist engagement with the state inevitably leads to co-option as radical feminists would suggest. Rather, a more nuanced argument emerges: that political institutions offer feminists different opportunity structures across place and time. . . .

Canadian Constitutional and Legal Institutions

Constitutional questions in general, and the issue of rights in particular, have long been a central concern within Canada. . . . The focus on the Constitution as a means to address political issues, which culminated in the entrenchment of the Charter [of Rights and Freedoms], can be seen to have provided a favorable opportunity structure for political actors in Canada—especially "equality seekers." On the one hand, the emphasis on the

Constitution, and the entrenchment of a bill of rights gave added legitimacy to the claims of rights activists, including feminists. Moreover, once the Charter was entrenched, these actors were provided with an instrument through which they could pursue rights-based claims in the courts.

The existence of other "enabling structures"—including financial support and access to the court system—made the political opportunity structure in relation to the constitutional/judicial realm even more favorable as far as equality seekers were concerned. Once the Charter came into effect, the Federal government was, at least initially, willing to provide some of the necessary financial resources to fund court challenges. . . . Moreover, interest groups in Canada have found it relatively easy to gain access to the Courts because of existing provisions in relation to legal standing and *amicus curiae* (a friend of the court) applications. The Supreme Court of Canada has frequently used its broad discretionary powers to allow public interest groups to intervene as a party in constitutional cases (Wilcox 1993: 242). . . .

Anglo-Canadian Feminist Constitutional and Legal Strategies

. . . Anglo-Canadian feminists responded to this structure by developing sophisticated positions in relation to the Constitution and the legal system more generally, and have been directly engaged in constitutional politics. It is important to note that there has not been one unified Canadian feminist constitutional position but a range of views, which tend to fall along broad linguistic and racialized lines. Francophone feminists have overwhelmingly supported the stance taken by the Quebec government to reject as far as possible the application of the Charter to the province. Aboriginal women's groups have adopted yet another range of positions: some argue strongly in support of the application of the Charter to native communities, others are more suspicious of an individual rights–based approach and fear the Charter will interfere with aspirations for self-government (for a full discussion see Vickers 1993: 266). . . .

The involvement of Anglo-feminists in the constitutional debates can be conceptualized as occurring in three distinct phases. The first phase, which occurred during the late 1970s and early 1980s, saw elite feminist legal groups lobby the government to include equality provisions in the proposed charter of rights. However, it soon became obvious that this elite-level approach was not in itself sufficient to secure the ironclad equality guarantees that many feminists were looking for. Problems with this approach came to a head when a forthcoming convention on women and the Constitution organized by Canadian Advisory Council on the Status of Women (CACSW) was canceled. . . . Members of the women's movement established the Ad Hoc Committee on Women and the Constitution and set about arranging their own conference (see Kome 1983: ch. 4). . . .

The Ad Hoc conference ushered in the second phase of feminist organizing around the Constitution. A distinguishing feature of this phase of intervention was the level of mass involvement by women's activists. While some feminists were circumspect about the usefulness of a Charter for advancing women's interests because it meant relying on "male dominated" courts (see Vickers 1993: 274), in general there was widespread support for entrenched equality guarantees within the Anglo-women's movement. . . . The conference agreed that it would support the Charter on the proviso that the Government accept its amendments including an overriding protection of equality rights (Ad Hoc Committee 1981: 165). . . .

The third phase of feminist engagement with the Constitution, which began after the entrenchment of the Charter in 1982, saw a return to an elitist approach, with feminist legal experts involved in developing a legal "project." This "project" had two components: "Charterwatching" and a litigation strategy. Charterwatching involved holding conferences and workshops, writing books and articles, and undertaking an "audit" of federal and provincial statues which aimed to "pinpoint what needed to be changed to avoid subsequent legal battles over equality and provide women with a catalogue of what may need changing through litigation" (Razack 1991: 39). When the equality provisions came into effect in 1985 legal activists enthusiastically shifted their effort from these activities toward the development of a litigation strategy. . . .

The Anglo-Canadian Feminist Litigation Strategy: An Assessment

. . . What a decade of litigation experience has taught Anglo-Canadian feminist legal activists is that on its own, this strategy cannot be relied upon to always bring about positive outcomes for women, but that it can sometimes achieve its aims. The lesson for Canadian feminists to draw from this experience is that their best chance of achieving positive outcomes for women is to adopt a multi-faceted strategy—one which enables them to take advantage of the opportunities in one institution when they are closed off in another. . . .

Some feminists, including those from non-majoritarian backgrounds, continue to express skepticism about the litigation strategy (see Fudge 1989: 449; Bacchi and Marquis 1994: 102). Nevertheless, the problems some feminists have had with the litigation strategy more generally cannot detract from the fact that the organization and the strategy have broadened the repertoire of the Anglo-Canadian women's movement in such a way as to enhance its capacity to make the most of existing institutional arrangements. While Anglo-Canadian feminists have been able to look to the parliamentary realm when blocked by the courts, the reverse situation has also been possible; the litigation strategy pursued by Canadian feminists has been able to provide women with protection against negative legislative decisions. . . .

Political Constraints in Australian Constitutional and Legal Institutions

In contrast to Canada, there has been a comparatively low degree of interest in Australia about general constitutional questions, including constitutional issues related to individual rights. Australia is one of the few liberal democratic nations that does not have either a legislative or constitutional bill of rights. . . . Support for parliamentary and common law rights protections, rather than an entrenched bill of rights, has remained strong since federation (see Connolly 1993; Maddox 1996: 243).[1]

To some degree, the reluctance to address rights issues can be seen to have been influenced by Australian political culture. From the time of white settlement, the question of individual rights has been subordinated to other issues. In Australia, the perception of government as "a source of services," or as a 'provider' has been far more common than one that sees it as a protector of rights (Colebatch 1992: 4). . . . The emphasis on responsible government in Australia has meant that, to the extent that individual rights protections do exist, they have been the product of executive and legislative measures, rather than the Constitution (Thompson 1997: 99). This situation has had a fundamental influence on the strategies of Australian rights activists, including the women's movement. To the extent that the Constitution and legal institutions have had an effect on the Australian women's movement, they have argu- ably had a negative impact: feminists have been encouraged to look elsewhere—primarily to the bureaucracy and to a lesser extent, the legislature— to advance women's rights issues.

Institutional Impediments to an Australian Feminist Litigation Strategy

Australian feminist activists have faced institu- tional constraints, rather than opportunities, in relation to the constitutional and legal realm. Without access to an instrument such as a bill of rights, women's rights activists have not had the same reason as their Canadian counterparts to look to the Constitution or the courts to pur- sue their objectives. Although feminists had ac- tively engaged in the debate on constitutional change, and participated in a Women's Constitu- tional Convention in February 1998, unlike their Canadian sisters, their voices had little impact on the outcome. The Government-sponsored Con- stitutional Convention that directly followed the Women's Convention paid little heed to feminist arguments for the inclusion of a bill of rights in the Constitution. . . .

Executive and Legislative Rights Provisions

In addition to these negative influences, the strategic decision of the Australian women's movement in relation to rights have also been influenced, in a more positive way, by existing opportunities in other institutions—especially the executive and to a lesser extent the legislature. Feminists, like other equality seekers, have ori- entated themselves toward these institutions for a number of reasons: first, in Australia rights have remained . . . in large measure the prerogative of the legislature; second, parliament has enacted rights legislation; and, finally, parliament has cre- ated executive machinery to enforce these acts. In targeting the parliament and the executive, women's groups can be seen to have adopted the traditional *modus operandi* of Australian social actors—which is to look to these areas of the state to satisfy their demands.

The Femocrat Strategy

The efforts of Australian feminists may have been stymied in the constitutional arena, but they have been able to make headway on gender equity is- sues through their efforts within the bureaucracy— in particular through a "femocrat" strategy. The femocrat is one of the distinctive personalities of the Australian women's movement. This neolo- gism originally referred to feminist women who entered the bureaucracy to work in designated women's agencies. Over time, the meaning of the term has shifted to reflect femocrat praxis. As femocrats moved out of women's policy po- sitions into the mainstream bureaucracy the term has expanded to refer to "a powerful woman within government administration, with an ideological commitment to feminism" (Eisen- stein 1996: 68). . . .

Since the 1970s, the fortunes of Australian femocrats at both the federal and state level have waxed and waned. . . .

Despite these difficulties, the femocrat strategy has been highly successful in terms of policy out- comes. Whereas Canadian feminists have been able to influence equity issues through the court system, Australian feminists achieved a similar degree of success through the bureaucracy. One of the most significant achievements of the fem- ocracy has been to expand the purview of govern- ment to encompass areas that were not previously seen to be the subject of public policy. Femo- crats have influenced the development of policies in relation to childcare, women's refuges, and women's health centers (Eisenstein 1996: 50). They have drawn government attention to the issue of domestic violence and secured budget allocations for the creation of programs in this area. . . . Femocrats have had significant input into federal legislation in the areas of Sex Discrimination (1984); Equal Employment Opportunity for public service employees (1984 and 1987); and Affirmative Action (1986, 1992, and 1993) (see Sawer 1990: ch. 7; Wills 1995: 126). The influence of femocrats has also extended to the international sphere. They helped to secure the Government's signature of the UN Convention on Elimination of All Forms of Discrimination against Women (CEDAW) and the International Labour Organization Convention 156, which deals with workers with family responsibilities. . . .

The success of the femocrat strategy is directly attributable to the favorable opportunity structure Australian feminists have faced within bureaucratic institutions. It is possible to identify three key opportunities that have helped to shape this strategy. The first of these is the presence of ALP governments. The success of the femocrat strategy has by no means been guaranteed under Labour governments, nor has it come without its costs. In return for support for the strategy, ALP governments have used femocrats to help "sell" its policies to women in the electorate (Eisenstein 1996: 174). Nevertheless, feminists have found that the commitment of federal and state ALP governments to gender equality (at least at a rhetorical level) has smoothed the path for them to work from within government agencies to advance their agenda.

The second factor that has had a positive influence on the Australian femocrat strategy has been the existing political culture. In Australia there has been a long-standing tradition of certain social actors, especially producer groups such as trade unions, manufacturers, and farmers, looking toward the bureaucratic arm of the state to meet their demands. Adopting a utilitarian view of the state, these social actors have not only lobbied from outside the bureaucracy to have their demands met, but have sought to have the state create agencies through which they could advance their claims. . . . Not only did this utilitarian tradition influence the orientation of social actors, including feminists toward the bureaucracy (Sawer 1991), it also helped to create a tolerance for partisanship within bureaucratic institutions—something which ran counter to the neutral public servant model followed in other Westminster parliamentary systems, including Canada. . . .

A period of administrative reform during the 1970s, when feminists were first entering the bureaucracy, gave the femocrat strategy an additional boost. The shift from seniority to merit-based promotion and the introduction of lateral recruitment enabled femocrats to gain entry to senior bureaucratic positions without the need to work their way up through the male-dominated career service. The introduction of equal employment opportunity (EEO) programs, which were themselves the work of femocrats, also added to the improvement in the number of feminists and women in general in the senior ranks of the public service (Conroy 1994: 94). . . .

It would be wrong to assume that Australian feminists have concentrated all their efforts on the bureaucracy, or that political opportunities for feminists only exist in that arena. Members of the Australian women's movement have also lobbied from outside political institutions to advance their claims, at times with success. . . .

The legislature has also provided opportunities for Australian feminists to advance their claims. The enactment of the Sex Discrimination Act (SDA) (1984) . . . is one example of this. With the passage of the SDA, Australian women were given a new avenue through which they could pursue discrimination claims. . . .

Conclusion

. . . One of the significant points to emerge from this comparison of two similar countries is that we cannot assume that similar political institutions in different countries will offer feminists the same opportunity structures. Although we might be able to argue that the constitutional/legal realm is a positive arena for Canadian feminists, the same cannot be said of these institutions in Australia. This comparison alerts us to the fact that we cannot assume that particular institutions are "good" or "bad" for feminists wanting to pursue their objectives. Rather, we need to understand that the nature of political institutions, and the opportunities they offer political actors, will vary across time and place. A second important point to emerge from this comparison is that we cannot assume that feminists operating in similar political systems will adopt the same political strategies. Feminists, like other political actors, make strategic choices to suit the particular institutional opportunity structure in which they are operating. Finally, and perhaps most important in terms of a future research agenda, what this analysis shows us is that the relationship between feminists and political institutions is both interactive and dynamic. Feminists are able to take advantage of opportunities within political institutions to advance their political agenda and, in choosing certain strategies over others, they help shape the very nature of this political opportunity structure.

Note

1. There are some signs that suggest this is changing. In the past decade, the High Court of Australia has shown a willingness to question the adequacy of parliamentary and common law rights protections and has increasingly cast itself in the role of the guardian of fundamental rights (see Walker 1995: 251).

References

Ad Hoc Committee of Canadian Women Conference on Canadian Women and the Constitution. 1981. "Resolutions Adopted at the Conference on Canadian Women and the Constitution," 14–15 February, *Atlantis* 6(2):62.

Bacchi, Carol and Vicky Marquis. 1994. "Women and the Republic: 'Rights' and Wrongs," *Australian Feminist Studies* 19 Autumn: 93–113.

Burgmann, Verity. 1993. *Power and Protest: Movements for Change in Australian Society.* Sydney: Allen & Unwin.

Colebatch, H. K. 1992. "Theory and the Analysis of Australian Politics," *Australian Journal of Political Science* 27(1):1–11.

Connolly, Peter the Hon. CBE, QC. 1993. "Should the Courts Determine Social Policy?," *Upholding the Constitution*, Vol. 2. Melbourne: Samuel Griffiths Society.

Conroy, Denise. 1994. "The Glass Ceiling: Illusory or Real?," *Canberra Bulletin of Public Administration* No. 76, April.

Eisenstein, Hester. 1996. *Inside Agitators: Australian Femocrats and the Australian State.* Sydney: Allen & Unwin.

Fudge, Judy. 1989. "The Effect of Entrenching a Bill of Rights upon Political Discourse: Feminist Demands and Sexual Violence in Canada," *International Journal of Sociology of Law* 17:445–63.

Kome, Penny. 1983. *The Taking of Twenty-Eight: Women Challenge the Constitution.* Toronto: The Women's Educational Press.

Maddox, Graham. 1996. *Australian Democracy in Theory and Practice*, 3rd edn. Melbourne: Longman.

Razack, Sherene. 1991. *Canadian Feminism and the Law: The Women's Legal Education and Action Fund and the Pursuit of Equality.* Toronto: Second Story Press.

Sawer, Marian. 1990. *Sisters in Suits: Women and Public Policy in Australia.* Sydney: Allen & Unwin.

———. 1991. "Why Has the Australian Women's Movement Had More Influence on Government in Australia than Elsewhere?" In Francis Castles (ed.) *Australia Compared.* Sydney: Allen & Unwin.

———. 1994. "Feminism and the State: Theory and Practice in Australia and Canada," *Australian Canadian Studies* 12(1):49–68.

———. 1996. "Challenging Politics? Seventy-Five Years of Women's Parliamentary Representation in Australia," Guest Editorial, *International Review of Women and Leadership* 2(1):i–xvi.

Thompson, Elaine. 1997. "The Constitution," in Rodney Smith (ed.) *Politics in Australia*, 3rd edn. Sydney: Allen & Unwin.

Vickers, Jill. 1992. "The Intellectual Origins of the Women's Movement in Canada," in Constance Backhouse and David H. Flaherty (eds) *Challenging Times: The Women's Movement in Canada and the United States.* Montreal & Kingston: McGill/Kingston University Press.

———. 1993. "The Canadian Women's Movement and a Changing Constitutional Order," *International Journal of Canadian Studies* 7–8 (spring/fall):261–84.

Walker, Kristen. 1995. "Who's the Boss? The Judiciary, the Executive, the Parliament and the Protection of Human Rights," *Western Australian Law Review* 25, December. 238–54.

Wilcox, Murray R. Justice. 1993. *The Australian Charter of Rights.* North Ryde: The Law Book Company Limited.

Wills, Sue. 1995. "Sexual Equality," in M. Hogan and K. Dempsey (eds) *Equity and Citizenship under Keating.* Sydney: Public Affairs Research Centre, University of Sydney.

Chapter 38

INTRODUCTION TO COMPARATIVE
STATE FEMINISM

Dorothy McBride Stetson

Amy G. Mazur

Social movements provoke official action, especially by democratic governments. Whereas movement activists seek real change and permanent access to arenas of power, government actions may be symbolic or even cosmetic, a way of damping the fires of reform. Second-wave women's movements in advanced industrial societies have generated an assortment of responses from their governments.[1] The most striking consequence of over 25 years of women's movement activism has been the array of institutional arrangements inside democratic states devoted to women's policy questions. Such a widespread change in institutions has the potential of turning the state into an activist on behalf of feminist goals,[2] embedding gender issues in national policy agendas and giving advocates for the advancement of women permanent access to arenas of power. . . .

The concept *state feminism* refers to activities of government structures that are formally charged with furthering women's status and rights. At issue is the extent to which these agencies are effective in helping women as a group and undermining patterns of gender-based inequities in society. To many women's movement activists, the idea that the state could further such a feminist agenda is problematic if not impossible. Their skepticism triggers the central questions of this comparative study. First, does state feminism exist? That is, do state structures assigned by political leaders to address women's inferior position in society contribute to policies that reduce gender-based inequities and provide an opportunity for women's movement activists to influence feminist policy

formation? Second, if state feminism exists, are there variations in the abilities of these state structures to promote feminist political agendas in the context of the different political, social, and cultural traditions of various countries? This chapter, therefore, has three major objectives:

1. To describe the range and diversity of state structures formally responsible for promoting women's position and rights in advanced industrial societies
2. To analyze the extent to which these state offices achieve feminist goals within the social, political, and historical context of each nation-state and the variations in achieving goals across different countries
3. To propose, based on this cross-national comparison, the combination of political and social factors that appears to produce state structures prone to pursuing effective state feminist action

Women's Policy Machinery

No single inventor claims to have developed the idea that the state could, through its institutions, become an actor in promoting equality between men and women. One of the first countries to have a permanent agency for women was the United States, where Congress established the Women's Bureau of the Department of Labor in 1920. Over the years, especially during World War II, women's agencies and officers appeared in other countries. More recently, successive governments have added offices, commissions, agencies, ministries, committees, secretaries, and advisers to deal with women's issues. A source of encouragement and advice to them has been the United Nations.

The United Nations has its own institutions devoted to women's agendas: the Commission on the Status of Women (CSW) and its administrative arm, the Division for the Advancement of Women (DAW). Through these structures, the United Nations has recommended, since the 1960s, that governments around the world establish similar structures. The CSW coined the term *national policy machinery for the advancement of women* to refer to agencies devoted to women's policy issues. Following this UN definition, this chapter will use the term *women's policy machinery*[3] to describe any structure established by government with its main purpose being the betterment of women's social status. Often set up in name only, formal women's policy structures may not actually achieve state feminist goals.

Both domestic and international influences have led states in advanced industrial societies to create women's policy machinery. Domestically, the second wave of the women's movement emerged in the context of social and economic changes after World War II. Stimulated by the rise of other movements, especially on the Left, activists used various strategies to protest against pervasive male dominance. The women's rights strategy focused on using conventional pressure-group tactics for seeking changes in policy and practice to promote antidiscrimination and equality. Other activists worked on leftist parties to include women's demands in socialist and social democratic agendas. Adding energy to the women's movement were the radicals of the women's liberation wing, inventing a variety of unconventional means to change gender relations at the personal level.

Whatever form the second wave took, political leaders were faced with a challenge to take action. Demands came from sectors they were used to working with, such as unions and parties. But they also came from formerly nonpolitical women's organizations and newly formed groups skillful at attracting media attention. In crafting a response or, in come cases, a diversion, most leaders found it useful to create some sort of office to be responsible for dealing with the movement's

concerns. At the time, many politicians believed that, at the very least, adding women's policy machinery would show the growing number of women voters that the state was responding with attention to some version of a women's policy agenda.

The CSW has viewed policy machinery as a means of implementing its resolutions on equality and opportunity for women at the national and local levels. As the UN activities on behalf of women have become more ambitious, especially with the International Women's Decade (1975–1985), its attention to policy machinery has intensified. Beginning in 1975, the Decade for Women: Equality, Development, and Peace conferences (Mexico City, 1975; Copenhagen, 1980; Nairobi, 1985) focused on setting a worldwide agenda for women as elaborated in *Nairobi Forward-Looking Strategies for the Advancement of Women* (United Nations, 1985/1993b). Central to the implementation of this agenda has been the establishment of a national policy machinery by each member state.

Since the Nairobi Conference in 1985, and leading up to the Fourth Women's Conference in Beijing in 1995, DAW has gathered information on machinery in many countries and studied the range, diversity, and effectiveness of various efforts. Leaders of UN member states are frequently called upon to report to DAW on the types of machinery they have established. Furthermore, since 1979, over 120 countries have ratified the UN's Convention for the Elimination of Discrimination against Women (CEDAW). Signatories must file periodic reports with the oversight committee on the "legislative, judicial, administrative, or other measures which they have adopted to give effect to the provisions" of the convention (Article 18). Pressure from domestic movements, together with monitoring by international agencies, has encouraged political leaders in many countries to establish and retain some sort of institution to treat women's issues.[4]

Reports to the United Nations about national machinery indicate a wide variety of forms: permanent national commissions on the status of women, ad hoc and regional commissions, advisory committees, permanent bureaus within departments and ministries, and, in Communist countries, administrative committees within ruling parties (United Nations, 1987). These structures vary by their level of organization, authority, and power and by their links to governmental and nongovernmental agencies. Women's issues are complex, affecting a cross section of conventional governmental activities from social and labor to economic and legal. As a consequence, machinery is also complex and adapts to fit the needs and political context of each country. The UN studies show that the national machineries do not lend themselves to easy categorization.

It is important to contrast this focus on policy machinery with other ways of looking at women's role in government. Policy machinery refers to structures in government—those agencies that are established by statute, administrative directive, or political resolution. Thus, studies of machinery are different from studies of women in government and political office. Participation of women in elective office is defined according to the rates of representation in legislatures, cabinets, and executive positions (e.g., Darcy, Welch, & Clark, 1994; Lovenduski & Norris, 1993; Randall, 1987). Studies of state feminist offices are also different from studies that look at the role of women in public administration of feminist scholarship on organizations (e.g., Ferguson, 1984; Guy, 1992; Staudt, 1990). The establishment of women's policy machinery does allow some women to work full-time inside government, designing and implementing projects devoted to the improvement of women's status rather than being restricted to a part-time role outside as supplicants. Unlike much research in this area, this study calls women who staff women's policy agencies *femocrats* to distinguish them from other women in government.[5] In this chapter, therefore, the term *women's policy machinery* refers to state structures established to advance the status of women; state feminist women's policy machineries are those agencies that concretely achieve their formal charge in some way.

State Feminism

. . . Many advanced industrial democratic states have established agencies ranging from equal opportunity commissions and councils to departments and ministries for women. Governments have given these institutions the responsibility to achieve what Hernes (1987, p. 11) calls "feminism from above," or state feminism. The meaning of the term *state feminism* has evolved in its brief public life. Originally, the Scandinavian literature refers to state feminists as "both feminists employed as administrators and bureaucrats in positions of power and to women politicians advocating gender equality policies" (Siim, 1991, p. 189). Then Australian writers coined the term *femocrat* (Sawer, 1990) to describe the individuals referred to by Siim. The creation of the notion of a femocrat allowed scholars like Eisenstein (1990) and Outshoorn (1992) to focus on the institutionalization of feminism in public agencies promoting a women's policy agenda and to analyze the women staffing them.[6] It is a logical step, then, to use state feminism to refer to this institutionalization of feminist interests. It is important to avoid, at this point, any assumptions about a universal definition of feminism. As we will see, the definitions of both *state* and *feminism* are questions for cross-national research.

The scholars who have begun to turn their attention to women's agencies offer a fresh look at the state and its capacity to achieve feminist goals. These writings on state feminism differ from previous feminist research in that they question the notion held by many critics that the state is a single entity acting in society in defense of its own interests. Whether influenced by postmodernism's obliteration of grand design or sobered by their encounters with the world around them, . . . writers of state feminist literature avoid such global definitions of the state (Pringle & Watson, 1992). A more useful approach is to conceive of the state as the site or location of a variety of internally differentiated structures and processes (Franzway, Court, & Connell, 1989). Furthermore, for purposes of comparative research, these analysts recognize that whatever the state means is relative; conceptions vary from political culture to political culture, and these differences affect the way the state agencies may intervene in women's lives (Pringle & Watson, 1992; Sawer, 1993).

Deconstructing the monolithic state has reconstructed the question of its impact on women. Until now, empirical research on state feminism has been limited to a few case studies (e.g., Sawer, 1990, 1993; Stetson, 1987; Walker, 1990).

Research in state feminism in Australia, for example, shows that through the intervention of femocrats and state offices, organizations have been successful in securing funds for many projects based on feminist collective ideologies. Sawer (1993) argues that the operation of these agencies cemented a bond between the state and women's groups that strengthened the nongovernmental bodies' influence over policy. Work on these structures in Canada, on the contrary, suggests that subsidies from women's agencies to feminist groups were limited and were seen by political leaders as too radical (Walker, 1990). Still, as Stetson (1987) has shown in the case of France, the Ministry of Woman's Rights under the first Socialist presidency of Mitterrand (1981–1986) took over the agenda-setting role that had previously resided in nongovernmental feminist groups.

These initial forays to explore the records of action by specialized agencies have led many to agree with Drude Dahlerup (1987) that in order to develop a feminist theory of the state, we need less abstraction and more studies of "the scope and context of government action and its consequences for the position of women" (p. 108). Theories about the state and feminism must be examined cross-nationally, given the cultural differences in the ways both these terms are understood. Eisenstein (1990) agrees that the question of whether the state has helped or hurt women requires comparative research to assess the impact in a variety of contexts. We offer the first systematic cross-national examination and analysis of states' records and potential to further feminist goals.

Selecting the Cases

The population from which the cases were drawn is composed of advanced industrial societies.[7] In selecting the cases, we used primarily the most similar approach, choosing countries that had many characteristics in common. Thus, we reduced our population to those advanced industrial societies with stable democratic political systems. Because we are studying a phenomenon that arose from the second wave of feminism beginning in the 1960s, we confine our cases to those countries that have had democratic governments continuously

since the 1950s.[8] From this population, we have selected 12 cases: Australia, Canada, Denmark, France, Germany, Great Britain, Ireland, Italy, the Netherlands, Norway, Sweden, and the United States.

Our study also includes two contrasting cases, representing political change among the advanced industrial societies: Spain and Poland. Spain, a member of the European Union and classified among the advanced industrial societies by the World Bank, has had continuous democratic rule only since 1975, when the authoritarian Franco regime was replaced. Poland, a member of the Communist bloc until 1989, represents the more recent trend of democratization in Europe: the transition of Eastern European countries from communism to market economies and democratic regimes. This set of 14 cases, therefore, simultaneously provides a solid foundation to develop propositions about cross-national variations in state feminism in democratic states and suggests explanations for the existence of women's policy machineries in systems that are not as prone to democratic stability. . . .

Dependent Variables: Criteria for State Feminism

Central to this study is the following question: Is women's policy machinery feminist? To answer this question requires setting forth categories of agency activities to study and criteria for determining whether they are feminist or not. To develop the categories of agency activities, we drew upon literature from comparative social science on the state, particularly the work of Skocpol (1985). She suggests two important categories for studying state action: the *capacity* of the state, through policy, to have an impact on society and the impact of the state on political relationships or *state-society relations*. Adapting these two analytical angles to the study of women's policy machinery yields two areas of inquiry:

1. State capacity: To what extent does women's policy machinery influence feminist policy?
2. State-society relations: To what extent does women's policy machinery develop opportunities for society-based actors—feminist and

women's advocacy organizations—to have access to the policy process?

When these questions are examined in a variety of different country case studies, problems of "conceptual stretching" may arise.[9] Most social science concepts are subject to various interpretations in different cultures and languages. And we have used two concepts—state and feminist—that are subject to intense debates both cross-nationally and within countries. The contemporary scholarly debates on the use of the state in political research have revealed one area of agreement: Conceptions of the state in society are grounded in history and political culture (Rockman, 1990). Such conceptions range from societies where the idea of the state has little political meaning, the so-called stateless societies, such as the United States, to nations where several ideas of state as actor in society coexist, such as Germany (Caporaso, 1989; Dyson, 1980; Joppke, 1992; Nettl, 1968). We seek to solve this problem by incorporating a country's conception of the state into the framework as a possible explanatory variable. . . .

The problem of defining *feminist* or *feminism* is especially important and thus especially difficult to resolve because these terms are central to the phenomenon we are trying to document and compare, namely whether the state can further feminist goals. There is much controversy among women's movement activists, self-defined feminists, and women's studies scholars about what is meant by these terms and whether a particular action is feminist. . . .

It is conventional in this literature to set forth a list of feminist ideologies limited to varieties of modified feminism: liberal feminism, Marxist feminism, socialist feminism, and radical feminism. Recent studies of gender and international relations have added ecofeminism and postmodern feminism to the list (Peterson & Runyan, 1993). The problem with this approach is that it tends to restrict the vision of researchers to a predetermined set of categories and cause them to overlook gender-based ideologies that are politically important but do not fit on the list. It thus denies the right of women in various countries to set forth their own versions of feminist agendas. . . .

. . . For the purposes of the comparison of the case studies we used the following working definition:

An ideology, policy, organization, or activity is feminist to the extent that it has the purpose of improving the status of women as a group and undermining patterns of gender hierarchy.

Independent Variables: Explaining State Feminism

In identifying factors that explain cross-national variations in state feminism, it was important in the design of this study to choose independent variables that would affect the two dimensions of state feminist offices: their policy influence and their ability to provide access to women's groups. Early in our research we noted that despite the common environment of the second-wave women's movements and the international impetus from the United Nations, the politics that led to the establishment of agencies seemed to vary. In some countries, political leaders, hoping to win over women voters, created an agency or appointed an adviser for women in the absence of any demand from outside the government. In other countries, the issue became part of party platforms pushed by women within party organizations. In still others, leaders sought to respond to increased activism from women's movement organizations. These observations suggest that a major area of explanation for the nature and degree of state feminism in a given country will be the circumstances of office creation. . . .

The form of women's policy offices also appears to have an important influence on cross-national differences in the effectiveness of their activities. The UN studies have shown a broad array of types of agencies and locations, from ministries of the national cabinet to ad hoc committees and regional advisers. There are equal opportunity agencies, bureaus, and autonomous commissions. As a consequence, the second area of explanation for divergences in state feminism will be the specific type of agency. . . .

Looking at the organizational forms alone might omit the effect of expectations of and cultural attitudes about state action in the political culture. Here is where the cross-national diversity of conceptions of the state can be included in the analysis. The capacity of the state to resolve social problems may be greater if the agencies operate in the context of cultural beliefs that define these agencies as the main vehicles for social action. Women's policy machinery would draw resources from this view to further feminist policy. At the same time, cultural traditions of a strong state, especially those embraced by state elites, may hinder efforts to strengthen nongovernmental women's advocacy organizations, by opening access to the policy process without making these society-based organizations dependent on the state or co-opting them. On the other hand, groups may not look to the state as an arena for social change in the so-called stateless societies such as the United States, where the government operates within a cultural context that does not recognize a coherent entity—the state—acting for social goals. In such societies, policy machinery would be seen as just another social agency with limited potential for changing anything. . . .

Finally, we must include variations in the politics of the women's movement as a possible explanation of patterns of state feminist action. Specifically, we focus on activists' views of the state, whether they see it as a possible vehicle to improve the status of women or as an instrument of male power that is not to be trusted. Also of interest is the pattern of organization that developed in the second-wave women's movement, whether it was a coherent national network sponsoring a professional women's lobby, a diverse set of small loose-knit women's liberation groups, or a combination of the two. . . .

Notes

1. Students of women's movements agree that there have been two major waves of feminist political activity in most Western democracies, with the first wave occurring around the turn of the century. The second wave began in advanced industrialized countries in the late 1960s and early 1970s, thus coinciding with the creation of new women's policy machineries. Historians note that in some countries, including the United States, the contemporary movement is, in fact, the third wave.

2. It is important to note that feminism is a highly contested concept that has different meanings in different political, social, and national contexts. The controversies over this notion and the way in which this study deals with the problems of defining the term will be discussed at further length in this chapter.

3. The use of the term *women's policy* raises questions about the existence of *women's interests*. Clearly there is no way to verify that a particular demand is in the interest of all women (see, e.g., Molyneux, 1985). However, the United Nations charges women's policy machinery with improving the status of women by identifying the needs of women in various situations. Similarly, the term *women's policy* is used here to include actions to promote women in various situations in advanced industrial societies. Such actions promote equality and respond to women's concerns about maternity leave and child care. This contrasts with the use of the term by Hernes (1987, Chapter 1), who separates equality policy from women's policy.

4. For the most recent official list of women's policy machineries worldwide see United Nations, 1993a.

5. Franzway et al. (1989, Chapter 7), for instance, state that the word *femocrat* is "sometimes spoken pejoratively, it refers to those women appointed to work in 'women's affairs' and women's units in the state apparatus, the bureaucracies" (p. 133). An invention of Australian feminists, the term is also used to refer to any feminist in a government bureaucratic job (Eisenstein, 1991; Watson, 1990).

6. Hatem, in a study of Egypt published in 1992, departs from the pattern of usage by Outshoorn, Eisenstein, and this chapter's authors by using state feminism to mean the same thing as welfare state policies and programs.

7. This does not mean that these are the only countries with active women's policy machineries; many less industrialized societies in the southern hemisphere have national policy machinery as well.

8. These include the following 20 countries: Austria, Belgium, Denmark, Finland, France, Germany, Iceland, Ireland, Italy, Luxembourg, the Netherlands, Norway, Sweden, Switzerland, the United Kingdom, Australia, New Zealand, Canada, the United States, and Japan.

9. For a discussion of the problem of conceptual stretching in comparative research and proposed solutions, see Collier and Mahon (1993).

References

Caporaso, J. A. (Ed.). (1989). *The elusive state: International and comparative perspectives.* Newbury Park: Sage.

Collier, D., & Mahon, J. E. (1993, December). Conceptual "stretching" revisited: Adapting categories in comparative analysis. *American Political Science Review, 87*(4), 845–855.

Dahlerup, D. (1987). Confusing concepts—confusing reality: A theoretical discussion of the patriarchal state. In A. S. Sassoon (Ed.), *Women and the state: The shifting boundaries of public and private* (pp. 93–127). London: Unwin Hyman.

Darcy, R., Welch, S., & Clark, J. (Eds.). (1994). *Women, elections, and representation* (2nd ed.). Lincoln: University of Nebraska Press.

Dyson, K. (1980). *The state tradition in Western Europe.* New York: Oxford University Press.

Eisenstein, H. (1990). Femocrats, official feminism, and the uses of power. In S. Watson (Ed.), *Playing the state: Australian feminist interventions* (pp. 87–103). London: Verso.

Eisentein, H. (1991). *Gender shock: Practicing feminism on two continents.* Boston: Beacon Press.

Ferguson, K. E. (1984). *The feminist case against bureaucracy.* Philadelphia: Temple University Press.

Franzway, S., Court, D., & Connell, R. W. (1989). *Staking a claim: Feminism, bureaucracy, and the state.* Sydney, Australia: Allen & Unwin.

Guy, M. E. (Ed.). (1992). *Women and men of the states: Public administrators at the state level.* Armonk, NY: M. E. Sharpe.

Hatem, M. F. (1992). Economic and political liberation in Egypt and the demise of state feminism. *International Journal of Middle East Studies, 24,* 231–251.

Hernes, H. M. (1987). *Welfare state and woman power: Essays in state feminism.* Oslo: Universitetsforlaget.

Joppke, C. (1992, July). Models of statehood in the German nuclear energy debate. *Comparative Political Studies, 25*(2), 251–280.

Lovenduski, J., & Norris, P. (Eds.) (1993). *Gender and party politics.* London: Sage.

Molyneux, M. (1985). Mobilization with emancipation? Women's interests, the state, and revolution in Nicaragua. *Feminist Studies, 11*(2), 227–255.

Nettl, J. P. (1968). The state as a conceptual variable. *World Politics, 20,* 559–592.

Outshoorn, J. (1992, April). *Femocrats in the Netherlands: Mission or career?* Paper presented at the European Consortium for Political Research Joint Sessions of Workshops, Limerick, Eire.

Peterson, V. S., & Runyan, A. S. (1993). *Global gender issues.* Boulder, CO: Westview Press.

Pringle, R., & Watson, S. (1992). Women's interests and the post-structuralist state. In M. Barrett & A. Phillips (Eds.), *Destabilizing theory: Contemporary feminist debates* (pp. 53–73). Cambridge, U.K.: Polity Press.

Randall, V. (1987). *Women and politics: An international perspective* (2nd ed.). Chicago: University of Chicago Press.

Rockman, B. A. (1990). Minding the state—or a state of mind? Issues in the comparative conceptualization of the state. *Comparative Political Studies, 23,* 22–55.

Sawer, M. (1990). *Sisters in suits: Women and public policy in Australia.* Sydney: Allen & Unwin.

Sawer, M. (1993, June). Reclaiming social liberalism: The women's movement and the state. *Journal of Australian Studies,* No. 37, 1–21.

Siim, B. (1991). Welfare state, gender politics, and equality policies: Women's citizenship in the Scandinavian welfare states. In E. Meehan & S. Sevenhuijsen (Eds.), *Equality, politics, and gender* (pp. 175–193). London: Sage.

Skocpol, T. (1985). Bringing the state back in: Strategies of analysis in current research. In P. B. Evans, D. Ruechemeyer, & T. Skocpol (Eds.), *Bringing the state back in* (pp. 3–37). Cambridge, MA: Cambridge University Press.

Staudt, K. (Ed.). (1990). *Women, international development, and politics: The bureaucratic mire.* Philadelphia: Temple University Press.

Stetson, D. M. (1987). *Women's rights in France.* Westport, CT: Greenwood Press.

United Nations. (1987). *The development of national machinery for the advancement of women and their characteristics in 1985.* Vienna: Seminar on National Machinery for the Advancement of Women.

United Nations. (1993a). *Directory of national machinery for the advancement of women.* Vienna: Division for the Advancement of Women.

United Nations. (1993b). The Nairobi forward-looking strategies for the advancement of women adopted by World Conference. New York: Author. (Original work published 1985).

Walker, G. (1990, Fall). The conceptual politics of struggle: Wife battering, the women's movement, and the state. *Studies in Political Economy, 33,* 63–90.

Watson, S. (Ed.). (1990). *Playing the state: Australian feminist interventions.* London: Verso.

Chapter 39

State Feminism or Party Feminism? Feminist Politics and the Spanish Institute of Women

Monica Threlfall

Introduction

Spain's return to democratic politics was accompanied by the rise of a women's movement which made a plethora of demands on the new polity and vowed to change Spanish society in the name of women's liberation and advancement in all walks of life. By the end of 1982, a government had been elected that was particularly sympathetic to such demands, headed by the Spanish Socialist Worker's Party (PSOE), a sister party of the social democratic Socialist International. The following year a proposal to set up an Institute of Women was passed by the parliament. The Instituto de la Mujer became the central government department responsible for promoting gender equality during four successive PSOE administrations which lasted until the party's electoral defeat by the conservative People's Party in March 1996. The Institute's functions were to promote the social advancement of women and gender equality in politics, employment, health, education, the family, and the media.

The Spanish initiative was by no means unique. It has been a characteristic tendency of the women's movement in various parts of the world to press governments to develop their general commitments to equal opportunities (where any have existed) with the aid of dedicated administrative bodies. Stetson and Mazur (1995) hold that the array of institutional arrangements inside democratic states devoted to women's policy questions is "the most striking consequence of over 25 years of women's movement activism" (Stetson and Mazur, 1995: 1). In the Spanish case, the founders of the Institute of Women are on record as seeing their initiative as part of the internationally sanctioned feminist strategy of ensuring that the appropriate machinery of state is in place to develop women's policy. . . .

This [chapter] puts forward two main arguments. First, it argues that it is no longer helpful to analyze recent strategies regarding the state used by feminists in countries such as Spain as examples of state feminism because the concept has been used in such widely different contexts, periods, and political strategies so as to now be misleading. The chapter discusses several cases of "state feminism" and shows that the term refers to such contrasting and even contradictory phenomena that it is in danger of having any real meaning sucked out of it altogether.

The second main argument of the [chapter] is that both the use of the term "state feminism" and the analysis of the various national experiences to which it refers severely underplay the role of the party in power and of what the chapter terms "party feminism" in shaping policy at the time in which "state feminism" is said to have occurred. To illustrate the role of party feminism, the chapter traces the genesis of the Spanish Institute of Women back to the first political commitments on sex equality made by PSOE, and shows how these developed steadily under pressure from organized feminists inside the party. . . .

State Feminism

First let us consider the term "state feminism." It comes from the literature on women and the state and is one of the terms used, but not the only term, to characterize the relationship between the feminist movement and the state. Other terms are, for instance, "institutionalized feminism" and "feminist bureaucracy," which has been shortened to "femocracy" by analysts of the Australian experience (Sawer, 1995). . . . "State feminism" has been used both as a characterization of a certain type of institution, state policy-making *bodies* for women, as well as of a certain type of *strategy*. . . .

"State feminism" has been used by Helga Hernes when referring to the context of Scandinavia. . . . Here state feminism is the outcome of the official response of the state to women's agitation. Both the latter, creating pressure from below, and the state's response in the form of state feminism, are held to have had lasting effects on Nordic welfare state development. . . . The term is used in order to differentiate the activities of the state from the voluntary mobilization of women and their interests and preferences. More particularly, state feminism is the outcome of negotiations and compacts between the state and women: "it represents the results of an alliance between the two" (Hernes, 1987: 162, 1988: 210). . . .

. . . Other authors use the term "state feminism" not to characterize a political experience, but a *strategy*. For Judith Chapman, as a strategy, state feminism had as its objective, at least in Scandinavia, to use the state in order to liberate women from dependence on men, by means of employment in the public sector and state social services. The state's intervention weakens family power and the status of men by increasing the economic independence and life-choices of women (Chapman, 1993: 248). In this sense the term is a strategy deployed by the women's movement, from below. This usage is crucially different in two ways: first, if a strategy, then the difference established by Hernes between the two actors—the movement and the state—and the two realms at which the activities in support of women are taking place—the unofficial grassroots and the official realm—becomes blurred. And if it is a strategy, it cannot also refer to outcomes, since the objective of a strategy may possibly not be fulfilled. A further complication is that if it is primarily

a strategy then the outcome may not warrant the accolade of being termed "feminist," whereas in Hernes's use it is the results which are understood to be feminist. . . .

A variant on the use of the term is to talk about "state feminists" referring to the women who have taken up posts in public administration, because many of them were once active in the women's movement or the parties (Van der Ros, 1994: 530; Chapman, 1993: 248). They are not career civil servants but feminists who participate in conventional politics and hold public office. . . . But there is further slippage in consistency here: state feminists are criticized by some for failing to produce state feminism, or for promoting insufficiently feminist policies.

. . . Femocrats are simply "Women appointed to work in women's affairs and women's units in the state apparatus, the bureaucracies" (Franzway et al., 1989: 133), that is, identical to "state feminists" discussed earlier, the state being synonymous with bureaucracy. This leads to further subtleties in usage: feminist bureaucracies in the state are not to be confused with the separate phenomenon of bureaucratization of feminism where the term suggests co-optation and depoliticization of the movement (Franzway et al., 1989: 134). . . .

Let us now consider how the term is used in the context of a state which does not preside over an advanced capitalist economy and society. In her analysis of Egypt during the Nasser regime, Hatem uses the term "state feminism" to refer in general to the new welfare state's policies toward women, and agrees that the product of these was, as in western Europe, patriarchal: "state feminism in Egypt, as in the advanced capitalist states, replaced the old form of patriarchy based on the family with a new form of patriarchy originating in state control—a state patriarchy" (Hatem, 1994: 230).

The problem resides in the fact that the process described as state feminism in Egypt refers to the Nasser regime during the 1950s and 1960s which are seen as "the golden decades of Egyptian state feminism" (Hatem, 1994: 231). Yet Hatem does not suggest that there was an independent women's movement in Egypt in those decades or that second-wave feminism occurred earlier there. The picture of activists pressuring the state and forming an alliance with it to advance women's policies by creating new machinery of state and appointing feminists to government jobs in order to advance the status of women . . . is absent from the characterization of the Egyptian experience of those decades.

In Hatem's view, state feminism was an alliance between *women*—not feminist movements— and the state, which only really functioned well in a period of economic growth, during which the state supported women's right to vote and to take paid employment, outlawing sex discrimination and requiring large companies to provide day-care centers. The Egyptian government created a state women's organization in an attempt to represent women. But it used this to mobilize women in support of the state's development policies, which included birth control (Hatem, 1994: 229). This is evidently a very different type of state feminism and appears to be a good illustration of a top-down process led by an enlightened or possibly simply manipulative political elite. . . . Furthermore while women became more dependent on the state for jobs, state feminism did not challenge the personal and familial views of women's dependency on men that were institutionalized by the personal status laws and the political system (Hatem, 1992: 233). . . .

Therefore it is possible to distinguish two broad models of processes of change for women, both of which are described as state feminist. One, where the term is used approvingly, refers to policies on the part of the machinery of government viewed as benign or beneficial, being mostly designed and led by feminists in a period in which the welfare state is already fairly well established. Despite this, the policies of state feminism, though viewed favorably by feminists working with the state, are open to challenge by autonomous women's organizations. In the second model, the term "state feminism" is in fact used to refer to rather general policies of the state toward women in several countries and decades. In Egypt, aspects of early state feminism such as the provision of employment, education, health, and other social benefits to sizable sections of the female population are seen as progressive (Hatem, 1992: 232), while other characteristics of state feminism, particularly visible during its decline, such as elitism, absence of a grassroots movement, political manipulation of women, and lack of complete freedom to organize, are presented critically. Consequently,

Hatem sees the need for a feminism from below, in the form of nongovernmental women's organizations, as an alternative to the failings of state feminism (Hatem, 1994: 237–40). . . .

Undoubtedly the most wide-ranging use of the concept of state feminism has been developed by Stetson and Mazur (1995). Yet the fourteen cases covered in their study are all from the advanced capitalist democracies of western Europe, North America, and Australia, with the exception of Poland. Such a selection already implies that state feminism is a phenomenon of "western" market economies. However, Stetson and Mazur argue that state feminism really only exists in a given state under certain conditions, such as when "state structures assigned by political leaders to address women's inferior position in society contribute to policies that reduce gender-based inequities and provide an opportunity for women's movement activists to influence feminist policy formation" (Stetson and Mazur, 1995: 2). The authors argue that state machinery must have feminist aims and must *achieve feminist goals* and should also increase the access of the movement to the political process (Stetson and Mazur 1995: 272).

In Stetson and Mazur's approach, state feminism is a phenomenon of politico-administrative structures and their performance, and although Norway and Sweden are included, the analysis is of a far less comprehensive phenomenon than that dealt with in Hernes's state feminism, which was a wider political project. Furthermore in Stetson and Mazur's analysis, two elements are privileged above all others: the aims and goals of the policy machinery, and second, the access to the policy sphere which it opens up for the women's movement. . . .

Given the profusion of elements in the accounts we have reviewed thus far, the discussion would benefit from an identification of the constitutive characteristics of the experiences of state feminism analyzed above. In constructing Table 39.1, I have used mostly elements from the sources themselves but I have established the categories and situated the elements within them. There may well be contested accounts of the experiences referred to which do not use the term "state feminism" at all. I would have no quarrel with them. The point here is not to reinterpret national experiences, but

Table 39.1. Summary of Experiences of "State Feminism"

	Type A	Type B1	Type B2	Type C
Definition:	A woman-led political project to create a woman-friendly society	A male politician-led political project	A male politician-led political project	Woman-led policy machinery of state
Context/historical period:	1970s, 1980s Sweden Norway	1950s, 1960s Egypt, 1920s Turkey	1980s Greece	Historical referent: 1970s–1990s, 13 advanced capitalist nations
Level of welfare state development:	Established welfare state	Pre-welfare state	Rudimentary/incipient welfare state	Established welfare state + expanding incipient welfare state
Political démarche:	Elected governments take on board feminist demands	Revolutionary or unelected leaders act on behalf of women	Elected leader launches measures for women	Creation of influential women's policy machinery
General outcome:	Steps taken toward women-friendly society	Women's rights granted	Women's rights granted	Influence on reduction of gender inequality
Relations with women's movement:	Feminists appointed to implement policies for women	No feminist elite involvement; no independent women's movement	Elite feminist involvement; independent women's movement marginalized	Increased access of feminist activists and organizations to policy sphere, and influence on it
Feminist view of relations:	Feminists take steps to feminize "patriarchal" welfare state	Women mobilized to support government's general aims	Party-dominated agenda	Dialogue or alliance established between women's groups and sympathetic governments

to show the wide range of situations which have been referred to as experiences of state feminism, and to question the conceptual precision and hence the usefulness of the term. . . .

The Role of Parties in Women's Policy Advocacy

The problem with using the term "state feminism" to encompass all these phenomena is not just one of excessive looseness. . . . Crucial elements of the political context have been either ignored or misunderstood. . . . In particular the presence of political parties both in the background and in the foreground of these national experiences should be given greater consideration, and the relationship between parties in power and feminism needs to be examined. . . .

It is our contention that, particularly in the cases of the advanced democracies, it is crucial to discuss the relationships of the women's organizations with each political party or coalition of parties that becomes elected because it is under their auspices and during their administration that the women's policy machinery operates. None of the above analyses gives sufficient consideration to the role of the party in power in facilitating or constraining the experience of feminists in state administration.

The issue is illustrated here by an analysis of the case of Spain. I use the term "feminist" to refer to any woman or man active on behalf of the advancement of women as a gender . . . and as understood in Spain at the time. The term "party women" refers to women active in political parties, here particularly the PSOE, who did *not* identify themselves as feminists at that stage, some of whom were generally sympathetic to women's advancement while others were unsympathetic to feminism as a whole. The term "non-party feminist" refers to feminists working for the PSOE administration who were not active members of the party.

The PSOE and Feminism

It is important to appreciate how clearly the foundations of the PSOE government's policy on women rest on the *party's* initial commitments to sex equality.[1] The party's first encounter with feminism can be traced back to the setting up, shortly before the party's 27th Congress held in December 1976, of a feminist grouping in the PSOE composed of the women who were actively raising the issue of women's rights in different parts of the party. . . . A resolution was passed which resolved to fight for a slate of demands, typical of women's liberation of the time, and committed the PSOE to obtaining "equal rights for women in all fields without restriction or discrimination of any kind" (PSOE, 1977: 8). The resolution also sanctioned the establishment of the Women and Socialism (Mujer y Socialismo) committee. From 1977 Mujer y Socialismo functioned as a subcommittee of the Federal Executive Commission's Secretariat for Political Education, at that time headed by Luis Gómez Llorente. This experience shows that it was not the fact of the 1975 [United Nations] Decade for Women nor was it a general awareness of the women's liberation movement that led the PSOE leadership to become receptive to the issue. Instead, it was the actions of the women members of the party and their use of elective and other decision-making party structures which were effective.

The key player in Mujer y Socialismo's foundation was Carlota Bustelo, a long-time member of the PSOE, who had been active in the party during the years of clandestinity and was elected to parliament in June 1977. Mujer y Socialismo brought together a number of party feminists

of varying intensity who started to work on developing specific public policies for the party to implement either directly or, as PSOE candidates steadily gained office, in town councils and regional authorities. This work had a snowball effect. It became evident that practical steps could be taken (particularly after the first democratic local elections of 1979 in which the left won many city and town councils), such as setting up family planning or advice centers for women, or drafting changes to the law. More women from inside and outside the party came out as feminists, drawn by the opportunity to contribute by virtue of their office—newly elected councillors—or of their expertise as lawyers or doctors. For instance, by late 1979 there were already four women's advice centers functioning in Andalucía. . . . This was mainly as a result of the presence of a PSOE feminist in the regional government, María Izquierdo, as neither the Andalusian party leaders nor the government were especially sympathetic to feminism at that time.

By the 29th PSOE Congress of 1981, the PSOE had adopted an extensive set of public policy commitments toward women, advanced in general by the Mujer y Socialismo group of party feminists (PSOE, 1981: 231–35) but fought for specifically by party feminists in the delegations sent in by each area of the country. Though party feminists demanded a Women's Secretariat of the Federal Executive Commission, this was not achieved, but a compromise was reached whereby the then coordinator of Mujer y Socialismo, Carmen Mestre, was included on Secretary-General Félipe González's slate of candidates for the Federal Executive Committee and duly elected for the awkwardly named portfolio of "Defence of Freedoms." Thus, a declared feminist who had been active in an independent feminist organization before joining the party reached the top of the PSOE hierarchy. . . .

The Genesis of the Spanish Institute of Women

The PSOE was hopeful of gaining office and from 1981 enjoyed a lead in opinion polls. Party feminists set their sights on obtaining an office to promote women's rights from within the next government. . . .

Though the following year the PSOE's 1982 general election manifesto itself did not pledge the creation of women's policy machinery, it was a group of feminists in the PSOE who mobilized to obtain one. González's first cabinet contained not a single woman, but in 1983 the new Minister of Culture, Javier Solana, had to decide what to do with a small office in his ministry called the Subdirectorate of the Feminine Condition [sic]. He appointed prominent feminist Carlota Bustelo to his private office to advise him. She put together the team who designed the machinery for women's policy, later acknowledging that they bolstered their requests by reference to the precedents in other European countries of a body in the administration charged with drawing up equality policies (Instituto de la Mujer, 1993: 35). Ms Bustelo was then appointed by the Minister to head the Institute of Women once parliament had approved its creation as a (technically) "autonomous body" of the administration, which closely resembled a ministerial department.

Feminists and the PSOE

In arguing for the role of the party in the emergence of official women's rights policy machinery, one should consider how far the existence and the functioning of the machinery is a reflection of an individual party's commitment to women's rights. In the case of Spain, the view taken here is that without the slow buildup of internal party support for women's rights outlined above, it is most unlikely that the Institute would have been created. True, the preexisting Subdirectorate of the Feminine Condition might have survived. But it can be argued that had there been no pressure from party feminists, or the political flexibility to yield to it, a small office of this type might have been to the minister's preference, since it would have sufficed to give the impression that something was being done. Instead, a much more ambitious initiative was launched.

Second, the nature of the appointment is also significant. It would have been possible to give the issue a veneer of political neutrality by appointing a career civil servant or a person with no connections to the women's movement to head the old or a revamped office for women. In addition,

a further possibility would have been for Minister Solana to appoint someone from the party political hierarchy, rather than the high-profile and independent-minded Bustelo who, though a prominent and historic member, did not occupy any internal party post and had ceased to be an MP in 1979. She had as much prestige outside the party as within it.

With hindsight, the appointment set a precedent for the relationship between the PSOE government, women's policy machinery, and feminism. For the permeability of the party in office was a crucial element in composing the alliance between PSOE and feminist elites, as explained later. In 1984, a feminist trade union leader, Matilde Fernández, was elected onto the party Federal Executive Committee and took charge of the newly created Secretariat for Women's Participation. Associated with the group around Alfonso Guerra, who had become Vice-President in Felipe González's government, Fernández was an important ally for party feminists.

Yet, in spite of operating in the arena of internal party politics, the new Institute did not become dominated or even strongly associated with any particular party tendency or current. It appears that in the PSOE feminists came from all sectors of the party, and each of the players earlier mentioned had political friends and allies in different sectors, as well as outside among feminists. Reinforcing the new Institute's autonomy from internal party structures, the bulk of Bustelo's appointments to head its departments (the only discretionary appointments allowed) were of non-PSOE feminists with professional or women's movement experience: Isabel Romero, Isabel Alberdi, Gracia Pérez, Vicky Abril, Regina Rodríguez—two of them formerly active in a socialist feminist group, one a former Communist Party feminist. This fluidity can be seen as a characteristic feature of the subtle political balance between state administration, party hierarchy, and feminist movement. . . .

. . . The PSOE government drew in selected pro-socialist feminists instead of party women to high-profile posts to run the women's policy machinery. The Institute was thereby able to maintain a certain autonomy from internal party debates, avoiding the pitfall of becoming a stepping stone for party women who focused mainly on advancing their political careers. The operation of the Institute can therefore be viewed as a successful bid on the part of a certain tendency in Spanish feminism to collaborate closely with a party for the purpose of using public institutions for the advancement of women. . . .

The Costs of Party Feminism

Nevertheless, the collaboration we have referred to between feminists and the PSOE had certain costs. It had the nature of an implicit compact, in which feminists accepted that at the end of the day the government as a whole rather than individual ministers would set the parameters of policy initiatives for women which could be achievable under a PSOE administration (Valiente, 1994: 41). Several illustrations of this acceptance can be advanced. The first is that the women's policy machinery, in spite of being run by feminists who were in no way party placewomen, avoided becoming the site of important political tensions over criticism that the government was failing to live up to its socialist credentials and falling short of its promises. . . . Second, the limits to the Institute directors' political autonomy from the PSOE party are visible in their general acceptance of the government's fiscal orthodoxy. . . .

Third, the costs of the compact show up in the Institute's inability to push through acceptance for its policy to extend abortion rights at the right moment (Valiente, 1994: 41). . . . With hindsight the directors of the Institute recognized the decision to go ahead with a new law was made when it was politically too late and thus never reached the statute books before the PSOE lost power in March 1996. . . .

Conclusion

So far this chapter has made a case highlighting the extensive opportunities afforded by the rise of a social democratic party to power and its prominence in local, regional, and national government over a period of over 13 years. It has shown how a group of feminists used the political opportunity structure to advance feminists' goals and bring the women's agenda to increasing levels of prominence in government. The purpose was

to clarify that if the term "state feminism" is to be applied to the Spanish experience at all, it is misleading unless the role of the party in power is duly recognized, and unless the compact between a sector of feminism and social democratic politics is acknowledged.

Notes

1. The following account is based on interviews and personal communications with prominent players in the field, as well as on my own archive and recollections. No accounts of this type have been published before.

References

Chapman, J. (1993) *Politics, Feminism and the Reformation of Gender.* London and New York: Routledge.

Franzway, F., D. Court and R. W. Connell (1989) *Staking a Claim: Feminism, Bureaucracy and the State.* Cambridge: Polity Press.

Hatem, M. (1992) "Economic and Political Liberalisation in Egypt and the Demise of State Feminism," *International Journal of Middle East Studies* 24: 231–51.

Hatem, M. (1994) "The Paradoxes of State Feminism in Egypt," pp. 226–42 in B. Nelson and N. Chowdury (eds) *Women and Politics Worldwide.* New Haven, CT and London: Yale University Press.

Hernes, H. M. (1987) *Welfare State and Woman Power: Essays in State Feminism.* Oslo: Universitetsforlaget.

Hernes, H. M. (1988) "The Welfare State Citizenship of Scandinavian Women," in K. B. Jones and A. G. Jónasdóttir (eds) *The Political Interests of Gender.* London: Sage.

Instituto de la Mujer (1993) *10 Anos del Instituto de la Mujer.* Madrid: Ministerio de Asuntos Sociales.

POSE (1977) *Mujer y Socialismo.* Madrid: POSE.

POSE (1981) "Resolución 7.5 Feminismo," pp. 231–35 in 29 *Congreso: Resoluciones.* Madrid: POSE.

Sawer, M. (1995) "Feminism in Glass Towers? The Office of the Status of Women in Australia," pp. 22–39 in D. M. Stetson and A. Mazur (eds) *Comparative State Feminism.* London: Sage.

Stetson, D. M. and A. Mazur (eds) (1995) *Comparative State Feminism.* London: Sage.

Valiente, C. (1994) *El Feminismo de Estado en España: El Instituto de la Mujer 1983–1994,* Estudios / Working Papers 1994/38. Madrid: Instituto Juan March de Estudios e Investigaciones. (Reprinted as "El Feminismo Institucional en España: el Instituto de la Mujer 1983–94," *Revista Internacional de Sociología* 13: 163–204.

Van der Ros, J. (1994) "The State and Women: A Troubled Relationship in Norway," pp. 527–43 in B. Nelson and N. Chowdury (eds) *Women and Politics Worldwide.* New Haven, CT and London: Yale University Press.

Chapter 40

WHEN POWER RELOCATES: INTERACTIVE CHANGES IN WOMEN'S MOVEMENTS AND STATES

Lee Ann Banaszak, Karen Beckwith, and Dieter Rucht

. . . This [chapter] investigates the pattern of change in women's movements in West Europe and North America as they interact with states that are reconfiguring state powers. Given this central theme, our task is twofold. First, we clarify the concept of state reconfiguration and outline its extent and evidence in three exemplary nations. Second, we demonstrate how state reconfiguration influences concrete interactions between states and women's movements and discuss the effects of these interactions on both states and women's movements.

The Reconfiguration of States in West Europe and North America

The fundamental character of the nation-state is undergoing change. . . . As was the case with the formation of nation-states (Anderson 1974a, 1974b; Bright and Harding 1984) and the creation and development of welfare states (Castles and Mitchell 1993; Esping-Andersen 1990; Rieger and Leibfried 1995), the process of reconfiguration is highly differentiated, starting at different time points, taking different guises, and evoking different levels of support and resistance depending on the specific context in which it takes place. . . . For the sake of analytical clarity, we describe reconfiguration as an *ideal-type* process, and illustrate the various dimensions and aspects of the process with empirical references to particular states and policies.

Reconfiguration is evidenced, first, by structural changes within the state and, second, by the changing relationship between the state and civil society. These changes are accompanied, and partly reflected, by a changing discourse about the role of the state. . . .

Structural Changes within the State

Structural changes imply a relocation of formal state authority and/or a transfer of state policy responsibilities from one governmental level or branch to another. This relocation can first occur in a vertical direction by shifting power, which was mainly concentrated at the level of the nation-state, upward or downward. Much state authority has been *uploaded* to supranational organizations such as the European Union (EU), various UN bodies, the International Monetary Fund (IMF), and the World Trade Organization (WTO). Member nations of the EU, for example, having relinquished independent formal state powers to the EU, are subject to "supreme legal powers residing in the European Court of Justice . . . and the autonomous capacity for action of the European Commission. . . . [T]he Treaties and Directives of the EU have a direct effect on every citizen of the EU" (Walby 1997: 120). . . . Other examples of uploading include the transfer of economic decision-making powers by the United States and Canada to the North American Free Trade Agreements and to the WTO. In these arrangements, nations have relinquished autonomy of decision making in

335

policy-specific areas, and hence, have ceded some state authority to supranational organizations.

Vertical reconfiguration of formal state decision-making powers is also evidenced by *downloading,* that is, by the relocation of national state authority or responsibility for specific tasks to substate, provincial, or regional governments. For example, the devolution of formal decision making from the British Parliament to the new Scottish Parliament constitutes a transfer of state power and authority and the formal empowerment of a national region. . . . In addition to downloading formal authority, national governments have been reducing their responsibility for tasks by downloading these to subnational territorial units, without transferring the authority over policy arenas. . . .

Parallel to these vertical changes in state authority and responsibility, shifts of power occurred across the traditional representative spheres of the state, particularly the legislative and executive arenas. As a rule, there has been a weakening of the power of elected state spheres and a growing reliance on other and partly nonelected state bodies to make policy. We refer to these changes in state responsibility as *lateral loading.*[1] The national state maintains its decision-making powers, yet policy decisions increasingly occur in the courts, quasi-nongovernmental organizations (quangos), and executive agencies of government. . . .

The movement of policy decisions to nonelected state bodies is important because each policy venue influences the specific characteristics of policy decisions (Baumgartner and Jones 1993; Kirp 1982). In particular, as Baumgartner and Jones note (1993: 32–33), electoral politics allow activists greater influence over the framing of issues. When issues move from the Parliament to the administration, they tend to become more invisible and depoliticized. Similarly, issues may become depoliticized when they move to the judiciary. . . . As governments have increasingly engaged in lateral loading, women's movements have been presented with an increasingly depoliticized and remote set of state policy-making agencies at the national level. Thus, the relocation of responsibility to nonelected state bodies eventually reduces social movement influence.

Structural Changes in the Relationship between State and Civil Society

States have not only shifted their power within their own realm but also have reduced their own power and authority vis-à-vis civil society. Perhaps the most visible part of such a shift in power and authority involves states' decisions to offload their traditional responsibilities onto nonstate venues such as the community, the family, the market, or intermediary organizations. In the United States, Germany, and Great Britain, for example, the state has shifted away from being the sole provider of welfare and the primary authority for equalizing economic inequalities. Instead, some of these responsibilities are now part of the economic market or, in the case of alleviating poverty, have become the charge of the community or of civil society (Birkinshaw, Harden, and Lewis 1990). . . . One result of offloading has been that families (particularly women) increasingly bear the burdens of caring for the aged and disabled (Bashevkin 1998).

Related to the rise in power of nonelected state bodies has been the proliferation of civil society representation within the state itself. Quangos, regulatory agencies, and corporatist institutions usually include representatives of civil groups. For example, beginning in the 1980s, educational policy in the United States was increasingly decided by quasi-governmental organizations (Fuhrman 1994). Members of these organizations are appointed by national or state political leaders, who usually seek representatives of business, teachers, and policymakers. Thus, as the number of such bodies has increased in the last ten years, so has the presence of certain parts of civil society within official state organizations (Levine and Trachtman 1988).

These changes in the institutions of the state reflect a new power relationship between the state and other actors. On the one hand, there is a decline of the traditional neocorporatist arrangements of the past (Schmitter 1989). . . . On the other hand, the structural changes described previously, particularly the offloading of state responsibilities, mean that an increase in public-private partnerships provides new power to particular private interests. Certain policy areas are increasingly seen as specifically geared to serving business interests (for example, education, health, security, prisons) and, as a result, private corporations have increased power over certain types of state policy. . . .

As the overall political and social power structure, including the organization and competencies of the state, is reconfigured, it affects a broad range of policy domains and social actors. To the extent that state reconfiguration is the result of large-scale transformations in the global economic structure and international world order, states will experience widespread and long-lasting structural alterations, to which nonstate actors such as women's movements will have to adapt and of which they can take advantage. We argue that these reconfiguration processes are crucial for women's movements insofar as they provide negative as well as positive opportunities that differ fundamentally from the state context that women's movements faced in the 1960s and early 1970s.

Structural changes in the state are accompanied by a rhetoric and discourse of the state that has provided the rationale for state reconfiguration. . . . This discourse helped to shift and justify citizens' perceptions from a vision of states as activist centers of policy initiatives to one of states as limited, morally and economically, in their responsibilities and to an image of citizens as customers. . . . In addition, states altered their discourse about citizen participation from a vision of individuals as citizens with basic rights and of political participation, particularly voting, as the basis for citizen equality in the 1970s to a neoliberal discourse in the 1980s where citizens are seen as clients or consumers whose primary legitimate demand upon the state is for the satisfaction of specific needs (Brown 1995: 194).[2] . . .

Examples of Reconfiguration in Three Nations

Although we argue that all nations in West Europe and North America have experienced state reconfiguration, we also recognize that not all nations reconfigured in the same ways, at the same pace, and to the same extent. We discuss the cases of Britain, France, and Germany, which serve as examples of different experiences with state reconfiguration from the 1970s to the 1990s, as follows.

Britain Britain's major reconfiguration of state powers is evidenced in its (1) program of radical privatization of state-owned enterprises, (2) shift of many former social welfare commitments and responsibilities away from the national state, by defunding and abolishing some programs, and by transferring implementation responsibilities to local venues, (3) transfer of responsibilities to nonelected venues within the state, and (4) devolution of some powers to Scotland. . . .

On the other hand, Britain has not been as active as France and Germany in uploading formal state powers to supranational organizations, specifically the European Union. Britain's membership in the EU has been marked by a series of fits and starts; since joining the EU, Britain has conditioned its membership by reserving for itself specific policy exceptions. For example, Britain signed the Maastricht Treaty but negotiated a series of "opt-outs" from workers' rights provisions in the Social Charter of the Treaty,[3] and from its unitary monetary and currency provisions. Britain's resistance to ceding these sovereign powers to the EU is shared by both the Conservative and Labour Parties (see, for example, Butler and Westlake 1995).

France The French state varies considerably in all reconfiguration dimensions from Great Britain. France's state reconfiguration has been limited; the French state has continued central state authority within national boundaries, and maintained its commitment to state social welfare provisions. Nonetheless, France has moved toward reconfiguration, decentralizing policy implementation to local governments and relinquishing some authority to the European Union. . . .

France's greatest step toward reconfiguration is its membership in the European Union, with commitments to monetary union and to the social and economic components of the Maastricht Treaty. As a founding member of the Common Market (1957), France has had long-standing political commitments to Europe as a unified entity as evidenced in its transfer of state power through the Single European Act (1987) and the Treaty of Maastricht (1993). In contrast to Britain, France has not reserved specific state powers for itself as a condition of EU monetary union or, obviously, as a condition of EU membership.

Germany Germany's degree of reconfiguration lies somewhere in between those of France and the United Kingdom; Germany has participated in the construction of a stronger European Union, has engaged in privatization, has downloaded some previous responsibilities to the states, and has offloaded others to the private sector. However, much of this reconfiguration has occurred within the context of continual support for a strong and active state. Thus, it has not gone as far as Great Britain in reducing the scope of state responsibility and authority. On the other hand, there have been more attempts to reduce state responsibility than in France.

Germany, like France, has been one of the strongest supporters of the European Union. Under Helmut Kohl, Germany signed the Maastricht Treaty and forged ahead with the Economic and Monetary Union. Under Gerhard Schröder, Germany has pushed for a stronger EU presence in social policy, particularly in the area of alleviating unemployment. Thus, both left and center-right governments have been responsible for shifting state authority from the national level to the European Union. . . .

Changing Interactions between Women's Movements and States in West Europe and North America

State reconfiguration, as a process of political restructuring and relocation of power, affects nonstate groups to the extent that these groups depend upon and interact with the state. How, in the context of state reconfiguration, have women's movements and states interacted? . . .

Conceptualizing Movement-State Interactions

The *strategies* of states and women's movements can be arrayed along a scale from assimilative to confrontational (see Kitschelt 1986). Women's movements may choose to use strictly persuasive and legal means to become confrontational and even potentially to employ physical violence. The choice of strategies may affect (although it does not determine) the reactions by the state. More disruptive strategies may provoke strong state reactions.

The issues at stake for women's movements and states may be classified as (1) those that do not fundamentally affect the existing distribution of power and (2) those that constitute direct and serious challenge to existing power arrangements. . . . The former . . . may engender strong resistance but they do not challenge systemic power arrangements. In contrast, issues that directly question the social and political order increase the stakes of the conflict for both the movement and the state; in these cases, movements risk harsh resistance by state authorities and other groups. . . .

. . . The interaction between women's movements and the state is also shaped by its context (Edmondson 1997; Hyvarinen 1997). The context of interaction can be conceived as a set of layers ranging from very general, deeply rooted, and relatively stable conditions to more variable, particular, and temporary settings which influence the form and outcome of interaction (Kriesi 1995; McAdam 1996; Tarrow 1998). Major components of the interaction context,[4] applicable to both movements and states, include political culture, the configuration of power, the policy agenda, and arenas and audiences.

The first and most general context variable is the *overall political culture* of a given society (Almond and Verba 1965; Johnston and Klandermans 1995; Laitin 1997; Steinmetz 1999). The political culture includes basic and widely accepted values to which women's movements and the state can appeal (Banaszak 1996). Moreover, the political culture sets evaluative standards about which kinds and forms of conflicts are legitimate and defines the roles and rights of certain kinds of actors in a given society. Although the character of the political culture does not determine the concrete strategies and reactions of women's movements and states, it makes some strategies and reactions more likely than others. . . .

A second contextual element that influences the interactions between women's movements and states is the *configuration of power* (Kriesi 1995: 179–192), that is, the cleavage structure as represented by major interest groups, the balance of power among political parties, and the composition of government. Conflicts between women's movements and states are shaped by the lines of established cleavages, the involvement of other actors as parties to the conflict, and governments' stances in opposing or supporting the movement. . . .

The third contextual element likely to shape the forms of interaction is the *forum*[5] where the interaction occurs. It consists of two components: (1) an arena where the interaction takes place and (2) a gallery or audience where bystanders observe and react to the interaction (Ferree, Gamson, Gerhards, and Rucht 2002; see also Schattschneider 1960). In interactions between women's movements and states, some major arenas are the mass media, parliaments, and courts. The choice of the arena has implications for the kinds of interactions that are possible, insofar as some arenas (for example, parliaments, courts) are regulated and controlled by the state, whereas others (for example, the streets) are open to a wider range of interactions. We can expect that states prefer to confine conflict to strongly regulated arenas. . . .

Women's movements and states act not only in relation to each other but also with regard to the gallery (Schattschneider 1960). The gallery may be defined as everything from the small number of those who are physically present during an interaction to the mass public observing events and processes via the media. In democratic societies the reactions of the gallery play a decisive role in many political struggles since the majority of the voters ultimately affect which groups get into positions of formal decision making. Because of this (and the potential mobilizing power of public opinion), movements and states calculate the effect of their actions on the gallery.

. . . We recognize the importance of feedback loops in understanding state-movement interactions. Earlier interactions structure subsequent ones. Movement and state experiences within the previous interaction and particularly their evaluations of its outcome are incorporated into the next round of interaction. For example, women's movements may change their strategies, reorganize, or redefine the stakes of the conflict based on past experiences. In this perspective, interactions between women's movements and states are episodes in an ongoing process that, at each stage, can only be fully understood in the light of the past.

The Dynamics of State-Movement Interaction

How has the interaction of states and women's movements in North America and West Europe changed over time? As our model suggests, the interaction between states and women's movements is structured by previous interactions as well as the characteristics of both actors and the political context. In this section, we present a rough overview of the shifting nature of this interaction since the 1970s, with the caveat that the generalizations presented here occurred in varying degrees in specific countries.

In the 1970s, women's movements' interactions with states were characterized in part by radical if not revolutionary rhetoric made by largely informally organized and locally based wings of the movements. The section of the second wave of the women's movement that grew out of New Left groups adhered to socialist and Marxist ideas and advocated revolutionary change in everyday life (see, for example, Echols 1989; Firestone 1970; Freeman 1975; Morgan 1970; Randall 1992; Salper 1972; Tanner 1971). . . . It was this section of the women's movement in particular that sought to eliminate patriarchal and capitalist institutions, demanding the creation of a new political system and economic order.

Other wings of the women's movement, such as those composed of trade union women or liberal movement organizations, were concerned with specific policy reforms of the state. Yet, even their demands (for example, regarding violence against women, reproductive rights, and sexuality) challenged established political arrangements and were not easily contained or captured by existing politics. While the exact character of these sections of the women's movement varied from state to state, in the 1970s they were relatively limited in size and scope. Despite a need for political allies, the women's movement had few inroads to established politics through political parties, trade unions, or governmental institutions. Moreover, during this period, the new women's movements tended to keep their distance from established parties, even those of the left, insisting on the movement's "autonomy" (Beckwith 1987; Ferree 1987; Hellman 1987; Jenson 1987). . . .

. . . In the beginning stages of the second wave, both the constellation of power and most bystanders were unreceptive to women's movements' demands. While different sections of the women's movement utilized different arenas, the early women's movement was characterized by greater reliance on venues outside of the state. Moreover, the issues at stake largely challenged the existing distribution of power. Particularly challenging were those demands that called for complete restructuring of the patriarchal system.

The novelty of the women's movement's demands and the lack of political allies or widespread public support allowed states to ignore most movement claims. Nonetheless, states did make some concessions to initial demands, although these varied depending on the specific historical and political context. Most West European and North American states acceded in very minimal ways to demands for equal opportunity, equal pay, and increased political inclusion, demands which were the least challenging to existing state structures and harmonized with the political norms of a liberal democratic state. In addition, many states also altered their policies in the issue areas of contraception and abortion, where women's movements' use of extrastate protest was greatest, and where larger changes in societal gender roles underlay movement positions. Outside the state, women's movements' activities over the decade led to increasingly sympathetic public opinion toward some of the less revolutionary demands of the women's movement.

In the 1980s and 1990s, as states began to reconfigure, the political context of state-women's movement interaction was different. Women's issues had permeated many social and political groups as well as a broad range of more formal organizations and institutions. For example, the issue of sexual harassment spread from the women's movement into even more conservative state institutions such as the military (Katzenstein 1998; Stiehm 1989). This does not necessarily imply that women's movements made outstanding substantial gains but rather that women's issues are raised and debated in many more and wider circles than ever before. Moreover, initial demands for inclusion in political institutions increased the links between women's movements and political parties. In some cases, movements established strongholds in left-libertarian parties, such as the Greens, which were likely to advance the movements' cause. Other left and left-center parties (and some center-right parties) offered organized women access to political office (see Darcy and Beckwith 1991; Studlar and Matland 1996).[6] Demands for

access to political institutions also contributed to the rise of feminists in public administration, even in traditionally "male" areas such as the military.

Increased public acceptance and links to other political allies made women's movements in many countries large, diverse, and multilayered. Women's movements now included loosely coupled networks that extended into many nonmovement areas, permitting the formation of broad alliances and the aggregation of heterogeneous resources (see Keck and Sikkink 1998). . . . However, in some cases, this meant that women's movements became so highly fragmented that they no longer exhibited an identifiable ideological and social core and hence jeopardized their ability to act strategically. . . .

These considerably altered women's movements faced a reconfigured state that had relinquished its authority in some areas, had actively empowered political decision making by other political actors through offloading and lateral loading, and had adopted an ideology that precluded some forms of action. On the other hand, the state was also more sympathetic to some women's movements' concerns and had adopted at least some forms of gender discourse. The resulting interactions for upper- and middle-class feminists were decidedly less conflictual although limited to issues that corresponded with state discourse and ideology. However, as Beckwith shows, parts of the women's movement and their issues continued to be excluded from this institutionalized interaction. Those segments of the women's movements that do not engage in institutionalized interactions with the state continue to engage in confrontational tactics. They are hampered in large part by a lack of resources and political allies. While public opinion and other bystanders are sensitized to some movement discourse and to more institutionalized interactions, the existence of these interactions has marginalized the other wings of the movement, giving them little opportunity to gain support of bystander publics or other political allies. . . .

The Effect of State-Movement Interactions on Women's Movements

As states have reconfigured their structures, relocated their policy responsibilities by delegating or abrogating them, and rearticulated their policy discourse, how have feminist movements responded? We argue that the effects of state-movement interactions on women's movements' development, tactics, discourse, and policy outcomes are both numerous and discernible. Some of the effects on women's movement organization have already been investigated; for example, the effect of shifting power to supranational levels in the specific case of the European Union (EU) has been examined by several authors (Elman 1996; Hoskyns 1996). In a limited number of policy areas, the increasing power of the EU has required women to organize collectively at that level (Hoskyns 1996: 16) . . . and to use that venue to wrest policy results from individual nations (see Carter 1988). We expect to see similar responses as feminist movements alter their organizing efforts to be consistent with other dimensions of state reconfiguration. For example, as states decentralize their power, feminist organizing, as well as feminist office seeking, is likely to increase at the local level. The offloading of state responsibility to private organizations may also lead women's movements to mobilize in ways that would allow them to acquire resources through offloading. . . . Such mobilization may encourage the transformation of local feminist groups into service organizations and self-help groups. Ironically, women's movements have solidified relationships with the national state and feminists have moved into state institutions and elected bodies at the same time as the traditional responsibilities afforded these institutions are dissipating through state reconfiguration.

We expect that these changes will affect women's movements' strategies, as well as their ability to articulate and to pursue their own agenda. For example, one interesting question is whether state-movement interactions played a role in the decline of radical feminist ideology and identity, and how differences in radical and autonomist stances of women's movements across nations might vary accordingly. We hypothesize that a revolutionary ideology and discourse was first abandoned in countries that traditionally lacked a strong left (most notably the United States and Canada), since these countries had no bystanders or political allies who might be swayed by such a discourse. Revolutionary ideology and discourse is also likely to disappear where states were relatively accessible and responsive to women's movements' demands. As women's movements had some initial policy successes in the 1970s (for example, divorce reform, liberalization of abortion), some strands within the movements learned to employ a neoliberal state discourse in achieving their ends. This is apparent in the successes of women's movements' emphasis on equality of opportunity and on equal access to employment, housing, social services, and legislative representation, even where equality may be posited on a male model. Finally, in nations where women's movements employed a state involvement rather than an autonomous political strategy, women's movements were unlikely to adopt revolutionary discourse.

We are also interested in how established party links and feminist presence within the state affect state-movement interactions. We hypothesize that strong links between women's movements and other social actors, including other movements, interest groups, and political parties, are likely to facilitate women's movements' access to the state and their influence on state policy making. Banaszak suggests that such links might facilitate policy successes during offloading and horizontal shifts to nonelected bodies because women's movements still receive less state recognition as a private interest than political parties and trade unions.

On the other hand, as women's movements establish such links and broaden their scope, they may also moderate their tactics, their demands, and their rhetoric. Movement action dependent upon alliances with other social groups and political parties may be constrained by the nature of the institutions themselves and by the (un)willingness of allies to engage in particular tactics. Such links also multiply the number of networks and organizations involved in the women's movement, making coordination among movement actors more difficult. In the creation and expansion of political alliances, the more radical components of the movement may find themselves marginalized.

Similarly, the changes in discourse wrought by state-movement interaction and by the process of state reconfiguration may alter the frames and issues of women's movements. While a moderate feminist discourse has gained a legitimate place within the political debate, the neoliberal, anticollectivist rhetoric of the reconfigured state also limits women's movements to issues that will resonate with a wider public. Moreover, the policy discourse of the state is itself limited to certain views of women (for example, as mothers or workers), which may again constrain the range of potential movement action. Thus, the interaction of states and women's movements, while providing legitimacy to some types of women's issues, restricts the acceptability of others and eliminates still others from the political agenda.

Effects of State-Movement Interactions on the State

Given the central role of the modern interventionist state, women's movements must engage the state to bring about political and societal changes. . . . Although hostility toward the state and a distaste for male-dominated national politics have been characteristic of some sectors of second-wave feminism (see Jenson and Sineau 1994; Lovenduski and Randall 1993; Randall 1998), feminist movements in the 1980s and 1990s have directed their efforts toward states, by becoming state authorities or agents (for example, elected or appointed officials, bureaucrats), by mobilizing for policy change, and by involving themselves in state reform projects.

Because the state is targeted by multiple and often conflicting groups, ranging from competing social movements to conventional pressure groups to political parties, the impact of women's movements on the general structures of the state remains limited. It is unlikely that any single social movement would be able to change the fundamental structure of the state. . . . Women's movements, in conjunction with other social forces, nonetheless contributed to structural changes; for example, new power constellations between state and nonstate actors developed as the result of the weakening, or even abolition, of corporatist arrangements in some countries. In other nations, the decentralization of state structures and downloading of state responsibilities may have been encouraged and supported by autonomous women's groups positioned to undertake control of these functions at the local level. In still other cases,

women's movements may have helped to shape new state structures in the making, for example, in the case of constructing new federalist arrangements in Canada . . . or in shaping the structure of devolution in Scotland (Brown 1995).

In which countries and in which respects have women's movements been most successful in effecting state changes and how can this be explained? Have feminist movements been able to cast these transformations in West European and North American states in forms and modes potentially more receptive to these movements, their issues, and their constituencies? We suggest that women's movements have been more likely to effect changes in state structures, institutional practices, policy priorities, state personnel and authorities, and state rhetoric—that is, to facilitate state reconfiguration—under the following conditions.

First, when women's movements are positioned to form an alliance with other movements, or when a sympathetic carrying agent (for example, a left, left-libertarian, or radical political party) seeks similar ends and can advance these issues within the state, women's movements are more likely to be able to influence state changes above and beyond specific policy achievements. . . . Conversely, where such allies were not available or did not share or pursue structural or policy changes, women's movements are not likely to contribute to state reconfiguration. . . .

Second, when policy arenas related to women's issues (for example, equal employment opportunity) or of specific concern to women (for example, schooling) have high saliency for the state, women's movements will be better positioned not only to shape the debate, but also to influence the locations of policy implementation and to direct the construction of new state agencies or quasi-nongovernmental organizations. In those policy domains that directly relate to most women's issues, women's movements are likely to have an impact by supporting an increase in women's representation within the state apparatus and by interjecting new women's issues, such as sexual violence, into the policy-making process. In several countries, this trend has even resulted in the establishment of women's state secretariats, women's bureaus, and other agencies that are geared to advancing the cause of women (Stetson and Mazur 1995). . . . As states abandon women's policy issues, or as such issues become less salient for states, women's movements are less likely to be able to influence or to resist state structural or implementation changes.[7]

Third, . . . where policy issues involve feminist struggles against implementation rather than active support for new policy initiatives, women's movements are more likely to be advantaged in their efforts by multiple centers of power. . . . Conversely, where state power is centralized and unitary, women's movements may be advantaged in attempts to advance policy initiatives which, confirmed by a central state structure, are then uniformly applicable nationwide (see Mink 1998). In addition, decentralization of state powers (implicated in but not coterminous with multiple locations of state power) may also open political opportunities for organized women.

Finally, state and feminist discourses have intersected in ways that also serve to feminize state discourse; that is, a shared discourse developed from the interaction between women's movements and states, as women targeted the state as a venue for issue resolution. States increasingly interact discursively with women's movements by employing a gendered discourse, that is, a discourse about women that is not necessarily feminist or change oriented. This has been evidenced in two ways. First, states have recognized gender as a legitimate and crucial venue for state rhetoric and discourse. Many controversies about rights and responsibilities now include discussions of gender, at least in the area of reproduction, work, and political representation. Moreover, reference to equality of the sexes is increasingly included in discussions around constitutional issues and basic rights. . . . In some cases, a feminized state discourse is purely symbolic and deflects state responsibility for policy change (for example, in the United States the gender-inclusive language of the 1984 Republican Party platform).

Second, states have employed a gendered discourse that relies upon neutral or inclusive language. In many cases gender has been recognized only in a few areas of state discourse and has been constrained by preexisting state and societal conceptions of gender. For example, in Britain, child-care policies continue to articulate concern with "heads of households," apparently neutral language that nonetheless functions as a male trope (Lewis 1998). Such feminized state discourse can serve to mask real differences in circumstance and power between women and men, despite face efforts to address women's issues. In these cases, while the state's focus on gender appears to be both a success of the women's movement and an opportunity for further activity, it also reflects the limits of and political constraints on women's movements. . . .

Notes

1. We thank Michael Lewis-Beck for suggesting this term.
2. Indeed, a vision akin to the "civic man" of Berelson, Lazarsfeld, and McPhee (1954).
3. The Social Charter, as it is referred to by other EU member states, is formally the "Community Charter of the Fundamental Social Rights of Workers."
4. Our concept of interaction context differs from the concept of political opportunity structure only in its applicability to the state as well as movements.
5. A forum is a visible place defined by certain roles and rules (Gerhards, Neidhardt, and Rucht 1998).
6. In other cases, however, changes in party competition and in party systems jeopardized women's movements' relationship with and reliance upon established parties to achieve movement goals (see Randall 1995). As left-wing parties lost elections, newly governing parties were unreceptive to organized feminists and their issues, and feminist movements found themselves without influence in government (for example, Britain, Canada).
7. Note that we recognize that potentially all policy issues and state formations are gendered insofar as male power and masculine attributes are actively, although not perfectly, enacted through state mechanisms, practices, and discourses (see Brown 1995: ch. 7; Dodson forthcoming).

References

Almond, Gabriel and Sidney Verba. 1965. *The Civic Culture: Political Attitudes and Democracy in Five Nations.* Boston: Little, Brown and Company.

Anderson, Perry. 1974a. *Lineages of the Absolutist State.* London: Verso.

Anderson, Perry. 1974b. *Passages from Antiquity to Feudalism.* London: Verso.

Banaszak, Lee Ann. 1996. *Why Movements Succeed or Fail: Opportunities, Culture and the Struggle for Woman Suffrage.* Princeton, NJ: Princeton University Press.

Bashevkin, Sylvia. 1998. *Women on the Defensive: Living through Conservative Times.* Chicago: University of Chicago Press.

Baumgartner, Sylvia. 1998. *Women on the Defensive: Living though Conservative Times.* Chicago: University of Chicago Press.

Baumgartner, Frank and Bryan D. Jones. 1993. *Agendas and Instability in American Politics*. Chicago: University of Chicago Press.

Beckwith, Karen. 1987. "Response to Feminism in the Italian Parliament: Divorce, Abortion and Sexual Violence Legislation." In *The Women's Movements of the United States and Western Europe*, ed. Mary Fainsod Katzenstein and Carol McClurg Mueller. Philadelphia: Temple University Press, pp. 153–171.

Beckwith, Karen. 2003. "The Gendering Ways of States: Women's Representation and State Reconfiguratoin in France, Great Britain, and the United States." *Women's Movements Facing the Reconfigured State*. Cambridge: Cambridge University Press.

Berelson, Bernard R., Paul F. Lazarsfeld, and William N. McPhee. 1954. *Voting*. Chicago: University of Chicago Press.

Birkinshaw, Patrick, Ian Harden, and Norman Lewis. 1990. *Government by Moonlight: The Hybrid Parts of the State*. London: Unwin Hyman.

Bright, Charles and Harding, Susan, eds. 1984. *Statemaking and Social Movements*. Ann Arbor: University of Michigan Press.

Brown, Wendy. 1995. *States of Injury: Power and Freedom in Late Modernity*. Princeton, NJ: Princeton University Press.

Butler, David and Martin Westlake. 1995. *British Politics and European Elections, 1994*. New York: St. Martin's Press.

Carter, April. 1998. *The Politics of Women's Rights*. London and New York: Longman.

Castles, Francis and Deborah Mitchell. 1993. "Worlds of Welfare and Families of Nations." In *Families of Nations: Patterns of Policy in Western Democracies*, ed. Francis G. Castles. Aldershot: Dartmouth, pp. 93–128.

Darcy, R. and Karen Beckwith. 1991. "Political Disaster, Political Triumph: The Election of Women to National Parliaments." Presented at the Annual Meeting of the American Political Science Association, Washington, DC, August 29–September 1.

Darcy, Robert, Susan Welch, and Janet Clark. 1994. *Women, Elections and Representation*, 2nd ed. Lincoln: University of Nebraska Press.

Dobrowolsky, Alexandra. 2003. "Shifting States; Women's Constitutional Organizing across Time and Space." *Women's Movements Facing the Reconfigured State*. Cambridge: Cambridge University Press.

Dodson, Debra. 2006. *The Impact of Women in Congress*. Oxford: Oxford University Press.

Echols, Alice. 1989. *Daring to Be Bad: Radical Feminism in America 1967–1975*. Minneapolis: University of Minnesota Press.

Edmonson, Ricca, ed. 1997. *The Political Context of Collective Action: Power, Argumentation, and Democracy*. London and New York: Routledge.

Elman, R. Amy, ed. 1996. *Sexual Politics and the European Union*. Providence, RI: Berghahn Books.

Esping-Andersen, Gosta. 1990. *The Three Worlds of Welfare Capitalism*. Cambridge: Polity Press.

Ferree, Myra Marx, 1987. "Equality and Autonomy: Feminist Politics in the United States and West Germany." In *The Women's Movement of the United States and Western Europe*, ed. Mary Fainsod Katzenstein and Carol McClurg Mueller. Philadelphia: Temple University Press, pp. 172–195.

Ferree, Myra Marx, William A. Gamson, Jürgen Gerhards, and Dieter Rucht. 2002. *Shaping Abortion Discoures: Democracy and the Public Sphere in Germany and the United States*. Cambridge: Cambridge University Press.

Firestone, Shulamith. 1970. *The Dialectic of Sex*. New York: Bantam Books.

Freeman, Jo. 1975. *The Politics of Women's Liberation*. New York: Longman.

Fuhrman, Susan. 1994. "Clinton's Education Policy and Intergovernmental Relations in the 1990s." *Publius: The Journal of Federalism 24,* Summer: 83–97.

Gerhards, Jürgen, Friedhelm Neidhardt, and Dieter Rucht. 1998. *Zwischen Palaver und Diskurs: Strukturen öffentlicher Meinungsbildung am Beispiel der deutschen Diskussion Zur Abtreibung* Opladen: Westdeutscher Verlag.

Hellman, Judith Adler. 1987. "Women's Struggle in a Worker's City: Feminist Movements in Turin." In *The Women's Movements of the United States and Western Europe*, ed. Mary Fainsod Katzenstein and Carol McClurg Mueller. Philadelphia: Temple University Press, pp. 111–131.

Hoskyns, Catherine. 1996. *Integrating Gender: Women, Law and Politics in the European Union*. London: Verso.

Hyvarinen, Matti. 1997. "The Merging of Context into Collective Action." In *The Political Context of Collective Action: Power, Augmentation, and Democracy,* ed. Ricca Edmondson. London and New York: Routledge, pp. 33–46.

Jenson, Jane. 1987. "Changing Discourse, Changing Agendas: Political Rights and Reproductive Policies in France." In *The Women's Movements of the United States and Western Europe,* ed. Mary Fainsod Katzenstein and Carol McClurg Mueller. Philadelphia: Temple University Press, pp. 64–88.

Jenson, Jane and Mariette Sineau. 1994. "France: The Same or Different? An Unending Dilemma for French Women." In *Women and Politics Worldwide,* ed. Barbara J. Nelson and Najma Chowdhury. New Haven, CT: Yale University Press, pp. 243–260.

Johnston, Hank and Bert Klandermans, eds. 1995. *Social Movements and Culture*. Minneapolis: University of Minnesota Press.

Katzenstein, Mary Fainsod. 1998. *Faithful and Fearless: Moving Feminist Protest inside the Church and Military*. Princeton, NJ: Princeton University Press.

Keck, Margaret and Kathryn Sikkink. 1998. *Activists Beyond Borders: Advocacy Networks in International Politics*. Ithaca, NY: Cornell University Press.

Kirp, David. 1982. "Professionalization as a Policy Choice: British Special Education in Comparative Perspective." *World Politics 34*: 137–174.

Kitschelt, Herbert. 1986. "Political Opportunity Structures and Political Education Protest: Anti-Nuclear Movements in Four Democracies." *British Journal of Political Science 16(1)*: 57–85.

Kriesi, Hanspeter. 1995. "The Political Opportunity Structure of New Social Movements: Its Impact on Their Mobilization." In *The Politics of Social Protest: Comparative Perspectives on States and Social Movements,* ed. J. Craig Jenkins and Bert Klandermans. Minneapolis: University of Minnesota Press, pp. 167–198.

Laitin, David D. 1997. "The Cultural Identities of a European State." *Politics Society* 25, September: 277–302.

Levine, Marsha and Roberta Trachtman. 1998. *American Business and the Public School.* New York: Teachers College Press.

Lewis, Jane. 1998. " 'Work,' 'Welfare,' and Lone Mothers." *Political Quarterly* 69(1): 4–13.

Lovenduski, Joni and Vicky Randall. 1993. *Contemporary Feminist Politics: Women and Power in Britain.* Oxford: Oxford University Press.

McAdam, Doug. 1996. "Conceptual Origins, Problems, Future Directions." In *Comparative Perspectives on Social Movements: Political Opportunities, Mobilizing Structures, and Cultural Framing,* ed. Doug McAdam, John D. McCarthy, and Mayer N. Zald. Cambridge: Cambridge University Press.

Morgan, Robin, ed. 1970, *Sisterhood Is Powerful.* New York: Vintage.

Randall, Vicky. 1998. "Gender and Power: Women Engage the State." In *Gender, Politics, and the State,* ed. Georgina Waylen and Vicky Randall. London and New York: Routledge, pp. 185–205.

Randall, Vicky. 1995. "The Irresponsible State? The Politics of Child Daycare Provision in Britain." *British Journal of Political Science* 25 (3), July: 327-348.

Randall, Vicky. 1992. "Great Britain and Dilemmas for Feminist Strategy in the 1980s: The Case of Abortion and Reproductive Rights." In *Women Transforming Politics,* ed. Jill M. Bystydzienski. Bloomington: Indiana University Press, pp. 80-94.

Rieger, Elmar and Stephan Liebfried. 1995. *Globalization and the Western Welfare State.* New York: Social Science Research Council, Center for Social Policy Research.

Salper, Roberta, ed. 1972. *Female Liberation: History and Current Politics.* New York: Knopf.

Schattschneider, Elmer Eroc. 1960. *The Semi-Sovereign People: A Realist's View of Democracy in America.* New York: Holt, Rinehart and Winston.

Schmitter, Phillipp. 1989. "Corporatism is Dead! Long Live Corporatism!" *Government and Opposition* 24: 54–73.

Stenmetz, George, ed. 1999. *State/Culture: State-Formation after the Cultural Turn.* Ithaca, NY: Cornell University Press.

Stetson, Dorothy McBride and Amy Mazur, eds. 1995. *Comparative State Feminism.* Thousand Oaks, CA: Sage Publications.

Stiehm, Judith. 1989. *Arms and the Enlisted Woman.* Philadelphia: Temple University Press.

Studlar, Donley T. and Richard E. Matland. 1996. "The Contagion of Women Candidates in Single-Member District and Proportional Representation Electoral Systems: Canada and Norway." *Journal of Politics* 58: 707–733.

Tanner, Leslie, ed. 1971. *Voices from Women's Liberation.* New York: New American Library.

Tarrow, Sidney. 1998. *Power in Movement: Social Movements and Contentious Politics,* 2nd ed. Cambridge: Cambridge University Press.

Walby, Sylvia. 1997. *Gender Transformations.* New York: Routledge.

CREDITS

Alvarez, Sonia E. 2000. "Translating the Global: Effects of Transnational Organizing on Latin American Feminist Discourses and Practices." *Meridians: A Journal of Feminisms, Race, Transnationalism* 1 (1): 29–67.

Bacchi, Carol Lee. 1999. "Taking Problems Apart." Pp. 1–13 in *Women, Policy, and Politics: The Construction of Policy Problems.* Thousand Oaks, Calif.: Sage.

Baldez, Lisa. 2003. "Women's Movements and Democratic Transition in Chile, Brazil, East Germany, and Poland." *Comparative Politics* 35 (3): 253–272.

Banaszak, Lee Ann, Karen Beckwith, and Dieter Rucht. 2003. "When Power Relocates: Interactive Changes in Women's Movements and States." Pp. 1–29 in *Women's Movements Facing the Reconfigured State*, ed. Lee Ann Banaszak, Karen Beckwith, and Dieter Rucht. New York: Cambridge University Press.

Beckwith, Karen. 2000. "Beyond Compare? Women's Movements in Comparative Perspective." *European Journal of Political Research* 37 (4): 431–468.

Caul, Miki. 1999. "Women's Representation in Parliament: The Role of Political Parties." *Party Politics* 5 (1): 79–98.

Chappell, Louise. 2000. "Interacting with the State: Feminist Strategies and Political Opportunities." *International Feminist Journal of Politics* 2 (2): 244–275.

Cunningham, Karla J. 2003. "Cross-Regional Trends in Female Terrorism." *Studies in Conflict and Terrorism* 26 (3): 171–195.

Dahlerup, Drude. 1988. "From a Small to a Large Minority: Women in Scandinavian Politics." *Scandinavian Political Studies* 11 (4): 275–297.

Dahlerup, Drude, and Lenita Freidenvall. 2005. "Quotas as a 'Fast Track' to Equal Representation for Women: Why Scandinavia Is No Longer the Model." *International Feminist Journal of Politics* 7 (1): 26–48.

Dominelli, Lena, and Gudrun Jonsdottir. 1988. "Feminist Political Organization in Iceland: Some Reflections on the Experience of Kwenna Frambothid." *Feminist Studies* 30: 36–60.

Dovi, Suzanne. 2002. "Preferable Descriptive Representatives: Will Just Any Woman, Black, or Latino Do?" *American Political Science Review* 96 (4): 729–743.

Fox, Richard L., and Jennifer L. Lawless. 2004. "Entering the Arena? Gender and the Decision to Run for Office." *American Journal of Political Science* 48 (2): 264–280.

Freeman, Jo. 2000. "Building a Base: Women in Local Party Politics." Pp. 149–178 in *A Room at a*

347

Time: How Women Entered Party Politics. Lanham, Md.: Rowman and Littlefield.

Goetz, Anne Marie. 2003. "The Problem with Patronage: Constraints on Women's Political Effectiveness in Uganda." Pp. 110–139 in *No Shortcuts to Power: African Women in Politics and Policy-Making*, ed. Anne Marie Goetz and Shireen Hassim. New York: Zed.

Hawkesworth, Mary. 2003. "Congressional Enactments of Race-Gender: Toward a Theory of Raced-Gendered Institutions." *American Political Science Review* 97 (4): 529–550.

Htun, Mala. 2003. "Sex and the State in Latin America." Pp. 1–28 in *Sex and the State: Abortion, Divorce, and the Family under Latin American Dictatorships and Democracies*. New York: Cambridge University Press.

Inglehart, Ronald, and Pippa Norris. 2000. "The Developmental Theory of the Gender Gap: Women's and Men's Voting Behavior in Global Perspective." *International Political Science Review* 21 (4): 441–463.

Kantola, Johanna. 2006. "Gender and the State: Theories and Debates." In *Feminists Theorize the State*. New York: Palgrave.

Katzenstein, Mary Fainsod. 1998. "Protest Moves inside Institutions." Pp. 3–22 in *Faithful and Fearless: Moving Feminist Protest inside the Church and Military*. Princeton, N.J.: Princeton University Press.

Lovenduski, Joni. 1993. "Introduction: The Dynamics of Gender and Party." Pp. 1–15 in *Gender and Party Politics*, ed. Joni Lovenduski and Pippa Norris. Thousand Oaks, Calif.: Sage.

MacKinnon, Catharine A. 1989. "The Liberal State." Pp. 157–170 in *Toward a Feminist Theory of the State*. Cambridge, Mass.: Harvard University Press.

Mansbridge, Jane. 1999. "Should Blacks Represent Blacks and Women Represent Women? A Contingent 'Yes.'" *Journal of Politics* 61 (3): 628–657.

Molyneux, Maxine. 1985. "Mobilization without Emancipation? Women's Interests, the State and Revolution in Nicaragua." *Feminist Studies* 11 (2): 227–254.

Niven, David. 1998. "Party Elites and Women Candidates: The Shape of Bias." *Women and Politics* 19 (2): 57–80.

Norris, Pippa, and Joni Lovenduski. 1995. "Puzzles in Political Recruitment." Pp. 1–19 in *Political Recruitment: Gender, Race, and Class in the British Parliament*. New York: Cambridge University Press.

Orloff, Ann. 1996. "Gender in the Welfare State." *Annual Review of Sociology* 22: 51–78.

Phillips, Anne. 1995. "Quotas for Women." Pp. 57–83 in *The Politics of Presence: The Political Representation of Gender, Ethnicity, and Race*. New York: Oxford University Press.

Sainsbury, Diane. 2004. "Women's Political Representation in Sweden: Discursive Politics and Institutional Presence." *Scandinavian Political Studies* 27 (1): 65–87.

Sarvasy, Wendy. 1992. "Beyond the Difference versus Equality Policy Debate: Postsuffrage Feminism, Citizenship, and the Quest for a Feminist Welfare State." *Signs* 17 (2): 329–362.

Squires, Judith. 2005. "Is Mainstreaming Transformative? Theorizing Mainstreaming in the Context of Diversity and Deliberation." *Social Politics* 12 (3): 366–388.

Stetson, Dorothy McBride, and Amy Mazur. 1995. "Introduction." Pp. 1–21 in *Comparative State Feminism*, ed. Dorothy McBride Stetson and Amy Mazu. Thousand Oaks, Calif.: Sage.

Strolovitch, Dara Z. 2006. "Do Interest Groups Represent the Disadvantaged? Advocacy at the Intersections of Race, Class, and Gender." *Journal of Politics* 68 (4): 894–910.

Tamerius, Karin L. 1995. "Sex, Gender, and Leadership in the Representation of Women." Pp. 93–112 in *Gender Power, Leadership, and Governance*, ed. Georgia Duerst-Lahti and Rita Mae Kelly. Ann Arbor: University of Michigan Press.

Threlfall, Monica. 1998. "State Feminism or Party Feminism? Feminist Politics and the Spanish Institute for Women." *European Journal of Women's Studies* 5: 69–93.

Yoon, Mi Yung. 2004. "Explaining Women's Legislative Representation in Sub-Saharan Africa." *Legislative Studies Quarterly* 29 (3): 447–466.

Young, Iris Marion. 2000. "Representation and Social Perspective." Pp. 121–153 in *Inclusion and Democracy*. New York: Oxford University Press.

Young, Lisa. 2000. "Theorizing Feminist Strategy and Party Responsiveness." Pp. 11–26 in *Feminists and Party Politics*. Vancouver: UBC Press.

INDEX

Abbott, Edith, 278, 279, 281
abortion policy, 25, 43, 268–270, 271, 273, 296
Abril, Vicky, 332
absolutist *vs.* technical policies, 267–268, 269
accountability, political representation, 188–190,
   194–195, 205
Acker, Joan, 223*n*10
Ackerman, Bruce, 296*n*1
Action for Development (ACDODE), Uganda, 108–109
activist hypothesis, parliamentary representation, 160,
   163–165
add-on method, Uganda, 109–110
administrative appointments, Uganda, 107, 109, 114
   See also state feminism
advantaged-subgroup issues category, intersectional
   typology, 56–62
Advisory Council, Sweden, 99–101, 104
affirmative action strategies, political party leadership, 84
Africa
   quota regulation trend, 178–179
   sub-Saharan representation study, 167–172
   See also specific countries
African Americans. *See* descriptive representation; racing-
   gendering processes
agenda-setting model, 284, 285, 286, 288
aggregative function, representative democracy, 201–202,
   203–204
Aid to Dependent Children (ADC), United States, 277,
   279–280
Akureyri elections, Iceland, 118, 119
Al-Aqsa Martyrs Brigade, 72, 75
Alberdi, Isabel, 332
Algeria, terrorist activity, 72
Aliyan, Etaf, 75
Al-Sha'ab, 75–76
Alvarez, Sonia E.
   chapter by, 63–70
   comments on, 20
AMNLAE, Nicaragua, 24–25, 27, 28*n*15
Al Amouri, Shahanaz, 78*n*28

apartisan movements, as political strategy, 88
Argentina, 130, 178, 180, 268, 271–272
Armey, Dick, 258
Asia, quota regulation trend, 178
   See also specific countries
associational activism, 48–49
association factor, experience category, legislative process
   study, 245
attitudes category, legislative process study, 245–249
Australia, 8, 84, 307, 308, 313–318, 322
Austria, welfare state characteristics, 308
authorization function, political representation, 194–195
autonomy argument, descriptive representative selection,
   216
awareness factor, resources category, legislative process
   study, 246, 247

Bacchi, Carol Lee
   chapter by, 263–266
   comments on, 241–242
balanced group, in critical mass arguments, 227
Baldez, Lisa
   chapter by, 37–45
   comments on, 19–20
Banaszak, Lee Ann
   chapter by, 335–345
   comments on, 292, 341
Bangladesh, quota regulations, 178, 179
Bannister, Don, 265
Barrett, Michèle, 300
Basu, Amrita, 33
Baumgartner, Frank, 336
Beard, Mary, 282*n*9
Beckwith, Karen
   chapters by, 29–36, 335–345
   comments on, 19, 292, 340
Beijing conference, 66–67, 69*n*8, 180
Belgium, quota regulations, 178, 181*n*5
Berry, Jeffrey M., 56
Besigye, Kiiza, 115*n*6

bias studies
    disadvantage group representation, 20, 55–62
    political party elites, 151–157
blacks. *See* descriptive representation; intersectionality;
        racing-gendering processes
Black Tigers, Sri Lanka, 72, 74
Blair, Emily Newell, 92–93
Bock, G., 307
Boëthuis, Maria-Pia, 102
Bogue, Mary F., 278
Bolivia, quota regulations, 180
boomerang pattern, transnational activism, 64
Bosnia-Herzegovina, quota discussions, 179
Boswell, Helen V., 91, 92, 94n10
Brazil
    electoral system impact, 272
    gender-related policy, 268
    quota regulations, 181n5
    transnational activism, 67
    women's movement, 30, 38–40
Breckinridge, Sophonisba, 278, 279, 281, 282n11
Britain
    candidate recruitment study, 135–140
    political parties, 81–82, 85
    reconfiguration and power shifts, 336, 337
    welfare state characteristics, 307, 308, 309, 310, 336
    women's movement, 30, 34
bureaucracy appointments. *See* state feminism
Burke, Edmund, 210n6
Burke, Yvonne Braithwaite, 261n1
Burkina Faso, electoral system, 171n8
Bustelo, Carlota, 331, 332
Butler, Sarah Schuyler, 91

Cable Act, 280–281, 282n11
California, local party activity, 94n4
Canada
    feminist political strategies, 313–318
    gender gap patterns, 130
    political parties, 85, 136
    state feminism impact, 322
    welfare state characteristics, 308
    women's movement, 33
Canadian Royal Commission on Electoral Reform, 210
candidate recruitment studies, 8–9, 135–140, 151–157
capitalist state theory, 300–301
Catholic Church
    and democratization, 38, 40, 41
    Eastern Europe democratization, 38
    feminist protests, 48–50, 51–52
    Latin American gender policies, 267–268, 269,
        272–273
Caul, Miki
    chapter by, 159–166
    comments on, 126
centralization component, political party organization,
        159, 161–162, 166n5
centralized systems, candidate recruitment, 136
Centre Party Communists, Sweden, 98
Chapman, Judith, 328

Chappell, Louise
    chapter by, 313–318
    comments on, 291
Charter of Rights and Freedoms, Canada, 314–315
Chase, Erica, 72
Chicago, political machine, 92
child care policies, welfare states, 309
Childs, Sarah, chapter by, 3–20
Chile
    family life regulation, 268, 272, 273n3
    gender gap study, 132
    transnational activism, 68
    women's movement and democratization, 38–39,
        40–41
China, women's activism, 32
Chinese women, U.S. citizenship ruling, 282n11
Chisholm, Shirley, 261n1
churches, Germany democratization, 38, 42
    See also Catholic Church
Citizen Political Ambition Study, United States, 142–148
citizenship, married women, 280–281, 282n11
city councils, Iceland, 118–119, 121–122
civic associationalism, 48–49
civil society, and state power reconfigurations, 336–337
class interests, 23, 220–221, 223n10
    See also disadvantaged groups, representation
        effectiveness; intersectionality
Clayton, Eva, 258, 259, 260
Cloward, Richard A., 52nn1–2
club approach, local parties, 90–91
Cohen, Cathy, 220
Collins, Barbara, 258
Collins, Cardiss, 261n1
Collins, Patricia Hill, 287
Colombia, terrorist activity, 72, 73
Colorado, local party activity, 90, 94n4
Commission on the Status of Women (CSW), United
        Nations, 320
commitment factor, attitudes category, legislative process
        study, 245–249
Communist Party, Italy, 31, 136, 161
Communist Party, Sweden, 98, 100
communist regimes, women's movements and
        democratization, 38–39, 42–43
Confederate flag controversy, 207
Congress, U.S.
    legislative process study, 243–249
    racing-gendering processes study, 251–260
Congressional Black Caucus, 255–256
Congressional Caucus for Women's Issues, 255–256
Congressional Members Organizations (CMOs), 255–256
Conover, P. J., 129
conservative-corporatist regimes, welfare states, 308–309
Conservative Party, Britain, 137, 140n9
Conservative Party, Sweden, 101–102, 104
Constituent Assembly (CA), Uganda, 109, 112
constitutional approaches
    as feminist political opportunities, 314–316
    quota provisions, 178–179, 180
Constitutional Commission, Uganda, 108, 109

content factor, experience category, legislative process study, 244
contingency argument, descriptive representative selection, 216
Convention for the Elimination of Discrimination against Women (CEDAW), 320
cosponsorship importance, legislative process, 246–247, 248–249
Costa Rica, 175–176, 179, 180
critical mass arguments, 10, 225–230, 236–238
cultural theories, gender gap, 129
culture variable, sub-Saharan Africa representation study, 168, 169–170
Cunningham, Karla J.
    chapter by, 71–78
    comments on, 20
Cunningham, Representative, 258

Dahl, Robert, 294, 297n3
Dahlerup, Drude
    chapters by, 175–182, 225–230
    comments on, 126, 184, 322
Dahlgren, Edesse, 94n13
Dawson, William, 95n15
deliberative function, representative democracy, 201–202, 203–204, 288–289
demand model, candidate recruitment study, 138–139
democracy quality argument, quotas, 185, 188
    See also Sweden
Democratic Party, U.S., 90, 93–94, 95nn15–16, 127
    See also Congress, U.S.
democratization, and women's movements, 37–43
Denmark, 130, 175–176
descriptive representation
    overviews, 201–202, 215
    benefits, 205–209, 210n5, 211n7, n11, n16
    cost factors, 202–205, 210n2
    institutionalizing considerations, 209–210, 211n17, n19
    selection criteria, 215–223
developmental theory, gender gap, 127–132
Dhanu (terrorist), 74
differentiated state theory, 302–303
disadvantaged groups, representation effectiveness, 55–62
    See also descriptive representation
discrimination variable, candidate selection study, 138–139
displacement, as mainstreaming strategy, 283–290
dispossessed subgroups. *See* descriptive representation
distribution effect, elite bias study, 152–157
diversity mainstreaming, 11–12, 287–290
divorce policy, Latin America, 268, 269–270, 271, 273
Djibouti, representation statistics, 167
Dobrowolski, A., 33
Dobyns, Winifred Starr, 92
Dock, Lavinia, 280
Dodson, Louise, 90
Dole, Robert, 93
domestic labor factor
    Iceland political parties, 118
    Latin America organizing, 38

political ambition study, 142, 145, 146
public policy interests, 23, 27
welfare state theory, 305
Domestic Relations Bill, Uganda, 112
Dominelli, Lena
    chapter by, 117–123
    comments on, 80
Dominican Republic, transnational activism, 65
double militancy dilemma, 7, 31–32
Dovi, Suzanne
    chapter by, 215–223
    comments on, 184
downloading processes, in state reconfigurations, 336

East Germany, 19–20, 33, 38–39, 42, 132
East Timor, quota discussions, 179
economic conditions
    as gender gap hypothesis, 129–130, 131
    sub-Saharan Africa, 168, 170
Ecuador, quota regulations, 180
education systems, Nicaragua, 27
education variable, sub-Saharan Africa representation study, 167, 169, 170, 171n4
Egypt, 75–76, 179, 328–329
Eisenstein, H., 321, 322
elections and electoral systems
    overview, 7–9, 125–126
    African countries, 168, 169, 171nn7–8
    candidate recruitment studies, 8–9, 135–140, 151–157
    Iceland, 119, 122
    Latin American countries, 272
    nomination routes summarized, 84–86
    as parliamentary representation hypothesis, 161, 163–165
    political ambition study, 141–148
    proportional *vs.* majority effects, 179
    Spain, 327
    Sweden, 102–103
    Uganda, 108, 109–110, 111, 114
    voting behavior patterns, 7–8, 127–132
    See also political parties; political representation *entries;* quotas
eligibility pool study, 141–148
elite bias, political parties, 151–157
employment patterns
    Iceland, 117, 121
    sub-Saharan Africa, 167–168, 169, 170
    voting behavior correlations, 129, 131
encuentros, Latin America, 63–68
Equal Rights Amendment, 278, 279–280
Esping-Andersen, G., 308
essentialism problem, descriptive representation, 204–205
Ethiopia, electoral system, 171n8
European Commission, gender equality approach, 284
European Union (EU), 335–336, 337–338, 341
    See also specific countries
experience category, legislative process study, 244–245
expertise factor, resources category, legislative process study, 246, 247

family life regulation, Latin America, 267–273
family responsibilities variable, political ambition study, 142, 145, 146
FARC (Revolutionary Armed Forces of Colombia), 72, 73
Farley, Jim, 93
fast track approach, political representation, 175–177, 181
Feickert, Lillian, 90, 91
feminism, and state theory, 293–294
feminist bureaucracy. *See* state feminism
feminist movements, institutional settings, 47–54
    See also women's movements
feminist welfare state, 277–282
femocrats, 13, 101, 316–317, 321, 324n3, 328
    See also state feminism
Ferguson, Kathy, 299
Fernández, Matílde, 332
Ferraro, Geraldine, 50
Fianna Fáil, Ireland, 161
Figueiredo, João Batista, 40
Finland, 8, 130
Ford Foundation, 41
formal systems, candidate recruitment, 136–140
Forthal, Sonya, 94n9
Foster, J. Ellen, 90
Fox, Richard L.
    chapter by, 141–149
    comments on, 126
France
    election routes, 84–85
    gender gap study, 131
    nominations process study, 136
    quota regulations, 178, 179
    reconfiguration and power shifts, 337
    representation statistics, 180
    state feminism impact, 322
    welfare state characteristics, 307, 308, 310
Frank, Barney, 211n12
Fransella, Fay, 265
Franzway, S., 324n3
Fraser, Nancy, 302
Fredrika Bremer Association, 97, 100
Freeman, Jo
    chapter by, 89–95
    comments on, 79
Friedenwall, Lenita
    chapter by, 175–182
    comments on, 126
FSLN party, Nicaragua, 24–26, 28n16

Gabon, electoral system, 171n8
Garofalo, Lucia, 72
gender, defined, 3
    See also specific topics, e.g., Britain; descriptive representation; political parties
gender gap, voting behavior, 8, 9, 127–132
gender interests
    overviews, 9–11, 21–23
    defining, 309
    strategic *vs.* political, 22–24, 25–27

gender quotas. *See* quotas
gender socialization, impact on political ambition, 141, 145–148
generational cohorts, as gender gap hypothesis, 129–130, 131, 132
Germany
    gender gap patterns, 128, 131
    political parties, 85
    reconfiguration and power shifts, 338
    welfare state characteristics, 307, 308, 336
Gingrich, Newt, 255–256
Githens, Marianne, 251
Goetz, Anne Marie
    chapter by, 107–115
    comments on, 80
Goodin, Bob, 189
Gordon, April A., 170
Gosnell, Harold F., 92
Great Britain. *See* Britain
Griffin, Susan, 297n10
Guerra, Alfonso, 332
Guinier, Lani, 210n5
Gustafsson, S., 309

Hacker, Helen Mayer, 226
Hall, Mrs. Frank, 94n1
Hall, Richard, 256
Hammond, Hilda Phelps, 92
Hartmann, Susan, 48
Hatem, M. F., 324n3, 328–329
Hawkesworth, Mary
    chapter by, 251–262
    comments on, 241
Hay, Mary Garrett, 91
health care, Nicaragua, 27
Helig, Peggy, 211n15
Helms, Jesse, 207
Hernes, Helga Maria, 301, 302, 321, 324n3, 328
Hill, Anita, 207
House of Commons, UK, nominations process study, 137
House of Representatives, U.S., legislative process study, 248–249
Htun, Mala
    chapter by, 267–275
    comments on, 242
Hurtado, Aida, 253

Iceland, feminist political organization, 117–123
ideology hypotheses
    feminist political strategies, 313
    gender gap, 129, 130–132
    parliamentary representation, 160, 162–165
ideology variable, political ambition study, 146
Idris, Wafa, 75
Illinois, 92, 211n17
Illinois Commission on the Status of Women, 211n11
inclusion, as mainstreaming strategy, 283–290
incremental track approach, political representation, 175–177, 181
incumbency advantage premise, 141, 148

Independent Women's League, East Germany, 42
India, 14*n*4, 74, 77*n*16, 178, 179
individuals as representatives, limitations, 231–233, 238
informal systems, candidate recruitment, 136
Inglehart, Ronald
    chapter by, 127–133
    comments on, 125
Institute of Women, Spain, 327, 331–333
institutionalization component, political party
    organization, 159–160, 162, 165*n*2
institutionalized feminism. *See* state feminism
institutional settings, feminist protests, 20, 47–52
institutions as representation, 231–239
Instituto de la Mujer, Spain, 327, 331–333
integrationist model, 284–285, 287
interest articulation argument
    descriptive representation, 206–207, 211*n*7, *n*11, 223*n*9
    quotas, 185, 186–190
international activism. *See* transnational activism
intersectionality
    and differentiated representation, 193–199
    and disadvantaged subgroup representation, 55–62,
        220–222
    and diversity mainsteaming, 11–12, 287–290
    double militancy dilemma, 7, 31–32
    and racing-gendering processes, 252
introspective representation, 206
Iowa, local party activity, 90
Ireland, 73, 161, 310
Islamic Action Group, Algeria, 72
Islamic Jihad, 75
Israel, 72, 75–76, 78*n*28
issue networks, Latin America, 268, 270–273
Italy
    female terrorist activity, 73
    gender gap patterns, 128, 130
    political parties, 31, 84, 85, 136
    regime change impact, 34
    representation statistics, 161
    welfare state characteristics, 308
Izquierdo, María, 331

Japan, political parties, 136
Jenson, J., 307
Jonasdottir, Anna, 191*n*5
Jones, Bryan D., 336
Jonsdottir, Gudrun
    chapter by, 117–123
    comments on, 80
Jordan, Barbara, 261*n*1
Jordan, representation statistics, 179
justice promotion argument, quotas, 185–186, 190

Kanter, Rosabeth Moss, 226, 227, 228
Kantola, Johanna
    chapter by, 299–304
    comments on, 291
Katzenstein, Mary Fainsod
    chapter by, 47–54
    comments on, 20

Keck, Margaret, 64, 69*n*9
Kelley, Florence, 278
Kennedy, Jackie, 95*n*15
Kennedy, John F., 95*n*15
Kennedy, Robert F., 93
KF (Kwenna Frambothid), Iceland, 117–123
Khaled, Leila, 75
King, Mae, 261*n*1
Kolinsky, Eva, 85
Koven, S., 306–307
Krook, Mona Lena, chapter by, 3–20
Kwenna Frambothid (KF), Iceland, 117–123
Kwenna Listin, Iceland, 119–120
Kymlicka, Will, 186, 202, 211*n*14

Labor Party, Norway, 161
Labour Party, UK, 30, 137, 140*n*9
Land Act, Uganda, 112
Lasswell, Harold, 294
Latin America
    gender-related regulation, 267–273
    quota regulations, 178
    terrorist activity, 72–73, 77*n*14
    transnational activism effects, 63–69
    women's movements and democratization, 38–39
    See also specific countries
law, in male state, 293–296, 305–306
Lawless, Jennifer L.
    chapter by, 141–149
    comments on, 126
Law Reform Commission, Uganda, 112–113
Lee, Sheila Jackson, 258, 259
left-oriented parties. *See* political parties
Left Party Communists, Sweden, 98, 103
legal quotas *vs.* party quotas, 178–179, 180
legislative process study, United States, 243–249
legitimacy benefit, descriptive representation, 208–209,
    211*n*15
Lesotho, 167, 171*n*8
Lewis, J., 309–310
Liberal Democrats, Japan, 136
liberal feminism, 5, 12, 34, 299, 306
Liberal Party, Ireland, 161
Liberal Party, Netherlands, 136
Liberal Party, Sweden, 99, 100, 103, 104
liberal regimes, welfare states, 308–309
Liberation Tigers for Tamil Eelam (LTTE)., 72, 73–74,
    77*n*8, *n*16
Liberia, electoral system, 171*n*8
Lila Offensive, East Germany, 42
Lindblom, C. E., 297*n*3
Lindsey, Ben, 280
literacy rate, Nicaragua, 27
literature overview
    elections, 8–10
    political parties, 6–7
    political representation, 9–11
    public policies, 11–12
    social movements, 5–6
    state relationships, 12–13

Livermore, Henrietta Wells, 91, 93
localized systems, candidate recruitment, 136
local party politics, 84–85, 89–95
Locke, Marnie, 253
Long, Huey, 92
lottery costs, descriptive representation, 202–203, 210n2
Louchheim, Katie, 95n15
Louisiana, local party politics, 92
Lovenduski, Joni
    chapters by, 81–86, 135–140
    comments on, 79, 125, 160
LTTE (Liberation Tigers for Tamil Eelam), 72, 73–74,
    77n8, n16
Lukes, Steven, 297n3

MacKinnon, Catharine A.
    chapter by, 293–298
    comments on, 291
mainstreaming, transformation question, 11–12,
    283–290
majoritarian representation, gender representations, 9,
    169, 170, 179
majority issues category, intersectional typology, 56–62
Mansbridge, Jane
    chapter by, 201–213
    comments on, 183–184, 216
Marxist feminism theory, 300–301
Maryland, local party politics, 90
maternalism, 306–307
Matland, Richard E., 168
Mauritania, electoral system, 171n8
Mayhew, David R., 94n1, n8
Mazur, Amy G.
    chapter by, 319–325
    comments on, 291–292, 327, 329
Meek, Carrie, 260
Merton, Robert K., 265
Mestre, Carmen, 331
Mexico, 132, 273n1
Mexico meeting, Latin American feminists, 64–66
Michel, S., 306–307
microcosmic representation, 202–203
middle-class bias, disadvantaged group representation, 56
Middle East, gender quotas, 178–179
military institution, feminist protests, 47–50, 51–52
military recruitment, terrorist recruitment, compared,
    77n7
Millett, Kate, 294
minimum requirement approach, quotas, 179–180
minimum wage legislation, 254–255
Mink, Patsy, 255, 257, 258, 259, 261n1
mirror metaphor, 294, 297n10
mirror representation. See descriptive representation
Molyneux, Maxine
    chapter by, 21–28
    comments on, 19
Morocco, representation statistics, 179
Moseley-Braun, Carol, 207, 259
mothers' pensions, United States, 277–282, 307
Mother Teresa, 52, 53n10

Movement Act, Uganda, 108
Mozambique, 167, 171n7
Mujer y Socialismo, Spain, 331–333
multipartisan movements, as political strategy, 87–88
Multi-Party Committee of Women, United States, 94n13
Mundt, Robert J., 211n15
Museveni, Yoweri Kaguta, 107, 109, 111, 112
Mussolini, 297n10
mutuality factor, experience category, legislative process
    study, 245
mutual relationship criteria, descriptive representative
    selection, 215, 217–222
Myers, Jan, 261n3

Nambia, 167, 171n8
Napoleon, 297n10
National Executive Committee (NEC), Uganda, 113–
    114
National Resistance Army (NRA), Uganda, 107, 113
National Resistance Movement (NRM), Uganda
    gender equity legislation, 112–113
    no-party system, 107–108, 113–114, 115n6
    women's patronage appointments, 108–111
National Women's Council, Uganda, 111, 113
National Women's Party, United States, 278,
    279–280
Navarro, Marysa, 65–66
Nelson, Barbara, 281n4
Nepal, quota regulations, 179
Netherlands, 84, 130, 136, 308, 309
neutral state theory, 299
New Democrats, Sweden, 101–102
New Jersey, 90, 91
New Mexico, local party politics, 90
New Orleans, political machine, 92
New York, 91, 93
New Zealand, women's suffrage, 8
Nicaragua, 19, 24–28
Niger, representation statistics, 167
Nigeria, 167, 171n8
Niven, David
    chapter by, 151–158
    comments on, 126
Njuba, Sam, 115n6
nomination level, political party organization,
    160, 162
nomination process, Britain study, 135–140
no-party system. See Uganda
Nordic feminism, 12, 301–302
    See also Norway
Norris, Pippa
    chapters by, 127–133, 135–140
    comments on, 125, 160, 168
Norway, 8, 14n4, 81–82, 130, 161
    See also Nordic feminism
Nzomo, Maria, 168

occupation test, elite bias study, 153–154
Odongo, Onyango, 115n6
offloading processes, in state reconfigurations, 336–337

Ohio, local party activity, 90
Olsen, Frances, 264
opinions, as representation aspect, 196, 197–198, 223*n*9
organizational structure hypothesis, representation study,
    159–160, 161–162, 164–165
Orloff, Ann
    chapter by, 305–311
    comments on, 291, 310
Otero-Warren, Nina, 90
outgroup effect, elite bias study, 152, 153–157
Outshoorn, J., 321

Pakistan, gender quotas, 178
Palestine, 72, 75–76, 78*n*28
Palme, Olof, 99
Paraguay, quota regulations, 180
parliamentary representation. *See* political representation
partisan movements, as political strategy, 87
party clubs, U.S., 90–91
party quotas *vs.* legal quotas, 178–179, 180
Pastor, Ed, 257
patriarchal culture, sub-Saharan Africa, 168, 169–170
patriarchal state theory, 299–300, 305–306
patriarchy, definitions, 28*n*2
pay equity example, problem representation, 265
pendejo game, 253
Penock, J. Roland, 201
Pérez, Gracia, 332
personality trait test, elite bias study, 154
perspective factor, experience category, legislative process
    study, 244–245
Peru, terrorist activity, 72, 73, 77*n*14
Petersen, Agnes L., 278
Phillips, Anne
    chapter by, 185–191
    comments on, 183, 210*n*3, 211*n*7, 217, 220, 223*n*10
Pinochet, Augusto, 40–41
Pitkin, Hanna, 194, 210*n*3
Piven, Frances Fox, 52*nn*1–2
Poland, 19–20, 38–39, 42–43, 322
policy agencies, women's, 233, 234, 235–238, 319–324
    See also social policies; state feminism
policy responsiveness, defined, 7
    See also social policies
political ambition study, United States, 141–148
political culture variable, political ambition study, 142,
    145, 146
political machines, 91–92, 94*n*8
political parties
    overviews, 6–7, 79–86
    Britain, 135–140
    candidate recruitment studies, 135–140, 151–157
    East Germany, 42
    gender support patterns, 127, 128
    Iceland, 117–123
    Latin America, 40, 41, 272
    as opinion representation, 196
    parliamentary representation study, 159–166
    Spain, 327, 331–333
    and state feminism, 330–331

sub-Saharan Africa, 168, 170
Sweden, 97–100, 101–103, 104
Uganda, 107–108, 113–114
United States, 89–95, 151–157, 161
and women's movements, 6–7, 30–31, 33, 82–83,
    87–88, 343*n*6
political representation
    overviews, 8–11, 183–184
    critical mass arguments, 10, 225–230, 236–238
    definitions, 82
    with multiple institutional sources, 231–239
    relationship model, 193–199
    See also descriptive representation; political parties;
        quotas; social policies
political representation, statistics
    African countries, 14*n*4, 107, 167
    Britain, 137
    Iceland, 117, 122
    India, 14*n*4
    Norway, 14*n*4
    in sub-Saharan Africa study, 167–172
    Sweden, 101
    United States, 141, 251
politics, definitions, 3–4
Popular Front for the Liberation of Palestine (PFLP), 75
pornography, 264–265, 295–296
Porta, Della, 34
A Portrait of Marginality (Githens and Prestage), 251
positive discrimination strategies, political party
    leadership, 84
postmodern feminism, 5, 12
poverty, Nicaragua, 27
poverty rates, limitations for theory, 306
    See also welfare state
power relocations, with state reconfigurations, 335–343
power theories, 294, 297*n*3
practical gender interests, 22–24, 27–28
Pratt, Ruth B., 91
Prestage, Jewel, 251
Pringle, Rosemary, 302
privacy law, in male state, 296
problem identification, framework impact, 263–266
Progressive Conservative Party, Canada, 136
proportional representation, gender representations, 9,
    169, 170–171, 179
prostitution, in male state, 296
protest activity, institutional settings, 47–52
PSOE (Socialist Worker's Party), Spain, 327, 331–333
public policies. *See* social policies
Putnam, Robert, 49

Quinn, Jack, 255
quotas
    arguments for, 185–190
    empowerment question, 180–181
    implementation factors, 179–180
    parliamentary representation hypothesis, 161, 163,
        164–165
    political representation impact, 175–178
    sub-Saharan Africa, 168, 169, 170, 171*n*7

quotas (*continued*)
  Sweden, 99–100
  types of, 178–180
  Uganda's system, 108, 109

racing-gendering processes
  overview, 251–252
  study methodology, 253–254
  theory, 252–253, 256–257
  types of, 254–256, 257–260, 261nn2–4
  See also welfare state
radical feminism, 5, 12, 293–296, 299–300, 305–306
Rajiv Gandhi, 74
ranking effects, quotas, 180
Ranney, Austin, 136
rape, 74, 211n11, 295, 296
recruitment studies, candidate, 8–9, 135–140, 151–157
Red Stockings, Iceland, 117
Rees, Teresa, 284
reformist feminism, Sweden, 97
relationship model, political representation process,
  193–199
religion, voting behavior correlations, 129
representation responsiveness, defined, 7
  See also political representation
Republican Party, U.S., 90, 91, 92–93, 94n4, 95n15, 127
  See also Congress, United States
Resistance Council system (RC), Uganda, 107–108
resource mobilization, as women's movement variable,
  38–39
resources category, legislative process study, 245–246
reversal, as mainstreaming strategy, 283–290
Revolutionary Armed Forces of Columbia (FARC), 72,
  73
Reykjavik elections, Iceland, 118, 119, 121–122
Reynolds, Andrew, 168
rhetorical strategies, political party leadership, 84
right-oriented parties. *See* political parties
Robinson, Martha, 92
Robles, Rosario, 273n1
Rodríguez, Regina, 332
role model argument, quotas, 185
roll call voting, legislative process study, 244, 246, 247,
  248–249
Romero, Isabel, 332
Roosevelt, Eleanor, 93
Ros-Lehtinen, Ileana, 255, 260
Rowbotham, S., 33–34
Roybal-Allard, Lucille, 259
Rucht, Dieter
  chapter by, 335–345
  comments on, 32, 34n4, 292
Rule, Wilma, 168
rules hypothesis, parliamentary representation, 160–161,
  163, 164–165
Russia, quota regulations, 178
Rwanda, 14n4, 178

Sabin, Pauline, 91
sacrifice theme, female terrorist activity, 74–76

Sahlin, Mona, 102
Sainsbury, Diane
  chapter by, 97–106
  comments on, 79–80, 309, 310
Saleh, Salim, 114
Samarasinghe, Vidyamali, 77n7
sanctions, quota non-compliance, 180
Sandistas, 19, 24–28
Sarvasy, Wendy
  chapter by, 277–282
  comments on, 242
Saudi Arabia, voting rights, 14n3
Sawer, Marian, 313, 322
Scandinavian politics, critical mass argument, 10,
  225–230
  See also Norway; Sweden
Schattschneider, E. E., 56, 135–136, 256
Scotland, parliamentary power changes, 336
selective form, descriptive representation, 202–203,
  211n14
self-perceived qualification variable, political ambition
  study, 142, 145, 146–147
Senegal, electoral system, 171nn7–8
sex, gender compared, 3
Sexual Assault Act, Illinois, 211n11
sexuality, in male state, 295–296, 298n12
Sexual Offences Bill, Uganda, 112–113
Seychelles, representation statistics, 167
Shaver, S., 307
Shining Path, Peru, 72, 73, 77n14
Sikh militants, 74
Sikkink, Kathryn, 64, 69n9
skewed group, in critical mass arguments, 227
Skjeie, H., 188
Skocpol, T., 322
Sniderman, Paul, 157n6
Snyder, Elizabeth, 94, 95n15
social bias, candidate selection study, 138–139
social-democratic regimes, welfare states,
  308–309
Social Democratic Women's Federation (SSKF), Sweden,
  99, 102
Social Democrats, Sweden, 98, 99–100, 102–103
socialist feminism, 5, 12, 300–301
Socialist Party, Senegal, 171n7
Socialist Unity Party (SED), East Germany, 42
Socialist Worker's Party (PSOE), Spain, 327, 331–333
socialization, impact on political ambition, 141,
  145–148
social meaning benefit, descriptive representation, 208,
  211n14
social movements
  overview, 4–6, 19–20
  issue networks compared, 270
  Nicaragua's experience, 24–28
  See also women's movement
social perspectives, as representation aspect, 196–198,
  223n9
social policies
  overview, 241–242

Latin American family life regulation, 267–273
legislative process study, 243–249
mainstreaming models, 11–12, 283–290
problem representation, 263–266
racing-gendering processes, 251–261
welfare state approaches, 277–282, 307–310
See also state feminism
Solana, Javier, 332
Solidarity, Poland, 38, 42, 43
South Africa, 167, 171*n*8, 178
South Korea, gender gap patterns, 130
Spain, 30, 130, 322, 327–328, 331–333
speechmaking importance, legislative process, 246–247, 248–249
Spivak, Gayatri, 259
sponsorship importance, legislative process, 246–247, 248–249
Squires, Judith
chapter by, 283–290
comments on, 242
Sri Lanka, female terrorist activity, 72, 73–74, 77*n*8
state feminism
meanings of, 13, 328–330
policy agency impact, 319–324
and political parties, 330–331
Spain's experience, 327, 331–333
Sweden's experience, 100–101, 103–104
See also state relationships
state reconfiguration, processes, 13
state relationships
overview, 12–13, 33–34, 291–292
double militancy dilemma, 32
feminism theories, 293, 299–303, 305–306
law as male, 293–296, 305–306
and maternalism, 306–307
political opportunities comparisons, 313–318
power theories, 294, 297*n*3
reconfiguration processes, 335–343
Sweden's approach, 100–101, 103
welfare state comparisons, 307–310
Stetson, Dorothy McBride
chapter by, 319–325
comments on, 233, 291–292, 322, 327, 329
Stevenson, Adlai, 93–94, 95*n*16
Stone, Deborah, 264
strategic gender interests, 22–23, 25–26
Strolovitch, Dara Z.
chapter by, 55–62
comments on, 20
Studlar, Donley T., 168
subordination assumption, in state relationships, 293–298
sub-Saharan Africa, representation study, 167–172
Sudan, representation statistics, 171*n*6
suffrage, women's, 8, 14*n*2
suicide terrorism, 72, 74–75
Supermarket Demonstration, Iceland, 121
supply model, candidate recruitment study, 139
support factor, attitudes category, legislative process study, 245
Support Stockings, Sweden, 101–103

Supreme Court, Canada, public interest groups, 314
Supreme Court, U.S., citizenship ruling, 282*n*11
surrogate representation, 205–206, 210*n*6
Swaziland, electoral system, 171*n*8
Sweden
appointment quota debate, 100–101, 103–104
election routes, 84, 85–86
representation debates, 98–99, 101–104
welfare state characteristics, 308, 309, 310
women's movement, 97–98

Tamale, Sylvia, 110
Tamerius, Karin
chapter by, 243–249
comments on, 241
Tanzania, representation statistics, 167, 171*n*6
Taylor, Charles, 209
technical *vs.* absolutist policies, 267–268, 269
Teresa, Mother, 52, 53*n*10
terrorist activity, female, 20, 71–78
Thatcher, Margaret, 138
Thomas, Clarence, 207
Thomas, Sue, 211*n*11, 261*n*2
Three Worlds of Welfare Capitalism (Esping-Anderson), 308
Threlfall, Monica
chapter by, 327–333
comments on, 292
tilted group, in critical mass arguments, 227
Togo, representation statistics, 167
tokenism, and racing-gendering processes, 253
topic extinctions, and racing-gendering processes, 253, 254
Towards Equality program, Sweden, 98
transformative model, 284, 286–287
transnational activism
and democratization processes, 39, 40, 41, 42, 43
Latin American impact, 63–68, 270–271
and quota trends, 180
Tripp, Aili Mari, 108

Uganda
gender equity legislation, 112–113
no-party system, 107–108, 113–114, 115*n*6
representation statistics, 171*n*6, 179
women's patronage appointments, 108–111, 178
uniform group, in minority size arguments, 227
unions, 32–33, 42–43, 104*n*2, 117
United Arab Emirates, 14*n*3
United Kingdom. *See* Britain
United Nations, 64–66, 68*n*4, 69*nn*7–8, 270–271, 320–321, 324*n*3
United States
civil society changes, 336
election routes, 84, 85
female terrorist activity, 72
legislative process study, 248–249
political ambition study, 141–148
political parties, 89–95, 151–157, 161
racing-gendering processes study, 251–260
representation patterns, 141, 243–249, 251
state feminism history, 319

United States (*continued*)
    union influences, 32–33
    voting behavior patterns, 127–132
    welfare state characteristics, 307, 308, 309, 336
universal issues category, intersectional typology, 56–62
unobtrusive mobilization, 48–49, 52n4
uploading processes, in state reconfigurations, 335–336, 337–338
Upton, Harriet Taylor, 90
Utah, local party activity, 94n4

Vargas, Virginia, 65
Vasquez, Roxana, 67
Velazquez, Nydia, 258
violence against women
    disadvantaged representation study, 58, 60, 61
    Latin American feminism, 65, 66–67
    multi-source representation study, 234–238
virtual representation, 210n6
voting behavior patterns, 7–8, 127–132, 243–249

Wadsworth, James W., 91
wage equity
    problem representation example, 265
    and welfare state theory, 305
Wales, 14n4, 181n4
Waters, Maxine, 257, 258, 260
Watkins v. Army, 298n12
Watson, Sophie, 301, 302
Weldon, S. Laurel
    chapter by, 231–239
    comments on, 184, 234
welfare policy, racing-gendering processes, 256–260, 261nn3–4
welfare state, 13, 277–282, 301–302, 305–310
West Germany, gender gap patterns, 130, 132
widow factor, as election route, 84
Williams, Clare, 93
Williams, Melissa S., 211n14, 221
Winberg, Margareta, 102
Woman Citizen's Union (WCU), Louisiana, 92
Women and Socialism committee, Spain, 331–333
Women and Welfare Reform conference, United States, 257

"Women as a Minority Group" (Hacker), 226
Women for Life, Chile, 41
Women for Peace, East Germany, 42
Women's Caucus, Uganda, 109, 111, 112
Women's Committee for Louisiana, 92
Women's Equality program, Sweden, 98
women's interests, overviews, 9–11, 21–23
    See also specific topics, e.g., racing-gendering processes; political parties; social policies
Women's League, Poland, 43
Women's List, Iceland, 117–118, 122
women's movements
    overview, 4–6, 29–36, 319–320, 324n1
    comparative analysis requirements, 19
    and democratic transitions, 37–43
    and gender gap patterns, 129
    institutional settings, 47–52
    Latin America, 24, 63–68, 268
    and political parties, 6–7, 30–31, 33, 82–83, 87–88, 343n6
    as source of political representation, 233–234, 235–238, 239n6
    and state relationships, 13, 338–343
    Sweden, 97–98
    Uganda, 108–109, 113
women's parties, 7, 31, 117–123
women's policy machinery. *See* state feminism
Woolf, Virginia, 297n10
Woolsey, Lynn, 257, 258
World Church of the Creator (WCOTC), 72
Wu, X., 32

Yoon, Mi Yung
    chapter by, 167–173
    comments on, 126
Young, Iris Marion
    chapter by, 193–199
    comments on, 183, 202, 221, 223n29
Young, Lisa
    chapter by, 87–88
    comments on, 79
Younger, Maud, 280

Zhang, N., 32

Made in the USA
Monee, IL
17 January 2020